THE
INFANTRY'S
ARMOR

THE
INFANTRY'S
ARMOR

The U.S. Army's Separate Tank Battalions in World War II

Harry Yeide

STACKPOLE
BOOKS

Essex, Connecticut
Blue Ridge Summit, Pennsylvania

"If I could I would always work in silence and obscurity,
and let my efforts be known by their results."
—Emily Brontë

STACKPOLE BOOKS
An imprint of Globe Pequot, the trade division of
The Rowman & Littlefield Publishing Group, Inc.
4501 Forbes Blvd., Ste. 200
Lanham, MD 20706
www.rowman.com

Distributed by NATIONAL BOOK NETWORK

British Library Cataloguing in Publication Information available

Library of Congress Cataloging-in-Publication Data available

ISBN 9780811705950 (cloth : alk. paper)
ISBN 9780811776585 (pbk : alk. paper)
ISBN 9780811743792 (ebook)

♾™ The paper used in this publication meets the minimum requirements of American
National Standard for Information Sciences—Permanence of Paper for Printed Library
Materials, ANSI/NISO Z39.48-1992.

TABLE OF CONTENTS

INTRODUCTION

This work tells the stories of the tank battalions that fought in North Africa, Sicily, Italy, and the European theater, as well as the tank, amphibian tank, and amphibian tractor battalions—all manned by armored force tankers—that battled in the Pacific. It is a portrait of those battalions as much as it is a history. The book explores how they fought the war, as often as possible in the tankers' own words. It is impossible to provide a running account of each armored battalion; it was a big war! To the extent possible, I have selected material that either illustrates experiences common to many battalions or highlights the more noteworthy experience of an individual unit or sector of the front. Readers interested in a day-by-day account of the eighteen "land tank" battalions that fought in the Pacific—albeit with no coverage of the armored amphibians—should consult Gene Eric Salecker's *Rolling Thunder against the Rising Sun.*

The quality of the surviving records varies tremendously from battalion to battalion. Some, such as the 743d Tank Battalion, left exhaustive records, while others left skimpy and uninformative files. The officers of some battalions, such as the 708th Amphibian Tank Battalion, wrote articles for professional journals that fleshed out their outfits' histories. Finally, veterans and interested members of succeeding generations have gathered information on a few battalions and made that available on the internet, such as the remarkable website dedicated as of this writing to the 192d Tank Battalion, created by the students of Proviso East High School in cooperation with veterans of the battalion. The disparity in surviving information largely accounts for the relative frequency of citations drawn from the experiences of the various units.

I recognize that even the original accounts are not always entirely accurate. Particularly in cases where something went wrong, such as a breakdown in tank-infantry teamwork, the various parties are likely to have come away with—and recorded—different views of reality. The reader should know that this book is as close as I could get to what actually happened.

I offer one suggestion to the reader: keep in mind that the success or loss of any given tank was a drama for the men inside. Newly arriving battalions generally kept close track of individuals. After all, these were men that the recording officers knew and had trained with for months. As the war dragged on and casualties became routine, the tank to some extent became the collective surrogate for the crew in the historical record.

This work is not a history of American military operations worldwide, although those operations are obviously the framework in which the story of the separate armored battalions unfolds. I have relied heavily on the excellent works of the U.S. Army Center of Military History to relate the big picture. Reliance on U.S. Army perspectives introduces certain biases, but that is a risk I willingly accept. Moreover, I note cases in which other accounts conflict with the official histories.

I do pay attention to the feedback readers give, and one critique of my earlier books is that I have not devoted much space to discussing doctrine. Here's why: the lesson I have drawn from looking at how armored and tank destroyer battalions and mechanized cavalry squadrons and troops actually fought the war is that doctrine generally went out the window in favor of a de facto doctrine developed on the battlefield and mixed with old, familiar patterns of doing business. The guy in the turret stopped caring very much about what the manual said. Modifications to standing doctrine eventually caught up, but not in time to be inculcated into units going into combat. Still, this work contains more on doctrine than did *Steel Victory*.

I have hewed as closely as practicable to the original text of the records where they are quoted but have taken some small liberties with texts drawn from the military records and personal accounts in order to correct grammatical errors and spelling mistakes and introduce some consistency in references to unit designations, equipment, dates, and numbers.

I have used the word "jeep" throughout to describe the quarter-ton truck because of the term's universal familiarity. Tankers called it a "peep." The Armored Force as an organization was renamed the Armored Command on 2 July 1943 and the Armored Center on 20 February 1944. I have used "Armored Force" to describe the totality of armored units throughout this book.

CHAPTER 1

General McNair's Offspring

"In August [1943], two weeks were spent out at Hell Cat Camp. It was a battle training camp and mighty rough. Dust lay all over a foot thick, and the men were perpetually covered in and out with it. There was usually so much dust in our throats that when we spit, a ball of dirt came out."

—*History of Company "C",*
44th Tank Battalion, 1942–1945

The U.S. Army's separate armored battalions in World War II labored in obscurity by comparison with the flashy armored divisions, but they overwhelmingly carried the heavier burden in the grim, global struggle to destroy the Axis Powers. The armored divisions were few in number; attracted war correspondents; frequently had dashing, well-known commanders; and flaunted memorable nicknames, such as the 1st "Old Ironsides," 2d "Hell on Wheels," and 3d "Spearhead" Armored Divisions. The separate battalions almost always worked for somebody else's division, were led by unknown lieutenant colonels, and were labeled like generic products, usually a forgettable three-digit number beginning with "7." If a battalion had a nickname, it was likely to be something like the "Seven-Five-Zero."

The separate tank, amphibian tank, or amphibian tractor battalions, though, were present at every amphibious assault that the U.S. Army conducted where armor was used at all, while armored divisions participated in landings only in North Africa and Sicily, which were also the only two campaigns in which the armored divisions played a preponderant combat role. The separate battalions did most of the bloody work in Italy and constituted the *entire* effort in the Pacific. The respective roles were most equally balanced in Western Europe, and the separate tank battalions fought everywhere the infantry divisions did. The men fought beside the foot soldier in dust, mud, and sand. They were the dirt-grimed tankers.

It is easy to forget how difficult it was to make this feat possible. On 1 September 1939, the day the largest and most destructive war in history ignited, the

1

United States possessed a small and obsolete armored force. The Regular Army's infantry branch had only the just-organized 66th Infantry (Light Tanks) and the 67th Infantry (Medium Tanks) based at Fort Benning, Georgia, plus one tank company in each of seven infantry divisions and eighteen National Guard infantry divisions. The 7th Cavalry Brigade was mechanized, but only two of its battalion-size squadrons were equipped with light tanks—and they carried nothing more lethal than machine guns. Other than World War I–era tanks, the total American tank inventory amounted to some 240 machine-gun-armed M1 and M2 light tanks, plus a single M2 medium tank prototype equipped with a 37-millimeter gun. There were tentative budgetary plans to allocate $7 million for additional infantry tanks, but the country had no tank in large-scale production.[1]

Adolf Hitler changed all that when he unleashed his *Wehrmacht* on Poland in the first stunning display of *blitzkrieg*. Distressingly for American planners, the Polish army was similar to the U.S. Army in terms of size, reliance on cavalry, and lagging mechanization. Hitler's legions broke the Polish army's back in about two weeks, the panzer divisions cutting through defenses with ease.

During the 1930s, the U.S. Army had decentralized authority over mechanization, and the cavalry and infantry branches had pursued tank development after their own visions. They were mired in rivalry, bickering over whether the tank should support the doughboy as it had in the Great War or join the horse in slashing maneuver, as well as over more prosaic matters of stature and resources. The cavalry called its tanks by a different name—"combat cars"—because Congress had decreed that it could not own tanks. Even within the branches, visionary advocates of armored warfare struggled to overcome resistance from old-school officers.

Brig. Gen. Adna Chaffee, who was in command of the 7th Cavalry Brigade (Mechanized) the day Hitler invaded Poland, led other mechanization advocates in calling for the establishment of "cavalry divisions, mechanized" built roughly along the lines of the German panzer divisions.[2] During Third Army maneuvers in May 1940, the 7th Cavalry Brigade formed part of a provisional armored division, along with the 6th Infantry Regiment (Motorized) and the infantry's Provisional Tank Brigade, which included the two tank regiments from Fort Benning. The provisional division dominated the exercise.[3]

At the conclusion of the exercises, Brig. Gen. Frank Andrews, the War Department's assistant chief of staff, G-3 (operations), met on 25 May in a high-school basement in Alexandria, Louisiana, with now-Maj. Gen. Adna Chaffee and other officers from cavalry and mechanized units.[4] As the men talked, the German armed forces were just beginning the third week of their dazzling campaign to destroy the French Army, as they had the Polish.

These officers called for a unified approach to mechanized development free of the chiefs of cavalry and infantry.[5] Within a month, U.S. Army Chief of Staff

Gen. George C. Marshall had approved a proposal to organize a separate armored corps that would incorporate most of the army's mechanized formations. A formal plan reached the War Department General Staff on 10 June. Detailed consideration followed, and despite resistance from the chiefs of cavalry and infantry, the War Plans Division altered mobilization plans to include armored divisions.[6]

The G-3 proposed to establish two mechanized divisions, one based at Fort Knox, Kentucky, and the second at Fort Benning, Georgia. Mechanized units would be redistributed among them to ensure that the divisions started from roughly the same basis. The infantry's light tank formations were to be reorganized along the lines of mechanized cavalry regiments, and cavalry officers would be spread among the two divisions, where they were expected to wield strong influence. On the other hand, the new divisions inherited the organization of distinct light and medium tank battalions, a concept approved by the War Department in 1938 to meet the declared needs of the infantry branch.[7]

On 10 July, the adjutant general authorized the creation of the Armored Force as a "service test," which sidestepped the need for congressional approval and allowed the War Department great flexibility in modifying the organization. The Armored Force consisted of the 1st and 2d Armored Divisions and the separate 70th Tank Battalion (Medium), a General Headquarters (GHQ) "reserve" battalion. The nucleus of GHQ was activated on 26 July, initially to oversee the training of tactical units in the States. The units were stationed, respectively, at Fort Knox, Fort Benning, and Fort Meade in Maryland.

ORGANIZATION OF THE BATTALIONS

Fittingly for the separate tank battalions, their most important patron during the early evolution of the Armored Force was the decidedly unglamorous, hard-of-hearing Lt. Gen. Lesley J. McNair, who, as commander of GHQ, lacked any clear authority over the newly created Armored Force. His views on the subject nevertheless carried great weight at the War Department. Along with senior infantry officers, McNair, an artilleryman, continued to champion the traditional infantry-support role of armor, which had a pedigree dating back to World War I.

As of 1940, the War Department planned to activate only fifteen GHQ tank battalions subordinated to three Reserve (later called Tank and then Armored) Group headquarters. Plans called for the activation in 1941 of the 71st through 75th Tank Battalions (Medium) and the 76th through 79th Tank Battalions (Light), though the War Department on 8 May ordered that these battalions instead receive designations in the series 751 to 759. The separate tank battalion of 1940 consisted of a Headquarters and Headquarters (H&H) Company and three tank companies, each consisting of three five-tank platoons and a two-tank headquarters section. By 1942, the battalion gained a service company.[8]

The 70th Tank Battalion (Medium) had some real advantages over outfits formed later. Manpower was entirely Regular Army personnel until August 1940, when several reserve officers joined the unit. Many of the men were drawn from the 34th Infantry, and the others were tankers from the 1st Battalion, 67th Infantry

(Medium Tanks), from which the 70th Battalion had been created. They merged infantry and armored thinking. The first draftees arrived on 11 December 1941.[9]

Decisions involving the armored divisions tended to drive how the separate tank battalions were organized until 1943, when establishment of amphibian and other specialized battalions created a remarkable diversity in non-divisional armored units. The GHQ tank battalions were the stepchildren of the Armored Force from the start. The 70th Tank Battalion (Medium) initially ranked last in priority for deliveries of new tanks.[10] Indeed, despite its formal designation, the outfit never received medium tanks, and it organized and trained with worn-out M2A2 light tanks beginning in the summer of 1940; it received new—by then obsolete—M2A2s in November. This fact was acknowledged with the reclassification of the outfit as a light battalion on 7 October 1941.[11] The 193d Tank Battalion (Medium), called into active service from the National Guard in January 1941 and attached to the 2d Armored Division for training, had to recondition hand-me-down M2A2 and M2A3 light tanks from the armored division for training. When alerted for movement overseas in December, the battalion was issued used M3 light tanks from armored regiment stocks.[12] The 191st Tank Battalion (Light), which assembled at Fort Meade in February 1941, possessed only eight old M2A2s. The 756th Tank Battalion (Light), activated on 1 June 1941, did not receive any tanks at all until February 1942.[13]

McNair was convinced that the Armored Force was the most wasteful of the ground arms in its use of men and equipment, and he argued in 1942 and 1943 that the armored divisions were bloated and unwieldy. Combat experience helped McNair make his case by showing that tanks frequently needed escort by foot troops to locate and destroy antitank defenses. In 1943, McNair wrote in a memorandum: "It is believed that our 1943 troop basis has entirely too many armored divisions, considering their proper tactical employment, and too few GHQ tank battalions. It is particularly important that the latter be available in quantities to permit all infantry divisions to work with them freely and frequently."[14]

In part because of McNair's influence, the armored divisions were reorganized twice, first in March 1942 and again in September 1943. The latter reorganization affected all but the 1st, 2d, and 3d Armored Divisions and released two tank battalions per division into the GHQ pool. Standard separate battalions were made identical to the divisional ones and thus could theoretically be attached to armored divisions—although that appears to have occurred only in Italy.

Prior to the reshuffle in 1943, a sharp distinction existed between medium and light tank battalions. The fighting in North Africa showed that light tanks operating alone were generally not effective against the Germans. Most tank battalions therefore reorganized to incorporate both types of armor. Each battalion now had three medium tank companies (seventeen tanks and one assault gun each) and one light tank company (seventeen tanks). Each also had a service company and an H&H company, which included a reconnaissance platoon, a mortar platoon with three 81-millimeter tubes, and an assault gun platoon with three guns and a small tank section that brought battalion strength to a total of fifty-four medium tanks.

Several outfits—including the 744th, 758th, 759th, 764th, and 767th—remained light tank battalions. They retained the old structure: only three tank companies, a three-vehicle assault gun section incorporated in H&H Company, and a service company.[15]

Six battalions—the 701st, 736th, 738th, 739th, 740th, and 748th—organized in great secrecy as special formations code-named "Leaflet" battalions that were equipped largely with M3 medium tanks mounting special searchlights code-named Canal Defense Lights (CDLs).[16] Developed by the British in 1939, the primary mission of CDL tanks was to provide illumination for aimed fire at night. Secondary missions included dazzling enemy soldiers with a flicker effect and protecting friendly foot troops in triangles of darkness formed between adjacent lights. No CDL battalion was used in combat as such, and in October 1944, the 701st, 736th, 740th, and 748th were converted to standard battalions; the 738th and 739th became mine-exploder battalions.[17]

Starting in October 1943, the renamed Armored Command reorganized nine tank battalions as amphibian tank ("amtank" or, less frequently, "amphtank") or amphibian tractor ("amtrac") battalions and raised more from other sources.[18] Nearly all served in the Pacific theater. The amphibian tank battalion had a headquarters and headquarters/service company (four amtracs) and four seventeen-tank companies organized into three five-tank platoons and a two-tank headquarters section. In January 1944, the number of amtanks per company rose to eighteen, and companies received two amtracs each; the headquarters company received three amtanks. The amphibian tractor battalion consisted of a headquarters and a service company, plus two line companies with fifty-one amtracs apiece. The battalions by 1945 were reorganized into three line companies, each with sixteen amtracs. Each company had two maintenance amtracs and its own mechanics, electricians, and radio repairmen.[19]

An oddball formation, the 28th Airborne Tank Battalion, was activated on 6 December 1943. The outfit had a headquarters and service company and three line companies lettered A through C. No theater commander ever requested an airborne tank battalion, so the 28th Battalion was converted to a standard tank battalion in October 1944. It shipped to the Pacific but never saw combat.[20]

The 44th Tank Battalion was separated from the 12th Armored Division in February 1944 and sent to the southwest Pacific while the remainder of the division prepared for Europe.[21] The 714th Tank Battalion, which had become a separate tank battalion when the 12th Armored Division reorganized as a "light" armored division in 1943, returned to replace it.

The 713th Tank Battalion reorganized on 1 January 1945 as the army's only "Tank Battalion, Armored Flamethrower." The battalion had three companies of flame-throwing medium tanks divided into three six-tank platoons, plus standard fighting tanks for the company and battalion commanders. The outfit deactivated the light tank company and mortar platoon to provide personnel for an expanded service company to handle increased supply problems.[22]

From the initially planned fifteen separate tank battalions, the number of such units rose to twenty-six by late 1942, forty-one by mid-1943, and sixty-five by late 1944. The separate battalions by that time outnumbered the fifty-four battalions incorporated into sixteen armored divisions.[23] Another seven amphibian tank and twenty-three amphibian tractor battalions filled out the armored force.[24] Not all of these outfits saw combat.

Several separate tank companies also served during the war. Company C, 70th Tank Battalion (Light), for example, was detached in January 1942 and deployed to Iceland, where it became the 10th Light Tank Company. It later rejoined the standardized 70th Tank Battalion as its Company D.[25] The 603d Tank Company fought in the Pacific with six different divisions.[26]

SEPARATE-BATTALION DOCTRINE

Beyond a substantial common base, specialized doctrines evolved for the use of tanks in armored divisions and separate tank battalions, as the latter outfits had to accommodate infantry doctrine. The infantry initially used a wave-attack concept that it had pioneered in 1938 and 1939. Doctrine in 1940 called for two echelons of tanks to work with the riflemen. The first would neutralize antitank guns, while the second worked closely with the infantry against machine guns, pillboxes, personnel in trenches, and so on.[27] But doctrine for the infantry-support tanks did not receive the attention that doctrine for the armored divisions did. *Field Manual (FM) 100-5* on tank operations, issued in May 1941, provided a little more than two pages on the use of GHQ tank battalions, with dubious guidance such as "Tanks should not be tied too closely to foot troops."[28] The 1942 Armored Force field manual on tactics devoted ten sentences to tank-infantry operations, and the army did not even issue a field manual on the use of tanks with infantry until 1943.[29] As a result, infantry and supporting armor were left to figure out many things on their own in battle.

The doctrine captured in the 1942 field manuals anticipated that light tanks would provide the main strike force in most cases and that medium tanks would support them. This was appropriate for armored divisions, which had both light and medium tanks, but not very useful to the separate battalions that were to be either light or medium. Medium tanks, meanwhile, were to form the leading echelon of attack against known enemy resistance when antitank defenses were strong and to support light tanks, other medium tanks, and infantry in tank-versus-tank action.[30]

Battle experience in North Africa, mainly that of the 1st Armored Division, led to the conclusion that light tanks generally could not operate alone against the Germans. The idea that medium tanks should lead the advance into the teeth of strong antitank defenses also proved a bloody failure. The organization in late 1943 of the standardized tank battalion and a modified doctrine sought to address these problems.

The mission of the standardized separate tank battalion was outlined in *FM 17-33* (19 December 1944) as follows:

- to lead the attack;
- to support by direct fire the advance of light tanks, other medium tanks, and ground troops;
- to feel out the enemy and develop weak spots;
- to serve as a reserve for exploiting a success or breaking up a counterattack against the supported unit;
- to accompany the infantry and assist the advance by destroying or neutralizing automatic weapons and pillboxes holding up the advance;
- to fight enemy tanks when necessary;
- to reinforce artillery fires; and
- to assist the infantry in mop-up.

Wayne Robinson, who served with and wrote the informal history of the 743d Tank Battalion, described a separate tank battalion's role in these terms (tankers during the war overwhelmingly used "doughboy" or "dough" as slang for the infantryman, as did many infantry officers; the postwar favorite "GI" never appears):

A separate tank battalion assigned to work with an infantry division fought at the foot soldier's pace. Its job was to give the doughboy's attack the added punch that tanks have, to bull ahead when the going got rough, to knock down houses Jerry tried to use as forts, to stop enemy tanks in the counterattacks, to spearhead a way for the doughboy and his rifle, his machine gun, and his mortar. . . . Often the doughboy regiment and its attached tank battalion slugged it out with the Jerry on the line for days, inching painfully ahead to engineer an opening in the enemy defenses through which the star ball carriers, the armored divisions, could do their free and fancy open-field running. When this happened, it became the job of the doughboy and his supporting tanks to follow up as fast as they could, moving behind the swift, surging, twenty-mile-a-day drives. The infantry moved and fought, mopping up the pockets of resistance always left in the wake of such drives. But mostly, while the big armor waited in reserve for the quarterback to call their number and set them going through the line, the infantry and the separate tank battalion were in the thick of the line play, fighting and getting hurt, always under fire, within enemy artillery range, doing their work ever at the front of the division's sector.[31]

Robinson's description held true for the tank battalions that fought in the Pacific, as well, except that there were no armored divisions to exploit an opening. The tankers and infantry had to do that, too. By the end of the war, infantry and tank commanders in Europe appended an additional role on the basis of combat experience: transporting infantry on tanks in fast-moving operations.[32]

The results of a doctrinal dispute over whether tanks should fight tanks was to result in tankers in the separate battalions and the armored divisions going into battle with machines designed mainly to destroy targets other than tanks. Maj. Gen. George Lynch, chief of infantry, in July 1940 argued, "[U]narmored antitank units cannot counterattack. . . . The best antitank defense lies in the defeat of hostile armored forces by our own armored units."[33] That same month, Lesley McNair, then a brigadier general soon to become chief of staff at GHQ, countered, "The [antitank] gun, supported properly by foot troops, should defeat hostile armored units by fire and free the friendly armored units for action against objectives which are vulnerable to them."[34] McNair was not hostile to armored forces; he just thought they should concentrate on their comparative advantages.

McNair and his allies ultimately prevailed on most counts, which resulted in the establishment in October 1941 of a separate Tank Destroyer Force charged with battling enemy armor. Tank destroyers were to carry high-velocity guns to kill tanks, while medium tanks would carry the lower-velocity 75-millimeter gun that fired an effective high-explosive round but had more modest penetrating power against armor. Ironically, the first stopgap tank destroyers were equipped with the same 75-millimeter and 37-millimeter guns found in medium and light tanks.

The notion that tanks were enjoined from fighting tanks has become somewhat overblown in the popular perception, as the matter was more one of emphasis. Armored Force *Field Manual FM 17-10*, published in March 1942, specified, "Against equal or superior hostile armored forces, friendly armored units will avoid frontal assault and maneuver to cut off or destroy armored units' supply facilities, followed by blows against the rear of enemy detachments." Tank destroyers were assigned the primary role in defense against hostile mechanized forces, but the manual acknowledged that medium tanks were to protect light tanks from enemy armor and could be "used offensively against hostile tanks."[35]

Moreover, for the infantry-support tankers, tank battles were the exception rather than the rule, and machine guns were usually the most important weapon in the vehicle. Tankers were happy enough with their .30 calibers, which fired more slowly than the German counterpart but were more accurate.[36] Most units carried 50 percent more .30-caliber ammunition than could be contained in organized stowage.[37] Tankers had mixed feelings regarding the .50-caliber gun mounted on the turret top: German soldiers were afraid of it, but a tank could carry only 500 to 600 rounds of .50-caliber ammunition.[38] Tankers in the Pacific and Italy generally viewed the weapon as useless.

Amphibian units appear to have adopted wholesale the doctrine being worked out by the U.S. Marine Corps—which pioneered the use of tracked amphibians—through often-bloody trial and error in the Pacific. When Col. William Triplet arrived at Fort Ord, California, in 1943 to organize the 18th Armored Group (Amphibious) to train amtank and amtrac battalions, he asked what manuals were available. "There are no manuals of any type," he was told. "The Marines are starting to train five battalions at Camp Pendleton, but all they have is the Navy stuff on boat landings. Training manuals will probably be written after a study of your experience."[39] Army manuals on amphibious operations did not even mention landing vehicles, tracked (LVTs)—navy terminology for both amtanks and amtracs. An army history of amphibian battalion training in the Pacific wryly described the instruction available to the first outfits to go into combat as "improvised."[40]

FROM ACTIVATION TO ACTION

As the separate tank battalions stood up, they often obtained cadre troops—those needed to form the organizational skeleton of a unit—from another battalion. An order from Headquarters, Armored Force, on 16 March 1942 indicated that ten of the twelve then-existing separate tank battalions were to be manned at their table-of-organization-and-equipment strength "plus a cadre equivalent over strength" in order to provide trained troops later to newly activated battalions.[41] The 746th Tank Battalion, for example, drew its activating officers from the 760th Tank Battalion and its initial cadre of enlisted men from the 70th Tank Battalion.[42]

William Duncan, who commanded the 743d Tank Battalion after D-Day, described the men who filled his outfit—a similar observation could have applied to most battalions—with regional variations regarding hunting knowledge: "The officers . . . were all products of the university ROTC (Reserve Officer Training Corps) or 90-day wonders of the OCS (Officer Candidate School). The enlisted men on the other hand were volunteers or draftees, but they were all great American youth. . . . A majority of the officers and men were from farms and small towns in the Midwest. When they joined the battalion, they brought with them knowledge of tractors, trucks, and other farm equipment which blended well with the tanks, half-tracks, jeeps, and trucks of a tank battalion. Most also had a basic knowledge of guns from their hunting deer, pheasants, ducks, and rabbits."[43]

Referring to its civilians-become-soldiers, the history of the 726th Amphibian Tractor Battalion records, "[T]hey weren't anybody in particular; they were everybody. . . . They were a cross-section of America."[44]

TANK BATTALION TRAINING

Newly formed battalions typically went through a basic-training regimen of about thirteen weeks and qualification on tank weapons, but the details varied from unit to unit. Most courses were at the battalion's home base, but some officers and men attended the Armored Training Center at Fort Knox. Some outfits had to conduct their own basic training for raw recruits received directly from replacement centers. First furloughs followed the completion of basic training, and for most men, this was the first opportunity to visit their homes as soldiers.[45]

The army's assumption was that six months was the time required to train a unit for combat.[46] Maneuvers followed, normally in combination with a permanent change of station for the battalion. Major maneuver areas included Camp Polk, Louisiana, and the Desert Training Center, which included Camp Young in Indio, California, and Camp Laguna, thirty miles north of Yuma, Arizona. Describing the

Desert Training Center, then-Lt. Raymond Fleig recalled, "The ever-present dust rose in choking clouds as vehicles moved at the pace of a snail. Dust was everywhere; in your eyes, nose, mouth, ears, in the food, your clothing, bedding, weapons, and worst of all the moving parts of machinery."[47]

Several battalions organized in Hawaii, where no such large-scale maneuvers were possible. The 767th Tank Battalion, activated on Oahu, trained there under the oversight of the 4th Armored Group, which as "near as possible," observed the battalion's history, complied with training requirements in the States.[48]

The training that the separate tank battalions underwent was to some extent appropriate for what would come. Brand-new outfits were able to learn the basics of firing and maneuvering as coherent units. Battalions in Hawaii went through weeks of jungle training, which gave men some appreciation for what they were going to face. The tankers in some cases were already learning critical lessons, such as the need to establish direct liaison contact with the infantry. There is no indication in the records, however, that such lessons were pulled together and shared among the tank battalions.

In other respects, the training did not give the soldiers in most outfits a realistic appreciation for—or preparation to handle—the realities they would face in battle. In the worst cases, the training appears to have been simply inadequate or to have created unrealistic notions about the likely course of battle.

Some of the earliest-formed battalions, such as the 193d Tank Battalion, were attached to armored divisions for training. So, too, were some battalions that separated from armored divisions in 1943 yet remained with the old division for training. This guaranteed that they would get little or no instruction on how to work with an infantry division.[49] The army also realized that even subordinating many separate battalions to armored groups removed the tankers from close contact with infantry divisions and that few infantry regiments had trained beside tanks.[50]

By 1943, the army concluded that tank-infantry training in the States was inadequate, and it was recommended that a separate tank battalion be activated jointly with each infantry division. Army Ground Forces mandated that separate battalions be attached to infantry divisions and corps as soon as they completed battalion-level training and anticipated that the reorganization of the armored divisions would release enough such formations to make the idea practical. Instead, the distractions caused by the reorganization prevented such attachments, and few infantry divisions had a chance to work with tanks before they shipped overseas.[51] Homer Wilkes, a lieutenant in the 747th Tank Battalion, recalled that for his outfit, there was no training with the infantry, artillery, or air support, and no amphibious training. Battalion officers on their own taught the men indirect fire with tank cannons.[52]

There were other major shortcomings. Training did not include the use of tanks in towns, which was common in combat.[53] Battalion records provide no evidence that units were given any practice in dealing with known enemy capabilities (beyond basic enemy vehicle identification training) in the tactical or technical sense.

Amphibious Training

Armored Force men engaged in two distinct forms of operations from sea to shore, amphibious and amphibian. Amphibious operations revolved around getting a land force from oceangoing transports to a hostile shore. Amphibian battalions were equipped so that they could conduct amphibious assaults, but they also were able to return to the water under their own power.

The army and navy anticipated that armor would play a role in amphibious assault operations as they geared up for what seemed increasingly likely involvement in a global war. As of 30 September 1941, the two services had obtained only 46 tank landing craft, but they had 101 under construction and 131 funded and awaiting contract; 300 amphibian tractors were under construction, and 188 more were awaiting contract. The number of landing craft of all types available or under procurement was sufficient for three army or marine corps triangular infantry divisions to land nine battalion combat teams each.

The army was deeply involved in obtaining the wherewithal—transports and landing craft—to mount its own amphibious operations to be supported by the navy, and as late as April 1942, it argued that it should be responsible for all amphibious operations in the Atlantic while the marine corps conducted those in the Pacific. Instead, the Amphibious Forces of the Atlantic and Pacific Fleets were established on 14 March and 10 April 1942, respectively, and the navy took responsibility for getting troops onto hostile shores and training the men needed to do that.[54]

Regular tank battalions destined for early amphibious operations practiced landing techniques well in advance. The army had trained one infantry division on each coast for amphibious operations, the 1st Division on the east and the 3d Division on the west. Company A, 70th Tank Battalion, participated in secret amphibious maneuvers with the 1st Infantry Division between 17 June and 16 August 1941, which was the first such training for an American tank battalion. Combat elements underwent additional amphibious training with the Amphibious Force in Norfolk, Virginia, during the spring and summer of 1942.[55]

At the same time, the 756th Tank Battalion underwent amphibious training at Fort Ord, California, with the 3d Infantry Division, with which it would land in North Africa.[56] Then-Lt. David Redle, a twenty-three-old ROTC graduate from Wyoming, recalled that his Company B was attached to the 3d Division on 1 October 1941 and first shipped to Tacoma to qualify all the men as swimmers and conduct initial training with light tanks in Higgins boats, also known as tank lighters. These plywood vessels had a ramp on the front that went down on the beach and allowed men or a vehicle to exit. Upon arriving at Fort Ord, odd-looking wading stacks or shrouds were attached to the backs of the waterproofed M5 light tanks in order to keep water out of the air intake and exhaust when in the surf.[57]

Amphibian outfits first began training at Fort Ord when the North Africa landings were a receding memory, and later battalions trained both there and in Hawaii. The 534th, 715th, and 773d Amphibian Tractor Battalions—the first a reorganized armored infantry battalion and the latter two converted from medium tank battalions—were all designated as such at Fort Ord in October 1943.

The 708th Amphibian Tank Battalion, which received orders for Fort Ord on 27 October 1943, underwent a massive mental and organizational reorientation. Only a month earlier, it had been the 3d Battalion, 69th Armored Regiment, in the 6th Armored Division, with which it had gone through the desert training center equipped with M3 medium tanks. The outfit had been transformed into a separate tank battalion for several weeks before being redesignated for an amphibian battalion.

Instructors from the Marine Corps provided training to the first outfits to reach Fort Ord, where the 2d and 18th Armored Groups were setting up operations. Drivers found that amphibian tanks handled similarly to the land tanks to which they were accustomed, and mechanics learned that the drive trains were about the same as those on light tanks. The former armored infantrymen in the 534th Battalion, however, had to learn everything from scratch.[58]

The 708th Amphibian Tank Battalion shipped out for Hawaii on 9 December, having gotten little more than a month of instruction, followed by the three amtrac battalions. They joined the 4th Armored Group, Combat Training Command, Central Pacific Area, which was organized to train land tank battalions and could provide little help. Upon arrival, the 708th Battalion was alerted for the invasion of the Marshall Islands, while the tractor battalions organized for subsequent landings on Saipan. The amphibian units snagged a Marine Corps veteran of Tarawa, and they patched together a training regimen.[59]

CHARIOTS OF IRON

On 14 June 1940, the army established a technical board to examine the material requirements of the divisions, which laid down several goals. All new tanks would be outfitted with 37-millimeter guns, thicker front armor, and power-traversing turrets while development began on a medium tank mounting a 75-millimeter gun. Diesel engines would power all new tanks (the army would pick gasoline instead). The board also addressed the possibility of mounting flame-throwers in medium tanks, upgrading radio sets, developing observation aircraft with short takeoff and landing capabilities, and improving air-ground communications.[60]

The army owned only sixty-six obsolete M2 and M2A1 medium tanks in June 1940, and ramping up tank production took two years. Ordnance received a $200 million appropriation in August 1939, mostly for tank production, but only

1,467 medium tanks of all types rolled off the assembly lines through 1941. By July 1941, the army still possessed enough tanks to equip only two armored divisions at a time when all branches—plus the British—were demanding scarce production resources to meet their needs.[61]

The first separate tank battalions went to war in the thirteen-ton M3 light tank (nicknamed the Stuart by the British), which was standardized in July 1940 just as the Armored Force stood up. Armor was one and a half inches thick on the front and one inch on the sides, while the turret walls were one inch thick. The vehicle had a 250-horsepower Continental radial aircraft engine.

Four men crewed the M3. The commander had to service the gun, as well as keep track of the battlefield and his own unit's maneuvers. The early M3 lacked an intercom system for the crew, which suggests that the army had not fully realized the vital importance of the men working together as a seamless team in battle.

The turret had a manual traverse system, which was not a terrible deficiency given its small size. The 37-millimeter main gun was installed with a coaxial .30-caliber machine gun. The M3 had stowage for 103 37-millimeter rounds, which would typically be a mix of armor-piercing, high-explosive, and canister shells. Canister, which spewed a cloud of steel balls like a shotgun shell, was highly effective against infantry to a range of 200 yards and could be fired on the move.[62] Four additional .30-caliber machine guns were provided: one in a hull ball mount for the assistant driver (bow gunner or "bog"), two in the side sponsons, and one on the turret roof for antiaircraft defense.

By the time the 70th Tank Battalion landed in North Africa in November 1942, it had received an improved model, the M5 (also called the Stuart). The M5, standardized in February 1942, introduced an improved welded, sloped armor layout and twin Cadillac engines that could move the tank at thirty-six miles per hour. The M5 had a gyrostabilized 37-millimeter main gun and coaxial .30-caliber machine gun, and the bog retained a .30-caliber machine gun in a hull ball mount. The crew could traverse the turret using either a hydraulic or manual mechanism. The vehicle had organized stowage for 123 37-millimeter shells.

The first separate medium tank battalions in both North Africa and the Pacific entered battle in the M3 medium tank (nicknamed the Lee by the British), as the limited number of M4 and M4A1 Shermans were going to the British and the armored divisions. Designers had started with an M2A1 medium tank hull and mounted a 75-millimeter gun on the thirty-ton M3 in a side sponson that allowed only fifteen degrees of traverse in either direction. Atop the tank, a fully traversing turret carried the same 37-millimeter gun used in the M3/M5 light tank series, a coaxial .30-caliber machine gun, and a rotating cupola with a .30-caliber for antiaircraft defense.

Frontal armor was two inches thick, sloped to provide the ballistic protection of four and three-eighths inches, and the sides and rear had armor a half-inch thinner. The nine-cylinder Continental (Wright Whirlwind) R-975-EC2 or R-975-C1 aircraft engine enabled the tank to attain a speed of twenty-six miles per hour on level ground.

Three members of the six-man crew—the commander, a gunner, and a loader—sat in the upper turret. The driver and a radio operator sat forward in the hull, while the 75-millimeter gunner perched to the left of his weapon. The crew had an intercom system.

The first assault gun issued to light and medium tank battalions was the half-track-based T30, a stopgap similar to the ad hoc first-generation M3 tank destroyer. The T30 consisted of an M3 half-track with an M1A1 75-millimeter pack howitzer mounted in the bed pointing forward over the cab.

CHAPTER 2

First Blood

"Good tankers cannot be pre-selected before combat. Only combat can make the selection."

—Pacific Warfare Board,
September 1945

The geostrategic flow of World War II was a healthy environment in which an American armored force could grow from a pup to a mighty beast. Armor is fundamentally about the attack, and American tankers had to spend less than a year playing defense before the United States and the Allies shifted to the strategic offense. The bad phase unfolded in the Pacific, the only place the Axis was able to engage American ground forces when Uncle Sam first entered the war.

DEFENSE OF THE PHILIPPINES

The first separate tank battalions experienced combat within twenty-four hours of the bombing of Pearl Harbor, and in the nation's hour of need, it is perhaps appropriate that the tankers came from the National Guard, called to the colors like their Minutemen forebears. The Guard's tank companies had been tentatively assigned to four tank battalions, the 191st through 194th, in September 1940 and joined those battalions after being federalized in February 1941. At that point, draftees joined the Guardsmen to fill out the ranks. When the shooting started, the only Armored Force battalions abroad were two Guard battalions on Luzon, the largest island in the Philippines.

Rated the best tank battalion in the Army by the training command after being tested at Fort Lewis, Washington, the 194th Tank Battalion drew its men from Guard units around the country. Company C's tankers were Californians, and Company B was filled with Missourians, while Company A hailed from Minnesota. The battalion—minus Company B—received orders for the Philippines

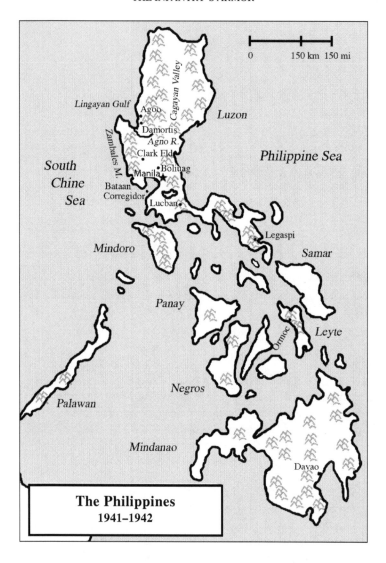

The Philippines
1941–1942

and boarded transports in San Francisco on 8 September 1941. The battalion had surrendered its obsolete M2A2 light tanks (armed only with machine guns) and received fifty-four brand new M3 light tanks with a 37-millimeter main gun. Company B, which was redesignated the 602d Separate Tank Company, Light, was dispatched to Alaska.

"All my life I'd dreamed of going to the South Seas," recalled Ken Porwoll, a tanker in Company A who had joined the Guard to look good in his uniform at its annual dance, the biggest social event of the winter in Brainerd, Minnesota. "So now I thought, 'Now I'm going to get a free trip.'"[1]

The outfit arrived in Manila on 26 September and drove to its new home at Fort Stotsenburg north of Manila. Maj. Ernest Miller tried to ready his troops for battle, but there was a general lack of urgency in higher quarters. The men had never trained on their M3 tanks, but Miller could not do much about that because there was little fuel until 14 November and spare parts took up to thirty days to arrive from depots in nearby Manila. The battalion received no live ammunition until 2 December, and it was able to fire its machine guns and unfamiliar 37-millimeter cannons for the first time only in combat. The only maps available for terrain study came from Atlantic Richfield service stations. Even the tank officers were uncertain about the cross-country limitations of their new M3s, which weighed a ton more than the M2A2s they had used during training.

The 192d Tank Battalion—Guardsmen from Wisconsin, Illinois, Ohio, and Kentucky—reached Manila in late November. Before sailing, men over twenty-nine and married men had been released and replaced by volunteers from the 752d and 753d Tank Battalions. M3 light tanks replaced M2A2s, but the battalion had no time to train on its new mounts. Everyone knew that the idea of one year of federal service was going right out the window.

The newly arrived battalion's Company D was attached to the 194th Tank Battalion to replace Company B so that each outfit had three line companies. The two tank battalions were subordinated to the Provisional Tank Group under Col. R. N. Weaver. Maj. Gen. Douglas MacArthur, who commanded U.S. Forces Far East, exercised direct authority over the tank group, not Maj. Gen. Jonathan Wainwright, who otherwise led ground forces on Luzon. MacArthur told Weaver that he had requested an armored division, but the group never received even the 193d Tank Battalion (Medium) that had been alerted for transfer to the Philippines.[2]

Japanese plans for war against the United States and its allies called for roughly simultaneous attacks on Hawaii, the Philippines, American-held Guam and Wake Islands, and British-owned Hong Kong and Singapore. The United States had foresworn building new fortifications on its Pacific possessions in the Washington Naval Treaty in 1922, and the Philippine government had taken primary responsibility for defense of the islands when granted commonwealth status in 1935. The American war plan for its forces on the islands, code-named Orange, therefore called only for the defense of Manila Bay and critical adjacent areas. The American garrison of about 31,000 men was to withdraw to the Bataan Peninsula and the fortress island of Corregidor. There were no plans for evacuation or relief, and senior commanders had already concluded that the Philippines would have to be sacrificed if Japan attacked. MacArthur convinced Washington to let him adopt a more aggressive strategy, but that hinged on a build-up that would not be completed until April 1942.[3]

The men and 108 tanks and 46 half-tracks belonging to the 192d and 194th Tank Battalions were dispersed around Clark Field, north of Manila, when the Japanese bombed the complex on 8 December. The tankers were guarding thirty-five B-17s and nearly 100 P-40s against paratroopers and saboteurs, blissfully ignorant of the fact that Washington considered them and all the troops around them expendable. The men that morning heard about the attack on Pearl Harbor and knew they were at war. Some of the tankers were just finishing lunch when they heard the sound of engines and spotted bombers far overhead. They thought the planes were reinforcements until bombs exploded among the American aircraft, which were lined up in neat rows to make them easier to protect against sabotage.

Men ran to their machine guns, and soon low-flying fighters strafing the airfield and dive-bombers gave them plenty to shoot at. During the air raid, T/Sgt. Zenon Bardowski of Company B, 192d Tank Battalion, manned a half-track-mounted machine gun on a hill near the end of a runway. A Japanese Zero fighter flew straight down the runway at his half-track, bullets kicking up chips from the surface, but Bardowski stayed in place, blasting away with his machine gun. The fighter burst into flames, passed overhead emitting a trail of smoke, and crashed to the rear. Bardowski had downed the tankers' first enemy aircraft. Private Brooks from the 194th Battalion that day became the first Armored Force soldier to die in combat. The air raids left most of the American air power on Luzon a gutted ruin.[4]

The Great Retreat

Japanese ground forces from Lt. Gen. Masaharu Homma's 14th Army landed at several points on Luzon on 9, 10, and 12 December, followed on 22 December by the main assault at Lingayen Gulf by a force of 43,000 men.[5] The American tanks were soon scattered over 150 miles in support four infantry divisions in the North Luzon Force (under Maj. Gen. Jonathan Wainwright) and two in the South Luzon Force (under Brig. Gen. George Parker Jr.). MacArthur had incorporated the Philippine Army's divisions and the Philippine Scouts into his defense forces, but other than the Scouts, most units were ill trained and poorly equipped. In just the first such tale of many, the tankers and infantry had no joint training, and infantry commanders—most of them American—little understood or even recognized the limitations of tanks. Indeed, at Damortis, one infantry officer approached a Japanese tank to speak to the crew, and several days later, American infantrymen fired on friendly tanks.

Being the most "experienced," the 194th Tank Battalion was sent to join the South Luzon Force. Reconnaissance parties contacted the 41st and 51st Divisions on 13 December, and combat elements arrived the next day. The Japanese had landed at distant Legaspi only the day before, and the tankers found they had no immediate missions.

The 192d Tank Battalion received battle orders upon the landing of Japanese forces at Lingayen Gulf north of Manila. The battalion rolled out to join elements of the 11th Philippine Army Division and the 26th Cavalry, Philippine Scouts, near Damortis, but most of the vehicles ran out of fuel en route. A single tank platoon commanded by Lt. Ben Morin—all that could be fueled for action—rolled north on 21 December to join the 26th Cavalry on orders from Wainwright. Most of the men in the tanks knew each other from Proviso Township High School, classes of 1935 to 1937. The tankers reached Rosario that evening.

The next morning, R. N. Weaver, now a brigadier general commanding the provisional tank group, ordered Morin to attack the Japanese at Agoo, some eight miles farther north. It was believed that the Japanese had not yet brought up artillery or tanks. The tanks departed about 1100 hours and were soon attacked by Japanese planes. Bombs exploded close to the tanks, but they were fragmentation bombs, and the shrapnel merely ricocheted off the armor. Japanese fighters were strafing the cavalry when Morin's platoon arrived, and wounded horses raced around in panic. This was the first view of war for the Guardsmen, and they were mightily upset.

Warned by a cavalryman that he was close to the Japanese, Morin ordered his gunner to fire a test shot from the new 37-millimeter gun, which locked in recoil and remained jammed during the coming engagement. The tankers first came upon Japanese infantry off to the sides of the road. Morin's driver had to maneuver the tank so the sponson-mounted .30 calibers could be brought to bear, and his bow gunner went through several belts of ammunition, despite repeated jams. Morin fired the coaxial machine gun, which was defective and eventually forced him to pull the bolt back by hand for each shot.

About two miles south of Agoo, a shell struck the left side of the hull on Morin's tank and knocked the door in front of the driver loose. The Japanese had indeed brought forward armor, and the first American tank battle of the war was under way. Morin moved his M3 out of the line of fire to fix the door, but a Japanese medium tank rolled from concealment and rammed the American tank, damaging the left front sprocket. When Morin's driver applied power, the tank swung off the road, where several shells hit the right side and rear. One shell set the engine on fire, but a crewman was able to douse the flames with an extinguisher.

The Japanese were using turretless tanks carrying 47-millimeter guns. The American tankers watched in dismay as their 37-millimeter rounds bounced off the sloped Japanese armor, and the platoon started to back to the south. Morin and three of his crewmen were captured, and one man had been killed. The other four tanks were disabled by Japanese fire.

The remainder of the battalion's tanks finally received fuel during the afternoon and deployed to Damortis with orders to cover the retreat of the infantry and cavalry. Cavalry mounts killed by air attacks littered the route forward. The tankers had orders to fight and then "peel off" after the foot troops had passed to the rear.

The situation was so perilous that the 194th Tank Battalion, which had been killing time chasing down flare activity and suspected fifth columnists, was ordered northward on 24 December, without its Company C, to join the 192d Tank Battalion and help stem the tide. By Christmas, two of the 192d Tank Battalion's company commanders had been killed and nine tanks destroyed.[6]

On Christmas night, the Japanese cut off the 194th's Company A when the infantry line to the tankers' right pulled back without alerting the battalion. The

Japanese established a roadblock at Carmen and sighted antitank guns on the road. Lieutenant Burke, who had just taken command, was on the point when the company withdrew toward its next position, and his tank and another fell prey to the ambush. Burke was wounded and taken prisoner. According to one participant, "the balance of Company A made a spectacular dash out, one tank at least going across the whole front, with hostile fire impact and its own return fire making a pyrotechnic spectacle." The infantry blew the bridge across the Agno River after the tanks passed.

Company D—attached from the 192d Tank Battalion—was less fortunate when it reached Moncada at 0800 hours. The infantry had already destroyed the bridges, and reconnaissance uncovered no way to cross because of the steep banks. The commander, Capt. Jack Altman, reluctantly ordered that the tank guns and radios be destroyed, and the men left their tanks and two half-tracks behind them. The Japanese managed to get a handful of the tanks running again and later used them against the Americans on two occasions. After returning to American lines, the crews were used as replacements for losses in other companies.[7]

On 26 December, MacArthur reactivated Plan Orange and ordered the withdrawal to Bataan, where his forces were to hold out and deny Japan the use of Manila Bay. MacArthur ordered Wainwright's northern force to delay the Japanese advance to cover the withdrawal of the southern force onto the Bataan Peninsula. Wainwright then planned a series of fallback lines that he would hold and relinquish in turn. The hasty withdrawal forced units to abandon most of their supplies, which was to have dire consequences.[8] These decisions evidently caused the diversion to Hawaii of the 193d Tank Battalion (Medium), still equipped with light tanks, which sailed on 27 December to reinforce the Philippine garrison.[9]

That same day, Company C of the 194th Tank Battalion joined South Luzon Force elements near Lucena, Paglibo, and Lucban, where they had become engaged. The Japanese 16th Infantry Division had come ashore in southern Luzon two days earlier and was pressing Brigadier General Parker's disorganized forces hard. From the very start, infantry use of the tanks was misguided. The 2d Platoon was ordered to reconnoiter down a trail near Lucban. An infantry major told the platoon commander he could expect to face nothing but small-arms fire, but the tankers instead ran into a roadblock defended by an antitank gun and several hidden field pieces. Antitank fire wrecked the platoon commander's tank and mortally wounded the lieutenant. The commander of the second tank in line pulled around the disabled vehicle and accomplished something called for by tactical doctrine but rarely executed in battle without fatal consequences: he ran over the gun. The four remaining tanks raced forward, but there was no escape other than the track over which they had advanced. The Japanese at the roadblock knocked out the lead tank in line and trapped the others. When the enemy's guns ceased fire, all five tanks were knocked out, and the crews had suffered heavy casualties.[10]

Company C's tankers learned that machine-gun fire striking the sides of their turrets, which were held together by rivets, could knock the rivets loose and send them flying around inside the tank. They also learned that an effective way to eliminate an enemy soldier in a foxhole was to place one tank track over the hole and pivot the tank on the track to dig into the ground. The men slept upwind of the tanks after such action. The Japanese, meanwhile, attacked the tanks with gasoline. A man would rush the tank and try to climb onto the deck, pour the fuel into the engine vents, and set it alight. Tankers at times had to shoot Japanese off the decks of neighboring tanks to protect them.[11]

The men in the Provisional Tank Group fought with rear guards at many points, playing the role of a cavalry delaying force. Each day, men reconnoitered the next fallback position to make sure it provided adequate fields of fire, and the tanks fell back in leapfrog fashion, generally moving at night to avoid Japanese air attack.[12]

The American tankers got in their licks, too, even if the overall situation was deteriorating. Early on 30 December, a Japanese bicycle battalion rode into the overnight bivouac of Company A, 192d Tank Battalion, only to be wiped out by the tankers. The next day, Company C had hidden its tanks among the huts of Baliuag except for two outposts when Japanese tanks approached. The gunners waited patiently while the Japanese closed to within 1,000 yards before opening fire. The first salvos scored no hits, and the Japanese tanks entered town only to be stalked up and down the streets by the American light tanks, which destroyed eight or nine of the attackers. After this action, Brigadier General Weaver, the tank group commander, judged the M3 superior to the Japanese mediums.[13]

On 6 January 1942 at Lubao, Capt. Fred Moffit led two 192d Battalion tanks and two half-tracks, and working with four 75-millimeter self-propelled guns and riflemen from the 31st Infantry, they ambushed some 800 Japanese troops attempting to cut the escape route onto Bataan. The bold action inflicted 50 percent casualties on the enemy and kept the road open for a few more critical hours.[14]

The Siege at Bataan

After suffering heavy losses, the tankers were the last Americans to retreat onto the Bataan Peninsula on 7 January. Just before the final bridge was blown, Maj. Theodore Wickord, commanding the 192d Tank Battalion, crossed it to make certain all the tanks were across. He found one of his platoons lined up along the road, the exhausted crews asleep inside.[15]

The 194th Tank Battalion at this point had lost twenty-six tanks, and the 192d Battalion was down ten. Companies were reorganized to consist of ten tanks, broken into three platoons of three tanks each, plus the company commander's vehicle. Tank tracks were worn down to the metal, and engines were far past their 400-hour maintenance. Now that the long moves were over the support troops were able to deal with these problems.[16]

Bataan juts south like a thumb from Luzon, Manila Bay to the east and the South China Sea to the west. The defense plan established two lines that stretched across the peninsula from bay to sea. The main battle position was located at the base of the peninsula, and the rear battle position was located about halfway to the tip. Wainwright's I Philippine Corps held the eastern half and Parker's II Philippine Corps the western.[17]

Plan Orange foresaw 80,000 troops and 26,000 civilians holding out for six months, but the loss of supplies now hit home. Half-rations were introduced, and Weaver recalled that the effects showed up quickly among his tankers, especially in the form of weakened eyesight.[18] "We were so weak," recalled Sgt. Ken Porwoll, "it took three men to do one man's job."[19]

A Presidential Unit Citation issued to the provisional tank group summarized its role on the peninsula:

> During the period from 6 January to 8 March 1942, after covering the withdrawal of the Luzon Forces into the Bataan Peninsula, this group was charged with the support of the I and II Philippine Corps, the cordon defense of the coasts of Bataan, and the defense of three major landing fields. These measures prevented a projected landing of airborne and paratroop enemy, as well as several abortive thrusts across Manila Bay, any one of which would have meant early disaster in Bataan. Under constant air attack, these units, despite heavy losses in men and material, maintained a magnificent defense and through their ability, courage, and devotion to duty contributed in large measure to the prolonged defense of the Bataan Peninsula.

The Japanese attacked in earnest on 9 January, and by 22 January, they had driven the defenders back to the second line. The tanks were used occasionally to support local attacks, but at times, heavy mining prevented their use. Commanders took steps to remedy the frequent breakdowns in tank-infantry cooperation that emerged during the fighting prior to the withdrawal onto Bataan. The most important step was battalion-by-battalion tank-infantry training to familiarize the infantry with the tanks and their limitations. Articles on coordination were printed in local military publications.

The tankers nevertheless felt that they never received the close infantry support they needed in battle. They found that the infantry did not really want them around except in an emergency because they drew too much artillery fire—a rifle-man's lament that was to recur throughout the war. Brigadier General Weaver identified other problems:

> Crews suffered accordingly from a lack of rest for extended periods, there being no covering troops—as organic to an armored division. The tanks were mistakenly considered invulnerable, self-sustaining fortresses; capa-ble of going anywhere, surmounting extraordinary obstacles; and perform-ing prodigies such as operations against snipers, flushing enemy out of cane fields, patrolling against infiltration—operations stymied by the inher-ent blindness of the tank, the noise of its operation, and its considerable dead space, permitting approach to it by enemy with mines, grenades, flamethrowers—particularly in heavy vegetation, and when the tanks were immobilized by blown tracks or bogging.[20]

From 27 January to 17 February, MacArthur's men fought to destroy Japanese troops who had penetrated the American line only to become lost in the jungle and cut off in what became known as the Battle of the Pockets. The Japanese had dug trenches and foxholes and were nearly impossible to see, much less shoot. From 2 to 4 February, tanks from Companies A and B of the 192d Tank Battalion worked with the infantry in an abortive attempt to wipe out the so-called big (or Toul) pocket. 2d Lt. Kenneth Bloomfield's platoon from Company A attacked with the tank sirens blaring beside riflemen from the 1st Battalion, 45th Infantry, Philippine Scouts, in a coordinated tank-infantry operation. They faced a maze of downed trees hiding snipers and machine-gun nests. The tanks and infantry became separated, the former progressing down a trail to the far side of the pocket with the loss of one M3, but the latter making little progress.

An attack the next day had nearly identical results, again with the loss of a tank. Lt. Willibald Bianchi, an infantryman, was awarded the Medal of Honor for his actions on 3 February while working with the tanks. A tank near Bianchi was having difficulty suppressing its 37-millimeter gun far enough to destroy a machine gun. Already wounded in the hand and chest by bullets, Bianchi climbed onto the deck of an M3 and fired the antiaircraft machine gun at the enemy strongpoint until he was knocked from the tank by a third severe wound.

Although left unmentioned in the army's official history, 2d Lt. John Hay's tanks from Company C also participated in the fight, and the lieutenant is credited with conceiving a nondoctrinal form of tank-infantry cooperation that foreshad-owed practice later in the war. The tankers were to support a group of air corps men who had been converted to riflemen but had no infantry training. By now, it was clear how well dug-in the Japanese were. Hay mounted six riflemen on the back of each tank and provided every man with a sack of grenades. When the tanks rolled forward, the Japanese ducked into their foxholes and dugouts to wait for them to pass. The men on the deck then dropped grenades into the holes. Hay was awarded two Silver Stars for his gallantry during the pocket fighting and was one of many tankers to die in Japanese captivity after the fall of Bataan.[21]

On 12 March, President Franklin Roosevelt ordered MacArthur to leave Corregidor by submarine for Australia, leaving Wainwright in command. That month, Wainwright estimated that 75 percent of his men were no longer fit for duty. The thinking man could see the end in this, and by the time the Japanese began their final attack on 3 April, the defenders were dispirited, as well as exhausted and malnourished.[22]

The 192d and 194th Tank battalions still had tanks in action on 7 April, when the Japanese delivered the coup de grace. When told on 8 April that the surrender order would come the next day, Zenon Bardowski, now a sergeant and tank platoon commander, directed his tank to the shore with the plan of going to Corregidor to fight on. Told there was no room on a barge for him and his men, Bardowski cocked his Tommy gun and convinced the other soldier he was wrong.

On 9 April, the men received the radio code message "Crash"—the order to destroy their vehicles and weapons.[23] Surrender was a hope-crushing fate. Officers' voices cracked as they delivered the news. Some tankers wondered what the folks at home would think of them, while others considered how terrible their fates might be in captivity.[24]

With the end of resistance, the remaining tankers joined the Bataan Death March into a miserable and inhumane captivity. Prisoners were forced to march sixty-five miles to Camp O'Donnell near Manila with almost no food or water and under mistreatment by Japanese soldiers. "Anybody who lagged behind on the first day was shot," remembered Sgt. Ken Porwoll. "After the first day, they just bayoneted you. They didn't think you were worth a bullet."[25]

Some 600 Americans and 5,000 to 10,000 Filipinos died during the march.[26] According to a veteran of the 192d Tank Battalion, tankers removed their Armored Force insignia once they saw that the Japanese were picking tankers out and taking them away, never to be seen again. The tankers had done the Japanese a great deal of damage.[27]

Control of Bataan gave the Japanese firing positions from which to pound the defenses on Corregidor. Nevertheless, the troops on the island, including a handful of men from the 192d and 194th Tank Battalions, held out for another month.

The Japanese began their final attack on 1 May and put troops ashore on 5 May. Sergeant Bardowski's captured tank, manned by Japanese, was the first enemy tank to land on Corregidor. Bardowski, fighting with the 4th Marines, was bayoneted and taken captive when the island fell on 6 May. The intrepid sergeant survived captivity and returned home. Many of his comrades did not. When the war ended and prisoners were liberated, the 192d Tank Battalion's loss became known: 325 of the 593 men who had sailed from San Francisco were dead, most at the hands of their Japanese captors.[28]

NORTH AFRICAN THEATER OF OPERATIONS

The Western Allies took the strategic offensive against Hitler on the periphery in North Africa because they lacked the wherewithal to challenge him yet at the walls of his so-called Fortress Europe. After a somewhat acrimonious debate, the Americans and British agreed to seize the North African possessions of Vichy France. With luck, the French colonial administration would jump to the Allied camp, and a quick push eastward would threaten the rear of Axis forces under the command of Lt. Gen. Erwin Rommel, who was giving the British a hard time in Egypt.

The separate tank battalions had a numerically small but tactically important role in Operation Torch, the Allied landings in North Africa on 8 November 1942. The army intended to use two light tank battalions in the role that amphibian tanks would play in the later stages of the war in the Pacific—to help secure an initial foothold through which following waves of troops and heavier tanks could pass to wage battle inland. It was imperative that troops rapidly clear the beach as they landed, which meant that the infantrymen would need all the firepower they could get to overwhelm initial resistance at the shore. That meant tanks. The aim was to establish a beachhead, which army amphibious doctrine—crafted jointly with the navy—defined as a position organized in depth, with a view to offensive or defensive operations, which protected the beach initially from enemy light artillery fire (range about 10,000 yards) and eventually from medium artillery (range about 15,000 yards).[29]

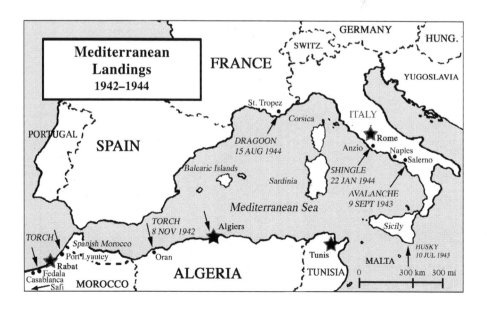

Amphibious doctrine as of 1938 specified certain requirements for landings, all subject to the general principles of war, such as the desire for surprise. The beaches had to be good from the landing fleet's point of view and the interior from the land force's perspective. Naval gun and aviation had to control the area of the objective, damage or weaken resistance on the shore, and support ground forces moving inland. The landing force had to have a reasonably secure line of communication. As soon as the action ashore moved from amphibious warfare to land warfare, the army was to relieve the marines. In the eyes of Adm. Richmond "Kelly" Turner, who commanded numerous operations in the Central and South Pacific, the only substantial change to occur in amphibious doctrine during the war was to the last element, because the army threw itself so deeply into amphibious operations.[30]

The sum total of Allied experience in assaulting a defended shore using tanks was the raid at Dieppe, France, in August 1942. In April of that year, Gen. George Marshall, the army's chief of staff, had sent an American team under Col. Lucian Truscott, a cavalryman who had served with the 1st Armored Division after the creation of the Armored Force in 1940, to London to join the British Combined Operations Command, led by Vice Admiral Lord Louis Mountbatten. The command was responsible for the Commando force and amphibious training. Marshall wanted some American officers to gain battle experience and learn British staff procedures in preparation for what he hoped would be a cross-channel invasion in 1943.

Promoted to brigadier general, Truscott in May and June organized the 1st Ranger Battalion under Maj. William O. Darby to participate in British Commando operations. On 29 June, Truscott and about sixty American officers and men were assigned to Commonwealth units that were to take part in the planned 5,000-man raid on the port of Dieppe. Four days earlier, Mountbatten had also designated a joint "syndicate" of planners to work with American and British planners for Operation Torch; this was soon expanded to four syndicates, including one headed by Truscott that ultimately did much of the planning for Lt. Gen. George S. Patton Jr.

Truscott participated in the Dieppe operation on 19 August, during which a mostly Canadian infantry force, supported by Commandos and the 14th Canadian Tank Battalion equipped with Churchill tanks, assaulted the beach under fire. A light naval bombardment preceded the landings, which also were provided air cover. The affair was viewed by many as bloody failure; 3,400 of the 5,000 men involved were casualties or taken prisoner, and twenty-eight tanks were lost or left behind.[31]

Then-Maj. Theodore Conway, who worked for Truscott and had participated in planning the Dieppe operation, recalled,

Churchill and [Field Marshal Lord Alanbrooke, Chief of the Imperial General Staff] and . . . Truscott all agreed on this point: that we had to learn something about the strength and nature of the German defenses. . . . If we were ever going to land on that defended coast, we had to learn how to undertake an operation against defenses. . . . I think the main lessons came in the area of types of equipment, what do we need to do to waterproof tanks and the like, communications. . . . Truscott's experience in Dieppe had had a great deal of influence on the North African landings. . . ."[32]

Technological limitations in sealift left few options for planners. The infant Allied amphibious force was capable of landing only light tanks aboard available tank lighters, as the medium tanks were too heavy. In the American fleet, the tanks had to be lifted from the holds of transports by cranes and lowered into the lighters waiting alongside.[33] The M5s available to the light tank battalions assigned to Western Task Force, which was to invade French Morocco, were waterproofed, with hooded shrouds attached over the air intake and exhaust so the tanks could run through four-to-five-foot-deep water after leaving the lighters.[34] Medium tanks had to be offloaded at dockside once the infantry and light tanks had secured port facilities.

David Redle of the 756th Tank Battalion (Light), who had experienced loading many times in training, described the process:

Each time the operation took place at night in blackout conditions. They used the ship boom and a winch. The winch operator watched the man next to the edge of the ship. He had to move the tank down to the waiting Higgins boat. He had to be in synch with the boat moving up and down with the swell. If they were out of synch, the thirteen-ton tank would smash the boat. The tank crew was in the bow of the boat. As soon as the tank was in the boat, they moved away from the ship.[35]

Casablanca, the prize in French Morocco, was too strongly defended to be taken by frontal assault, so planners selected from among the small ports north and south of Casablanca two just big enough to handle medium tanks unloaded from transport ships—Port Lyautey and Safi. As Safi was 150 miles southwest of Casablanca and Port Lyautey fifty miles to the northeast, infantry and light tanks were to land at Fedala, only eighteen miles northeast of Casablanca, and wait for the medium tanks to arrive.[36]

Planners adopted another strategy for the landings by Task Force Center at Oran, Algeria, where no ports would be immediately available in the target areas of coast. The 1st Infantry Division was to clear the way for the 1st Armored Division's Combat Command B to land its men and light tanks from Maracaibo transport ships (converted oil tankers).[37] The Maracaibos required seven feet of draft, so pontoon bridges were to be constructed—a task requiring three hours—over which vehicles were to drive to shore.[38] Once the port of Arzew was captured, the medium tanks, which were too large for the Maracaibos, were to disembark.[39]

For the easternmost Allied landings around Algiers, the 9th and 34th Infantry Divisions had contributed one regimental combat team each—the 168th and 39th, respectively—to what was a British-majority enterprise.[40] One company from the 70th Tank Battalion (Light) was attached to the 39th Infantry for the operation, but no American medium tanks were to participate.

The armored force that was to land in Morocco was the best equipped in the Allied invasion force, despite being farthest from the ultimate objective in Tunisia, because its components deployed from the States and had been able to absorb new equipment until shortly before departure. Where the 70th and 756th Tank battalions had new M5s, the 1st Armored Division, which had shipped out from the United Kingdom, retained M3s. The 2d Armored Division fielded the new M4 Sherman medium tank, as well as the M5 light tank. The 1st Armored Division went into battle with M3 medium tanks.

Fleet Tactical Publication No. 167, the bible of landing operations doctrine published by the U.S. Navy in 1941, had stipulated that the landing area was to be prepared by air and naval bombardment so that troops could seize the shore with confidence. On 7 August, at Guadalcanal, the first American amphibious offensive of the war, three cruisers and four destroyers—nearly all the firepower available for the operation from the overstretched, post–Pearl Harbor Pacific Fleet—had bombarded the invasion beaches for seven minutes before the landing craft reached the sand.[41] For political reasons, Operation Torch, the second amphibious offensive, violated this basic tenet of doctrine. Planners hoped the French would not resist vigorously, and there would be no massive bombardment of French soil. Naval units were to fire only when requested to do so by ground forces, at any searchlights, and at any shore batteries that began shooting.[42]

The 70th Tank Battalion entered Africa with the widely scattered regiments of the 9th Infantry Division. The division was split between the eastern and western task forces, and its 39th Infantry was to land nearly 600 miles east of the 47th and 60th Infantry Regiments. Even within the western task force's zone, the 9th Division was spread out, and its regiments were to land well to the north and south of Casablanca. So, too, were the tankers, parceled out one company to each regiment.

Maj. Gen. Ernest Harmon, commanding general of the 2d Armored Division, directed the sub-task force that was to capture Safi, which included the 47th Infantry Regiment. Company B, 70th Tank Battalion, was attached to the 47th Infantry's assault wave, which was to clear the way for Combat Command B of the 2d Armored Division to disembark medium tanks at the docks in Safi. Combat Command B included M4 Shermans from the 2d Battalion (reinforced) of the 67th Armored Regiment.[43]

Landing operations commenced shortly after midnight. The limited training and inexperience of the Western Naval Task Force combined with a heavy swell off shore to cause delays in hoisting the light tanks and other gear into lighters. One platoon of Company B's light tanks joined the 1st Battalion Landing Team, which sailed into Safi Harbor to seize control of high ground just outside of town while special landing groups secured the wharves. Only three of the tank lighters managed to reach Green Beach, and all three tanks were immobilized—one by a drowned motor, one by a faulty battery, and one by soft sand—and the riflemen had to advance under fire without their tank support.[44] The 1st Platoon's tanks, however, reached shore at 0500 hours with the 47th Reconnaissance Platoon; half the command moved into Safi, seized the telephone and telegraph exchange, and knocked out an antitank gun near the post office.

The 9th Division's 60th Regiment, meanwhile, was to land well northeast of Casablanca. At 0130 hours off Port Lyautey, Company C of the 70th Tank Battalion left the transports with the 60th Infantry Regiment as part of Force Goalpost, the main objective of which was to capture an airfield near the port. Twelve tanks were put ashore—one tank was swamped with the loss of all crewmen—and the Americans easily established a beachhead.

Planners knew that the French regiment defending the airfield could be reinforced by a battalion of forty-five light tanks by late on D-Day and by another half battalion the next day. Brig. Gen. Lucian Truscott, commanding the 60th Infantry, had known he would need tanks of his own, and in addition to Company C, he had a battalion-size landing team from the 2d Armored Division's 66th Armored Regiment assigned. The armor was to guard the south flank, which was effectively Truscott's rear once he was able to drive on the airfield.

The 60th Infantry Regiment was unable to secure all of its D-Day objectives, notably the Kasba, a walled fortress straight out of *Beau Geste*. A shortage of lighters had allowed only seven M5s from the 66th Armored Regiment to reach the beach. Ominously, French troops appeared from the direction of Rabat before nightfall, supported by Renault light tanks.[45]

Companies A and C, 756th Tank Battalion (Light), landed with the 3d Infantry Division at Fedala—the main landing for the capture of Casablanca—to be followed by the 1st Battalion, 67th Armored Regiment. Company B had been left at Camp Pickett for lack of shipping space. The command collectively was known as Brushwood Force. Then-Col. Ben Harrell, who functioned as the G-3 of the II Corps and then the 3d Infantry Division during the planning phase, said, "Well, of course this was the first time any of us had done it, and we made our mistakes in our plans and carrying them out. . . . I made the small boat employment plan, and on paper it looked pretty good, but the thing was too damned complicated. . . . When we were coming in to land, the whole task force was scattered all over hell."[46]

Indeed, the plan called for each battalion landing team to be supported by between forty-three and forty-five personnel landing craft and from five to nine tank lighters.[47] The landing craft were loaded with tank-infantry teams rather than just vehicles. Each had a single M5 tank aboard, plus fifty infantrymen.[48] As it turned out, the navy and army commanders agreed that the convoy was too disarranged for the plan to ever work, and they ordered transports to unload troops into whatever landing craft were available, which meant that most formations arrived on shore incrementally.

The neophyte character of the American amphibious capability became clear to the tankers almost immediately. 2d Lt. John Rutledge, commanding the 2d Platoon of Company A, heard the wave commander and the coxswain talking at the back of the landing craft, and by and by, the coxswain asked Rutledge whether any of his men could read a compass. Fearing he might lose a man to the navy, Rutledge disingenuously replied no. The navy turned the assault wave 180 degrees about and started, the commander imagined, toward the beach. A destroyer loomed out of the dark, and its crew warned that the assault wave was headed toward South America. A turnabout put the landing force in the right spot, but late and in a confused state.[49]

The landings were a disaster in terms of lost landing craft at the hands of inexperienced crews and drowned infantrymen dragged to the bottom by their heavy loads.[50] Only five light tanks reached shore, but fortunately, the French had few tanks of their own in the area.[51]

Those five tanks—Rutledge and his platoon—rolled off the tank lighters at about 0830 under fire from coastal defense guns on and near Cape Fedala and quickly became engaged just as the army had intended the infantry tanker to be. The tanks drove off the beach, crossed a low hill, and stopped so the crews could remove the waterproofing. Col. William Wilbur, the commander of the 7th Infantry Regiment, drove up. He introduced himself and said there were some guns in Fedala that were shooting up his boys and asked what the tankers were going to do about it. Some readers will be relieved to know that there ensued a brief discussion of doctrine and its relationship to real-world battlefield needs. Rutledge described what happened:

> I informed him that our 1st Platoon was supposed to be handling that part of it, and that Armored Force tactics frowned upon taking tanks into towns. He said that we were the only tanks on shore at that time, and that we were the only ones to do the job. He outlined the situation and said, "Lets go get them."
>
> One of my tanks had strayed away after landing. However, the remaining four tanks proceeded toward Fedala. Colonel Wilbur rode on the outside of my tank. . . . We proceeded into town, where we met Lt. Col. [Roy] Moore, 1st Battalion, 7th Infantry Regiment. Watches were coordinated and arrangements made to meet the infantry battalion in front of the guns in twenty minutes. . . .
>
> At this time, my platoon sergeant's tank "shorted" out. The remaining three tanks proceeded to a point in the formal gardens back of the church there, where we took up defilade positions behind the hedge and opened fire on some guns in the southwest portion of Fedala near the harbor master's house. . . .

Colonel Wilbur and I went forward on foot to some houses just west of Rue de Reims to reconnoiter. While climbing atop a house in order to better observe the situation, we were fired on by an enemy machine gun, the bullets passing between Colonel Wilbur's feet and over my head. We returned to the ground. . . .

Upon arriving at the last row of buildings in front of the guns, I lost track of Colonel Wilbur. I looked over the situation and found the infantry under fire from pillboxes. Two of the three tanks reduced the pillboxes and snipers' positions, while the remaining tank crashed through the barbed wire barricade, thus opening the position to the infantry.[52]

The French 100-millimeter gun battery surrendered. Wilbur was awarded the Medal of Honor for this and several other acts of bravery during the landing.[53]

The 7th and 15th Infantry regimental landing groups received orders at 1600 hours to advance on Casablanca. In the 7th Infantry's zone, the light tanks from the battalion landing teams were pulled back into regimental reserve near the command post, and nine more from Company C were shifted there from the 30th Infantry Regiment.[54]

The importance of having even a few tanks present during an assault landing became apparent in the one place the tanks did not arrive as planned. A lighter-borne landing by Company A of the 70th Tank Battalion east of Algiers with the 9th Infantry Division's 39th Infantry Regiment took place belatedly because the ship carrying the company was disabled by a torpedo before it reached the objective.[55] Beach conditions prevented the deployment of antitank guns by the infantry. As a result, when both the 1st and 3d Battalions encountered small numbers of French tanks, they had no weapons to deal with them. The threat of attack by a mere three tanks stopped the 1st Battalion's advance on Algiers. Fortunately, when the 3d Battalion approached its initial objective at an airfield, French tanks there fired a few token rounds and withdrew.[56]

Like everyone else on the American side in Morocco, the tankers were somewhat more organized by D+1. Companies A and C of the 756th Tank Battalion were attached to the 7th Infantry Regiment, which formed the main effort of the 3d Division's advance that day along the coast toward Casablanca.[57] They do not appear to have engaged the enemy, however, and one of the few references to their activities was a lament in the report of the 10th Field Artillery Battalion: "Wire was continually being torn up by tanks or by natives cutting out sections for clothes lines."

At 0800 hours, the 70th Tank Battalion's Company C, along with the 9th Division's 60th Infantry Regiment at Port Lyautey, attacked a French armored column five miles south of Mehdia, which itself lies just west of Port Lyautey. Seven light tanks from the 2d Armored Division—no more had been able land overnight because of strong surf—had driven off an earlier attack by French light tanks and infantry, but Truscott realized they needed help and sent Company C to join them. The French were well camouflaged in a cactus patch, and one M5 tank was lost and all crew members seriously wounded. Lieutenant Herbert, commanding Company C's tanks, rallied his men and dispersed the enemy. This was a hard first lesson in the effectiveness of camouflage.

After the French armor drew off, the company headed across country to an assembly area with the 1st Battalion, 60th Infantry, to support the attack on the airfield. The tankers chanced upon two companies of French infantry approaching the 1st Battalion from the rear and pounced. The outmatched French drew off after a sharp exchange of fire but left behind many prisoners.

The next morning, 10 November, the company successfully neutralized machine-gun nests, assault guns, and antitank guns near Port Lyautey. The tanks then moved into defensive positions at the airport outside the city.[58]

French commanders ended resistance in Algiers late on 8 November and ordered a ceasefire throughout North Africa on 10 November. Days of political disarray and confusion followed, but the French in North Africa had cast their lot with the Allies.[59]

The first Allied offensive had achieved its initial objectives, but it was already clear that the Americans had much to learn. Patton told observers from Washington that had the landings been opposed by Germans, "we never would have gotten ashore."[60] Major General Harmon wrote to a friend in December, "Really, I wonder how we will do against real opposition. I am greatly worried."[61]

The deployment of light tanks with the assault wave had gone poorly at most locations, and the need to capture docks to off-load medium tanks made the heavier armor unavailable for hours even in the best of circumstances. The fact that the French had been ill equipped with armor in the areas where American tanks had been unable to support the assault infantry had obscured the lesson. At the one place that French armor appeared in force—Port Lyautey—fortune dictated that the handful of 70th Tank Battalion and 2d Armored Division light tanks were just enough to deal with them.

German combat aircraft and a handful of troops began landing at an airfield near Tunis on 9 November, the first of 15,500 reinforcements—including 130 tanks—that arrived by the end of the month. Nine thousand Italian troops also moved in, most having shifted west from Tripoli. British forces, meanwhile, advanced from Algiers by land and by short seaborne and airborne hops. Thanks in part to the Axis incursion, the Allies persuaded the French in North Africa to join their cause formally as combatants on 13 November. On 17 November, a German parachute battalion encountered French holding forces and the British spearhead at Medjez el Bab. The bold German commander bluffed the Allied forces into pulling back.[62]

The real war for North Africa was about to begin. Eisenhower noted in his after-action report on Operation Torch that Prime Minister Winston Churchill had anticipated as much during the planning phase, commenting, "Well, if the enemy rushes into Tunisia, where he can probably forestall us if he so determines, where is a better place to kill Germans?"[63]

On 4 December, Hitler ordered that all Mark VI Tiger tanks that had been shipped to Italy be sent to the newly formed Fifth Panzer Army in Tunisia rather than to the German-Italian Panzer Army fighting Montgomery's Eighth Army.[64] American tankers were destined to find out that there was a top league of tank design that their own side had not even considered when designing their machines.

By 10 December, a combination of German resistance and horrifically wet weather had combined to stop the Allied advance toward Tunis. None of the separate tank battalions were involved in this phase of the campaign. One reason for this was probably the inability of the logistic chain to sustain more American tanks than those of the 1st Armored Division at the far end of the rickety, British-run French colonial rail line. For about the first six days of December, Eisenhower reported to the War Department, tank losses amounted to approximately forty, and the accumulated need for replacements at the front equaled a tank battalion. The U.S. Army in North Africa lacked a tank transport unit able to move even a single battalion of medium tanks, a shortfall that would not be remedied until spring 1943.[65] A War Department observer reported that as of January 1943, Combat Command B of the 1st Armored Division was still short on vehicles and was cannibalizing those destroyed by enemy fire to obtain spare parts.[66] That same month, the 1st Tank Group, which had just arrived at Oran from the United Kingdom with the 751st, 752d, and 755th Tank Battalions, had to surrender fifty-four M3 medium tanks to be rushed to the front as replacements.[67]

A dowdy band of American tankers nevertheless was about to stake one small claim to the war in Tunisia on behalf of the separate tank battalions.

A Very Separate Tank Company
On 13 December, Company A, 70th Tank Battalion, in Algiers received orders to head to the front, where on 26 December it was attached to the 16th French Infantry Regiment along with Company A, 601st Tank Destroyer Battalion. The first action the next day was something of a debacle, as seven tanks were stranded on the far side of a river and abandoned. Fortunately, the company was able to recover them the following day.

The French XIX Corps, despite a hodge-podge mixing of national units that developed, can be said to have held what became the central stretch of the Allied line, with the British on the left along the coast and, from mid-January 1943, the U.S. II Corps to the right. On 27 December, French forces launched a limited offensive along the Eastern Dorsal mountain chain that ran like a wall before most of the Allied front. Company A's tankers had only slightly better luck than in their

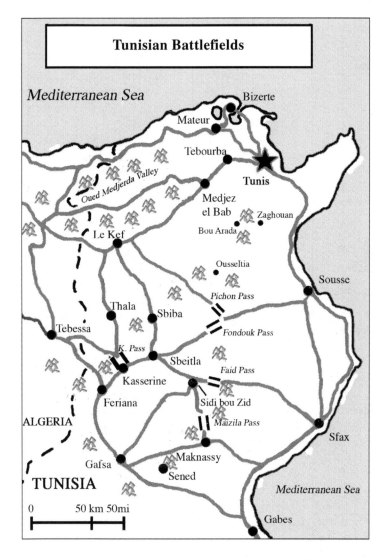

first engagement when, on 29 December, they attacked 200 Afrika Korps troops supported by mortars and antitank guns near Pichon Pass, Tunisia, under cover of a bombardment by two batteries of French 75s. The tanks achieved a penetration of 3,000 yards, but the inexperienced tankers learned a hard lesson. For reasons no one could reconstruct later, two M5s veered off and headed for a hill where the Germans had hidden an antitank gun. Antitank fire claimed both M5s, as well as the T30 assault gun, which was picked off unnoticed at the back of the column along with its entire crew.

Lt. Franklin Anderson recalled, "We didn't know where [the two tanks] had gone because of our maintaining radio silence. This was . . . a mistake, and one we didn't make again. We were new to combat, and I guess were afraid of our radio communications being intercepted. This was our baptism of fire, and we were up against veterans. We learned from our mistakes, but it was a costly lesson."[68] According to a hand-written manuscript in the battalion's records, probably drafted by company commanding officer Capt. Ralph Lennon, "During this period, our tanks came under heavy air and artillery attack. The Pichon-Ousseltia road was strafed constantly."

Sparring along the French line continued through mid-January, as the Germans sought to reverse local French gains. On 5 January 1943, the Germans attacked the French and Company A at Fondouk with thirty-two medium and light tanks and drove the defenders out. When the Allies fought their way back two days later, the graves of three crewmen from one lost tank were found with a note reading, "Here lie three valorous American panzer soldiers who fell on 29 December 1942."[69]

The Germans mounted a substantial counterstroke against the southern end of the British zone and against the French on 18 January. Three groups, each backed by panzers including Mark VI Tigers, made little progress against the British but punched a hole in the French line. The next day, reconnaissance revealed that German armor and motorized infantry were entering the Ousseltia Valley.[70]

Eisenhower had counted on the French being able to fight in the mountains, where German armored strength counted little, and viewed French forces as too ill equipped to fight in the valleys. A program to rearm the French had gained approval from the Joint Chiefs of Staff only two days earlier, but the execution would require months. The British 6th Armored Division sent a squadron of tanks and some artillery to aid the French, and a battalion of the 1st Guards Brigade had already moved into the area.[71]

On 20 January, about fifteen miles northeast of Ousseltia, six M5 tanks from the 70th Tank Battalion's Company A were used as bait to draw German panzers into range of the tank destroyers and some British 6-pounder antitank guns. This was, in fact, a sound tactic according to existing doctrine, but the tankers evidently found the experience so harrowing that the battalion never again risked its tanks as bait for panzers or antitank guns.[72]

The situation had become sufficiently alarming that Eisenhower's forward command post arranged to put the 1st Armored Division's Combat Command B at the disposal of the French XIX Corps, and the combat command drove into the Ousseltia Valley on 21 January.[73]

Capt. Ralph Ingersoll was passing through the II Corps' rear headquarters at Tebessa in late February when he encountered a supply-gathering team from the 70th Tank Battalion and received a quick oral history of the company's fight in the Ousseltia valley—and of the arrival of Combat Command B.

The other guest in the mess tent was a second lieutenant with a story. . . .
The lieutenant was about twenty-five, sunburnt and solid. . . . He was the executive officer of the only American company of light tanks in action

in Africa [*sic*]. . . . It had been attached to the French at the beginning of the campaign. . . . It got neither mail nor orders; it drew neither pay nor supplies—and it ate French food. . . .

The American light tanks had made ten attacks, and every fourth man in the little company had been decorated by the French government. It was all the Frenchmen could do to show their appreciation. The Americans had been fighting German Mark IVs and, lately, some 60-ton Mark VIs. The solemn, sunburnt lieutenant shook his head between mouthfuls and said:

"It's discouraging. The fellows are awful good shots, but when they make direct hits, the shells just bounce off. . . ."

So the officers at the mess asked the lieutenant what he did about it, anyway.

He said, "Oh, there's always something you can do about it, but it's discouraging. You can hide most of the tanks, and if the Mark IVs will chase the others, you can get in behind and blow up a few trucks before you have to beat it."

And then he cheered up and said brightly, "We got a Mark VI last week."

"How did you do it?" I asked.

"Well," he said, "we tried running like hell when they chased us and dropping antitank mines behind us as we ran. We tried dropping them off in bunches. One of those big bastards ran on three mines all at once and it blew off a tread. Then we sneaked around the other side and kept popping at it until it went up."

The American company had lost about one-fourth of its tanks. The others, we gathered, were kept running by sheer ingenuity and spare parts salvaged from the battlefield.

The month before, the Germans . . . had wedged and chivied and herded the Americans down into [the Ousseltia] valley. There the Americans had a little Arab village to hide in, but the German tanks were all around them now and could sit out of range and blow up the village, house by house.

"And, by God," said the lieutenant, "what do you suppose happened then . . . ? It was just like a wild-west movie. Just exactly. There was a road from east to west across one end of the valley, and that afternoon the whole damned 1st Armored Division of the United States Army came up that road. . . . [W]e didn't know they were coming, and they didn't know we were there, and the Germans didn't know they were coming, either. We would have liked to have gone along with them," he said ruefully, "but after they went by, we had to go back to that French chow."[74]

Joined by elements of the 1st Infantry Division, Combat Command B threw the Germans back into the mountains by 29 January, but the Germans retained the passes. The Allies that day decided to pull most French units back from the line to reorganize and reequip.[75]

On 14 February 1943, the Axis launched a crushing counterattack against the II Corps that came to be known as the Battle of Kasserine. In five days, mainly German forces sent American troops reeling back to the west side of Kasserine Pass and destroyed almost half the tanks possessed by the 1st Armored Division. Only the threat posed to the German rear by Montgomery's Eighth Army forced an end to the Axis rampage.[76]

The 1st Armored Division, which had fought while broken up into four combat commands scattered across the battlefield, admitted that it had suffered defeat in detail.[77] The battle was the hardest lesson an armored division would suffer in the school of hard knocks, and it provided some of the key lessons that the army drew from North Africa. The separate tank battalions, however, had not gone through that school yet.

Company A continued to fight beside the French in the Ousseltia Valley in March, buttressed by a squadron of British Churchill tanks that had enough armor and firepower to stand up to German panzers. On 26 March, the company carried French infantry into the attack against some high ground near Sidi Bou Rhrib in the Ousseltia Valley, which appears to have been the first use of tank-borne infantry tactics by an American armored unit outside the Pacific.[78]

Often within the U.S. Army, it seemed that the infantry commanders and tankers spoke different languages. Company A was fighting beside a French-speaking force in which the colonial troops sometimes did not even speak much French. A French-speaking Canadian in the tank company acted as interpreter, and while the Americans found his English difficult to understand, the French doubtless were having similar problems grasping his Canadian French. Everyone did the best he could to understand orders given and comply with them, but it was not easy.

French colonial forces, moreover, like many of their American counterparts, had apparently never trained with tanks, and officers tended to misuse them as forward outposts or pillboxes with no infantry support. Captain Lennon evidently protested these incidents to the point where the French asked that he be relieved.

On 30 March, Capt. Atlee Wampler assumed command. In his first encounter with the French infantry commander, he was ordered to attack at dawn but was not even told from where. A liaison officer led the tanks into position after dark. The tankers emerged from the attack unscathed, but Wampler realized he had to do something. He confronted the French infantry colonel and demanded that henceforth he be included in planning for all operations involving his tanks. After threatening to sack Wampler, too, the Frenchman backed down, and coordination improved markedly.[79]

All this while, the tank company had been an orphan of the U.S. Army, forced to rely on the French for rations and on long hauls to the American rear for military supplies. In late February, a colonel from the U.S. II Corps headquarters agreed to let the company send its one remaining truck in weekly to pick up supplies.[80] On 11 March, the II Corps finally attached Company A for administration and supply. Patton, commanding the corps and a tank man himself, took pity on the company and told his staff to do what it could. The company received its first five replacements for tanks lost in battle on 5 April, and the first personnel replacements arrived five days later. This improvement lasted only until the third week of April, when the II Corps shifted north to the coast to attack toward Bizerte.[81]

The final phase in the battle for Tunisia began in April. The French XIX Corps, however, played a secondary role in Allied plans, and relegated to holding the wall of a Fifth Panzer Army salient, its advances in late April were largely the result of German withdrawals caused by British gains farther north.[82]

On 6 April, the British 6th Armored Division relieved the American tankers, but they were attached to the British to protect their left flank during the advance. Company A counted the loss of one more M5 to antitank fire and another to a mine. On 22 April, the tankers were sent to rejoin the French four miles southwest of Bou Arada and became part of the Oran Division's *Groupement Blindé Français*, commanded by Colonel Le Coulteux de Caumont. The armored group, formed on 13 April, additionally consisted of three French tank squadrons (companies) equipped with 1940-vintage Somua S-35 tanks and British Valentines.[83]

Here, the company again experienced frequent strafing and bombings. Beginning four days after its attachment, the tankers supported a French offensive that led to the capture of Zaghouan, where the company accepted the surrender of the German garrison.

On 11 May, with the last German resistance in Tunisia collapsing, Company A shared the glory of taking prisoner 7,000 troops from the Hermann Göring Division and 1,500 Italian troops.[84] The company finally rejoined the 70th Tank Battalion in late May. The battalion's history recorded, "The first echelon arrived during the afternoon meal, and the men finished quickly and ran to talk with their friends in Company A. 'How was it?' everyone wished to know. The answer was written all over their faces. It was good to get back to the battalion."[85] In June 1943, the 70th Tank Battalion finally gathered all of its strength in one place for the first time since September 1942.[86]

An Infantry-Support Battalion in the Desert

In the midst of the Battle of Kasserine, the 751st Tank Battalion (Medium) was sent to the front, departing Algeria on 18 February and moving its vehicles by rail and water. The battalion had arrived at Oran a month earlier, and the other two separate tank battalions in the 1st Tank Group had had to pool equipment to bring the 751st Battalion up to authorized strength.[87]

On the first day of March, the 751st Tank Battalion moved into bivouac with the 34th Infantry Division in what came to be known as "Stuka Valley" near Rohia, Tunisia.[88] Three times a day at chow time, a dozen Stukas would appear overhead and attack the area. The first time this happened, the tankers dove into their M3 medium tanks, which they realized was a mistake. They next day, machine guns on fifty-four mediums blazed away at the aircraft and shot down four. Thereafter, the *Luftwaffe* avoided the 751st Tank Battalion and went after less dangerous targets.[89]

In the atmosphere of recent crisis, the battalion was told it would be used defensively or for limited counterattacks. Once the Allies regained the initiative, it would provide close support to the infantry.

Battalion men saw action for the first time on 5 March near Pichon Pass, when Company A covered the withdrawal of a 135th Infantry Regiment task force, during which one man was killed and two wounded and a half-track destroyed. On 30 March, Company C and the mortar and assault gun platoons worked with a company from the 109th Engineer Battalion and some tank destroyers to clear a slope near Fondouk. The mission succeeded, but German fire set two medium tanks on fire. These were sobering first contacts with the enemy.[90]

As the Allies did retake the initiative, the 34th Infantry Division, attached to British 9 Corps for the operation, sought to capture a strategic gap at Fondouk through the Eastern Dorsal Mountains, which would give the Allies access to the Tunisian coastal plain on the far side and present an opportunity to sever Rommel's supply line. A regiment of the 999th Africa Division, consisting largely of German soldiers who had been court-martialed but allowed to redeem themselves in combat, defended the area. An assault on 27 March by the 135th and 168th Infantry Regiments to capture the high ground south of the gap came to naught.[91]

On 8 April, the 751st Tank Battalion supported the 34th Infantry Division's 133d and 135th Infantry regiments in a second attack to take the high ground, Djebel El Aouareb, south of the Fondouk Gap. The British 128th Infantry Brigade was to make a simultaneous assault on the heights north of the pass, and the British 6th Armored Division was to enter the gap once both sides were secure. Although the 135th Infantry Regiment had entered the line in the Pichon sector on 14 February, the failed attack on 27–28 March had been its only offensive operation, so while the regiment was not quite green, it was close, and it had not yet worked with tanks. The neighboring 133d Infantry, just to the south, was in similar circumstances.

This operation was not going to be easy, experience aside: the Germans held the high ground in strength, amply supported by artillery and mortars, and apparently unknown to the Americans, they had arrayed machine-gun and antitank positions protected by minefields on the flat area before the slope from which they could unleash grazing fire. The Americans, attacking nearly due east, would have to cross more than three miles of level ground with only occasional cactus patches and hummocks to provide concealment.

The difficulties that inexperienced outfits often encountered became visible fairly quickly. The 135th Infantry Regiment's artillery started a barrage at 0630 on that April morning, and three hours later, division artillery joined the action and pounded the rightmost company of the 3d Battalion, which was to conduct the assault. The regiment was evidently surprised that a promised air strike failed to materialize, although the 9 Corps had informed the 34th Division of the cancellation hours before the start time. At 1130 hours, the 3d Battalion reported that it was making slow progress, and the division headquarters ordered the attack to continue "at all costs." Still, the attack stalled—as did the 133d Infantry's—and Col. Robert Ward, the regimental commanding officer, decided to commit his 2d Battalion next to the 3d Battalion.

Shortly before the new kickoff, Brig. Gen. Benjamin Caffey, the assistant division commander, drove to the 135th Infantry's command post, called the battalion commanders, and told them the objective had to be taken that day. So far, the 751st Tank Battalion had been held in reserve. PFC Francis Sternberg recalled the day's events:

[A]t 0545, our artillery opened up on Fondouk Gap. They shelled the mountain all morning. In a little while, we would get our orders. We checked everything and for the thousandth time wiped the sand out of our guns. All of us were eager to get going. We had grown tired of hiding in the cactus patches for the past two weeks. We were excited, but nobody was scared. . . .

At about 2 o'clock in the afternoon. . . I heard the battalion commander's voice on our loudspeaker: "Turn 'em over and roll out!" That is the tank corps' informal assault order. We grabbed the camouflage net and yanked it off the tank, jumped in, and buttoned up. The driver, Sgt. John Lippert, kicked the motor to life and rolled us up into line formation.[92]

At 1715 hours, tanks were committed to the attack for the first time, and events suggest that no real effort was made to coordinate operations with the infantry. Lt. Col. Louis Hammack was going to fight his tanks as a battalion—a rare experience for a separate tank battalion commander, as things turned out. The tanks moved out, Companies A and B in the lead with Company C following, all arrayed in wedge formation with Hammack's command tank positioned between the two waves, and they reached the base of the objective, where the tanks fired at suspected targets.[93]

Sternberg continued his tanker's eye story:

Our . . . tanks, one following the other with a distance of 100 yards in between, moved up past the infantry and headed on toward the base of the mountain. . . .

The Germans are coming through the pass in great numbers. I can see their guns spouting fire. Stukas appear overhead, zooming every which way. [Lieutenant Bruce] Foster turned to us.

"Hold your fire, fellows. Wait until they come within range. . . ."

Our first burst of fire was terrific. The ground shook. . . . The valley is so full of smoke now it is obscuring our vision. Onward we move. Our big guns are really laying it on, the sounds are deafening. . . .

I can see some of our tanks hit, the crews jumping out and beginning to dig foxholes. Ugly red flames dart through the hatch, then mysteriously flash from the sides until it is a molten mass. Through my peep hole, I can see some of our tanks moving up on the right side of the pass in an attempt to cut off the Jerries. . . .

The tanks reformed into a horseshoe formation as they drew near the base of the mountain. When we were almost there, the Nazis opened up. It came from all sides. They had everything trained on us, including powerful 88s. The first shell tore off one of our tracks, and the tank swerved and came to a stop.[94]

More shells struck the crippled tank and set it on fire. The gunner fell dead across the breach of his 75-millimeter. Sternberg, already wounded and with his uniform burning, climbed through a hatch that had been blown open. Foster followed, only to be killed by machine-gun fire. The other crewmen made it out, but all the survivors had suffered serious injuries and burns.

Only the infantry on the right wing was able to follow, two other companies being thrown back, and the tankers had to withdraw. During the attack, six tanks struck mines and one was disabled by antitank fire, resulting in five men killed and six wounded. Ward lost contact with all of his infantry battalions after dark, probably because tanks had cut the phone lines.[95]

The events of 9 April are somewhat confused, and the official U.S. Army history sheds no light on the matter. The tankers supported two attacks that day, and they reached the objective both times, but tank-infantry cooperation was nonexistent where and when it was needed.

At 0640 hours, according to the infantry account, the 1st Battalion, 135th Infantry, clawed its way to the top of its first objective, Hill 254. None of the tanks had been assigned to support this attack, however, and the doughboys were left to their own devices. The Germans counterattacked, and by 1015, the GIs had been forced back off the hill. Soon the 1st Battalion was being shelled and hit by Stukas and reported heavy casualties.

The tank battalion's after-action report indicates that the M3 Lees, meanwhile, attacked at about 0900 out of the 133d Infantry Regiment's zone. Lt. Thomas Rutledge said several days later,

One thing that I have learned: The next time we move up, before we close up on the objective, it is a good thing to look down on the ground in front of the objective, and if you see anything that looks like the enemy or enemy guns, fire away at it with canister. We were so close that with keen observation, even two or three rounds or some machine-gun fire would have downed many machine guns. I believe this would save us a lot of grief afterwards. We know there are lots of mines, but when approaching the objective, we seem to forget those machine guns. So instead of covering the ground in front of the objective with machine-gun fire, we thought only of the objective, which was on the hill.[96]

The tanks reached the base of the hill bereft of infantry support, in great measure because of the German machine-gun nests that the tankers had ignored. Rutledge had also bypassed several antitank guns, and he spotted one thirty yards away. His gunner put a 75-millimeter round into the German position. The tanks could not climb the 200-foot height and pulled back after exchanging fire for some twenty minutes. Two tanks hit mines, and another two collided and were disabled. The intact German machine guns kept the crews that bailed out pinned down until dark.[97]

According to tanker records, the afternoon attack began at 1215. The 135th Infantry's journal refers vaguely to a "tank battle" being underway during the afternoon. The 34th Infantry Division's soldiers were supposed to follow the tanks but once again could not because of machine-gun fire and mines. The remaining tanks pulled back, and the division did not take the pass until 10 April.[98]

The 751st Tank Battalion had lost sixteen tanks during its first big fight—nearly the strength of one of its companies.[99] Fortunately, replacement crewmen who arrived were good ones, drawn from the 2d Armored Division, which was sitting idle on occupation duty on the border of Spanish Morocco.[100]

The 751st Tank Battalion next saw action with the 9th Infantry Division, to which Company A was attached on 4 May, during the II Corps' drive on Bizerte. The 9th Division had not worked with infantry-support tanks since the Torch landings, and it showed. Shortly before noon on 7 May, the tankers along with the 894th Tank Destroyer Battalion were given the mission to reconnoiter some hills to the east and north and "overcome any opposition found therein." Sending armor alone off on such a mission showed no grasp of combined-arms operations.

The 9th Division again ordered the armor to advance alone into Bizerte, which the vehicles entered at about 1550 hours; they were the first Allied troops to enter the town. Maj. Gen. Manton Eddy, the 9th Division's commander, gave an attached French brigade the honor of sending the first foot soldiers into Bizerte, and photographic evidence indicates that the tanks helped the infantry root out a few die-hard defenders. The tanks withdrew that night because they had attracted artillery fire.[101]

Lessons Learned

The army had drawn some lessons about its tanks, largely from the experience of the 1st Armored Division, which had seen the lion's share of the action in North Africa. Interviewed by a War Department observer, the executive officer of the 1st's Combat Command B, commented in January 1943, "The light tank is excellent for reconnaissance in force, exploitation, wide harassing attacks, and hit-and-run attacks. It is no good for tank-versus-tank combat."[102] Maj. Gen. Ernest

Harmon, who had taken command of an armored corps controlling the British 6th and U.S. 1st Armored Divisions after Kasserine, had recommended as early as March that all light tanks be removed from the line regiments and given to reconnaissance troops to replace half-tracks and scout cars.[103]

By August 1943, the Army Ground Forces well understood that a light tank mounting a 75-millimeter gun was needed. It had considered putting one on the M5A1 but concluded that the M24 light tank could be put into production just as quickly and ordered that project expedited.[104]

Harmon also pleaded, "I wish our tanks were diesel operated instead of gas. Practically all of our tanks that are hit catch on fire, which is caused by the high-velocity 75 shell, which is red hot, igniting the leaking gasoline which comes from ruptured tanks when the vehicle is hit. This is a very serious morale factor, and the men want diesels."[105] North Africa had provided one more lesson that was to torment the tankers fighting the Germans throughout the war: a majority of wounds suffered were burns.[106] (A British survey of burned Shermans in Italy indicated that most fires were actually caused by main gun ammunition stored in the vehicles.[107] The eventual introduction of wet stowage, which encased the ammunition racks in fluid, dramatically reduced the number of tanks that burned.[108])

The separate tank battalions had seen such limited use that few lessons emerged of direct relevance to the infantry-support tankers. Allied Forces Headquarters, for example, issued a training memorandum that devoted several pages of analysis to the use of an armored division. It concluded that "the outstanding general lesson of the campaign was failure to use the armored division in sufficient strength or concentrated mass."

The memorandum drew only a vague and brief conclusion regarding tank-infantry cooperation, and even that appears to have been based on the employment of the 1st Armored Division's tanks to support infantry divisions:

> The campaign has demonstrated that excellent results can be obtained through the use of tanks with the troops of the infantry division, as distinguished from the normal action of the armored infantry. It has been found that their employment should follow the principles of cooperation, teamwork, and coordination required for the infantry-artillery team. Two types of infantry cooperation were effective, as determined by the situation: Preliminary preparation for the breakthrough of the tanks, and close support of the tanks in their own breakthrough. In either case, infantry support has been indispensable to the tank action, especially in consolidating the ground overrun by the tanks.[109]

CHAPTER 3

Beachheads and Mountains

The "rush-to-battle" idea is wrong. Here we creep *up. Each tank
should overwatch another tank; each section should overwatch another
section; each platoon another platoon.*
—Lt. Col. Percy Perkins,
191st Tank Battalion

The Allies decided to follow up the victory in North Africa by invading Sicily in the hope of driving Italy out of the war, which would force the Germans to occupy Italy and pick up Italian military commitments in the Balkans. President Roosevelt also wanted to keep American troops active in the European war during the remainder of 1943. The plan for Operation Husky ultimately called for two corps to land under the British Eighth Army on the southeastern corner of the island. The U.S. Seventh Army's II Corps, under Lt. Gen. Omar Bradley, controlled the 1st and 45th Infantry Divisions and assaulted beaches somewhat farther west around Gela. Lt. Gen. George Patton Jr., who commanded the Seventh Army, retained personal control over the 3d Infantry Division, which landed on the left at Licata.

Two Italian corps defended the island, the XII Corps in the west and the XVI Corps in the east. Field Marshal Albert Kesselring, responsible for German forces in southern Italy—while Field Marshal Erwin Rommel commanded those in the north—had buttressed the Italians with the Hermann Göring Panzer Division assigned to the XII Corps and the 15th Panzergrenadier Division attached to the XVI Corps. At Kesselring's insistence, the two German divisions were positioned close to likely landing areas on the south coast so that they could counterattack quickly to drive invaders back into the sea.[1]

The Hermann Göring Panzer Division, which had responsibility for the area where the Americans were going to land, would earn a fearsome reputation, but as of early July 1943, the division was green, as few of its soldiers who had fought in Africa had been rescued. It had just organized as a panzer division and had few seasoned tank officers. The division was equipped with about thirty-five Panzer IIIs and Panzer IVs, and the *Luftwaffe* division had attached to it a company of Tiger tanks from the army.[2]

The Allied landings on 10 July 1943 constituted the largest amphibious assault of the war and put seven divisions ashore in Sicily. In the American zone, Combat Command A of the 2d Armored Division landed at Licata to support the 3d Infantry Division's beachhead on the left of the American assault zone, while the 753d Tank Battalion (Medium) supported the 45th Infantry Division on the right around Scoglitti. Ten of the 753d Battalion's Shermans were to help the 1st Infantry Division in the center around Gela until the 2d's Combat Command B and the 70th Tank Battalion (Light) came ashore. The two combat commands were initially to fill the role normally accorded separate battalions—that is, infantry support.

The invasion fleet was equipped with new models of landing vessels that were designed to speed the delivery of vehicles and men to a hostile shore. The landing ship, tank (LST); landing craft, tank (LCT); landing craft, infantry (LCI); and landing craft, vehicle or personnel (LCVP), saw action for the first time. No longer would tanks have to be hoisted over the sides of transports into landing craft; now they would arrive off the invasion coast aboard their ride to the beach.

The potential revolution of delivering tanks to a spot nearly on the sand did not fully pan out at Sicily, however. False beaches or sandbars off the selected landing areas gave way to fairly deep water before the true shore. As a result, pontoons had to be used between an LST's bow doors and the beach as during the

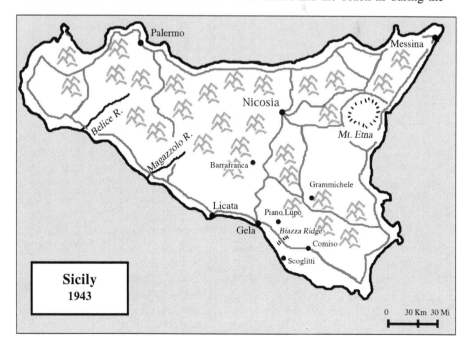

Sicily 1943

0   30 Km 30 Mi

Oran landings—though this time they were prefabricated for speedy installation—or a cumbersome LCT relay had to be employed.[3] Moreover, there were not enough of the new craft to equip the entire force. The 45th Infantry Division arrived combat loaded from the States in traditional fashion. As had inexperienced divisions and fleets similarly equipped during Operation Torch, the landing force suffered high losses in landing craft—up to 50 percent off some transports and 20 percent overall.[4] The bulk of the 1st Infantry Division's vehicles arrived aboard transports from North Africa. Only the 3d Infantry Division (code-named Joss Force) received enough landing craft to mount a shore-to-shore operation from North African ports.[5]

Yet despite the success in landing some light tanks with the assault wave during Torch and the availability of LCTs to Joss Force, for unknown reasons no tanks were assigned to the assault wave in Operation Husky. The assault force commanders imposed a set of rules that applied to all regimental combat teams landing on all beaches, which included several stipulations regarding tanks. The first wave of LCTs was not to hit the beach until H plus ninety minutes (with one exception), and five of those were to carry medium tanks towing antitank guns and followed by the latter's prime movers. All LCTs were to be loaded to permit tanks to fire as they approached the shore. All transports were to be tactically loaded, with no more than one tank company on any given vessel.[6]

Maj. Gen. Lucian Truscott, commanding the 3d Infantry Division, evidently was the one exception. Truscott assigned the 3d Battalion, 66th Armored Regiment, to land one company of medium tanks by LCT immediately behind the last battalion of each infantry regiment, which would put tanks on the island within sixty minutes of H-Hour. The remainder of Combat Command A was to remain in floating reserve and land on call.[7]

It is unclear how far behind the 45th Division's assault wave the 753d Tank Battalion landed, but it went ashore with the 157th Infantry. The tank battalion's records for Husky are missing. As of midnight on D-Day, the division's G-3 was unaware of any action involving the tanks, and the tanks' presence is first reflected in 45th Division message traffic about combat operations on D+1.[8]

Tank destroyers had gotten a bad reputation in North Africa with some senior officers, including Patton. The Seventh Army had assigned no tank destroyer battalions to the Sicily operation, which meant that Patton was relying on tanks to fight tanks in situations of maneuver.

The 753d Tank Battalion was the first separate battalion to use the M4A1 Sherman in combat. The M4A1 was distinguishable from the M4 by the rounded contours of its cast hull, whereas the M4 had a welded and angular hull. The two models were mechanically identical.

The Sherman inherited the chassis, suspension, and power train of the M3, but the gyrostabilized 75-millimeter gun moved to a fully traversing cast turret powered by hydraulic and manual systems. The thirty-four-ton vehicle had a crew of five (commander, gunner, cannoneer/loader, driver, and assistant driver/bow gunner). Tank commanders, who had a simple steel sight on the turret top, could override the gunner's control of the turret rotation, but their switch lacked fine calibration, which meant the gunner usually had to make final adjustments on the target. The turret turned quickly, a trait crews came to value highly because it often meant the Sherman got in the first accurate shot against heavier panzers that had manual traverse systems.

The decision to stick with the 75-millimeter main gun rested on the fact that it fired an excellent high-explosive round—in keeping with the doctrinal assumption that tanks should generally leave fighting other tanks to the tank destroyers—but it nevertheless had plenty of armor-piercing punch for the battlefield of mid-1943. The main gun fired an armor-piercing round at a muzzle velocity of 2,030 feet per second and could penetrate 3.1 inches of face-hardened plate at 1,000 yards, which provided a considerable comfort margin over the two-inch-thick armor on the front of Germany's Mark IV medium tank. A combination gun mount incorporated a .30-caliber coaxial machine gun.

The executive officer of Combat Command B of the 1st Armored Division had told a War Department observer in North Africa flatly, "The M4 tank is the best tank in the theater."[9] After an inspection tour in North Africa from December 1942 to January 1943, Lt. Gen. Jacob Devers also asserted, "The M4 medium tank (General Sherman) is the best tank on the battlefield."[10] A visit by then-Maj. Gen. Omar Bradley to the 1st Armored Division revealed that crews had a more nuanced view. They had learned that most turret penetrations occurred where the armor was thinned down on the inside to accommodate fittings. The plexiglas in the direct vision slits on older tanks could be blown into the driver's face by even a near miss, and many crews had removed it. They thought their gun sights were too weak and should be illuminated for night fighting.[11]

The naval bombardment began only fifteen minutes before the assault boats reached the sand because Patton wanted to achieve tactical surprise.[12] Indeed, even though the Italian coastal defenses had an hour's tactical warning because of airborne drops inland, the 1st and 3d Infantry Divisions rolled ashore against virtually no opposition.

The 45th Division landed three regiments abreast, with destroyers providing the close support against targets on the beach that tanks might otherwise have provided. The tin cans followed the assault troops to within 3,000 yards of the beach, blazing away. "Sometimes," recalled Maj. Ellsworth Cundiff, the S-2 for the 179th Infantry in the division's central zone, "it seemed as if the destroyers themselves were making the assault."

The GIs paid the price for not having tanks sent in with them. Resistance on the beaches in the 45th Division's zone ranged from spirited in the 180th Infantry's area to nothing elsewhere. Once the regiments moved toward their objectives inland, a combat group from the Hermann Göring Panzer Division consisting of

Mark IV and Mark VI panzers, infantry, and artillery badly mauled the 180th's 1st Battalion, pushed the regiment back, and created a potentially dangerous gap between it and the 179th Infantry, which was advancing on the Comiso airfield.[13]

At Gela, two Ranger battalions attached to the 1st Infantry Division without any armor support fought off Italian counterattacks backed by tanks. At Piano Lupo crossroads, 82d Airborne Division paratroopers and the first advancing doughboys from the 1st Division's 16th Infantry needed naval gunfire to beat back Italian tanks, and then much of the Hermann Göring Panzer Division.[14]

The following day, Axis forces threw more tank-heavy counterpunches at the American beachhead, and the slow arrival of friendly armor almost had fatal consequences for the 1st Infantry Division. Two tank platoons from Combat Command B had landed late on D-Day but got stuck in soft sand. Four Shermans got loose on D+1 in time to help fend off a large armored attack that nearly overran the 1st Division's beaches.

That same day, two platoons of Company B, 753d Tank Battalion, came to the aid of 82d Airborne Division paratroopers near Piano Lupo, but only after their epic close-range fight against counterattacking Tigers from the Hermann Göring Panzer Division at Biazza Ridge. The tankers supported an evening attack against the Germans and claimed the destruction of a Tiger and a Mark IV, two 88s, and five machine-gun emplacements while losing four Shermans.

Tank support was finally playing a role in the 45th Division's zone, where the 157th Infantry ordered Company C, 753d Tank Battalion, to seize the Comiso airfield and hold it until the arrival of the infantry—an order that reflects no grasp of combined-arms tactics. The tankers moved out, with company commander Capt. George Fowler's Sherman in the lead. After crossing a ridge west of Comiso, Fowler spotted five Italian Renault tanks, which he engaged at only 200 yards; 75-millimeter rounds ripped through the light armor and destroyed all five tanks in short order. The regiment had overrun the airfield by evening.[15]

The 179th Infantry pushed northward toward Grammichele on 12 July, shoving back delaying forces from the Hermann Göring Panzer Division. The German division had begun a staged withdrawal through three defensive positions. That evening, a sharp counterattack disorganized Company K, but the advance resumed, and the exhausted infantrymen were not allowed to stop and rest until midnight. The next day, German resistance flared at every hill, and counterattacks greeted every success.

Late in the morning, two Sicilians who had once lived in the States reported that there was a concentration of thirty-five panzers and 500 infantry ahead, information that another informant corroborated. Division dispatched Company A, 753d Tank Battalion, to support the advance planned for the next day. In the meantime, the 179th Infantry's 3d Battalion stopped again at midnight on a rolling hill cut by a sunken road. Large olive groves and geranium plants eight feet high covered the hill. Knowing they would be there only a short time, the exhausted doughs dug their slit trenches only a foot deep. Nobody told the company commanders about the enemy force not far ahead. The tanks from Company A arrived and laagered for the night in the battalion's motor park.

On the morning of 14 July, a light fog cloaked the hill. At 0600, the battalion's commanding officer gathered the company commanders to issue his orders for the day's attack. Most of the men were still asleep.

Just then, a Mark III tank appeared out of the fog and overran the security squad, killing two and wounding four men. Two Mark IVs appeared behind it, accompanied by panzergrenadiers on foot. A GI pelted back toward the 3d Battalion, yelling, "Tanks!" The tank company commander, Capt. George Fowler, who was at the officers' call, had his radio with him and immediately ordered his Sherman crews to turn the engines over. Fowler then ran back to his tanks.

As the fog lifted, yet two more panzers with infantry appeared on the next hill, covering the three slowly advancing on the 3d Battalion. The Mark III stopped thirty-five yards from the forward slit trenches.

Mortar crews at that moment dropped a barrage of 60-millimeter rounds on the panzergrenadiers, and "all hell broke loose," recalled the regimental S-2, Maj. Ellsworth Cundiff. The Germans fired all weapons, and the three lead panzers ground forward again. American heavy machine guns opened up on the infantry, but tank fire quickly destroyed one. The panzers shot into individual slit trenches with cannons and machine guns, and German fire scattered the crews of a 57-millimeter antitank gun and a self-propelled 75-millimeter gun from Cannon Company. As the tanks rolled over the 3d Platoon of Company K, the rifle-grenade man hit the Mark III in the flank and set it on fire.

Now 81-millimeter and 4.2-inch mortar shells dropped around the Germans, who pulled back to an olive grove. Two platoons of Shermans mounted a flanking attack and destroyed three of the retreating panzers. The tanks became separated among the olive trees during the shooting, however, and Fowler crested a rise only to find his Sherman behind two Mark IVs and two Tigers, all of which were driving off with their guns pointed away from the battle.

Fowler's gunner put two rounds into one Tiger's engine and set it alight, and he picked off a Mark IV as his driver backed frantically away from the panzer cannons that were now turning toward the Sherman. Two 88-millimeter shells penetrated the front armor, but the Tiger drove off without finishing off the crew.[16]

The fight had exhibited none of the niceties of tank-infantry cooperation, but it had amply demonstrated how much better battles went when the army could get tanks to the infantry when they needed them. Indeed, a day earlier, the 180th Infantry had waged a desperate struggle around the Biscati airfield without any tank support at first, relying on bazookas and antitank grenades to disable Italian and German tanks at point-blank range until friendly tanks arrived to join the fight.[17]

After the first few days, tank operations began to take on the vague outlines of what would be the standard practice in Europe. Once the Allied foothold was secure, the reassembled 2d Armored Division went into reserve until it provided the tank muscle to Patton's famous sweep around the western side of the island to Palermo.

The two separate tank battalions, meanwhile, worked through the mountains with the 1st and 45th Infantry Divisions. The 70th Tank Battalion (Light) landed on 13 July and was attached to the 1st Infantry Division, and the tankers barely had time to get oriented before they were thrown into one of the outfit's roughest fights of the war. On 16 July, the tankers joined the 3d Battalion of the 26th Infantry Regiment in its attack on Barrafranca. The day started badly when Companies B and C attacked abreast at the right end of the infantry battalion's line and, forced to use a single road because of rough terrain, ran into a crushing artillery and mortar barrage. The battalion withdrew, at which time sixteen Mark IV medium tanks counterattacked behind an artillery barrage.[18] A Mark IV could easily destroy an M5 with a single round.

The battalion's commander, Lt. Col. John Welborn, arrayed two companies of his M5s and the T30 75-millimeter assault guns on high ground above the road the panzers were using, one company to each side. Tanker Carl Rambo explained: "We would run up to the crest of the hill, fire a shot or two, back off, then go to the right or left, run up again, and fire another shot."

The Mark IVs could not elevate their guns far enough to shoot at the light tanks, and the American tankers knocked out five panzers by hitting tracks and thin top armor. Battalion personnel directed artillery fire on the enemy and accounted for an additional four panzers. The battalion's history observed, "That tactic isn't in the books. You don't throw a light tank armed only with a 37mm cannon and a few machine guns up against a heavily armed Mark IV. Especially not at 1,000 yards range. It takes guts plenty. But these tank men knew what the odds are."

The infantry and tankers regrouped and captured Barrafranca late in the afternoon. The 70th Battalion's losses for the day were eight tanks damaged and two destroyed, one man killed, and eleven men wounded.[19]

The Shermans from Company A, 753d Tank Battalion, were attached to the 70th Battalion for most of the campaign, an acknowledgement that the light tanks alone could not provide effective support to the riflemen. In exchange, the 70th Battalion's own Company C was sent to the 753d Tank Battalion, operating attached to the 45th Infantry Division.[20] The practice foreshadowed the army's sweeping reorganization only two months later that largely eliminated light tank battalions in favor of combining medium and light tanks. Still, sometimes the light tank could do more than a medium on narrow mountain roads.

The 1st Infantry Division took another step to increase the 70th Tank Battalion's usefulness on the battlefield when it transformed the outfit into a task force. The 1st Engineer Battalion; Cannon Company, 26th Infantry; Company A, 26th Infantry (motorized in tank battalion trucks); and the 1st Cavalry Reconnaissance Troop were attached on 21 July. Such ad hoc combined-arms operations were repeated occasionally, but generally, the light tanks worked closely with the infantry in the assault, while the attached medium tanks and the battalion's three assault guns provided supporting fire.

The relationship that developed between the 1st Infantry Division troops and the tankers was an early indication that extended education together in the school of hard knocks was essential to fostering effective cooperation in battle. When the 70th Battalion was detached to refit and train on 10 August, Maj. Gen. Terry Allen, who led the 1st Infantry Division, praised the "intimate relationship" that had developed between his division and the battalion.[21] This lesson might have seemed obvious later, but the three-and-a-half weeks that the 1st Division and 70th Tank Battalion had just spent together was the longest period an American separate armored and infantry unit had worked together daily during the war.

Things were not so good everywhere. One infantry captain observed, "The infantry should be given practical training in cooperation with tanks. . . . I know our regiment didn't have any training with tanks in preparation for combat. At Branieri [*sic*, unidentified] we just didn't know how to work with the attached tank unit. When our tanks came up to support us after we had broken up the German attack, we did not follow up the tanks properly as they went forward. Had we done so, we could have cleaned out almost a battalion of Germans."[22]

Sicily was a foretaste of the fighting tankers would face in Italy, as the often-mountainous terrain canalized movement and gave immense advantages to the defender. Blown bridges stopped the advance as often as did enemy resistance. In praising the 70th Tank Battalion's service during the campaign, Lt. Gen. Omar Bradley, commanding the II Corps, noted, "As long as the terrain permitted, some of your tanks were always well up to the front and played a major part in the advance of the infantry."[23]

Benito Mussolini was deposed on 26 July, and the Germans took overall command of Axis forces on Sicily several days later. On 5 August, Kesselring, now facing pressure from Patton's drive eastward along the northern coast toward Messina, decided to evacuate Sicily after consultations with Hitler and the German High Command. The withdrawal began the night of 12 August, and patrols from the 3d Infantry Division entered Messina on 16 August, just behind the last Germans slipping away.[24]

Sicily was the last campaign in Europe in which the infantry more often than not fought without tank support. After parting ways with the 2d Armored Division, the 3d Infantry Division—with but minor exceptions near the end of the campaign—had no tanks attached to it, and the 9th Infantry Division never saw a friendly tank.

ITALY: THE TANKERS' BANE

The Italians had begun making peace overtures after Mussolini's ouster, but they were unwilling to surrender without a substantial Allied force moving to the mainland. For once, Gen. George Marshall backed an operation in the Mediterranean, if it would get Italy out of the war; he foresaw capturing Naples followed by a rapid advance to Rome. Churchill had even bigger aspirations and saw the Italian peninsula as the route to Austria or the Balkans.[25]

U.S. Fifth Army forces landed at Salerno, Italy, on 9 September 1943 in Operation Avalanche. Allied Forces Headquarters had selected that site rather than

a place farther north in part because it was just in range of fighters based in Sicily that could provide air cover.[26] The assigned mission was "to seize the port of Naples and secure airfields in the vicinity of Naples with a view toward preparing a firm base for further offensive operations."[27] Six days beforehand, the British Eighth Army had crossed the Straits of Messina from Sicily to the toe of the Italian boot and was advancing with deliberate speed toward a junction with the Salerno beachhead.

Only about twelve hours before the landings, Eisenhower publicly announced the surrender of Italy, which the Allies had secretly negotiated over the preceding weeks. Perhaps these momentous events had created an excessive optimism in American ranks. Maj. Gen. Lucian Truscott recorded in his memoirs that on 5 September, Lt. Gen. Mark Clark, commanding the Fifth Army, told him at a meeting in Algiers that there was not likely to be much opposition and that Truscott should be ready to land with his 3d Infantry Division as far north as Rome.[28]

The impact of the Italian surrender was not as great as Clark expected, but it did force the German High Command to shift from a strategy of trying to hold Italy to one of delaying defense up the peninsula. German commanders viewed the anticipated invasion of Italy as a training ground for fighting the inevitable Allied landings on the west European coast.[29] Still, Field Marshal Gerd von Rundstedt, who commanded German forces in France, groused to interrogators at the end of the war, "[I]t was madness to continue the war in Italy. . . . After the collapse of Italy, that frightful boot of a country should have been evacuated . . . and we should have held a decent front with a few divisions on the Alpine frontier, and they should not have taken away the best divisions from me in the west in order to send them to Italy."[30]

Clark's Fifth Army was a showcase of Anglo-American integration. It included two corps, Maj. Gen. Ernest Dawley's U.S. VI Corps and Lt. Gen. Sir Richard McCreery's British 10 Corps, and, along with the British Eighth Army, was part of the 15th Army Group, commanded by Gen. Sir Harold Alexander. Both corps participated in Avalanche, with the British landing to the north of the Americans. By the time Allied troops set foot on Italy, the capture of Sicily had already effectively cleared the Germans from the Mediterranean, and the theater had become a subsidiary one to the great invasion being planned for France.

Italy was to become arguably the most frustrating of the many theaters in which the tankers fought. In some ways, combat for tank battalions resembled that faced by outfits in the Pacific. The campaign involved two full-blown amphibious landings. The long battle up the peninsula, with the Apennine Mountains running up it like a dragon's spine, required repeated assaults across rivers to establish "beachheads," and much of the action involved rooting defenders out of fortifications that might have seemed familiar to soldiers engaged in "cave warfare" on Peleliu, in the Zambales Mountains on Luzon, or on Okinawa. The battles in which tanks were able to play much of a role stand isolated almost like islands: Salerno, Cassino, the Anzio breakout, the Po valley.

In between, as the official U.S. Army history put it, "The American mechanized forces for the most part fought the terrain rather than the enemy. . . . [T]he artillery, tank destroyers, and tanks were often a liability rather than an asset."[31] While the terrain in Sicily had foreshadowed mountainous Italy, Sicily had been dry, and engineers could easily build bypasses around destroyed bridges; Italy was going to be wet, very wet.[32]

Decision-making by commanders regarding the use of armor appears to have been unusually bad, starting with a failure to provide adequate armored support to the assault force at Salerno. The 36th Infantry Division, a green outfit fresh from the States, was to conduct the landing. Follow-on troops were to include the 45th Infantry Division, one reinforced regiment of which was in floating reserve; the 3d and 34th Infantry divisions; and the 1st or 2d Armored Division. The 82d Airborne Division stood ready on Sicily if needed. Allied intelligence assessed that the Germans had a panzer division in the vicinity of Salerno and that the landing force could expect to encounter panzers early.[33]

The first American tanks were not even scheduled to land until the sixth wave—or H-Hour plus 140 minutes. According to the plan, the 751st Tank Battalion (Medium) was to put a single platoon ashore before daybreak with each of the 141st and 142d Infantry Regiments. Company A's 1st Platoon, assigned to the 141st Infantry, was to support a "flying column" that was to enter the village of Agropoli. The remaining combat elements of the battalion were to land throughout

D-Day. Maj. Gen. Fred Walker, commanding the 36th Division, believed that this timetable would get tanks ashore in time to deal with any armored counterattack, though his total armored strength at first light was to be only ten medium tanks.

The first tank destroyers, roughly two companies of M10s from the 601st Tank Destroyer Battalion—which according to doctrine were actually supposed to fight tanks—were not to land until 1630, thirteen hours after the first GIs. This was better than the initial plan, which foresaw no tank destroyers arriving until D+2. To cap Salerno's status as the antithesis of amphibious warfare doctrine, Walker decided to forego a preliminary naval bombardment and indeed hoped the shelling of the British beaches would draw off any panzer units in his area.[34]

Why planners for Operation Avalanche strayed so far from the emerging amphibious doctrine—shell the beach, storm the beach (with armor along to protect the infantry), secure the beach—is a mystery. The assaulting division's commander exercised his judgment regarding the bombardment. Who scheduled the belated arrival of armor is less clear. The Salerno beaches were optimal for landing craft up to the size of LSTs, the exits were suitable for tanks and vehicles, and the only known obstacle was an antitank ditch behind the beach. Other nearby beaches were appropriate for tanks, although some were defended by pillboxes.[35] Fifteen LSTs were available for the landings, and Clark had demanded an increase from the three initially allocated in part to land tanks and tank destroyers.[36]

The 16th Panzer Division, which defended the landing area, received warning a day before the invasion that an Allied fleet had sailed from Sicily for Salerno, and it was put on alert. At 1600 hours, its status was raised to "ready for battle." Warning orders had also reached other panzer and panzergrenadier divisions south of Rome. As the Fifth Army history records, once the landings began, "German motors began to roar, and column upon column swung out onto the roads of Southern Italy, driving rapidly [toward] the plains of Salerno."[37]

At one minute after midnight on 9 September, riflemen of the 141st and 142d Infantry Regiments clambered down rope nets from troop transports twelve miles off shore into waiting landing craft. Stubby landing craft prows turned toward Italy, and at 0330 hours, the initial wave hit the beach. Miraculously, all was quiet. The rumble and flashes of gun and rocket fire to the north, where two divisions of the British 10 Corps were conducting their assault closer to Naples, told a different story.

As the first squads pushed inland, a loudspeaker called out in English, "Come on in and give up. We have you covered!" Suddenly, German flares popped in the night sky. A furious rain of mortar and machine-gun rounds struck the men now crossing the beach. The infantry assaulted German positions among the dunes, and by dawn, most units were approaching their initial objectives.

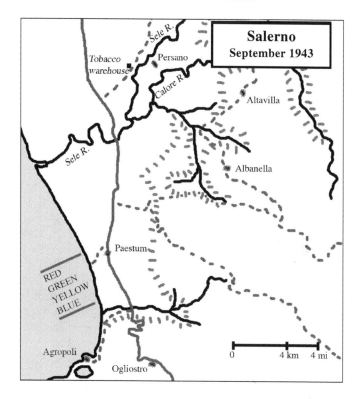

Shortly after daybreak, the first two company-size German tank groups counterattacked. One, striking from the south, overran assault troops of the 142d Infantry and sewed confusion. The second group appeared to the front of the 141st Infantry and kept the men pinned down much of the day. A third tank attack at 1020 hours was stopped only one half mile from Paestum on the sea by field pieces firing over open sights and 37-millimeter guns on weapons carriers manned by the 36th Cavalry Reconnaissance Troop. More panzer attacks followed, and the GIs held them off with bazookas, grenades, and supporting naval gunfire.[38]

The rate at which American tanks were reaching shore, meanwhile, was falling far short of even modest plans. The landing crafts, mechanized (LCMs), carrying the 1st Platoon, Company A, 751st Tank Battalion, twice tried to reach Blue Beach and failed for reasons that are not clear. One tank finally managed to land at 1500 hours, and the remaining four did not arrive until 1730 across a different beach.

The 2d Platoon beat the designated assault platoon to the beach, but it, too, arrived piecemeal. One tank landed at 0800, followed by a second at 1000, and a third at 1100. A general officer commandeered the second of the tanks to use as his transportation, but the other two went into action with infantry working toward Yellow Beach. The rest of the platoon did not get to Italy until the next day.

The 3d Platoon got its first tank to the beach at 0930, and Sgt. Thomas Glasheen moved smartly inland to support the doughboys. He soon found that the Germans were already counterattacking, and his gunner knocked out two Mark IV Specials (equipped with a long-barreled 75-millimeter gun) and an antitank gun. As Glasheen's tank approached the main highway, a high-velocity round penetrated the turret, killed the gunner, and wounded the rest of the crew.

The platoon's second tank did not arrive until 1330, and the remainder after nightfall. Because of an insufficient number of landing barges, Company B did not start landing until afternoon, followed by Company C and other battalion elements.[39]

The 191st Tank Battalion was having no better luck. The battalion's intended lead elements, including the command tank, reconnaissance platoon, assault gun platoon, and Company A, had sailed from North Africa aboard LCTs, while the remainder of the outfit followed in two LSTs. The LCTs had arrived at 0330 and been guided through a minefield into Salerno Bay. The LCTs headed for the beach around 0600 hours and immediately drew German artillery fire. Three LCTs were driven back by fire twice before putting two platoons of tanks and the assault guns ashore at 1130, one vessel listing and with wounded on board. Immediately on landing, an unknown general ordered the 3d Platoon to secure some high ground near the beach and prepare to fend off an expected panzer attack.

A shell struck the ramp of a fourth LCT, and then a second round hit a tank, glanced off, and exploded in the pilothouse, where it killed a naval officer and an entire gun crew. The LCT, only 600 yards from shore, turned to head back to sea, and a third round penetrated the side of a tank, killed two men, and set the Sherman alight. With great difficulty, the smoldering tank was pushed off the damaged ramp into the water. This LCT began to take on water and does not appear to have reached the beach. The remaining two reached shore at 1345 and 1540 hours, respectively, each on its third attempt.

The LSTs experienced difficulties, as well. One lowered its pontoon well out to sea at 1030 and headed in. About a mile from shore, it was struck twice by guns located near Paestum, and several men on the pontoon were wounded. Debarkation began at 1505 under intense artillery fire. The second LST failed two times to reach its assigned beach and was sent to another, where the tanks off-loaded at 1530 with nary a friendly GI to be seen. There were some Germans, but they took off when the tanks appeared.

The tankers de-waterproofed their vehicles under artillery fire and strafing from German fighters. The exhaust and intake shrouds on most tanks had to be pulled off by other tanks or hacked free with axes. They had been designed to fit the M10 tank destroyer, but that was what the army had provided.

The battalion rallied, and led by Company C, it drove westward to the Sele River, where the Germans destroyed the bridge as the tanks appeared. The battalion's after-action report records that in the course of the afternoon, it knocked out at least eight Mark IV tanks, four antitank guns, a pillbox, and an unknown number of infantry while losing not a man or vehicle. "It is apparent that the defense of the highway from Paestum to the Sele bridge was not too carefully planned," wrote the recording officer. "The enemy withdrawal was not an orderly one."[40]

By day's end, Allied units had reached their D-Day goals, with the exception of most of the 141st Infantry Regiment. The next day, the VI Corps experienced almost no opposition as the 143d Infantry landed, and the 36th Division occupied positions in the hills overlooking the beachhead.[41] Doubtless stung by the preceding day's events, the 36th Infantry Division employed its armored strike force in a most peculiar fashion. Companies B and C of the 751st Tank Battalion were ordered to take up defensive positions on either side of the main highway to defend against any armored attack from the south. The Company C tanks fired artillery missions from their positions near the road.[42]

On 10 and 11 September, the British 10 Corps faced bitter resistance, and on the night of the tenth, Clark ordered the VI Corps to reinforce the American Rangers operating on the British right.[43] On the eleventh, Major General Walker instructed Lt. Col. Louis Hammack to supply a company from his 751st Tank Battalion to join a task force rapidly organized to go. Built around an infantry battalion, the task force sailed that day to join Darby's Rangers—who had been fighting beside the British Commandos since D-Day—at Amalfi Peninsula. Hammack selected Company B.

Hammack did not hear another word about Company B until 16 September, when he learned that his boys had fought beside the Rangers for two days, been attached to British 10 Corps for two more, and then sent to the 141st Infantry Regiment, which at the time was attached to the 45th Infantry Division.[44] For a man who had fought his outfit as a battalion in speedy maneuver across the desert at Fondouk, this was a new and probably unsettling experience. He was to find that watching his command be scattered hither and yon was to be his lot in Italy.

Indeed, on 12 September, the 36th Infantry Division ordered the battalion—minus Companies B and C—to support the 143d Infantry Regiment east of Paestum. While trying to bypass a heavily mined road by working over a twisting mountain path, the tankers were strafed by American A-36 bombers. Fortunately, the flyboys were not good shots, and only two men were wounded. Mined fields thwarted the maneuver, and the battalion had to repair to defensive positions.[45]

Meanwhile, the 191st Tank Battalion had been detached in place from the 36th Infantry Division on 10 September, attached to the 45th Infantry Division, and sat on its haunches the entire day. The next day, Company B received orders to cross the Sele, head north, and move cross-country—all without the benefit of supporting infantry. Upon approaching what became know as the tobacco warehouse, the tankers spotted panzers.

Captain May directed his company forward cautiously. As the tanks approached the building, an apparent trap was sprung, and heavy-caliber and small-arms fire swept over the Shermans. Gunners returned fire and knocked out several half-tracks, antitank guns, and machine-gun nests. May pulled back just long enough to deploy his tanks for battle and charged back in. May's tank was hit, and May was wounded, then captured while trying to escape. One platoon commander was missing, and another severely injured. Four men were known to be dead and thirteen missing. Seven tanks were lost, including five that burned.

Infantry officers who viewed the clash declared the attack had been courageous. But this was a hard lesson for a green outfit in how *not* to use tanks with infantry.[46] The problems cut both ways. A War Department observer reported that a tank company commander who was ordered to attack Persano, which consisted of a dozen buildings, objected that the manual said that tanks were not to attack towns. The debate about the attack lasted all afternoon, and finally, it was decided that the tanks would attack under cover of artillery airbursts. That assault never materialized, though the town was shelled.[47]

Momentum on the VI Corps' front shifted abruptly on 12 September with the arrival of the 26th Panzer and 29th Panzergrenadier Divisions, which had rolled north to escape being cut off by the Eighth Army. The first sign of trouble was a counterattack that drove the 36th Division's 1st Battalion, 142d Infantry, off key high ground at Altavilla. Elements of the Hermann Göring Panzer and 15th Panzergrenadier Divisions had appeared in front of the 10 Corps a day earlier.[48]

On September 12, the 45th Infantry Division's 157th and 179th Infantry Regiments had taken up positions on the VI Corps' left wing, captured Persano, and crossed the Sele River, putting the division in striking distance of the 10 Corps' beachhead. The 36th Division's 2d Battalion, 143d Infantry, shifted leftward on 13 September to man the lengthening line.

That day, the 79th Panzergrenadier Regiment of the 29th Panzergrenadier Division aimed a powerful counterattack at the juncture between the two divisions. A tank-infantry force drove the 157th Infantry back across the Sele at Persano and hit the 2d Battalion, 143d Infantry, from the front and rear, smashing the battalion. The attack rolled toward the beach, and only heroic efforts by the 189th and 158th Field Artillery Battalions stopped it from reaching the sand.[49]

Two companies from the 191st Tank Battalion were attached to the 157th and in the evening supported counterattacks that reclaimed lost ground near the tobacco warehouse and to the south. Operations were again poorly coordinated, and the tankers said that uncertainty about the location of friendly troops had nearly caused needless casualties.

German counterattacks continued on 13 September, and the 45th Infantry Division appears to have made no plan to use its tanks. The only indication of a coherent order reaching the 191st Tank Battalion took place at 1600 hours, when, in response to the first reports of German attacks, the 45th Division operations officer ordered Company C to support the 1st Battalion, 157th Infantry. Evidently acting on his own, Lt. Col. Percy Perkins arrayed his three companies in a wide semicircle to cover three fronts. The mortar and assault gun platoons were deployed behind the tanks. At the time of the action, Companies A and C were at full strength, with seventeen M4A1s each; Company B had ten M4A1s available; the headquarters section had two Shermans, and the assault gun platoon fielded three M8s.

At one point, German troops struck both flanks simultaneously, but the battalion's heavy fire broke up the attack. Tanks shot at targets of opportunity and, when the ammo ran out, backed out one-by-one to resupply from an ad hoc dump set up behind a hedgerow. Gunnery also stopped a German attempt to move down the Sele River and get behind the battalion's line. Fighting continued until 2100 hours; infantry surrounded some of the tanks in Company A, and the nervous crews had no idea whose side they were on.[50]

As of 14 September, the 751st Tank Battalion had provided the 36th Infantry Division with very little close support. At 0510 that morning, Major General Walker ordered one company to take positions to defend against armored attack from the north. Ten Company A tanks and one from the headquarters section took up their prescribed positions, and a German tank attack developed. Well positioned, the American tanks knocked out eight panzers, five of which burned. The Germans disabled one Sherman in the exchange.[51] Meanwhile, Company B was sent to the hard-pressed 45th Division at about 1000 hours.[52]

The 191st Tank Battalion characterized its situation as desperate on the morning of 14 September, although its initial report to the 45th Division reflected at most the loss of a single Company A Sherman in the preceding twenty-four hours. Its tanks were strewn across the front line and under nearly constant artillery fire. The battalion and Company B of the 751st Tank Battalion screened the withdrawal of the infantry during the morning. Company B of the 191st had lost four more tanks by the time panzers attacked its sector in the afternoon, but fortunately, the tanks were well concealed. Gunners claimed to have destroyed four Mark IVs and one Tiger tank.[53]

The tankers' efforts were not in vain. "The contributing factor that probably prevented the invasion from being a failure on the 45th Division front," recorded the division's after-action report, "was the defensive employment of artillery and of tanks and tank destroyers."[54]

Field Marshal Albert Kesselring had tried to drive the Fifth Army into the sea and very nearly succeeded, but on 16 September, he ordered a slow fighting withdrawal to the Volturno River line, which he intended to hold until 15 October. Beyond that, his engineers were preparing more fortified belts across the isthmus.[55] On 18 September, VI Corps troops found nothing to their immediate front.

The Cooperation Conundrum

The Salerno beachhead had survived, but the fighting had provoked some officers to think hard about whether the army's approach to tank-infantry cooperation was working all that well—in truth, the first time anyone had devoted much attention to the question. Perhaps the near destruction of the beachhead had had one positive effect.

Maj. Gen. W. H. H. Morris Jr., an Army Ground Forces observer, suggested that attaching the 191st and 751st Tank Battalions to the VI Corps instead of to the infantry divisions would have made a great difference during the first desperate days of fighting. The 45th Infantry Division on the left occupied in part the Salerno plain, which was good tank country and was where the G-2 had expected the main German counterattack to come. On the right, the 36th Infantry Division occupied very mountainous terrain, yet it in effect immobilized the 751st Tank Battalion when it could have been used against the German counterstroke in the 45th Division zone.

This same observer put his finger on the way separate tank battalions were going to fight the war, no matter what doctrine said about the use of armor en masse. Morris criticized the allocation of tank companies to each infantry regiment and the further dispersal of platoons to the battalions. Even platoons were dispersed, and individual tanks acted as "mobile pill boxes" or roadblocks. This meant that the tank battalion was never concentrated enough to counterattack the enemy.[56]

"As a general rule," commented Morris, "I found that the [infantry] commanders to whom [tank] battalions were attached had no conception as to their correct employment. This is borne out by the fact that several field officers and one general officer frankly admitted that they were ignorant of tank tactics and asked the writer to advise them on same." Another observer agreed and noted that an infantry battalion had been sent across flat ground north of Altavilla without any tank support, only to be counterattacked by panzers against which they had no defense, and that heavy casualties were the result.

The problem, again, cut both ways. "There is a great tendency among junior tank officers," Morris noted, "to use tanks in an assault-gun role, that is, to support attacks from the rear rather than in front.[57]

The 756th Tank Battalion (Light), which had disembarked at Salerno on 17 September, had an exemplary experience of these problems when attached to the 45th Infantry Division. On 20 September, the battalion was attached to the 180th Infantry Regiment along with Company A, 191st Tank Battalion (Medium), to support an attack on Oliveto Citra. The regiment's plan envisioned a night advance by the 1st Battalion without tank support along the road into Oliveto. At 0500 hours, the medium tank company was to drive down the road into the presumably secured town to support the GIs, followed by the 756th Tank Battalion, less one company. Once in Oliveto, the medium tanks were to be attached to the 756th. Two artillery observers able to control five battalions of guns were also attached for the operation.

Lt. Col. Harry Sweeting, who commanded the 756th Tank Battalion, personally reconnoitered the ground his tanks were expected to cross. Sweeting was to prove himself an extremely aggressive officer who exposed himself frequently to extreme danger. His only contact with the infantry was to be a radio-equipped liaison officer at the regimental command post.

At 0500 hours, the tankers learned that the infantry had not reached the objective but that the tanks were to advance as planned. Sweeting ordered the tanks forward. Soon the medium tank commander reported that he was drawing artillery fire and had stopped. Sweeting went forward to investigate, but the thick morning haze made it difficult to see. As it turned out, the infantry was pinned down along an aqueduct by artillery and automatic-weapons fire. The operation ground to a halt while the regimental commander tried to reorganize his troops.

A new plan was devised by which, under cover of artillery, assault guns, and smoke, a light tank company was to advance, followed by a platoon of medium tanks and the second light tank company. The other mediums were to provide covering fire, and the infantry was to follow the tanks closely. The tanks advanced through artillery fire and were soon in a maze of terraces and buildings, engaging targets of opportunity. Fortunately, two antitank guns discovered later were not manned. Sweeting ordered the remaining mediums forward, and noticing that automatic-weapons fire was coming from structures now behind the tanks, he sent the light tanks back through town, blasting every enemy position. Eventually, enemy fire petered out.

Friendly infantry was nowhere to be seen. The attack had succeeded, but at no point during the day had an actual tank-infantry operation taken place.[58]

On 23 September, Company A, 191st Tank Battalion, lost two tanks to antitank fire outside Oliveto. The battalion's after-action report complained, "[C]ommunications with front-line infantry would give us information of enemy antitank gun positions without our first blundering into them and drawing their fire. . . . Many [infantry officers] appear to have little realization of a tank's limitations and capabilities."[59]

The First Hurdle: The Volturno Line

The German XIV Panzer Corps had orders to fall back on the Volturno River, holding the mountain passes as long as possible to allow time for the destruction of port facilities in Naples. At the Volturno, the corps would form a bow-shaped line pointing south tied into the LXXVI Panzer Corps, which was fighting its own delaying retreat in front of the Eighth Army. Within the Fifth Army, the 10 Corps was to make the main thrust toward Naples, while the VI Corps advanced on its right.

The terrain was so mountainous in the VI Corps' zone that by the last week of September, the 3d Infantry Division was turning to pack animals and human pack trains to supply some of its elements. Nevertheless, there was little German resistance. The British encountered much stiffer delaying actions but captured Naples on 1 October. By 6 October, the Fifth Army had reached the Volturno along most of its length, and here the forward movement stopped.

This was not tank country. As the Fifth Army lamented in its history, "The terrain, together with rainy weather, severely limited the opportunity for varied tactics. Armor, wide envelopments, and swiftly striking spearheads could not be used to speed up the advance." The VI Corps planned to pierce the German line on 13 October, with the 3d Infantry Division making the main effort across a section of the river defended by *Kampfgruppe* Mauke, part of the Hermann Göring Panzer Division.[60]

Still, tanks could be useful, even if only in small numbers. In preparation for the crossing, the 3d Infantry Division waterproofed a company from each of the 751st Tank and 601st Tank Destroyer Battalions to accompany the GIs from the 7th Infantry Regiment, which was to constitute the division's main effort in the center of the line. The rain-filled Volturno was chest-deep at the crossing site and flowing quickly, but patrols had found a spot at which vehicles would be able to ford the river.

Shortly after midnight, infantrymen from the 1st Battalion crossed the Volturno in rubber boats or by wading with one hand on a guide rope in what fortuitously turned out to be a dead space in the German fields of fire, which was filled with enemy machine-gun fire as soon as the operation was detected. The 2d and 3d Battalions gained the far bank shortly thereafter, and the regiment crossed what would have been a killing field in the daytime to assault their objectives on the high ground ahead.

Day came, and with it increasingly accurate German fire. The waterproofed armor was to have crossed with daylight, but German fire prevented engineers from digging an access route through the bank to the water's edge. Dug-in tank destroyers drove several panzers back into the hills, but at about 1000 hours, a radio intercept indicated that a counterattack by a panzer battalion of the Hermann Göring Panzer Division was imminent. Orders flashed to the 751st Tank Battalion to get Company A's waterproofed tanks over to the far bank to support the infantry. Men grabbed picks and shovels and carved out an access route through the riverbank by hand.

The first Sherman reached the infantry at 1100, and by noon, fifteen tanks and three tank destroyers were across. Artillery and tank destroyer fire had already broken up the counterattack, and backed by armor, the 7th Infantry drove forward and gave the Germans no time to reorganize. Although some hard fighting remained, the 7th Infantry had poked an irreparable hole in the Volturno defenses.[61]

With the Volturno line forced, the Germans fell back slowly and in good order through the mountains to what became known as the Winter Position or Winter Line, which the Germans called the Bernhard Line. German resistance was determined and took advantage of every ridgeline. Demolished bridges slowed the American advance as much as the Germans, and delivery of supplies was difficult. Rains became more frequent, the weather became colder, and the Fifth Army exhausted itself in weeks of steady combat against an elusive enemy.[62]

There was an odd asymmetry to the forces engaged. For the Americans, each fight to clear a roadblock or a ridge was mainly an infantry action, conducted by an infantry division; American tanks could contribute only occasionally. Within the Fifth Army, the 10 Corps' 7th Armoured Division was the only large armored formation, and it operated on the more tank-friendly coastal plain. The U.S. 1st Armored Division arrived only in November and at first sat largely unused in reserve to exploit any breakout.

The German forces were largely mechanized. The VI Corps faced the Herman Göring Panzer, 26th Panzer, and 3d Panzergrenadier Divisions (the last replaced in November by the 29th Panzergrenadier Division), and the 10 Corps faced the 15th Panzergrenadier Division; all were part of the German XIV Panzer Corps, along with the 94th and 305th Infantry Divisions. One reason may have been that German commanders unanimously expected the Fifth Army to strive for mobile warfare by striking in the center of its line through the Mignano Pass and driving into the Liri Valley past Cassino, where the Fifth Army could make best use of its tanks. The Germans could not understand why the Allies instead sought to advance on a broad front through the mountains. The XIV Panzer Corps' commander, Gen. of Panzer Troops Frido von Senger und Etterlin, viewed the panzer division as completely unsuited to the mountain warfare that unfolded because it lacked the rifle strength to hold much of the front.[63] The Germans nevertheless were able to use their tanks effectively in small-scale counterattacks and as artillery.

German Maj. Gen. Martin Schmidt noted from the perspective of the panzer crews:

> The German panzer units, in regard to organization, equipment, and training, were intended primarily for action on terrain like that of western, central, and eastern Europe. . . . It was of decisive significance that the panzer organizations were fighting on the defensive during the whole campaign [in Italy], whereas they were intended for offensive action. Almost all the panzer and panzergrenadier divisions that came to Italy in 1943 had gained their combat experience during campaigns in France and Russia. . . . In Italy, these divisions had to change their tactics considerably and sometimes paid dearly for their lessons."[64]

The Second Hurdle: The Winter Line

By the end of the first week of November, the Fifth Army was coming up against the so-called Winter Line, which the Germans had intended to use only as a temporary delaying position until they realized how effective it was. The defenses ran across the peninsula between the Volturno and Garigliano/Rapido Rivers. The Germans held prepared positions that, though generally simple fieldworks protected by mines and barbed wire, combined with the mountainous terrain to pose a daunting challenge. On 15 November, Clark ordered a halt to offensive operations. His exhausted men had to recuperate before they could smash through the Winter Line.[65]

A skimming of the after-action report for November of the 751st Tank Battalion—which was attached to the 3d Infantry Division at the Mignano Gap, through which ran Highway 6 to Rome—captures the essence of the obstacles to effective use of tanks on this front: "During the afternoon [of 1 November] the 1st Platoon, Company C, moved to [map coordinates] to support 15th Infantry in attack to northwest, but upon [arrival] was stopped by impassable terrain. . . . Company A was forced by the rains to move to higher ground on 8 November. . . . Engineers worked continuously constructing tanks routes across wadis and ravines. . . . Hard rains made it impossible to reach [one] platoon with vehicles, and the platoon was not able to get out of the small valley in which it was located." When the tanks were able to help at all, it was usually direct or indirect firing at distant targets. The battalion was pulled back for rest and refitting on 16 November.[66]

On 18 November, the II Corps took charge of the 3d and 36th Infantry Divisions in the center of the Fifth Army's line, while the VI Corps retained the 34th and 45th Divisions on the right. More manpower was on the way, as the French Expeditionary Corps was scheduled to arrive with its first two infantry divisions in December.

The Fifth Army's drive to bore through the Winter Line and reach the Liri Valley—the pathway to Rome—fell largely on the shoulders of the American infantry divisions. The VI Corps' 34th Infantry Division launched preliminary attacks on 29 November, and the main offensive, Operation Raincoat, began four days later. Once again, the push was largely an infantry fight through the mountains.[67]

For tankers, the key event during the offensive was the 36th Infantry Division's fight to take San Pietro from the 29th Panzergrenadier Division, which lasted from 8 to 17 December, as it became another classic lesson in how not to employ tanks. Much of the struggle took place on the cliffs towering above the little village, where American and Italian troops bled profusely while taking the commanding heights. On 15 December, the 143d Infantry Regiment attempted to capture the town itself.

Company A of the 753d Tank Battalion was committed to clear the way for the 2d and 3d Battalions. A single narrow road wound down a slope into San Pietro, lined for much of its length by rock-walled terraces three to seven feet high and covered with olive trees and scrub. Visibility was limited to about twenty-five yards in most places. The road was mined, and rain-soaked ground, streambeds, and gullies made cross-country movement impossible.

The column of Shermans moved out about noon under covering fire from a company each of medium tanks and tank destroyers. Four tanks were knocked out by artillery that opened fire on the exposed column, four tanks struck mines, two threw tracks, and two turned over trying to maneuver onto terraces. Only two tanks made it to the outskirts of San Pietro, where one was destroyed. Only four tanks returned to the assembly area. The infantry attack was no more successful.[68]

The 191st, 751st, and 756th Tank Battalions were moved out of the line for rest and rehabilitation in December, at which time they reorganized into standard tank battalions. The 751st Tank Battalion replaced its three 75-millimeter M8 assault guns with six 105-millimeter M7 Priest self-propelled howitzers, as the medium tank companies were now allocated one assault gun each.[69] The 756th Tank Battalion appears to have adopted the M7 as well. With the guns concentrated, a tank battalion now had the equivalent of an armored field artillery battery at its immediate disposal. Each battalion also organized a light tank company as Company D. During the reorganization, the 191st and 751st Tank Battalions were required to deploy a composite company each to hold defensive positions as infantry attached to the 45th Infantry Division.[70]

Beyond the Winter Position was Kesselring's next fortified line across the peninsula, the Gustav Line, which he intended to hold indefinitely. Operations against the Winter and Gustav Lines overlapped, and the Fifth Army considered the former to be ended only on 15 January 1944—a six-week slugfest that netted a mere five to seven miles of progress at a cost of nearly 16,000 battle casualties.[71]

CHAPTER 4

The Battle for Rome

As soon as I could I gathered a company of Roger's tanks and took off,
in the rapidly deepening twilight, for the center of [Rome]. . . .
—Hamilton Howze,
A Cavalryman's Story

The 15th Army Group optimistically entitled its operation instruction issued on 12 January 1944 "The Battle for Rome." Alexander told his subordinates:

The enemy has suffered considerable losses in recent operations especially on Eighth Army front. . . . Fifth Army have now started upon a series of operations on their present front designed to break through the enemy's main defensive positions in the area south of Cassino, and to draw in his reserves. These operations will culminate with an attack by II Corps across the Rapido River on or about 20 January. Fifth Army are also preparing an amphibious operation to land a corps of two divisions and the necessary corps troops, followed by a strong and fully mobile striking force based on elements of a third division, in the Nettuno area. The object of this operation will be to cut the enemy's main communications in the Colle Laziali [Alban Hills] area southeast of Rome, and to threaten the rear of German XIV [Panzer] Corps. Weather permitting, this amphibious operation will be launched on 22 January. . . . Commander Fifth Army will conduct his operations as to force the enemy to withdraw north of Rome, and at the same time inflict the maximum losses on the German forces in the area south of Rome.

Commander Eighth Army will maintain sufficient pressure on the enemy forces on his front to prevent the enemy from moving any troops from LXXVI [Panzer] Corps to reinforce those opposing Fifth Army.[1]

FIRST CRACK AT THE GUSTAV LINE

The Gustav Line resembled a vast medieval fortress, with the Germans manning battlements in the mountain fastness, and the Rapido and Garigliano running before them like a moat from the Apennines to the sea. Many emplacements were blasted from the living rock and could withstand direct hits by heavy artillery. German observation and fields of fire were superb.

The Fifth Army's plan for penetrating the Gustav Line envisaged simultaneous attacks by the British 10 Corps on the left out of bridgeheads to be established along the Garigliano River, by the U.S. II Corps in the center across the Rapido River, and by the French Expeditionary Corps on the right into the upper Rapido Valley.[2] In the event, the 10 Corps was unable to establish its bridgeheads as planned on the night of 19 January because the swift river current prevented the launching of assault boats. Likewise, the attack mounted by the French Expeditionary Corps on 20 January slowed to a standstill the next day.[3]

The 36th Infantry Division had attached to it the 760th Tank and 636th Tank Destroyer Battalions for its crossing of the Rapido River. At 2000 hours on 20 January, the 141st Infantry Regiment was to make the assault across the river from east to west near Sant' Angelo and establish a bridgehead into which Combat Command B, 1st Armored Division, would move on the night of D+1. The 1st Tank Group, with the 753d and 755th Tank Battalions, was attached to the combat command, as were two tank destroyer battalions. The 760th Tank and 636th Tank Destroyer Battalions were to move into positions on the east bank from which they could provide direct-fire support against targets across the river at daylight on the twenty-first.[4]

The 34th Infantry Division was to cross the Rapido four days later to the right of the 36th Division near Cassino, a town at the base of Monte Cassino, a mountain that dominated the battlefield and access to the Liri Valley. The division, supported by the 756th Tank Battalion, was to seize the high ground northwest of town and then continue to the northwest. The tanks were to concentrate in the 133d Infantry Regiment's zone.[5] The 45th Infantry Division was to reinforce Combat Command B in the event of a breakout.[6]

Debacle at the Rapido River

The 36th Infantry Division's attempt to cross the Rapido River was one of the most infamous incidents of the Italian campaign and has led to decades of finger pointing over who was responsible. What can be said is that the affair was another case in which the division failed to use effectively the armored power it had been given.

In the 36th Infantry Division's zone, the Rapido was between forty and fifty feet wide and rushed between raised banks between four and five feet high. The Germans had mined both banks and strung barbed wire along the west bank, and patrols learned that the defenders from the 15th Panzergrenadier Division were extremely alert. The Germans occupied fortifications, some of which would be able to place attackers in the division zone under flanking fire. The 760th Tank and 636th Tank Destroyer Battalions' armor was held back from the river in positions from which it was to support the GIs by direct fire against known positions.

The 1st and 3d Battalions of the 141st Infantry pushed off on the evening of 20 January after a three-minute artillery barrage. A little more than two companies reached the far bank across a single footbridge that had been carried forward to the river, while artillery fire and mines claimed other footbridges and men, and the rapid waters prevented the launching of assault boats. The 143d Infantry, which worked in thick fog in addition to all the other problems, managed to get a battalion across via two footbridges, but panzers pounded the men with direct fire on top of a rain of mortar and artillery rounds, and the battalion withdrew by 1000 hours.

The tanks that were to have fired in direct support were completely out of the action. The 760th Tank Battalion devoted but a single sentence to its activity: "Throughout the day of 21 January, Companies B and C remained in position but were unable to fire because of poor visibility, the entire area being smoked to aid the infantry crossing." Company A was immobile because the engineers could not build a bridge across the Rapido for the tanks to cross.

A second attempt by the two regiments that evening encountered similar problems, but most infantry elements were across by 0530 on 22 January. When German fire again prevented engineers from installing a Bailey bridge to get tanks across, smoke was employed to cover the engineers. Unfortunately, it also prevented artillery observers and tankers from seeing German targets, too.

The GIs managed to advance across exposed ground only 600 yards or less before they dug in under fire from the German fortifications. Nearly all company and battalion officers became casualties, resupply was nearly impossible, and communications were bad. That day, only a single platoon of Shermans from Company C, 760th Tank Battalion, was able to get into a position from which to fire across the river. When the Germans counterattacked at 1600 hours, the 141st Infantry barely held onto its tenuous foothold, and most of the 143d Infantry was driven back across the Rapido. That night, the division withdrew the survivors. The 141st alone had suffered casualties of 48 officers and 1,002 enlisted men.[7]

By 25 January, it had become apparent that there would be no armored breakout into the Liri Valley, which would have witnessed the first employment in battle by an armored division of attached separate tank battalions. Combat Command B received orders to move to Naples and from there to the Anzio beachhead. Those orders were soon cancelled, and the combat command took on a coordinating role overseeing the activities of several attached tank and tank destroyer battalions.[8]

The Futile but Classic Fight at Cassino
The town of Cassino and the mountain that towered above it with its famous Benedictine abbey was the linchpin of Kesselring's Gustav Line. It was also by far the best fortified town that the Fifth Army had encountered to date—or would face thereafter. The 34th Division's ultimately fruitless struggle to capture the town alongside the 756th Tank Battalion took place on a crazy-quilt battlefield that favored an enemy adept at using his own tanks, infantry, and artillery in sweet har-

mony. It stands as a superb illustration of how American infantry and tankers learned to cooperate under fire, with both flashes of brilliance and breakdowns in teamwork, and embodies perhaps the best case one could hope for as long as the two elements of the team had no good way to communicate directly at the tactical level.

The 756th Tank Battalion's first fire missions in the sector were actually conducted to support the neighboring 36th Infantry Division during its attempt to force the Rapido River line on 20 January. Medium tanks fired indirectly as artillery, and the battalion consolidated its six assault guns into an artillery battery. As in the Pacific, assault gun crews suffered considerably from the build-up of gun fumes in the tank. "Sometimes [the crews] would get sick and have to stop and vomit during the heavy firing on account of the gasses from the powder smoke," recalled Roy Collins. "They'd bail out of the tank, vomit, and climb right back in and continue firing."[9]

The 34th Division was to cross the Rapido north of the town of Cassino, capture Monte Castelleone, and then take Monte Cassino from the rear. The Rapido flowed through the division's zone between stone walls four to five feet high. Although the river was fordable at this point, the Germans had dammed the river in such a way as to create a muddy swamp on the American side.

The Germans had mined the approaches to the river as well as the ground between the water and their defenses, and bands of barbed wire ran along the west bank. The enemy had constructed intricate fortifications at key points along the Caira-Cassino road and on a series of hills that commanded the river valley. As noted, the town of Cassino was also fortified, and tanks and self-propelled guns covered all its entrances. German artillery observers had superb views from the mountainside. Intelligence reported that much of the 71st Panzergrenadier Division (actually an infantry division) had just arrived to reinforce the 44th Infantry Division in the sector.

The tankers had learned some lessons about tank-infantry cooperation, and battalion commander Lt. Col. Harry Sweeting now ordered company commanders to plan liaison and communications with the infantry battalion commanders before the attack. Radio-equipped liaison officers were placed at regimental and battalion command posts. A tentative crossing site was identified north of some barracks on the west bank.[10]

Companies A and B were to work with the 135th Infantry, initially supported by fire from Company C in the 133d Infantry Regiment's zone. It was bitterly cold, and snow hung in the air. The GIs were to move out at 0200 hours on 24 January, and the tanks were to follow once it became light. In the event, requests for fire support and for tanks to run through minefields to explode antipersonnel mines began almost at once, and the tankers tried to comply. Where targets could be seen at all in the dark, gunners bore-sighted on them and engaged each target with an initial round. Thereafter, fire was adjusted through liaison radios, which was not very effective.

With daylight, Companies A and B engaged targets on the far side of the river. After surveying the terrain and seeing artillery shells pounding the engineers

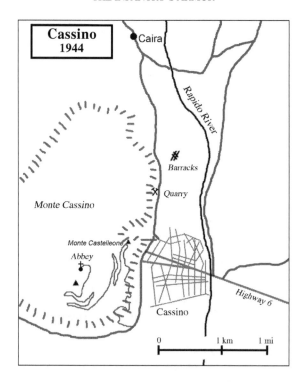

trying to prepare a river crossing for his tanks, Lt. Col. Harry Sweeting told the
infantry that it looked like the engineers would be unable to finish their work until
the infantry cleared a substantial bridgehead, but his tanks could move laterally
along the river and would support the GIs with direct fire.[11]

On 25 January, tank patrols probed down the road toward Cassino. Companies A and B shelled targets across the river, and more engineers appeared to work
on the roads and crossing. This stalemate continued the next day, so Sweeting
sent a tank section forward to see whether his vehicles could pass without the
engineers finishing the job. One tank got stuck and blocked the route, but it had
gotten far enough to show that the maneuver might be possible with a little more
engineering work.[12]

Nevertheless, when the tankers tried again, more tanks got stuck, and it was
not until 0730 on 27 January that the 2d Platoon's commander, Lt. Wayne Henry,
slipped across a small bridge with two tanks to the far side of the river. They immediately set about destroying barbed wire and creating paths through antipersonnel
minefields. By 0915, two more Company B tanks got across, including the one
temporarily commanded by Capt. Charles Wilkinson, the determined company
commander. Wilkinson recalled, "I spotted a house out there on the flat between
the lines in no-man's land. I could see a firing position. . . . We blew it away with
an HE round. We were communicating with hand signals at this time [because
Henry's radio was out]."

According to the official account, stuck tanks blocked the rest, but veterans recall that a platoon commander—who ultimately was relieved for incompetence—refused to move his tanks forward. Sweeting directed some of those tanks to fire on suspected gun positions across the river, and the fire evidently was effective enough to draw crushing counterbattery fire that disabled one Sherman.

The Germans apparently had thought no tank could cross the river at that point, and there were no antitank guns. One tank struck a Teller mine on the road toward Caira, and the crew manned it until dark, when they crawled back overnight along the tank tracks because they were clear of mines. Sweeting ordered the remaining three to proceed deeper into the German defenses to keep the Germans' heads down so the infantry could move forward. Just as Wilkinson was about to fire on some field fortifications near the barracks, he spotted a German on foot racing toward the tank with a *panzerfaust*. He ordered his gunner to traverse and fire, but the action came just too late. The bazooka round penetrated the armor, and the tank filled with flame and smoke. "Fire!" yelled Wilkinson again, but then he saw that his gunner was either dead or unconscious.

By 1300, three tanks on the far bank were out of action. Lieutenant Henry tried to back his tank—the last one moving—to safety, but one track hung on the bridge, and Henry was shot when he climbed from the turret, dead on his first day of combat. The infantry had failed to move up to the location of the tanks, and Wilkinson and Henry's crews were captured. The infantry, at least, had cleared enough ground to shield engineers from most small-arms fire at the crossings.[13]

Sweeting and the infantry commander agreed that there would be no attempted tank crossing on 28 January to give the engineers time to work. The battalion spent the day extracting Company B's remaining tanks from the muck under frequent shellfire. Each tank was manned and fired at targets of opportunity until its turn came to be pulled free. A route to the crossings through the neighboring French zone was now available, which allowed the tireless engineers to concentrate on the crossings. Company C, 760th Tank Battalion, was attached to reinforce the armor.[14]

Maj. Edwin Arnold, the battalion's S-3, conducted a personal reconnaissance into enemy territory to find routes for the tanks through the mud and icy water. And find one he did.[15]

On 29 January, Capt. French Lewis led six of his Company A Shermans across the Rapido before two tanks got stuck and blocked the crossing. During the crossing, a shell exploded in front of one tank and wounded the driver, T/4 Earl Hollon. In order not to block the path, Hollon drove the tank another 700 yards, despite a shell fragment that had pierced one eye and blood running down his face from head wounds.[16]

Mist limited visibility, and the tankers were surprised when one or more self-propelled guns opened fire.[17] A high-velocity round struck Lewis's Sherman and killed his loader, and a second strike wounded the captain, gunner, and driver. "Abandon tank!" shouted Lewis. As the captain bailed out over the deck and to the ground, he saw the next tank in line take a hit. Two more were struck in quick succession, and one burst into flames.

Lewis helped his surviving crewmen escape to the rear but refused to follow them. Finally, Sgt. Mack Corbitt spotted the self-propelled gun hidden beside the wall of a cemetery, and his gunner destroyed it. But only two tanks remained in action. Lewis directed them into firing positions where they could do the infantry the most good.[18]

Not long before dusk, tanks from the two Company Cs crossed in numbers at a newly discovered path across the riverbed, turned left, and headed down the Rapido to reach the infantry. "Get those guys alerted that the cavalry is coming so they will be ready to move when we get there," an elated Sweeting radioed from his turret. Twenty-six Shermans suddenly appeared on the 168th Infantry's front and headed for the Germans. The frozen, miserable GIs were slow to follow at first, but once they sensed the dramatic shift in momentum, they rose from their holes and followed the armor in its tracks, where all the antipersonnel mines had been detonated. On the flanks, Germans opened up, and tank turrets rotated, cannons barked. The German fire withered away, and under cover of smoke fired by the mortar platoon across the river, the tank-infantry team reached the "Pimple," the high ground on the far side of the Rapido.[19]

On 2 February, the 756th Tank Battalion became the first Allied unit to enter Cassino. The battalion employed a composite company of the running tanks from the three medium companies in what was initially a well-coordinated operation with the 3d Battalion, 133d Infantry Regiment. Lt. David Redle commanded the tank force and was given charge of the mortar and assault gun platoons, which were to provide smoke and supporting fire. Artillery provided a smokescreen for the command when it moved out southward along the Rapido, with the infantry sticking close to the tanks.

At 0730, the 3d Battalion reported to regiment, "We jumped off. The tanks are moving up with us."

"Keep your men off the road for the tanks. Are the tanks firing?"

"Yes, sir."

The force advanced in bounds, placing smoke 300 yards ahead, clearing the area, and repeating the procedure. The tanks advanced some 500 yards without contact until Germans in a bunker just beside the road threw some hand grenades. Redle's gunner took care of the problem, but Redle guessed that they had bypassed other camouflaged field works. Redle backed the column up and started again. Sure enough, this time the Americans flushed out about 150 German soldiers.

Whenever a machine gun opened fire on the GIs, the tanks dealt with it. The force reached a stream about four feet deep, and engineers moved in to construct a tank crossing. When the infantry moved a bit ahead of the tanks, Redle ordered his crews to fire only machine guns and solid-shot armor-piercing rounds to avoid causing friendly casualties.

As the tanks neared Cassino, they became channeled onto narrow paths—one along a blacktop road between the high riverbank and the mountain, the other in the riverbed—so that only the front vehicles were able to fire. This became a problem when the smoke dissipated, and at about 1100 hours, accurate fire screamed in from a camouflaged self-propelled gun in hull defilade on the outskirts of Cassino. The self-propelled gun shot the turret hatch off the M4A1 in the riverbed and wounded the commander. A second shot passed so close to Redle's head in the lead tank on the road that he was deafened in one ear for hours. Redle's tanks backed into a quarry for protection, and the infantry's attempts to knock the gun out with artillery and mortar fire were fruitless.

At 1630 hours, Sweeting instructed that the 34th Division was going to fire a heavy barrage at Cassino, and he ordered the reserve force—four or five Company A Shermans—into town. At this point, coordination with the infantry broke down because the infantry officers had gone back several hundred yards to their battalion command post for orders, and Company K had pulled back to an assembly area. Moreover, the Company A tank platoon commander's radio was on the fritz. The tanks charged alone into Cassino, where the Germans—who had been ordered to withdraw until their officers realized the tanks had no infantry support—waited in ambush.

Point-blank fire destroyed the last tank in line, and the remainder were trapped. The tanks sought a way out, and the Germans pursued them with bazookas, grenades, and dynamite. Three or four antitank rounds slammed into one tank but did not penetrate the armor. Close assault by infantry claimed one after the other, however. Redle was ordered to pull back because of advancing darkness, and he directed his driver to town to pass the order personally because of the radio problem. All he found was an empty tank from Company A.

The next morning, a company of medium tanks from the 760th Tank Battalion was again attached to the 756th Battalion to reinforce its striking power after its heavy losses. Maj. Welborn Dolvin, the executive officer, commanded the tank force assigned to enter Cassino alongside the 3d Battalion, 133d Infantry Regiment. Dolvin's tank took a high-velocity round in the final drive and burst into flames. Dolvin bailed out and sprinted to Redle's tank, which had a radio on the battalion net, and directed the attack from the back deck.

"What's holding you up?" queried Sweeting over the radio.

Dolvin looked around. "I don't know, colonel, but I think it's the Germans."

Another artillery barrage fell on Cassino, and the 760th Tank Battalion's Company C and the infantry tried again. Lt. Leo Trahan's 2d Platoon, followed by about fifty infantry, managed to capture the first four or five buildings in Cassino, and after some confusion between the tankers and infantry that nearly resulted in a withdrawal, the team got its act together and settled in to protect one another. Trahan's tank was hit and burned during the aborted withdrawal, and a second tank became immobilized. Joined by other Company C tanks, the men from the 760th slugged it out in the streets of Cassino beside the tankers of the 756th Battalion until 7 February, when the detached company returned to its parent battalion.

For the next month, the medium tank companies in the 756th Tank Battalion each kept a platoon—which by now usually meant no more than three tanks—in Cassino to work with the infantry. The GIs attacked mainly at night because German observation was so good that any movement drew heavy fire during the day.

The tankers' main job was to blast holes in the walls of fortified buildings that the riflemen could pass through, and gunners made heavy use of concrete-piercing ammunition.

Advances were measured in tens of yards, and tankers learned that working with the infantry in the confusing urban battlefield could be tough. Lt. Howard Harley lost his tank to bazooka fire on 12 February and later related, "It was because the fight was so wild that we got ahead of the infantry. You get lost in your intent sometimes and pursue targets with intent so strong you can get up ahead without realizing it."[20]

A British observer who witnessed the Cassino operation commented,

> In the initial advance, the tanks work in mutual support. Once inside the town, however, it becomes a personal matter, and each tank must fend for itself. . . . An enemy behind solid walls is difficult to dislodge. . . . By continuous firing at heavily fortified buildings, and chipping a few inches with each shot, the 75mm HE shell with a delayed-action fuse has finally reduced the strongest building. . . . There have been many occasions when, at the request of the infantry, close tank support has been given from the immediate vicinity of the forward troops; each support naturally increases the danger to the tank. Casualties to crews have been caused by the penetration of enemy rifle grenades and [antitank] bombs of the rocket type fired on the upper surfaces of the tank from upstairs windows. . . . During a sortie, as many as 200 shells have been directed against [the tanks] in town. Despite this, the infantry still prefer to have them in close proximity.

Sweeting told the observer that his use of tanks as close as five yards to the infantry was "an improvised use . . . which should not become a habit." The British officer noted that the Germans used their self-propelled guns aggressively in the town's streets—they would advance to point-blank range, fire, and withdraw—and that chance engagements with American tanks were frequent. There were few long streets, and local commanders had to designate streets for use by friendly tanks; any other vehicular movement was met immediately by fire. The Germans generally used their Mark IV tanks outside the town but occasionally employed them much as the Americans used their Shermans.[21]

Redle described one such encounter, when Sgt. Haskell Oliver's tank was crossing a street to knock holes in the wall of a building near the town jail. A ball of fire streaked past the nose of the tank, and Oliver backed off. Sweeting was in a nearby observation post and reported that a Mark IV had fired at Oliver. Get the panzer, he said.

The infantry watched as Oliver dismounted with his crew to look the situation over from behind a boulder using binoculars so that each man knew where the Mark IV lurked, and they put their heads together to come up with a plan. The crewmen climbed back through their hatches and settled into their seats. Oliver asked if everyone was ready.

Redle recalled:

> At Oliver's command, [Roy] Anderson thrust down on the throttle, and the Sherman suddenly roared around the granite shoulder; he yanked the sticks to align the tank on that Mark IV and heaved back on the sticks to lurch to a stop. [Bert] Bulen, with his head pressed into the sight rest, saw the ground as the 30-ton hulk rocked forward, and as it reared back and the sight came level, he swung the turret and squeezed off the first shot. His hand-eye coordination allowed him to place that first shot as the sights still moved across the target. [Ed] Sadowski slammed shell after shell into the recoiling breech as fast as Bulen fired, Bulen spinning the elevation/deflection wheels quickly and firing again and again. The German was out-maneuvered and was knocked out immediately."[22]

The 34th Infantry Division never did take Cassino. Still, Sweeting's aggressive leadership had so impressed Maj. Gen. Charles Ryder, the commander of the 34th Infantry Division, that he put Sweeting in command of one of his regiments, only to see him captured because of the folly of his personal bravery.[23] Three more bloody Allied assaults would fail to capture the town, which was to fall only when the Allies unhinged the Gustav Line in May. The American tankers kept their hand in for the next round, and in March, the 760th Tank Battalion and several tank destroyer battalions supported the 4th Indian and 2d New Zealand Divisions in their unsuccessful attempt to capture Cassino.[24]

END-AROUND STOPPED AT THE LINE: ANZIO

Discussion of a possible end run had ebbed and flowed from the time Eisenhower had first raised the possibility as German resistance solidified after the Salerno landings. Several strategic considerations were in play. The first was pressure from the Joint Chiefs on Eisenhower to release landing craft on schedule for the invasion of France. The second was an Allied assessment that even in the best case, available transport would support only a small expeditionary force. Alexander identified Anzio as the landing site as early as 8 November, but commanders viewed the entire enterprise as contingent upon making sufficient progress up the peninsula to guarantee a rapid link-up with the landing force. The virtual stalemate in the Winter Position persuaded Clark to recommend scrubbing the operation on 18 December.[25]

By December, Eisenhower had received the nod to take command of the invasion of northwestern Europe, and Gen. Sir Henry Maitland Wilson had been named to take command of a combined Mediterranean and Middle Eastern theater. The British were now unquestionably the senior partners in Italy, and Churchill wanted to pursue the Anzio option. On Christmas Day, Churchill obtained Eisenhower's backing.[26]

The U.S. VI Corps would make the assault. The corps commander, Maj. Gen. John Lucas, would have the American 3d and British 1st Infantry Divisions, the American Ranger Force of three battalions, a British Special Service brigade with two Commando battalions, an American parachute infantry regiment, and an additional parachute battalion. A week before the landings, Clark promised Lucas elements of the 45th Infantry and 1st Armored Divisions, with more to come if needed.[27]

Lucas wanted more time, but the deadline for surrendering landing craft for Operation Overlord permitted no delay. Preparations were rushed. The VI Corps did not fully extricate itself from the line until 3 January 1944, and then the final landing rehearsal, on 19 January, was a fiasco. Lucas recorded that he feared he was in for another Battle of the Little Big Horn and noted on another occasion, "[T]he whole affair has a strong odor of Gallipoli."[28]

The 15th Army Group's Operation Instruction No. 32, issued 2 January 1944, clearly specified, "Fifth Army will prepare an amphibious operation. . . with the object of cutting the enemy lines of communication and threatening the rear of German XIV [Panzer] Corps."[29] Lucas, however, viewed his job as establishing and defending a beachhead at Anzio. He judged his initial assault force to be too weak to risk penetrating the Alban Hills that dominated the landing site from a dozen miles inland, although by doing so he could have cut the main highway—and supply route—from Rome to the Gustav Line as the Fifth Army had been instructed to do.[30] Even the hard-charging 3d Infantry Division's commander, Maj. Gen. Lucian Truscott, did not seem to think that striking out for the Alban Hills would be a good idea.[31] Lucas's decision decided the terms under which the battle at Anzio would be fought.

The Fifth Army's G-2 assessed that the Germans would be able to respond on D-Day with a panzergrenadier division, a tank battalion, four battalions of paratroopers, an antitank battalion or equivalent, and miscellaneous naval and air defense units. On D+1, they were expected to bring to bear a second panzergrenadier division, a tank regiment of the Hermann Göring Panzer Division, an SS infantry regiment, and an infantry regiment.[32] The assault plan anticipated heavy resistance at the beaches and heavy counterattacks as soon as the enemy became aware of the extent of the landings.[33]

All of the beaches in the American zone would require engineering work, such as laying steel mats, to get armored vehicles inland. A sandbar offshore blocked access by LSTs, which would demand the use of pontoons.[34] The lessons of Salerno evidently were fresh enough that this time ways would be found to get the infantry tank support from the start using LCTs, which could land at spots.

The VI Corps also took steps to address the shortfalls that had emerged in tank-infantry cooperation. At Naples, the 3d Infantry Division and the attached 751st Tank Battalion underwent vigorous training and joint exercises.[35]

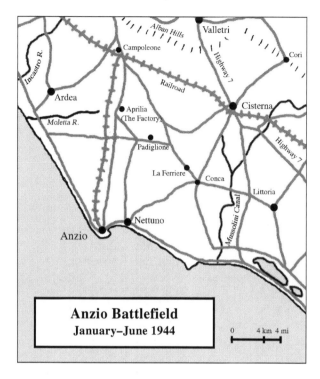

Anzio Battlefield
January–June 1944

0   4 km 4 mi

H-Hour was 0200 hours on 22 January, the amphibious operation was picture-perfect, and the assault troops were astonished to find that there was no enemy to meet them—the operation had caught the Germans completely by surprise. A few antiaircraft batteries on the coast fired several rounds, but only two battered battalions from the 29th Panzergrenadier Division were anywhere near Anzio.[36] By 0240, the 751st Tank Battalion had its Company A on land, with a platoon moving to support each of the three regimental combat teams of the 3d Division. Resistance, as it turned out, was virtually nonexistent off the beach, as well, and the infantry quickly occupied its initial objectives and dug in against counterattack. Company B and the mortar platoon were ashore by '0700, and the rest of the battalion shortly after noon.[37]

The British 1st Infantry Division landed to the left and also made easy progress inland; engineers and the navy had the port of Anzio open by mid-afternoon. By midnight, the VI Corps had 36,000 men and 3,200 vehicles ashore. It had lost only thirteen men killed and ninety-seven wounded.[38]

The first tank-backed patrols from the Hermann Göring Panzer Division, rushing to contain the landing zone, appeared at the Mussolini Canal at about 1800 hours but were driven off, and the American tankers worked with the GIs against German infantry elements through 24 January. Things changed dramatically the next day, when the 15th and 30th Infantry Regiments tried to push into Cisterna and were thrown back by the Hermann Göring Panzer Division, which was now present in strength.[39] On the twenty-seventh, a platoon of Company C, 751st Tank Battalion, engaged an enemy force including tanks and knocked out one panzer.[40]

Far from abandoning the Gustav Line, the Germans were moving reinforcements toward Anzio at incredible speed and showed every sign of being determined to throw the invaders back into the sea. The 29th Panzergrenadier Regiment and 4th Airborne Division concentrated opposite the British, and the 1st Airborne and 26th Panzer Divisions were on their way from the Adriatic side of Italy.

The German command had anticipated such a landing as this in late 1943 and had issued requirements to commanders in France, the Balkans, and the Replacement Army in Germany to have formations ready to go to Italy should the need arise. Detailed deployment plans were in place. Construction had also begun on the Gothic Line across the top of the boot before the Po Valley in case an Allied landing rendered lines in central Italy untenable.[41]

Major General Lucas judged that the beachhead was secure enough to attack toward the Alban Hills on 30 January, by which time the 1st Armored Division's Combat Command A had arrived to give him a powerful strike force. The 45th Infantry Division had debarked and taken responsibility for part of the 3d Division's line.

Lucas was too late. On 24 January, a ring was completed around the beachhead, and German commanders concluded that the danger of a breakout had passed. The 1st Airborne and 26th Panzer Divisions arrived in time to blunt the attack, and elements of the 3d Panzergrenadier, 715th Motorized Infantry, 65th and 71st Infantry, and 90th Panzergrenadier Divisions appeared on the front, along with battalions from other formations. By 2 February, the threat of a massive counterattack was so stark that Clark ordered the VI Corps to go over to the defensive.[42]

Greeted by rocket fire, the 191st Tank Battalion had arrived off Anzio on 31 January with elements of the 1st Armored Division. On 1 February, the outfit was attached to the 3d Infantry Division. "The new attachment was purely a defensive measure," recorded the battalion's after-action report. "The 3d Infantry Division had reason to expect an enemy armored attack. Its 751st Tank Battalion was already thinly deployed along a wide front, and additional antitank defense was necessary."[43]

Conditions were about as bad as they could be from a tanker's perspective. "The battalion occupied a bald area south of Le Ferriere," the after-action report continued. "In only a very few sections of the beachhead would the terrain permit movement of tanks off the roads. A good many vehicles bogged down during combat and had to be abandoned. Frequent rains did little to alleviate the difficulty. Cover and concealment were at a minimum. Much of the land was perfectly flat. Houses, haystacks, and an occasional fold or gully were the only means of concealment."

Tanks were deployed in depth alongside the infantry holding the main line of resistance. The battalion's six new M7 Priest assault guns, grouped as a battery, tied into the 41st Field Artillery Battalion, while one platoon of each medium tank company registered for indirect fire missions with the 39th Field Artillery.

The defensive action cost a tank here and a tank there, and on 10 February, the battalion shifted to support the 45th Infantry Division's fruitless attack toward "the Factory" at Carroceto. The British had just attacked up the same road and reported the area was crawling with panzers. They had lost seven tanks but could say little about where the Germans were hiding.

Companies A and B rolled out at 0630 on 11 February. Almost immediately, direct fire set one Sherman ablaze. Disabled British tanks blocked the road, and gunners could spot no targets. Immobilized, the tankers expended all of their ammo against possible enemy positions and then withdrew around midday under intense enemy fire. Each company had lost five tanks. When the attack sputtered out the next day, the tankers reverted to a defensive role.[44]

The story was the same everywhere in the beachhead. The cessation of the VI Corps' forward movement left it holding a zone some seven miles deep and fifteen miles wide, where the terrain was generally flat. Meanwhile, the Germans held the high ground inland, from which they could observe and shoot at almost anything within the Allied lines. The Fifth Army observed that bound on the flanks by the Moletta River on the left and swamps and the Mussolini Canal on the right, it was a strong defensive beachhead.[45] But in Alexander's eyes, that had not been its purpose.

Lieutenant Colonel Hammack of the 751st Tank Battalion concluded in early February that effective tank-infantry cooperation was not possible without continuous communication. The placement of a liaison team with an SCR-509 radio at the infantry battalion command post had proved satisfactory, in his view, but he judged that tanks should never be attached to units below a battalion because of the lack of communications.[46] This was allowing communications to drive tactical employment of tanks rather than the other way around. On the far side of the world at Kwajalein, some of his counterparts at this very time were experimenting with ways to establish communications at the lowest tactical level.

On 16 February, the Germans launched their last attempt to annihilate the beachhead. The Hermann Göring Panzer Division joined the 3d Panzergrenadier and 715th Motorized divisions in a thrust against the sector held by the 45th Division's 157th and 179th Infantry regiments, on the American left just south of Aprilia and east of the Anzio-Campoleone road.[47]

This time, the enemy suffered the consequences of being unable to move off the roads, and gunners in the 191st Tank Battalion picked panzers off one by one. The assault guns got the drop on six Tigers mired in mud and destroyed them all. The German attack ran out of steam by 1800 hours, by which time the 191st Tank Battalion counted fifteen panzers positively destroyed at the cost of seven Shermans.

That night, the tanks remained in place with the infantry. Three Shermans from Company C were supporting Company E, 157th Infantry, when German infantry supported by a few panzers assaulted the position. The enemy was able to surround the tanks, which blazed away with all weapons into the dark. Crewmen added Tommy gun and carbine fire from the turret ports and expended 15,000 rounds of small-arms ammunition. Panzers crawled within fifty yards of the American tanks, and two were dispatched.[48]

About midnight, persistent German attacks tore a hole at the seam between the two American regiments, and by dawn, the enemy had created a two-mile-deep salient that threatened the survival of the beachhead. Massive use of artillery and air strikes, and the commitment of elements from the 1st Armored Division, destroyed the German spearhead over the next several days. By 22 February, the counterattack had petered out.[49]

As the Anzio beachhead settled down into stalemates, the tank battalions—against all doctrine and the expressed views of battalion commanders—largely became providers of antitank defenses. The 751st Tank Battalion's medium companies, for example, were usually deployed in defensive positions, often dug-in firing points, alongside the infantry. The outfit's after-action report notes four platoon-size tank-on-tank fights during February, with about even losses for the two sides. Attempts to advance even to support patrols usually drew lethal antitank fire. Morale and health declined as crews spent weeks on end sitting in their immobile tanks on the line. The assault gun platoon, with the three line-company assault guns attached, was attached to a field artillery unit.[50]

The 191st Tank Battalion organized nocturnal "shoots" starting in March, which were designed mainly to harass the enemy. "Aside from whatever material benefit the 'shoots' produced," recorded the after-action report, "they were excellent morale stimulants for the tank crews, who spend so many weary hours 'sweating out' enemy fire without delivering any in return."[51]

In April, the 34th Infantry Division, just transferred from the southern front, relieved the 3d Infantry Division, but the 751st Tank Battalion remained in the line with the new command, despite seventy days of continuous action. The 34th Division made greater use of the tanks as a reserve and to fire artillery missions.[52]

On 25 April, the 34th Infantry Division experimented with a small-scale tank-infantry raid. The objective was a German-held house. Two tanks fired fifteen 75-millimeter rounds apiece at the structure, and then four tanks with infantry on the decks rushed it, all guns firing. The infantry jumped off a short distance from the building and stormed it, taking six prisoners, and the raiding party withdrew.

"Tank-borne infantry has been tried and is successful," observed Maj. Roue Hogan, now acting commander of the 751st Battalion. "It got the infantry to their objective with great speed. The doughboys did not have to worry about antipersonnel mines. He protected himself from enemy fire by crouching behind the turret."[53]

STATE OF THE ART

By early 1944, infantry commanders knew there were serious problems with tank-infantry cooperation. As to the importance of the tank to the infantry, Col. W. Shephard, assistant division commander in the 3d Infantry Division, told a War

Department observer, "I have determined since I have been here that it is the consensus of the officers that these infantry will not go forward without tanks, and will not stay in a defense without tanks. They just won't do it."

His boss, Brig. Gen. John "Iron Mike" O'Daniel, said, "Tanks and infantry must be trained together. . . . The same tank battalion should be attached to an infantry division all the time. The planning of the tanks into the attack with the infantry should be normal. We will have to do much more tank-infantry fighting when we get to France."

Frequent reattachment of separate tank battalions to unfamiliar infantry commands had remained a problem. "My battalion was attached so many times that I almost lost count," complained Lt. Col. Glenn Rogers, the commander of the 756th Tank Battalion. "In one case, the battalion was attached to three different organizations within a period of twelve hours."[54]

Lt. Gen. Jacob Devers, the deputy supreme commander-in-chief in the Mediterranean, tried to improve the situation. He told a War Department observer in March, "The Army Ground Forces should consider including the tank battalion as an organic unit in the infantry division. . . . The teamwork required of the infantry and tanks is so close that it cannot be effectively carried out if the tank battalions are continuously shifted from division to division. . . . All the infantry division commanders in this theater have expressed their urgent desire to have the tank battalion permanently attached. I am attaching the tank battalions available in this theater to the infantry divisions on a permanent basis."

The observer who interviewed Devers recommended that some means of allowing tanks and infantry to communicate by radio be perfected. He proposed as an interim measure that an infantry SCR-300 radio be mounted in each tank platoon commander's vehicle, an idea that would bear fruit after several months.[55]

Nevertheless, at the time of the spring offensive in May 1944, headquarters of the Mediterranean theater of operations still found general agreement among the Fifth Army's units "that there has been a definite lack of coordination and teamwork vitally necessary . . . particularly between infantry and tanks."[56]

Extremely lethal Panther medium tanks had been encountered for the first time at the Anzio beachhead, which marked a sudden shift of technological advantage to German tankers. The Mark V mounted a high-velocity 75-millimeter cannon that could hole the front armor of a Sherman at ordinary combat ranges while presenting well-sloped front armor nearly three inches thick that was impervious to the M4's 75-millimeter gun. Moreover, the American tankers were fighting in old vehicles; new ones were being shipped to units in the United Kingdom preparing for the invasion of France. A War Department observer on armor matters who visited North Africa and Italy in early 1944 reported, "The medium tanks in this theater are all of the old 1942 manufacture [M4 and M4A1]. They do not incorporate the modifications and corrections for deficiencies discovered in combat and testing in 1942 and 1943. . . . Even when fully modified, these tanks will be greatly below the standard of 1944 production tanks." All tanks available as replacements had already seen heavy use in training or combat.[57]

Another War Department observer who visited Italy in March 1944 found tankers hungry for the reported M4 models with a 76-millimeter gun. Indeed, as a result of his visit, Allied Forces Headquarters cabled the War Department requesting the replacement of 75-millimeter models with the 76 millimeter. Tankers also expressed great interest in tanks with the Ford V-8 engine in place of their radials. Tank users expressed general dissatisfaction with the M5 and M5A1 light tanks because of the 37-millimeter gun's lack of punch and the large percentage of dud 37-millimeter rounds received.[58]

By early 1944, tankers had found "field solutions" to the complaint that armored men had raised about the M4's gun sights in North Africa. One Army Ground Forces observer reported, "All types of sights are used on the medium tank. They vary from old machine-sights to captured sights. Some standard sight is needed."[59]

CRACKING THE GUSTAV LINE

In April, the Allies had repositioned forces on the southern front to concentrate all Commonwealth divisions and the Polish Corps on the 15th Army Group's right under the Eighth Army, while the Fifth Army held the left end of the line with the II Corps adjacent to the sea and the French Expeditionary Corps to its right. The II Corps now contained the 36th, 85th, and 88th Infantry Divisions, the 34th Infantry Division having joined the VI Corps at Anzio. The IV Corps had joined the Fifth Army and was to take possession of part of the front in June. The inter-army boundary ran along Highway 6, and the Eighth Army had responsibility for the Cassino sector and the Liri Valley.[60]

The 15th Army Group planned to drive north past Rome with its two armies advancing in parallel. At 2300 hours on 11 May, the II Corps, the French Expeditionary Corps, and the British 13 Corps attacked the Gustav Line in full strength from the Garigliano River to Cassino. The objectives were two: to crack the German defenses and to draw German divisions away from Anzio to ease the planned breakout there. The offensive succeeded on both counts.[61]

Les Chars Americaines!

The Fifth Army had been supplying the French with considerable armor, artillery, and antiaircraft support because the French lacked such separate battalions.[62] In May, the 2d Armored Group was attached to the French Expeditionary Corps, which included the French 1st Infantry Division (1st DFL or 1st DMI), 2d Moroccan Infantry Division (2d DIM), 3d Algerian Infantry Division (3d DIA), and 4th Moroccan Mountain Division (4th DMM). The French divisions each fielded a battalion-size light tank element called a regiment, but the French had no battalions equivalent to the medium-tank-heavy American formations. The 2d Armored Group had first worked with the French in January, when usually one company at a time from the 755th Tank Battalion had been attached to the 2d DIM and 3d

DIA; the 757th Tank Battalion had joined the rotation in February. By late May, the 2d Armored Group grew to include the 753d, 755th, 756th, and 757th Tank Battalions.[63] This was the largest commitment of separate armored battalions to a foreign command during the war.

Clark intended to hit the Germans hard in the French sector, where they least expected it, and elements of all four French divisions were included from the very start. The initial French objective was Mount Majo, whose seizure would fall to the 2d DIM.[64]

The French plan of attack against the Gustav Line in the vicinity of Castelforte, which lay on the French left near the boundary line with the II Corps, incorporated the use of mobile forces and a regiment (brigade) each from the 1st DMI and 3d DIA. The 757th Tank Battalion was attached to Gen. Diego Brosset's 1st DMI, while the 755th Tank Battalion was held in reserve to exploit any breakthrough. Brosset conceived an employment of the American tanks that was idiosyncratic. He created three waves of armor, each consisting of an American medium tank company, a light tank company (one American and one each from the 1st DMI and 2d DIM), a company of French tank destroyers, a company of infantry, and a platoon of engineers. An infantry regiment was to advance parallel to the armored thrust across high ground too rough for the tanks. The French and Americans spent the first eleven days of May working out tactical plans and communications schemes.

A French barrage commenced at 2300 hours on 11 May, and the tanks rolled unheard by the enemy into attack positions by 0300 hours on the twelfth. While it was still dark, the first wave of the 4th Brigade of the 1st DMI forded the Garigliano River with the infantry riding the medium tanks, crossed an antitank ditch that French engineers had bridged during the night, and attacked German positions southeast of San Andrea. The next two waves followed.

Jack Hay, a Company A driver in the first wave, recalled

> The [French] infantry would ride on our tanks, with about ten soldiers on each tank. We also had a company of chemical mortars. They would cover the valley with smoke and camouflage us from the enemy. . . . On the morning we started the offensive, it was foggy mixed with smoke from the chemical mortars. . . . As we traveled through no-man's-land in the valley, we came closer to the German defenses. Then things started really happening. Machine guns were rattling, and mortars were exploding. The [French] soldiers left our tanks in a hurry.

The French infantry started up a hill, and the American tankers, unable to follow, watched them fall.[65]

At 0615, Company A of the 755th Tank Battalion was thrown into the attack on Castelforte alongside the 4th Tunisian Infantry Regiment, 3d DIA, while the French tank destroyers provided overwatch and the tank battalion's six assault guns, working as a platoon, fired in direct support.[66] Late in the afternoon, the tanks closed to within 100 yards of Castelforte and fired to cover the infantry, who stormed the town. Gen. Goislard de Monsabert, commanding the 3d DIA, watched the assault and then called the 755th Tank Battalion's command post to express his admiration for the action of the tankers.

In two days, the 2d DIM seized its objective and tore a hole in the Gustav Line that the Germans could not mend. The 4th Brigade of the 1st DIM and its attached 757th Tank Battalion Shermans made a nearly simultaneous penetration near Sant' Andrea. The French corps was off and running, outpacing the Americans and British on the flanks. By 19 May, the 1st DMI and 3d DIA had surrounded and captured Mount d'Oro, which rendered the Germans' Hitler Line—the fallback position to the Gustav Line—untenable. "The operations of the [French] during the period 11–19 May," recorded the Fifth Army history, "form one of the most spectacular and most important parts of the entire drive on Rome."[67]

The 756th Tank Battalion was attached to the 2d Armored Group on 19 May, and the 753d Tank Battalion was attached the next day. This allowed a tank battalion to work with each attacking French infantry division, per American practice.[68]

Despite having received American training in North Africa, the French apparently lacked a well-developed doctrine for the use of separate tank battalions with the infantry, and in fact, they used separate commanders for the infantry and armored components of an operation rather than subordinating supporting tanks to the infantry commander on the scene. Lt. Col. Glenn Rogers, who had taken command of the 756th Tank Battalion, observed,

> The habitual practice of the [4th DMM] was to detach a small tank force and put it under the command of a French officer. The tank battalion commander was usually not consulted regarding the employment of the tanks, and precise information was difficult to get because of the system of having one officer (French) in charge of all armored operations, one officer in charge of infantry operations, another officer to coordinate the plans, and, on top of this, a *groupement* commander in charge of the entire operation. Generally, an attempt to find out the precise plans resulted in a fruitless visit from one officer to another, each referring the inquirer to someone else. For instance, a visit to the general generally resulted in being referred to a major, who referred me to another major, who referred me back to the general. As a result of uncertainty, our troops became dubious and hesitant, even over perfectly proper orders.[69]

The battalion had fought beside the 1st DMI and then the 3d DIA before joining the 4th DMM. Capt. French Lewis, who commanded Company A, recalled, "Naturally, being in the mountains, most tank actions were restricted to a one-tank front with a steep mountain on one side of the road and a deep valley on the other. Most actions were conducted by platoons. Most often, the lieutenant or his platoon sergeant would be in the lead tank. That would be fighting at 100-percent efficiency, wishing for 200 percent. The second tank was at about 50–75 percent efficiency, due to restricted visibility and terrain." The other tanks were out of play. Captain Lewis found that the French inevitably wanted the tanks to go down every road first, whether or not infantry was going to follow them. The battalion executive officer, Major Dolvin, and a French-speaking lieutenant spent most of their time keeping the tanks out of trouble.[70]

The 2d Armored Group's after-action report summarized the experience of all its battalions:

> The ground around the Gustav Line and Hitler Line was very mountainous and rugged, pierced by narrow roads. . . . The attacks were limited to road nets, which were easily defended by antitank guns, mines, and roadblocks. It was impossible to use flanking tactics to reduce these threats. Of necessity, a system of well-coordinated teamwork was developed between the tanks and the infantry. . . . After the penetration of the Gustav Line, the attack moved forward very rapidly. . . .
>
> The burden of the attack was carried by the medium tanks. Light tank companies were used mainly to mop up and neutralize enemy units that had been cut off. They were also used for reconnaissance and flank protection. The six self-propelled 105-millimeter assault guns (M7) in each battalion were grouped into one battery and gave direct fire support to the leading elements of the battalions.[71]

One solution worked out with the French to overcome language and technical barriers to communication was to place a French interpreter equipped with an SCR-300 walkie-talkie infantry radio in the tank of each platoon leader during an attack. The tankers also established a close relationship with field artillery units attached to the French, using their Cub light planes to spot panzers and strongpoints along the route of advance. The tankers had also gained a real respect for French M10 tank destroyers, especially after encountering Panther and Tiger tanks that were impervious to the 75-millimeter guns on their Shermans. Whenever possible, concluded the 2d Armored Group, tank destroyers should overwatch any tank advance.[72]

The 753d and 756th Tank battalions were detached from the 2d Armored Group on 30 and 31 May, respectively, to support the American drive on Rome, while the 894th Tank Destroyer Battalion, equipped with M10s, joined the group in June. Some of the tankers' French partners would soon have a campaign to fight for the liberation of France.

Linkup

With the Fifth Army's separate tank battalions concentrated on the wings in the French sector and the Anzio beachhead, the 760th Tank Battalion shuttled between the 85th and 88th Infantry Divisions mounting the II Corps' drive across the Garigliano and along the coast.

The II Corps assaulted the Hitler Line on 20 May and cut through it with relative ease, as the Germans had lacked time to get set and bring up reinforcements. By the time the 29th Panzergrenadier Division arrived on 21 May to strengthen the line, it was too late.[73]

Minefields and antitank guns claimed a steady, low-level attrition from the 760th Tank Battalion, as the corps captured a series of urban strong points along the route to Anzio: Santa Maria, Formia, Gaeta, Itri. At dusk on 21 May, Company B reached a point on Highway 7 some 500 yards short of the port of Terracina, the last stronghold separating the II and VI Corps.

The German roadblock outside town defied efforts to overcome it, and the advance seemed stymied until an engineer on 22 May discovered a mule trail that looped around the town through the hills. The engineers went to work, and about 1600 hours, Company D's light tanks set off through the "impassable" terrain, followed by Company B's mediums. The tankers brushed aside some infantry and took positions from where they could overlook the town and cut the road north of Terracina by fire. Friendly infantry joined the tankers on their perch.

The Germans threw in the towel and pulled out, blowing up bridges behind them. But the way ahead was open all the way to the Pontine Marshes. On 24 May, the 91st Cavalry Reconnaissance Squadron was unleashed to make contact with the Anzio beachhead forces. Troop A made first contact near Borgo Grappa on the morning of 25 May. Lieutenant General Clark, who had been in the Anzio beachhead during the breakout, was able to personally greet the troops from his reunited Fifth Army, because the VI Corps had not been idle during May.[74]

THE ANZIO BREAKOUT AND CAPTURE OF ROME

The weather in the Anzio beachhead had turned suddenly to summer during May, and swampy fields that had stopped tanks during the winter had turned hard and firm. Tanks no longer would be limited to the road net.[75]

Operation Buffalo, the breakout from Anzio, commenced at 0545 hours on 23 May with a crushing artillery barrage. Forty-five minutes later, the 1st Armored Division, supported by the 3d Infantry Division and the Canadian-American First Special Service Force (FSSF, known as the Devil's Brigade by the Germans), launched the main attack into the surprised German ranks. The 45th Infantry Division shielded the VI Corps' left, and the 36th Infantry Division waited in reserve, ready to exploit any breakthrough.[76]

The 751st Tank Battalion, attached to the 3d Infantry Division, ran into numerous mines on the twenty-third. The battalion attempted to employ an explosive "snake," a long tube that exploded to clear mine fields. A snake had been used successfully that day by the 1st Armored Division's Combat Command A, but the system now failed because it was assembled too far from the line of departure. Eight tanks and a tankdozer fell prey to the mines and two more to antitank fire. Company A destroyed a single Mark IV, which was small compensation.

The 751st Tank Battalion was involved in a second clever but ineffective idea with the use of "battle sleds," which were towed by tanks and carried specially trained infantry. Each regiment was issued ten sleds and two platoons of medium tanks to tow them. Only the 15th and 30th Infantry regiments decided to send forward a platoon each of tanks towing sleds, and both attempts proved failures when the tanks encountered obstructions and stopped and the Germans responded with a mortar or artillery barrage.

The tank-infantry team came within a whisker of the solution to tactical communications that would, one day soon, dramatically improve teamwork. The battalion had drawn five SCR-300 radios but, for reasons unknown, found that in most cases the link was unsatisfactory. Liaison officers equipped with SCR-509s at infantry battalion and regimental command posts carried most of the communication load.[77]

Every one of the four National Guard tank battalions experienced a particular hell, and for the 191st Tank Battalion, that battle was the breakout from Anzio. The tankers participated in two supporting thrusts rather than the main effort, but the outfit suffered the worst losses of all the separate battalions that participated in the breakout. This came on top of months during which the battalion had received many unqualified replacements and been unable to adequately train the men.

Worthy of passing note, the battalion employed two tankdozers—Shermans with bulldozer blades mounted on the front—before and during the assault, which appears to have been their first use in combat by a separate tank battalion. The dozers created bypasses and stream crossings, cleared brush, and created dug-in firing points for the tanks.

For Operation Buffalo, Companies A and D were attached to the 645th Tank Destroyer Battalion to work with the FSSF, which pushed out on the right flank toward Cori. The infantry and tankers trained together intensively for the three days before the attack. The battalion, with Companies B and C, joined the 45th Infantry Division and attacked toward the northwest between Aprilia and Campoleone through heavy minefields.

In the FSSF's zone, the assault force crossed prepared bridges over the Mussolini Canal in a peculiar order—light tanks, medium tanks and tank destroyers, and then infantry. Two battalions of the German 1028th Infantry Regiment, 362d Infantry Division; an Italian SS battalion; and a company of tanks held the enemy line. "Resistance was fanatical, and casualties mounted fast," recorded the tank battalion's informal history. The American tanks plowed into minefields covered by high-velocity fire from panzers and guns, and the mines alone disabled ten light tanks and four mediums. Two light tanks reached a point 200 yards south of Highway 7 but had to withdraw because the infantry did not arrive. The North American doughboys were pinned down by the same fire and were suffering heavy casualties.

At 1530 hours, medium tanks took the lead, and Company A's 1st and 3d Platoons crossed Highway 7 only to run into seventeen panzers identified as Tigers, though it is more likely they were Mark IVs as the Shermans knocked out two with their 75-millimeter guns. Withdrawal was in order. One tank in the 3d Platoon fired smoke to cover the 1st Platoon's retreat, but it was hit and set afire. None of the 1st Platoon tanks made it out of the inferno, and only two 3d Platoon tanks managed to escape. The FSSF pulled back 600 yards south of the highway, but some elements were cut off and continued to fight for two days until reached by the 34th Infantry Division.

2d Lt. Thomas Fowler, erroneously identified as belonging to the 1st Armored Division by most sources, was awarded the Medal of Honor for his actions when the tank-infantry team started to come unglued. His citation reads,

> In the midst of a full-scale armored-infantry attack, 2d Lieutenant Fowler, while on foot, came upon two completely disorganized infantry platoons held up in their advance by an enemy minefield. Although a tank officer, he immediately reorganized the infantry. He then made a personal reconnaissance through the minefield, clearing a path as he went, by lifting the antipersonnel mines out of the ground with his hands. After he had gone through the 75-yard belt of deadly explosives, he returned to the infantry and led them through the minefield, a squad at a time. As they deployed, 2d Lieutenant Fowler, despite small-arms fire and the constant danger of antipersonnel mines, made a reconnaissance into enemy territory in search of a route to continue the advance.
>
> He then returned through the minefield and, on foot, he led the tanks through the mines into a position from which they could best support the infantry. Acting as scout 300 yards in front of the infantry, he led the two platoons forward until he had gained his objective, where he came upon several dug-in enemy infantrymen. Having taken them by surprise, 2d Lieutenant Fowler dragged them out of their foxholes and sent them to the rear; twice, when they resisted, he threw hand grenades into their dugouts. Realizing that a dangerous gap existed between his company and the unit to his right, 2d Lieutenant Fowler decided to continue his advance until the gap was filled. He reconnoitered to his front, brought the infantry into position where they dug in and, under heavy mortar and small-arms fire, brought his tanks forward.
>
> A few minutes later, the enemy began an armored counterattack. Several Mark VI tanks fired their cannons directly on 2d Lieutenant Fowler's position. One of his tanks was set afire. With utter disregard for his own life, with shells bursting near him, he ran directly into the enemy tank fire to reach the burning vehicle. For a half-hour, under intense strafing from the advancing tanks, although all other elements had withdrawn, he remained in his forward position, attempting to save the lives of the wounded tank crew. Only when the enemy tanks had almost overrun him did he withdraw a short distance where he personally rendered first aid to nine wounded infantrymen in the midst of the relentless incoming fire.

Fowler was killed on 3 June at the age of twenty-two. He was not alone among the men of the 191st Tank Battalion.

Both the battalion commander and executive officer were wounded on the first day of the breakout. From 23 May to 5 June, all but five of nineteen battalion officers became casualties, most to aimed sniper fire directed at tank commanders, along with seventy-five enlisted men. An officer from the 601st Tank Destroyer Battalion assumed temporary command of the battalion on 28 May, until Maj. Welborn Dolvin moved from his executive officer job in the 756th Tank Battalion to take command of the battered outfit on 3 June.[78]

We now make a slight detour to another part of the armored force, the 1st Armored Division, which for a few hectic days in early June implemented the doctrinal vision of attaching separate tank battalions to an armored division—sort of. Most of the separate tank battalions in Italy at one time or another had been attached to the division for training during periods out of the line. But none had yet fought under its command.

On 26 May, the 13th Armored Regiment's commanding officer, Col. Hamilton Howze, was given his regiment's light tank battalion and one of its medium tank battalions, along with orders to slip behind Combat Command B and attack northward. The division's operational plan had not anticipated using the reserve in combat as a unit, but division commander Maj. Gen. Ernest Harmon saw an opportunity and took it. While most of the Fifth Army expended its strength against determined German defenses in the Alban Hills and west thereof along Highway 7, Harmon saw a chance to slip around the Alban Hills to the east, cut Highway 6 (the main supply route to the German Tenth Army in the Gustav Line), and swing west along the highway into Rome in short order.

This plan did not pan out because Lt. Gen. Mark Clark at the Fifth Army insisted on battering away at the German line from the Alban Hills west with the 1st Armored Division and the 34th and 45th Infantry Divisions. Nevertheless, the task force had nearly reached Highway 6 when, on the night of 30 March, the 36th Infantry Division found a soft spot in the German line among the slopes of Colli Laziali. The resulting penetration over the next three days unhinged the German defenses south of Rome.[79]

On 1 June, the 756th Tank Battalion, which had just shifted into the Anzio sector of the newly unified front, was attached to Task Force Howze for the advance on Rome. Howze and Lt. Col. Glenn Rogers were old friends from cavalry days. Howze's task force at this point otherwise included the 7th Infantry's 1st Battalion, the 59th Field Artillery Battalion, and a British outfit equipped with 105-millimeter guns.

On the morning of 2 June, the 88th Infantry Division asserted a claim to the 756th Tank Battalion and removed it from the task force.[80] Lt. David Redle, commanding Company B, got his tanks to the right sector, found the infantry commander, and proposed that some of the infantry mount the tanks for the operation.

Working from hill to hill along Highway 6, the tank company advanced by fire and movement, one of the rare occasions it was able to do so in Italy. One platoon advanced on the objective, while the other two fired on it. Once the lead platoon was on the objective, the other two advanced, and one of those two set off for the next hilltop. Progress was so rapid that the doughboys on foot fell behind.[81]

On 2 June, meanwhile, Howze was given even greater strength: the 1st Battalion, 349th Infantry, 88th Infantry Division, plus a company of tank destroyers. That evening, Howze received orders to get to Rome as fast as possible.

On 3 June, the 88th Division gave Rogers the same instructions Howze had received—get to Rome as quickly as possible—which led to Howze's and Rogers's tanks becoming snarled along Highway 6 early that morning. Howze tracked down Rogers, and the latter—regardless of his instructions—agreed to put himself under Howze. During the day, the 88th Division first attached him to the 85th Infantry Division and finally to Howze. Howze shifted Rogers's battalion to a parallel road south of the main highway and attached to it the 1st Battalion, 7th Infantry. The two tank-infantry columns, the GIs perched on the back decks of the tanks, plowed forward abreast through frequent German delaying positions. When Rogers was pinched out by the road net, Howze shifted him north of Highway 6, and his men captured crossings on the Aniene River and roared across.

Howze recalled:

From time to time I became dissatisfied with our speed and the caution with which our tanks would size up each bit of terrain before going over it—so I would issue orders to put a platoon on the road and barrel down it at ten miles an hour. I would watch this platoon—in a few minutes the lead tank would stop and burst into flames. Here again was a dilemma— it was difficult and unpleasant to dispatch an element in what amounted in part to a suicide mission, but on the other hand such a maneuver frequently resulted in our gaining 2,000 or 3,000 yards in thirty minutes, at the cost of a single tank.

Howze led from the front and shared the danger; at one point, he and Rogers found themselves crouched in a ditch under fire waiting for the tanks to come up.[82]

The tankers' experience during the advance into Rome the next day demonstrated that they could work effectively with an unfamiliar infantry outfit if even five or ten hours were devoted to coordinating operations before an attack. On 4 June, the 756th Tank Battalion was ordered to work with the First Special Service Force, which the preceding evening had come up and taken control of the task force. Task Force Howze was to attack during daylight hours and the FSSF during the night.

Despite strafing attacks by Allied P-40s and Spitfires on the 756th Tank Battalion that shot some of the infantry off the tanks, the task force was soon fighting in the outskirts of Rome. The FSSF had carefully coordinated its planning with Rogers, even to the point of delaying its attack an hour rather than sacrificing teamwork. Tank-infantry cooperation went off like "clockwork," reported Rogers, despite having to rely on hand signals and runners, and casualties were very light among tankers and infantry.

Redle recalled one example of that working with a battalion commanded by a Canadian: "A runner came back to my tank and climbed up on the tank. He said they were getting machine-gun fire from the top of a silo on our right flank. Sergeant Frank Mielcarski knocked off the top of the silo. The messenger had a big grin as he headed back to his unit. A few minutes later he was back to inform us that another machine gun was firing from the bottom of the silo. Frank just knocked down the entire silo."

At 1530 hours, Howze led an ad hoc command that included the 756th Tank Battalion, the 2d and 3d Special Service Force Regiments, and the 7th Infantry's 1st Battalion to objectives on the Tiber River. The 2d Regiment led with the tanks, which were attached by section to each rifle platoon. Howze recalled, "Immediately resistance was encountered, and no matter what its character, the infantry whistled up a tank that blasted it out. This attack made fine progress against considerable resistance; we lost two tanks but knocked out five, plus some guns, and killed [many] and captured a good batch of prisoners."

Redle's Company B encountered four of the panzers and learned of their presence when high-velocity rounds suddenly knocked out two Shermans. Bert Bulen, the gunner in one of the disabled tanks, spotted a flash, fired at it, and destroyed a panzer. His tank commander realized the problem and radioed that the panzers were camouflaged as haystacks. Bulen dispatched a second panzer, and other gunners claimed two more.

A battalion of the 3d Regiment operated in small patrols without tank support once the command entered the built-up city center, each team equipped with a typed note in Italian instructing the recipient to lead the men to a specific bridge on the Tiber. The scheme worked well, and by 0200 hours on 5 June, the 756th Tank Battalion had joined the infantry at five bridges, a tank at each end.[83]

Company A of the 191st Tank Battalion, despite its heavy losses in the breakout, also reached the Tiber not far away early on the fifth. The company formed part of the 34th Infantry Division's Force A, along with a company of infantry, a reconnaissance company, a field artillery battery, and an engineer detachment. Scouts found an intact bridge, and just before dawn, the task force crossed the Tiber and pressed on five miles north of the river.[84]

In the meantime, the 760th Tank Battalion had penetrated Rome from the south with the II Corps' 85th Infantry Division. The 3d Platoons of Companies A and D were assigned to a 338th Infantry Regiment task force with orders to drive up Highway 6 into the city to secure bridges across the Tiber. Antitank fire stopped the column on the outskirts at about 1500 hours, but the infantry eventually outflanked the guns, and the tanks were able to move on at about 1830 hours. At 2025 hours, the light tanks reached the Coliseum, and heretofore quiet streets filled with excited crowds. The task force reported it had captured the bridges intact at 0030 hours on 5 June.[85]

The 756th Tank Battalion had no time to rest and was attached to Task Force Ellis, formed around the 1st Armored Division's 91st Cavalry Reconnaissance Squadron (itself attached to the 88th Infantry Division) and commanded by that outfit's Lt. Col. Charles Ellis. The task force pushed northward on 6 June immediately parallel to a reduced Task Force Howze. The tankers learned from Ellis that the Allies had landed in Normandy, which they hoped would take some of the load off the soldiers fighting in Italy. The advance encountered no resistance until heavy artillery fire brought the column to a halt at Formello. Subsequent investigation suggested that the fire originated from the 88th Infantry Division, competently adjusted by the 117th Cavalry Reconnaissance Squadron.

The structure of the task force revealed how far American forces had come in learning to build task-based commands incorporating divisional and non-divisional armor, infantry, and artillery. In addition to the cavalry squadron and the 756th Tank Battalion, the task force consisted of the 88th Infantry Division's 3d Battalion, 351st Infantry; the 804th Tank Destroyer Battalion; the 93d Armored Field Artillery Battalion, and the 313th Engineer Battalion.

Ellis divided his task force into two columns, each commanded by the senior infantry officer present. A reconnaissance troop scouted ahead of each, followed in turn by a company each of tanks and tank destroyers carrying infantry. A reserve force of tanks, tank destroyers, and engineers was ready to reinforce either column as needed. The 93d Armored Field Artillery Battalion, with the tank battalion's six assault guns attached, supported both advancing elements.[86]

The 752d Tank Battalion, which had entered the line only on 27 May and was attached to the 88th Infantry Division, recorded in its after-action report, "From 6 June until 13 June, the battalion spent chasing the Germans at full speed with nothing but token resistance."[87] The 1st Armored Group, which had been functioning as an armor staff for the II Corps, formed the headquarters of Task Force Ramey, commanded by Brig. Gen. Rufus Ramey, which relieved Task Force Ellis on the twelfth. This marked a rare tactical use of an armored group in Italy.[88]

The speedy charge ended north of Rome. Four fresh German divisions rushed to the front, and Field Marshal Albert Kesselring employed delaying tactics while he slid the 3d, 29th, and 90th Panzergrenadier and 26th Panzer Divisions to block the Fifth Army.[89] Once again, the odd asymmetry of mainly mechanized German formations fighting mainly infantry divisions on the Allied side characterized the fighting among the mountains.

On 9 June, the 756th Tank Battalion was withdrawn into Fifth Army reserve and enjoyed some R&R. Soon, the outfit would head to Naples to undergo amphibious

assault training, for another theater lay in its future.[90] Likewise, the battered 191st Tank Battalion withdrew into corps reserve and began reorganization, rehabilitation, and training. Then the outfit moved to the Invasion Training Center at Salerno.[91]

By June, tank battalions had been in action with the infantry in Italy for nearly nine months.

Despite earlier pledges by senior commanders to keep tank battalions attached to the same division, Lt. Col. Rogers complained in June 1944, "During [thirty-one] days of combat, this battalion changed its attachment eleven times, not including about four abortive attachments not carried out." He noted that with each reattachment, the battalion had to recall between four and seven liaison officers, each with a radio and two men, and hook them up with the new infantry formation. He also observed that his battalion had frequently been committed to support infantry attacks already in progress after being given only the vaguest notion of the plan and that this invariably rendered the tanks nearly ineffective.[92]

Another problem was that trained Armored Force personnel were not available to replace casualties. From 11 May to 11 June, the 756th Tank Battalion had six officers and sixty-nine men evacuated and received only eight enlisted replacements. The battalion had to put mess, supply, and maintenance personnel into the tanks to maintain combat strength. Moreover, during that period, the battalion had advanced 300 miles and seen combat every single day. Exhaustion had taken a toll, evidenced in misunderstanding of orders, slowness in organizing, and hesitation in execution.[93]

One step taken to resolve the replacement problem was that the 760th Tank Battalion's Company D, less one platoon, was detached to run an armored replacement center in Eboli under the North Africa (soon renamed Mediterranean) Theater of Operations Training Command.[94]

On 1 July 1944, Lt. Gen. Lesley McNair forwarded a memorandum to all divisions and the commanders of all separate tank battalions attached to which was a letter from an unidentified tank battalion commander in Italy who had wanted to help prepare formations headed for France. The officer offered a summary of lessons learned to that point in Italy on the tank-infantry-artillery team. He observed that there were times that the infantry supports the tanks—such as an action where the enemy is not dug in or protected by a minefield, when the tank can lead—and others when the tanks had to support the infantry. He noted that when the tanks led, his infantry division's artillery observers rode with the assault and had called down artillery as close as sixty yards from the armor and that the shrapnel caused no harm. Artillery, he said, was the cure for antitank guns.

The tank battalion had experimented with loaning radios to the infantry to improve tactical communications. The officer wrote that this enabled a rapid reversion of control over tanks from the infantry to the tank battalion commander when the situation changed suddenly from slugging to breakthrough. Tanks had to withdraw at night behind a protective infantry screen.

The officer stressed that medium tanks could not duke it out with Tiger tanks unless they caught them from the flank and that close cooperation with tank destroyers was necessary. His battalion normally used tank destroyers to provide covering fire for advancing tanks.[95]

These were excellent observations, and they might have helped the troops who landed at Normandy had they reached them in time. But it was too late. They were going to have to learn many of these things the hard way.

With the Overlord landings in Normandy on 6 June, Italy became a secondary theater for the Allies. The Germans also considered Italy to be a secondary front, and it was allotted supplies, equipment, and troops accordingly.[96]

The Allied advance stopped on 4 August after covering 270 miles in sixty-four days. The Americans, who viewed France as the decisive theater, had prevailed in a strategy debate with the British over whether to keep forces in Italy strong enough to drive into the Balkans. For now, the mission of the 15th Army Group in Italy was to pin German forces in place so they could not shift to more critical fronts elsewhere, while the VI Corps and the French divisions invaded southern France in Operation Dragoon.[97]

As Lt. Col. Theodore Conway, then on the Fifth Army's staff, put it, "[W]e were looking at Italy. You know, there is nothing soft about this underbelly, and the question finally came down to twenty some odd German divisions and twenty some Allied divisions in Italy. Who was pinning down whom? You might say it is a stand-off."[98]

The 15th Army Group took one stab at throwing the Germans from the Gothic Line into the Po Valley, with the Eighth Army attacking on 25 August and the Fifth Army on 1 September. Progress was slow and egregiously costly, and by late October, an undeniable stalemate had emerged on the Italian front. Much like troops in the European theater at the same time, Allied forces—thinned by attrition, short on supplies, and subject to increasingly harsh weather—simply lacked the punch to defeat German defenders who held well-prepared positions in advantageous terrain. For the tankers, this meant turning almost entirely to firing artillery missions, punctuated by occasional limited-objective attacks. During November alone, the 752d Tank Battalion consumed 12,000 rounds on indirect fire.[99]

CHAPTER 5

Lethal Sea Turtles

"Assault landings were awesome. Noise unbelievable. Confusion all around. Fear."

—T/5 Clair Polites, 788th
Amphibian Tractor Battalion[1]

After the debacle in the Philippines, Army tankers returned rather late to the war against Japan, after their comrades half a world away had fought across North Africa and Sicily and were just bogging down in the Winter Position in Italy.

The Pacific was divided into area commands, the two most important being Gen. Douglas MacArthur's Southwest Pacific Area and Admiral Chester Nimitz's Pacific Ocean Area, which included as subtheaters the South, Central, and North Pacific. In both areas, island-hopping campaigns would play out in which naval and air power, rather than large and heavy ground forces, dominated.

Armor operated on a much more limited scale in the Pacific theater than in Europe, but some campaigns fielded as many tanks as were used in North Africa. Twelve tank and amphibian tank battalions fought in the Philippines, and the Ryukyus campaign, including Okinawa, involved nine tank and amphibian tank battalions. Specialized battalions played a substantially larger role than they did in North Africa or Europe, particularly amphibian units.

The Japanese had swept across the Pacific after Pearl Harbor, seemingly unstoppable until checked in the naval engagement in the Coral Sea from 7 to 8 May 1942 and then defeated in the Battle of Midway from 3 to 6 June 1942. It was time to recover the initiative, and the U.S. Joint Chiefs of Staff on 2 July 1942 ordered the reconquest of the Solomon Islands to deny the Japanese the use of the huge naval and air base at Rabaul.

The U.S. Marines took the first step in the South Pacific when they landed at Guadalcanal on 7 August, but stalemate ensued. The army joined the fight in

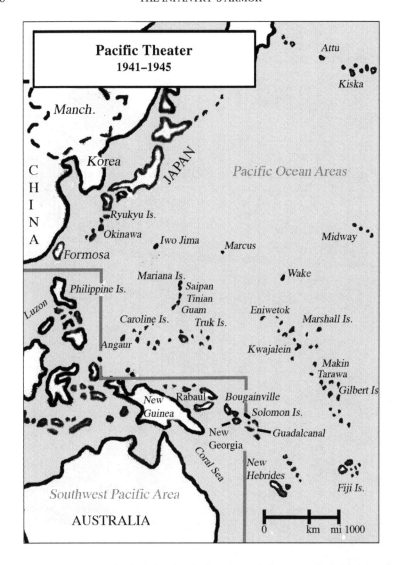

November with the arrival of the lead elements of the Americal Division.[2] No army tanks were dispatched to the jungle-cloaked island.

The army nevertheless got a few chances to work with U.S. Marine Corps light tanks on Guadalcanal, which was enough to get a taste for the differences from the school solutions taught back in the States. Maj. Gen. O. W. Griswold, who took command of the XIV Corps in April 1943, wrote to General McNair, "We used [the tanks] to advantage on some terrain here. Jap suicide squads went after them with magnetic mines, but our infantry kept them pretty well protected. . . . *Infantry must be trained to support tanks closely in this terrain.* It's rather like putting the cart before the horse, from an orthodox viewpoint."[3]

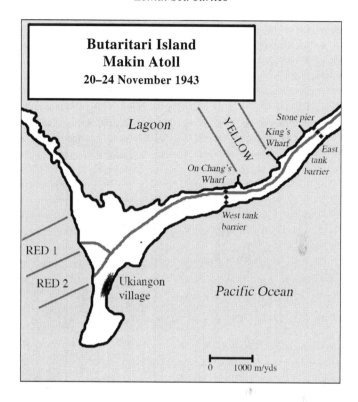

**Butaritari Island
Makin Atoll
20–24 November 1943**

Lagoon

YELLOW

Stone pier

King's Wharf

East tank barrier

On Chang's Wharf

West tank barrier

RED 1

RED 2

Ukiangon village

Pacific Ocean

0　　　1000 m/yds

Griswold was evidently sufficiently unimpressed with the tankers' contribution that he included no army armor in his operations when the XIV Corps moved on to take New Georgia, which was secured in October, nor when it initially deployed to Bougainville in November.

BACK INTO BATTLE: MAKIN ATOLL

In November 1943, Nimitz's island-hopping campaign began with assaults on the Tarawa and Makin Atolls by the marines and army, respectively. The first separate tank battalion to take the war back to the Japanese did so at Makin, and it was fitting that the outfit was the 193d Tank Battalion (Medium), which had been formed from National Guard tank companies, just like the two battalions lost at Bataan. The 193d Tank Battalion, which joined the defenses on Oahu in January 1941, had arrived there with secondhand M3 light tanks, two companies of which had been replaced with M3 Lees. The M3 had not seen service on the far side of the globe for half a year.

For its first operation, the battalion reorganized as a strange hybrid bearing no relationship to any formal table of organization and equipment. The battalion was the first army outfit in the Pacific to receive amphibian tractors, forty-nine of which arrived in October. These appear to have been T33/LVT(1) Alligators, which were unarmored and constructed of sheet metal. The cargo area had room for twenty-four men with packs and rifles or 4,500 pounds of cargo. Gun rails ran around the sides and rear, and the vehicle usually had one .30-caliber and one .50-caliber machine gun mounted to the sides. A six-cylinder Hercules WLXC3 gasoline engine powered the LVT(1), and tracks that used blocks with scoop-shaped blades provided the motive force in the water as well as on land. The tankers learned during exercises with the LVTs that concertina barbed wire invariably jammed the bogies and tracks and that rock and coral could easily knock holes in the bottom.

The LVTs were formed into a provisional company for the assault. Company C was still mounted in its M3A1 light tanks, leaving only Company A equipped with medium tanks. LCMs were to carry the tanks to the beach.

Communications at the tactical level between infantry and tanks in Company A consisted of an SCR-509 radio mounted on an infantry mountain pack for use by a liaison officer. The division's reconnaissance troop supplied three more SCR-509s for use by the infantry. The LVTs were equipped with SCR-508s only the night before the landings.[4]

The Makin operation saw the first use of an amphibious ship that was to haul armored battalions to many Pacific destinations—the landing ship, dock (LSD). In the formula of shore-to-shore operations suggested by Maj. Gen. Lucian Truscott in his account of the Sicily landings, the LSD provided an originating "shore" for smaller craft. Each LSD had a massive dock well accessed by two rear doors into which loaded landing craft could maneuver. Once they were inside the vessel, the well was pumped dry for ocean transit and refilled once the fleet was off the landing area. For example, the USS *Belle Grove*, LSD-2, could ferry, over a distance of 8,000 miles, three LCTs (Mark V or VI) with five medium tanks apiece, two LCTs (Mark III or IV) with twelve tanks apiece, eighteen LCMs with one tank on each, or forty-one LVTs.[5]

The 27th Infantry Division was bringing an overwhelming force to bear on Makin Atoll. Two regiments were to make the assault. The small Japanese garrison on Butaritari Island—commanded by a lieutenant—possessed no weapons heavier than machine guns and a few antiaircraft guns. Troops had constructed pillboxes and an antitank ditch at each end of their defensive zone.

Upon arrival in the transport area on 20 November 1943, LSTs opened their bow doors, lowered their ramps, and disgorged the 193d Tank Battalion's LVTs carrying detachments from the 105th Infantry, while the 1st and 3d Battalions of the 165th Infantry quickly debarked into small boats in time to make H-Hour at 0830. The critical requirement for the assault wave was the unloading of the light tanks from transports, which was accomplished more rapidly than had been the case during exercises. Once in the LCMs, the tankers turned over their motors, turned on their radios, and tested the turret traverse and gyrostabilizers. The tankers buttoned up except for the commanders, who would watch the beach through field glasses until 100 yards from shore.

The 105th Infantry's assault company in LVTs, followed by the 1st and 3d Battalions in boats, landed at H-Hour on Beaches Red and Red 2 on Butaritari Island's sea side against light opposition and quickly reached their objectives. Red Beach turned out to be a clutter of coral just below the water's surface, and the alligators managed to reach the sand, whereas the landing craft could not. After discharging the infantry, the alligators shuttled cargo from landing craft to the sand. One medium tank landing at Red Beach got stuck in a shell hole; when the crew abandoned the tank, the men came under fire from a Japanese machine gun and returned to it twice as fast. "The Red beaches were just plain stinko profundo," commented Adm. Richmond Turner. The navy learned to have a human reconnoiter every landing beach rather than rely on aerial photos.

The 2d Battalion, 165th Infantry, preceded by a company from the 105th Infantry mounted in LVTs and by medium tanks, at W-Hour, or 1030, stormed Yellow Beach on the lagoon side of the island, where it was hoped they would catch the Japanese fighting the first landing from the rear. The M3 Lees had been waterproofed and equipped with wading stacks that kept sea water away from the engine's air intake and exhaust. The battalion commanding officer, Lt. Col. Harmon Edmonson, reported, "We experienced no difficulty in the water, but after reaching the beach, we were held up by taro pits and shell holes in addition to the coconut trees and a fuel dump that was on fire." Two M3 medium tanks tipped into a pit and had to be abandoned, and another got stuck in a shell hole off shore. Several of the LVTs were "shot full of holes" and had to be welded later by maintenance men.

On Beach Yellow 1, the medium tanks were to destroy known heavy positions, and their 75-millimeter guns did the job. Meanwhile, the infantry advanced rapidly inland, anchored its right flank, and pushed westward to link up with the 1st Battalion. One platoon leader's tank in Company A was knocked out, but in response to orders from the infantry, the remaining four tanks progressed to King's Wharf and shelled the Japanese. By 1700, only a small pocket of resistance remained on the north side of the island, and Company C's light tanks at Red Beach had linked up with Company A's mediums at Yellow Beach.

On D+1, the 2d Battalion resumed the advance eastward, supported by tanks, until it encountered a heavily fortified position to the south of the lagoon road. The ground was too marshy for the tanks to help, and the Japanese limited the GIs to 600 yards that day.[6]

Company A's tanks were in action along the lagoon, as reported by Cpl. Charles Meyer, who commanded Tank #7:

We proceeded up the road on the lagoon side and came upon a bomb shelter [emitting] enemy gunfire. We blasted the doorways with 75mm. We then came back about 200 yards to Wharf "C" and proceeded to ride out on the wharf, machine-gunning small wooden houses on the left of the pier. We shelled the barricade at the end of the pier with 75mm gunfire. Rode back up to the area of the bomb shelter we had blasted and under direction of foot troops who pointed out enemy positions, mostly pillboxes, proceeded to shell and strafe many of same. The 75mm fire was very effective. Enemy positions in pillboxes were silenced.

Our next mission was to take out a large house. . . . Shelled house with 75mm and 37mm gunfire. House was left in flames. Tracer ammunition was seen coming from house while it was burning.[7]

The light tanks from the 1st Platoon of Company C were meanwhile helping the doughboys from the 1st Battalion. The tankers were enthusiastic to learn how easily one could knock a sniper out of a tree with one round of 37-millimeter canister, and five Japanese with light machine guns were dispatched by doing so.

The 3d Battalion relieved the 2d Battalion overnight and attacked the next morning supported by Company A, 193d Tank Battalion. Company A, 165th Infantry, simultaneously mounted LVTs and advanced along the coast to a village 3,000 yards beyond the 3d Battalion's line, where the GIs established a blocking position. Few Japanese were caught by this hammer and anvil, and natives reported that the enemy had left before Company A's arrival.

By 0800 hours on D+4, all Japanese resistance had ended. A reconnaissance detachment toured the neighboring islets in an LVT and reported that none were occupied.

The division's commanding general, Maj. Gen. Ralph Smith, reported, "Light and medium tanks were employed continuously throughout the operation and are considered invaluable both for their combat strength and the morale effect on the troops. . . . The problem of reliable means of communication between the tanks and the close supported infantry is not yet solved. It was extremely difficult to transmit information from outside the tank to the tank crews." Smith blamed, in part, the absence of small-unit infantry training with tanks.[8]

Capt. Wayne Sikes of the 193d Tank Battalion agreed: "For operations in close terrain, there should be available to the infantry platoon leader or even squad leader a means of communication with the individual tank commander that would enable the infantry leader to point out specific targets and coordinate the forward movement of the smallest unit."[9]

The Battle for Bougainville

On 1 October 1943, the 3d Marine Division had landed on the west coast of jungle-cloaked Bougainville in the Solomons. In November, the 37th Infantry Division joined the marines. The 754th Tank Battalion arrived on 6 January 1944, and the Americal Division, with which the tankers had partnered while training on New Caledonia, disembarked a week later. The tank battalion was subordinated to the XIV Corps rather than either of the infantry divisions, and initially, it deployed to secure the perimeter at Empress Augusta Bay as corps reserve.

Soldiers on the scene were going to have to come up with a way to use tanks with the infantry on the fly, largely through trial and error. The XIV Corps' planners drew on lessons learned during tank-infantry training conducted on Guadalcanal before the operation and had gathered what information they could on the prior use of tanks to support infantry in the Pacific. They implemented a training program for the tank-infantry-engineer teams the corps intended to use in Bougainville's rain-soaked jungles. "This [combat] experience has been limited both in number of times tanks have been used and in number of tanks used in any one attack," the corps noted in a training memorandum issued on 20 January. "Therefore, the principles enumerated cannot be considered as final."

Some of the concepts taught on Bougainville were old-hat, such as using tanks only on appropriate terrain. Others were novel: "In the jungle, the firepower of the tank assumes far greater importance due to the inherent limitations of maneuver and shock action. Therefore a portion of the tanks must be formed in line in order to exploit maximum firepower." Combat experience had shown that 37-millimeter canister rounds and machine guns could clear jungle growth to reveal pillbox openings. High-explosive rounds and flamethrowers could then be fired through the opening, or failing that, armor-piercing rounds often created a hole big enough for high-explosive fire.

Formations had to be extremely simple to permit any control, and tanks were to be pre-positioned behind the line of departure. Advances had to be short and by bounds with frequent halts for reorganization and reorientation.

The corps mandated that tanks be used en masse, at least one company at a time. This notion doubtless reflected the hand of some unrecorded armored officer, trained in Fort Knox notions of tank warfare, and it was so inapplicable in the jungle that it was among the first to be ditched in practice. Planners said the infantry had to protect the tanks during approach, attack, and withdrawal, and the tanks had to support the doughboys by fire. This insight was the heart of armored warfare in the jungle.

Training emphasized that the infantry and tanks maintain constant communication, but the means were primitive. The armor and the infantry commanders were to establish a radio link at the tank company-infantry battalion level, which was possible only if the tankers loaned a radio to the doughboys. At the tank platoon level, a sound-powered or field telephone was to be run between each tank and the local infantry commander by taping the phone wire to a light cable towed by the tank.

Engineers were crucial to the team to help tanks overcome terrain obstacles, such as by using bulldozers to clear paths or by bridging streams. In cases where mutually supporting pillboxes could be bypassed, small engineer-tank-infantry teams were to destroy them.[10]

The tankers saw their first action on 30 January with the American Division's 132d Infantry, before any of the new training could take place. The operation featured massed use of armor—twenty light tanks—to support the GIs. The regiment's journal indicates that the tanks advanced some 200 yards beyond the perimeter, stopped, and shelled Japanese positions, accounting for eleven pill-boxes. A Japanese 90-millimeter gun destroyed one tank, and a second bogged down and was abandoned. At least on one flank, a squad of infantry provided effective cover for a platoon of tanks.[11]

The infantry and tankers had undergone the XIV Corps' training regimen and received their allotment of Sherman tanks by early March, when the Japanese Seventeenth Army launched a desperate and ultimately pointless counterattack to eliminate the XIV Corps' lodgment, which was only 8,000 yards deep. The Japanese confronted a daunting objective, for the American line consisted of fortified pillboxes and firing positions, protected by barbed wire and minefields. The first serious Japanese attacks hit before dawn on 9 March. On the twelfth, elements of the Japanese 45th Infantry Division attacked the 37th Division's 129th Infantry on a narrow front. The American regiment held a stretch of low ground in the center of the division line, where the Japanese established a salient 200 yards deep and 100 yards wide into the 2d Battalion's line. The Japanese drove the GIs out of seven pillboxes, and efforts to retake the ground recovered only two pillboxes.

The next morning, the Japanese attacked again and grabbed another pillbox. At 0945 hours, the 1st Platoon, Company C, 754th Tank Battalion, which consisted of three Shermans and two light tanks, arrived to support a counterattack using the new tactics. Maj. Gen. Oscar Griswold, the XIV Corps' commander, had released the tanks with the stipulation that they be used in an attack rather than defense. The tanks moved out as expected, but the infantry failed to stay close or to designate targets, and the sally broke down. The tanks had difficulty firing at the Japanese, who were hunkered down in ravines with steep slopes. The team tried again at 1315 hours, and again the infantry failed to stick close. Japanese infantry surrounded two tanks for a few nail-biting minutes but were driven off.

The 2d Platoon—also consisting of three medium and two light tanks—arrived to relieve the 1st Platoon, and at 1700 hours, the team made its third attempt. This time, the infantry stuck close to the tanks and designated targets by telephone and colored smoke. The tanks approached within fifteen yards of the Japanese positions and hit them with 75-millimeter and machine-gun fire. One 75-millimeter round killed eighteen enemy soldiers sheltering in the roots of a Banyan tree. The combined assault reclaimed the former line with hardly any losses among the doughboys.

On 15 March, the Japanese again penetrated the line in the 2d Battalion's sector and seized a pillbox. A counterattack supported by the 2d Platoon's tanks failed because even infantry NCOs riding in the tanks could not distinguish between the pillboxes held by friend and foe. The tanks fired at visible targets from a distance, but the Japanese had moved in heavy weapons and held firm.

The tank-infantry team tried again at 1635 hours. A corps report related: "Coordination between infantry and tanks was good until several telephones were shot away. Although infantry accompanied the tanks, close-in protection was not continuous, and the enemy succeeding in exploding two mines on the tanks. . . . At one point, a group of enemy swarmed onto one of the assault tanks; several well-placed charges of canister from the support tanks swept them away without damage to the assault tanks. When the fierce fighting ended at dark, our forces had completely annihilated the enemy." One hundred ninety Japanese dead were counted within the original American line.

The whole cycle repeated itself on 17 March. The XIV Corps reported that in the American counterattack,

> ideal coordination between the tank platoon and its supporting infantry platoon was realized. Infantry squad leaders could see the fresh dirt which indicated enemy entrenchments, halted the tanks just short of these, tossed out colored smoke grenades, and gave directions for fire. 75mm and 37mm shells blew the enemy from the ground. Jap machine guns delivered a stream of fire against the tanks but inflicted no damage. Infantry quickly spotted the gun positions, some of which were only fifteen yards off on the flank. These were designated as targets to the tanks and were quickly knocked out. By 0950, our [main line of resistance] was restored, and 200 enemy dead were counted within our wire.[12]

(The 754th, like most battalions in the Pacific theater, put rubber block or rubber chevron tracks on the tanks. These proved better than steel chevron tracks for gripping mud.[13])

On 4 April, after having tested its ideas in combat, the XIV Corps issued a memorandum that concluded that most of its doctrine had proved sound. It had nevertheless refined its model attack formation. The new infantry-tank-engineer team consisted of one "platoon" of tanks (in fact an ad hoc platoon consisting of three medium and three light tanks), a platoon of infantry, and a few attached engineers. Three medium tanks led the assault spread across a frontage of fifty yards. Their mission was to advance slowly, firing cannons and machine guns to drive the enemy to cover and to strip camouflage from pillboxes. A second echelon of two light tanks followed by twenty-five yards, each behind a medium tank on one flank. The light tank could fire the extremely useful canister round, which the medium tank could not. Their mission was to knock out bypassed pillboxes, shoot snipers from treetops, and protect the medium tanks using machine guns and canister fire from attack by foot troops carrying magnetic mines or charges. Two GIs acting as target designators, a telephone orderly from the tank battalion attached to the squad leader and talking to the tank crew through a field telephone, a squad of riflemen and BAR men, and a few engineers with demolitions and flamethrowers walked immediately behind in a wedge formation to avoid canalization in the tracks of the tanks. The designators showed the tankers what to shoot, while the others rooted out enemy infantry and protected the tanks from close infantry assault. The platoon reserve and a third light tank came last. An entire infantry company could be arrayed with three such formations side by side.

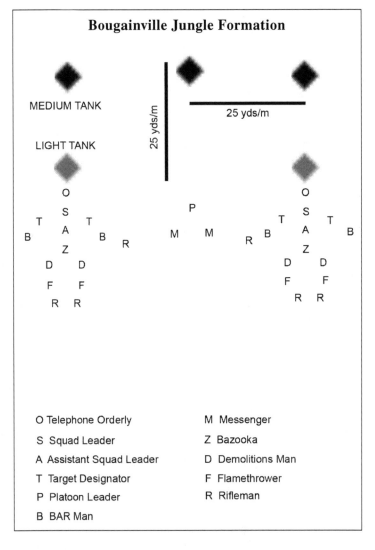

Bougainville Jungle Formation

MEDIUM TANK

LIGHT TANK

25 yds/m

25 yds/m

O Telephone Orderly

S Squad Leader

A Assistant Squad Leader

T Target Designator

P Platoon Leader

B BAR Man

M Messenger

Z Bazooka

D Demolitions Man

F Flamethrower

R Rifleman

The target designators were an effective invention. "Tanks proved to be almost blind in thick jungle," the corps noted. Tracer fire proved inadequate for designating targets such as well-hidden pillboxes. A red or violet smoke grenade only obscured the target. Trial and error showed that if the grenade's fuse was unscrewed and half the charge removed, the level of smoke was just right. Target designators either tossed the modified grenades by hand or fired rifle grenades at longer ranges.

In a jungle advance, tanks could operate for about three hours before needing reservicing. Typically, the tanks could conduct two such sorties during the day. The pace of jungle combat—tanks advanced in first gear for only twenty-five to seventy-five yards before stopping—was tough on the engines and could result in vapor lock.

Communication plans had fallen short of needs. Only one fix had worked under fire on Bougainville: placing an EE-8 field telephone inside the each tank's turret and running a wire to a handset mounted on the rear of the tank. The soldiers had learned that if the box itself were strapped outside the tank, enemy fire would damage it. The telephone orderly from the tank battalion, armed only with a pistol, could translate the wishes of each infantry squad leader into words the tank crew would understand.[14]

KWAJALEIN: THE ARMY ADOPTS A WHOLE NEW APPROACH

The invasion of the Kwajalein Atoll, the westernmost of the Marshall Islands, marked the debut of the amphibian tank units of the army and the marine corps. The Kwajalein Atoll consisted of flat coral islands connected by underwater reefs and was roughly seventy miles long and thirty miles wide. Two main assault forces—the 4th Marine Division to the north and 7th Infantry Division to the south—arrived the morning of 31 January.

The 708th Amphibian Tank Battalion had joined the 7th Infantry Division in December 1943 to train in the Hawaiian Islands for an amphibious assault somewhere in the Central Pacific. Company D was detached from the battalion and sent to join the 27th Infantry Division.

The 7th Division's plans had not originally called for the use of amphibian tractors, but the lessons learned at Tarawa convinced planners that the infantry would have to ride amtracs to shore.[15] Tarawa, the chief bastion of the Gilbert Islands, lay some 1,000 miles northeast of Guadalcanal. It was the first atoll to be assaulted by American forces when the 2d Marine Division attacked Betio on 20 November 1943 while army elements landed at Makin Atoll. The marines had insisted that they be partially equipped with LVTs for the operation because they were skeptical—rightly so—that landing craft would be able to cross the coral reef offshore. Japanese heavy machine guns, mortars, and artillery claimed about 80 of the 125 unarmored amtracs used to carry the first three waves, and LVT machine gunners suffered disproportionate casualties because they had to expose themselves in order to fire back. As bad as that was, landing craft in later waves hung on the reef, and the marines had to wade up to 800 yards to reach the sand under intense fire, which caused a bloodbath.[16]

Only seventeen of the battalion's authorized seventy-five LVT(A)(1) amtanks had arrived with the men, but amtracs would become available. The antitank companies of the three infantry regiments were pressed into service to help man them. The resulting 708th Provisional Amphibian Tractor Battalion included one company of LVT(A)(1) amphibian tanks and four provisional amphibian tractor groups. As equipment arrived, each of the groups received fourteen armored LVT(A)(2) amtracs and twenty unarmored LVT(2)s. Each company had two platoons with seventeen vehicles apiece, enough to fill two LSTs. Each platoon was broken into two waves of eight LVTs, with the extra amtrac available for command or air-ground liaison. The armored LVT(A)(2)s were to form the first wave and part of the second.

Training was intensive, as it was clear that not much time remained before the operation. The men practiced landings day and night, first a battalion at a

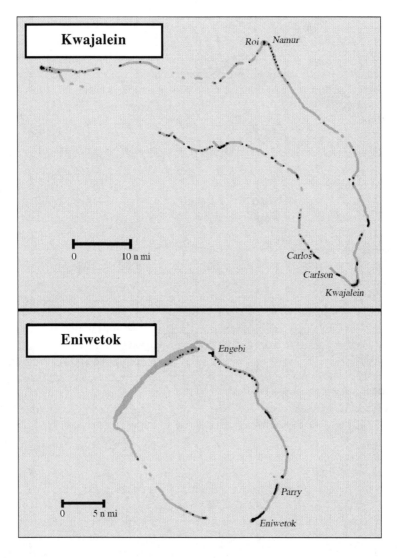

time and then two abreast. The scenarios involved D-Day and D+1, which was appropriate because the amphibian armor was to get the troops to shore, after which standard tanks—called "land tanks" by amphibian units—took over. This was the first amphibious assault for both the tankers and the infantry, and they made many mistakes during practice that they were able to correct before the real thing.

Rather than the army, the navy, through its Bureau of Ships, procured amphibian tanks and tractors. The navy designed the vehicles to crawl across coral reefs off Pacific island beaches and then to move out of the water and over the beach without having to stop.[17]

The amtrac was first developed for rescue work in the Everglades and was initially adapted to military use by the U.S. Marine Corps. The nomenclature was changed to landing vehicle, tracked (LVT), to match the navy's designation for landing craft, but the "amtrac" shorthand remained in general use. The LVT(2), LVT(A)(2), and LVT(4) Water Buffalos descended directly from the LVT(1) Alligator first used by the marine corps at Guadalcanal and outfitted the army's amtrac battalions. The LVT(2) was constructed of sheet steel while the LVT(A)(2) was made of armor plate, which increased the weight slightly from 30,900 to 32,000 pounds. Both vehicles had gun rails forward and to the sides and rear, which allowed machine guns to be mounted to fire in any direction, and twin forward-facing machine guns protected by shields became a common configuration. Thirty fully equipped infantrymen could be ferried to the beach, and they had to exit by clambering over the sides, often under fire. The LVT(4)—by the end of the war the most common model in army use—closely resembled the LVT(2) but had an armored cab and an armored rear ramp that could be lowered with a hand crank to allow the vehicle to carry a jeep, small antitank gun, or field piece and enabled riflemen to debark in greater safety. The LVT(4) had two swinging and two stationary machine-gun mounts.

These models were longer and wider than the Alligator, had an improved and highly flexible suspension system, and used the same seven-cylinder aircraft engine that powered the M3 light tank. The amtrac could reach speeds of about twenty-five miles per hour on land and six miles per hour in the water. It made a stable enough boat, but a large wave or rough surf greater than five feet could swamp or overturn one.[18]

A crew of three men managed the LVT(2) and LVT(A)(2). The commander/driver, assistant driver, and radio operator sat in the cab. The LVT(4) often had a fourth crewman assigned to operate the rear ramp.

In light of experience on Tarawa, the 708th Provisional Amphibian Tractor Battalion modified its LVTs for the assault. Two .50-caliber machine guns were mounted on the cab rail, and welders fitted them with improvised shields to protect the gunners. Men piled sandbags on top of the vehicles for yet more protection. An additional .30-caliber was mounted on each side, and flamethrowers—all destined to drown out in action despite application of condoms over the nozzles— were installed in five LVTs in ad hoc ball-and-socket arrangements in the bow.[19]

Amphibian tanks were built on the LVT(2) amtrac chassis and were designed to provide the assault wave with tank gun support on the beach. They had the same drive train as the LVT(2) and reached similar top speeds on both land and water but were more stable at sea because of their greater weight and could likewise bull through up to eight feet of surf.[20] Armor ranged from a quarter of an inch on the flanks to half an inch on the front.

The sixteen-ton LVT(A)(1) was basically a covered amtrac with an M5 light tank turret mounted on top. As on the M5, the amtank had a 37-millimeter main gun and a .30-caliber coaxial machine gun, and the roomy vehicle carried 104 shells for the cannon and 6,000 machine-gun rounds. The turret had both hydraulic and manual traverse systems, and twin hatches were provided. Twin hatches on the rear deck had scarf mounts for .30-caliber machine guns. The six-man crew included commander, driver, assistant driver/radio operator, 37-millimeter gunner, and two scarf machine gunners. The vehicle had a radio and intercom system.

The 767th Tank Battalion had also joined the 7th Infantry Division, and the land tankers, too, had drawn lessons from earlier operations. Following the Makin and Tarawa operations, military officers put their heads together to consider the lessons learned regarding troubled communications experienced there between the infantry and supporting tanks. A solution emerged that would be tried at Kwajalein: attaching a TS-7 phone in a metal box to the rear of the tank, through which an infantryman could talk to the commander buttoned up inside. An army combat lessons report indicates that some tanks still used the original Bougainville method of trailing a wire behind the tank to an infantry EE-8 field telephone.

Moreover, every effort was made to ensure that tank units were able to exercise and train with the infantry beside whom they were going to fight. Tankers were advised that, based on experience elsewhere in the Pacific, the infantry would follow them by about thirty yards. Crews also received instruction at jungle training facilities to give them a better appreciation for the difficulties faced by the GIs.

In December 1943, the 767th Tank Battalion had received orders from the 7th Infantry Division to design a flamethrower kit that could be installed in its light tanks in the bow gunner's position. It did so through trial and error and fitted every M3A1 tank in Company D with a flame unit. The battalion, which had been equipped with M7 105-millimeter self-propelled howitzers to use as assault guns, traded those in for M10 tank destroyers mounting 3-inch guns because they had proved so good at destroying fixed emplacements.[21]

On D-Day, 31 January, the provisional amtrac battalion loaded the 2d Battalion, 17th Infantry, aboard Group Able's LVTs and landed on Carlson (Enubuj) Island, where five battalions of artillery were to deploy to support landings the next day on Kwajalein Island. Eight LVT(A)(2)s flanked on each side by a platoon of amtanks headed for shore, which proved to be undefended. The operational plan called for the first wave to hit the beach, unload the infantry, and move 100 yards inland to establish a perimeter defense, into which subsequent waves of infantry and tanks would land. Unbothered by enemy fire, the first wave instead pushed a third of the way across the island and set up a line, where four disembarking land tanks—M3A1 light tanks from Company D, 767th Tank Battalion—relieved the amphibians.

A similar assault group captured nearby Carlos Island (Group Dog and the 1st Battalion, 17th Infantry), which served as an LVT base for the remainder of the operation, while four LVTs carried a hydrographic party to survey the beach on Kwajalein Island's southwest end, where the chosen landing beaches were located. The vehicles drew small-arms fire, but the passengers suffered no casualties.[22] The gunfire signaled that the main island would not be an uncontested walkover.

For the main assault, the provisional battalion loaded two battalions from each of the 32d and 184th Infantry Regiments into the LVTs. The first wave consisted of two infantry battalions, with an amtank platoon arrayed on each flank and the third platoon plus the company headquarters deployed in a wedge formation in the center.[23] Medical detachment personnel (two doctors, a dentist, and nineteen enlisted men) were distributed among the groups to handle casualties on the spot except for three enlisted men who remained aboard an LST.

Amphibians started into battle by leaving an LST, and as one report commented, "the difficulty of such movement can be fully appreciated only by an eyewitness. The LST is not a readily maneuverable vessel, and it is peculiarly subject to rolling and pitching. The heavy amphibian tank must be driven off the ramp without damaging ship or tank. Its return is even more complicated."[24] The fact that the driver could not quickly stop an amphibian in the water—the scoops on the tracks faced only one way, so reversing thrust only slowed the ungainly vessels slightly—helps explain why.[25] Recovering onto a landing ship involved coasting to an open bow door, catching and securing guide lines tossed from the ship, and backing the amphibian up the ramp.[26]

As Kwajalein shuddered under the last salvos of a devastating barrage delivered by the navy, artillery on Carlson Island, and heavy bombers flying from Tarawa, the amtanks and amtracs gathered along the line of departure some 3,000 yards from shore. Navy aircraft roared through the sky to give the Japanese a final strafing. At a flag signal from the navy, the lumbering amphibians churned forward like light-blue, lethal sea turtles, and one official observer reported, "LVTs displayed excellent discipline and at no time got out of control as they had in previous operations." LCI(G)s—landing craft loaded with rockets and 40-millimeter guns—led the formation, adding to the mayhem on shore, and then peeled off to the flanks. The amtanks opened fire with cannons and machine guns about 100 yards from shore. Rounds fired by the batteries on Carlson Island were still landing when the amphibians were thirty-five yards from the sand.

The LVT(A)(1)s clawed their way across the beach at 0930 hours, and the scarf gunners concentrated their fire in the treetops to kill any snipers who might be hidden there. Gunners quickly learned that their 37-millimeter cannon was able to knock out coconut palm field works, but one had to blast a hole into a concrete bunker with armor-piercing rounds and then follow up with high explosives.

The amtracs offloaded their infantry, and the armored LVT(A)(2)s moved forward to support the amtanks with fire from their multiple machine guns while the unarmored LVT(2)s turned around to pick up a new load. Even a .25-caliber round could penetrate the LVT(2)'s steel walls. Within minutes, some 1,200 infantrymen were on the ground, having suffered not a single casualty getting there.

On Beach Yellow 2, Lt. Frank Tallman commanded a platoon of LVT(A)(1)s supporting the 184th Infantry; the after-action report recorded:

> They received considerable small-arms fire while in the water and also after reaching the shore at the western tip of the 1,200-yard long island. Lieutenant Tallman's tank and two others crossed to the lagoon side of the island, leaving the two remaining tanks of the platoon to move down the seaward side. . . . Tallman took his three tanks to the reef and escorted the infantry as far as a pier about halfway down the island. They received bursts of small-arms fire at intervals during their slow progress, and on one occasion Lieutenant Tallman was wounded slightly when, after raising his head from the turret to talk to an infantryman who had asked for assistance, he was cut on the cheek by a ricocheting bullet.

Tallman was wounded again the next day when, after he breached a pillbox with his 37-millimeter gun at close range, he was burned by a flamethrower that was fired to clear out the occupants.

Capt. John Straub, who commanded the LVTs of Dog Group, described the landings:

> While proceeding to shore [on Beach White 2], we drew only scattered rifle fire, and that was ineffective. We landed on the [southwest] end of the island and found no opposition on the beach. The first [LVT] wave moved inland to the right while the later waves landed on the beach and returned to the rendezvous point [out to sea] for more troops. Our tanks helped the infantrymen through the heavy underbrush for a distance of about 150 yards. We found no strongly held positions, and the few Japs encountered were quickly disposed of by fire from our tanks and infantry.

Japanese resistance became more determined as the morning wore on. Rounds from .25-caliber machine guns and occasionally 20-millimeter guns scored the thin armor on even the amtanks, as did shrapnel from artillery fire, but none penetrated. "Many times," the battalion's after-action report records, "individual tanks were assaulted by enemy troops and were saved by the scarf guns. Most of the casualties were among the scarf gunners, who do not have adequate armor protection to their sides and rear." The LVT(A)(2)s proved somewhat more vulnerable, and one had so many holes that it later sank when it reentered the water.[27]

The 767th Tank Battalion's vehicles disembarked onto the beach beginning roughly fifteen minutes after the assault wave had touched dry ground. Company A's M4A1 medium tanks joined the infantry on the line in direct support at 1205 hours.

The handoff completed, the amtanks were released and reloaded onto LSTs. The amtracs were kept busy shuttling men and supplies until after dark, which resulted in some confusion because crews could not discern their assigned LSTs.[28]

The U.S. Marine Corps' 1st Armored Amphibian Battalion (amtanks), meanwhile, landed on Roi and Namur Islands with the 4th Marine Division. Seizure of offshore islands on which to place artillery met no opposition on D-Day, and the main assault proceeded simultaneously with that at Kwajalein on 1 February.[29] The surf on the beaches was so bad that several tanks overturned, and the outfit lost more men to drowning than to enemy action.[30] This was not to be an unusual problem. A postwar survey of army amphibian battalions indicated that the leading causes of vehicle losses were rough surf and mechanical deadlining, while losses to enemy action ranged from only 5 to 50 percent, depending on unit.[31]

A Study in Tank-Infantry Coordination

The 7th Infantry Division had divided the boomerang-shaped Kwajalein roughly down its middle, with the 184th Infantry on the left (lagoon) side and the 32d Infantry on the right (ocean) side. Lt. Col. S. L. A. Marshall organized intensive interviews of participants after the battle to capture the fine details of the action, and his published account of the activities of Company B, 184th Infantry, on 2 February provide insights into the challenges probably experienced throughout the island that day regarding tank-infantry cooperation.

The infantry jumped off at about 0700 hours following an artillery barrage, having waited until the last minute because the M4A1 medium tanks from Company B, 767th Tank Battalion, that were to support the advance had not shown up. Despite pre-landing efforts to match tankers to their infantry partners, these two outfits had never worked together before. Immediately, the GIs encountered Japanese troops occupying bunkers, air-raid shelters, blockhouses, and the ruins of a concrete warehouse. Under building fire, the two assault platoons sought cover, and the outfit broke down into small clumps with little cohesion. Just then, the tanks arrived. The GIs had no way to communicate with them, and the tanks "became part of the scenery" and contributed no help.

After two hours, it became clear that the infantry had reached the core of the island's defenses, and the company regrouped to attack with tanks and satchel charges at 0945. Capt. Charles White, commanding Company B, ordered the tanks to fan out ahead of the infantry and advance slowly, firing all weapons at any target in sight. The infantry was to follow and use satchel charges against surviving emplacements. Marshall recorded:

> At first, the tank artillery was used in the least profitable way against the shelters and blockhouses. The fire was put on the entrances. This gave the Japanese the choice of remaining inside or charging directly into the

cannon. Some time passed before White realized that if the fire was directed at the walls, the enemy would spill out of the entrances and could be shot down.

Yet it was difficult to get an understanding on even these fundamental problems. The TS-7 telephones on the rear of the tanks were not working, and the tanks remained buttoned up after they got forward. White could get his orders to the tank men only by scrambling up the outside of the tank and hammering on the armor with his rifle until someone looked out. When the fire became too thick, he couldn't do that. So cohesion failed and could only be restored for brief intervals. Such was the chaotic state of the ground and such the nature of the fighting that the infantry frequently could not see their own elements at distances greater than fifteen or twenty yards; the tanks, having even less vision, were not always aware when our men advanced into fresh ground and sometimes fired toward targets in their midst.

Lt. Frank Kaplan was leading his 2d Platoon along the lagoon shore. Three medium tanks approached from behind them and, the crews evidently having not seen the GIs, opened fire over the heads of Kaplan and two other men, who crawled for safety into a nearby shell hole. The muzzle blasts lifted the men clear off the ground, and Kaplan recalled that every round made them feel like "our guts were being turned around inside."

White managed to get everyone stopped and repeated his earlier orders, emphasizing to the tankers that they needed to move at the pace of the riflemen. They got ten yards before one tank's gun jammed, and it pulled back and the others halted. "As invariably happens in atoll fighting," recorded Marshall, "the moment the tanks stopped, enemy sniper fire increased all along the fronts and flank." The remaining tanks expended their ammunition and stayed in place to await resupply. The riflemen clustered in the lee of the tanks and fired every weapon at every debris pile and rise of ground. Japanese resistance broke, and Marshall commented that the mere physical presence of the tanks had given the GIs the confidence to stick it out to the end.

The advance continued, and by now, the infantry and tankers had figured out what worked best. White designated specific targets for the tanks, and the infantry advanced in half-squads behind the armor, clearing each bunker or shelter with grenades and satchel charges.[32]

Two more days of bitter fighting followed. So much smoke and debris filled the air that at times men ten yards apart could not see one another. Finally, on 4 February, Maj. Gen. Charles Corlett announced to his division that Japanese resistance had ceased on Kwajalein Island as of 1535 hours. American casualties amounted to 142 dead, 845 wounded, and 2 missing. These included 19 men killed and 26 men wounded from the 767th Tank Battalion. An estimated 5,000 Japanese troops had been killed.[33]

From 3 to 7 February, the 708th Provisional Amphibian Tractor Battalion, the infantry, and elements of the 767th Tank Battalion jumped from islet to islet around the atoll, clearing out a few remaining Japanese. The battalion, less Group Able, reboarded the LSTs and performed maintenance, for on 15 February the vessels set sail for the next destination.

On to Eniwetok

The battalion and the 7th Infantry Division's 106th Infantry Regiment, less a battalion, were now subordinated to Tactical Group 1 of the V Amphibious Corps, which had orders to seize Eniwetok Atoll, located at the northwest corner of the Marshall Islands. The atoll is approximately twenty-one miles in length and seventeen miles across and contains some seventy islets. The original plan for the landings had not included Eniwetok because of uncertainty over what part of available troops would be absorbed by Kwajalein, but tentative plans had been prepared in case Kwajalein fell rapidly. Otherwise, operations at Eniwetok were to begin on 1 May.[34]

Intelligence estimates of Japanese strength were rather vague, as there were unconfirmed reports that the 4,000-man First Mobile Seaborne Brigade, an army formation, might be in the area. The estimate given the expeditionary force commander put the number at between 2,900 and 4,000 men, and this was to be the first time in the Central Pacific area that the Americans faced Japanese Army troops rather than naval infantry. The three islands in the atoll had been under continuous bombardment during the Kwajalein operation, and reconnaissance photos showed that most installations had been destroyed. Nevertheless, well-camouflaged concrete and other defensive works survived.

On D-Day, 17 February, battleships and heavy cruisers commenced shelling Japanese-held islands, lifting fire only to permit attacks by carrier-based aircraft. Minesweepers cleared the channels into the lagoon, and soon shallow-draft vessels from the Southern Group and the entire Northern Group steamed straight into the lagoon. At 1150, six amtanks from the 708th Provisional Amphibian Tractor Battalion carried a marine assault force to Rujiyoru Island, where no Japanese were found. DUKW amphibian trucks carried 75-millimeter and 105-millimeter artillery batteries to shore without interference from the Japanese.[35]

Two battalions of the 22d Marines landed on Engebi Island the next day, courtesy of 708th Battalion's LVTs. As at Kwajalein, LCI(G)s led the assault wave toward shore and then peeled away to the flanks. The army amtanks advanced in line with the first LVTs, five echeloned on each flank and seven arrayed in an inverted V in the center. Smoke and dust from the bombardment drifted over the water and obscured the view of naval guide officers, and the formation drifted about 300 yards too far to the left. The gunners aboard the amtanks and amtracs unleashed a hail of 37-millimeter, .50-caliber, and .30-caliber rounds into the obscuring cloud when about 500 yards from the beach.

Engebi was a triangle-shaped island some 1,500 yards long, which was about 100 yards too short for the airstrip the Japanese built there, so they had constructed a cement abutment that jutted into the lagoon. The drift leftward caused the left-most battalion to arrive at the abutment instead of a beach, and when the marines from Company F clambered up to the flat airstrip, machine guns in concrete pill-boxes along the edge laid down a withering fire. Seeing this, the LVT crew maneuvered into dead space under the pillboxes and destroyed them by heaving hand grenades through the apertures.

Meanwhile, the five amtanks on the left wing landed alone on the northern tip of the island. Fire was heavy, but the crews were able to extinguish local resistance on their own.

There was little resistance at the beach. The amtracs were supposed to carry the marines inland 100 yards, where they were to establish a perimeter to protect the arrival of the next wave, but they stopped along the beach, which caused congestion on the sand. Japanese troops in camouflaged foxholes allowed the first wave of riflemen to pass inland and then opened up a sporadic fire from the rear, while fire from small arms and howitzers increased to the front. The marines, supported by a company of medium tanks, nevertheless were able to secure the island by 1600 hours, and most hurriedly reloaded to form the reserve for the next day's landing on Eniwetok.

Army troops from two battalions of the 106th Infantry Regiment formed the assault force for Eniwetok—twice the strength originally planned. Prisoners had indicated that there was a large force on both Eniwetok Island and nearby Parry Island.[36]

LVTs from the 708th Battalion landed elements of the 5th Amphibious Reconnaissance Company on two small islets on 17 February. The next day, the 1st and 2d Battalions of the 106th Infantry loaded onto the LVTs for the main assault on Eniwetok. The amtank company deployed on the left wing of the landing force, less a platoon and the company headquarters that took up position between the battalion landing teams. The amphibian crews were surprised to encounter a cliff ranging from six to ten feet in height about ten yards from the water's edge, which had not been visible in air reconnaissance photos. All amphibians had to stop until reconnaissance parties found gaps through which they could move and continue their missions. Unlike at Kwajalein, the amphibians were used to provide close support during operations in the island's interior.[37]

The GIs were able to cut the island across its middle within an hour and deployed to attack both ends, reinforced by a battalion of the 22d Marines that had been in reserve. Captured documents had confirmed the presence of the mobile brigade, and in light of the determined resistance on Eniwetok, commanders decided to commit the remainder of the 22d Marines to capture Parry Island the following day, a landing then postponed until 23 February because of slow progress on Eniwetok.

Indeed, on 20 February, the 3d Battalion, 106th Infantry, was still engaged in full-scale assault operations on the northern part of the island, supported by light tanks from Company C, 766th Tank Battalion. The 1st Battalion, 106th Infantry, and 3d Battalion, 22d Marines, were mopping up on the southern half, backed by Marine medium tanks from the 2d Separate Tank Company. "They moved barely fifteen yards at a time, tanks leading the way," recorded a Yank reporter, "flanked on each side by infantrymen—BAR men spraying every foot, and riflemen throwing grenades into each mound."[38] Resistance finally ended late on 21 February, and Parry Island fell after the 22d Marines overcame determined resistance two days later, with transportation again provided by Maj. James Rogers's army amphibians.

In its after-action report, the V Amphibious Corps complimented the 708th Provisional Amphibian Tractor Battalion, which it said played a creditable role in support of all landings.[39]

Lessons Learned

The 708th Amphibian Tank Battalion, which reverted to its normal organization after operations ended, concluded that the 37-millimeter gun on the LVT(A)(1) had been sufficient to disable light tanks encountered but lacked the punch to reduce pillboxes and other strongholds.

The arrival five days before the Saipan landings of the first sixteen LVT(A)(4)s filled the need. The LVT(A)(4) was similar in design to the LVT(A)(1) but carried the turret from the M8 howitzer motor carriage assault gun mounted farther toward the stern for proper trim (which eliminated the scarf gun positions) and weighed nearly seventeen tons. The open-topped turret had a short-barreled 75-millimeter howitzer and a .50-caliber machine gun mounted to the rear, and the vehicle carried 100 rounds for the main gun and 400 for the machine gun. The vehicle had a crew of six men, including commander, driver, assistant driver-radio operator, gunner, assistant gunner, and ammunition handler. The vehicle had a radio and intercom system.

The 776th Amphibian Tank Battalion's command staff would later argue that while the LVT(A)(1) was an amphibious light tank, the new model was a self-propelled artillery piece—no longer a tank—and should be used as field artillery in amphibious operations.[40] As there was no doctrine distilled in a field manual, different battalions wound up following different paths. While the 708th would eventually use the "A4s" as artillery to some extent, it never stopped thinking of the vehicle as a tank.

Crews that had served in the old tank battalion assault gun section in M8s had helped train other gunners in anticipation of the new model's arrival, and many gunners found the weapon easy to learn after having fired 75-millimeter cannons in their old M3 medium tanks. The battalion realized quickly that the amtank's lack of a coaxial machine gun and scarf guns nevertheless presented a new tactical problem that had to be solved: warding off close infantry attack. The only automatic weapon was the .50-caliber antiaircraft machine gun on the turret rear, and a man had to expose himself to fire it at a ground target. The immediate solution was to assign one LVT(A)(4) to each tank platoon and one to each company headquarters so that the LVT(A)(1)s could provide covering fire with their machine guns.

The battalion constructed a crude but effective course on which to train scarf gunners. Firing took place at ranges of between 50 and 100 yards, which had been typical in combat.

The battalion had learned that amphibian vehicles were much more demanding in terms of maintenance than were land tanks. The thin underbellies were prone to puncture by rocks and coral. The clutch and gears were overtaxed and required constant overhaul. Salt water and sand also played havoc with moving parts. The result was that the outfit had to completely overhaul each LVT every 200 hours and maintain strict first-echelon maintenance in between.[41]

The commander of the V Amphibious Corps expressed his views on the use of amtanks on Kwajalein, judging that they had provided excellent support to the initial waves of infantry. He warned, however, that they should not be used as tanks on land, but rather as "supplementary fighting vehicles" because of their thin armor. He concluded that the 708th Battalion had demonstrated the durability of the amphibian tractor, and preliminary reports from the marine amphibian units suggested the same.

The navy conceded that it had to work out much better methods for reloading LVTs onto LSTs. Under good sea conditions, two hours were required to get seventeen LVTs back onto a vessel. One idea considered was to install railroad-style turntables in the bow so that vehicles could drive in nose first and then be turned around.[42]

The land tankers in the 767th Battalion had been pleased with the flamethrowers mounted in the light tanks, which had been used against buildings, debris piles, and, in a few cases, pillboxes. About half had been rendered inoperable by seawater, so the outfit planned to refine the design. The use of M10s had also been deemed a great success. Regarding tank-infantry cooperation, the battalion judged that its crews had been overly cautious in their well-meant efforts to stay with the doughboys. Still, by the end of the battle, the tanks had been engaging targets up to 300 yards in front of the infantry line. Because there were so many obstructions on the ground, the tactic that had gained the greatest favor in battle was for the tanks to pound any possible target in front of the GIs, even if no enemy could be seen, after which the infantry would advance. White-phosphorus rounds had proved extremely effective when fired into emplacements through a breach, inevitably persuading the enemy to exit in haste.[43]

CHAPTER 6

Saipan: Bookend to Normandy

"The conquest of Saipan was, among Pacific operations up to that time, the most clear-cut decisive triumph of combined arms of the United States over the Japanese."

—Gen. C. B. Cates, Commandant
of the Marine Corps

The capture of the Marshall Islands had guaranteed the U.S. Fleet protected forward-area anchorages. The conquest of the Mariana's would penetrate the inner perimeter of Japan's defenses and provide bases for B-29 long-range bombers to hit the home islands. The key islands in the Marianas for military purposes were Saipan, Tinian, Rota, and Guam. Saipan hosted two airfields, a naval fueling station, and a seaplane base, and nearby Tinian had two airfields.

On 15 June 1944, LSTs belonging to the Fifth Fleet's Northern Attack Force and bearing the Northern Troops and Landing Force massed some 6,000 yards off the west side of Saipan, the second largest of the Mariana Islands at fourteen miles long north to south and six miles across at the widest point. Mount Tapotchau dominates the island and gives way to a coastal plain to its west and south. The landing beaches along the southwest corner of the island were protected by a coral reef approximately 500 yards from the sand, so amphibian vehicles once again were a must. The Japanese-built Aslito Airfield, a key objective, was located roughly a mile from the southern coast, and a small half-finished fighter strip lay close to the landing beaches.

Lt. Gen. Yoshitsugu Saito, the commanding general of the Northern Marianas Army Group, had available to defend the island the 43d Division (reinforced), the 47th Mixed Brigade, an infantry battalion, a tank regiment, an antiaircraft regiment, and two regiments of engineers. Total army strength was approximately 22,700 men, supported by about 7,000 naval personnel.[1]

Elements of the Marine Corps' V Amphibious Corps were to pry those troops off the island. Lt. Russell Gugeler, who gathered oral history of the action from army amphibian crews using the techniques of Lt. Col. S. L. A. Marshall, summed up Operation Forager:

> Briefly, the plan called for the landing of two Marine divisions [2d and 4th], attached units, and necessary supplies within a few hours. This plan was dependent upon the amphibious vehicles and their capability of movement on land and in the water. Prior to the landing, the naval and air bombardment would neutralize defensive positions in the landing area. This fire would lift as the amphibious tanks and troop-laden tractors neared the shore and the shock action of a large number of these vehicle should extend the neutralization long enough to allow the first waves to push inland several hundred yards to the initial objective [with the infantry still mounted in LVTs]. This would provide a beachhead sufficiently large for the assault battalions to deploy on the ground and organize for the continuation of the attack. Subsequent waves would debark from the tractors at the beach and mop up resistance that was bypassed by the first waves. This plan to by-pass the beach defenses would also afford defiladed areas inland where troops could debark with greater safety.

The 27th Infantry Division was in Expeditionary Troops reserve and prepared to land on Saipan, Tinian, or Guam; in the event, it was to enter the Saipan beachhead once it was secured.

Four battalions of the 4th Marine Division were to land on the right and four battalions of the 2d Marine Division on the left. The 4th Division had attached to it the 708th Amphibian Tank Battalion, which was to form the first wave and land seventeen amtanks on each of the division's four beaches. The 773d Amphibian Tractor Battalion was to carry the 25th Marines to the two yellow-coded beaches, while Marine amtracs from the 10th Amphibian Tractor Battalion carried the infantry to the two blue-coded beaches. The 534th Amphibian Tractor Battalion (launching from the LSD USS *Belle Grove*) was also attached to carry marine reconnaissance parties and reserve troops to division beaches and to land artillery reconnaissance parties for both the 4th Marine Division and the 27th Infantry Division. Marine amtanks, meanwhile, were to lead the 2d Division's assault, but the army's 715th Amphibian Tractor Battalion was attached to carry the infantry to the two green-coded beaches in the division's zone.[2] The Marine Corps' 2d and 5th Amphibian Tractor battalions provided the remainder of the division's amtracs.

An amphibian tractor battalion had enough LVTs to carry two assault battalions to shore. Normally, each company was attached to and under the operational control of the commander of the infantry battalion to be carried by the company. The amtrac battalion commander and his staff would typically join the staff of the

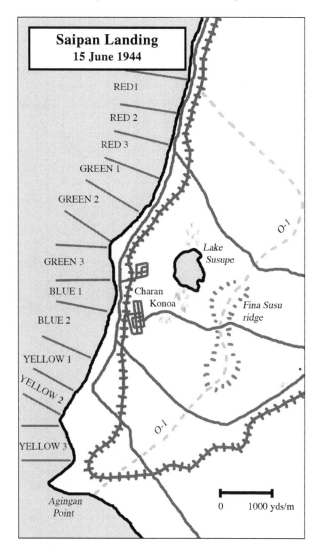

Saipan Landing
15 June 1944

RED 1
RED 2
RED 3
GREEN 1
GREEN 2
GREEN 3
BLUE 1
BLUE 2
YELLOW 1
YELLOW 2
YELLOW 3

Charan Konoa

Lake Susupe

Fina Susu ridge

O-1

Agingan Point

0   1000 yds/m

infantry regiment on its control vessel for the operation, which enabled the navy, infantry, and armor to coordinate closely.[3]

Naval aircraft had been pounding Saipan, Tinian, Rota, and Guam since 11 June, and warships commenced bombardment of Saipan and Tinian two days later. The Japanese certainly knew the Americans were coming.

Army Tankers and the 4th Marine Division

The army's amphibian tankers do not appear to have yet grasped the importance of working and communicating with the infantry that had emerged in land tank formations. The 708th Amphibian Tank Battalion had conducted extensive exercises at Maui with the 4th Marine Division, which it concluded did more harm than good because of the extensive wear on the LVTs. Liaison officers equipped with army SCR-510 radios at the battalion, regiment, and division levels on the marine side were the only communications link between the armor and the infantry.[4] None of these channels were going to matter during the fierce company and platoon action on the beaches.

By the time of Operation Forager, the 708th Amphibian Tank Battalion was organized into four companies, each consisting of four LVT(A)(4)s and thirteen LVT(A)(1)s. After the experience at Kwajalein, the battalion had scraped together extra armor plate to cover the side pontoons on as many vehicles as possible and added extra armor for the scarf gunners. Maintenance men cut vision slits in the front armor for drivers and their assistants.

The battalion—minus Companies C and D—was attached to the 23d Marines, and the other two companies were attached to the 25th Marines. The battalion was to form the first wave for the entire 4th Marine Division front, with each company leading an LVT-mounted assault battalion. The amtanks were to help the marines seize and secure a phase line designated O-1 and then assist the infantry as ordered. If the advance inland occurred rapidly and with few casualties, a mechanized attack with marines mounted in their LVTs and supported by the amtanks was to take place before day's end.

On 15 June, the armored force crews aboard the American fleet were awakened between 0145 and 0230 hours and served chow. The men then trooped to the cavernous tank deck to start the engines. Lt. Harry Semmes, a platoon commander in the 708th Amphibian Tank Battalion, recalled, "From past experience it had been found that for morale purposes it was better to have the engines warmed before the infantry loaded on."[5]

At about 0700, the LSTs dropped anchor, and within minutes amphibian vehicles splashed off the lowered ramps into the ocean. The amtanks and amtracs formed by waves at the line of departure about 5,000 yards off shore while the navy pummeled the landing area with a preparatory bombardment.[6] LVT commanders sorted themselves out by looking for flags on the platoon commanders' vehicles, and then a small naval craft led each company in a column to the line of departure. The ungainly vessels had difficulty remaining in line, but the wait was not long.

At about 0800 hours, the word reached the amtanks over the radio: "The flag is down. Move out!" The rough line became somewhat more chaotic as drivers proceeded at slightly different speeds, and heavy traffic on the radio net blocked officers' attempts to straighten the line again.[7] Fortunately, the sea was calm except for a few spots at the coral reef, where waves would cause some problems. The 773d Amphibian Tractor Battalion's amtracs, augmented by the lead LVT(2)s from Company B (reinforced), 534th Amphibian Tractor Battalion, carrying the first wave of marines, set off behind the amtanks after a three-minute delay, which created a space of about 300 yards between the first and second lines.

Rocket- and gun-firing LCI(G)s preceded the amphibians, giving the beach a final working over and peeling off to the flanks just before the coral reef. When the amtanks reached a line about 600 yards from shore, heavy artillery and mortar fire crashed around the vehicles. Marines crouched in the amtracs not far behind the amtanks, hoping and praying that none of the shells would find them. A moment later, the amtanks opened fire in return, although the gunners could see nothing through the cloud of dirt and debris raised by the naval bombardment. Indeed, fire from 5-inch naval guns continued until the assault wave was 300 yards from the beach.[8]

"Observation was limited to about fifteen yards," recalled Lieutenant Semmes, who was with Company A's amtanks, "and it is a frightening thing to go into something you cannot see, so the tanks stopped momentarily. The beach, however, was receiving a lot of shellfire, and it was urgent that the tanks move inland. The platoon started ahead ten yards at a time, halted, fired a few rounds, and then moved another ten yards."[9]

Company A landed on Beach Blue 2 in front of the 2d Battalion, 23d Marines, leaving one tank burning in the surf. Many trees had survived the bombardment, and the Japanese had exploited natural obstacles and created numerous tank traps; seven amtanks became stuck while crossing the first 200 yards under small-arms fire. After 600 yards, the remaining tanks ran into a curtain of accurate artillery and mortar fire that demolished three vehicles. The remaining six made it to the O-1 line and waited for the infantry to arrive, and eventually, a single platoon did so. The tanks spent the remainder of the day shooting at targets on and beyond the ridge from which they were receiving artillery and mortar fire.

Capt. John Straub's Company B amtanks landed nearby on Beach Blue 1 with the 3d Battalion, having lost one vehicle that hung up on the coral reef. The remaining tanks crawled through the village of Charan Konoa under small-arms and artillery fire and then advanced to the Fina Susu ridge by 0930. Amtracs followed, and marines manned the machine guns and exchanged fire with Japanese riflemen who were firing from drainage ditches perpendicular to the road. The tankers say they held the O-1 line the entire day without contact with the infantry, except for brief exchanges with nothing larger than a platoon. The marines assert that they ascended to the crest, where they were pinned down by direct artillery fire, and that the amtank crews failed to follow to provide support. As both accounts are probably substantially true, communication had clearly broken down.

Once the tanks were in place (wherever that was), Straub set off in his amtank to reconnoiter his right flank. According to his interview with Lieutenant Gugeler, about 400 yards south of the company's position, he encountered what he believed to be about thirty enemy infantrymen. The Japanese were armed with rifles but made no attempt to fire at Straub's tank then or while he was turning it around, which he did in order to be in position to move if the force proved to be larger than he then thought. When the tank had reversed its position, Straub halted it and waited while the Japanese walked toward his tank, rifles in their right hands, their left hands aloft. Some carried pieces of white cloth. The soldiers continued to walk toward the tank, but Straub, uncertain of their intentions and in no position to care for that many prisoners, ordered his scarf gunners to kill them. Straub had just started back when he noticed another group of similar size following in the same manner. Straub believed they must have seen the first group killed, but they continued to walk toward his tank and all but one of these were dispatched. During the afternoon, he met other smaller groups that displayed the same strange behavior.

Meanwhile, fire was so heavy on Beach Blue 1 that the 534th Amphibian Tractor Battalion's LVTs—which were bearing elements of the 1st Battalion, 23d Marines, arriving in the second echelon—diverted to Blue 2, which itself was so hot that six amtracs were knocked out with the loss of four men killed and nineteen wounded. The remaining vehicles advanced east of Charan Konoa 1,500 yards inland, unloaded, and returned to the beach to transport casualties.

Company D of the 708th Battalion and the 2d Battalion of the 25th Marines had a relatively easy experience at Beach Yellow 1, where the company lost four vehicles to obstacles and artillery fire before encountering a railroad embankment that stymied the tanks. The amtanks had moved off the beach so briskly that the amtracs of Company B, 773d Amphibian Tractor Battalion, were able to proceed to the railroad. At the rail line, the marines decided to disembark and fight on the ground rather than wait and ride to the O-1 phase line. One tractor was lost to enemy fire at this point. The amtracs turned around and carried casualties back to the beach.

The 3d Platoon's amtanks on the right of the 2d Battalion's zone finally drove into the neighboring zone, crossed the railroad tracks, and cut back to establish a base of fire. The remainder of the company thereupon crossed the rail line following the same route. Three concealed 75-millimeter guns destroyed two amtanks before the concentrated fire of the 2d Platoon and company headquarters destroyed them. After the survivors were rescued under cover of smoke, five amtanks from the 3d Platoon knocked out several machine-gun nests for marines on the left, who by day's end occupied the ridge in sufficient strength. "I shall always remember the excellent support given to my battalion by the Army LVT(A)s," commented the 2d Battalion's commanding officer, Lt. Col. L. C. Dudson.

At Beach Yellow 2, Company C ran into antitank fire that destroyed Sgt. Harold Gabriel's vehicle at the water's edge. T/5 John Dombrowski was blown into the water, the crewmen in the front of the tank killed, and the other crewmembers wounded. The wounded Dombrowski tried three times to get to the badly injured Gabriel, but each time, the Japanese gunner slammed another round into the tank and dislodged Dombrowski, who was finally pulled away by comrades.

The trailing 773d Amphibian Tractor Battalion's amtracs carrying the 1st Battalion, 25th Marines, had closed to within fifty yards of the amtanks by the time the latter reached the beach, and the first wave of amtracs jammed up onto the sand beside them because they stopped for a few moments. Sgt. James McLean's tractor (Company A) halted just behind Gabriel's tank, where it received three direct hits from a mortar that killed thirteen of the twenty-eight men in the vehicle and left only the driver unscathed.

PFC Peter Wilson, who commanded a nearby amtrac, spotted the gun that had knocked out Gabriel's tank and destroyed it with his machine gun. Incoming small-arms fire incapacitated the tractor commanded by Sgt. Steven Spradley, who fired his machine gun until the grips were shot from his hands.

When the tanks moved inland, heavy and accurate small-arms fire picked off several tank commanders, and six amtanks hung on obstacles. The remaining ten traversed nearly a mile of ground to the Fina Susu Ridge, where four tanks crossed the crest and were presented with a splendid target: some of the artillery and mortar positions that were firing at the beach. Direct fire killed some enemy crews and caused others to retreat. The marines who were supposed to follow them in their tractors were back at the beach, however, where they had dismounted and dug in after the amtrac Company A commander—having witnessed the immobilization of many tanks by obstacles—told the marine commander that he could proceed no farther. According to marine accounts, the LVTs left hurriedly after the men had jumped clear, carrying much of their equipment— machine guns, mortars, ammunition, and radios—back off the beach. Japanese soldiers who were bypassed by the amtanks unleashed a fusillade of frontal and enfilading fire across the sand, and after an hour, the 1st Battalion had gained only twelve yards of beach depth while casualties mounted alarmingly.

Meanwhile, Lt. Dean Coulter's platoon of amtanks moved ahead of Company B's marines, who were to seize the ridge at Agingan Point on the right flank of the beachhead, and reached the objective. Guns in a honeycomb of defenses on the point were laying down flanking fire on the beach, which drove the marines to ground. Coulter had already lost Gabriel's tank, and three more stuck in tank traps, so Coulter was alone when he neared the objective. After drawing heavy artillery fire, he returned and found that two tanks had extricated themselves, and the three amtanks rolled onto the objective by 0945 hours. Heavy naval gunfire from the battleship USS *Tennessee*, directed by the marines at an imagined counterattack, drove the tankers back, and they joined the marines who were supposed to have reached the ridge. The three running tanks now supported the marines' attempted drive toward the point. The marines had no machine guns, and those on the amtanks were instrumental in scattering the enemy infantry. Nevertheless, resistance was so persistent that the infantry officer on the scene judged it impractical to press all the way to the point.

By 1100, the four tanks on the Fina Susu Ridge were joined by a handful of riflemen. Behind them, most of the marines were pinned down by fire along a line parallel to the beach. At 1330, a heavy barrage drove the infantrymen back, so the amtanks followed them and joined the force trying to reach Agingan Point, which had also obtained infantry reinforcement. The Japanese nonetheless pushed this marine line back 500 yards by evening. Communications by then had broken down even within Company C as most radios failed, some because of saltwater damage and others because the antennae had been shot off.[10]

Lieutenant Semmes summed up the platoon-level experience on Saipan: "Hitting an enemy-held beach in the leading waves might best be described by a single word, 'confusion. . . .' During the move inland, the platoons did little fighting as a unit. Each tank commander would check periodically to see that his tank was in proper position of the platoon, but most firing was done on his own volition or when foot troops called for it."[11]

Progress in the 4th Division's zone had been too slow, and the losses too heavy, for an attack on Aslito Airfield on D-Day. The fallback plan anticipated a ground assault the next day.[12]

The 773d Amphibian Tractor Battalion's amtracs returned to the transfer lines after they unloaded the assault waves and thereafter shuttled men and supplies until late afternoon. The surf at that point increased from eight to seventeen feet, which resulted in eight tractors swamping, including one that turned over and drowned most of the Marines on board. At that point, the battalion suspended operations to reboard the LSTs.

The 534th Amphibian Tractor Battalion's Company A began delivering reserve troops from three 27th Division field artillery battalions and elements of the 14th Marine Artillery Regiment to the 23d and 25th Marine Regiments at about 1000 hours. The tractors did not engage in combat, but artillery fire knocked out several amtracs, and many others hung up on obstructions when they tried to move inland.

The rising surf had played havoc with the marines' efforts to land a battalion of M4A2 tanks during the afternoon, and many drowned out. Nevertheless, several platoons' worth joined the line by the end of the day, including a platoon that arrived during yet another attack on the endangered right flank just in time to turn the tide.[13] The marines were going to need tank support the next day, and candidates were scarce.

The majority of amtanks were released to refuel that evening. Only nine amtanks remained on the O-1 line overnight, seven of them with Lieutenant Coulter on the shaky right flank of the beachhead.[14]

Tankers and the 2d Marine Division

In the 2d Marine Division's zone, the amtracs of the 715th Amphibian Tractor Battalion formed part of the first wave. The marines had arrayed thirty-six amtanks from the 2d Armored Amphibian Battalion in platoon-size, inverted-V formations to the flanks of and in between the amtrac companies. The LVTs were to proceed in line across the beach to a tractor control line some 200 yards inland, where the marines would dismount to fight. The amtracs were to provide fire support and, when appropriate, return to the control vessel. The second through fourth waves, following at five-to-eight-minute intervals, were to unload troops on the beach, execute a flank movement to the edge of the beach, and immediately return to sea in column formation to reload without interfering with the next wave.

The plan came unglued quickly. The navy guide boat on the right flank drifted left and forced both amtanks and amtracs to shift until that wing of the formation consisted of three sub-waves, with amtracs in front, which prevented the tanks from firing as they approached the beach. An unexpected northern current also encouraged leftward shift. Marines urged crews to steer right, and crews tried to get the guide boat to steer right, all to no effect. Despite heavy artillery fire that began when the amphibians reached the reef, all but 2 of the 100 tractors made shore. The entire formation had moved leftward, and all elements landed the equivalent of one beach too far over.[15]

Capt. Richard Adams, who commanded Company B and a dozen attached amtracs from Company C of the 715th Amphibian Tractor Battalion, had a ringside seat from the third wave of the assault force of the 3d Battalion, 8th Marines. The troops, whose amtracs debarked from LSTs 6,000 yards offshore at about 0700, were headed for Beach Green 1, barely visible because of the dust raised by naval fire. The run would take about twenty-five minutes:

As the third wave crossed the line of departure at 0828, the beach seemed strangely quiet and inactive, and nothing seemed to be firing toward the first wave, which was now approximately 1,500 yards from the beach and beginning to cross the coral reef. . . . When the leading wave was approximately 800 yards from the beach, naval and Marine fighters came in strafing the beach, and this attack continued along the beaches until the leading wave approached within 100 yards of shore. . . .

Then the enemy opened fire. This happened as the first wave hit the beach and the third wave hit the reef at 1,500 yards. Suddenly, the entire reef seemed to be one mass of exploding mortar and big shells. A heavy barrage was laid down between the reef and the beach. Several amtracs took direct hits and went down. Men were blown into the water by direct hits and later [were] picked up by the amtracs returning seaward.

All control that had persisted up to this point ceased. Nothing could be accomplished by radio, and it was almost impossible to see anything, much less make contact with the other waves. Evidently the enemy fire was coming from positions 1,000 to 2,000 yards back of the beach. It was later established that this was true, most of the shelling was coming from caves and along the ridges of Mt. Topatchau, caves that contained artillery pieces on steel tracks that were moved up to the cave entrances, fired, then were pulled back into the caves and sliding steel doors shut. . . .

Also, artillery fire from Tinian, 5,000 yards to the southwest, was falling along the beaches.

To get back to the first wave, as it hit the beach it was discovered that the beach was only about thirty feet in [depth], and that directly to the front the terrain rose steeply to a height of four or five feet. Not only was this too high in most places for the amtracs to negotiate, but trees and thick brush constituted an unsurpassable obstacle in crossing the beach.[16]

This confronted the amtanks and amtracs on the left wing with a tree-covered bank that blocked passage. The marines disembarked in the water and dug in along the bank, and as subsequent waves arrived, they found themselves squeezed between a growing number of armored amphibians to the rear and the Japanese to the front. Captain Adams observed, "By the time the infantry jumped from the amtracs and got out their equipment, the second wave was upon them, and the massing of vehicles and troops on the beach gave the enemy a target that was hard to miss."

By noon, the landing teams had scrabbled their way only a few hundred yards inland. The division had established a toehold, not a beachhead.

Only two tractors were able to leave the beach; they reached the edge of an airstrip just beyond. One ran into three Japanese tanks, and the driver stalled his vehicle in the excitement. Crew and marines bailed out and ran back to the beachhead. The driver of the second eventually reappeared, disoriented, and no further word was heard of the other men's fate.

Despite confusion and a breakdown in radio communications, the amtracs found ways to get back to the control vessel and thereafter ferried more men and supplies to the beach. All crews had been well briefed on what had to be done in anticipation of radio problems and the Japanese history of concentrating artillery and mortar fire on groups of LVTs, which might then have to split up. The battalion suspended operations at 1830 because of the rising surf. Some LSTs had been converted to hospital ships and could not take the LVTs on board again, and others had closed their doors and refused to re-open them, so much of the battalion spent the night in the water.[17]

Continuing Infantry Close Support

D-Day losses in the 708th Amphibian Tank Battalion amounted to eight amtanks destroyed and six damaged by enemy fire, plus seven put out of action for other reasons. Twelve men were killed and eighty-three men wounded, and five men were listed as missing. Over the next eleven days, losses of men and equipment would nearly double.[18] The three tractor battalions combined on D-Day lost roughly the same number of men as the 708th Battalion, eleven amtracs destroyed by enemy fire, forty-two damaged by fire, and twenty-seven swamped or sunk.[19] The marines' 2d Armored Amphibian Battalion had lost three of sixty-eight amtanks in the water and twenty-eight between the beach and the tractor control line.[20]

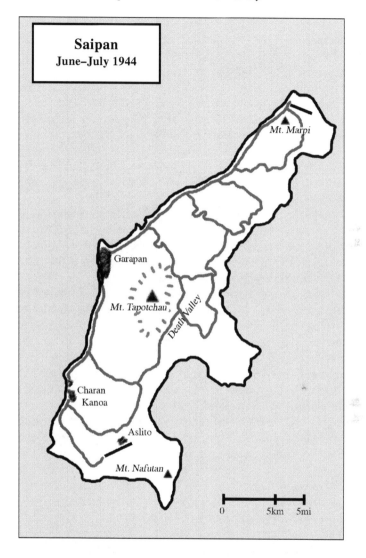

The amphibian tank companies refueled and conducted repairs aboard the LSTs on D+1. Coulter's amtanks were relieved from the line on the 4th Marine Division's right flank at about noon, and the weary crews returned to the LSTs. Company B, which had refueled overnight, was attached to the 25th Marines but remained in reserve under frequent shellfire.[21]

Adm. Raymond Spruance, the Fifth Fleet's commander, had learned the previous night that the Japanese fleet was approaching from Philippine waters, and on the morning of D+1, he made several decisions that led to the battle commonly called the Great Marianas Turkey Shoot after the large number of Japanese naval aircraft destroyed. One command was to affect the army amphibians and the marines on shore: unloading would continue at Saipan until daylight on 17 June, and then all vessels not critically needed would withdraw to the east of Saipan for safety. As it was clear that a grim fight was in store, the 27th Infantry Division began to land before the transports pulled off. The 165th Infantry debarked at dusk.[22]

The first army land tanks to come ashore were four light tanks from Company D, 766th Tank Battalion, which were attached to the 165th Infantry. These tanks were landed at 0830 on 17 June. The company was subordinated to the 762d Tank Battalion, which was also preparing to disembark, as a third company. The 762d for this operation consisted of only its headquarters element and Companies B and D and was called the 762d Provisional Tank Battalion. In the event, the medium tank company was carried off with the fleet and did not return for several days.[23]

On D+2, all companies of the 708th Amphibian Tank Battalion were committed to the drive on Aslito Airfield, which was overrun by the 25th Marines. Companies A and B again worked with the 4th Marine Division on the left, while Company C joined the 165th Infantry (as did several light tanks from Company D, 766th Tank Battalion), which had relieved the right wing of the marine line. Only on the left, where the 24th Marines fought over broken ground toward a ridge designated O-2, did the tankers of Company A have much trouble. Captain Bonner led five tanks out on a reconnaissance and ran into Japanese fire—possibly from anti-aircraft guns east of Aslito that were firing at ground targets—that knocked out his tank and one belonging to one of his lieutenants, and both suffered heavy losses among the crew. Lt. Paul Silberstein led the other three tanks forward to help, but his tank also was struck and the lieutenant wounded. With that, all officers in the company had been killed or disabled, total casualties had reached roughly 50 percent, and a staff sergeant rallied the company's five remaining tanks on the beach.[24]

On D+3 in the 4th Marine Division's zone, Company D of the 708th Amphibian Tank Battalion was assigned to support attacks by the 23d Marines beyond the O-1 line. During the action, the company commander was killed, and enemy guns knocked out two amtanks. Companies B and C worked with Marine medium tanks, supporting them by fire and followed by the infantry. The 75-millimeter guns on the LVT(A)(4)s proved very effective against all targets and fired high-explosives against artillery positions and small emplacements, and high-explosive antitank rounds against concrete fortifications. The 37-millimeter guns on the LVT(A)(1)s were ineffective against most targets except when the gunner could use canister against exposed infantry. Once again, the scarf guns proved the most useful weapons on the amtanks.

The amphibian battalions first heard about the withdrawal of the transports and LSTs that afternoon. The battalions rushed to get their maintenance men to shore, but when the ships pulled out, the 534th Amphibian Tractor Battalion still had twenty-two LVTs and 182 officers and men aboard. Some did not reappear for three weeks.[25]

The light tanks from the 762d Provisional Tank Battalion continued to work with the 27th Infantry Division, blasting caves and field positions. The tankers quickly adjusted their ammo loads to carry a minimum of armor-piercing rounds and boost the amount of high explosive and canister. They also learned that unless the ground of a Japanese gun position were physically occupied by the infantry after the tanks had knocked it out, the Japanese would repair the piece over night and open fire the next morning. The medium tanks of Company B went into action on 22 June, the day that most of the 27th Division was ordered into corps reserve and then into position between the 2d and 4th Marine Divisions in the central part of the island.

On 23 June, the light tanks began a six-day fight with the 2d Battalion, 105th Infantry, to clear the Nafutan Valley, a brush-filled area only 200 yards wide sandwiched between steep hills. The brush was so tall that it stood above the tank periscopes, and crewmen could hardly see a thing, which made it nearly impossible to spot and destroy the many machine-gun positions the Japanese has set up throughout the valley. The infantry and tankers adopted the tactic of having the tanks advance twenty-five yards to clear a path, and then the infantry would move forward.

On the first day of the operation, the 105th Infantry sent three light tanks on their own a mile into the valley. The tankers rolled along, firing into caves, houses, brush, and dugouts and returned safely despite attempts by Japanese mortars to disable them. The next day, after the infantry pointed out two dual-purpose guns with tracer fire, several light tanks staged another raid, cutting through the brush to overrun the guns from behind.[26] It may be that these successful cases of tank action without infantry support contributed to the 105th Infantry's disastrous use of the 193d Tank Battalion later on Okinawa.

More typically, though, the infantry and tanks sought to work together because the doughboys on their own might never have rooted the Japanese out of the island's tangled terrain. A report on the use of army tanks on Saipan said regarding fighting on the Nafutan Peninsula on 25–26 June:

[Lt. John] Phalon's tanks [from Company D, 762d Tank Battalion] . . . supported Lieutenant Greenwell's 3d Platoon, Company F. The Japanese positions were in rocks and bad places for tanks to approach. Nevertheless, the infantry credited Phalon's tanks on this day with knocking out six Japanese heavy machine guns, several mortars, a dual-purpose gun, of destroying dumps of various kinds of ammunition and grenades, and of killing more than 100 Japanese soldiers. Their bodies were found later. While all this was happening, not one live Japanese had been seen by the infantry, who were only a short distance away.

The same kind of tank-infantry fighting on Nafutan was resumed the next day. The infantry had been pinned down for several days and had been able to make little or no progress. The tanks were the only means available with which to break up the stubborn enemy resistance in this jungle of coral rock and brush. Phalon's tanks advanced through the brush and cane fields with the infantry following immediately behind them. On one hurry-up call from the infantry, the tanks fired high explosives and canister into a position where the Japanese were in the act of setting up a 75mm pack howitzer and killed twenty-four of them.[27]

The difficulty of tank-infantry communication loomed large:

Good communication between tank commanders and infantry required that the tank men open their turrets, raise up, and talk with the infantry. This was very dangerous for tank men in enemy territory. The Japanese frequently would allow infantry to pass without firing on them, but the moment a tank man showed himself he was the object of all the enemy fire that could be brought to bear on him. Killing or seriously wounding a tank commander or member of the crew usually meant the tank was immobilized or that it would have to withdraw.[28]

Five hundred Japanese tried to break through the 105th Infantry's line across the Nafutan Peninsula the night of 26 June. Most died in confused fighting in the dark or were hunted down by patrols the next day.

Medium tanks from Company B, meanwhile, were committed to the fight in Death Valley on 23 June, when the 27th Infantry Division's 106th and 165th Infantry Regiments joined the two marine divisions battling to clear the central part of Saipan. Lt. Dudley Williams's platoon underwent its baptism of fire on 24 June, when a section of three tanks commanded by Williams was attached to Company C, 165th Infantry. The tankers got an immediate lesson in the critical importance of cooperating with the infantry, given Japanese close-assault tactics.

The plan was for the infantry to lead, while the tanks were available nearby on call. The tankers lost sight of the GIs and wound up driving along a narrow road where a light tank had been destroyed a day earlier by Molotov cocktails.

Williams arrived at the spot where the light tank was still burning and stopped, whereupon, in the words of Cpl. Howard Myers, gunner in the third tank, "the entire little knoll to the left seemed to move." Japanese infantry charged Williams's tank, and Myers cut loose with his coaxial machine gun, cutting down men within arm's reach of the Sherman. Myers went through 1,400 rounds of ammunition before the surviving Japanese pulled back.

After one tank broke down and was taken in tow, the tankers went in search of the infantry. They stumbled instead onto a position of the 4th Marine Division. While Williams was speaking to the marines, a shot rang out, and one of the marines dropped like a sack. Williams spotted a Japanese soldier who had crawled underneath his tank and placed two grenades on one track. Williams raced to the deck and asked for the Tommy gun. His gunner suggested grenades would be better, but after two failed to kill the intruder, Williams killed him with a burst of .45-caliber slugs.

Almost immediately, new excitement ensued as three Japanese tanks appeared. The two running tanks joined antitank guns in dispensing a broadside that turned all three into piles of junk.

Elsewhere in the valley, the other two platoons were running into high-velocity antitank fire that destroyed or immobilized all but two tanks by nightfall. This had truly been a baptism of fire, and one platoon commander was evacuated as a combat fatigue case. Men were wounded, but the tankers were just lucky enough not to sacrifice any lives to Death Valley that day.

Vicious fighting raged through the valley and onto the slopes of Mt. Tapotchau. Heavy rains drenched the battlefield on 25 June, and the tankers were unable to find the infantry they were supposed to support. Tankers vainly tried to spot Japanese guns emplaced on high ground, and one crew engaged and destroyed two Japanese tanks. Lieutenant Williams's tank engine was penetrated by an antitank round, and over the next several days, other Shermans and light tanks fell prey to direct fire and artillery.

At least some of the medium tanks had field telephones attached to the rear by now. The value became clear on 27 June, when Williams's section was supporting the 3d Battalion, 106th Infantry, on Mount Tapotchau. The riflemen were pinned down, and only 75-millimeter gunfire could knock out the Japanese positions that were causing trouble. Williams directed one of his tanks to a hill from where it could engage the enemy. An infantry major trailed the Sherman, at considerable risk to himself, calling for fire over the telephone. Corporal Myers, in the gunners seat, engaged the strongpoint and destroyed a dug-in tank and machine-gun nest. Job done, the tanks ferried sixteen wounded doughboys to the rear.

At one point, a single platoon of medium tanks operated as a fixed artillery battery under the fire direction of the infantry. This appears to have been the first recorded use of tanks as artillery in the Pacific.

By 30 June, Death Valley was strewn with knocked out tanks, both American and Japanese. Maintenance men stripped the most damaged tanks of parts to keep the rest running, and service company men took casualties while making runs onto the battlefield to reach wrecks. So many tanks were out of action that the 762d Battalion abandoned the platoon structure and formed a pool of "runners," from which as many tanks as a mission required were dispatched.

Many tank men complained that during the inland fighting, they received little if any guidance from the infantry, that they often had to decide their own missions, and that it was hard to distinguish friendly from enemy infantry. The use of SCR-536 radios to tie the infantry and tanks together was deemed a consistent failure.

The battle moved out of Death Valley on 1 July. More tough fighting remained, and mines, antitank guns, and suicide squads claimed more American tanks. At the end of twenty-two days of battle, the 762d Tank Battalion had lost seventeen light and five medium tanks destroyed beyond repair. The three tank companies had suffered eighty-eight casualties, including eighteen killed in action. The continued combat utility of light tanks under conditions in the Pacific had been amply demonstrated; the two companies of light tanks had expended

24,000 rounds of high explosive, as compared with 2,204 rounds fired by the mediums, as well as 18,900 rounds of canister.[29]

The 708th Amphibian Tank Battalion had also conducted close-support missions, losing a trickle of men and equipment, until 26 June, when it was able to pull back to perform maintenance. The tractor battalions, meanwhile, settled into a routine of hauling. In early July, 708th Battalion tanks helped the marines clear caves along the coast by firing into them from the sea. Saipan was declared secure on 10 July.

The battle was not quite over, as Companies C and D were ordered on 23 July to board LSTs for transfer to Tinian, where they were attached to the 23d Marines. On the twenty-fourth, the 773d Amphibian Tractor Battalion, augmented by Companies A and C and a platoon of Company B of the 534th Battalion, carried the 25th Marines to the beach. From 25 to 27 July, amtanks from Company D of the 708th Battalion conducted sorties ashore from the LSTs and provided fire support to the infantry. The battalion was then ordered back to Oahu.[30] During the Marianas operation, it had suffered a casualty rate of roughly 31 percent in personnel and lost sixteen tanks destroyed and fourteen badly damaged.[31]

Lessons Learned

The 708th Amphibian Tank Battalion judged that the use of its amtanks beyond the beachhead had been a mistake because they lacked sufficient armor and mechanical stamina. The battalion therefore proposed that its 75-millimeter howitzers be put to use as artillery once a beach had been secured. The Central Pacific Base Command and the Tenth Army endorsed the idea, and because only one officer in the battalion had training in indirect fire, the outfit turned to other units, including the marine corps, for manuals, education, and equipment. Some officers and men left their tanks to become forward observers as there was a shortage because of the slow arrival of replacements for men lost on Saipan. Those that did arrive had no experience with an amphibian unit and needed extensive training.

The battalion also recommended that LVT(A)(4)s be equipped with scarf guns and the gunners and commanders with bullet-proof vests. It urged that the amtanks be camouflaged for land instead of painted light blue, as the dust raised by bombardment obscured the enemy's view of the vehicles when in the water.

While amtanks left naval control once on the beach, amtracs often spent days shuttling from shore to ship and back. Operations on Saipan had shown that when navy officers delivered orders directly to LVTs, platoon, company, and battalion cohesion broke down. The navy adapted by changing policy so that all orders would go through the amphibian units' officers.[32]

In its lessons-learned report, the 762d Tank Battalion concluded, "Probably the greatest single obstacle with which the battalion was confronted was the problem of understanding the infantry and making them understand us. Only toward the end of the twenty-three days fighting, and after many mistakes were made, was a relationship achieved between tanks and infantry that approximated harmony and permitted efficient operation."

The tankers argued that one battalion of tanks was too little to support an infantry division and that a regiment would be more appropriate. Specific lessons included removing white stars from everywhere but the top of the turret because they served Japanese gunners so well as aiming points. And tankers wanted some solution to keep Molotov cocktails from setting engines on fire.[33]

The Saipan operation is far eclipsed in the popular memory by the landings that had taken place in Normandy, France, only nine days earlier, but for the men of the armored force, the Pacific assault was a bigger show. Sixty-eight army amtanks participated in the assault wave at Saipan, as compared with 102 amphibious and 59 wader-equipped tanks at Omaha and Utah Beaches, but to that must be added 200 army-crewed amtracs at Saipan.

CHAPTER 7

DDs at D-Day

"The British Second Army on the left, the American V Corps in the cen-
ter, and American VII Corps on the right, together with combined
Allied Naval and Air Forces, land simultaneously on the coast of
France with the mission of establishing a beachhead on the continent
from which further offensive operations can be developed. . . .

"[The 741st Tank Battalion] will land on Beach OMAHA–Easy Red
and Fox Green in direct support of the 2d and 3d BLTs [Battalion Land-
ing Teams], CT [Combat Team] 16, Companies B and C (DD) landing
at H-5, D-Day, and Company A landing at H-Hour, D-Day. . . ."

—Field Order #1, 1st Infantry
Division

Operation Overlord was to be the symphony of the "Atlantic style" of amphibious operation, developed from the painful learning experiences in North Africa,
Sicily, and Italy. Dependence on the infantry to clear landing areas for tanks in Operations Torch, Husky, and Avalanche had weakened the assault waves' ability to handle counterattacks, and commanders determined that the doughs would enjoy close
tank support on the Normandy beaches. The Allied armies would shell the beach,
storm the beach with infantry *and* tanks, and secure the beach.

The first separate tank battalions destined to participate in the invasion of
France—including the 70th, 743d, and 745th—arrived in the United Kingdom
between August and November 1943. Preparation before D-Day included refresher
training, exercises with partner infantry divisions, familiarization with landing
craft, waterproofing of equipment, and orientation with special equipment built for
the invasion. Three battalions selected to go ashore with the first invasion wave in
Operation Overlord received special and secret training for a scheme that embod-
ied the purpose of the separate battalions: giving the infantry close-in gun support
throughout combat operations. Two companies each of the 70th, 741st, and 743d
Tank Battalions were to land minutes before the first infantry, riding special
amphibious duplex-drive (DD, also known as "Donald Duck") M4A1 Sherman
tanks to shore. The third medium tank company and battalion tankdozers would
follow in landing craft.

Developed by the British, the DD conversion to the M4 Sherman series added
a collapsible screen and thirty-six inflatable rubber tubes or pillars attached to a

boat-shaped platform welded to the hull of the waterproofed tank. When inflated, the tubes raised the screen, which was locked into position by struts. The assembly acted as a flotation device, allowing the tank to displace its own weight in water and giving the vehicle about three feet of freeboard. The tank was driven through the water at seven to eight miles per hour by two eighteen-inch movable screw propellers, which also acted as rudders, attached to the back of the hull and powered through a bevel box off the track idler wheel. Between 15 March and 30 April 1944, the 743d Tank Battalion conducted 1,200 test launches from landing craft at Slapton Sands, losing only three M4A1 tanks and three lives.[1] The DD-equipped battalions exercised on a restricted beach to maintain secrecy until D-Day, which meant that the men had no opportunity to practice with their infantry partners.[2]

Maj. Gen. Charles "Cowboy Pete" Corlett, who in April had taken command of the XIX Corps and had led the 7th Infantry Division in its assault on Kwajalein, was appalled that planners were ignoring the lessons of the Pacific War. Why was the first wave of infantry not riding to the beach in armored LVTs? he wanted to know. His observations were brushed off, as if anything learned in the Pacific was "bush league."[3]

Moreover, training for all battalions focused on getting ashore in France rather than what to do afterward, and crowded conditions in the British Isles precluded any extensive tank-infantry training.[4] For example, even though the 70th Tank Battalion exercised in an inland area that somewhat resembled the hedgerow country of Normandy, all training was invasion related; infantry and tanks had no opportunity to work on coordination or tactics in hedgerow country or anywhere else.[5] Capt. Charles Kidd of Company M, 116th Infantry, recalled that the 29th Division's three pre-invasion exercises covered concentration, marshalling, embarkation, sea voyage, debarkation, ship-to-shore, and assault on the beach.[6] The unit history of the 746th Tank Battalion suggests that maneuvers with the partner 4th Infantry Division routinely ended on the same day of or the day after landing exercises.

Nevertheless, pre-invasion maneuvers gave the army forewarning that the tank-infantry team was going to have trouble once ashore in France, but commanders took no steps to remedy the situation. American forces conducted a series of landing exercises on the beaches of Slapton Sands. One of these, called Beaver, took place on 28 March 1944. Following preparatory fire from all classes of ships of the Royal Navy, Companies B and C of the 746th Tank Battalion hit the beach in the leading wave. The assault troops moved toward objectives several miles inland, and the unit history reported that "the attack was resumed on the second day ashore and terminated in the afternoon. During this phase of the exercise, a new difficulty arose: that of infantry-tank communication. Up to this point the infantry-tank teams had worked with close coordination, due to a prearranged system of smoke signals, but the unexpected situations arising after the successful assault landing created some disruption in contact between infantry and tanks. This was temporarily solved by the use of radio."[7] The infantry and tanks, however, did not use interoperable radio equipment; in the above case, one partner physically loaned a radio to the other.

Here again, solutions that had already been found in the Pacific and could have saved lives were unknown on the vast troop carrier that was the British Isles. Tank-infantry tactics worked out in jungles that more closely resembled what men would face in the hedgerows than did terrain assumed by doctrine never reached the ears of men headed for Normandy. Use of the EE-8 field telephone for communications between the doughboy and the tanker had been proved on Bougainville by the spring. Mid-twentieth-century communications technology—and perhaps military bureaucracy—kept this wisdom from soldiers who needed it.

INTO THE MAELSTROM

After delays caused by awful weather, the date was set: D-Day was to be 6 June 1944, with H-Hour at 0630. A massive flotilla off the coast of Normandy readied itself to launch the largest amphibious operation in history (if all air, land, and sea components are taken into account). At 0400 hours, soldiers of the assault wave in the 743d Tank Battalion awoke and prepared equipment and vehicles for landing. At 0430, hot coffee and K rations were issued to all men.[8] Tankers in the 741st were getting ready, too, and at 0445 turned over their engines.[9] In the 70th, men downed their last cup of hot java in the galley at 0530.[10]

The invasion plan called for elements of one corps to land at each of the two American beaches: the V Corps at Omaha and the VII Corps at Utah. Later, the XIX Corps would become active in the area between the two lead corps, and the 116th Infantry of the XIX Corps' 29th Infantry Division had accordingly been attached to the V Corps for the assault.[11]

Weather conditions at H-Hour were actually somewhat better than predicted, with fifteen-knot winds and eight-mile visibility. Heavy bombers struck coastal defenses on the British beaches and Utah Beach, but low clouds forced bombing on instruments at Omaha, which resulted in most ordnance being dropped to the rear. At 0550, the naval flotilla opened its bombardment of the Omaha and Utah Beach defenses. The battlewagons and cruisers fired until just before the troops hit the sand, at which time rocket gunships and other close-support vessels took up the task.[12] A vast armada of landing craft headed for the coast of France. The German Seventh Army's war diary noted, "Strong seaborne landings of infantry and tank forces beginning at [0615] hours."[13]

THE GOOD NEWS: UTAH BEACH

Utah Beach offered advantages to the Germans, who had 110 emplacements with guns ranging from 75 to 170 millimeters. Immediately behind the beach was a stretch of sand dunes between 150 and 1,000 yards deep, and behind that the terrain had been flooded back to one to two miles, forcing all traffic onto causeways.[14] These advantages did the Germans no good.

Except for a standard military issue of screw-ups, such as putting troops ashore far away from their assigned landing spots, the Utah Beach assault went as planned. The water was relatively calm when the 70th Tank Battalion's DDs launched 1,500 yards offshore rather than the planned 5,000 yards and puttered to the beach. All but five made it to the sand. Because of the late arrival of the LSTs carrying the DD tanks and the loss of a primary control vessel, Company C's tanks, which were supposed to land after the DDs of Companies A and B, actually hit the beach first, becoming the assault wave. The company lost four tanks on the way in when the LCT they were on was sunk.

Little fighting occurred at the water's edge.[15] Invading troops encountered only light artillery fire, and by 1000 hours, six infantry battalions were ashore.[16] While Company C's tanks took over the mission of suppressing defenses laterally to the left and right of the beach, the DD tanks landed and moved quickly inland to link up with paratroopers of the 101st Airborne Division who had jumped the previous night. The relative ease of the landing was reflected in the fact that as of midday, the tanks required no resupply of ammunition. Nevertheless, by day's end, seven medium tanks had been lost. The light tanks of Company D landed late on D-Day and also joined the 101st Airborne Division. Tankers were "unprepared" for the hedgerow terrain they encountered, but initially, they faced little resistance beyond shelling and mines.[17]

The 746th Tank Battalion crossed Utah Beach late in the morning in the second wave, although the 1st Platoon of Company A had landed more than two hours earlier in support of the 3d Battalion, 22d Infantry, 4th Infantry Division. Company C of the 746th Tank Battalion formed part of Howell Force, the seaborne component of the 82d Airborne Division, which rolled out of its landing craft at about H plus 3 hours. Commanded by Col. Edson Raff, a daring veteran of the North Africa campaign, the force consisted of the 3d Platoon, Troop B, 4th Cavalry Reconnaissance Squadron; ninety riflemen from the 325th Glider Infantry Regiment; and Company C's medium tanks. Together, they were to drive inland to Ste. Mère-Église to link up with the 82d Airborne Division and secure the landing zone for the 325th Glider Infantry Regiment, which was scheduled to land at 2100 hours.[18] Howell Force failed to overcome the 352d Infantry Division's defenses. The gliders carrying the 325th Glider Infantry swooped in to land as scheduled, and some came down in the German positions. Many others crashed, which resulted in high casualties.

THE BAD NEWS: OMAHA BEACH
Omaha Beach was about 7,000 yards wide and flanked by cliffs, and defensive obstacles covered the sand. Next came a shingle shelf, which presented a problem for vehicles, and then either a seawall or sand dunes. After a flat, somewhat marshy stretch of ground, bluffs honeycombed with German defensive positions rose 170 feet. A mere four draws offered exits from the beach.[19]

Off Omaha Beach, winds of ten to eighteen knots caused waves averaging four feet high in the transport area, with occasional waves up to six feet. Breakers were three to four feet.[20] The DD rigging provided about three feet of freeboard.

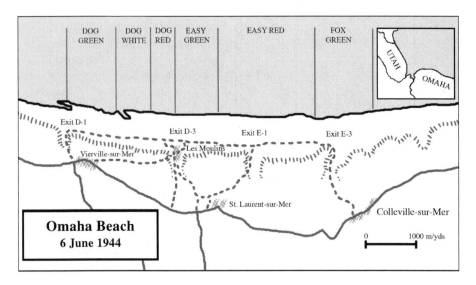

At approximately H minus 60 minutes, LCTs bearing DDs of Companies B and C, 741st Tank Battalion, attached to the 1st Division's 16th Infantry, reached position about 6,000 yards from the regiment's zone at the left end of Omaha Beach. In view of the rough weather forecast for D-Day, the commanding general of Task Force O and the admiral commanding Force O Naval had agreed that the senior naval commander in each LCT flotilla carrying DD tanks would decide whether to launch them at sea or carry them to the beach; the senior DD tank unit commander was to advise the flotilla commander on the matter.[21] Capt. James Thornton Jr., the commander Company B, was able to reach his counterpart from Company C, Capt. Charles Young, by radio. The two discussed the advisability of launching the DD Shermans in the extremely rough seas—much rougher than any they had tackled during preparatory training. Thornton was an extremely brave man; a product of The Citadel and deeply respected by his noncommissioned officers and men, he was always eager to take the lead.[22] The officers agreed that the advantage to be gained by launching the tanks justified the risk, and they issued orders for launching at approximately H-50.[23]

Soon Thornton was standing atop his strange armored boat. His head, more than ten feet above the deck, swung through wild arcs as the LCT pitched and yawed. The bow door opened, and it was action time. Thornton could see the beach four miles away and explosions from the naval bombardment churning the bluffs just beyond. Yellow launch flags went up, and Thornton ordered his driver, who could see nothing over the DD's canvas wall, to ease forward into the choppy water.

The tank following Thornton's off the LCT bow swamped immediately, as did the fourth Sherman to launch. Thornton's DD began to suffer damage after only a few yards; struts snapped and canvas tore, and water eventually flooded the engine compartment. He could see other tanks from his company and Company C suffering similarly alarming problems, but he could do nothing for any of them. After sailing only 1,000 yards, Thornton's tank foundered.[24] The beach—the object of Thornton's planning, training, speculation, and apprehension for months—still seemed so very far away. The crew scrambled to escape, and Thornton found himself bobbing amid the waves and bustle of assault landing craft headed for shore.

Of the Company B DD tanks launched, only two survived the full distance to Omaha Beach. The rest of Company B and all of Company C sank at distances from 1,000 to 5,000 yards from shore.[25] Small craft maneuvered to rescue the freezing tankers, and Thornton and his crew were pulled aboard a small landing craft. The boat pointed its bow back toward the long line of transports. Once aboard ship, tankers gratefully changed into dry clothes. The crews were told that they would be evacuated to England.[26]

S/Sgt. Turner Sheppard commanded one of the two tanks that reached shore and saw Thornton's tank go down on his way in. When the tracks hit sand, he told his driver to keep moving forward. It was smoothest landing the crew had ever managed. He deflated the screen and only then climbed from the deck into the comparative safety of the turret. To his left, he could see the other surviving DD Sherman commanded by Sergeant Geddes on the sand.

Sheppard's gunner fired at bunkers and pillboxes. Two concrete-piercing rounds slammed into the mouth of a tunnel and produced a satisfying secondary explosion, evidently from the ammunition reserve for a nearby 88-millimeter gun.[27]

Three other DD tanks aboard one landing craft were carried all the way to the beach after a wave sank the first DD to exit the vessel and smashed the remaining tanks together, which damaged their screens. Sgt. Paul Ragan, the senior tanker on board, convinced the skipper to take the remaining Shermans to the beach.[28]

"When we drove off the LCT," recalled Ragan, "I couldn't see much in front of me except smoke, but there was a clear spot in it, and through here I could see a pillbox. We fired at least forty rounds of 75 ammo at this." These tanks had landed too far to the right, and they moved left along the beach, weaving past obstacles, skirting a minefield, and firing as they went. Ragan spotted a mortar lobbing shells from behind some drums, and his gunner blew it sky-high. Two of the tanks remained stuck on the beach for seven hours; one pushed ahead to try to knock out a gun but was hit itself and burned.[29]

The 1st Infantry Division assault had landed in the teeth of a defense mounted by eight battalions of the well-trained German 352d Infantry Division.[30] Heavy fire greeted the 16th Infantry's assault wave, and casualties mounted quickly as the men left their landing craft. The loss of all Company C tanks in the water meant that the GIs on Fox Beach had no armored support at all. The handful of Company B tanks and four boat sections of infantry were the only assault troops on Easy Red Beach for the first half hour of the invasion, and at first, some GIs reported later, the tanks drove up and down the beach but did little shooting.

It all depended where you were. PFC Alfred Whitehead II was one of a handful of combat engineers and infantrymen seconded from the 2d Infantry Division

to the Special Engineer Task Force for the assault on Easy Red. He recalled, referring to one of the five DD tanks that seemed to him to have appeared from the sea
but were already ashore:

> I looked around and the picture on the beach was staggering to the imag-
> ination. It looked like the end of the world. There were knocked-out Ger-
> man bunkers and pillboxes, cast-off life preservers and lost gas masks,
> plus piles of all kinds of equipment; wet, waterlogged and ruined. Sher-
> man tanks, halftracks, and other vehicles littered the shoreline, partly
> submerged and sinking deeper with the rushing tide. More men were
> still struggling through tremendous forms of twisted steel and shattered
> concrete, right over broken, lifeless bodies littering the beach-bodies
> which only a short time before had been living, breathing beings. It was
> so rough that I thought we had lost the beach three or four times. . . .
>   For a long time it looked hopeless. The enemy was slaughtering our
> men with an 88 housed in [a] huge bunker. But just when things looked
> darkest, one of our Sherman DD amphibious tanks managed to crawl in
> to the beach and not get knocked-out, probably because there were so
> many wrecked vehicles the enemy missed spotting it. It moved in close
> to the bottom of the slope, and I ran over and directed it to that 88. The
> terrain was such that our tank could creep up close enough to where its
> gun barrel was just barely sticking its nose over the top of a little rise to
> fire. I told the tanker that he'd have only a few seconds to move over the
> rise and shoot, then hit the reverse gears before that 88 could return fire.
> The first two rounds missed their mark, chipping chunks of concrete out-
> side its massive structure. On the third try the round hit home-right
> through the bunker's narrow gun slit.
>   What a relief![31]

The tankdozer platoon of four vehicles and all but three tanks from Company
A reached shore in the second wave. The tanks blazed away with their 75-
millimeter guns as they neared the beach, although the odds of hitting anything
with aimed fire from a pitching landing craft were remote. Nevertheless, one
Sherman on a drifting LCT disabled by German fire had the good fortune to
destroy with a single 75-millimeter round the artillery piece that had done the
damage. Three Shermans went down with an LCT sunk by enemy fire.[32]
    Staff Sergeant Fair commanded one of the Company A tanks in the 741st
Tank Battalion that made it to the beach aboard an LCT, along with another Sherman and a tankdozer. Sergeant Fair reported his experience shortly after landing:

> [We were] supposed to land at 0630 hours about two hundred yards right of
> Exit-3, but due to weather conditions and other landing craft we beached at
> Exit-1 near to 743d Tank Battalion. The ramp was dropped in pretty deep
> water and we left the craft. I was in No. 1 tank, Sergeant Larsen No. 2 tank,

and the dozer No. 3. The water was up over our turret ring. We finally pulled up on the beach but still stayed in the water enough for protection. Our bow gunner and gunner started spraying the trees and hillside with .30 cal. while, not helped by the snipers and shrapnel, we looked for antitank guns and pillboxes. It wasn't long until we spotted one, which no doubt was a machine-gun emplacement. I put my gunner on it, and he fired. His first shots went low, but after the correction was made the next shots entered straight through the opening and put it out of action.

We had to keep moving up with the tide, for it was coming up pretty fast. All of a sudden hell broke loose in front of us; they had made a hit on the boat obstacles on which were Teller mines. We moved to a new position to the left and began firing in the direction we thought it came from. I noticed the tide was closing in on us and we had no exit to escape from in case we had to move, for there was a hill in front of us, a good tank obstacle, and casualties were piling up all around us. I started down the beach to look for our platoon leader, who was Lt. [Gastano] Barcelona. The going was slow, for we had to weave in and out among bodies and sometimes stop till the medics cleared them from our path. On our way down, we accounted for two machine-gun nests that the infantry located for us. We finally located the 1st Platoon, so we got in firing position, as we were firing at gun positions located below Exit-3. Sergeant Larsen's tank was hit by 57mm [*sic*; not actually used by the defenders] AP between the gun shield and extra armor plate, wounding his gunner. It also smashed the breach mechanism and recoil. Sergeant Larsen got a few powder burns on the face. He gave orders to abandon tank.

About that time, Lieutenant McDonough came moving up the beach. I was sitting crossways in his path, so I pulled up on the bank and got stuck in the pebbles. I heard someone call me and I looked over the side. I saw Private First Class Robinson of Company A, 741st Tank Battalion. He was wounded. I couldn't hear what he was trying to tell me, so I dismounted. He wanted a cigarette and told me to give him morphine. I took him on up where Sergeant Larsen's crew was and gave him morphine and covered him up. Coming back I tried to unhook our trailer [holding extra ammunition] so we could back up. It was in our way all of the time. If I had known what an obstacle it was in the first place, I would have left it on the LCT. I finally got it unhooked and we tried to get off the bank again, resulting in breaking about ten connectors and threw the track. We were out of HE and all the heavy firing was about over with so we dismounted and got behind our tank. All told we fired, Sergeant Larsen and our tank, 450 HE and an uncounted number of .30 cal.[33]

The LCT bearing Sergeant Holcombe's tankdozer was struck and caught fire but was able to unload its tanks. Holcombe followed a Sherman and a tankdozer in front of him from the burning LCT. They were in water almost up to the Shermans' back decks. Suddenly, the first tank lurched to a halt after being struck by an 88-millimeter shell. The men bailed out and clambered aboard Holcombe's tank, which carried them to the sand. By this point, Holcombe had had enough of his first time under fire and ordered his crew to abandon tank. Realizing that their sergeant was in shock, the crew refused. The bow gunner climbed into the turret, took command of the Sherman, and helped load the 75-millimeter gun. Once ashore, the dozer began clearing obstacles and pushing sand into berms to shield the pinned-down infantry. The dozer crew decided to share blankets and food with the wounded and pulled the machine guns out of the tank for the infantry to use while the dozer went about its work.[34]

Meanwhile, because the command radio had been ruined by seawater, battalion command personnel had to move from tank to tank to direct fire and move vehicles into more advantageous positions. Both technical sergeants and the radio operator in the group were wounded.[35]

By the time the badly shot-up Company L, 16th Infantry, attacked the German strongpoint assigned to it in a draw through the bluff, two medium tanks were providing covering fire from the beach under the direction of an infantry lieutenant, and the GIs by 0900 captured the objective and moved to the top of the bluff. Likewise, a DD tank appeared at an opportune moment and destroyed several machine guns that were holding up Company F. At about this time, a British destroyer pulled within 400 yards of the sand, and under cover from its broadsides, Company F and the rest of the 3d Battalion were able to reach the crest. We can only imagine the Sherman gunner's reaction to this display of one-upmanship.[36]

The first tanks crawled off Omaha Beach at about 1700 hours via exit Easy-1, having spent almost twelve hours on that steel-raked sand. Three tanks were knocked out on the road to Colleville-sur-Mer when they tried to exit the beach with the infantry, two of them at the top of the bluff near the 16th Infantry's command post. S/Sgt. Turner Sheppard commanded one of them. At the infantry's request, Sheppard led the way up the road in his DD tank. There was a fortified house at a sharp bend, but the tanks had worked it over fairly well, and Sheppard pulled past it. Suddenly, he spotted an antitank gun in the road about 600 yards away. The German gunners had the drop on him, and their first round penetrated the front armor, killed the bow gunner, and wounded Sheppard. The survivors bailed out. Sheppard was evacuated the next day but returned to the battalion and earned its first battlefield commission.

At 2000 hours, four battalion tanks were still supporting the infantry against machine-gun nests in the vicinity of St. Laurent-sur-Mer. The outfit's remnants laagered in a field two miles from the water and watched a canopy of red tracers slice the air overhead to drive off *Luftwaffe* raiders. The battalion's first daily tank status report, submitted to the V Corps at 2315 hours on 6 June, indicated that it had three battle-ready medium tanks, two tanks damaged but reparable, and forty-eight tanks reckoned lost.[37]

In the 116th Regimental Combat Team's zone on the right end of Omaha Beach, the officers in charge of the DD-loaded LCTs decided not to risk the sea conditions, so all thirty-two DDs of the 743d Tank Battalion were carried nearly to the beach.[38] The unit's S-3 journal recorded: "Company C landed on Dog White and Easy Green beaches at H minus 6 [minutes]. Upon approaching beach we were met with fire from individual weapons, 155mm, 88mm, and machine guns. . . . Air support missing." Company B landed simultaneously, and Company A's tanks followed the DDs ashore as planned.[39] Navy navigation errors deposited some of the tanks on beaches intended for use by the 741st Tank Battalion, which was not such a bad outcome, given the losses suffered by that outfit.[40]

The infantry arrived after the tanks. Lt. Jack Shea, who landed with the 116th Infantry's regimental headquarters, recalled,

Our particular LCVP did not draw direct fire until we were within 200 yards of the beach. . . . Moderate small-arms fire was directed at our craft as the ramp was lowered. . . . The first cover available was the partial screen provided by a DD amphibious tank of Company C, 743d Tank Battalion, which had landed at H minus 6. There were about eighteen of these tanks standing just above the water line of Dog Beach. They were faced toward the mainland at an interval of 70–100 yards, and about twenty-five yards from the breakwater. They were firing at enemy positions to their immediate front. Two tanks, near the Vierville exit, had been hit by enemy fire and were burning.

The tank that screened us was firing to its front right, rather than engaging its previously assigned target—the enemy strong point and gun positions atop the cliff at Point et Raz de la Percee. This was necessary for the tank evidently was seeking to protect itself from the fire of several antitank guns that had survived the air-and-naval pre-landing bombardment. . . .

Both [assistant division commander Brig. Gen Norman] Cota and Col. [Charles] Canham expressed the opinion that the fact that these tanks were not firing at Point Percee permitted those enemy gun positions to profitably employ their fires.[41] [Indeed, the German commander of that strongpoint at first judged that the landing had been crushed on the beach; he saw ten burning tanks and infantry hiding behind obstacles, and he noted that his guns were causing heavy losses.[42]]

The tank battalion's commander, Lt. Col. John Upham, who had put the battalion together, directed operations from an LCT a few hundred yards offshore until he landed ninety minutes after the assault wave. Upham moved from tank to tank, directing fire and movement. Sometime during the morning, a sniper's slug destroyed his right shoulder, but he continued to exercise personal leadership until Green Beach was cleared. Only then did he finally allow medics to evacuate him— an action for which he was awarded the Distinguished Service Cross.[43]

The seawall kept the tanks penned on the beach, where Company A lined up along the promenade under fire; two Shermans burst into flames. The infantry under Cota's leadership reached the top of the bluff by 1000 hours. Cota was concerned that the riflemen had no tank support and turned to a colonel of engineers. "Can you blow up the antitank wall at the exit?"

"We can, sir, just as soon as the infantry clears out those pillboxes around there."

"We just came through there. There's nothing to speak of there. Get to it!" Cota ordered.

Still lacking tanks, Cota spotted two Shermans from the 741st Tank Battalion headquarters section, which had landed at 1530 and climbed up exit Easy-1 to the bluff, parked next to a hedgerow. Cota commandeered one of them from the 1st Infantry Division and sent it to support his men in St. Laurent-sur-Mer. A sergeant from the 115th Infantry, which had come ashore on the heels of the 116th Infantry, took the assistant driver's position to guide the driver into position. The tank had just passed between two farm buildings when a high-velocity round whizzed by. Unable to spot the source, the gunner fired ten 75-millimeter rounds and some machine-gun bullets in the direction of the enemy, and the tank backed away.[44]

The first Shermans from the 743d Tank Battalion did not exit the beach until about 2200 hours through exit Dog-1 and moved to a bivouac point about 200 yards from Vierville. Approximately eighteen DD tanks from Companies B and C got off the beach, as well as half of Company A. The tankers continued to receive sniper and machine-gun fire until dark. The battalion lost sixteen tanks destroyed or disabled during the day.[45] Company A alone had lost eight of sixteen tanks and six dozers; the confusion was such that, at the end of the day, the company commander was not sure how many men had become casualties. Company B had lost seven tanks with three officers and six enlisted men killed in action. Company C was luckier, suffering the loss of only one tank disabled and five men wounded.[46]

The U.S. Army Center of Military History concluded that, regarding the importance of the tanks on the beach that day, "[t]heir achievement cannot be summed up in statistics; the best testimony in their favor is the casual mention in the records of many units, from all parts of the beach, of emplacements neutralized by the supporting fire of tanks. In an interview shortly after the battle, the commander of the 2d Battalion, 116th Infantry, who saw some of the worst fighting on the beach at Les Moulins, expressed as his opinion that the tanks 'saved the day. They shot the hell out of the Germans, and got the hell shot out of them.'"[47]

The importance of the tanks was also underscored by what happened when they could not get to the point of decision to help the doughboys. By noon, the 116th Infantry's 3d Battalion had worked its way into the draw between Les Moulins and St. Laurent-sur-Mer, where it encountered stiff resistance. The battalion commander decided to flank the Germans and advance on St. Laurent. As Company L's attack got underway, the navy shelled the village church, which had a demoralizing effect on the troops. German soldiers in town blasted the advancing GIs with automatic weapons and small-caliber antiaircraft guns. The battalion suffered more casualties than it had getting across the beach and, after one more futile push, pulled back to "button up" for the night.

Capt. Charles Kidd would not forget one key factor: "Tanks were not able to get off the beaches."[48] Tanks would have shrugged off machine-gun and 20-millimeter or 37-millimeter antiaircraft fire.

Meanwhile, engineers had cut several roads to the top of the bluffs, and landing schedules were adjusted to take advantage of this. The first tanks of the 745th Tank Battalion landed on Fox Green about 1630 and made it to the high ground by 2000, with the loss of three Shermans to mines.[49] Because of the high losses suffered by the 741st Tank Battalion, Maj. Gen. Leonard Gerow, the commanding general of Task Force O, decided to commit the 745th Tank Battalion to battle immediately.[50] (Only one company landed on 6 June, with two more coming ashore on 7 June.[51]) The arrival of the 745th raised to five the number of separate tank battalions in France by the end of D-Day. The 747th Tank Battalion (in V Corps reserve) would disembark on Omaha at 0700 on 7 June,[52] and at the height of the Normandy campaign, twenty-one separate tank battalions were employed.[53]

The assault on Omaha had succeeded, but ground units there made less progress than planned. The beachhead was one and a half miles deep at its deepest point. At Utah Beach, in contrast, casualties had been low, and the 4th Infantry Division's 8th Infantry Regiment had advanced all the way to its D-Day objectives.[54]

CHAPTER 8

The Bocage: A School of Very Hard Knocks

"That was no country for tanks. And we never trained with infantry, always tanks against tanks. We had a hell of a time for a while learning how they fought. It's a wonder we didn't shoot each other."
—William McFadden, veteran,
749th Tank Battalion[1]

The hedgerow country—or bocage—of Normandy is much like the Gallic persona in general: quaint in its way, but a source of unending frustration for any outsider. The *Tactical Study of Terrain* in the Neptune package offered this anodyne description: "The eastern section, which is our immediate area of operation, is featured by rolling hills, more-or-less open fields, and wooded areas. Cultivated areas consist principally of rectangular fields and orchards bordered by hedges." It almost sounds nice.

Tankers knew that they would be fighting in hedgerow country, but men from more than one unit say that the reality came as a rude surprise to them upon landing in Normandy. The separate tank battalions would bloody themselves in this morass from 6 June until after the Operation Cobra breakout, starting 25 July. Wayne Robinson describes the bocage from the tanker's perspective:

> The open sun-baked stretch of beach was bad; now it was the green hedgerows, and those were very bad, too.
>
> The hedgerows divided the battlefront into hundreds of separate small boxes, each box a separate battle, a lone tactical problem on a checkerboard of fields, each in itself a single objective to be fought for, gained, or lost.
>
> South of St. Jean de Daye, the hedgerows were spaced so close together that a man could sometimes run from one to another across an open stretch of field in four or five seconds—if nothing stopped him.

There was plenty to stop him.

The hedgerows were perfect field defenses for a holding army, and the Germans, never slothful in military matters, took every advantage of this tough terrain to build a defense in depth that, to break through, would take all the fighting spirit, and many of the lives, of "a soft generation," as German propaganda mistakenly plugged American youth.

Dirt embankments and deep natural ditches were standard accessories with every hedgerow. Those embankments and ditches gave the German fighter protection—ready-made trenches on all four sides of each field, so that parallel hedgerows covered each other, and one hedgerow linked with another to form a system of communicating trenches. . . .

Behind the leafy screens were such unseen targets as machine guns, big and little antitank guns, tanks, self-propelled guns on tank chassis, infantrymen equipped with bazookas—all waiting, playing a deadly cat-and-mouse game.

There was only one way to fight the hedgerows—one at a time, expecting the worst at each (and almost always finding it) and thinking of each row as a fortress from which the enemy must be routed, field by field. And that was how it was done.[2]

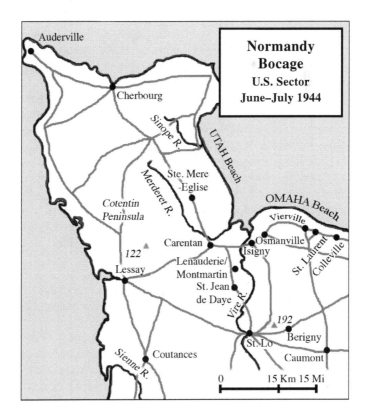

The German defenders did not simply sit still; they employed an active defense, launching many local counterattacks supported by tanks. Indeed, the Germans used their armor almost entirely for infantry support in a role similar to that of the American separate tank battalions. They also became increasingly aggressive in firing their artillery in battery and battalion volleys.[3]

On D+1, Gen. Dwight Eisenhower, the supreme commander of the European theater; Bernard Montgomery, the commander of Allied ground forces; and Omar Bradley, the commander of American ground forces, agreed to adjust plans somewhat to put more emphasis on linking the beachheads. They feared that the isolated toeholds were vulnerable to counterattack. Although the Germans had few reserves immediately available, this issue was not moot.[4]

A CRITICAL CONTRIBUTION

The weight of American armor began to influence the battle on 7 June. The Germans were gathering their armored strength under the I SS Panzer Corps in the vicinity of Caen, in the British zone, leaving the defenders in the American zone with little tank support.[5] Nevertheless, the 746th Tank Battalion was called to Ste. Mère-Église to support the 82d Airborne Division in driving off one armored counterattack. Here, only twenty-four hours after D-Day, was an assignment that according to doctrine should have gone to tank destroyers. The battalion's S-3, Maj. Richard Langston Jr., recalled, "I was told to block the crossroads [there] with my three headquarters tanks and let them burn right there if necessary."[6]

Company B and the assault gun platoon, equipped with normal 75-millimeter Shermans for the invasion, accompanied Langston. Lt. Houston Payne, commanding the assault guns, was in the lead and was the first to spot the German armored column at about 1500 hours when he crested a rise a few hundred yards north of the center of town. Payne was surprised to see five panzers and other vehicles only 400 yards away. The Germans evidently were equally surprised, as Payne's gunner was able to knock out an antitank gun beside the road and set the first Mark IV on fire with armor-piercing rounds before the Germans responded. The opening return salvo knocked the antiaircraft machine gun and periscope off the top of the turret and injured Payne, but Payne's gunner calmly set a second Mark IV on fire. Payne had expended all the rounds in the ready rack and pulled back, motioning for the second tank to fire. This one's gun jammed, but the German column by this time was pulling back toward Neuville au Plain, a village just northwest of Ste. Mère-Église.

Capt. Asher Pay, commanding Company B, led two platoons of tanks to flank the Germans and reached Neuville au Plain. A German gunner knocked out two Company B tanks, but a Sherman nailed the panzer for its troubles. Company B had cut the enemy column.[7]

Tankers from one of the damaged Shermans ran to a farmhouse as the tanks blazed away at one another. Inside, they saw about twenty German soldiers guarding a like number of American paratroopers. After the tanks fired a few 75-millimeter rounds into the house, the guards became prisoners, and the paratroopers made ready for battle—just in time. German infantry attacked the Americans, trying desperately to close with the tanks to destroy them with grenades, but the tankers and paratroopers fired into their ranks. Once the enemy troops realized the odds they faced, sixty of them surrendered.[8]

While this action was unfolding, the 4th Infantry Division's 8th Infantry Regiment arrived in the area north of Ste. Mère-Église with two companies of tanks from the 70th Tank Battalion. Lt. John Casteel of Company B reported, "We went into the town from the south and cut across to the west side and across fields until we made contact with two battalions of parachutists holding the north and west of town. The Germans were still holding a large part of the town, and we had to go through the streets firing and got out into the open as quickly as we could. Besides the enemy in the town, there seemed to be a large force of Germans to the north across the creek. That's where the 746th was fighting."[9]

For the men from the two tank battalions, the fight in Ste. Mère-Église had been a pure tank action with no coordination demanded with the other arms. The impact of shock action by tanks even in fairly small numbers was illustrated by the outcome. Under pressure from two armored thrusts, the German 1058th Regiment panicked and withdrew.[10]

Except for some veterans in the 70th Tank Battalion, which had fought in North Africa and Sicily, combat was new and confusing. Homer Wilkes, a tank platoon commander, realized that on 8 June, when his 747th Tank Battalion, less Company B, was attached to the 29th Division's 175th Infantry, which was going into action for the first time. Wilkes had been a cowboy before joining the army, where he had risen through the ranks to become platoon sergeant before going to Officer Candidate School in 1942. Always ready to apply the jaundiced eye of practicality and common sense, he recalled:

The column . . . formed up at Vierville in terrain curiously free of hedgerows. We started out in column on the road with Company C leading. I know not what others thought, but I thought we were marching to the front. This impression was corrected minutes later by the appearance of an infantry skirmish line. Although it was my first taste of battle, I knew what that meant. . . .

[One] strong point was Osmanville. And there on a clear day this village was attacked by a dozen British fighter-bombers. The Company C platoon leader of the advance guard was killed trying to display his identification panel. Other officers threw out smoke grenades. But the strike was pressed home until the pilots had dropped all their bombs and expended all ammunition. As a result, thirty-two infantrymen were slain, plus our officer, and Company C lost an entire platoon of tanks. . . .

This seemed to paralyze the infantry command group, as well it might. Omaha was their first combat too. After sitting on the road a while we were notified to attend officers call in a field. There we found Major General [Norman] Cota (the assistant commander [29th Infantry Division]), officers of the 175th [Infantry] Regiment and 747th Tank Battalion officers.

The general asked for a situation report upon which the regimental commander told him he could not get through the enemy line by any means, frontal or flank. He would have to wait for artillery support, which probably wasn't ashore.

The general replied, "All I can tell you, Colonel, is the commanding general told me this attack has to get moving."

He then addressed the 747th's commander. "Colonel Fries, can you get us through this strong point?"

To which the Colonel replied, "Yes, Sir."

"Who will be your leading officer?"

The colonel indicated the 3d Platoon [Wilkes's platoon], Company A, would be in the van, whereupon the general was introduced to the officer [Wilkes], who promptly received a pep talk.

"Is there a place for me in your tank?" asked Cota.

The reply was a crewmember would have to be dismounted. And if the general rode, it would be as assistant driver, which entailed handing ammunition up to the turret.

"I can do that. Which is your tank?" he replied. . . .

Cota's request (actually an order) made me nervous. The general had to serve as a crewmember. Hence I as commander gave him several orders during the night, all of which he obeyed with alacrity. . . .

Now, the plan as [I outlined it to my] tank commanders was to drive along the road until targets were encountered (meaning buildings. We had found out the enemy would be in buildings.) Then the first tank would ease left while the second tank, commanded by Lt. George P. Gale, then an enlisted man, would pull alongside. The commanders would engage targets on their respective sides of the road. . . .

An infantry captain accompanied by a Browning Automatic Rifle-man came up to report that his company was attached to the platoon. The BAR-man was an alert, clear-eyed soldier, an encouraging sign under any circumstance. The captain said they would be right behind the lead tank any time [I] needed them.

At one hundred yards, the first buildings were successfully attacked. The advance continued. . . .

Coming upon a mined place, the point stopped. The division had not placed engineers forward with the advance guard. No one present knew how to remove the mines.

The infantry captain suggested firing the coaxial machine gun at them. This was done, but no mines exploded. Therefore it was thought the mines were inactive. The march continued and the platoon sergeant's tank was blown up by the mines. . . .[11]

"There was no particular effort for the foot troops to keep in contact with the tanks," observed an army combat-interview on the action. "The mediums just rolled along with about a 50-yard interval between them, and thundered on towards the town." Isigny fell without resistance.[12]

The tanks, under Cota's leadership, had made all the difference. The 175th Infantry's drive collapsed the left flank of the 352d Infantry Division and opened a hole in the German line that cleared the path to the merger of the V and VII Corps beachheads.[13]

Meanwhile, the 741st and 743d Tank Battalions committed their remaining tanks beside the foot soldiers of the 1st, 2d, 29th, and 30th Infantry Divisions and recovered what tanks they could from the surf. On the morning of 7 June, Capt. James Thornton strolled into the 741st Battalion's transit area. Rather than return to England, he had hitched a ride to the beach, where he fell in with an infantry platoon heading inland. He eventually found someone who knew where the battalion had set up, and he parted ways; now he had a tank company to rebuild.

The assault battalions inland from Utah Beach encountered the enemy in strength and began to suffer heavy losses after their easy landing. The 70th and 746th Tank Battalions were the only armor available to the 4th Infantry and the 82d and 101st Airborne Divisions inland from Utah Beach for the first six days of fighting.[14] By 9 June, Company C of the 746th Battalion assessed its combat efficiency at only 33 percent and reported that most tank machine guns were burned out from overuse and that many of the tank guns were ineffective. On 11 June, the company had only two officers, seventy enlisted men, and six tanks in action. By 10 July, the battalion would lose half its tanks to enemy fire.[15] From D-Day to 31 July, the 70th Tank Battalion would lose forty Shermans and six M5A1s.[16]

On both beachheads in the first few days, a pattern emerged of rapid resubordinations of tankers that complicated early efforts to grapple with the new experience of combat. The 746th Tank Battalion, for example, had elements attached to both the 4th Infantry and 82d Airborne Divisions on D-Day.[17] Company C was attached to the 82d Airborne Division from 6 to 11 June; Company A was attached to the 101st Airborne Division on 7 and 8 June; and the rest of the battalion was assigned to the 4th Division until 11 June, when the entire battalion was attached to the 90th Infantry Division. On 13 June, the outfit was attached to the 9th Division, with the exception of Company A, which went to the 82d Airborne Division.[18]

TACKLING THE BOCAGE

At Omaha, hedgerows reached to the bluffs above the beach.[19] At Utah, the hedgerows began just beyond the inundated area behind the beach.[20] There were, on average, fourteen hedgerows per kilometer in Normandy.[21]

Incredibly, the invading forces had no tactics worked out for dealing with the terrain, nor equipment tailored to the situation. The hedgerows were not wholly impenetrable to tanks, but in the first few days, they often enough channeled armor onto narrow roads where defenders could focus their antitank and artillery pieces. The first Sherman from one battalion that tried to ram through a hedgerow was flipped onto its back and lay there like an upended turtle.[22] The infantry had to attack across fields, however, which meant that tankers had to figure out a way to get their tanks to places where the infantry needed support. There was one benefit, at least, although it probably did not seem so at the time. The bocage provided terrain relatively advantageous to the Shermans in the sense that few engagements occurred at the long ranges that maximized the advantages held by German armor. Tanks generally engaged at ranges between 150 and 400 yards.[23]

Thus began a period of trial-and-error progress. As the 737th Tank Battalion's commander, Lt. Col. James Hamilton Jr., put it retrospectively, "We've spent years studying the book and practicing, and then in our first action we had to throw away the book, and everything we learned in practice was no good to us at all."[24]

Early Challenges

In order to use tactics, the tanks had to be able to move. The first approach to overcoming the challenge posed by the terrain itself was to have a tankdozer punch a hole through the hedgerow, which the tanks would pass through to support the infantry. This occurred to tankers as soon as they saw the hedges.[25] Experience showed that dozers were capable of breaching about 50 percent of hedgerows.[26]

The main drawback to the dozer approach was that the Germans quickly figured out the procedure; when a tankdozer created a gap, tanks were likely to follow. The Germans sighted their antitank guns on the hole and waited.

At the tactical level, the tanks and infantry were not even organized as a cooperative venture, and they quickly learned to create ad hoc task organizations. Capt. Charles Kidd of the 116th Infantry, 29th Infantry Division, noted, "Initial operations in Normandy indicated that insufficient training had been conducted in infantry-tank cooperation prior to entry into combat. After the fall of Grandcamp [on 8 June], tank and infantry teams were organized. The tanks would support the advance of the infantry by firing in the trees and along the hedgerows. An infantry squad would protect the tank and assist its advance through the hedgerow by blowing a hole with TNT."[27]

Tankers and their infantry partners were finding they were unprepared to communicate effectively, just as pre-invasion exercises had foreshadowed. In the first hours after the troops moved inland, operational planning was scant, and commanders on the scene often made up their plans as they went. As had been the case on the beach, communications between the infantry and the tank initially were of the mouth-to-ear variety. This method had one major drawback that had already become apparent to tankers on other fronts: it was insanely dangerous under fire. The risk meant that often communication simply did not occur when things got hot. Oral communication was also rather haphazard, in part because tank crews

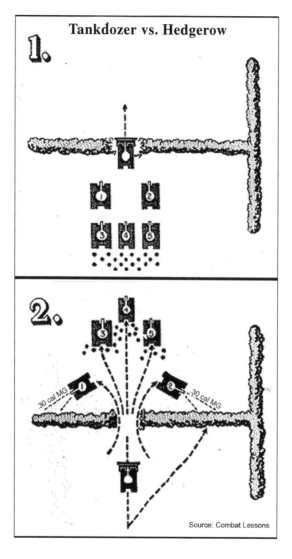

Tankdozer vs. Hedgerow

Source: Combat Lessons

could not see well through their periscopes, and the infantry had to get the crew's attention amidst the roar of battle and the tank's engine. Riflemen guiding tanks sometimes had to get in front and jump up and down to get the crew's attention.[28] Tankers eventually figured out that the doughs often did not understand how blind they were when buttoned up and tried to teach them.[29]

Tankers were particularly concerned about coordination with the doughs on those nights when tanks remained in forward positions and were vulnerable to attack by infiltrating German infantry. Tank gunners could see nothing whatsoever through their sights at night. Tanker complaints on the subject started early and recurred throughout the war. Company C of the 743d Tank Battalion, for example, reported on 15 June, "Infantry left us without protection and under fire of enemy in darkness."[30]

The dough, of course, had his own point of view about all this. For one thing, tanks drew enemy fire, both direct and indirect.[31] And not only the doughs on the line worried about this fact. Two platoon leaders from the 741st Tank Battalion who attempted to find out how their tanks would be used in one day's attack, for example, found that "the infantry commanders were very vague about the situation, and confessed a reluctance to use the tanks at all, because of tanks drawing artillery fire."[32] For another thing, the infantry concluded that the poor-sighted friendly tanks could sometimes be just as dangerous as the enemy. One 6th Armored Group liaison officer reported, "1st Division troops do not like to precede tanks. Claim our tanks shoot them. Prefer to go alongside or behind our tanks."[33] But when the fighting got heavy, the infantry usually wanted as many tanks around as possible. A report filed by the 746th Tank Battalion captured this moth-and-flame dilemma of the infantry: "9th Inf[antry] Div[ision] still says tanks are no good but won't allow them back for rest or training."[34]

Experiments were undertaken to provide a radio link between the tanks and infantry, at first very indirectly. On 12 June, for example, the 747th Tank Battalion kept two company command tanks at the regimental command post to provide radio liaison with the platoons in action. Clearly, nobody was aware that radio liaison had already been pushed down to the level of the infantry battalion in the Pacific and Italy. The company commanders relied on jeeps to make quick personal trips to visit their tanks.[35]

Breakdowns in tank-infantry teamwork were commonplace in the first weeks after D-Day. On 16 June, for example, the 2d Infantry Division began a series of futile attacks to capture Hill 192, which dominated the approach to the strategic road hub of St. Lô and was defended by two battalions of the 3d Airborne Division. The paratroopers had just arrived at the front, and the men had never before tasted battle. Nonetheless, German morale was high, and these men resisted fanatically. A 2d Division history described the objective: "[Hill 192] was studded with foxholes, machine-gun nests, and expertly camouflaged observation points. Hedgerows sprouted along its gradual slope. Behind these, Germans huddled in dugouts. Every crossing and road in the vicinity had been zeroed in by enemy artillery emplaced on the rear slope. German camouflage suits blended softly with the foliage so well that one Nazi sniper remained in a tree only 150 yards from American lines an entire day before he was . . . killed."[36]

The battered 741st Tank Battalion supported the division. Their joint attacks showed a lack of infantry-tank cooperation and a misunderstanding on the part of the doughboys regarding what they could expect from tanks. The infantrymen believed that tankers had been too reluctant to take advantage of their armor protection to press forward to destroy emplacements and fire into hedgerows. The tanks, however, suffered high losses when they tried to do just that, as German antitank guns, *panzerfausts*, and antitank grenades could easily get the drop on them, especially when they were trying to clamber over a hedgerow.[37] The paratroopers were surprised that the American infantryman refused to give up his tank support in hedgerow terrain and turned to stealth instead; the defenders could usually anticipate an attack because of the noise of the tanks.[38]

Even when the tanks took the lead, things went wrong because the tankers and infantry could not communicate, and because basic groundwork like terrain reconnaissance was left undone. On 16 June, for example, Capt. Cecil Thomas led eight running M4A1s from the 741st Tank Battalion to a rendezvous with Company E, 23d Infantry, to conduct an assault on Berigny. Thomas and the infantry captain decided to attack straight down a road, four tanks on each side, each group followed by a platoon of infantry. The team set off about noon, and soon intense machine-gun fire from pillboxes and fortified houses lashed the riflemen, who dropped to the ground with many casualties. The tanks returned fire and advanced alone to cover the infantry and destroy the German emplacements. Thomas discovered, however, that marshy ground prevented his advance into Berigny. One tank was lost to a bazooka when the force finally gave up and pulled back about 1700 hours.

Three days later, five Shermans and a tankdozer were ordered forward to support the 1st Battalion of the 23d Infantry. The tanks advanced, spraying hedgerows with machine-gun fire and shelling houses. An American colonel ran up and ordered the tanks to halt. They had been shooting at the 1st Battalion.[39]

"Such situations," noted a combat interviewer who spoke with both the tankers and infantrymen, "bred mutual distrust. The fault was due to the lack of coordination in the larger sense, rather than the fault of either the tankers or the infantry."[40] For the German paratroopers, the success in stopping the 2d Division and destroying a number of tanks boosted self-confidence enormously.[41]

The 29th Infantry Division launched its own assault on high ground north of St. Lô on 16 June to assist the 2d Division, and similar breakdowns occurred. The 747th Tank Battalion's after-action report recorded for 20 June, "At 0600, Company B moved forward 800 yards. Engineers were blowing gaps in the hedgerows. The infantry was following. The infantry had been pinned down. . . . Tanks were withdrawn due to bazooka and 105mm fire. One tank was knocked out. The tank burned, and the whole crew was wounded. . . . On order of the regiment commanding officer, four tanks forced their way through the fire to the objective. No infantry followed. Two tanks returned. . . ."[42]

The Exceptional 743d Tank Battalion

Perhaps the 743d Tank Battalion, commanded by Lt. Col. William Duncan after the wounding of Upham, had learned wisdom on the sands of Omaha Beach. Perhaps it was a lucky outfit. Perhaps Duncan had a knack for war. Whatever the cause, the battalion showed during the early going that there was hope for American combined arms in the European theater.

The battalion had the good fortune to be attached, from 11 to 13 June, to the veteran 1st Infantry Division, which had learned a few things about working with tanks on Sicily. Wayne Robinson captured a model of how tank-infantry cooperation was supposed to work in describing the attack on Caumont on 12 June, when all three medium tank companies supported the 1st Division's 26th Infantry Regiment:

> An occasional house or a bush or a position suspected of harboring undesirable tenants was given a treatment of lead by trigger-happy machine gunners and riflemen. Tanks joined the spraying parties whenever the infantry called for it. In working with infantry, a separate tank battalion learns not to shoot at everything in sight. It might turn out to be a platoon of friendly infantry. Tank-infantry coordination is a difficult operation. . . .
>
> As the evening wore along [Companies B and C] began receiving heavy concentrations of artillery fire mixed in with customary mortars. Direct fire from antitank guns worried tank commanders. Machine-gun fire pinned down the doughboys. The attack, however, kept moving in toward the objective. It was slow and cautious work. The tank-infantry coordination of the 26th Infantry Regiment, veterans of the proud and battle-hardened (in Africa and Sicily) 1st Division, remained extremely good on this attack as strong point after strong point was reduced and overrun with the minimum of casualties to the doughs. The infantry efficiently infiltrated antitank gun positions; a tank cannot bull its way past an antitank gun without somebody getting hurt—a sorry lesson learned in Africa by Armored Force men. Machine-gun positions, deadly to the doughs, were another story to tanks. A few rounds of HE from the 75mm fired into the laps of the crews usually was all that was required. An antitank gun was almost always protected by flanking machine-gun nests. Each was a tactical problem to be worked out by infantry and tankers.[43]

The 1st Division certainly deserved its share of the credit for the effective cooperation with Duncan's tanks, as illustrated by its handling of the 745th Tank Battalion, which would fight with the Big Red One for the rest of the European campaign. The tankers had been attached to the division on 21 April, though like other outfits, no real effort was made to develop a tight tank-infantry team before D-Day. Immediately after the landings, the division attached one medium tank company to each regiment, and each regiment attached a platoon to each battalion. These assignments were retained through the end of the war—with occasional exceptions to strengthen an infantry assault with more tanks—which allowed the tankers and infantry to become intimately familiar with one another. The tankers even drew their rations from the infantry, which encouraged further mingling. Tank platoons took their orders from the infantry company commanders.

The Company D light tanks were usually attached to the 16th Infantry Regiment in addition to Company A, as were the mortar platoon and assault gun platoon. The three tanks from the battalion headquarters were split up among the three medium tank companies, and the company assault guns were consolidated with the assault gun platoon to form a six-gun battery.[44]

After its brief attachment to the Big Red One, the 743d Tank Battalion was shifted to the Old Hickory Division. The 30th Infantry Division and 743d Tank Battalion were to have an unusually harmonious relationship and were to soldier together for most of the European campaign. Their promising future became amply visible during the 120th Infantry Regiment's attack to clear an area north of the Vire River on 15 June. Granted, the tankers by now were veterans, but the operation was the GIs' first taste of combat.

The 120th Infantry Regiment was to attack straight down the road running from Cherbourg to St. Lô, its 2d Battalion on the left and 3d Battalion on the right, each supported by tanks and tankdozers. The assault began as scheduled at 0800 hours, and both battalions quickly ran into stiff resistance. The regimental commanding officer, Col. Hammond Birks, exercised firm personal control over the operation, racing from spot to spot in his jeep.

A platoon advance party and a rifle squad led Company E down a small, curving road, followed by two tanks 200 yards ahead of the main party, and six tanks bringing up the rear. Rifle and machine-gun fire from both sides of the road drove the point men to ground. The lead platoon deployed into the fields while the two trailing Shermans attacked the machine guns. The doughboys worked their way through the hedgerows with grenades, grenade launchers, BARs, and bayonets, while the tanks crushed dugouts and knocked out the machine guns, and the German line gave way. The advance continued until 88-millimeter fire at Lenauderie stopped the Americans again.

Meanwhile, the 3d Battalion pushed down the St. Lô road for half a mile until it, too, encountered 88-millimeter fire and machine guns. Artillery took care of the problem, and the Americans pressed forward again. Company F moved up from reserve to tackle Montmartin-en-Grainges, the main objective. Colonel Birks, following the attack, noticed that the supporting tanks were not in action, and he personally directed them into the battle. The doughs had run into German infantry in dugouts and zig-zag trenches outside town, and seven tanks rolled forward to crush the resistance. A tankdozer pushed dirt over the firing embrasures of several dugouts.

Company F took Montmartin but came under fire from a nearby ridge. Birks ordered a barrage down on the hill, and then Company E and its supporting tanks attacked and secured it. Birks also sent a rifle platoon mounted on the decks of tanks into action against Germans in Le Comte, an early example of such tactics in Normandy.[45]

REGROUPING AND REASSESSING

After roughly two weeks of nonstop fighting, the infantry and tankers from the assault units in the VII Corps had a chance to catch their breath and assimilate some of the hard lessons they had learned regarding hedgerow tactics and tank-infantry communications. Several tank battalions withdrew from the line to perform critical maintenance on their vehicles and train with the doughs. The 743d

Tank Battalion went into bivouac from 17 June to 7 July, the 747th Battalion from 21 June to 10 July, and the 741st Battalion from 20 to 30 June.

Replacement tanks and crews began to arrive (by 17 June for the 741st and 20 June for the 743d Tank battalions), but not in numbers adequate to make up losses.[46] Some other developments were encouraging. On 20 June, kitchen trucks served hot meals to the men of the 743d Tank Battalion or the first time since the invasion.[47]

The 747th Tank Battalion and 29th Infantry Division built on their first ad hoc tank-infantry approach to beating the bocage. The battalion welded two prongs made of iron pipe cut four and a half feet long to the final drive housing at the nose of thirteen battalion Shermans. The tank poked holes in the hedgerow, into which engineers placed prepared TNT charges and then blew a gap.[48]

Meanwhile, at the tactical level, tankers and infantry worked out the following drill: using high-explosive shells with fuse delay, tanks blew out the corners of the opposite hedgerow where the Germans often put their machine guns. The tanks then skipped fuse-delay shells above the hedgerow, causing airbursts, and fired machine guns. The infantry advanced under this protection to the next hedgerow, over which they would throw hand grenades.[49]

Commanders tried to help. On 25 June, the 29th Infantry Division sponsored a conference on coordination of tanks, infantry, and engineers in the assault of

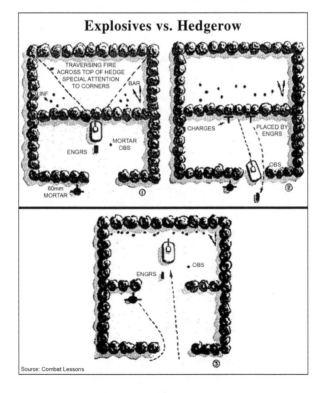

hedgerows, and it published a memo entitled "Infantry Coordination of Tanks, Infantry & Engineers in Hedgerow Tactics." Two days later, a booklet arrived at the front, courtesy of the XIX Corps, entitled *The Tank and Infantry Team.*[50] If these publications had anything helpful to say, it had doubtless come from the guys on the ground painfully working it out.

The 741st Tank Battalion began training in rear areas with the 2d Infantry Division on 20 June. Rifle platoons or entire companies pulled back from the line to practice for a half day with tankers and combat engineers.[51] This partnership adopted the following plan:

> [A]ttach a tank to an infantry squad, together with four engineers. . . . Since the tank would encounter great difficulty in negotiating the hedgerows, the engineer group would blow a hole in the hedge of sufficient size to enable the tank to get through. The team play of this group was to be as follows: The squad leader of the infantry would form a base of fire with his squad along the hedgerow to be used as a line of departure. The tank would take up a firing position along the same hedgerow with the engineer personnel near the tank, the explosives to be carried on the rear deck of the tank where the engineers could obtain them. Since sufficient personnel were not available to cover all the fields within the zone of advance, the fields on either flank of the field covered by a team had to be covered by fire, in some cases this fire was furnished by light or heavy machine gun, emplaced in the corner of the field at the line of departure to sweep the adjacent fields. A reserve tank would be directly behind the assault tank for over-watching purposes and to provide a reserve tank in case the assault tank became stuck or was knocked out. After the base of fire neutralized the enemy fire in the first hedgerow past the line of departure, the squad leader would send the scouts of the squad forward along the hedgerows parallel with the line of advance on each side of the field. Then the BAR-man and the Tommy gunner would move forward. In short, the infantry squad infiltrated to the next hedgerow. The squad leader, when he went forward, would pick a spot suitable for the tank to secure a fire position and would signal the tank forward. If necessary, the hedge at the point of departure would be blown. In some cases, the tank was able to push through the hedge. . . .
>
> When the tank moved forward, the engineer group went with it to protect the tank from the fire of bazookas and antitank grenades. Upon reaching the next hedgerow, the tank would again go into firing position, the squad would form a base of fire with the tank, and the entire process of advance would be repeated. . . .[52]

The 743d Tank Battalion began practicing hedgerow tactics with the 30th Infantry Division on 2 July.[53] In that partnership's approach, engineers blew three holes simultaneously in a hedgerow. At a signal from a tank's siren, everybody in the operation rushed through the openings simultaneously, thus preventing German gunners from picking tanks off one by one. In the 737th Tank Battalion, which arrived a few weeks later, teams also relied on the rush tactic. Engineers blew holes in the hedgerow using twenty-second fuses, and then tanks, infantry, engineers, and any other assault elements would pelt through before the dust settled and the Germans could sight their antitank guns on the gaps.[54]

Men were also trying to solve the riddle of tank-infantry communications, without which tactical improvements might help little. The chief of the First Army's armor section fired a message back to Army Ground Forces on 18 June flagging the "positive need in separate battalions and armored divisions of a quick means of communication between tanks and infantry. We are trying to get the [SCR-]300 series for the purpose. I understand AGF had authorized them. Can you send me the dope?"[55] The infantry's standard tactical radio was the SCR-300 walkie-talkie. It is an intriguing possibility that the AGF approval was the result of the war observer's proposal from Italy some months earlier.

While the military bureaucracy chewed on that one, soldiers turned to the field solution that had already proved itself in the Pacific: installing a standard EE-8 field telephone, at first ensconced in an empty ammo box hung under the Sherman's rear deck overhang, which was wired into the intercom system of the tank. Installation of such rigs began by about 20 June and became standard operating procedure in most separate tank battalions. Despite the demonstrated usefulness of the phones on the tanks, battalions were not so outfitted before being committed to combat. The 749th Tank Battalion, for example, did not incorporate the boxes until 22 or 23 July, three weeks after entering battle.[56] The 712th Tank Battalion did not receive phones until February 1945.[57]

Some battalions turned to light tanks for liaison with infantry command posts because they could tie into the tankers' radio net and were less useful than Shermans in combat. On 9 July, for example, the 749th Tank Battalion sent one light tank to the command post of each of the three infantry battalions the unit was supporting that day.[58] The 747th Tank Battalion also used light tanks in this capacity.[59] This at least signaled that communications links were getting down to the infantry battalion-tank company level.

The first efforts to get radios into the hands of the infantry that could link directly to tanks began by July. On 18 July, the 3d Armored Group ordered its battalions to supply their partner infantry battalion command post with a jeep carrying an SCR-510 tank radio, as well as jeeps carrying the similar SCR-509 to work with the infantry platoons.[60] This was essentially the same approach battalions in both Italy and the Pacific had adopted months earlier.

It would be some time after American forces broke out of Normandy before tankers and infantry hit upon a more or less satisfactory solution to radio communications at the platoon level. On 16 July, the 745th Tank Battalion received a message from the U.S. First Army foreshadowing what, months later, would become the standardized solution: the battalion would receive four extra SCR-509 radios for tank-infantry communications on a loan basis, which would eventually be replaced by the "300 series tank set." The official U.S. Army history asserts that signal companies in Normandy installed infantry-type radios in the tanks, but the battalion records suggest that such installations did not take place in any numbers—if at all—until the autumn.[61]

Communications aside, the record suggests that the only route to a solid partnership between the doughs and the tankers was for them to spend time together taking the same classes at the school of hard knocks. The stream of units flowing into France made lasting attachments rare. For the tank battalions that landed early, this meant that now veteran tankers sometimes had to teach new infantry outfits the ropes—or die trying. The now seasoned 746th Tank Battalion, for example, was attached to the virgin 83d Infantry Division on 5 July. That division was badly mauled over the next several days, and tank-infantry cooperation was especially bad. The infantry accused the tankers of refusing to fight at night and disobeying orders, and one infantry commander threatened to shoot a tank officer for refusing to advance in support. One tank commander, meanwhile, threatened to shoot infantrymen who appeared ready to bolt and abandon the tanks.[62]

When an enduring partnership could take hold, tankers grew to respect infantry commanders who learned how to use their tanks effectively. In some cases battalions came to be treated as members of the infantry division to which they were attached for months.

Over the course of the fighting in Europe, tank battalions experienced the extremes of shared time with infantry divisions and everything in between. Enjoying a continuity similar to that experienced by the 745th Tank Battalion and 1st Infantry Division, the 70th Tank Battalion spent most of the campaign attached to the 4th Infantry Division. The 90th Infantry Division considered the 712th Tank Battalion a virtually organic component.

In contrast, the 761st Tank Battalion rarely spent more than a few weeks attached to any one unit, a circumstance that forced it to fight under the least advantageous circumstances for most of the war; the modern observer may be drawn to the conclusion—perhaps unfairly—that the nearly all-black 761st had to fight under such ultimately dangerous circumstances because of racist distrust within the still-segregated army in its fighting abilities. The 740th Tank Battalion or its companies at one time or another were attached to seven different divisions.

CONTINUING THE FIGHT

While much of the VII Corps gnawed at the problems of tank-infantry cooperation during late June, the focus of the American effort in Normandy was northward out of the beachhead with the goal of capturing the port of Cherbourg. The 70th (attached most of the time to the 4th Infantry Division) and the 746th (attached by late June to the 9th Infantry Division) Tank Battalions were committed to the V Corps' drive on Cherbourg.

The 746th Tank Battalion recorded two firsts during the attack on Cherbourg. On the outskirts of the city, tanks lobbed 75-millimeter rounds into the fortress, marking the first mass use of a tank battalion in its secondary role as artillery in the European theater. While this was a common practice in Italy, a study conducted by the General Board of U.S. Forces for the European theater at the end of the war concluded that tank units found it increasingly difficult later in the campaign to use tanks in the indirect-fire role. The reason was that replacements for casualties almost never had received artillery training.[63] After-action reports indicate that battalions often grouped the three-vehicle 105-millimeter assault gun platoon and the assault guns from each of the three medium tank companies into an expanded platoon the same size as an armored field artillery battery to fire indirectly under direction from a field artillery unit. On occasion, the battalion's three assault guns were attached to the cannon company of an infantry regiment, which also fielded 105-millimeter howitzers.[64]

The tankers also were the first in the theater to help capture a major city. Company A supported the 79th Infantry Division's attack on the left, while Companies B and C worked with the 9th Division's 47th and 60th Infantry regiments on the right. Cherbourg was surrounded by fortifications facing land and sea, and tank action mainly involved destroying bunkers, pillboxes, and antitank positions, rather than waging the street-by-street, house-by-house urban battle that would characterize the fighting in Cassino, many German cities, or Manila.[65] Indeed, in almost Napoleonic fashion, one tank supporting Company A of the 47th Infantry was knocked out on 26 June by a 75-millimeter gun firing from the parapet of the arsenal.[66]

The tank battalion's after-action report records:

> By the morning of the 27th [of June], all of the city was in our hands except the highly fortified arsenal. At 0600 the three platoons of Company B moved up to shell the arsenal before they would withdraw, allowing our air support to bomb the fort at 1000 hours. After the tanks fired but before time for the air bombing, the general in charge of the German fortifications said that he would surrender the fort only if we would show our forces. So Lieutenant Kegut's platoon of tanks moved up to the gates of the arsenal and actually stuck the tank guns into the doors of the fortifications. This convinced the general that we had force, and he surrendered his entire command.

APPLYING THE LESSONS

After the capture of Cherbourg on 26 June, Lieutenant General Bradley tried to get an attack moving southward and inland. As of the beginning of July, Bradley's expanding forces included four corps headquarters and thirteen combat divisions (nine infantry, two armored, and two airborne). To the south, however, lay the heart of the bocage. And, on the Carentan plain, five large swamps and numerous slow-moving rivers and streams further broke up the terrain. Frequent rainfall turned fields to mud; indeed, the amount of cloud, wind, and rain in June and July was greater than that recorded at any time since 1900, and this cut air support in half.[67]

The going was horrendous for the infantry, particularly the units tasting battle for the first time. Using twelve divisions over seventeen days in July, the First Army was able to advance only about seven miles in its western zone and little more than half that in its eastern zone. It suffered 40,000 casualties during July, most of them infantrymen.[68]

The push southward brought back into action the divisions and tank battalions that had invested time in trying to figure out how best to fight together in the hedgerows. Preparatory to a planned First Army breakout from Normandy in late July, the V Corps attacked southward on 11 July to seize St. Lô and the terrain to the east, striking with the 2d Infantry Division in conjunction with the XIX Corp's 29th Infantry Division to its right.

The 2d Infantry Division and 741st Tank Battalion, once again charged with capturing Hill 192 and reaching the Berigny–St. Lô highway, implemented the tank-infantry-engineer techniques they had been practicing. Commanders had learned that patience and preparation, rather than the audacity of armored cavalry, generally paid off in bocage fighting. Battalion and company commanders were flown over the terrain on which they would fight, and in-depth planning sessions using aerial photos took place at battalion and regimental command posts. The division conducted extensive reconnaissance, and the engineers drew up extremely detailed maps at 1:10,000 scale showing every hedgerow, sunken road, building, trail, and crossroads, and a coded number assigned to every field, copies of which were given to the infantry and to every tank commander.[69] The use of numbered fields enabled the tank battalion to control the action by radio once the attack had started, facilitated the use of supporting artillery fire, and expedited the recovery of damaged tanks.[70]

Defying armored doctrine that frowned on use of individual tanks alone, the division assigned a tank to each rifle squad on the line, with the remainder held back to provide overwatch and replacements. The tank and rifle squad trained intensively together three times before the looming operation so the men could get to know one another. The same was true of the engineer demolition men assigned to the team. The tanks all had EE-8 phones installed to improve communications, most of which worked during the coming fight. "According to the men who fought the battle," noted a combat interviewer, "the training paid off."[71]

The day of the attack, tanks eased forward one at a time through the darkness at hourly intervals using first or second gear to avoid alerting the enemy. The tactic worked, and this time the paratroopers were not alerted to an impending attack by the noise of tanks. Engineers had scooped out the friendly side of the first hedgerows so gaps could be blown quickly, and elaborate signs indicated which tank was to pass through which gap. The tanks carried satchel charges on the

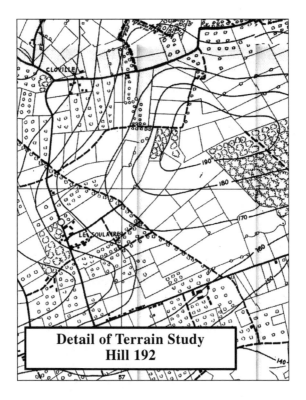

**Detail of Terrain Study
Hill 192**

decks for use by the engineers. Tank commanders and drivers had walked the routes to the line of departure to familiarize themselves with the path.[72]

At 0600 on 11 July, the 38th Infantry Regiment's 2d Battalion and the 741st Tank Battalion's Company B assaulted a nettlesome strongpoint nicknamed "Kraut Corner." Engineers blew their holes, and tanks fired high-explosive rounds into the two facing corners of the next fields and any other suspicious spot. Riflemen from Company E then advanced along hedgerows supported by suppressing fire from BARs, heavy and light machine guns, and the machine guns on the Shermans. The tanks' guns fired so continuously, reported participants, that they sounded like threshing machines, and they became so hot that the gunners had to lift the covers when not firing in order not to accidentally discharge into friendly infantry. A tankdozer covered die-hard German paratroopers in their firing positions when they shot at passing doughs from the flanks.

Cpl. Jack Boardman, Company B, recalled some hedgerow action during the attack that showed how the field telephone helped in battle:

[W]e rolled through the opening with both our machine guns blasting at the enemy hedge. The squad of doughs scrambled and tore their way through the jungle-like shrubbery on the high bank and desperately ran down the field to gain the shelter of the opposite bank. . . . Suddenly the doughboy I could see in front of me dropped to the ground. I strained my eyes into the gunsight and traversed the turret back and forth trying to pick up the gun that was firing on them. The doughs' squad leader began yelling over the telephone on the back of the tank, "We're getting heavy fire from the left corner! Hit 'em, hit 'em!" I snapped the turret to the left and put an HE on delay into the corner of the hedge. It passed through the bank and exploded in the middle of a machine-gun nest. The Jerry gun that had been pointed through a small slot on the bottom of the hedge fired no more.[73]

Company F hit the German flank, and it buckled. Company E pressed on toward Cloville, on the flank of Hill 192, where a Sturmgeschütz III assault gun and a Mark IV tank lurked in the rubble of buildings destroyed by shelling. S/Sgt. Paul Ragan engaged and destroyed them both after a brief duel, which opened the door to the infantry to mop up in the village.

Soon the 2d Battalion crossed the St. Lô road and reached its objective. "Without the tanks, I doubt we could have made it," conceded one infantry sergeant. The battalion's commanding officer added, "In many cases, the tanks were leading the infantry, and they did a fearless job." A captured letter from a paratrooper commented about the tanks, "They shot with their guns through the hedgerows as through cake dough!"[74]

Things initially went less well in the zone of the 38th Infantry's 1st Battalion, which kicked off on the regimental left at 0620, supported by tanks from Company A. When the infantry pulled back 400 yards for the preliminary artillery bombardment, the German paratroopers infiltrated behind them despite the shelling, and the GIs had to fight hard to get back to the line of departure. The Germans had zeroed in the line of departure with mortars and artillery, and shells struck the decks of two tanks carrying satchel charges and destroyed them both. A bazooka disabled a third, and three others were damaged or forced to withdraw. The infantry pressed ahead without the tanks. By afternoon, replacement tanks had reached the doughboys, and the team fought just as it had trained.[75]

The 2d Infantry Division's tank-infantry team threw the German 3d Airborne Division off Hill 192 by 13 July, despite the commitment of the Germans' last reserves. The paratroopers never did execute a coordinated withdrawal and fought in place until destroyed or captured.[76]

The 29th Infantry Division also struck toward St. Lô on 11 July, and the time invested in tank-infantry training paid off there, too. Col. Philip Dwyer, commanding the 116th Infantry, judged that "the success of the 116th Infantry's attack on 11–12 July 1944 was due primarily to its being a well-planned tank-infantry attack. It is unquestionably true that the tanks draw artillery fire, but certainly on 11 July they contributed to the excellent advance of [the 2d Battalion]."[77] The commanding officer of the 2d Battalion agreed:

One platoon of medium tanks from the 747th Tank Battalion was teamed with each assault platoon, with another tank platoon in reserve. . . . The first 500–600 yards were tough. The infantry and tanks worked well together, however, and Lieutenant Colonel Fries's ramrods [that poked holes for TNT] on the front of his tanks made things go faster than they would have otherwise. Their great merit is that they saved on the use of TNT, which draws artillery and usually necessitates waiting while the charges are being set and blown.[78]

Regarding an attack on 15 July by the 1st Battalion of his 115th Infantry, Col. Godwin Ordway Jr. observed, "The tanks and infantry worked well together. The tank company commanding officer said the men of the 1st Battalion were the only ones not to run when the tanks got 88 fire."[79] On 18 July, a platoon of medium tanks joined Task Force C, commanded by Brigadier General Cota, which finally pushed into St. Lô and secured the town.

Crews turned to field solutions in hope of adding protection against *panzerfausts* and other light antitank weapons. The first expedient was sandbagging. The bags were initially held on with chicken wire or some other quick fix, but service companies later welded brackets intended for the purpose onto many tanks. The 743d Tank Battalion, for example, sandbagged all of its tanks between 18 and 22 July 1944, and its records show that the unit re-sandbagged old tanks and outfitted newly received tanks during down times for much of the rest of the war.[80] There is considerable debate as to whether sandbagging was all that effective. Some field tests suggested not.[81] But some showed promising results: a day after test-firing a German bazooka and antitank grenade against a sandbagged Sherman on 28 July in the 3d Armored Group, trucks headed back to the beach to collect sand.[82] If nothing else, as the commander of one battalion noted, "Sandbagging the front of the tank greatly improves the morale of the crew."[83]

With a month or more of experience, tankers learned that they faced one last problem: the infantry divisions typically rotated the units doing the actual fighting, with two regiments in combat and one held in reserve. The tank battalions remained on the line for weeks, supporting whichever infantry units happened to be engaged on a given day. This was extremely hard on both machines and men.

Regrettably, all these lessons being learned in battle were not even being shared across the short distance to England. When the 35th Infantry Division entered the XIX Corps' line on 9 July, its job was to capture Hill 122, the anchor of the German Mahlman defense line across the base of the Cotentin peninsula—no easy task. Maj. Budd Richmond of the 137th Infantry recalled, "Hedgerows and more hedgerows, and [we] wondered just how the hell we were going to mount a successful attack, from and through them. . . . During our intensive training phase of preparation in England, no instructions or suggestions were issued on the tactical application of such weird terrain."[84]

Likewise, green tank battalions still were being committed without meaningful training in tank-infantry cooperation in the bocage.[85] The armored groups ashore did what they could to arrange a briefing by experienced commanders and perhaps a few days of demonstrations and training, but that was not always possible.

That meant learning in the school of hard knocks, and experience related directly to casualties. Tank battalions tended to suffer a substantial portion of their total losses for the war in their first few weeks of combat, after which the tankers who survived evidently learned how to fight more effectively. The 737th Tank Battalion joined the 35th Infantry Division in combat on 14 July and lost twenty-three Shermans in its first three days of fighting—35 percent of its losses for the war.[86]

Maj. Budd Richmond, the operations officer of the 137th Infantry's 3d Battalion, conceded that the destruction in just two hours of four out of five of the 737th Battalion's tanks that were supporting one rifle company during an attack on 15 July was due to "improper employment in unsuitable terrain, and lack of infantry support. . . . [T]his was the first such tank-infantry team action, in training or in battle. And what prior planning and coordination that did exist between the infantry and the tanks on the ground was pure chance and individual initiative."[87] Capt. Don Rubottom, a company commander in the 134th Infantry, recalled, "There was no way of communicating with the men in the tank. Time after time, it was necessary to crawl upon the tank, beat on the buttoned-up hatch until it was opened, point out targets, and change the direction of the tank as it was guided through the hedgerows."[88]

Observers with the XIX Corps, in a report to Army Ground Forces covering the July period, summed up,

> The operation of the tank-infantry team in Normandy was definitely poor. Cases are know wherein due to confusion, poor coordination and lack of common understanding, American tanks were blasted apart by friendly antitank weapons, and American tanks fired upon friendly troops with considerable casualty effect, with the result that there developed an unhealthy feeling of animosity and recrimination between the infantry and tanks. Communication between the two was poor generally. . . . Simple standard means of communication between tanks and infantry must be devised.[89]

CHAPTER 9

Open-Field Running

*Now we began to roll—long marches and shorter bivouacs. This was
the happier type of fighting, the blitzkrieg style. No endless days of
sweating out a battle within earshot of the enemy, although we were
often less than six hours behind them. It meant more work, and less
sleep, but everyone knew he was getting somewhere.*

—Al Heintzleman, *We'll Never Go
Over-Seas*

Operation Cobra, which ripped the threadbare German defenses in Normandy,
unleashed the kind of fluid campaign tankers dream about, one that even the
dirt-grimed infantry tankers could enjoy. The attrition in the bocage had hurt the
Germans badly. In all of Normandy between 6 June and 9 July (including the
British sector), the Germans lost 2,000 officers and 85,000 men and received only
5,210 replacements. They also lost 150 Mark IVs, 85 Panthers, 15 Tigers, 167 75-
millimeter assault guns and antitank guns, and almost 30 88-millimeter guns.[1]

Lt. Gen. Omar Bradley conceived Operation Cobra as a way to end the
bloody hedgerow war with a major breakthrough on a narrow front west of St.
Lô.[2] J. Lawton Collins's VII Corps was to make the main effort in the American
center immediately west of St. Lô, with the 83d and 9th Infantry Divisions on the
left, the 30th Infantry Division in the center, and the 29th Infantry Division on the
right. Once a penetration had been achieved, the motorized 1st Infantry Division,
with Combat Command B from the 3d Armored Division attached, was to exploit
four miles southward to Marigny and then turn west ten miles to Coutances on the
coast to cut off the German left wing. The rest of the 3d Armored Division, with
a 1st Infantry Division rifle battalion attached, was to secure the southern exits
from Coutances. The 2d Armored Division, with the motorized 22d Infantry Regiment attached, was to drive through the gap and establish more blocking positions. The XIX and V Corps were to launch smaller attacks to pin the Germans in
place along their fronts east of the VII Corps, while the VIII Corps pushed southward down the coast to the west to destroy the German left wing after delaying

just long enough for the VII Corps' action to be felt.[3] To the rear, Lt. Gen. George Patton Jr.'s Third Army bided its time, ready to explode into France.

Cobra experienced an inauspicious false start on 24 July. Bad weather forced commanders to cancel the air operation, but the word did not reach some of the heavy bombers already in flight. American troops had withdrawn 1,200 yards from the bomb zone, but some bombers released their loads early and hit soldiers of the 30th Infantry Division some 2,000 yards north of the Periers–St. Lô highway "no-bomb" line. Twenty-five American soldiers were killed and 131 wounded. Cobra was postponed for twenty-four hours.

American forces tried again on 25 July, and once more, the initial signs were inauspicious. Flying north to south over American and then German lines despite the previous day's mishap, 1,500 B-17 and B-24 heavy bombers from the U.S. Eighth Air Force dropped more than 3,300 tons of bombs, while 380 B-26 medium bombers unloaded more than 650 tons of high-explosive and fragmentation bombs. Theoretically the only aircraft attacking in the zone closest to American ground troops, more than 550 fighter-bombers from the IX Tactical Air Command dropped more than 200 tons of bombs and a large amount of napalm.

Roughly 75 of the bombers dropped their loads within American lines due to various errors, killing 111 troops and wounding 490. This time, tankers were under the bombs, too. One officer in the 746th Tank Battalion was seriously wounded.

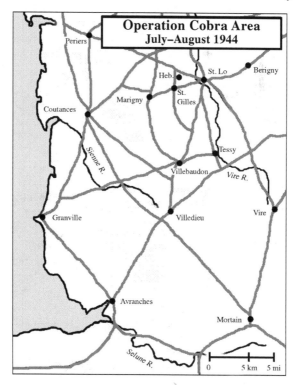

**Operation Cobra Area
July–August 1944**

Medics in the 743d Tank Battalion raced among burning fuel trucks to help doughs hit or buried by the bombs, and two battalion tanks were knocked out.[4] Lt. Gen. Lesley McNair, the head of the Army Ground Forces and father of the separate tank battalions, was killed while observing the attack. So was the entire command group of the 47th Infantry Regiment except the commander, and many soldiers were in deep shock.

There would be no more delays, however. Assault elements were ordered forward.

The bombing had dealt German units in the assault zone a shocking and crippling blow, although that was not immediately apparent to the tankers. The German commander, Lt. Gen. Fritz Bayerlein, had organized a tank defense in depth and thought his position strong; he had not reckoned on being carpet-bombed. His *Panzer Lehr* armored division—already badly depleted—and small attached elements from *Kampfgruppe* Heinz and an airborne regiment were shattered. About one-third of the combat effectives manning the main line of defense and the immediate reserve line were killed or wounded, and the remainder left in a daze. Forced to throw their remaining armor reserves into the line to stop Operation Goodwood, launched by Montgomery in the British sector a week before Cobra, the German command had almost nothing with which to fill the gap. By that evening, Field Marshal Günther von Kluge, the German theater commander who had recently replaced Gerd von Rundstedt, had to conclude, "As of this moment, the front has . . . burst."[5]

Advancing American troops, however, were surprised to find groups of enemy soldiers fighting stubbornly despite the saturation bombing. In the center, the 30th Infantry Division attacked generally toward St. Gilles. Company B of the 743d Tank Battalion worked with Col. Edwin Sutherland's 119th Infantry on the division's left, which was to capture Hebecrevon and the high ground on which the village was located. While two companies from the 1st Battalion and the entire 3d Battalion attacked the town frontally, the tanks carried the doughs of Company A, 1st Battalion, in a hook around the left and into the village. Resistance against the main attack was fierce, and at 2200 hours, the flanking force, which encountered little trouble, slipped into Hebecrevon. Enemy fire was heavy for a few minutes but then dropped off as the Germans pulled out.[6]

On the division's right, the 120th Infantry Regiment had orders to punch through the German main line of resistance and capture St. Gilles, after which the 2d Armored Division's Combat Command A was to pass through the regiment. Col. Hammond Birks attacked south down the St. Gilles road in a column of battalions—with the 2d Battalion, which had been heavily bombed, in the lead—and he planned to deploy the following battalion to the left if he ran into firm resistance. Companies and platoons were to use this same scheme of maneuver. Companies A and C of the 743d Tank Battalion and two platoons of light tanks supported the regiment's drive.

At the very first crossroad, the 2d Battalion ran into a strongpoint formed by three Panthers flanked by infantry and machine guns. High-velocity fire knocked out one Sherman and killed a platoon leader in the turret of a second. The 2d Battalion tried to overcome the resistance, but the fighting was bitter, and the battalion's S-3 was killed. Birks sent his 1st Battalion to the left, and when progress there slowed, he sent the 3d Battalion to the right. Birks and Lt. Col. William Duncan, who commanded the 743d Tank Battalion, met behind a hedgerow to figure out what they could do about the strongpoint.

In the meantime, Lt. Ernest Aas of Company A had dismounted from his tank and conducted a stealthy foot reconnaissance of the German position. Aas reported to Birks and Duncan and proposed sending five Shermans across the fields to the left of the road, which was mined, to take out the Panthers that formed the core of the defense. Duncan observed that three of the five Shermans might be knocked out, but it seemed like the only thing to be done.

Aas led his tanks off the road toward the first panzer he had spotted. The gunners destroyed the Panther, and the other two took off westward toward La Picauderie. Aas and his tankers cornered one there and destroyed it. "The infantry-tank cooperation was working smoothly," observed Aas. Returning to the main road, the tankers saw the third Panther firing from the west and knocked it out. The way was clear for the 2d Battalion.

During the fight, the light tanks had been unable to play any role, because, in Duncan's view, their 37-millimeter guns were wholly inadequate. One tank commander had engaged one of the Panthers but radioed dolefully, "Good God, I fired three rounds, and they all bounced off!"[7]

Wayne Robinson's history of the 743d records, "It did not seem like the battle was getting any place in that welter of confusion, with the attack beginning under the ill-starred bombing, with the roads heavily mined, with direct-fire weapons hidden in the hedgerows, with the enemy shells falling constantly, and with the infantry disorganized. It did not seem that anybody was getting anywhere."[8] Nevertheless, with the loss of Hebecrevon, the German Seventh Army recorded in its war diary, "The various small penetrations in the area of the *Panzer Lehr* Division and to the left of it have developed into a breakthrough."[9]

The 9th Infantry Division, attacking toward Marigny, generally fell short of its initial objectives on 25 July.[10] The 746th Tank Battalion encountered stiff resistance through 29 July as the doughs advanced. Beginning on 1 August, however, the division pushed through to St. Pois, and the 746th Tank Battalion's after-action report recorded, "The operation was characterized by more open hilly terrain with increased visibility and faster movement from high ground to high ground. The operation was one of mopping up heavy centers of resistance and fighting delaying actions accompanied by local counterattacks. Losses were considerably lighter than in the previous period. Employment of tanks with the 9th Infantry Division during this period was generally good."

During the initial phase of the attack, the tankers finally were permitted to exploit the mobility afforded by their Rhino attachments or "Culin hedgerow device." History has linked the name of Sgt. Curtis G. Culin of the 102d Cavalry Reconnaissance Squadron to the device, although other inventors produced their own variants. The contraption (the 3d Armored Group referred to them as "Rube Goldbergs") was made of steel girders from German beach defenses. It amounted to a set of steel teeth protruding from the nose of the tank, and it could be mounted on M4s and M5s. The teeth allowed the vehicle to grip and plow through a hedgerow with hardly any loss of speed.[11] Tankers found that approaching the typical hedgerow in third gear at about fifteen miles per hour usually worked.[12] A similar device that looked more like a blade was referred to as the "green dozer." By the time Cobra began, 60 percent of the tanks involved had been fitted with Culin devices.[13] The use of the Rhino in combat had been barred until the launch of Cobra in order to maintain tactical surprise.[14]

Generally, the devices allowed tankers to better execute standard hedgerow tactics. The 709th Tank Battalion, attached to the 8th Infantry Division in the VIII Corps' zone, for example, was able to support the infantry by side-slipping German positions and putting enfilading fire on hedgerow defenses.[15]

The Cobra breakout was a rough execution of theory: The infantry divisions and their supporting tanks created the hole through which the armored divisions could exploit. Collins sent two armored columns driving south into the guts of the disintegrating German defenses on the afternoon of 26 July. On the right, Maj. Gen. Clarence Huebner's 1st Infantry Division (motorized), with the 3d Armored Division's Combat Command B attached, was to pass through the 9th Infantry Division and capture Marigny. Maj. Gen. Edward Brooks's 2d Armored Division, with the 4th Infantry Division's 22d Infantry Regiment attached, was to drive south and east on the left, passing through the 30th Infantry Division to seize St. Gilles.[16] By 27 July, it was clear to American commanders that they had broken open the German defenses.[17]

Combat Command B of the 3d Armored Division formed one spearhead aimed initially at Marigny, and the 18th Infantry Regiment was attached to provide rifle strength. The infantry regiment brought along Company B, 745th Tank Battalion. Almost immediately after crossing the Periers–St. Lô road on 26 July, the 1st Battalion found it could not advance along the roads because they were ripped up by bomb craters. It therefore struck off cross-country, led by tankdozers to cut through the hedgerows and followed by tanks, which fanned out on the far side until the next hedgerow was reached.[18]

The 1st and 3d Battalions, 16th Infantry, followed Combat Command B's charge. Each battalion mounted a company of infantry on tanks from the 745th

Tank Battalion, while the remainder followed on foot. The GIs almost immediately learned the risks inherent in mounting men on tanks when on 27 July eight Company I soldiers were shot off the decks at a strongpoint near Marigny.[19]

General Patton and his Third Army followed. On 28 July, Bradley temporarily named Patton deputy army group commander and gave him charge of the VIII Corps on Collins's right flank. Patton immediately threw the 4th and 6th Armored Divisions and the already attacking 8th and 79th Infantry Divisions against the Germans, who by now were trying to "advance to the rear" to avoid complete encirclement. This advance passed through Avranches at the base of the Cotentin Peninsula on 1 August. That same day, Patton's Third Army officially became operational.

The doorway to France was ajar. Said Patton, "Those troops know their business. We'll keep right on going, full speed ahead."[20] On 2 August, the 749th Tank Battalion, attached to the 79th Infantry Division, pushed forward more than thirty-three miles, and on the seventh, it advanced forty miles.[21] Patton's spearhead first cut right into Brittany. The next wave—the XV Corps, composed at this time of the 5th Armored Division and the 83d and 90th Infantry Divisions—hooked eastward toward Paris and Germany.

On the left shoulder of the breakout, the 4th Infantry Division initially had trouble maintaining contact with supporting tanks. Nevertheless, each time resistance brought the advance to a halt, 70th Tank Battalion Shermans eventually showed up and hammered a way through.[22] At the end of 25 July, the battalion had advanced only 2,000 yards but despite what it considered stubborn opposition, it had lost no tanks. The next day, the battalion advanced rapidly, and by 2 August, it was at Villedieu—about twenty-five miles from St. Lô—an objective the German commanders viewed along with Avranches as the keys to any American success.[23] Maj. Gen. Raymond Barton, the commander of the 4th Infantry Division, told his commanders, "We face a defeated enemy, an enemy terribly low in morale, terribly confused. I want you in the next advance to throw caution to the winds. . . destroying, capturing, or bypassing the enemy, and pressing recklessly on to the objective." His troops did just that.[24]

The breakout ended the bloodiest chapter in the history of the separate tank battalions. Attrition in the bocage had been grim. The 747th Tank Battalion, for example, lost 8 men killed and 34 wounded between 7 and 17 June alone. In late July, the 741st suffered 16 men killed and 64 wounded—more than 10 percent of its strength—in just over two weeks. In June and July, the 743rd lost at least 25 officers and men killed in action and another 116 wounded—nearly 20 percent.

For the separate tank battalions, once clear of the bocage, breaking out offered a rare opportunity to act like armored divisions in slashing maneuver. The main difference was that, whereas the armored-infantry battalions had organic transportation, the tanks carried the infantry to whom they were attached. The infantry divisions "motorized themselves," using not only tanks but mortar carriers, artillery prime movers, fuel and ammunition trucks, and anything else that would roll. The doughs loved it.[25]

After starting slowly because of congested roads, advancing troops broke into open ground, and hastily organized task forces formed spearheads that struck toward distant objectives. Ad hoc by nature, task forces could vary substantially in size. In the 5th Infantry Division, for example, Task Force Thackery, commanded by the division's intelligence officer, consisted of the reconnaissance troop, one infantry company, one light tank platoon from the 735th Tank Battalion, an engineer platoon, and medics. On 7 August, this small band was ordered to race roughly 100 miles to Angers at the base of the Brittany Peninsula to capture the bridge there intact and prevent German movement into or out of the region. Unfortunately, the bridge had been blown.[26] At the larger end of the spectrum, Task Force Taylor, activated on 1 September by the 4th Infantry Division to drive for Brussels, consisted of the 22d Infantry Regiment, the entire 747th Tank Battalion, Company C of the 893d Tank Destroyer Battalion, a company of engineers, the 44th Field Artillery Battalion, and the division antitank company.[27]

As American forces broke free, combat tended to consist of short, often sharp, engagements against delaying forces and strongpoints. This was a new style of warfare for the tankers for which, again, they and the doughs had not trained. Adaptation came easily, however, because an entire village often posed no greater challenge than had a well-defended hedgerow. This account from the after-action report of 741st Tank Battalion is typical:

Company D, with Company A, 1st Battalion, 23d Infantry, [2d Infantry Division,] mounted on the tanks' decks . . . by 0250, 1 August, had reached the village of St. Amand without encountering resistance. By 0430, this company had penetrated still further on, to the railroad station near Les Bessardierre. At this point the advance was halted to await the coming of daylight.

At 0730, the advance was continued, with the infantry still riding the tanks until, at 0900 near the village of Cour de Precuire, a bazooka projectile slammed into the lead tank of the 1st Platoon, and the fight was on. Withdrawing slightly to permit the attack to be organized, the tanks and infantry attacked before noon, facing a concentration of artillery and mortar fire in addition to fire from machine guns and rifles. The attack pressed on steadily, in spite of steady opposition, and at last reached the village of Lovdier, where the action ceased at 2030.

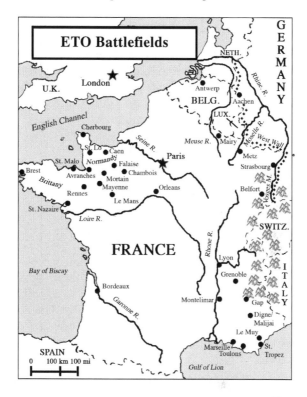

The Near Destruction of the German Seventh Army

Near Caen on 9 August, the Canadian First Army launched a massive attack southeast toward Falaise, about thirty miles behind and west-northwest of the German line at Mortain, where, on the night of 6 August, the Germans had launched an unsuccessful offensive to pinch shut the hole at Avranches. On 10 August, Patton ordered the XV Corps, which had captured Le Mans seventy miles behind and southeast of the enemy's Mortain line, to attack north across the German rear toward Argentan and Falaise.[28] The entire German Seventh Army was in danger of encirclement. As the situation became clear, Hitler finally agreed that the Seventh Army must withdraw.

Punching through desperate German resistance at Alençon on 11 August, the French 2d and U.S. 5th Armored Divisions, followed closely by the U.S. 79th and 90th Infantry Divisions, reached Argentan. Patrols reached Falaise only ten miles to the northwest. But on 13 August, Supreme Headquarters Allied Expeditionary Force ordered the 90th Infantry and French 2d Armored Divisions to stop in Argentan and wait for Montgomery's troops, who were pushing south to close the gap; the rest of the XV Corps was ordered to turn east toward Paris. Unfortunately, the Canadian attack stalled halfway to the objective, and Montgomery's troops did not close the trap until 19 August, which allowed perhaps one-third of the German troops to escape.[29] The collapse of the Falaise Pocket was nonetheless a disaster for the German army. It left behind 50,000 prisoners, 10,000 dead, as many as 500 tanks and assault guns destroyed or captured, and most of the transportation and artillery of the troops who fled.[30]

The 90th Infantry Division advanced to Chambois on 18 August to crimp the escape hole out of the Falaise Pocket, and the 712th Tank Battalion fought with the doughs as usual. On 15 August, the 359th Infantry spread out along the line from Le Bourg-St.-Leonard to Le Merlerault, small villages south and east of Chambois. The next day, German artillery shelled Le Bourg-St.-Leonard, which was held by Company A, 1st Battalion, and the tanks of Company A's 1st Platoon. German infantry attacks followed, and at 1700 hours, panzers joined the fray. The elements of many different divisions were piling up against the 359th Infantry's holding position, and the Germans briefly captured Le Bourg-St.-Leonard.

The Germans struck with renewed fury on 16 August, as a dozen panzers and parts of two panzergrenadier regiments of the 2d SS Panzer Division *Das Reich* sought to break free of the pocket. The attack successfully enveloped Le Bourg-St.-Leonard, and the 359th Infantry threw a platoon of reserve tanks into the fight, with the 1st Battalion's commander, Maj. Leroy Pond, standing atop the lead tank and the Ammunition and Pioneer Platoon of the 1st Battalion mounted on the decks, which restored the situation and carpeted the field with dead SS stormtroopers. Commented one participant, the only thing that stopped the German thrust was "our tanks and American guts." Nevertheless, the Germans, having no alternative, came on again, and control over the town passed back and forth. By 2300, the Americans held it for good.

From 17 through 21 August, the 359th Infantry stood in the Germans' path like a stone wall. Artillery smashed column after column as they approached Chambois. The watching GIs cheered and cheered. Soldiers from the 90th Division linked up with Polish troops under Canadian command at 1600 hours on 19 August, and the pocket was closed.[31]

In his oral history of the 712th Tank Battalion, Aaron Elson records tank commander Jim Gifford's recollection of the immense scene of chaos and slaughter as the pincers closed:

[I]t was just daylight, I took my field glasses and went up the hill so I could see out over this valley. . . . I see all these little sparkles, little sparkles all over the valley, what the hell is that? I looked through the field glasses and I'm telling you, I couldn't believe the sight I saw. It was thousands of bayonets flashing in the early morning sun. These guys, these infantry guys, were walking toward us, now they're about three miles away up that valley, and they're dispersed among hundreds of tanks moving along. Holy shit, I saw this, this was coming toward us, this is it. So I ran down, I got on the radio and I started hollering over the radio what's coming. And it wasn't twenty minutes later a bunch of our

P-47 Thunderbolts were flying towards them, at treetop level, those guys were our saviors, they were our angels up there, they were there all the time so we felt secure. They used to run in groups of four, and they came flying in one group after another. They'd go and the next thing there'd be more of them coming, they were knocking the shit out of them, and shells started flying over us, big shells. . . .

Well, these poor bastards out there three miles away, they were catching bloody hell, I'll tell you, they were getting it. We were firing at them from a mile or two away. . . . Companies A and B were spread out across the valley [with] the 773d [Tank Destroyer] Battalion. . . . And this monolith, whatever you want to call it, was slowly rolling, with all the destruction that was going on, it was coming right along by us—and Jesus, it wasn't stopping—and we were hitting everything. They had hundreds of horses drawing artillery. And instead of turning and coming up the hill toward us, they continued to head toward the gap with our [Companies] A, B, and 773d [Tank Destroyer] Battalion dispersed there, and those two companies were catching hell because the Germans started rolling through them. And when they hit these two companies plus the 773d they started piling up, and the next thing they turned and started to go back and started running into themselves.

By two o'clock in the afternoon, airplanes had been flying over dropping leaflets . . . saying surrender, wave the leaflet, you'll be okay. We got orders, they kept coming over the radio, stop firing at two o'clock. . . . Then at two o'clock it stopped, and they started coming up, out of the gap. Their equipment was burning all over the place, as far as you could see. . . . I looked down from the tank, and these guys were all dusty, dirty and filthy, and tired. They were a bedraggled army, it was a defeated army. They were just so goddamn glad to just be alive.[32]

The 90th Division's G-2 estimated that the 712th Tank Battalion had destroyed 50 tanks, 123 self-propelled guns, and 408 other vehicles—numbers that simply are not credible. The G-2 estimated that the 773d Tank Destroyer Battalion had knocked out 104 tanks and 51 self-propelled guns—several times the figure claimed by the battalion itself.

Nevertheless, it had been a killing field for the Germans. One infantry officer commented upon entering Chambois that it was the first time he had seen the proverbial river of blood.[33]

Getting a Better Tank

With the arrival of the 774th Tank Battalion in August, the first Shermans armed with a 76-millimeter gun reached the pool of separate tank battalions. A few 76-millimeter Shermans made it to England in time for D-Day, but commanders were not enthused until stung by the bad experiences of tankers in France, where gunners learned that their 75-millimeter rounds simply bounced off the front armor of Panther tanks. Initial plans called for one-third of tanks eventually to mount the 76-millimeter gun, but by the end of hostilities, the proportion would climb to more than half.[34]

Like many equipment upgrades, the appearance of 76-millimeter Shermans in the separate tank battalions varied tremendously. At one extreme, the 774th Tank Battalion entered combat fully equipped with 76-millimeter Shermans, and the 70th Tank Battalion drew 76-millimeter Shermans on 10 August (all of which went to Company A).[35] On 19 October 1944, the 737th Tank Battalion received a single tank with a 76-millimeter gun, which it decided to use as an assault gun attached to Headquarters Company and shuttle among the line units as needed.[36] The 741st Tank Battalion did not draw its first 76-millimeter Shermans until 1 January 1945,[37] and the 743d Tank Battalion received its first five M4A1s with 76-millimeter guns on 2 January.[38] It was not until February 1945 that the separate tank battalions moved to the top of the list, ahead of armored divisions, for allocation of 76-millimeter tanks arriving in theater.[39] In January, the 756th Tank Battalion, for example, had 75-millimeter and 76-millimeter tanks in a ratio of two to one, and by the end of February, the proportions had reversed.[40]

Although better against armor than the 75 millimeter, the 76-millimeter gun was not the solution for which tankers had hoped. It, too, proved to be generally ineffective against the frontal armor of the Panther and Tiger, except at close ranges, thanks to a botched assessment of the gun's penetration ability by the Ordnance Department during development.[41] The gun's effectiveness improved significantly with the introduction of tungsten-core hyper-velocity armor-piercing (HVAP) rounds, with which the Sherman finally gained the ability to kill Panthers from the front at 300 yards.[42] Once again, deployment of equipment in the pipeline caused the Sherman to remain weaker than it had to be. HVAP rounds began to reach separate tank battalions by September 1944 at the latest,[43] but the new ammunition remained extremely scarce for the entire war. In late March 1945, when the Ninth Army notified the 3d Armored Group that HVAP would henceforth be available as a standard issue, it indicated that one-half round per tube per month could be drawn.[44]

A drawback to the 76-millimeter gun was that it fired a far less effective high-explosive round than did the 75 millimeter. For infantry-support tanks, this was a major sticking point. At least some infantry commanders seemed to want to keep a preponderance of 75-millimeter guns around. Indeed, Maj. Gen. Alvan Gillem, who became commander of the Armored Force in May 1943, was an infantry officer and believed that no more than one-third of Shermans should have the 76-millimeter gun because of its less effective high-explosive round.[45]

The 76-millimeter gun also produced a muzzle blast so large that crews had trouble tracking the rounds in order to correct their aim. It was not until the M4A3E8 "Easy 8" was delivered in early 1945 that a muzzle brake—a pineapple-shaped device on the end of the gun tube with vents that diverted blast force to the sides—corrected the problem.

PARIS AND BEYOND: THE PURSUIT

After the closure of the Falaise Gap, the road race eastward truly began. On 19 August, Eisenhower made another major adjustment to the plan. Instead of stopping at the Seine River for three months in order to build up supplies, open ports, and build airfields, he decided to pursue the retreating Germans relentlessly on a broad front.[46] The First and Third Armies were to charge ahead. Eisenhower's decision to advance on a broad front led to months of friction with Montgomery, who wanted to stage a single thrust in the north all the way into Germany and cut off the Ruhr industrial basin.

The official U.S. Army history describes this period almost entirely as a series of movements rather than clashes. Contact with the enemy, whose forces were in disarray, was sporadic. The Germans tried to make a stand in only a few instances, usually at river crossings. Otherwise, American units faced scattered roadblocks or small rearguard actions that rarely lasted even a few hours. Many bridges were captured intact, and the Germans defended few towns and villages.[47] Only the armored division spearheads ran into serious fighting—even then highly localized—once the race began.

For the separate tank battalions, the action was essentially one of rapid pursuit of the enemy, who threw up defenses in the form of mined roadblocks, demolitions, and mobile strongpoints consisting of infantry, tanks, and self-propelled artillery.[48] The 743d Tank Battalion, for example, raced 123 miles on 19 and 20 August.[49] At one time, the battalion's point was only eight minutes behind the enemy's rear guard. The retreating column was frequently shelled, and the highway was littered with knocked-out vehicles and abandoned equipment. So fast was the advance that the Germans had no time to lay mines or do more than construct the simplest roadblocks.[50]

Aside from such occasional run-ins with German troops, the race eastward was a triumphant experience for the tankers. Locals mobbed them in every village, eager to greet their liberators with flowers, cheers, wine, and kisses from the girls. For once, fear was far away. Lt. Homer Wilkes recalled that on one occasion, none of the gunners in another 747th platoon were able to hit an escaping Tiger tank in full view because they were all inebriated.[51]

Paris fell on 25 August. Eisenhower had hoped to bypass and surround the city, but the French Resistance launched a rebellion that quickly got into trouble. They called for help. Free French leader Gen. Charles de Gaulle insisted on intervention, and he and the French 2d Armored Division commander, Maj. Gen. Jacque Leclerc, gave every indication that French troops under U.S. First Army command would disobey orders not to take the city. Eisenhower gave in.[52] For political reasons, the French 2d Armored Division was officially the first unit to enter Paris; Patton's Third Army had been poised to move earlier, but it had been ordered to stay to the south. Simultaneously, the 4th Infantry Division moved into the French capital, providing the 70th Tank Battalion with the unmatched opportunity to perform two days of "guard" duty in the center of a joyous and momentarily generous Parisian public. The tankers enjoyed the time—a great deal.[53]

The 741st Tank Battalion also got to Paris, and Capt. James Thornton and his men had great expectations when the word went around. "Paris was on everyone's lips," recalled Sgt. Bill Merk. "Paris, the ambition of any vacationer, playboy, or fashion expert!"[54] The tankers reached the city at 1015 on 29 August, where they formed up to participate in a parade through the city center. Along with doughs of the 28th Infantry Division, they rolled four tanks abreast down the Champs Elysee—and straight out the other end of Paris. They had orders to attack at 0730 the next day.[55]

Meanwhile, the 70th Tank Battalion sadly left the City of Light and was fully recommitted to battle on 27 August, a day during which it lost seven Shermans, one of its highest loss rates of the war. Perhaps hangovers played a role.[56]

On 8 September, the 712th Tank Battalion was in bivouac around Mairy, a village near Landres and not far from Metz, when it experienced the only real tank battle in the separate tank battalion annals during the race across northern France. At 0200 hours, about thirty-five Panthers and Mark IVs belonging to the 106th Panzer Brigade, accompanied by half-tracks bearing panzergrenadiers, stumbled into the bivouac area. George Bussel, whose Company A platoon was guarding the division's artillery position, watched in amazement as the column appeared out of the dark and the commander in the first German panzer leaned over the turret to read the sign pointing toward the 90th Infantry Division artillery command post. The Germans were on their way to Briey and had taken a wrong turn, though a bright moon lit the night. Four or five panzers, accompanied by about ten half-tracks, had approached the command post, while the rest of the column halted.

Lt. Lester O'Riley, commanding Company A, reported the German incursion to the battalion command post but said he was not opening fire because he was unsure of the enemy's strength and his tanks were poorly positioned. Nevertheless, shortly thereafter, Lt. Harry Bell's section of three Shermans fired on the Germans, who immediately replied. At least one Sherman exploded in flames (some accounts say two were knocked out), as did two Panthers.

The panzergrenadiers dismounted and attacked the American position, while the crew of the destroyed Sherman joined the artillerymen in a small-arms defense of the command post. When the Germans mounted a second attack at 0345 under cover of panzer cannon fire, Pvt. George Briggs climbed atop the crippled Sherman and fired the antiaircraft machine gun at the Germans. After an exchange of grenades around the artillery message center, the Germans drew off.

A confused fight flared until daybreak, during which time the division command post evacuated its nearby bivouac and ordered two rifle battalions into action. A platoon of Company C tanks moved into the division command post area, where two were hit and burned.

After daybreak, the German column ran into the 1st Battalion, 358th Infantry, which was responding to the summons to engage the enemy. The battalion had been told there were 100 German tanks, and because all the enemy vehicles were camouflaged with brush, the GIs at first thought that number to be true. The battalion commander called for all the artillery he could get, no matter how close it fell to his own positions. While shells ripped the German column, a heroic bazooka man worked his way to the head of the column and disabled the lead vehicle, which blocked the Germans on a sunken road. Three panzers and thirty-one half-tracks were destroyed in the trap.

At 1000 hours, two Panthers broke past the American tanks and headed for the tank battalion's command post. Guns from many directions turned on the panzers and knocked them out. Captured crewmen said that by this time they were trying to break out, not in.

About noon, three more panzers advanced on the glade where the Service Company was repairing tanks. As men scattered, maintenance officer Forrest Dixon and another man clambered into one of the Shermans. Doubting that the sights and main gun were aligned, Dixon waited until the lead German tank was only fifty yards away. The enemy's turret began to turn in his direction, so Dixon let him have it and called for help over the radio. The shell hit a bogie on the Panther, and it skewed to the left. Two other Shermans pumped 75-millimeter shells into its flank, and the German commander waved a white handkerchief and dismounted from his now burning panzer with his two surviving crewmates. Meanwhile, a towed tank destroyer crew that happened along unlimbered the gun with the help of some GIs and dispatched the other two panzers, though the tankers were firing on one of them, too, and also claimed the kill.

By the time the fighting finally died down, the 712th Tank Battalion and 90th Division had knocked out thirty German tanks and fifty-four half-tracks and had captured ten tanks, at least fifty half-tracks, and 764 enemy soldiers. The 712th Tank Battalion's own losses that day were a handful of men and four Shermans.[57]

The rapid advance across France took a tremendous toll on the equipment of the tank battalions despite the Sherman's remarkable durability. On 10 September, for example, the 749th Tank Battalion, advancing with the 8th Infantry Division, could muster only a composite platoon of five operational Shermans; all its other tanks were out of action for maintenance reasons. The battalion that day dispatched thirty trucks to Utah Beach or Cherbourg to find tank tracks, engines, and other needed spares. On 12 September, one of the battalion's five tanks hit a mine and a second broke down.[58] The First Army reacted to the shortage of tanks throughout armored formations by adopting a provisional table of organization and equipment that reduced the size of armored divisions and the separate tank battalions—in the latter case to fifty medium tanks.[59]

But while steel suffered, for a change human flesh did not to any great degree, except perhaps for those portions that sat in bouncing tank seats for hundreds of miles. During the entire race across France after 20 August, for example, the 743rd Tank Battalion lost only one man killed and two wounded.[60] The 741st Tank Battalion had only one man lightly wounded in the first two weeks of September.

The race across northern France ended by mid-September because of supply problems and successful German efforts to rally the shards of the Seventh Army along the German frontier, boosted by fortress battalions and other scanty reserves from inside the Reich. Patton's advance elements reached Metz on 1 September,[61] but Eisenhower's decision in August to throw most of the available logistic support behind Monty's advance along the coast starved the Third Army of fuel and other necessities, and the tanks ground to a halt. Patton improvised a bit by using captured German fuel.

Farther north in the First Army's zone, American columns had similar supply problems. By early September, the 743d Tank Battalion, whose tanks were the first to enter Belgium and the Netherlands, was rationing tank fuel and sending supply trucks far to the rear in search of more; on 12 September, the point halted because it had no more gas.[62] The 702d Tank Battalion noted in mid-September that the distance to its various supply points ranged from 100 to 500 miles.[63] That any fuel at all was reaching the advance elements was due to the tireless efforts of the famous Red Ball Express, which moved gasoline forward in five-gallon jerry cans on quartermaster trucks. By September, however, the Red Ball was approaching the point at which it burned more gas to reach the front than the trucks could carry.[64]

In any event, First Army elements reached prepared defensive positions in the Netherlands and the Siegfried Line along the German border by 11 September. There they slowed or stopped in the face of re-emergent German resistance.[65]

OPERATION DRAGOON: THE OTHER SHOE DROPS

On 15 August, the U.S. Seventh Army's VI Corps, drawn from the Italian campaign, landed on the southern coast of France. German forces in southern France under Army Group G, almost stripped of effective armored units and many of the best infantry divisions to help hold the line in Normandy, already confronted an untenable position as Patton raced across their rear toward the German border.

American forces faced generally light opposition from several infantry divisions belonging to the German Nineteenth Army as they came ashore near St. Tropez.[66] The three infantry divisions of the VI Corps—the 3d, the 36th, and the 45th—made up the invasion force, which was to be followed by four French divisions. Three tank battalions—the 191st, 753d, and 756th—were each equipped with the rough equivalent of one company of DD Shermans for the invasion. On D-Day, all three of the 191st Tank Battalion's DD platoons puttered to shore safely, although an entire platoon was immobilized by mines on Blue Beach after landing. Three DDs were total losses, and the platoon drew standard replacement tanks. In the 753d Tank Battalion, Company A's DDs were floated 4,000 yards offshore, and only one was lost temporarily when its screen was pierced by an antitank round, flooding the engine as the tank neared the beach.[67]

The 756th Tank Battalion lost two DDs from Company A when they hit underwater objects and their canvas tore. The commander of a third tank was killed

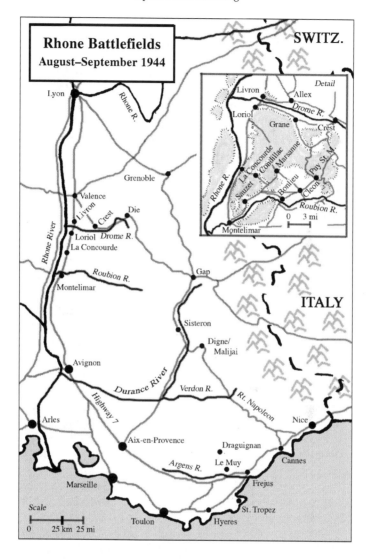

Rhone Battlefields
August–September 1944

by friendly fire as he perched atop the turret. All of Company B's DDs reached the beach, although one drowned out when the wake from a passing small vessel swamped the vehicle, which had dropped its screen to fire with the water halfway up the hull.[68]

Lt. Col. Glenn Rogers, the commander of the 756th Tank Battalion, opined that the DD tank's screen was far to vulnerable to enemy fire and that because the commander had to remain fully exposed, he was likely to be a casualty if resistance was fierce. "I believe that a different type of tank should be used in the assault waves—probably the 'amphtank' used in the Pacific."[69]

Lessons learned in Italy about the need for effective tank-infantry communications gave the Dragoon tankers a leg up. Each company commander's tank in the

191st Tank Battalion went ashore with an infantry SCR-300 radio installed in an armored box behind the turret. A shortage of such radios, however, prevented their use in platoon leaders' tanks. Meanwhile, the battalion gave the infantry regiments to which it was attached SCR-509 radios as a backup. The records of the 753d and 756th Tank Battalions provide no evidence that they adopted the same system.

The lesson of lasting partnership had also taken root. Maj. Gen. John "Iron Mike" O'Daniel, commanding the 3d Infantry Division, had put into practice the sentiments he had expressed to the War Department observer back in Italy. He had "claimed" the 756th Tank Battalion as his own. He required the tankers to wear the 3d Division patch on the shoulder opposite their armored force patch. David Redle recalled, "When we started with the 3rd [Division] in southern France, we had basic cooperation. As time went on, tankers had more and more concern about helping the infantry, and the infantry really developed a concern for our tanks' well being."[70]

On 17 August, Hitler instructed Army Group G to disengage from the enemy except for units occupying Marseille and Toulon and to withdraw northward to link up with the southern wing of Army Group B, which was reeling back before the Overlord forces. An initial order to withdraw elements not committed to the battle reached Army Group G on 17 August, and instructions for a total withdrawal arrived the next day. The 11th Panzer Division was to protect the Rhone Valley and serve as rearguard for the Nineteenth Army.[71]

The Seventh Army's plan called for an advance westward with two corps abreast to capture the major ports of Toulon and Marseille. But Maj. Gen. Lucian Truscott, the commander of the VI Corps, had his eye on a spot 100 miles to the north where high ground east of the Rhone River created a bottleneck near the town of Montelimar through which the Nineteenth Army would have to pass. Truscott expected the Germans to concentrate their forces to stop the Seventh Army's push westward, and he saw an opening to send a strike force toward Grenoble and from there to the high ground just upstream from Montelimar. No plan had foreseen such early exploitation, but Truscott had.[72]

Even before the landings, Truscott—denied an American armored division for the invasion—had decided to improvise a combat command, and on 1 August, he created a provisional armored group led by his assistant corps commander, Brig. Gen. Frederic Butler. This formation, generally referred to as Butler Task Force, consisted of the 2d Battalion, 143d Infantry Regiment; the 117th Cavalry Reconnaissance Squadron; the 753d Tank Battalion (reduced to two companies of medium tanks), under the command of Lt. Col. Joseph Felber; Company C, 636th Tank Destroyer Battalion; an armored field artillery battalion; and assorted other units. In strength, Butler Task Force closely approximated an American combat command, which was usually built around a battalion each of tanks and armored infantry. The command would form at Le Muy on order once the VI Corps was established ashore. Butler and his hastily gathered staff set to work planning for various contingencies, including an advance up the Route Napoleon toward Grenoble to block roads east of the Rhone River near Montelimar.[73]

Task Force Butler charged north toward Grenoble on 18 August. When the cavalry's light reconnaissance tanks and armored cars encountered too much German resistance to handle in Malijai and Digne the next day, a company of medium tanks and infantry lumbered up to provide the weight necessary to overcome the problems. The lead elements reached the town of Gap on 20 August, just as Truscott ordered Butler to move seventy miles westward through rough terrain to cut the highway along the Rhone.

Lt. Col. Joseph Felber, commanding the main column of armor and infantry, received orders at 0600 hours on 21 August to pass through Die and then, operating behind a reconnaissance screen, take the high ground overlooking the Rhone approximately three miles south of Livron. The lead reconnaissance elements—Troop B, 117th Cavalry Reconnaissance Squadron—reached the high ground by mid-afternoon.

Meanwhile, Felber Force rolled toward its objective over steep and winding roads, dropping elements here and there along the route to secure key junctions, and closed on Condillac at about 2145. After examining the terrain, Felber concluded he lacked the manpower to hold all of the high ground and decided to occupy hill masses to the north and south of the road running from Condillac down to La Concourde, where it intersected Highway 7 near the Rhone a few miles north of Montelimar. Felber had only a rifle company (less one squad), a heavy weapons company, a few antitank guns, a company of fourteen medium tanks, a handful of tank destroyers, an armored field artillery battalion (less one battery), and a company of noncombat engineers. Felber deployed his limited resources on the high ground and at a few strategic roadblocks, positioning four tank destroyers to command the Rhone road by fire. M7 Priests clanked into firing positions while forward observers made themselves comfortable, peering down on the German Nineteenth Army snaking northward below them. Felber obtained Butler's permission to outpost several more hills with Troop B of the 117th Cavalry Reconnaissance Squadron and met with the local Resistance commander, who supplied 200 men to assist in manning outposts and roadblocks.

By 2300 hours, Felber Force was in position.[74] The tankers and their comrades from the cavalry, infantry, and artillery had beaten most of the Nineteenth Army to the pass.

The sky gradually lightened enough on the morning of 22 August that the tank and tank destroyer gunners of Felber Force could see through their sights, and the men were delighted to observe a target-rich environment of German vehicles below them crawling past hulks destroyed by shelling during the night. Gunners gleefully added so much new wreckage that it temporarily blocked the highway.[75] There were many smaller paths parallel to the highway, however, so that German movement never ceased entirely.

Slowly, additional formations swelled the ranks of Butler Task Force—the missing armored field artillery battery, plus another column including six more tank destroyers. But as Butler later observed, "the Germans were building up against me faster than were our own forces building up."[76]

Artillery, tanks, tank destroyers, armored cars, and even the infantry's 57-millimeter antitank guns rained death on Highway 7 during the long daylight hours. The 59th Armored Field Artillery Battalion smashed several trains, which blocked the rail line on the east bank of the river. Two trains carried munitions and put on a display of amazing pyrotechnics as they burned.

Butler's main concern that day turned out not to be the Rhone highway, but rather German efforts to advance along the north bank of the Roubion River and thence northeastward across his rear, which Felber now protected with a small reserve force. Five Panthers supported by panzergrenadiers smashed a roadblock at Cleon and rolled toward Puy St. Martin, where Felber had his command post. Felber had only a few tank destroyers at hand, which engaged the Germans, but the Shermans and tank destroyers on the road from Gap—which were to form the core of his reserve—had not yet arrived. A cub artillery plane was dispatched to drop a message of dire need to the column. Butler described what happened next: "[O]ur rescue column arrived for a movie finish. The German tanks that had crossed the Roubion were destroyed, the infantry were driven back, and on the south bank several fires burned merrily where our guns had found trucks and light vehicles. It was a good honest fight. The reserves had arrived in the nick of time."

The arrival of Panthers and panzergrenadiers was a sure sign that the 11th Panzer Division was joining the battle. Receiving word that infantry was on the way from the 36th Division, Butler assured Felber that he would soon have help for his overextended reserve. But after the day's combat, Butler Task Force was down to twenty-five rounds of artillery ammunition per tube—half Butler's desired minimum. Fire ceased until supplies arrived after dark.[77]

When the tired GIs from the 141st Infantry finally arrived late that day, Felber's tanks and Company C, 636th Tank Destroyer Battalion, were attached to the regiment to provide general support.[78] The stage was set for the battle of Montelimar.[79]

Butler Task Force was dissolved at 0900 on 23 August, and at 1530, Felber turned command of his sector over to the 141st Infantry.[80] The tankers thereafter shuttled about supporting the doughboys where needed.

Although the 36th Infantry Division never completely blocked the escape route up the Rhone, by the time the 3d Infantry Division and 756th Tank Battalion pushed up Highway 7 to Montelimar in the wake of the retreating enemy, the Americans had badly hurt the Germans. Army Group G would report on 22 September that 209,000 men had left southern and southwestern France and that only 130,000 of them had escaped.[81] The Nineteenth Army had lost 1,316 of its 1,480 guns.[82]

The "Champagne Campaign," as critics called it, cost the U.S. Seventh Army 2,733 men killed, wounded, or captured to reach Lyon on 2 September. Casualties in the tank battalions were correspondingly modest despite an assault landing and 500-mile advance. The 756th Tank Battalion, for example, lost twenty-five men killed and thirty-seven wounded between 15 August and 15 September. During August, the 191st Tank Battalion had lost twenty-four tanks and fifty-four men killed, wounded, or missing.[83]

On 20 September, the VI Corps set out to force the Moselle River but found that the Germans were no longer running. They now held the VI Corps, dangling at the end of a long supply line, before the Belfort Gap in the Vosges Mountains west of the German border.[84] The 756th Tank Battalion reported in September, "Enemy defended approaches to Belfort Gap. . . . As enemy moved back into the hills, he began using considerable numbers of antitank mines. Enemy used few tanks, but employed considerable numbers of antitank and SP [self-propelled] guns. Enemy resistance stiffened as the terrain grew more favorable for defense, and artillery fire increased in intensity."[85]

Weather and terrain aided the Germans. The 191st Tank Battalion's after-action report recorded in October, "Continued rainfall rendered the surrounding territory unfit for cross-country maneuver. In addition, much of the action took place in densely wooded areas, where the employment of tanks was extremely dangerous."[86] It was just like being back in Italy.

The tankers had tangled with the Mark V Panthers of the 11th Panzer Division nearly all the way up the Rhone Valley, the first time they had encountered the deadly panzer in any numbers. The experience was sobering, as it had been for tankers in Normandy. Maj. Welborn Dolvin, the commanding officer of the 191st Tank Battalion, summarized the tanker's point of view in August 1944 after his outfit had been in action in France for only two weeks: "The Sherman tank, equipped with the 75mm gun, is no match for . . . the German Mark IV, V, or VI. On numerous occasions, hits were obtained on German tanks with no noticeable results. On the other hand, German high-velocity tank guns never failed to penetrate the Sherman tank. This situation has a tremendous effect on the morale of the tank crews. This was evidenced by reluctance of crews to fire on German tanks, feeling that it would do no good and would result in their being promptly knocked out."[87]

On 1 September, the 191st Tank Battalion expressed concern that long road marches and shortages of spares were forcing the battalion to continue using worn-out tank tracks.[88] By the second week of September, fuel shortages were hampering the advance.[89] The 753d Tank Battalion also reported near-critical shortages of tracks, support rollers, bogie wheels, and tank engines during September. On 6 September, the battalion's commander warned the commanding general of the 36th Infantry Division that his tanks would not be operational after two more days of movement unless parts could be obtained. At mid-month, Company C had only three tanks that would run.[90] But the problem was supply, not the tank. The 756th

Tank Battalion concluded, "The M4 tank has proved itself very reliable mechanically. Our tanks traveled some 1,200 miles between 15 August and 15 October, with relatively few mechanical failures."[91]

As German resistance toughened, the 753d Tank Battalion was hit in September by another shortage that soon would trouble tank battalions farther north: qualified replacement personnel. Since the Dragoon landing through September, the battalion had lost sixteen tank commanders and seventeen drivers; these positions required crucial skills, and the battalion had shifted its surviving veterans to fill them after heavy losses in Italy during May and June. In September, the battalion had to "deadline" operational tanks because of crew shortages.[92] According to the 756th Tank Battalion, "Replacements continue to be poorly trained. Approximately fifty percent of replacements have to be trained for their jobs after being received."[93]

CHAPTER 10

Hitting the West Wall .

"The reality of war was grimly present once more. . . . [T]he Germans showed a frantic—and fanatical—determination to throw up some semblance of a line. . . . By 12 September, the First Army's sustained drive had been stopped. The war settled down to a foot-soldier's walk again. Ahead was some of the bitterest fighting of the war."
—Wayne Robinson, *Move Out, Verify*

The officially recognized U.S. Army campaigns in northern and southern France, characterized by rapid movement, ended on 14 September 1944; on 15 September, the Rhineland Campaign began, a slugfest that dragged on, by official count, until 21 March of the next year.

The First Army's three corps butted up against the Siegfried Line between 13 and 19 September. Gen. William Simpson's Ninth Army, shifted from Brittany, took over control of the northernmost part of this sector on 22 October. In the Third Army's zone, Patton's troops had just breached the Moselle River line by 14 September but faced a shortage of most supplies and an order to go onto the defensive as of 25 September. Patton nevertheless was determined to knock through the fortifications around Metz that stood between him and the Siegfried Line.[1] On Patton's right flank, Seventh Army troops were stuck in the rough, forested terrain of the Vosges Mountains.

From north to south, the separate tank battalions faced broadly similar challenges in the next phase of the conflict. Tanks were committed against prepared—and often fortified—German positions where, lacking room for maneuver and heavy punch, they were at their least effective. Infantry and tankers had no training to deal with this and found themselves enrolled in another school of hard knocks.

The weather was horrible, which magnified most other problems. The fall and winter of 1944 produced weather of near-record severity, first in the form of mud-producing rain and then snow and unusually harsh temperatures.[2]

Instead of fighting a hedgerow-by-hedgerow battle, the doughs and tankers found themselves embroiled in a fortification-by-fortification, strongpoint-by-strongpoint struggle. Having experienced—and mastered—the first type of warfare, they quickly adapted to the new circumstances. Moreover, a more tightly integrated and effective combined-arms team was emerging in units that had spent time together in battle; the team integrated infantry, tanks, artillery, tank destroyers, and airpower into a package that could bore through the defenses. For example, with ever-greater frequency, after-action reports show tanks and tank destroyers working together (a great rarity in Normandy). More battalions began to put officers in artillery planes from which they could spot German tanks, guns, and other elements and coordinate action on the ground.[3] And a tank battalion could now expect to have its commanding officer at the front and officers equipped with tank radios at the infantry's battalion, regiment, and division headquarters. The worst experiences occurred in circumstances, such as the dense Hürtgen Forest, where the entire package could not come into play simultaneously.

The U.S. Army's official history goes too far, however, in describing the infantry-tank-artillery teams at this time as "close-knit families, into which had been adopted the fighter-bomber," that possessed an "almost reflexive knowledge of how to fight this kind of war."[4] American troops were frequently shot up by their own planes.[5] Disconnects between infantry and tanks continued to occur, and infantry commanders still sometimes made bad calls on the use of tanks.

Units had to work at keeping the team functioning because there was no reflexive knowledge. The main change from Normandy days was that both infantry and tankers better understood that they had to work out solutions together in order to survive and win.

THE SIEGFRIED LINE

The West Wall, construction of which began in 1936, ran nearly 400 miles from north of Aachen along the German frontier to the Swiss border. The Germans had neglected the defenses after 1940, so Hitler now worked furiously to put together a scratch force of 135,000 men to partially rebuild and man the line as the Allies approached the border. The strongest portion faced Patton along the Saar River between the Moselle and the Rhine. The second most formidable section was a double band of defenses protecting the Aachen Gap, with the city of Aachen lying between the two. Immediately behind the West Wall in this sector was the Roer River, which gave the Germans a backstop that they could flood from three dams farther south near Schmidt.[6]

Pillboxes in the West Wall typically had reinforced concrete walls and roofs three to eight feet thick and were generally twenty to thirty feet wide, forty to fifty feet deep, and twenty to twenty-five feet high, with at least half the structure underground. In some areas, rows of dragon's teeth—reinforced concrete pyramids—acted as antitank obstacles. In other areas, defenses relied on natural features—rivers, lakes, forests, defiles, and so on—to provide passive antitank protection.[7]

The woods that covered most of the Siegfried Line could work to the advantage of the tankers. Maj. William Campbell, who fought with the 745th Tank Battalion in the Aachen area, observed that the trees dramatically reduced the fields of fire available to German antitank gunners, and tanks could often safely work their way as close as fifty yards to the fortifications they were to bombard.[8]

LEARNING TO TACKLE THE WEST WALL

On 11 September, the First Army authorized the V Corps on the right and the VII Corps on the left to conduct a "reconnaissance in force" with the aim of breaching the Siegfried Line before the Germans could fully prepare their defenses. The V Corps' operation committed three divisions, the 28th and 4th Infantry and 5th Armored, which were spread out over a wide front and feeling the effects of the long advance across France. They faced rough terrain in the Schnee Eifel, a thickly forested highland. The VII Corps threw the 1st Infantry and 3d Armored Divisions, paralleled by the 9th Infantry Division, against Aachen from the south in anticipation of an eventual pincer move from the north by the 30th Infantry Division.[9]

Another unwelcome learning experience began. American tankers had never trained to assault fortifications before actually seeing them. The tankers discovered that their cannons were unable to knock out most bunkers. Even the 105-millimeter howitzers on the assault guns proved unable to destroy the pillboxes.[10] After trying, they soon realized that their main contribution was to keep the defenders down by firing at embrasures and using tankdozers to cover up the doors and embrasures of captured pillboxes. Here was another puzzle to be solved along with the doughs, the tank destroyers, and the artillery. Air support would prove practically worthless.

In the 28th Infantry Division's sector from 14 to 16 September, the attack painfully poked a pencil-like hole through the West Wall at the cost of 1,500 casualties—losses so high that they precluded exploitation.[11] Tanks had a great deal of trouble maneuvering off the roads because of the torrential rains that had fallen.[12]

The attached 741st Tank Battalion participated in one of the first assaults on the West Wall. On 14 September at 0930 hours, Capt. James Thornton ordered two platoons of Company B into motion to support the 2d Battalion of the 109th Infantry. His goal, the high ground southeast of Harsfelt, lay 1,500 yards ahead. Thornton deployed one platoon on each side of the road ahead, knowing that it was sure to be mined. Heavy fire from pillboxes and two sturdy houses swept the area. His crews advanced methodically, taking each strongpoint under fire. Then came an unexpected setback: an antitank ditch barred the way. Thornton radioed for one of the tankdozers to fill in a space wide enough for his Shermans to cross. This was soon accomplished. Thornton, looking around, realized that the enemy fire had become so heavy that the infantry had gone to ground. He ordered the Company B tankers to press ahead alone. Soon the high ground was his, and the infantry was able to join the Shermans on the objective.

At 1600 hours, Thornton's radio crackled to life. Regiment wanted him to lead a platoon of tanks to support his 3rd Platoon in the neighboring battalion's sector, where his boys had already lost two Shermans. Thornton quickly decided that the quickest route lay through the German defenses, so he set off to shoot his way past. His gamble cost him two tanks and three men, but Thornton made it. The ranking infantry officer ordered Thornton to lead an attack over the next hill. Thornton took the point and ordered his tanks to advance once again. The Shermans crested the rise. Suddenly, Thornton's tank rocked under a massive blow, followed by two more in quick succession. Fragments of the antitank shells and armor ricocheted like angry hornets inside the tank. Thornton was blown from the turret and badly injured. An infantry captain—an old friend and classmate from The Citadel—saw Thornton, pulled him away from the burning tank, and left two men to protect him. The Germans counterattacked, however, and that was the last Thornton was seen alive.[13] Only one crewman, the gunner, would make it back to American lines.

Not too far away, 2d Lt. Joseph Dew, commanding the 1st Platoon of Company C, 741st Tank Battalion, led his Shermans toward the staggered rows of dragon's teeth. The bocage fighting had claimed every one of the company's platoon leaders; Dew—a tall, straightforward man—was one of the replacements. Dew recorded his first major engagement in an after-action report:

On 14 September, [we] moved into position at 0840 hours southeast of Grosskampenberg. The 1st Platoon moved up on the right side of the road to the edge of the dragon's teeth and placed direct AP [armor-piercing] and HE [high-explosive] fire on two pillboxes at four hundred yards. We then placed a few HE on a small clump of trees just over the dragon's teeth and then placed fire on three pillboxes to the left front at ranges from 700 to 1,200 yards.

We waited until 0915 for the engineers to come up and blow a way through the dragon's teeth, and when they failed to arrive my tank pulled within a few feet of the concrete pillars and fired AP point-blank at them. About 0925 my tank went through and the rest of my platoon followed. We moved up to the pillboxes and fired AP and HE at them, point-blank. Then we moved ahead and over the hill. There were two pillboxes on our right at about two o'clock, and we fired on them. I heard AP whistle around the tank and then saw an antitank gun directly ahead of us by a building about eight hundred yards away. We blew that one up and swung towards the town. We saw another antitank gun by the corner of the building and blew the corner off the building firing at it, but I'm sure we didn't hit the gun for I saw it pull back. Then Captain Young called me and said an antitank gun had knocked out one of my tanks behind me,

Crewmen of a 192d Tank Battalion M3 light tank watch the 26th Cavalry, Philippine Scouts, pass in December 1941. Both outfits would soon give battle to Japanese invaders. SIGNAL CORPS PHOTO

The Army knew before the United States entered the war that it would have to put tanks on hostile shores. Tank lighters, such as this one participating in a 1st Division landing exercise in August 1941, could only carry light tanks, in this case an M2A4, which had to be hoisted from transports. SIGNAL CORPS PHOTO

M5 light tanks belonging to the 756th Tank Battalion (Light) await loading for the journey to North Africa for Operation Torch. They are waterproofed and fitted with wading stacks much like those that will be used in amphibious landings for the rest of the war. SIGNAL CORPS PHOTO

An M3 medium tank belonging to Company A, 751st Tank Battalion (Medium), engages in street fighting in Bizerte, Tunisia, on 8 May 1943. The separate tank battalions saw little action except during the first and last days of the North Africa campaign. SIGNAL CORPS FILM

Mountainous terrain such as this near Mistretta, Sicily, in August 1943 greatly limited the use of tanks on the island and the Italian mainland. Usually, German artillery observers had views like this over Allied troops below. SIGNAL CORPS PHOTO

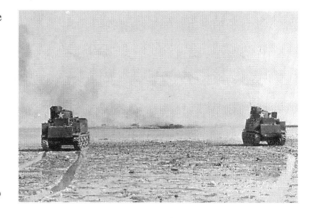

M3 tanks shell the Japanese at King's Wharf, Makin Atoll, on 21 November 1943. These Lees belong to Company A, 193d Tank Battalion. The first tank battalion to go on the offensive against Japan, the outfit equipped one company with M3 mediums, one with M3 light tanks, and one with amtracs. SIGNAL CORPS PHOTO

Tanks from the 191st or 751st Tank Battalion debark across a pontoon from an LST at Salerno on 9 September 1943. This method, also used in the Sicily landings, was slow and vulnerable to enemy fire. SIGNAL CORPS PHOTO

A 767th Tank Battalion Sherman works with 7th Infantry Division doughs on Kwajalein in February 1944. A field phone is mounted on the left-rear fender, one of the first experiments in improving tank-infantry communications. U.S. ARMY PHOTO

GIs from the 37th Infantry Division on Bougainville advance behind a Sherman belonging to the 754th Tank Battalion on 16 March 1944. They are using a formation developed on the island for jungle warfare, with target designators at the rear corners of the Sherman and riflemen, BAR men, and engineers in a wedge behind. SIGNAL CORPS PHOTO

An Army amtrac carries Marines toward what appears to be the O-1 phase line on Saipan on 15 June 1944. More armored force men participated in the Saipan landings than in D-Day.
MARINE CORPS PHOTO

70th Tank Battalion Shermans load onto a landing craft, tank (LCT), in Kingswear, England, on 1 June 1944. These Company C tanks beat the amphibious duplex drive tanks to Utah Beach in Normandy on 6 June, a screw-up that worked out well. SIGNAL CORPS PHOTO

Infantrymen shelter behind a hedgerow while an M4A1 tank fires at the next one. For both partners, the bocage was a checkerboard hell. SIGNAL CORPS FILM

LVT(A)(1) (left) and LVT(A)(4) amtanks belonging to Company D, 708th Amphibian Tank Battalion, line up to attack with the Marines on Saipan in June 1944. MARINE CORPS PHOTO

Amphibious duplex-drive M4A1s from the 70th Tank Battalion sit on Utah Beach on 6 June 1944. The Allies used DD tanks in Operations Overlord and Dragoon and in the Rhine crossing.
SIGNAL CORPS PHOTO

All six M4A3 105-millimeter assault guns from a tank battalion fire in battery in France in mid-July 1944. The 105-millimeter assault gun served in standard tank battalions, though outfits in Italy and the Pacific made do with the M7 self-propelled howitzer until late 1944.
SIGNAL CORPS PHOTO

GIs take cover as advancing troops encounter fire at the Siegfried Line near Aachen on 15 September 1944. Supply lines are stretched to the breaking point, and this crew hauls along spare gasoline. SIGNAL CORPS PHOTO

Lieutenant General George Patton Jr. takes a picture of a demonstration of the E4-5 hull-mounted flamethrower that began reaching tank battalions in September 1944. The flame unit was also used in the Pacific theater. SIGNAL CORPS PHOTO

LVT(A)(4)s fire indirectly. From the Leyte landings in October 1944, doctrine increasingly favored using amtanks as artillery after the initial assault, but reality kept pulling them back into combat. SIGNAL CORPS FILM

Two 12th SS Panzer Division Panthers knocked out during the fighting in Krinkelt, Belgium, beginning 17 December 1944. SIGNAL CORPS PHOTO

M8 75-millimeter assault guns, which replaced the half-track-based T-30 in 1943, fought with the light tank battalions, briefly with medium battalions in Italy, and with a few standard battalions in the Pacific. These are firing in battery near Hürtgen, Germany, in December 1944. SIGNAL CORPS PHOTO

LVT(4)s of the 658th Amphibian Tractor Battalion carry 40th Division assault troops ashore at Lingayen, Luzon Island, on 9 January 1945. Troops encountered virtually no resistance at the shoreline. SIGNAL CORPS FILM

The mortar platoon in light, medium, and standard tank battalions used half-track-mounted 81-millimeter mortars such as this M4A1 mortar carrier, at work in Belgium in early 1945. Some outfits made good use of the platoon, but many did not. SIGNAL CORPS PHOTO

M4A1 Shermans roll through Manila on 23 February 1945. In ten days of street fighting, Company B, 44th Tank Battalion, expended 3,500 rounds of 75-millimeter and 183,000 rounds of .30-caliber ammunition.
U.S. NAVY PHOTO

The M24 Chaffee light tank and the M5 that it replaced, both belonging to the 744th Tank Battalion (Light). The 740th Tank Battalion first used two M24s in battle when it found them at a replacement depot during the Battle of the Bulge. SIGNAL CORPS PHOTO

A barely recognizable 740th Tank Battalion Sherman attacks toward Heeresbach, Belgium, on 28 January 1945 with the 82d Airborne Division's 504th Parachute Infantry Regiment. "At a distance of fifty yards it was impossible to tell what kind of a vehicle it was—even if you determined that it actually was a vehicle," said the battalion commander. SIGNAL CORPS PHOTO

A 750th Tank Battalion Sherman works with 415th Infantry Regiment doughs in Cologne on 6 March 1945. Tankers and GIs time and again disproved early-war doctrine that tanks should not fight in cities. SIGNAL CORPS PHOTO

78th Infantry Division doughboys ride Shermans from the 741st Tank Battalion toward the Rhine River on 9 March 1945. SIGNAL CORPS PHOTO

702d Tank Battalion Sherman tanks with new sixty-tube rocket assemblies attached operate near the Siegfried Line with the 80th Infantry Division on 17 March 1945. Launchers were also used in Italy, but not in the Pacific. SIGNAL CORPS PHOTO

The M4A3E2 Jumbo assault Sherman appeared only in the European theater. The 750th Tank Battalion added a layer of concrete to the Tiger-tank-thick front armor on this Jumbo, seen on the road to Halle in April 1945. SIGNAL CORPS FILM

A 757th Tank Battalion M4A3 (76-millimeter) crosses the Po River on 26 April 1945. After soldiering with the oldest tanks in the arsenal into 1944, tankers in Italy caught up with their counterparts in the European theater by early 1945. SIGNAL CORPS PHOTO

781st Tank Battalion Shermans reach the frontier in Brenner Pass, where the Seventh Army linked up with the Fifth Army, on 4 May 1945. The Easy 8 (left) was the final stage of the Sherman's development, but tankers still resorted to sandbagging for better armor protection. SIGNAL CORPS PHOTO

A 713th Tank Battalion flame tank sprays down a Japanese position on Okinawa on 17 May 1945. Flame tanks played a larger role on Okinawa than in any other campaign. SIGNAL CORPS PHOTO

A Sherman from Company B, 775th Tank Battalion, works with 37th Infantry Division doughs on 12 June 1945 in Luzon's Cagayan Valley in the Philippines. The tankers proved they could work in rugged jungle terrain that nobody had ever imagined at the start of the war. SIGNAL CORPS PHOTO

so we pulled back to get him. The gun that got the tank was in the woods to the right and we put three rounds of HE at it at four hundred yards and blew it up. We covered the wounded until they were dragged behind the pillbox where they were temporarily safe. One of my tanks pulled back across the dragon's teeth to get a round out of his 75mm gun, and my tank sat by one pillbox and the other tank of [my] platoon sat by the other one. We waited until 1230 for the infantry to come up and take the pillbox, because they were full of Heinies. But the infantry didn't come and it finally got so hot with AP that Captain Young pulled us out of there.

The following account from the 3d Armored Group's after-action report for September captures the nature of the battle and the attempts on both sides to adapt to it:

On 15 September this headquarters with two tank battalions, the 741st and 747th, was attached to the 28th Infantry Division and on 17 September, with the support of the 110th Infantry and Division engineers, was designated as Task Force M and given the mission of widening the gap forced in the Siegfried Line between Heckhuscheid and Groskampenberg, Germany; the 108th Field Artillery Battalion provided artillery support. Due to the reduced strength of the infantry at this time the bulk of the force was to be composed of tanks, with one infantry company (at very reduced strength) in support of each tank battalion. Each of the tank battalions had an average of thirty-five medium tanks. Each was formed into composite companies. To these assault companies in each battalion were attached the tankdozers, and all available assault guns were placed in support in direct-fire position.

The general plan of attack was for the tanks to assault a position and, as soon as the fire superiority had been gained, the infantry would move out and occupy the position until a tankdozer had covered the embrasures and entrances to the pillbox. An artillery observer from the 108th Field Artillery Battalion accompanied the group commander and group S-3 to the forward OP [observation post] in the Siegfried Line in order to direct supporting artillery fire; it had been found that direct radio communication between the forward OP and fire control headquarters was unreliable, so one of the three SCR-508s at the group CP [command post] acted as a relay station. . . .

The enemy had all the advantages that go with a well-planned defensive line: terrain favorable to the defenders, direct observation, thick concrete pillboxes, and underground telephone communications. The mutual support provided by enemy pillboxes was particularly effective against the attacking troops. Yet, notwithstanding the many important disadvantages it faced, Task Force M made progress, and reduced the enemy line pillbox by pillbox.

The first day's operation, on 19 September, resulted in the capture of twenty-nine enemy pillboxes. Very heavy accurate enemy mortar and artillery concentrations were received by the attacking units throughout the day; it was evident that the enemy had direct observation and excellent communications between pillboxes. The captured pillboxes were either blown up by engineer demolition squads or locked and covered up with dirt by tankdozers to prevent the enemy from reoccupying them should he reinfiltrate the position.

On 20 September, twelve enemy pillboxes were captured and rendered unusable; heavy enemy mortar and artillery fire again caused trouble. On 21 September, Company I, 110th Infantry Regiment, replaced Company L; during the day's operations ten pillboxes were captured, under extremely heavy mortar and artillery concentrations, which pinned down the attacking infantry time after time. Dive-bombers supported Task Force M on 22 September, but poor visibility caused the results to be unsatisfactory; the first strike missed the pillbox targets by at least one thousand yards, and two near-hits on the second strike did not damage the pillboxes at all. Although hindered by antitank mines and the usual heavy, accurate enemy mortar and artillery fire, the task force succeeded in capturing and sealing five pillboxes.

In four days of operation this task force covered forty-nine pillboxes, sixteen of which were either unoccupied or previously taken and located in the area held by the infantry, and the remainder of which were captured by the task force and destroyed by the engineers. The bulk of these were captured during the first two days of combat for, as objectives were limited, the enemy grasped our method of operations and stationed men armed with bazookas in foxholes in the vicinity and on top of pillboxes.

Bunker-busting was dangerous work. During the fighting between 23 and 25 September, the 747th Tank Battalion lost probably ten men killed (crew members in tanks that burned were often listed as missing in action because they left no remains) and four wounded. After losing only one man during the last two weeks of the race across France, the 741st Tank Battalion suffered the loss of eighteen men killed and twenty men wounded during the first two weeks on the Siegfried Line.

South of the 28th Infantry Division's sector, the 4th Infantry and 5th Armored Divisions rolled through the West Wall in areas that were either weakly held or undefended by German units that were, in some cases, just arriving at the front. Both thrusts pulled up, however, because the rough and forested terrain and the villages behind the fortifications offered nearly as good a position to the gradually jelling German resistance and and because the still-critical logistic situation compelled the First Army and the V Corps to call a halt. On 22 September, the V Corps went over to the defensive. The relative inactivity that followed lasted until mid-December.[14]

A HOT IDEA

The U.S. Army had put some thought into equipment that might make tanks more effective against the fortified line that loomed ahead. Presumably inspired by the British Crocodile flamethrower tanks mounted on the Churchill chassis, the army decided to install flamethrowers in tanks already in combat. It had first investigated the idea during the Normandy fighting, but delays put the concept on hold.[15] In fact, U.S. Headquarters in the European theater had received four Crocodile-style Shermans built for it by the British in early 1944; eventually, these were deployed by the 739th Tank Battalion (Special, Mine Exploder [MX]), but the project had been dropped by August.[16]

The E4-5 equipment selected for use by most outfits put a nozzle in the place of the hull machine gun, and the storage tanks containing compressed air and fifty gallons of the fuel sat behind the bow gunner, who operated the weapon.[17] This system was capable of using crankcase oil mixed with gasoline, Naphthaline mixed with gasoline, or British fuel.[18] The E4-5 had first been used in combat by marine corps tanks on Guam in July.[19]

On orders from Maj. Gen. J. Lawton Collins of the V Corps, the 3d Armored Group recommended on 4 September that the 70th Tank Battalion serve as the test bed for the new flamethrowers.[20] The battalion received its first four units on 11 September, and the hardware spread gradually through other outfits.[21]

Tankers were divided over the utility of the American-style flamethrowers, which an after-action report of the 743d Tank Battalion described as "calculated to make the enemy burn with more than embarrassment." One tanker who fielded the hardware in the 70th Tank Battalion recalls having used it to good effect against pillboxes.[22] The after-action report for the 741st Tank Battalion, however, records for 18–19 September, "A flamethrower tank was used on one pillbox, but flamethrower had to approach within twenty yards of the box, and even then the flame was very unsatisfactory." Tankers in the 747th Tank Battalion realized that the flamethrower and the German bazooka had similar ranges, which made them loath to use the gear in battle against strongpoints. Another drawback of the system was that the equipment eliminated the ammunition rack behind the assistant driver.[23]

The army finally conceded that there was virtually no evidence that the E4-5 had made a contribution in battle that could not have been achieved with the bow machine gun or a white phosphorous round.[24] Nevertheless, battalions continued to be issued flamethrowers for months.

THE AUTUMN STALEMATE

October marked the beginning of a bitter war of attrition that would characterize the fighting in Europe until mid-December. Lt. Gen. Omar Bradley focused on two priorities: pushing the First Army forward near Aachen, Germany, with the goal of reaching the Rhine River at Cologne; and using the Third Army to reduce the fortifications at Metz, France.[25]

Painful Aachen

Aachen would be the first major German city to fall to the Allies as well as a superb demonstration of the fact that one could, in fact, use tanks effectively in urban warfare. The First Army's VII Corps attacked from the south, while its XIX Corps formed the other jaw of a pincer to the north. Once the two corps had encircled Aachen, the 1st Infantry Division was to storm the city.

To the north, in the XIX Corps' sector, the attack to break through the Siegfried Line and envelope Aachen kicked off on 2 October, spearheaded by the 30th Infantry Division and the attached 743d Tank Battalion. The 2d Armored Division stood by as the exploitation force.[26] The doughs moved forward and easily penetrated the fortifications. The tanks, however, sank into mud just across the narrow Würm River, which they crossed using a culvert-type hasty bridge designed by the battalion's own Captain Miller and the engineers, and it was not until nightfall that the Shermans were able to close with the infantry. By 7 October, the division had carved out a bridgehead beyond the West Wall that was four and a half miles deep and six miles wide.[27]

The good news ended there, and the struggle around Aachen became the bloodiest experienced by the 743d Tank Battalion after the battle of the hedgerows in Normandy. German resistance became ferocious as reinforcements arrived. Nine more days of heavy fighting were necessary before a 30th Infantry Division patrol hooked up with 1st Infantry Division troops on Ravel Hill, completing the encirclement of Aachen.[28] During October, the 743d Tank Battalion lost twenty of its Shermans, one light tank, and one assault gun while destroying three Tigers, eleven Panthers, five Mark IVs, twenty antitank guns, two armored cars, and two heavy artillery pieces. The battalion suffered thirteen officers and sixty-two enlisted men wounded in action, twenty enlisted men killed in action, and seven enlisted men missing in action during the period—nearly all from the medium tank companies.[29]

In the VII Corps' zone, the 3d Armored Division attacked in the center, with the 1st Infantry Division (with the 745th Tank Battalion attached) on the left oriented to envelop Aachen from the south and the 9th Infantry Division (with the 746th Tank Battalion attached) on the right. Seeking to regain momentum, the 1st Infantry Division launched its drive to close the ring around Aachen on 8 October. Hitler ordered the defenders—about 4,000 men backed by assault guns—to hold the historic city, the seat of Charlemagne's First Reich, at all costs.

Once the 1st and 30th Infantry Divisions closed the ring around Aachen, subduing the city fell to Col. John Seitz's 26th Infantry Regiment, which had only two battalions available for the job. The assault force was substantially outnumbered in terms of men, but it enjoyed a huge advantage in armor, artillery, and air support. The regiment attacked from east to west through the city.

Lt. Col. Derrill Daniel's 2d Battalion of the 26th Infantry—backed by tank destroyers from Company A of the 634th Tank Destroyer Battalion and tanks from the 745th Tank Battalion—had the dubious honor of clearing the south and center of Aachen. While dug in on the outskirts prior to the assault, Daniel had used the tanks as "snipers" against machine-gun nests and the tank destroyers to blow up buildings suspected of harboring observation posts.[30] But now he had to take the buildings.

Daniel's battalion had been conducting limited attacks for days to clear structures along the outskirts before moving into the city itself. Initially, Daniel assigned a mixed force of three or more Shermans and two tank destroyers to support each infantry company. The armor's job was to blast ahead of the infantry, drive the enemy into cellars, and generally "scare the hell out of them." Tanks and tank destroyers had prearranged infantry protection, but small-arms fire forced the doughs to move cautiously, dashing from door to door and hole to hole.

Meanwhile, Lt. Col. John Corley's 3d Battalion cleared a factory district on the east side of the city, and Shermans and M10s played backup. When the doughs came under fire, a tank or tank destroyer returned fire until the riflemen moved in and cleared the building with grenades.

The two battalions launched their attack on the city proper on 13 October. Companies F and G from the 2d Battalion each had three Shermans and one M10 attached, while Company H had three tanks and two tank destroyers. The armor had difficulty negotiating embankments along the main rail line that cut across the 2d Battalion's front. Several successfully slid down a ten-foot bank, while others went under the tracks near the Aachen–Rothe Erde train station only fifteen yards from the main underpass, where the men could see German demolitions installed.[31]

Daniel soon developed a more frugal tactical approach for the urban fighting: one or two tanks or tank destroyers went into action beside each infantry platoon. The armor would keep each successive building under fire until the riflemen moved in to assault it. The crews normally fired high-explosive rounds on fuse-delay through doors, windows, or thin walls to explode inside. They usually shot with no target visible, just in case a foe lurked there. Each armored vehicle expended an average of fifty rounds of high explosive daily.

The GIs would then advance about 100 yards ahead of the armored vehicle to protect it from *panzerfaust* attack, searching buildings on both sides of the street for enemy troops. When the riflemen spotted an antitank gun, they gave the tank commander precise details so he could pull swiftly into position and dispatch it. Four doughboys were assigned to each tank commander to provide close-in support and act as runners to keep the tankers informed as to the infantry's position.

At each intersection, the armor fired on all four corners before the infantry crossed the street. The presence of tanks gave the GIs greater confidence, as they knew that cannon and machine-gun fire were available in only seconds if the Germans opened up on them.

Only when a building was cleared and the doughs were safe from the muzzle blast would the tank or tank destroyer fire on its next target. The process quickly produced tremendous teamwork. Meanwhile, light artillery crept two or three blocks ahead of the advancing troops, while heavy artillery dropped beyond that.[32]

Daniel established checkpoints at intersections and in larger buildings so that adjacent units could keep track of one another and stay in line. Each company was assigned an area, and each platoon usually was given a single street to clear. At cross streets, platoons worked about halfway down each block until they made contact with their neighbor.[33]

George Mucha, a BBC correspondent following Daniel's men, reported:

> The Americans were advancing methodically from street to street. Ahead of us, a few yards ahead, a Sherman tank sprayed the buildings with machine-gun fire.
>
> Suddenly it stopped. There was a German machine-gun nest. We squeezed against the wall until the tank had dealt with this by firing its gun at point-blank range into the house. The street was shaking with the thunder of reports. Above our heads mortar bombs were whining through the air. It was raining. . . . Every ten yards a new house had to be searched from top to bottom for snipers; doors broken in, grenades thrown into suspect rooms.[34]

Because some structures, including many apartment buildings, were proving impervious to fire from tanks and tank destroyers, the 3d Battalion requested the help of a self-propelled 155-millimeter gun. Division artillery agreed to send one forward. The first test of the 155-millimeter rifle was most successful; one shot leveled a structure that had shrugged off tank and tank destroyer rounds. An enthusiastic Colonel Seitz decided to obtain another gun for the 2d Battalion.

The Germans finally surrendered on 21 October. Corley's troops had reached the German command post and were using a 155-millimeter gun against the outer walls. Col. Gerhard Wilck, the garrison commander, surrendered at 1205 hours, commenting, "When the Americans start using 155s as sniper weapons, it is time to give up."[35]

BLOODY HÜRTGEN

On the VII Corps' right, the 9th Infantry Division was the first of several American divisions to sink into the evil horror of the Hürtgen Forest, which commanders concluded had to be cleared in order to protect the flank of the anticipated advance to the Rhine.[36] Using tanks in thick forest proved to be much more difficult than deploying them in city streets. The attached 746th Tank Battalion recorded in its after-action report, "Operations during the period up to 27 October were in very rugged terrain, consisting of hilly, heavily wooded ground, principally the Rötgen and Hürtgen Forests, not suited to normal tank operation. Offensive activities consisted of closely coordinated tank-infantry teams employed against concrete and field fortifications within the forests in the Siegfried Line. Replacements in personnel were green and due to the tactical situation had to be put into tanks without the benefit of prior orientation in the unit."[37]

The informal history of the 70th Tank Battalion, which followed the 746th into gloomy evergreen woods, offers a pithier description:

No soldier who was there will ever forget Hürtgen Forest—it was simply hell. The 70th moved into the Hürtgen in mid-November. The air was damp and bitter cold, especially inside of a moving tank. Snow covered most of the ground but underneath was soft, slippery mud that hampered a tank's every move. There was danger everywhere: danger of bogging down, danger of ambush in the dense woods, and danger of moving along the mined roads. Enemy artillery and mortar fire was almost incessant. Great tall trees were stripped and chewed to shreds by the continuous pounding of artillery from both sides. Every time a shell burst among the trees, the explosion sent a deafening roar echoing throughout the forest. Tanks entering the thick woods were road-bound and extremely vulnerable to mines and bazooka fire. Oftentimes infantrymen were not available to lead them through, so tankers had to advance alone, sweating it out every inch of the way.

The 70th fought twenty-four separate engagements with the enemy in the Hürtgen death trap from 16 November to 12 December 1944. The tanks were used both offensively and defensively, depending on the situation, which at the time was most unpredictable. The Jerries counterattacked every night in an attempt to regain the ground they had lost during the day. . . . The entire Hürtgen fighting cost the 70th a total of ninety battle casualties and twenty-four tanks (twelve of which were later repaired).[38]

Bradley, who ultimately bears some responsibility for the fact that the battle took place at all, years later conceded, "What followed . . . was some of the most brutal and difficult fighting of the war. The battle . . . was sheer butchery on both sides."[39]

Indeed, the fighting was bitter for the doughs and tankers. During the period from 6 to 25 October, the 9th Infantry Division suffered 4,500 casualties for the gain of a mere 3,000 yards. The 746th Tank Battalion, meanwhile, lost ten Shermans, one M4A3E2 Jumbo assault tank, and one light tank while claiming two Mark IVs, four Panthers, two Tigers, eleven antitank guns, sixteen large bazookas and rocket guns, fifty pillboxes with machine guns, thirty-five pillboxes without machine guns, and 134 machine guns in open emplacements.[40] The following entry from the 746th's S-3 journal gives some flavor for a typical day in action during the period:

October 12: Battalion, less service and combat elements, in position northeast of Zweifall. . . . Assault Gun Platoon of three two-gun sections attached to each of three regimental combat teams in close support with indirect-fire missions. Mortar Platoon attached to 298th Engineer Battalion in support of roadblocks between the 60th and 39th Infantry combat teams. Mortars wearing out and replacements difficult to secure. One mortar (81mm) unserviceable after 750 rounds. Division is reducing allotment of mortar ammunition. Company A, attached to 47th Infantry Combat Team, continues to hold its position in the Schevenhutte area, continuing to absorb mortar and artillery concentrations. At 0615 1st Platoon, Company A, moved from 47th sector to 39th sector with Company C for contemplated attack with Company C on Vossenock [Vossenack]. Company B, attached to 60th Infantry Combat Team, supported attack to southwest on Vossenock. First Platoon reduced to three tanks, of which one is inoperative mechanically, in a very sensitive position at [map coordinates]. Supply and maintenance of this platoon very difficult. Lieutenant Hayden returned from hospital and took over his platoon at 1000. Was again evacuated at 1400. After procuring some personnel replacements (one sergeant and two crewmen), the two tanks of the platoon and two [tank destroyers] plus one platoon infantry assaulted from the flank the three pillboxes closely opposing them. One pillbox taken and the position improved somewhat.

Second Platoon held up by mined tank blocking the road. Retriever from company headquarters cleared road at 1500. By that time tanks had found way around. Crewmen from one tank of this platoon that was isolated from rest of the tanks fought off the enemy by dismounted [Thompson submachine gun] action. Machine guns of tank could not be brought to bear because vehicle had been mined. By 1630 other three tanks of platoon had joined it. Third Platoon of three tanks with Company I, 60th Infantry, at [map coordinates] were cut off for most of the day by counterattack. Two tanks of this platoon lost previously to mines. Company B drew four new thirty-nine-ton tanks (Ford engines and heavier armor) [Jumbos]. Personnel losses in Company B heavy due to both casualties and illness. One officer and five enlisted men evacuated. Company C plus one platoon Company A in position preparatory to launch massed tank attack on Vossenock. Before this could be accomplished, the 39th Regimental Combat Team's positions one thousand yards north of Germeter were strongly counterattacked by two companies of infantry reinforced with observed fire from SP [self-propelled] artillery and mortars. Communication lines to the platoons attached to battalions of 39th severed. Lieutenant Heinemann, [seriously wounded in action] and evacuated. One platoon leader left in Company C at close of period. Third Battalion of 39th, with tank platoon, had withdrawn from positions north of Vossenock and east of Germeter to positions north of Germeter. One platoon tanks plus one infantry company secured Germeter. Two tanks in Company C lost. Company D, attached to 9th Infantry Division Reconnaissance Troop, maintained one platoon at division CP [command post] as guard. This platoon alerted at approximately 0930 for possible use against counterattack in 39th sector. Use did not materialize. One platoon dismounted on the left flank of the 39th Combat Team in a defensive position was overrun by the attacking enemy. Later reassembled and reestablished its lines. One platoon remained in support of roadblocks in 298th Engineer sector. Weather fair to good, visibility fair to good. Light air activity on both sides.

More Equipment Improvements

The M4A3E2 Jumbos referred to in this report were among the first to arrive in the separate tank battalions. In March 1944—even before the hard lessons of Normandy—Army Ordnance ordered a limited production run of M4A3E2 assault tanks, nicknamed Jumbos. The Jumbo carried nearly six inches of armor up front (the lower hull was somewhat thicker than the upper hull) and, combining armor and the gun mantlet, thirteen inches of protection on the turret front.[41] The extra armor reduced the top speed slightly to twenty-two miles per hour. The records of the separate tank battalions demonstrate a certain futility in this armor race; although the Jumbos clearly took more punishment than stock Shermans, they nevertheless regularly fell prey to guns of 75-millimeter and higher, bazookas, and mines.

The 746th Tank Battalion drew fifteen Jumbos in October, and the 743d received five. In November, the 70th, 735th, and 737th Tank Battalions received various but smaller quantities. In December, the 774th obtained five.[42]

Mines were a serious problem for tanks everywhere along the front. In November, the army gave a hard look at special mine-exploding tanks, which had been used on a limited scale since Normandy. The British Crab flail tank (which detonated mines with chains attached to a spinning drum mounted on the front of the vehicle) was found to be far superior to the roller-style detonators T1E1 and T1E3 in American production. Beginning that month, the army placed orders with British authorities for growing numbers of the Crabs. The 738th and 739th MX Tank Battalions each had a company of mine-clearing Shermans, initially including both flail and roller style. The roller style units were abandoned for good, at least in the 739th, in February 1945.[43]

In late October, a large-scale program to install AN/VRC-3 radio sets (the tank version of the SCR-300) in infantry-support tanks finally kicked off.[44] In November, the 3d Armored Group recorded that "higher headquarters" had decided that twenty-eight tanks in each battalion should be fitted with the sets, but that they were in short supply.[45] The records of the 743d Tank Battalion, for example, indicate that sets were installed in the tanks of the company commanders and the platoon commanders and sergeants, and the 709th Tank Battalion had nineteen AN/VRC-3 radios installed that same month, a number that suggests a similar policy.[46]

The army judged that these radios achieved "relatively efficient" radio contact between tanks and infantry.[47] Some battalions viewed the radio link as a godsend. The 781st Tank Battalion, for example, recorded that "There are two SCR-300

radios in each platoon of tanks, and the importance of making SCR-300s available
to any infantry unit, no matter how small, that has a mission with tanks, cannot be
overestimated."[48] Other tank officers saw the improved communications as a mixed
blessing, because infantry officers could issue orders directly to individual tanks,
thereby undermining control by the battalion's command structure.[49]

Chaos at Kommerscheidt
One fight in the Hürtgen demonstrated that even a tank–tank destroyer–infantry–
artillery–tactical aircraft team in which all elements did their part could not win in
the face of command folly. The First Army's commander, Courtney Hodges,
ordered the 28th Infantry Division to replace the battered 9th Division on 26
October and push eastward through the Hürtgen Forest toward Schmidt. Thus
began an ill-conceived operation that would end in the mauling of the division,
particularly its 112th Infantry Regiment and the supporting 707th Tank Battalion.
From the German perspective, an attack in the direction of Schmidt could mean
nothing but an effort to seize the Roer River dams on which the defenders
depended to block an assault across the river downstream. American success
would also menace plans underway for a counteroffensive in the Ardennes. American commanders, however, were thinking primarily in terms of flank protection
and did not commit the resources that would be necessary to handle the likely
German response to a threat to the dams.

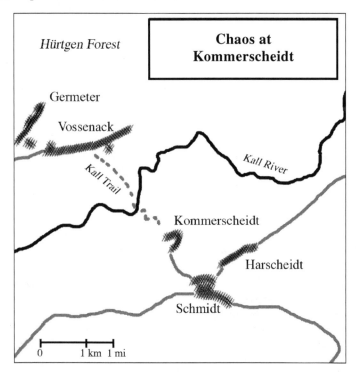

The division attacked in bad weather on 2 November, and the 112th Infantry's 2d Battalion, supported by Company C, 707th Tank Battalion, seized the first objective, Vossenack, with little difficulty. This was the tankers' baptism of fire, and cooperation with the seasoned GIs went remarkably well. The infantry battalions on the north and south flanks, however, became embroiled in confused and bloody fighting in the thick forest and made little progress. On 3 November, the 3d Battalion of the 112th Infantry pushed up the Kall Trail—little more than a cart track across the Kall River gorge—and thence over rough, forested terrain to high ground. At the far end, the doughs first reached the village of Kommerscheidt and then Schmidt just beyond, meeting little resistance. The 1st Battalion moved into Kommerscheidt on its heels.

One hour before dawn on 4 November, the M4A1s from 1st Platoon, Company A, commanded by Lt. Raymond Fleig, warmed up their engines and made ready to attempt the Kall Trail to reach the doughs. Fleig's tank entered the trail and immediately struck a mine. Using a winch, Fleig and his men carefully maneuvered the second tank past the blockage. Taking command of the point Sherman while his men performed the same maneuver with the remaining three Shermans, Fleig pressed on, his left track chewing the edge of the trail above a sharp drop into the forest.

The Germans counterattacked the Americans in Schmidt with the 1055th Infantry Regiment, 89th Infantry Division, which happened to be passing through the vicinity of Schmidt when American forces took the town. Twenty to thirty tanks of the 116th Panzer Division supported the regiment. The Germans quickly recaptured Schmidt and headed for Kommerscheidt.

When Fleig pulled into town at about 0900 hours, he could hear panzer fire from the direction of Schmidt. The infantry commander told him, "Get out there and stop those tanks!" About 1100 hours, ten panzers and 100 infantrymen attacked toward Kommerscheidt. Just as Fleig's M4A1 reached the eastern edge of Kommerscheidt, the lieutenant spotted a Mark IV seeking concealment in an orchard. "Gunner, tank, shot, 300, fire!" ordered Fleig. The cannon roared, and a 75-millimeter round struck the panzer. "Target, shot, fire!" This time, the Mark IV burst into flames, and two crewmen bailed out and ran for safety as .30-caliber rounds chased them.

Fleig moved his tank back and forth along the edge of town and fired at several Panthers. Even at a range of only 800 yards, his rounds glanced off the thick German armor. Fleig hoped more of his tanks would arrive soon.

Meanwhile, near the bottom of the gorge on the Kall Trail, the last 1st Platoon Sherman became stuck in mud and threw a track. After a heart-pounding journey over the precarious trail, two Shermans joined Fleig in Kommerscheidt about noon. To the rear, more tanks entered the path after daylight only to experience similar difficulties, made all the worse by the two crippled Shermans and the damage caused to the surface by each passing tank. Three more would slide off the path entirely.

At about 1400, five panzers and infantry attacked from the direction of Harscheidt. Fleig had positioned his tanks in defilade, and his gunners picked off three of the panzers.

Fleig spotted a Panther overrunning the infantry's positions in an orchard and ordered his driver in that direction. He told his gunner to fire the round already in the main gun, which unfortunately was high explosive and failed to harm the panzer. The Shermans had been firing high explosive over the heads of the infantrymen who first entered Kommerscheidt. "This was our baptism of fire," recalled Fleig, "and we didn't know we should have had a mix [in the ready rack]." A second round of high explosive frightened the German crew into bailing out, but once they realized there had been no harm done, they scrambled back aboard.

Unfortunately, all of the remaining armor-piercing rounds were in the hull sponson racks, and Fleig had to turn his turret away from the target in order for the crew to pass the ammo up. As he did so, the Panther's high-velocity 75-millimeter gun roared, but the first shot missed. Working feverishly, the American loader slammed an armor-piercing round into the chamber as the gunner spun the turret back into line. The gunner fired. His first shot cut the barrel of the Panther's main gun. Fleig pumped three more rounds into the side of the Mark V, which caught fire.

An infantryman, meanwhile, destroyed a fifth panzer with a bazooka. Close air support arrived, and a P-47 knocked out a panzer the pilot spotted near Schmidt. Artillery and mortar fire crashed into the German ranks. The Germans pulled back at 1600 hours.

On 5 November, the Germans struck shortly after dawn through a freezing rain with eight tanks and two self-propelled guns followed by infantry. The 707th Tank Battalion's assault guns to the rear combined with field artillery and stopped the German infantry. Fleig and his men knocked out one of the panzers, and the Germans pulled back again, but their tanks took up positions on high ground near Schmidt and began firing into Kommerscheidt from long range.

Six more Shermans and nine M10s from the 893d Tank Destroyer Battalion that had finally made it across the trail joined Fleig during the day. Fleig personally coordinated the tanks' actions with the tank destroyer commander, Lt. Leonard Turney, when the Germans struck again.

Under the German pounding and a foray by a dozen panzers early on 6 November, two-thirds of the tanks and tank destroyers were knocked out by midday. A plan cooked up by Fleig and Turney to draw panzer fire with the tanks so the tank destroyers could spot and kill them came to naught when Turney was badly wounded and the Germans found the range of both the American tanks and destroyers. The exhausted doughs huddled miserably in their foxholes and in ruined buildings. Lt. Col. Richard Ripple, who commanded the 707th Tank Battalion, also appeared with some 200 infantrymen, all that could get up the trail from a task force formed by Cota for the unachievable end of recapturing Schmidt.

The Germans attacked again during the afternoon on 6 November. Sgt. Tony Kudiak recalled, "There were five tanks and two self-propelled guns this time. They came in, and this time, German infantry came in fast with them. They seemed to come right through our artillery concentrations. Along about dusk, about seven P-47s came over and started strafing the German infantry and tried to hit a [Panther] tank out in the field in front of us. I went back to get one of our tanks to fire on it, and it fired seven rounds. They bounced off."

By 6 November, moreover, German infantry bypassed Kommerscheidt to interdict the nearly undefended trail. To the rear, American troops near Vossenack, pounded by artillery, panicked and broke.

On 7 November, striking out of a cold winter rain, eighteen German tanks and infantry overran Kommerscheidt. Fleig's and another tank engaged in a shootout that claimed three panzers, but an armor-piercing round penetrated the sponson of Fleig's Sherman, killed the driver and bow gunner, and set the tank on fire. The survivors leapt to the ground and climbed into the other M4A1. Elsewhere in town, panzers destroyed two more Shermans. American infantry began to bolt for the trail. Sergeant Kudiak recalled, "We saw quite a few men taking off over the hill to the rear on our left. . . . I looked around the corner of the barn and could see a German tank firing into the battalion CP [command post]."

Facing an untenable situation, the surviving tanks and tank destroyers withdrew toward the wood line as well, but two of the Shermans threw tracks and had to be abandoned. That afternoon, Maj. Gen. Norman Cota, commanding the 28th Infantry Division, ordered his troops to withdraw behind the Kall. The crew of the last Sherman destroyed its vehicle and walked back with the doughs.

The 707th Tank Battalion's losses amounted to seven men killed, twenty wounded, and thirty-seven missing. Lieutenant Fleig survived the debacle. By 8 November, the battalion had only nine operational tanks. An inspector from the 3d Armored Group who visited the front that same day recommended to the V Corps that the battalion be given time to rest and reorganize. The tankers withdrew with the 28th Infantry Division to the Ardennes on 20 November for intensive rehabilitation in a peaceful sector of the front.[50]

MUD AND FORTS

Being forced to hunker down did not sit well with Patton, so he ordered part of the Third Army back onto the offensive in late September. The XX Corps—including the 5th, 83d, and 90th Infantry Divisions, with the 735th, 774th, and the 712th Tank Battalions, respectively—jumped off first on the north flank. The 83d Infantry Division pushed northeast on the road to Trier. The 90th Infantry Division passed easily through the Maginot Line, where the 712th Battalion tankers used the fortifications to practice for the imminent attack on the West Wall.[51]

The most dramatic action, and most egregious display of how *not* to use infantry-support tanks, was the 5th Infantry Division's attack on the first of the Metz fortifications, Fort Driant, beginning on 27 September. The main works stood on a hill 360 meters tall and consisted of four casemates with reinforced concrete walls seven feet thick and a central fort shaped like a pentagon. All the elements were connected by tunnels. Each casemate mounted a three-gun battery of either 100- or 150-millimeter guns, and the southern side received additional cover from a detached fort mounting three 100-millimeter gun turrets. The central fort was surrounded by a dry moat running up to thirty feet deep. Barbed wire surrounded the fortification and wove among its individual elements. The gun turrets, as it turned out, could shrug off repeated hits by American 8-inch guns.[52]

The first battalion-size infantry attack received artillery, air, and tank destroyer support, all of which proved ineffective against the walls. The infantry became pinned down by small-arms, machine-gun, and mortar fire, and the effort was called off after about four hours.[53]

After the failure of the first operation, the 735th Tank Battalion (which would develop a specialty in attacking forts) was brought into the fight as part of a carefully constructed assault plan. For the special operation, on 30 September, the battalion assembled a composite company consisting of its eleven tanks with 76-millimeter guns, four 105-millimeter assault guns, and a single 75-millimeter Sherman for an artillery observer. They trained in the use of the explosive "snake," designed to blow a path through barbed wire much like the bangalore torpedo, and the use of concrete-piercing ammunition. (This would be the only tactical use of the snake on record in the European theater of operations.[54]) From 5 to 8 October, tanks tried to work in the confined space of the complex with the doughboys, subject to repeated close assaults by German infantry. Their snakes and guns made absolutely no difference to the outcome, which was failure.

On 9 October, American commanders decided that the attack—which thus far had cost 21 officers and 485 men killed, wounded, or missing in action—was too costly to continue. This decision ushered in a period of relative quiet in most of the Third Army's zone.[55] In some areas, however, October saw limited-objective advances against heavy German resistance marked by counterattacks so frequent that at times it was debatable who was on the offensive.[56] The 90th Infantry Division spent nearly an entire month taking the town of Maizieres-les-Metz; the army's official history records that men of the 712th Tank Battalion played little role in the battle, but battalion veterans remember tough street fighting.[57] During one sixteen-day "break" in offensive operations, moreover, tanks of the 737th Tank Battalion fired approximately 14,000 75-millimeter rounds in indirect-fire missions from static positions. By the end of the month, Patton's troops had breached the Moselle River line to a depth of a dozen miles.[58]

Almost stymied since September, Patton—with Bradley's blessing—resolved to launch a major offensive by 6 November that he hoped would quickly cross the Saar River, breach the West Wall, and reach the Rhine. Patton's plan was to capture the Saar-Moselle triangle and Trier, the major stronghold. Success would turn the flank of the Siegfried Line in the Third Army's sector and open the route to the Rhine at Koblenz, fifty miles distant.[59] Incessant rain during the days before the attack, however, forced delays and turned the entire front into a quagmire. Every bridge on the Moselle save one was knocked out by floodwaters, and movement across fields for even tracked vehicles became virtually impossible. Patton would not be dissuaded and ordered his troops ahead on 8 November.

The Germans, judging that no one in his right mind would attack under such conditions, were initially caught by surprise. They quickly recovered, fell back on prepared positions, and turned the conditions to their advantage on the defensive. The Third Army clawed forward only fifteen miles in eight days. The XII Corps battered its way across the Saar and finally came close to the Siegfried Line in early December when it captured Sarreguemines. The XX Corps took on Metz and its ring of thirty-five forts; Metz had not been taken by assault since the year 451.[60]

In the XII Corps' zone, the 737th Tank Battalion (attached to the 35th Division) fought through prepared enemy defenses, extensive mine fields, unfavorable weather, mud-soaked terrain, and moderate-to-heavy resistance. The battalion lost eighteen tanks, including two of the new Jumbos, in the first half of the month.[61] On a typical day, Company A's commander reported that his men had "moved from Laneuville to Fonteny starting with fifteen tanks—two stuck in mud, then two were hit by [antitank] guns and burned, one broke down in Fonteny, and one was hit by [antitank] fire, breaking the sprocket. Enemy tanks in Fonteny held north portion of town and [Company A] rallied at 1800, remaining all night under artillery with no doughs—only three tanks remain in shape to move. . . . The infantry knocked out a German tank with a bazooka. Now I have seen everything."[62] Tanks from the 737th Battalion were the first in the corps to enter Germany in early December.[63]

The 26th Infantry Division attacked with support from the newly committed 761st "Black Panthers" Tank Battalion, the first African-American armored unit to see combat. The battalion also recorded rough going through rain, mud, cold, and driving sleet. Upon the battalion's arrival in France in October, Patton had told the outfit, "Men, you're the first Negro tankers to ever fight in the American Army. I would never have asked for you if you weren't good. I have nothing but the best in my Army. I don't care what color you are as long as you go up there and kill those kraut sons of bitches. Everyone has their eyes on you and is expecting great things from you. Most of all, your race is looking forward to you. Don't let them down and damn you, don't let me down!"[64]

Most of the battalion was allocated to two task forces. The larger, Task Force A, consisted of Companies B and C and a platoon of Company A; a company of the 602d Tank Destroyer Battalion; a squad of engineers; and Company K of the 101st Infantry Regiment. Company C and two platoons of Company A supported the opening attacks by the 101st and 104th Infantry Regiments, and Moyenvic fell on 8 November, which opened the road toward Morville. The next morning, Task Force A rolled out, with the infantry riding the tanks. As the column approached Morville, artillery crashed around it. The infantry dismounted, and the tanks went into partial defilade and fired into the buildings some 600 yards away. Then Company B's tanks rolled forward across open ground, with the infantry sheltering behind the armor and exchanging shots with enemy gunmen in the buildings.

The infantry fanned out once inside Morville, while a Sherman led an advance up the main road until struck by a bazooka. The commander bailed out and fell dead in a rattle of machine-gun fire. The infantry went after the shooters, and by 1500, the town was secure.

Disaster struck Company C as it attacked toward high ground overlooking Morville, and the 761st Tank Battalion wrote its own chapter in the old story of suffering its heaviest losses in the first days of battle: twenty-seven of the thirty-four men who died in the war did so in November, fifteen of them on the eighth and ninth. Company C fell into a trap set by the 11th Panzer Division at an anti-tank ditch northeast of Morville, and seven tanks were destroyed.[65]

The XX Corps' attack on Metz, meanwhile, involved four parts: a wide envelopment to the north by the 90th Infantry and 10th Armored Divisions, a close-in envelopment from the south by the 5th Infantry Division, a containing action west of the Moselle by the 95th Infantry Division, and a final assault on both sides of the river.[66]

Despite grave difficulties of getting tanks across the flooded Moselle River (the first Shermans of the 712th Tank Battalion followed the infantry across after a two-day delay), the 90th Infantry Division advanced steadily through the muck

and fortifications. The only stiff challenge came in the form of an infantry-armor counterattack by the 25th Panzergrenadier Division at Distroff on 15 November. American troops had to call friendly artillery down on their own positions, because German infantry penetrated so deeply. Losses were heavy on both sides.[67]

The 5th Infantry Division slugged its way through strongpoint after strongpoint. The infantry crossed the Seille River early on 9 November, but the torrent prevented engineers from finishing a Bailey bridge capable of holding tanks until early the next day. That day, Companies A, C, and D of the 735th Tank Battalion supported the 2d Infantry's attack toward Vigny. The soggy ground was just firm enough to allow the medium tanks to operate across fields and stick with the infantry, although a platoon of light tanks bogged down. One platoon of medium tanks conducted evacuation and supply runs because wheeled vehicles could not move through the muck.

The 6th Armored Division's Combat Command B entered the bridgehead during the morning, passed through the 2d Infantry, and attacked toward the Nied River. The 2d Battalion's infantry mounted their supporting tanks and followed, while the other two battalions secured the flanks. The 2d Infantry and Combat Command B repeated this tactic the following day; when the combat command reached Aube, two infantry companies mounted on 735th Battalion tanks peeled off to the left and right to seize the high ground flanking the town.

The 5th Division and Combat Command B then crossed the Nied River at Sanry, and the Germans began a fighting withdrawal from the outer ring of fortifications. The Americans found the forts themselves abandoned but had to assault town after town. Company C tankers, who were using several M4A3E2 Jumbos for the first time, and doughs of the 11th Infantry Regiment spent two days beginning on 13 November clearing the airfield at Frescaty. In a single engagement against a German counterattack at Sanry sur Nied, three Company B tanks expended 27,000 rounds of .30-caliber ammunition.

Patrols reached the city limits of Metz on 17 November, and the 5th Division worked its way into the city against scattered resistance. On the eighteenth, a bazooka round hit one of the Jumbos, penetrated four inches of armor, and bounced off.[68]

Hostilities formally ceased in Metz on 22 November, although several forts continued to hold out. The official U.S. Army history asserts that because the XX Corps' commander, Maj. Gen. Walton Walker, had forbidden direct assaults on the forts and because artillery shells had to be conserved to support a projected drive on the Saar River, the isolated forts were left to "wither on the vine."[69] In fact, tanks of the 735th Tank Battalion were employed in a new approach to fort-busting.

On 24 November, the battalion received an initial allocation of 600 rounds of French-made 75-millimeter white-phosphorous shells to fire at the fortifications. On 25 November, tank crews that lobbed two hundred shells into Fort de Saint-Privat reported no appreciable results. Forts Jeanne d'Arc and Driant received similar treatment over the following days; the battalion poured hundreds of rounds daily into the German garrisons. Initial skepticism among the tankers gradually gave way as the results of sustained white-phosphorous bombardment became apparent. Fort de Saint-Privat surrendered on 29 November, with more than 10 percent of the troops suffering from burns. Artillery observers reported on 30 November that they could hear German troops inside Fort Driant screaming.[70] Fort Jeanne d'Arc was the last to capitulate, which it did on 13 December.

Alarmed by the threat that the Third Army posed to the planned Ardennes offensive, the Germans moved several divisions in to reinforce the front. More-over, German forces fell back into one of the most extensively fortified parts of the West Wall. Patton's planned dash ground to a halt. The 90th Infantry Division, for example, had barely crossed the Saar and succeeded in clearing the steel town of Dillingen after bloody house-to-house fighting when the Third Army had to turn north to deal with the Bulge.

FIRST TO THE RHINE
At the extreme south of the front, the 6th Army Group (which had been activated on 15 September under Gen. Jacob Devers to exercise control over the U.S. Seventh and French First Armies) made the most significant Allied gains in November. On 13 November, Lt. Gen. Alexander Patch's Seventh Army launched an offensive through the Vosges Mountains toward Strasbourg. Spearheaded by the French 2d Armored Division, Seventh Army forces liberated Strasbourg on the Rhine on 23 November.

To the south, the First French Army struck on 14 November and rolled through the Belfort Gap to the Upper Rhine. By mid-December, the army group occupied positions from south of Bitche through Wissembourg to the Rhine and thence south along the river to the Swiss border. The Germans retained only one sector west of the Rhine, which became known as the Colmar Pocket.[71] Hitler insisted that the pocket be held and gave Heinrich Himmler command.[72]

MORE NEW EQUIPMENT
In early December, ordnance began to equip some tanks in select battalions—including the 702d, 712th, 743d, 753d, and 781st—with turret-mounted multiple rocket launchers intended to provide high-volume area-saturation fire.[73] The fairly common T34 Calliope model consisted of a sixty-tube 4.5-inch rocket launcher mounted on a frame above the turret. Typically, about one company per battalion was outfitted with the launchers. The crew controlled elevation by using the main gun, which was connected to the launcher above by an extension. Much to the annoyance of the crews, initial models prevented firing of the main gun unless the aiming arm was removed.[74] Captured German soldiers reported that they found the rocket fire worse than artillery and extremely demoralizing.[75] But more than one tank battalion objected to the loss of tanks in their primary role, the vulnerability of the launchers to damage, and the additional supply and maintenance headaches. Several battalions, with the backing of infantry commanders, dumped the launch-ers after only weeks of use.[76]

The tank battalions saw the first army effort to improve mobility during the winter of 1944, when grouser kits, also known as "duck bills," became available. The duck bills were attached to the edge of the tracks, making them wider and thus better distributing the tank's weight. This expedient proved only somewhat successful, however, because the grousers were prone to snap off or bend.

CHAPTER 11

Hitler's Last Gamble

"The enemy is at present fighting a defensive campaign on all fronts; his situation is such that he cannot stage major offensive operations. Furthermore, at all costs he has to prevent the war from entering a mobile phase; he has not the transport or the petrol that would be necessary for mobile operations, nor could his tanks compete with ours in the mobile battle."

—British 21st Army Group
appreciation, 15 December 1944

By early December, Hitler had assembled twenty-eight divisions for his Ardennes offensive, Operation *Wacht am Rhein* ("Watch on the Rhine"). This was the largest reserve Germany had been able to accumulate in two years, albeit much weaker than the strike force available when German troops had rolled through the same area in 1940. Factories and repair shops, working furiously, had supplied 1,349 tanks and assault guns in November, and another 950 were delivered in December.[1] Troops below the level of officers and NCOs, however, often were new to battle.

Delivered to Field Marshal Gerd von Rundstedt complete to the last detail with "NOT TO BE ALTERED" scrawled across it in the Führer's own handwriting, Hitler's plan called for a three-pronged offensive along a seventy-five-mile front between Monschau and Echternach.[2] In the north, the Sixth SS Panzer Army was to strike to and then across the Meuse River before heading northwest for Antwerp. In the center, the Fifth Panzer Army was to attack through Namur and Dinant toward Brussels. The German Seventh Army was to reel out a line of infantry divisions to protect the southern flank of the operation.

Despite elaborate German safeguards, Allied intelligence picked up many signs of the build-up but, by and large, dismissed the possibility of a German offensive because of a false preconception: such an attack would be doomed to defeat and therefore irrational to undertake. Hitler was rolling the dice in a bigger game. He hoped that he could drive a wedge deep enough in the Allied camp to induce his enemies to come to terms rather than insist on unconditional surrender.

At its greatest penetration, the Bulge extended sixty miles deep and forty miles wide. By the end of the six-week battle, 600,000 American troops had fought 550,000 Germans. For the most part, the fighting did not turn on the well-planned movements of large formations. Instead, much of it unfolded at the level of small units and individuals—what generals and commentators at the time described as "fluid."[3] In a sense, it was the war with which infantry tankers were well familiar.

ABSORBING THE BLOW:
THE STORY OF THREE TANK BATTALIONS

Three separate tank battalions, two of them D-Day veterans, were in the thinly held Ardennes sector when *Wacht am Rhein* blasted out of the fog on 16 December. By the end of the month, another dozen would arrive as the Allies scrambled to block the expansion of the Bulge and lay the groundwork for its annihilation. Most of these battalions were by now experienced outfits with battle-hardened men. The tankers had learned their lessons and paid their tuition in blood. Now they were ready to teach the Germans a thing or two.

Facing the Sixth SS Panzer Army, the 741st Tank Battalion was split between two divisions on the northern shoulder of the German attack zone. The battalion itself was attached to the 2d Infantry Division, but one platoon—expanded to Companies C and D on 16 December—was attached to the neighboring 99th Infantry Division. In the center and directly in the path of the Fifth Panzer Army, the 707th Tank Battalion and 28th Infantry Division were recovering from the trauma of the

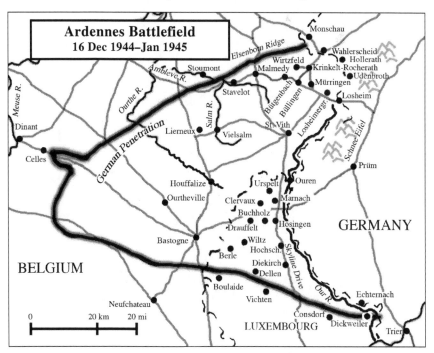

Ardennes Battlefield
16 Dec 1944–Jan 1945

failed operation at Schmidt the previous month. On the southern shoulder facing the German Seventh Army, the 70th Tank Battalion and 4th Infantry Division were also recuperating from the battering they had suffered in the Hürtgen Forest. The one other infantry division in the line, the untested 106th, was supported by Combat Command B of the 9th Armored Division.

Locked and Loaded

The 741st Tank Battalion was supporting offensive operations toward the Roer River dams by the 2d Infantry Division near Wahlerscheid, Germany, when the Sixth SS Panzer Army struck, so the battalion was well prepared for battle.[4] The I SS Panzer Corps' plan of attack foresaw three infantry divisions breaking the American lines and opening the road net for the 1st SS Panzer Division *Leibstandarte* and the 12th SS Panzer Division *Hitlerjugend* ("Hitler Youth"), which were to dash for the Meuse River.

The 277th Volksgrenadier Division was to open the path for the Hitler Youth in the Losheimergraben area. The 277th Division had been fighting in the Hürtgen Forest and was battle seasoned, but it was rated fit just for defensive operations, and only several companies had been trained for offensive operations in small-scale counterattacks. The division's orders were to clear roads through the forest from Hollerath and Udenbreth to the so-called twin villages of Krinkelt and Rocherath and then to capture them.

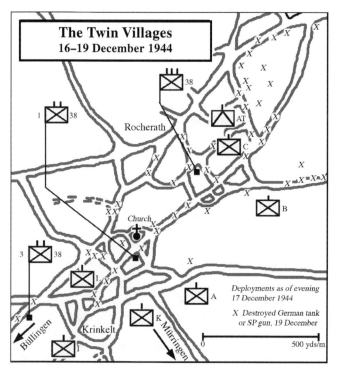

The 12th SS Panzer Division's main strike force was the 12th Panzer Regiment, which consisted of the 1st Battalion outfitted with Panthers and Mark IVs, and the army's 560th Heavy Tank Destroyer Battalion, which was equipped with a mix of Jagdpanther tank destroyers mounting an 88-millimeter gun and Jagdpanzer IVs, which carried a long-barreled 75-millimeter gun. The division also fielded a tank destroyer battalion armed with Jagdpanzer IVs. The 25th and 26th Panzergrenadier Regiments provided the division's infantry strength.

The division had been badly chewed up during the summer and fall, and it had been rebuilding inside Germany. When the division's commander, SS Lt. Gen. Hugo Kraas, received his orders for the Ardennes offensive, he informed the High Command that his mostly inexperienced men were not up to the tasks they had been assigned. The young volunteer replacements he had received had undergone very short training, a problem particularly acute among the ranks of the panzergrenadiers. The panzer crews, at least, were mostly seasoned, but fuel shortages had prevented any field training for the infantry with tanks.[5]

The 277th Volksgrenadier Division attacked toward the twin villages as planned before dawn on 16 December, but even with the commitment of its reserve regiment, it made scarcely any progress against a stiff defense mounted by the U.S. 99th Division's 393d Infantry. About mid-afternoon, the I SS Panzer Corps ordered the 12th SS Panzer Division to commit a reinforced battalion along the road toward Krinkelt to support the 991st Infantry Regiment, which it subordinated to the SS division. Nevertheless, by evening, only the 989th Infantry Regiment had gained much ground into the forest—at a high cost in men. The task of taking the twin villages was turned over to the 12th SS Panzer Division, and the 277th Volksgrenadier Division, minus the 991st Infantry Regiment, was ordered to reorganize.[6]

While the battle raged in the forest, the 741st Tank Battalion spent the day responding to initial reports of the German offensive. At 1520 hours, the 2d Infantry Division requested that the battalion deploy two platoons of Company A to critical points held by the 2d Battalion, 38th Infantry Regiment. At 1724, Division instructed that all of Company C was to operate with the 99th Infantry Division under formal attachment to the 2d Infantry Division's 23d Infantry Regiment. At 2030, Company D was ordered to proceed to Camp Elsenborn to join Company B of the 612th Tank Destroyer Battalion. At 2249, Company B and the remaining platoon of Company A were alerted and sent to the area north of Rocherath, where they were to constitute the division reserve.

On 17 December, the 741st Tank Battalion met the full force of the 12th SS Panzer Division attack in the fiercest armor battle experienced by a separate tank battalion during the war. The fight proved that battle-savvy American tankers—all still operating the 75-millimeter Sherman—could take on and beat concentrated German armor, particularly when they enjoyed the advantages of being on the defensive.[7]

Maj. Gen. Walter Robertson, who commanded the 2d Division, learned from the V Corps at 0730 on 17 December that the Germans had broken through the 99th Division on his right and threatened the rear of his own division. He was ordered to withdraw from the Wahlerscheid area, adjacent to the Siegfried Line, where his assistant division commander, Col. John Stokes, already was working to extricate the 38th Infantry Regiment. The sole escape route for the 2d and 99th Infantry Divisions ran westward through the twin villages and Wirtzfeld and then along a trail to Elsenborn Ridge, which made Krinkelt and Rocherath critical to both sides. Robertson was then to form a defensive line along Elsenborn Ridge, which ran like a wall along the northern shoulder of the German route of advance.

Robertson ordered the 9th and 38th Infantry Regiments to pull back; instructed Stokes to take command of units in Rocherath and Krinkelt; and dispatched the 2d Battalion of the 23d infantry, a company of tank destroyers, and a company of medium tanks to Rocherath, Krinkelt, and Wirtzfeld. Only four tanks and three tank destroyers showed up to meet the infantry, and a company of doughboys climbed aboard. The GIs perched atop the back decks of the tanks and tank destroyers as the column churned southward from Sourbrodt.

About 1100 hours, the tanks or tank destroyers (both groups claim the kills) sent by Robertson knocked out three Mark IVs near Wirtzfeld, where earlier in the day panzers and panzergrenadiers had threatened the 2d Division's command post from the south but had been dispersed by antitank guns and tank destroyers already located there. This apparently had been a flank guard of the 1st SS Panzer Division's *Kampfgruppe* Peiper, and the Germans shied away from Wirtzfeld after encountering sharp resistance there. The American column halted here and set up defensive positions south of Wirtzfeld. Fortunately, by 0825 hours, four platoons from the 644th Tank Destroyer Battalion had arrived in Krinkelt, where German troops had begun to infiltrate about 0950, to provide the infantry some means of antitank defense.

As the 38th Infantry Regiment moved south toward Krinkelt and Rocherath, so did the rest of the 741st Tank Battalion. The battalion had been stripped of its light tanks, which were sent to the 1st Infantry Division. With panzers and panzergrenadiers reported massing in Büllingen, all tanks available were instructed to report to the 38th Infantry in the vicinity of Krinkelt. The battalion spread its medium tanks in a rough arc east and south of the twin villages.

As one platoon from Company A and two from Company B moved southwest of Rocherath to a crest overlooking the road to Büllingen, the tanks ran into German armored reconnaissance elements and destroyed an armored car and a half-track. Arriving at the crest, the tanks found defiladed positions and settled down to watch for panzers.

Lt. Victor Miller, a recently arrived replacement platoon commander, led his platoon of Company C to the positions of the 3d Battalion, 23d Infantry, northeast of Rocherath. A second Company A platoon deployed southeast of Krinkelt; this platoon stayed in place only for several hours before it was pulled back to guard the road from Krinkelt to Wirtzfeld.

Inside Rocherath, every available man was thrown into hasty defenses erected around the tank battalion's command post. The infantry was preparing the bridges on the road to Elsenborn for demolition, which was definitely not a good sign. The twin villages, which merged into one community about the point of the shared church, offered a promising spot for a defender. The villages sat on high ground overlooking the approaches from the south and west, though the terrain was flatter and rolling toward the forest to the east. The streets formed a spider web in which a tank or a man with a bazooka could get the draw on an enemy, and stout houses offered shelter and second-story perches for gunmen.

At midday, the 741st Tank Battalion's S-3 recorded that the situation was developing favorably as American troops recaptured Büllingen, which the 1st SS Panzer Division left ungarrisoned as it drove westward. By the middle of the afternoon, reports were pouring into the 741st Tank Battalion's command post of heavy German tanks supported by infantry approaching from several directions. As the battalion's records dryly state, there was "much shifting of tanks" in order to meet anticipated enemy attacks.

Lt. Joseph Dew and his platoon sat in defensive positions on the northeastern perimeter of Rocherath. The weather was cold and bleak, and eighteen inches of snow blanketed the ground. As frantic messages inundated the radio net, Dew knew that as of 1450 hours, Lt. Victor Miller was engaging Panther tanks a couple thousand yards east of town.[8]

The 991st Infantry Regiment, still attached to the 12th SS Panzer Division, had fought its way nearly to the edge of the woods outside Krinkelt by daylight on 17 December, and at 0600 hours, it assembled for its first attack on the objective.[9] Holding the last stretch of woods before the village was the 3d Battalion, 23d Infantry Regiment. Company I, commanded by Capt. Charles MacDonald, held the trail running toward the twin villages, supported by two of Miller's tanks. Withdrawing soldiers from the 393d Infantry told MacDonald's men that panzers had joined the attack, and it took little imagination to realize they would soon be coming this way.

At about 1100 hours, they did, along with a passel of infantry. Miller told MacDonald he was pulling his two Shermans back to take up better firing positions. Fortunately, the first German attacks were mounted by the foot troops without any artillery or tank support, and they were thrown back. Eventually, however, five Panthers moved forward.

The panzers commenced pounding and driving back Company I, approaching within a few feet of dug in positions and firing directly into foxholes. MacDonald called for Miller's tanks, but they had fallen back all the way to a crossroads at the edge of the forest, and the 3d Battalion's commanding officer agreed with Miller's assessment that the Panthers would make mincemeat of the Shermans. By afternoon, the GIs were running low on antitank munitions and were falling back.

Miller called the 741st Tank Battalion command post for help against three approaching panzers but was told that he was on his own. The Panthers approached the road junction. "There," MacDonald recorded, "the two Shermans . . . gave battle."

Soon both Shermans and the lives of Miller and most of the crewmen had been lost, but they had exacted a steep price: two of the hulking panzers were burning, too. Staff Sergeant Crisler assumed command of the platoon on Miller's death and advanced to the spot of the firefight, where he could see the two pairs of knocked-out tanks. Crisler spotted a third Panther and destroyed it while the infantry fell back toward the twin villages.[10]

As darkness approached, the 38th Infantry aligned its 3d Battalion on the ground overlooking the slopes to the south and southeast of the twin villages, while the 2d Battalion, strengthened by a company from the otherwise disintegrating 3d Battalion of the 23d Infantry, formed the left wing northeast of Rocherath. The 1st Battalion, which was badly shot up by artillery while still on the road, was in poor shape when it took up the center of the regiment's line facing generally eastward. The regiment failed to establish contact with a battalion of the 9th Infantry that was supposed to be to its right.[11]

Panzers were on the prowl. That night, Jagdpanzer IVs and infantry attacked from the east and drove Companies B and C of the 38th Infantry, which had not had time to dig in or deploy heavy weapons, out of their positions. At least two jagdpanzers with grenadiers riding on the decks drove toward the church across the street from the 1st Battalion's command post. Regiment denied a battalion request for tank support.[12]

It appears that a second group of five panzers and panzergrenadiers simultaneously penetrated Rocherath from the south and headed for the church. At about 2100 hours, the SS troops approached the positions of the 3d Battalion's Company K not far from the church. Lt. Col. Olinto Barsanti had ordered his men not to shoot without positive identification because 99th Division troops were still believed to be pulling back through his line.[13]

Sergeant Dixon's tank, belonging to the 2d Platoon of Company B, was part of a roadblock on the edge of town. Dixon spotted the silhouette of an approaching tank. His gunner was already traversing the turret and the loader hefting a shell when a GI called out not to fire because those were American tank destroyers and infantry withdrawing into town. Seconds later, the tank reached the intersection, and Dixon saw it was German. He saw more panzers behind it and realized it was wisest not to fire because the Americans were outnumbered. The lead Panther and some grenadiers passed by the roadblock into town and penetrated to within 150 yards of the 741st Tank Battalion's command post in Rocherath. Other German infantry set up a machine gun beside the road and sprayed the area of the roadblock. With bullets bouncing off the turret, Dixon pulled his tank back.[14]

Men in the tank battalion command post could hear German voices, but the enemy moved off. At the command post, Lt. Turner Sheppard gathered tankers who had lost their mounts to form a guard and to spell crews in nearby tanks so they could get some sleep. At 2120 hours, the 3d Battalion's Company K reported that a panzer was firing on it at point-blank range in the vicinity of the church, where its line tied in to that of the 1st Battalion. At 2130 hours, Company K reported that it was being shelled and that tanks and infantry were advancing against it from the east.

By 2145 hours, German troops had reached the 3d Battalion's command post, and a panzer—from which group is unclear—was firing at it with its main gun after having unsuccessfully tried to ram through the wall. Company K called down artillery that destroyed one Panther, and a bazooka team knocked out another. After a forty-five-minute fight, the remaining panzers retreated with the grenadiers, less fifty-two SS men whose corpses Company K counted after the engagement. The attacks at the church had driven a hole between the 1st and 3d Battalions, and the latter was reported disorganized and of doubtful combat value. Companies B and C had retreated all the way to the area of the regimental command post in Rocherath.

Meanwhile, the Jagdpanzer IVs destroyed three Shermans, two from Company A and one from Company B, which were near the church on the highest point of ground. The battalion's after-action report says the tanks were knocked out while on their way to help Company K, but Cpl. Kelly Layman, who was there, tells a different story. The Company B tank was a sitting duck, having run out of fuel. The tankers could hear panzers approaching, and one of the Company A tanks moved out, only to be hit after some fifty yards. The tank caught fire, and the crew bailed out.

The men in the last tank could see the panzer that had done the shooting straight ahead, which seemed like a big problem. An unseen German tank only thirty yards away to the right rear proved to be a bigger one. The Sherman had just backed up ten yards when a 75-millimeter high-explosive round blew off the right track. A second round of high explosive rattled the turret, and when a round slammed through the engine compartment and set the tank on fire, the crew bailed out and ran.

In the midst of the nighttime fight, the headquarters element of the 38th Infantry drove into town, heading for the regimental command post. The column made a left turn and came into full view of a panzer crew, who could see quite well by the light of a burning Sherman. The panzer blasted the lead vehicle, and the headquarters personnel bailed out and crawled to the command post through ditches.

The night of 17 December belonged to the 12th SS Panzer Division, and the I SS Panzer Corps was under the misimpression that the division had taken both of the twin villages. The only incident anyone could recall of shooting a panzer ended in disappointment, as the armor-piercing round bounced off the German armor at a range of only seventy-five yards.[15]

There was no let-up on 18 December, as three panzers crawled within 100 yards of the 38th Infantry's command post at about 0900 hours. The infantrymen hit two of them with bazookas to no effect, but they finally disabled one Mark V, and M10s from the 644th Tank Destroyer Battalion accounted for the other two; the Germans retreated.[16]

More generally, the day belonged to the 741st Tank Battalion and the other defenders. The tankers' radio net again crackled with furious traffic at 0920 hours. Panzers were grinding into Rocherath down a street approximately 150 yards from the tank battalion command post. Fog and smoke from burning buildings reduced visibility to almost zero.[17] Two deadlined Company B tanks placed in a lane just east of the command post for antitank defense opened fire on the panzers' flanks with devastating effect. When the smoke cleared, these two "disabled" tanks had destroyed five panzers. One surviving German tank continued through town and down the hill on the road to Büllingen, but Sergeants Angelletti and Padgett of Company B maneuvered behind the panzer and destroyed it.

At almost the same moment as the drama near the tank battalion command post, Lieutenant Dew spotted seven enemy tanks advancing toward his position. He ordered his gunner to open fire. Soon one German tank was disabled and four others had been hit, and the enemy withdrew. Dew's crew counted their remaining ammo. They had only four rounds of armor-piercing ammunition left. With visions of six German tanks reappearing, Dew thumbed the radio and reported his plight. Within minutes, crews from other Company C tanks rushed some of their rounds to his position, and the battalion placed a hasty request to the division for three truckloads of ammo—70 percent armor piercing. The battalion called back to Rocherath those of its tanks still scattered in the direction of Büllingen, and by 1100, it had its three medium companies deployed along the edge of the twin villages facing the enemy.

Both the 1st and 2d Battalions of the 38th Infantry reported their command posts to be under tank attack at about the same time. "The fighting was at such close quarters," recalled regimental executive officer Lt. Col. Tom Morris, "that men were throwing hand grenades across the street into buildings that the enemy were occupying opposite to them. Men were captured and recaptured." The 1st Battalion now had some tank support. Shermans from Company B opened up on three Panthers that were menacing the 1st Battalion's command post and destroyed two of them. An infantry officer guided a third Sherman into position 200 yards from a Panther that had been immobilized by a bazooka, and the gunner put a round through the side of the turret. Two other Panthers moved on, and one of them was later knocked out by a Sherman near the 3d Battalion's command post.

Early that afternoon, the Germans came on again, and Dew's crew accounted for two more tanks. But Company C was losing Shermans, too—three that day— and in the confusion, nobody knew how many men from those crews had survived. Major General Robertson, visiting the 38th Infantry's command post, told his assistant division commander by phone at about 1800, "This is a tank battle. If there are any replacements, we could use them as the crews are pretty tired. We could use the [M36 tank destroyers] mounting a 90mm."

At dusk, the tankers were told that they would begin servicing and refueling a few vehicles at a time and would drape bright air-recognition panels across the front armor when pulling back to avoid misidentification. Dew knew that soon his crew would be called out. Shooting and shouting from the forward infantry positions snapped him back to watchfulness; it sounded like a tank moving in his direction, and Dew made sure that the gunner had armor-piercing rounds loaded. A dark bulk gradually separated itself from the gloom, and Dew brought his gun to bear and ordered the gunner to open up. Another burning wreck joined his day's tally, but only after Dew's gunner had fired eighteen rounds at it.

Elsewhere in northeast Rocherath, where two Company B platoons had moved, the tankers were surprised by searchlights stabbing out of the dark and seeking their positions. A spotlight fell on a Sherman, and a high-velocity round followed. The lights were mounted on panzers! The Shermans fired up their engines, slammed into gear, and moved to less exposed venues. By now, several buildings nearby were burning, making the task of staying hidden more difficult.

Northeast of the twin villages, the 1st Battalion of the 9th Infantry Regiment, with Company K attached, had for two days battled panzers and grenadiers pushing through its positions toward Rocherath. With no tank or tank destroyer support, the GIs had destroyed nearly a dozen panzers during the vicious fighting, which at times played out at ranges of twenty yards, using bazookas, antitank mines, and well-directed artillery barrages. With its companies overrun, the battalion was told to pull back at 1300 hours on 18 December. The commanding officer, Lt. Col. William McKinley, thought it would be impossible because his men were too tightly engaged. That is when a lieutenant from the antitank platoon spotted four Shermans from Company A, 741st Tank Battalion, and asked Lt. Gastano Barcelona, the tank platoon commander, if he would help.

"Hell yes!" replied the tanker, and the infantry lieutenant directed him to the crisis point. McKinley was pleasantly surprised when the tanks arrived, and he quickly sketched out a tank counterattack to cover his men's withdrawal. He knew where four panzers lurked, barring the escape route. He told Barcelona to send two tanks to the right to attract their attention and the other two to the left. The plan worked. The two tanks on the left hit one panzer with three rounds and a second with two. The other two panzers moved off toward Rocherath, and one of the gunners knocked out a third panzer with shots to the rear. The last one "ran like hell" toward the twin villages. The infantry battalion slipped away, reduced in the battle from 600 men to 197 exhausted survivors.[18]

On 19 December, the 12th SS Panzer Division staged one final push before it withdrew its remaining tanks from the twin villages to join a division drive toward Bütgenbach. The attack began at 0800 hours supported by a heavy artillery barrage. Sergeant Dixon tangled with some of the last Panthers to enter the narrow streets of Rocherath, as he later recalled:

> We found a kraut tank on the opposite side of the building that we were behind. It had two tanks supporting its flanks. To attract the kraut's attention, [Sergeant] Case fired on the left flank from a covered position, while we moved up on the right flank between two buildings, about forty-five yards from the enemy. Corporal Kroeger fired four rounds of AP [armor piercing], which ricocheted off the kraut armor like pebbles

falling on a tin roof. Then one of the enemy's supporting tanks fired on us but missed us and hit the building. A piece of shrapnel knocked a hole about the size of a half-dollar in my steel helmet. We immediately backed up and took cover behind a building, and the krauts started an encircling movement on us. We soon found out we were under observation and direct fire from any direction in which we tried to move. We started sweating blood. We called for artillery and additional support, but we thought we'd never get it in time. . . .

The building on our right was in flames, which was to our advantage, as we were hoping for a smoke screen. It finally got fairly thick, and I decided to make a break for it. We took off like a bat out of hell under the cover of smoke. Luckily we reached cover without drawing fire. As we reached cover, the enemy [tank] on our right completed his encirclement by breaking through a stone wall, which put him in direct [line of] fire from Sergeant Mazzio's tank. Mazzio's gunner, Corporal Snike, immediately knocked the tank out, and the situation was relieved entirely. During the excitement, our artillery dropped a round on the turret of a Tiger tank, knocking it out. With the additional support of a Company A tank, the three remaining kraut tanks were knocked out. . . .[19]

At 1440 hours, the division ordered the 741st Battalion's commander, Lt. Col. Robert Skaggs, to withdraw behind Wirtzfeld. The division also put Company C of the 644th Tank Destroyer Battalion under his command and ordered the armor to act as rear guard to screen the infantry's withdrawal. Skaggs was to destroy all equipment left behind.

Skaggs instructed his companies to ensure protection of the critical Krinkelt-Wirtzfeld road. The tankers fended off German attacks throughout the afternoon and reported the destruction of several more panzers. As if the battalion did not have problems enough, German planes bombed its rear positions at 1600 hours.

At 1810, Dew helped a tank destroyer locate and dispatch yet one more panzer. About two hours later, the rear guard began to extricate itself from Rocherath. At 2030 hours, Company B reported that the last tanks had cleared the town and that the engineers who laid antitank mines behind them were riding the Shermans to safety. The tankers did not withdraw far, and the line held with little flexing in this area.

The 741st Tank Battalion's after-action report recorded:

In the fierce three-day action at Rocherath, tankers of the 741st Tank Battalion proved themselves adept at the art of way-laying and killing Tigers. From well-camouflaged positions, by expert maneuvering and stalking, tank after tank of the enemy forces was destroyed by flank and tail shots of the battalion's gunners. Recapitulation at the end of the encounter showed the battalion as having knocked out twenty-seven enemy tanks, (mostly Mark VIs), one SP [self-propelled] gun, two armored cars, two half-tracks, and two trucks.

In contrast to the number of enemy vehicles destroyed, our tank losses were comparatively small. A total of eight tanks were lost to enemy action.

The recapitulation was a study conducted by the 38th Infantry Regiment's S-3, who concluded that seventy-eight German tanks and self-propelled guns had been destroyed by tanks, tank destroyers, antitank guns, bazookas, and artillery during the period from 17 to 19 December.[20]

A word about "Tigers" should be added here. In the course of the fighting, tankers, infantrymen, and tank destroyer men repeatedly identified Mark VI Tigers on the German side, and the official U.S. Army history agrees. The 12th SS Panzer Division, however, had no Tigers, only Mark IVs, Panthers, and some Jagdpanther tank killers that, like the Mark VI, mounted the 88-millimeter gun. One must conclude that the American observers were mistaken, though that in no way diminishes the remarkable success of the 741st Tank Battalion.

Amazingly, only eight battalion men died and six were wounded during the furious December fighting.[21] The outfit, which had been similarly honored for its heroism on Omaha Beach, received a Presidential Unit Citation for its actions around Rocherath. Equally remarkable, while the 12th SS Panzer Division was throwing itself at the heart of the 2d Division's defenses in the twin villages, the division's flanks had been completely exposed. The 1st Infantry Division's 26th Infantry first closed on the right the afternoon of 18 December, and the arrival of the 9th Infantry Division covered the left on 19 December.[22]

The lopsided American victory had several causes. The tankers and GIs were combat wise and, on average, far more experienced than the enemy. The twin villages had acted as the spider web that their streets resembled, trapping panzers in vulnerable places where the superior range and killing power of their guns meant little. American artillery support had been available in quantity. Finally, the 12th SS Panzer Division had shown little skill at tank-infantry cooperation, doubtless in part because the members of the team had been unable to conduct field exercises together before the offensive. The panzers and infantry appear to have become separated frequently.

Shattered

Almost everything had gone right for the 741st Tank Battalion—a full swing in the fortunes of war from the battalion's washout on D-Day. But fortune had no such plans for the 707th Tank Battalion, which was now rebuilding after its misadventure at Kommerscheidt.[23] The outfit was still training new men and readying replacement equipment. Some of the veterans were on three-day passes.[24]

Unfortunately, most of the tanks and assault guns in the German Seventh Army and two panzer corps from the Fifth Panzer Army hit the 28th Infantry Division's sector.[25] The 28th Division had all three of its regiments in the line to hold its extended front of some thirty miles.

At about 0630 on 16 December, tanks and infantry struck the 110th Infantry, holding in the center of the division's zone along Skyline Drive, and most frontline companies were soon practically surrounded as grenadiers in half-tracks headed toward the regiment's artillery positions. The 26th Volksgrenadier Division had orders to infiltrate around strongpoints, avoid major fights, and head for Clervaux, where the 110th Infantry's headquarters was located. The 2d Panzer Division, attacking to its right, was to charge to Bastogne, and by late afternoon, the first tanks belonging to the *Panzer Lehr* Division would be across the Our River and fighting on the 26th Volksgrenadier Division's left. The entire 352d Volksgrenadier Division, meanwhile, struck the 109th Infantry Regiment, which held the southern end of the division line, but the volksgrenadiers had no armored support, and the defenders handily repulsed their assaults. On the 28th Division's northern wing, a battalion of infantry from each of the 116th Panzer and 550th Volksgrenadier Divisions—the former supported by seven Panthers—attacked the 112th Infantry Regiment but were driven off.[26]

The 707th Tank Battalion was in 28th Infantry Division reserve. Assembly areas for direct support of the doughs had been reconnoitered, but no definite assignments to the regiments had been made, so none of the company or platoon commanders had made personal visits to the frontline positions.[27] Division alerted the tankers at 0600 hours and reported that the enemy had infiltrated the main line of resistance and attacked at dawn in several sectors. The battalion commander was away, so Maj. R. S. Garner, the executive officer, ordered the battalion to deploy. Garner drove to Clervaux, where the 110th Infantry Regiment's command post was located, and reported to its commander, Col. Hurley Fuller.

Companies A and B were attached to the 110th Infantry Regiment, Company C to the 109th, and Company D to the 112th. The Assault Gun Platoon was tied in with division artillery and ready to fire indirect missions. Fuller ordered Garner to deploy his platoons to reinforce the strongpoints that were still holding out along the front, including the one in Marnach, which lay in the path of the 2d Panzer Division. Two platoons of Company A, one commanded by Lt. Raymond Fleig, set off with a platoon of infantry to fight their way into town. Small-arms fire drove the doughboys to cover in woods along the road, and the tanks rolled right through Marnach without spotting the GIs of Company B and left, much to the dismay of the infantry.

Lt. Richard Payne led his 3d Platoon, Company A, to Hosingen, where he joined Company K, 110th Infantry, in defense of the town, which happened to lie athwart the 2d Panzer Division's intended route of advance and supply line. This small command would hold up the German advance for a critical two days.

Meanwhile, Company B made contact with the enemy in the vicinity of Buchholz, as did Company C in the Diekirch area. Fighting on the first day was mainly against infantry formations, and all 28th Infantry Division strongpoints remained intact when night fell. Only one 707th Battalion tank was temporarily knocked out of action.

Panzers and self-propelled guns belonging to the 3d Panzer Regiment overran Marnach at about midnight, and Fleig was ordered to counterattack with his 1st Platoon and a platoon of infantry. Fire from tanks, *panzerfausts*, and automatic weapons greeted the Americans when they reached Marnach at 0230. After a thirty-minute fight, Fleig was told to pull back. A second attempt to enter Marnach at 0700 hours also failed.

Two platoons of Company D, which had shifted to help the 110th Infantry Regiment, advanced down Skyline Drive toward Marnach in conjunction with Fleig's attacks from the southwest and ran into direct fire from Mark IVs and Panthers that knocked out eight light tanks on the spot. Most of the men who survived were captured. The company's third platoon was badly shot up when it drove to Urspelt.

The Germans threw tanks into the battle in growing numbers on 17 December, and the 707th Tank Battalion recorded "[h]eavy fighting throughout the sector against overwhelming odds." Lt. Col. Richard Ripple rejoined his battalion to find it hard pressed. Companies A and B battled armor and infantry the entire day, during which the Germans overran Urspelt, Drauffel, Hosingen, and Hoscheid. The 2d Platoon of Company A in Clervaux lost three Shermans in exchange for four Mark IVs when the two forces encountered each other rather suddenly and engaged in a brief, fierce shootout. Called to Clervaux by Colonel Fuller to replace the losses, Fleig had to take a round-about route along the small Clerve River, which runs through Clervaux, and nevertheless ran into a Mark IV before he reached the town. Fleig recalled, "The infantry aboard the tanks dove for cover while the two tanks slugged it out. [My] gunner found a vulnerable spot, and the wreckage of the Mark IV formed an impassable roadblock preventing any German vehicle from getting into Clervaux along the road from Marnach."

In Hosingen, Lieutenant Payne's tankers shuttled to every point of danger, often watching in frustration as their rounds bounced off Panthers. By dusk, German infantry had gotten into the buildings and were attacking from house to house. The tanks set up a perimeter defense around Company K's command post. About 2000 hours, a *panzerfaust* struck one Sherman, and panzer gunnery set a second ablaze. The remaining tanks were almost out of fuel and ammunition. That night, exfiltration being clearly impossible, the remaining officers decided to surrender.

Company C still faced only infantry in the 109th Infantry's zone. Nevertheless, at 2200 hours, heavy enemy pressure forced the battalion headquarters to withdraw from Wilwerwiltz, which lies just northeast of Wiltz. The 707th Tank Battalion claimed a total of six Mark IV and V tanks and four self-propelled guns knocked out that day. But by evening, the battalion had lost all of its light tanks, sixteen Shermans, and one T2. Wounded enlisted men totaled 14, but 5 officers and 111 enlisted men were listed as missing. Company C was the only line unit that had not been badly mauled.

The remnants of Companies A and B, the battalion's headquarters, and the Assault Gun Platoon were withdrawn to Wiltz on the road to Bastogne and combined into a composite unit on 18 December under the commanding officer of

Company B. This force amounted to nine Shermans, all damaged in some way, and five assault guns. Together with the remnants of the 110th Infantry and 28th Division headquarters personnel, the tankers fought off constant heavy attacks throughout the day. Fleig's tank was knocked out during the fighting. Company C and the 109th Infantry withdrew slightly to Diekirch, which was also under heavy pressure. The battalion reported having knocked out one Tiger tank and a half-track, but it had lost another seven Shermans, with four enlisted men wounded and two officers and twenty enlisted men missing in action.

On 19 December, the defenders of Wiltz found themselves surrounded. The assault guns had been committed to a fierce battle at the Erpeldange crossroads, engaging panzers with their 105-millimeter guns. The tank crews were exhausted, and men fell asleep at any pause in the action. When the assault guns pulled back into town at 1700, three ran out of gas, and there was no more to be had. The other two were sent to defend a bridge, and their crews were never heard from again.

At 2400 hours, Lieutenant Colonel Ripple mounted an unsuccessful effort to break out, after which he ordered all vehicles destroyed and organized personnel into groups under officers with orders to exfiltrate to Boulaide. Company C was ordered to cover the withdrawal of the 109th Infantry to Ettelbruck, a mile and a half southwest of Diekirch, which mission it accomplished at 2330 hours. The 707th Battalion lost fourteen Shermans, six assault guns, and eleven half-tracks, as well as 2 enlisted men wounded, and 15 officers and 131 enlisted men missing in action that day. Lieutenant Colonel Ripple was among those captured while trying to escape from Wiltz.

The battalion's few remaining tanks supported the defense of Vichten, and then Neufchateau, over the next few days, but the 707th Tank Battalion had ceased to exist as a fighting force, as had the 28th Infantry Division.[28] In Raymond Fleig's Company A, only a handful of man had escaped death or capture.[29] Company B was down to some twenty-five men. Their sacrifice had not been in vain, though, because their tenacious defense had disrupted the German timetable for the capture of the key road junction at Bastogne.[30] On 31 December, Lt. Col. H. S. Streeter assumed command of the remnants of the 707th Tank Battalion.

Playing a Tricky Hand

On the Bulge's southern shoulder, the German offensive caught the 70th Tank Battalion with its pants down, but the battalion had the good fortune to face virtually no enemy armor, and its combat experience enabled the tankers to recover quickly.[31] The battalion had just arrived in Luxembourg after the rugged fighting in the Hürtgen Forest, and many of its tanks were stripped down for complete maintenance and parts replacement. Spares, however, were difficult to come by, which precluded some needed repairs.

All companies of the 70th Tank Battalion were alerted at 1100 on 16 December. Service Company men at once speeded up work on the disassembled tanks, and the few that were ready to roll immediately deployed to support the 12th Infantry Regiment, which was under attack by the 212th Volksgrenadier Division.

The 4th Infantry Division line already was beginning to sag under German pressure. Company D was in the best shape, so it moved two platoons forward. Company A contributed a platoon. Company B could field only three Shermans. The tankers found that several companies of the 12th Infantry had been cut off at separate points, and the first day was spent trying to reopen communications lines with mixed success. Company D's M5A1s proved useful for hauling doughs and fighting off German infantry that had no armor support.

The battalion reported on 17 December in its after-action report, "Today was a gray foggy day, and the situation was extremely vague." Tankers had difficulty spotting enemy activity through the dense fog. All communication had been lost with the 3d Battalion, 12th Infantry, in Osweiler and Dickweiler. Three tanks from Company B were out of radio contact, their fate unknown.

The battalion continued efforts to reach the surrounded doughs, each tank carrying five infantrymen—all that were available. The tanks fought their way into Bergdorf, where the GIs of Company F were isolated. Spotting a large hotel that had been the company command post, the lead tank pumped several 76-millimeter rounds into the building before noticing an American flag being unfurled on the roof. The sixty grinning GIs still holding the hotel met the tankers at the door.

A relief attack on Echternach failed because of a lack of infantry support. At Consdorf, one Sherman manned by two crewmen, assisted by seven cooks, MPs, and stragglers, formed the defense as a German regiment approached. A Sherman from Company B and two light tanks, accompanied by a handful of infantry, arrived just in time to help beat back the first German probe.

On 18 December, task forces from the 9th and 10th Armored Divisions (the latter advancing from the Third Army's zone) arrived to assist the 4th Infantry Division. The 70th Tank Battalion remained committed, and much of the time, the tank radios provided the only means of communication between infantry companies and their battalion command posts. The 70th Battalion deployed half-tracks to strategic locations to act as relay stations, which enabled the battalion to maintain contact with all its tanks.

By 19 December, many 70th Battalion tankers found themselves making tactical advances. The greatest setback was a bazooka ambush that knocked out two and damaged one tank from the 3d Platoon of Company A. Artillery and mortar fire were intense. Two Company B tanks in Osweiler, which lies a mile west of Dickweiler, rocked as buildings collapsed around them. One bathroom—less its tub—was blown away, and the commode and sink came to rest on one tank's rear deck. The crew immediately complained about the lack of bathing facilities.

On 21 December, the 70th Tank Battalion was transferred from the First Army's control to Patton's Third Army. Company C's three remaining tanks moved to the top of a hill north of Consdorf, where they would remain for the next four days; they were so badly in need of maintenance that they could no longer move.

The 70th Tank Battalion fought until 24 December, when it was relieved. The battalion's losses during the Bulge were comparatively light: five Shermans, one M5A1, one half-track, one officer and five enlisted men killed, and three officers and twenty-one enlisted men wounded. Col. R. H. Chance, the commander of the 12th Infantry, praised the battalion for providing "the most outstanding tank support that this infantry regiment has ever witnessed."

HELP ARRIVES

Almost immediately after the German offensive struck, additional tank battalions moved to the threatened sector. Most arrived with their partner infantry divisions, but others were reattached to divisions already in the area.

Staunching the Wound

One of Patton's most famous gestures took place on 18 December when he boldly promised Eisenhower that he would have three divisions moving north to the Ardennes within forty-eight hours (he made good). But the first units to redeploy in response to the crisis came from the north—well-seasoned outfits all, if lacking Patton's fame. The 30th Infantry Division and 743d Tank Battalion arrived on 16 December, and the 1st and 9th Infantry Divisions (with the 745th and 746th Tank Battalions attached, respectively) followed the next day. The newly arrived 740th Tank Battalion also entered the fray on 19 December.

The 743d Tank Battalion was engaged in rocket-launcher training near Höngen, Germany, on 16 December, when it was alerted to move to the Ardennes.[32] Through a cold rain, the battalion conducted an all-night road march south the night of 17 December to take up immediate fighting positions in the vicinity of Malmedy, Belgium. During the march, the column was on the alert for German paratroopers. Enemy aerial activity was intense, and antiaircraft fire speared upward on all sides. As they arrived in Malmedy, companies were divided among the battalions of the 117th Infantry Regiment, which were moving into defensive positions around Malmedy, Masta (a cluster of houses halfway between Malmedy and Stavelot), and Stavelot. Lt. Col. William Duncan, the battalion's commander, set up his command post in a large hotel room. Asked the situation by one of his officers, he replied, "I don't know what the situation is beyond this: The Germans are on the loose and can be expected anywhere anytime. It's our job to find out where they are and then stabilize a line to stop them and hold them." The men knew no more, and rumors spread like wildfire.

When the first tankers from Company B—with three assault guns attached—arrived in Stavelot to join the 1st Battalion, 117th Infantry, they found the Germans already there and in control of the northern half of the town. Lt. Jean Hansen's 3d Platoon moved in and spent the night on one side of the main square with the infantry; the Germans were only about eighty yards away on the other side. Hansen told a battalion officer that he knew nothing about what was going on around him except that the Germans were mighty damn close because they kept shooting at him. The boys of the 1st SS Panzer Division appeared to be suffering some confusion of their own. During the first several hours, three halftracks loaded with German infantry drove into the square; the Americans easily dispatched all these "attacks."[33]

In Masta, the 743d Battalion's tanks were strafed by friendly P-47s. At 1900, Duncan was ordered to send a company to Stoumont in support of the 119th Infantry—a task he assigned to Company C.

The tankers from Company B and C in Stavelot and Stoumont bore the brunt of the fighting on 19 December as the 30th Infantry Division extended the wall sealing off the northern edge of the German salient westward. Not that Company A was having an easy time; as its Shermans maneuvered toward La Gleize—halfway between Stoumont and Stavelot—they encountered Panther and Tiger tanks. One M4 was lost to 88-millimeter fire, but tankers helped a friendly antitank gun knock out a Mark V.

In Stavelot, Hansen's tanks moved up a street to support the doughs, who were trying to eject the SS from the northern part of town. A Tiger tank rounded the corner a mere fifty yards ahead. A friendly tank destroyer fired one ineffective round and scuttled to safety. The lead Sherman fired four armor-piercing rounds at the panzer, but none penetrated even at this close range. The American crew fired a smoke shell and backed around a corner.

Hansen deployed his Shermans to flank the Tiger and gain a side or rear shot, but this German commander knew his business, too. The Mark VI maneuvered constantly to counter the Shermans. Stalemate ensued. The American tanks established an ambush roadblock in case the German decided to come out and fight, but the next day, the two sides were still locked in a Mexican standoff.[34]

Unfortunately, when Company C arrived in Stoumont, the American line was under fierce attack by SS troops of *Kampfgruppe* Peiper. The tankers ran into advancing Germans almost immediately upon entering town, as recorded in the after-action report:

The 3d Platoon, Company C, was attached to the 2d Battalion, 119th Infantry, and made an early morning move to Chevron. At about 0615 hours the 1st and 2d platoons with the company commander moved to join the 3d Battalion, 119th Infantry, at Stoumont, Belgium. The tanks reached Stoumont at 0700 hours and went into immediate defensive positions. The 1st Platoon deployed into a position on the high ground at the eastern edge of the town where they joined Company I, 119th Infantry. The 2d Platoon moved into a position at about [map coordinates] and supported Company L, Infantry.

Within the quarter-hour, the enemy counterattacked from the south and east with about forty tanks plus a battalion of infantry with half-tracks. Heavy enemy fire consisting of direct, mortar, small-arms, and automatic-weapons fire became intense during the three-hour fight that followed.

Infantry companies I and L began withdrawing toward the north and west. The 2d Platoon, 743d Tank Battalion, knocked out three enemy tanks, two half-tracks, and many enemy doughs as the enemy tried to advance from the east. The 1st Platoon, meanwhile, accounted for two enemy tanks, one half-track, and many enemy infantry who were advancing from the south.

As the 3d Battalion, Infantry, withdrew, the tanks laid down intense fire on the enemy; then the 1st Platoon pulled back by sections with some of the infantry riding on the rear decks of the vehicles. The 2d Platoon supported with fire during the withdrawal of the 1st Platoon, and then it, too, withdrew by sections. As the tanks moved to the rear, they exchanged direct fire with the enemy.[35]

Company C's tanks were desperately low on ammunition and fuel. The 743d Battalion's tanks withdrew to a makeshift defensive line to the west of Stoumont established by the 119th Infantry.[36] At this point, the histories of one of the army's most experienced tank battalions crossed with that of an untested outfit, the 740th, which was engaged in writing its own incredible story.

Can Anybody Spare a Tank?

Back in the States, the 740th Tank Battalion had been organized as a special battalion to be issued top-secret CDL spotlight tanks.[37] The battalion never actually received its CDL equipment despite a considerable amount of special training. So Lt. Col. George Rubel, a veteran of North Africa and the battalion's commander, stressed standard tank battalion instruction—especially accurate gunnery—a decision that probably saved the lives of many of his men in December 1944.[38] The 740th Tank Battalion arrived in Belgium in November having no tanks but with an order to convert to a standard tank battalion. The outfit did sport a bold new code name: Daredevil. Rubel borrowed nine Shermans, three M5A1s, and two assault guns from the tank-short First Army to begin retraining. None of the men had ever used the M5A1 or fired a 105-millimeter howitzer.

The battalion, which expected its first combat to take place in January, had tentative orders to join the 99th Infantry Division in the Ardennes. When the German attack struck on 16 December, however, several things occurred. First, the battalion was ordered to turn over all its Shermans to the 745th Tank Battalion. Second, on 17 December, Rubel was informed that the battalion might have to enter battle with its three M5A1s and two assault guns—and with the remainder of the personnel fighting as infantry. Third, on 18 December, the battalion was ordered to the front but was told to salvage what vehicles it could from an ordnance repair depot in Sprimont, Belgium. Upon arrival at the depot, the battalion was shocked to find that only three Sherman tanks were on the "ready for issue" line and that they were short of essential equipment. Of the twenty-five tanks in the park, only fifteen could be made operable, and even these were missing generators, starters, breech parts, radios, tools, rammer-staffs, and other items. None had a basic ammo load. Battalion personnel worked all night and until noon the next day cannibalizing tanks to put the fifteen selected into running condition. One tank crew nevertheless headed to battle from Sprimont without a breech-block, ammunition, or .30-caliber machine guns.

Rubel put crews into anything that could fight: M4s, M5A1s, M8 assault guns, two M24 light tanks, two DD Shermans, M7 self-propelled 105-millimeter howitzers, and M36 and M10 tank destroyers. The M24, featuring an improved suspension and a low-velocity 75-millimeter main gun, had begun arriving in the European theater in late 1944 as a replacement for the M5 series, but only a minority of the separate battalions ever received any.

S/Sgt. Charlie Loopey was one tank commander. Loopey had the reputation of being a bit of a playboy back in the States, but he would prove a fearless and steady man in combat.[39] He and his crew picked out one of the M36s. Although they had not trained on the equipment, the M36 was a tank-like self-propelled gun mounted on a Sherman chassis. It had a 90-millimeter converted antiaircraft cannon, which was the best antitank weapon in the American arsenal.

Lt. Charles Powers, Loopey's boss and leader of the 2d Platoon of Company C, picked a 75-millimeter Sherman for himself. Powers was a quiet, likeable gentleman who nevertheless was always ready to stand up for his men.[40] Powers's platoon moved out for Remouchamps in the late hours of 19 December, following company commander Capt. James "Red" Berry in his jeep. They soon encountered the S-2 of the 119th Infantry, 30th Infantry Division, who was on his way to the regimental command post. He related that one battalion of the regiment had been overrun and that the other two were under 50 percent strength and slowly losing ground. He requested assistance and did so again when Lieutenant Colonel Rubel arrived. Rubel noted that he had orders to stay where he was, so at 1400 hours, Maj. Gen. Leland Hobbs, the division's commanding general, appeared with authority from the First Army to attach the 740th Tank Battalion. The tankers moved out immediately.

As they arrived at the 119th Infantry's positions west of Stoumont, the tankers encountered the withdrawing Shermans of the 743d Tank Battalion, whose crews reported that five Panthers were advancing up the Ambleve River road about 1,000 yards distant. "We're low on ammo and fuel!" shouted one withdrawing tanker above the noise. "It's holy hell up there," called another. "Good luck!"

After consulting with regimental commander Col. Edwin Sutherland, it was agreed that the lead tank platoon would attack thirty minutes later at 1600 hours. The infantry were to advance as the tanks came abreast. Sutherland had learned a few things about how to use tanks, and Rubel would comment later, "[T]he cooperation between the battalion and the 119th Infantry was perfect."

Rubel added, "I never had such misgivings in my life. I hated to commit the battalion, and my fears were doubled when I saw the 743d Tank Battalion pulling out with more tanks than we were putting in." Rubel thought the other outfit's tankers just lacked the heart to keep on fighting; surely they could obtain more ammunition. He knew neither the men of the 743d Tank Battalion, nor what they had just been through. Captain Berry observed, "Of course, we were nervous as hell."

Powers and the 2d Platoon spearheaded the attack and advanced up the road toward Stoumont with supporting infantry arrayed to the sides, advancing by bounds as the armor clanked slowly up the road through the drizzly fog. The vehicles ground past two knocked-out panzers. After advancing 800 yards, Powers's loader, who also had his head out a hatch, realized that what he had thought was a brush pile was actually a Panther. He excitedly pointed it out to Powers, who ordered his gunner to fire. The first round hit the shot trap under the gun mantlet, ricocheted downward, killed the driver and bow gunner, and set the Mark V on fire. Another 100 yards on, Powers spotted a second Panther in the fog. This panzer got off several inaccurate rounds. Powers's first shot glanced off the front plate, and his second round jammed in his gun.

Powers desperately waved for Sergeant Loopey to move up, and his M36 tank destroyer advanced just as the Panther clawed closer to get a better shot. "I called [my gunner] for an AP, HE, hell, ANYTHING! Whatever you've got in there!" recalled Loopey. "Our first round hit him on the gun shield and kept him from getting down on us. We threw in several more rounds and blew a hole in his front left edge down low. Sparks flew, and flames shot twenty-five feet in the air!"

Meanwhile, Powers's gunner climbed out of the tank and cleared the jam with a ramrod. Powers resumed the lead and spotted a third Panther. The gunner's first shot blew the muzzle brake off the Mark V, and his next two shots set it on fire as the Panther tried to back away.

After this brisk thirty-minute firefight, the tide turned. The doughs, supported by the 740th Battalion armor spraying German infantry on the hillsides with machine guns, advanced 1,000 yards. Peiper's spearhead would not use this road. Both Powers and Loopey were awarded the Silver Star for their actions.

That night, the tankers ate K rations with cold-numbed fingers, hacked shallow trenches in the frozen soil, and parked their tanks over them to give them shelter as they slept. Surrounded by dug-in doughboys, the men felt secure even as they swapped rumors about Germans in the forest around them.

On 20 December, the battalion and the 119th Infantry attacked to retake Stoumont. One platoon of Company C (which still constituted the battalion's entire tank strength, though a platoon each of Companies A and B were nearly ready), working with the 1st Battalion west of town, ran into a Panther almost immediately. The lead Sherman knocked it out with a round that "opened its muzzle up like a rose." Another tank working with doughboys north of town fell prey to a concealed antitank gun. The infantry reached a sanitarium overlooking Stoumont, where fanatical SS troops screaming "Heil Hitler" backed by panzers

counterattacked and recaptured the facility. Three of Captain Berry's tanks helped stop the charge at that point, but after dark, the Germans illuminated the Shermans with flares, and direct fire destroyed two of them.

The next day, Combat Command B of the 3d Armored Division was attached to the 30th Infantry Division to help it clear the Stoumont–La Gleize pocket. During operations that day near a chateau at Stoumont, Lieutenant Powers nailed another Panther from the flank.

That night, Captain Berry conducted a personal reconnaissance to find a way to get tanks up to the sanitarium. Berry found a route and recruited some infantrymen to help construct a makeshift corduroy road. At about midnight, Lieutenant Powers, Loopey, and the commanders of two other tanks negotiated the path to a spot where they could fire through the windows of the sanitarium. This they did, with Berry running from tank to tank to direct the fire. The infantry cleaned out the last resistance on 22 December.

Rubel engaged in another bit of unorthodox equipment requisition and employment several days later during fighting near La Gleize. On 23 December, he dug up a 155-millimeter self-propelled gun, augmented the crew with his cooks, radio operators, and jeep driver, and positioned the weapon on high ground where it could fire into the German defenses over open sights. He ordered his 105-millimeter assault guns to keep the Germans' heads down. As he stood on a wall and directed fire, the gun pumped 192 rounds into La Gleize. Prisoners later said they had never experienced anything so terrible.[41]

The Northern Jaw Gains More Teeth

Between 16 and 18 December, the 1st Infantry Division moved into defensive positions between the 99th Division and the 30th Infantry Division. This added one more well-fired brick to the wall along the northern edge of the Bulge.

The 745th Tank Battalion moved into the line with the Big Red One, as usual, and encountered the strongest armor attacks it had yet faced. During the period from 20 to 22 December—when twelve German divisions, seven of them armored, threw a ferocious fresh attack against the northern shoulder defenses along the Malmedy-Bütgenbach-Monschau line—Company C alone destroyed thirteen tanks and one self-propelled gun near Bütgenbach.[42]

The 750th Tank Battalion left the 104th Infantry Division behind in defensive positions along the Roer and rolled into the Ardennes on 22 December after an all-night road march. Now attached to the untried 75th Infantry Division, the tankers spent most of their time until mid-January providing a mobile reserve to the infantry regiments. At no time during this period was even an entire company committed to action.[43]

Meanwhile, Lieutenant Colonel Rubel was learning that tank and infantry communities did not always become the tightly knit family portrayed in the official history. On 28 December, he reported to the headquarters of the 82d Airborne Division, to which the 740th Tank Battalion had been attached for an assault southward toward Lierneux, and met with a universally chilly reception. The paratroop officers told him that tanks had usually been more of a hindrance than a help to them because tankers refused to keep up with their men. Rubel, who evoked memories of Patton among some of his men, replied that his boys had come to fight.[44] At Rubel's urging, the paratroopers and tankers ran exercises together before attacking on 3 January. Within a few days, the tankers and doughs knew each other's first names, and after their first engagement together, the paratroopers told Rubel that his was the first outfit that *they* couldn't keep up with.[45]

The Southern Jaw Clamps Tight

Beginning on 18 December, Patton turned the weight of the Third Army more than ninety degrees and tore into the southern flank of the Bulge. His men moved 125 miles through a blizzard to accomplish this feat, and through 23 December, 133,178 motor vehicles traversed a total of 1,654,042 miles. The III Corps, including the 4th Armored and 80th and 26th Infantry Divisions, attacked on 22 December to relieve the surrounded "Battling Bastards of Bastogne," primarily paratroopers from the 101st Airborne Division. German commanders who calculated that Patton would never be able to react so quickly were wrong.[46] On the other hand, German intelligence easily detected the Third Army's shift, and by the time Patton's spearhead arrived, the Germans had deployed strong blocking forces on all approach routes.[47]

The 735th Tank Battalion took part in Patton's remarkable redeployment.[48] On 20 December, Companies A and C were on the east bank of the Saar supporting doughs of the 2d Infantry Regiment, 5th Infantry Division, fighting in Saarlautern. Patton had been calling around to get separate tank battalions on the move to the Ardennes.[49] At 1230 hours, the battalion received warning orders to move to the vicinity of Stuckange, where the commander was to report to the headquarters of the XX Corps. The battalion was told to move as a unit, which was impossible to do because its elements were engaged with the enemy and spread out across one hundred square miles. The companies were given their routes by special couriers and told to join up as quickly as they could. Sometime after 1500 hours, the battalion halted briefly at a bridge near Bouzanville, which was the first opportunity to discover if all companies had formed up. They had.

The 735th Tank Battalion's march orders were for Luxembourg, where a liaison officer from the 26th Infantry Division informed the battalion of its attachment to that unit and sent the tankers on to Arlon, Belgium. In about twelve hours, the outfit had arrived in its new sector after a sixty-mile, overnight, blacked-out road march that passed through parts of Germany, France, Luxembourg, and Belgium. The tankers reached their partner units on 21 December and engaged the enemy the next day as the 26th Division pushed northward toward Wiltz, initially meeting light resistance from elements of four volksgrenadier divisions. To the division's left, the 4th Armored Division strove to break through to Bastogne. By 24 December, the infantry and tanks had run into fierce resistance. In a single action on 27 December, German assault guns claimed three of the 735th Tank Battalion's M4A3E2 Jumbos.

Redeployment of tank battalions to unfamiliar infantry divisions reintroduced some of the old problems experienced in Normandy when fighting beside new partners. Despite a concerted effort by the 735th Tank Battalion's commanding officer, Lt. Col. Abe Bock, to work out the terms for tank-infantry cooperation with the headquarters of the 26th Infantry Division, problems due to unfamiliarity arose almost immediately. On 23 December, Company B supported a drive by the 104th Infantry Regiment toward Dellen. The battalion's after-action report described the problem and the tankers' reaction to being forced to risk their lives with strangers:

Very little resistance was met, and the tanks did little firing. The town of Dellen was taken by the tanks as the infantry would not go into it ahead of them. This attitude seemed to be prevalent among the infantry units here. Apparently they do not realize the ease with which tanks can be knocked out in restricted areas such as towns and that they could easily be left without any tank support whatsoever by running them into a trap such as that. . . .

Transfer of the 735th Tank Battalion and its attachment to a new division led inevitably to a feeling of doubt and in some cases to downright confusion on the battlefield. This doubt and confusion is directly traceable to the fact that the two units have different histories and have been confronted by different problems for which they have arrived at different solutions. Infantry-tank cooperation has suffered greatly by the change in attachment—which can only be regained by long association.[50]

The infantry saw it differently. According to the 104th Infantry, the tanks were completely road-bound. "[Tank] platoons were used in close support of attacking elements of the infantry and not to spearhead the attack."[51]

The 737th Tank Battalion also participated in the Third Army's counteroffensive. Attached to the 35th Infantry Division near Sarreguemines, the battalion was ordered north on 21 December. The battalion assembled in the vicinity of Detrange, Luxembourg, at 0300 hours on 23 December following a grueling 120-mile road march. The equipment was not in its best shape, and tankers worked frantically to perform what maintenance they could in the bitter cold and snow. By noon, the tanks were committed in support of 5th Infantry Division soldiers near Echternach. The 737th Tank Battalion had an unusually positive experience in terms of the rapid integration of tanks and infantry even though the battalion had never fought before with the "Red Diamond" Division. S/Sgt. Clint O'Davaney, a platoon sergeant in Company B, exclaimed, "These guys from the 5th are fighting bastards. Ain't it the truth!"[52] Maj. Gen. S. Leroy Irwin, commanding the division, recorded in his diary, "New tank battalion is in fairly good shape."[53]

By Christmas, *Wacht am Rhein* was spent as an offensive operation. That day, the 2d Armored Division stopped the 2d Panzer Division at Celles, four miles from the Meuse River. The same day, the 3d Armored Division blocked the 2d SS Panzer Division's drive on Namur. Bastogne still held, and on 26 December, the lead elements of a relief force from the 4th Armored Division punched through. The American lines along the shoulders of the Bulge held firm.[54] Hitler had coal in his stocking.

Interestingly enough, the tank battalions that had not borne the brunt of the initial German assault suffered low losses during the December fighting, probably because they for once held the advantages of the defender. The 743d Tank Battalion, for example, saw plenty of tough fighting—it knocked out at least six Panthers and Tigers—but lost only one crew of five men killed (and their Sherman) and four men wounded during late December.[55]

DENOUEMENT

On 3 January 1945, Hitler admitted that his Ardennes offensive no longer offered promise of success. He had shot his last bolt. On 8 January, he authorized a withdrawal to the Ourthe River. Although Operation *Nordwind* ("North Wind"), a counterstroke against the Seventh Army launched with New Year's, was still unfolding in Alsace, it would burn out within two weeks. The Allies could now turn to the task of overrunning the heart of Germany.[56]

Field Marshal Montgomery had carefully hoarded the First Army's VII Corps to spearhead the inevitable counterstroke against the German line from the north, an operation that he ordered to commence on 3 January in the general direction of Houffalize—about the midpoint of the Bulge. The corps commander, Maj. Gen. J. Lawton Collins, planned to strike with two armored divisions, the 2d and 3d, and follow through with the 84th and 83d Infantry Divisions, which would mop up bypassed resistance. Attached to those divisions were, respectively, the 774th and 771st Tank Battalions. The 75th Infantry Division (with the 750th Tank Battalion attached) would act as the corps reserve. The II SS Panzer Corps, made up of the 2d SS Panzer Division and two volksgrenadier divisions, barred the way.[57]

Confronting snow or rain, snowdrifts up to four feet deep, bad roads, rough terrain, and German resistance, the armored divisions failed to break through, and the infantry divisions became deeply embroiled in the same frustrating fighting.

Meanwhile, Patton was pressing northward with his III and VIII Corps against similar physical conditions and fierce resistance. In addition to the 6th Armored Division, the III Corps had two veteran infantry divisions—the 26th and 35th, with elements of both supported by the 735th Tank Battalion.

The veteran 90th Infantry Division and 712th Tank Battalion soon joined them after being withdrawn from the Saar region. The tankers moved into the Ardennes on 7 January 1945, arriving at Rippweiler, Luxembourg, after a forty-nine-mile road march over snow-covered roads. The battalion was committed again on 9 January near Berle, Luxembourg. Once again, battle-honed American tankers proved they could beat German armor. On 12 January, for example, camouflaged Shermans of the 2d Platoon, Company B, knocked out six tanks and six self-propelled guns, netting 150 prisoners. The next day, the same platoon knocked out three Panthers and three assault guns. Only three days later, two platoons from Company A, firing from defensive positions on good ground, destroyed eight Panthers and crippled a Tiger.[58]

On 15 January, troops from the First and Third Armies finally met at Houffalize. On 17 January, the First Army was returned to Bradley's 12th Army Group; it could now turn eastward to erase the remnant of the Bulge, adding the V Corps' 30th Infantry Division and 743d Tank Battalion to the effort.

Physical conditions remained atrocious for the men, many of whom had been in the line for nearly a month. The 743rd Tank Battalion's after-action report for 17 January noted that the battalion "had a number of [nonbattle casualty] illnesses not requiring hospitalization, most of these a result of the extreme cold and difficult operating conditions in the tanks which one man, with grim humor, referred to as 'Armored Frigidaires.'" Advancing in deep woods, the 750th Battalion tankers found that the snow from the trees fell into the open turrets of the tanks in such quantities that crewmen were unable to extract ammunition from the floor racks. Commanders had to keep the hatches open because periscopes were frosted over.[59]

The crews did the best they could to adapt to these miserable conditions. Lieutenant Colonel Rubel offered a description of the combined affects of carrying infantry and gradually accruing minimal creature comforts:

> In [the] attack a tank was a strange looking object. There were usually from ten to twenty men riding on top of it. It was usually towing a trailer loaded down with rations, machine guns, tripods, and the usual miscellany of gear that a combat soldier takes along with him. In addition, the tankers had placed sand bags on the front slope plate of the tank, the sides, and sometimes around the turrets for protection against panzerfausts. Add to this conglomeration the tankers' housekeeping tools, which usually included a liberated heating stove, three or four joints of stovepipe, two or three frying pans, and two or three ordinary black pots. The pots were multipurpose articles. They were used for converting snow into drinking water, washing clothes, cooking food, and pouring gasoline. They were also used as carriers for other smaller articles while en route. The load on the back of the tank usually included, in addition to all the other items mentioned, several extra boxes of .30- and .50-cal ammunition and occasionally the carcass of a deer or cow that had been killed while attacking the tank. The tank thus laden turned out to be an excellent camouflage job. At a distance of fifty yards it was impossible to tell what kind of a vehicle it was—even if you determined that it actually was a vehicle.[60]

American tankers also adapted to the wintry landscape once the U.S. Army finally began to provide the necessary whitewash. Generally, supplies came very late. The 741st Tank Battalion was notified on 10 January that calcimine had become available.[61] The 743d Tank Battalion was first able to apply coats of lime to its tanks of the line on 11 January 1945.[62] The 749th was not able to apply winter camouflage until 19 January.[63] The 753d Tank Battalion noted one problem with the improving use of white camouflage by American forces: in fighting on 8 January near Mackwiller in the Seventh Army's zone, tankers experienced difficulty distinguishing between the infantry of the two armies.[64]

Despite—or perhaps because of—the terrible weather, January generally proved to be a time of relatively low battle casualty rates for the tank battalions in the Ardennes sector. The 743d Tank Battalion, for example, lost seven men killed and three officers and sixteen men wounded, as well as four M4s and four M5A1s, despite being on the attack and encountering German armor with some frequency (the battalion destroyed nine and captured four Mark IVs and knocked out two Mark Vs).[65] The 750th Tank Battalion also attacked during the period and lost only two Shermans and two M5A1s, all to mines.[66] The 741st Tank Battalion lost two enlisted men killed and one officer and two enlisted men wounded—and lost no vehicles—during its push south near the Elsenborn Ridge.[67] And the 737th Tank Battalion recorded in its after-action report, "Our tanks destroyed one Royal Tiger, two Panthers, eight Mk IV tanks, ten SP vehicles, eight half-tracks, four 75mm [antitank] guns, one 75mm howitzer . . . [a]s against a total of eight casualties and five tanks being disabled by enemy action. . . . All of our tanks had covered thousands of miles and all were equipped with the 75mm gun."

The 740th Tank Battalion, however, lost thirteen Shermans and one M5A1 and was down to an average of seven operational tanks per company at month's end. It also suffered proportionate losses in men (seven killed and twenty-eight wounded).[68] The tendency of inexperienced battalions to suffer high losses early in their deployments may account for these figures in part, but the battalion's destruction of four Tigers, one King Tiger, and five other tanks and assault guns underscores the tough fighting the men endured. The 712th Tank Battalion also suffered heavy losses during its deployment into the area, including that of battalion commander Lt. Col. George Randolph, who was killed by shellfire.

Patton, meanwhile, launched an attack he had been pressing Bradley to approve on the base of the Bulge with the XII Corps. He pushed the 4th, 5th, and 80th Infantry Divisions (supported by the 70th, 737th, and 702d Tank battalions, respectively) across the Sauer River on 18 January.[69] Commanders had to lead their tanks forward on foot over the icy roads in some cases.[70]

Because towns offered protection and shelter from the elements, they became the centerpieces of the fighting. The official U.S. Army history credits tanks and tank destroyers during this period with playing an invaluable role for the infantry by blasting German defenders from the sturdy structures. Minefields again became a constant menace, particularly when hidden by a new layer of snow.[71]

Although Hitler had finally recognized that his offensive in the Ardennes had failed, he authorized a withdrawal only as far as the West Wall (except for SS units he transferred to the crumbling Eastern Front) despite the pleas of Rundstedt and Army Group B commander Field Marshal Walter Model that they be permitted to retreat to the east bank of the Rhine. This stubborn decision set the stage for the annihilation of much of the remaining German resources in the West.[72] The separate tank battalions would again play their part.

CHAPTER 12

The Reich Overrun

"We spent February licking our wounds. There were new men to be trained, battle lessons to be passed on, and new tanks to be processed. We all knew what we were getting ready for. The Germans had thrown their Sunday punch, now we were going to throw ours."
—*Up From Marseille, 781st Tank Battalion*

Late January found American commanders once again contemplating plans to breach the West Wall and capture the Roer River dams. This time, however, Lt. Gen. Omar Bradley decided to work around the Hürtgen Forest. The advance during late January and early February was limited far more by deep snow, icy or collapsing roads, and freezing temperatures than it was by patchwork—albeit sometimes spirited—German resistance.

On 1 February, Eisenhower ordered Bradley to throttle back the effort, because he wanted to shift the emphasis northward to the Ninth Army in support of Montgomery. The British field marshal's 21st Army Group launched Operation Veritable on 8 February. The Germans had sabotaged the Roer River dams before they were captured by the Americans on the ninth, and the flooding of the Roer River delayed the Ninth Army's Operation Grenade—supported by the First Army's VII Corps—until 23 February. For that crossing, the 739th Tank Battalion supplied twenty-seven tank drivers to operate LVTs, which ferried personnel and equipment across the Roer River during the assault. The swift current forced the battalion to discontinue use of the LVTs. The Germans had fought the British and Canadians hard, but their defenses gave way under the twin pounding, and the Ninth Army's XIX Corps reached the Rhine on 2 March.

One day earlier, the remainder of the First Army launched Operation Lumberjack, and on the seventh, the 9th Armored Division captured the Ludendorff railroad bridge across the Rhine at Remagen intact. Patton's Third and Patch's Seventh Armies struck in mid-March, and by the twenty-first, the Allies had destroyed most of the German Army west of the Rhine and held the near bank from Switzerland almost to the sea.[1]

Once resistance broke down, the race to the Rhine was another welcome period of low casualties for most separate tank battalions in the north. The 741st Tank Battalion, for example, lost seven men killed and eighteen wounded during all of March. The 743d Battalion suffered only seventeen casualties of all types for the month.[2]

About this time, some tank battalions hit upon a new method to improve armor protection by pouring concrete on the front plates of their Shermans. The 750th Tank Battalion, for example, had to use jackhammers at the end of hostilities to remove six inches of reinforced concrete it had added during combat.[3] Experiments conducted by the 709th Tank Battalion in February 1945 indicated that poured concrete did not stop bazookas from penetrating the armor plate but that it did reduce the splash of molten steel inside the tank caused by the warhead to "negligible" proportions.[4] Based on combat experience, tankers in the 753d Tank Battalion concluded that antitank rounds that hit concrete-reinforced armor had a reduced chance of killing the crew, even if they knocked the tank out of action.[5]

The 12th Army Group had concluded that the M5A1 light tank was not useful in combat. In February, it recommended to Eisenhower that medium tanks replace light tanks in all standard tank battalions and in light tank battalions.[6]

Central and Southern Germany

CROSSING THE RHINE: A THREE-TURRET-RING CIRCUS

The Rhine River was supposed to pose a major defensive obstacle to the Allies, but four separate operations easily forced the river during March. Eisenhower had agreed that Monty would make the big push across the Rhine in the north. Things did not work out that way.

As noted above, on 7 March, the First Army's 9th Armored Division had captured the Ludendorff railroad bridge at Remagen. The 746th Tank Battalion crossed the Remagen bridge on 8 March—the first separate tank battalion to cross the river.

On 22 March, Patton beat Monty to the punch and slipped across the Rhine at Oppenheim, a small barge harbor halfway between Mainz and Worms. The 5th Infantry Division crossed at the cost of only eight killed and twenty wounded, and the 737th Tank Battalion joined the doughs on 23 March. Within thirty-six hours, the bridgehead was five miles deep and seven miles wide. The 90th Infantry and 4th Armored Divisions crossed unmolested and headed east. By 28 March, tanks of Company C, 737th Tank Battalion, had crossed the Main River and entered Frankfurt.[7]

When news of this stroke reached Hitler, he called for immediate countermeasures, but German commanders had nothing with which to respond. The only "reserve" was an assortment of five panzers under repair at a tank depot 100 miles away. The bottom of the barrel had been scraped.[8]

On 23 March, Montgomery finally launched his operatic assault, complete with massive air strikes, airborne assaults by two divisions, and well-organized media coverage. He had slowly amassed twenty-five divisions and a quarter-million tons of ammunition and other supplies on the west bank of the Rhine. Opposing him in the thirty-five-mile stretch of river that he planned to cross were only five exhausted German divisions. The Ninth Army, which furnished half the assaulting infantry, lost only forty men killed during the crossing. Still, nervous about the Germans despite the near total absence of serious resistance, Monty would authorize no general advance eastward until he had moved twenty divisions and 1,500 tanks into the bridgehead.[9]

But first the bridgehead had to be enlarged. The 743d Tank Battalion had crossed the Rhine with the 30th Infantry Division as part of the assault wave, and it ran into a last-gasp German effort to staunch the wound as the 116th Panzer Division shifted into the tankers' path from the Canadian front. Several days of renewed limited-objective fighting against stiff resistance ensued. But the German effort was futile, because two American armored divisions were crossing the river behind the infantry. On 29 March, having again opened the door, the doughs and tankers settled down as the big armor passed through the lines and swept over the defenders.[10]

On 26 March, the Seventh Army forced the Rhine near Worms. One assault division, the 3d Infantry, had a tough time, but the second, the 45th Infantry, faced only modest resistance. The lead elements of the 756th Tank Battalion crossed the river at 1615 hours, mostly on pontoon rafts, to support the 3d Infantry Division doughs. Within three days, four more divisions, including two armored, had crossed—and more would follow.[11]

The Rhine assault featured an almost circus-like use of the good and not-so-good special capabilities that had been foisted on some of the separate tank battalions—almost as if higher command decided it needed to use the whole panoply to justify the cost.

DD tanks had proven themselves already, and Monty had a veritable naval task force of them ready: sixty-six British and seventeen American. The use of the 70th, 741st, and 743d Tank Battalions, which had used DD tanks in the Normandy landings, was considered. The losses among the tank crews had been so high since Normandy, however, that those outfits would have required as much training as those that had never used the equipment. Company C of the 736th Tank Battalion was instead trained and fitted out with DD tanks and attached to the 743d Battalion for the actual crossing, during which the tankers faced virtually no resistance. Prior to the Seventh Army's crossing, Company C of the 756th Tank Battalion—the only medium tank company in the battalion that had *not* used DD tanks in Operation Dragoon—had received hurried training on DD Shermans. The DD tanks participated in the crossing in support of the 3d Infantry Division. Launching at daylight, three successfully made the crossing in the 7th Infantry Regiment's sector, but three sank, and one was destroyed by artillery; in the 30th Infantry Regiment's sector, six made it, and one sank.[12] Technically, Patton in late March also used DD tanks that were supplied to the 748th Tank Battalion. Eight of the fifty-one DD Shermans actually entered the Rhine, but one sank. Most of the rest were so badly damaged by road march that they could no longer maintain buoyancy. The river crossing was not an assault crossing, however; the battalion was merely moving up to support the 65th and 89th Infantry Divisions.

The 747th Tank Battalion was issued LVTs, and between 24 and 26 March, it made 1,112 round trips across the Rhine in support of the Ninth Army. The Water Buffaloes carried elements of the 30th and 79th Infantry Divisions, including infantry, artillery, antitank guns, and ammunition. Two LVTs were damaged by artillery fire.[13] For Homer Wilkes and the rest of the battalion (except, briefly, for Company B and the assault guns), the Rhine crossing was the last action under fire of the war.

The Ninth Army reequipped Company B of the 739th Tank Battalion (Mine-exploder) with CDL tanks to illuminate bridging sites beginning 23 March. The First Army had been using a handful of CDL tanks from the 738th Tank Battalion (Mine-exploder) for the same purpose at the Remagen bridgehead since 9 March and deployed additional CDL tanks on the twenty-first and twenty-third. The Third Army also used three platoons of CDL tanks from the 748th Tank Battalion at St. Goar, Bad Salsig, and Mainz.[14]

POCKETING THE RUHR

The envelopment and capture of the Ruhr industrial basin, which lies on both banks of the river of that name, was the last large-scale battle facing American troops in Europe. The Ninth Army—still under Monty's command until 4 April, when it was returned to Bradley's 12th Army Group—raced around the north, while the First Army, in concert with the Third, looped around the south. The encirclement was mainly a story of the 2d Armored Division, which spearheaded the northern sweep, and the 3d Armored Division to the south. The infantry divisions and attached tank battalions played only a supporting role.

On 1 April, American forces linked at Lippstadt. The defenders in the Ruhr Pocket held out for eighteen days, but when the fighting was over, 325,000 Germans had surrendered. Field Marshal Walter Model chose to kill himself rather than give up.[15]

Mopping up the Ruhr Pocket was no cakewalk, although some areas fell almost without a shot.[16] The 8th Infantry Division, in a typical example, was ordered to cut the pocket in half by driving north through Olpe to Wuppertal, but without tank support. Pushing out of Siegen in the last days of March, the doughs were thrown back with heavy losses. On 8 April, the 740th Tank Battalion was sent to support the frustrated infantry. The tanks spearheaded the renewed attack, with infantrymen mounted on the rear decks. Their orders were to race ahead, with the doughs dismounting only to clear roadblocks; these usually comprised a log barricade defended by two or three bazooka teams, one or two machine guns, and two or more antitank guns. Unfortunately, if the Germans chose to fight, the first indication that a roadblock lay ahead was usually the destruction of the lead tank. In a growing number of cases, however, the dispirited defenders surrendered when the tanks rolled up.[17]

The 3d Platoon of Company C, 740th Tank Battalion, was under new management. Charlie Loopey had taken over the platoon when Lieutenant Powers had received his "million-dollar wound" after the Roer River crossing and received a battlefield commission to second lieutenant. On 9 April, Loopey and his men supported the 2d Battalion, 121st Infantry Regiment, in its advance through Rahrbach just east of Olpe. As Loopey approached the village of Welschen Ennestt, two enormous seventy-ton Jagdtiger tank killers mounting 128-millimeter guns came out of the forest ahead. Either could have obliterated Loopey's Sherman with a single round, and he stood no chance of penetrating the thick frontal armor of the German vehicles at any range. Fortunately, the Jagdtigers were evidently trying to escape because they turned the other direction and headed north. No one will ever know why the escape hatches on both were open. The escape hatch was a circular hole in the back of the superstructure normally covered by an armored door and was about two feet in diameter. Loopey's gunner put a couple of rounds of high-explosive through these holes on both vehicles and knocked them out, killing their crews.[18]

The doughs pushed forward relentlessly; the American infantry regiments were able to leapfrog one another, but once more, the tankers went into the line every day. The 740th Tank Battalion again experienced considerable friction with infantry commanders.[19] Nevertheless, American forces were in Olpe by 11 April.

On 12 April, only four days before the 740th Tank Battalion would experience hostile fire for the last time, Lieutenant Loopey's platoon jumped off at 0800 hours from Hombert. In Oberbrügge, some twenty miles east of Wuppertal, the tankers spotted a roadblock but also noticed a bypass that appeared to lead around the obstruction. Easing forward, Loopey realized that the Germans had set a bazooka ambush on the bypass, and he opened fire. The ambushers dispersed, and the tanks pressed ahead and swung back to take the roadblock from the rear. They found a target-rich environment and destroyed one self-propelled flak gun, one half-track, and many wheeled vehicles. Per standard practice, Loopey had his head protruding out of his hatch. A shell struck the turret, showering Loopey's face and neck with fragments. He was evacuated at about 1130 hours. The war was over for him, too. But the military machine clanked on: Staff Sergeant Fleming assumed command of the 3d Platoon.

On 14 April, the 8th Infantry Division linked with the 79th Infantry Division, which had pushed southward from the Ninth Army at Wetter on the Ruhr River. Lieutenant Colonel Rubel recorded: "The battle of the Ruhr Pocket was over. In many ways it had been a steeplechase, and from the infantry's standpoint, it was an easy operation. From the tanker's standpoint, it was a hundred miles of spearheading, and a grueling, exhausting battle. We had lost as many tanks here as we had lost in the Battle of the Ardennes. We hoped that the war would soon be over."[20]

On 18 April, Rubel received orders putting his battalion on occupation duty in Düsseldorf. Rubel himself took on the duties of lord mayor of the city. The colonel delivering the orders chuckled and added, "The last Lord Mayor of Düsseldorf was killed a few days ago, you know. Don't let it become a habit."[21]

RACE TO THE FINISH LINE

The tankers of the separate battalions were now among the most savvy graduates of the school of war. They knew how to storm cities and deal with small groups of defenders in villages or at crossroads. They could slog through fortifications and run like the cavalry of old. By and large, they had worked out effective teamwork strategies with the infantry, tank destroyers, and artillery, even if still a bit ambivalent about their friends in the fighter-bombers above them. They had learned to beat better tanks and worked out a series of pragmatic technical solutions to problems ranging from communication to moving on ice.

They had to do it only a little while longer before they could return to their lives and families.

Cornelius Ryan captured the essence of the final push: "The race was on. Never in the history of warfare had so many men moved so fast. The speed of the Anglo-American offensive was contagious, and all along the front the drive was taking on the proportions of a giant contest."[22] So fast, indeed, that between 24 and 30 April, the 737th Tank Battalion moved 520 miles.[23] A detailed accounting of the actions of each battalion during this period would be a dull recitation of long lists of towns passed through, sometimes involving a firefight but often not.

The Ninth Army pounded in the direction of Berlin all the way to the Elbe River. Just to the south, the First Army advanced to the Mulde River. Patton's Third Army drove toward Czechoslovakia, and the Seventh Army pushed through Bavaria toward the rumored Nazi National Redoubt in the Bavarian Alps and Austria.[24]

The tankers rolled past columns of German POWs heading for the rear, often with no supervision. Increasingly, displaced persons and released Allied POWs also appeared.

Spearheads

There were not enough armored divisions to sweep everywhere, and some infantry divisions with their attached tank battalions joined the spearheads. Doughs piled onto the tanks. In some cases, artillery observers rode with the forward elements. Tank battalions attached to the infantry divisions in the following wave spent their days scooping up wandering German soldiers and clearing out the scattered towns and villages where German forces refused to give up.

The 736th Tank Battalion (attached to the 83d Infantry Division) was one of the units leading the charge. Their column became engaged in an intense rivalry with the 2d Armored Division to see who could move farther faster. The doughs requisitioned every vehicle they came across—even one German Me 109 fighter plane, on which they painted "83d Inf. Div." across the underside—and soon became known as the "Rag-Tag Circus." The two divisions reluctantly conceded a tie at the Weser River. Then they pelted on. The 2d Armored reached the Elbe River late on 11 April and slipped armored infantry across; doughs of the 83d Division reached the east bank of the river on the thirteenth. The 736th Battalion's tanks crossed the Elbe on the twentieth, but Eisenhower had already decided that his troops would press no closer to Berlin.[25] This would be the farthest penetration for a separate tank battalion in Germany.

The 702d Tank Battalion, dashing through central Germany with the 80th Infantry Division, described in its after-action report the conditions tankers of most units encountered much of the time:

> Throughout the month of April, enemy attempts at resistance were marked by their continued feebleness. At only two periods was there any show of strength, and by late in the month our assault had lost its character, and the only proper description for operations engaged in by the battalion was "road march."
>
> The cities of Kassel and Erfurt were the focal points of resistance, and in the defense of the former, tanks were used in limited numbers. Flak units were the manpower basis for this defense. But these fanatical sacrifice operations served to no value, for the miscellaneous grab-bag units crumbled before our organized assaults after only a token-plus resistance. . . .

The attitude of the German soldier was one of complete abandonment to his fate. He found his fate lay only in two directions, death or the PW camp, and with a little physical persuasion, generally chose the latter. PW figures grew astronomically, and interrogation degenerated into a simple counting of those who passed through the tills of the PW cage. The German people were completely confused and confusing. Many of them went out of their way to be hospitable to the conquering American, and overt acts by the civilians against our military forces were rare.[26]

Not all German forces had abandoned the fight. Advancing columns frequently encountered small units that fought briefly, claiming a few more American lives, before giving up, running, or dying. The SS were a particular problem. American troops had a simple rule: if a town showed white flags and offered no resistance, they rolled through. If American troops came under fire, they smashed the community. Indeed, any sympathy for the civilian populace declined as advancing forces began liberating the concentration camps. The 70th Tank Battalion's informal history recorded that "[t]he tanks swept across open fields from village to village, blasting relentlessly at every sign of resistance. Any town or city that tried to delay the advance soon became a raging inferno. The German landscape was dotted with burning villages. More white flags began to appear."[27]

Lieutenant Dew in the 741st Tank Battalion was fighting a series of these small but deadly engagements as his battalion advanced with the 2d Infantry Division through central Germany. On 8 April, after crossing the Weser, his tankers had to destroy 20-millimeter antiaircraft guns that were firing on the column near Klein Lengden. They suppressed small-arms fire in a few small villages during the next several days. On the thirteenth, the column again encountered antiaircraft fire at Dörstewitz. The division was nearing Leipzig, and it was running into flak batteries disposed to defend synthetic rubber and gasoline plants in Shkopau and Leuna. Dew decided to rush the town and outflank the gun positions, and he ordered his platoon forward. As the Shermans swung into the village, an unseen enemy soldier fired a bazooka. The round easily punctured Dew's tank, wounding the lieutenant and killing his driver. The battalion would experience its final hostile fire only five days later. It seemed so senseless to lose a man at this stage. Dew would return to duty on 5 May after the battalion had fired its last shot.[28]

Now and again, the fights were big and dismaying. For example, after crossing the Rhine, the 100th Infantry Division and the 781st Tank Battalion advanced rapidly until reaching the west bank of the Neckar River in the vicinity of Heilbronn on 3 April. The doughs crossed the river in assault boats the next day to find themselves battling a remarkably effective defense made up of Wehrmacht, Volkssturm, Hitler Youth, and SS—so effective that the Germans counterattacked and almost threw the doughs back into the Neckar. Accurate artillery fire disrupted every American attempt to erect a bridge and get the tanks across. Higher headquarters frantically arranged for the delivery of ten DD Shermans to the 781st Tank Battalion, and crews were given a day of training. The tanks entered the water but were unable to climb the other side, and three sank. Finally, on 8 April, two platoons made the trip across a temporary bridge that was immediately knocked out by enemy artillery. On 12 April, American doughs and tanks pushed the German artillery out of range of the bridging sites, and on the next day, Heilbronn fell.[29]

On 17 April, the 756th Tank Battalion rolled into the Nazi citadel of Nürnberg, and with the doughs of the 3d Infantry Division, for three days, it fought street to street against determined resistance in the form of antitank, bazooka, and small-arms fire. The 191st Tank Battalion and 45th Infantry Division pushed in from the south. SS and mountain troops, backed by thirty-five tanks brought from the Grafenwoehr Proving Grounds, defended the city. German snipers with *panzerfausts* picked off tanks from the rooftops, and it became standard practice for the tanks to blast any building that even looked as if it might hide such a sniper. On 22 April, with victory finally at hand, the 756th Tank Battalion patrolled the streets of the city in a show of strength.[30]

THE UNDER-BELLY FINALLY GOES SOFT

The Fifth Army in Italy had spent nearly five months with almost no forward movement, but it had used that time wisely. Replacements joined the battle-thinned ranks, new vehicles replaced those worn out, and ammunition reserves piled up. Equipment on the Italian front finally began to catch up with that being used in the European theater. M4A3s with 76-millimeter guns reached the 760th Tank Battalion in October and the 751st Tank Battalion by November 1944, and both outfits allocated five to each medium tank company. Seventeen M24s arrived at the 751st Tank Battalion in March 1945, but the following month, the battalion had to turn those over to the 1st Armored Division, getting in exchange worn-out M5 and M5A1 tanks.[31] The 752d and 757th Tank Battalions similarly drew M24s only to have them taken away.[32]

The 752d and 757th Tank Battalions finally received M4A3 105-millimeter assault guns to replace their M7 Priests in December 1944. The first M4A3s with 76-millimeter guns arrived at the 752d and 757th Tank Battalions by February 1945, and the 757th Battalion had enough to fully equip Company A in March, while the 752d Battalion re-armored all three medium tank companies. "The boys were strictly in favor of the new high-velocity weapon," the 752d Tank Battalion recorded. (The battalion later re-issued M4s to one platoon in each company to take the lead crossing minefields, with the surplus M4A3s to be available as replacements; there is no record of what the crews issued M4s thought of that.) While swapping the new tanks for the old M4s, the crews experienced some exciting times on the icy mountain trails, because many of the tanks had been dug in without moving for four months, but installing grousers helped.

Back in August, the 760th Tank Battalion had received T27 4.5-inch rocket launcher kits to be installed on four medium tanks but had not used them. The 752d Tank Battalion was issued launchers for about four tanks during December and 7.2-inch T40 launchers—a point-blank weapon that rendered the main gun unusable until the launcher was jettisoned—for about the same number of tanks. The II Corps had viewed the 4.5-inch launchers as impractical and, in December, told the Fifth Army that it did not want them. Nevertheless, the 752d Tank Battalion put its 4.5-inch launchers into sustained use in March, firing 1,300 rockets over twelve days. The battalion also drew one Scorpion mine-clearing flail tank.[33]

By 1 April, the Fifth Army's rehabilitation was complete.

On 12 April, the crews of the 751st Tank Battalion pulled into positions behind the doughs of the 10th Mountain Division. The 755th Tank Battalion likewise moved forty Shermans into prepared positions, from which they were to support the 91st Infantry division. The 752d Tank Battalion deployed its rocket and medium tanks where they would do the most good for the 34th Division's GIs. Other battalions made ready, too.

In March, meanwhile, the 755th Tank Battalion had reequipped with LVTs and reorganized into three squadrons. After practicing on the waters of Lake Trasimene, the outfit moved to the Ravenna area and joined the Eighth Army. In one of the opening moves of the final offensive in Italy, on 11 April, the battalion ferried two battalions of the British 56th Infantry Division across flooded terrain south of Lake Comacchio to flank the German line. The next day, the battalion conducted a similar attack with troops from the 24th Guards Brigade, which succeeded despite determined German resistance. Of some interest, when most of the battalion reequipped with tanks after the operation, an entire company received British Fireflies, Shermans armed with the deadly 17-pounder main gun.[34]

At dawn on 14 April 1945, the Fifth Army attacked all along its line. To the east, the British Eighth Army had launched five days before, and diversionary attacks by the IV Corps near the western coast had started even earlier. At first, the going was tough. "The attack was proceeding slowly," recorded the 752d Tank Battalion, because of "heavily mined terrain and fanatic resistance by infantry and tanks." In the battalion's sector, the terrain proved too rough for the Scorpion mine-clearing tank to work effectively, and mines and antitank fire claimed several Shermans during the first few days.[35]

After cracking through the initial crust of resistance, American forces swept into the Po River Valley and crossed the river itself within ten days. By 21 April, Shermans and light tanks from the 752d Tank Battalion were churning down the road into Bologna, accompanied by tank destroyers and with a battalion of 34th Infantry Division GIs perched on the back decks. Bologna fell by 0730 that morning. Reattached to the 88th Infantry Division, the battalion reached the Po River on 23 April; Company A was credited with capturing 3,070 prisoners and destroying 1,800 vehicles that day.[36]

Company C of the 755th Tank Battalion was still equipped as an amphibian unit and transported troops from the 34th, 85th, and 91st Infantry Divisions across

the Po River in LVT(4)s on 24 April.[37] Drivers from the 752d Tank Battalion operated additional LVT(4)s that carried 88th Infantry Division GIs across the river.
Most tank battalions had to wait a day or two to be ferried across or for the engineers to build pontoon bridges. There was resistance here and there north of the
river, but German troops began to surrender en masse.[38]

The integration of tank destroyers and tanks was nearly complete by now, as
illustrated by the model adopted by the 10th Mountain Division. The 701st Tank
Destroyer Battalion was attached to the division along with the 751st Tank Battalion. Initially, the armor attached to each regiment was split into two forces under
the commands of the tank and tank destroyer company commander. Each medium
tank company attached a platoon of Shermans armed with 75-millimeter guns to
the tank destroyer company and received, in exchange, a platoon of M10s. The
mixed companies combined the armor-piercing firepower of the 3-inch guns and
the better high-explosive and automatic-weapons capabilities of the Sherman.

On the other hand, fragmentation reared its ugly head again. For days on end,
two tank companies at a time were attached to the 85th Infantry Division and
operated beyond the battalion's control.

In late April, the 10th Mountain Division formulated a system that allowed it
to advance around the clock. It rotated its three regiments every eight hours and
two reorganized armored task forces every twelve hours.

Rather than combine tanks and tank destroyers at the regiment–armored company level, it organized the armor at the division–armored battalion level. Force
Madden fell under the control of the 751st Tank Battalion's commanding officer,
Lt. Col. C. J. Madden, and included Company A and the tank destroyers of Company B, 701st Tank Destroyer Battalion. Headquarters of the 701st Tank Destroyer
Battalion controled Force Redding, which included Companies B, C, and D of the
751st Tank Battalion. Furthermore, each tank destroyer company swapped one platoon with its correspondingly lettered tank company. Company A of the tank battalion, for example, had two tank platoons and one tank destroyer platoon, while
the ratio was reversed in the tank destroyer company. The units also exchanged
radios and aligned crystals to ensure perfect communications.

One mixed company supported each of the six assault infantry battalions. The
tank destroyers provided a base of fire while the tanks advanced in direct support
of the doughs. Despite the installation of SCR-300 radios in many infantry-support
tanks in northwestern Europe, the armor and infantry components in the 10th
Mountain Division still could not communicate by radio at the tactical level.[39]

The 752d Tank Battalion, operating with the 88th Infantry Division, found
that the tank–tank destroyer–infantry team made such rapid progress that the main
threat turned out to be German forces appearing from the "rear" and trying to
escape. The team reached the outskirts of Verona on 25 April and spent the night
fending off attacks by German formations trying to get through town toward the
north. Still, stiff fights in a few places such as Vicenza on the twenty-eighth cost
the battalion more tanks and men.[40]

By the end of the war in Italy, American tankers had won the respect of the
enemy. Senior German officers judged that the tankers had learned to exploit their

mobility and the terrain and were impressed with the climbing ability of American tanks. By contrast, they concluded that German tank engines and tracks were not up to the demands of fighting in difficult terrain, especially mountains. They also praised the skillful use of fire and movement, excellent tank-artillery teamwork, and flexibility in fighting under fire. On the other hand, they believed that American armor rarely exploited tactical opportunities.[41]

Resting Arms

The war had effectively ended for a growing number of the tank battalions in the European theater. As early as 8 April, the 747th Tank Battalion started military-government duties around Wulfen. After two days of street combat in Magdeburg, the fighting was over for the D-Day veterans of the 743d Tank Battalion on 19 April. The 735th Tank Battalion halted at the advance limiting line by the twentieth and saw no further action. Another D-Day outfit, the 745th Tank Battalion, wrapped up fighting in the Harz Mountains on the twenty-second.

On 16 April, the strategic-bombing campaign was suspended for want of targets in Germany. On 25 April, the First Army linked with Soviet troops at Torgau.[42] On the thirtieth, Hitler shot himself in the Führerbunker in Berlin. When word reached German troops in the field, resistance virtually ceased.[43]

Nevertheless, other American battalions continued to push forward through Germany and into Austria and Czechoslovakia. On 4 May, tankers of the 781st Battalion and doughs of the 103d Infantry Division traversed the Brenner Pass and linked up with the U.S. Fifth Army eight miles inside Italy.[44]

In Italy, the Germans had surrendered, effective on 2 May. Tankers in Company C, 752d Tank Battalion, learned of the armistice from German soldiers who approached to surrender. Official word arrived at 1900 hours that evening.[45]

German formations north of the Alps continued to surrender en masse, and it was clear that the end was near. On 6 May, Capt. David Redle of the 756th Tank Battalion was driving along in a jeep on the *autobahn* toward Salzburg when about ten vehicles approached from the opposite direction with their headlights on. Each car had multiple stars on the front, and Redle could see that there were both American and German generals inside. "We knew it was over," recalled Redle.[46]

German representatives signed documents of capitulation in the early hours of 7 May. To the world, Dwight Eisenhower declared simply, "The mission of this Allied Force was fulfilled at 0241, local time, May 7, 1945."

At midnight on 8 May, the war in Europe was over for everyone. On 9 May, the 774th Tank Battalion recorded simply in its after-action report, "The entire battalion gathered for memorial services, paying tribute to the memory of our departed comrades." About that same day, the 756th Tank Battalion—which had been in direct combat for 420 days in North Africa, Italy, and the European theater—took a group picture of the men who had joined the outfit back at Fort Lewis, Washington, in 1941. Only forty-two men remained.[47]

CHAPTER 13

Jungle Heat

*"In small-island jungle-type warfare, the relation of tanks and infantry
should be comparable to that of Siamese twins."*
—Lt. Col. W. M. Rodgers, 710th
Tank Battalion

While vast amphibious operations were taking place at Saipan and Normandy
in June 1944, separate tank battalions were just reaching the southwest and
central Pacific in growing numbers. Like a boxer hitting with his left and then his
right, the Southwest Pacific forces under MacArthur drove toward Formosa, while
the Pacific Ocean forces under Nimitz carved a path directly toward the Japanese
home islands.

NEW GUINEA: HELL IN THE HEAT
The New Guinea operation was the first stepping stone to MacArthur's planned
reconquest of Leyte in the Philippines. "The campaign on New Guinea," observed
a U.S. Army history, "is all but forgotten except by those who served there." The
island had everything a soldier might hate: heat, torrential rains, thick jungle, dis-
ease, and a tenacious enemy. Australian and American forces had never been
ejected from the island, and by mid-1944, they had reclaimed considerable
ground from the Japanese invaders.[1]

The 44th Tank Battalion was the first separate battalion to arrive in the southwest Pacific and the first to join Lt. Gen. Walter Krueger's Sixth Army, which by
June 1944 had pushed up the New Guinea coast to the offshore island of Biak,
some 900 nautical miles southeast of Mindanao in the Philippines.[2]

The 44th had become a separate tank battalion when the 12th Armored Division released it upon its arrival at its port of embarkation in Vancouver in March
1944. The battalion had arrived at Milne Bay, Dutch New Guinea, on 21 April

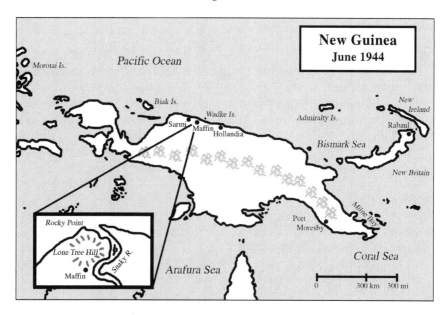

1944, having adopted the unit slogan "Wolf Pack" after learning the signature wolf call used by the Dutch crew that carried them across the Pacific.

During the last week of May, the battalion sent a composite tank crew to fight on Biak with the 603d Tank Company to gain battle experience. On the twenty-eighth, the 603d Tank Company fought the first tank battle in the Southwest Pacific when a platoon of Shermans chased off some Japanese light tanks. The next day, the American Shermans destroyed seven of the flimsy Japanese tanks.

On 3 June, Company C parted from the battalion—after strenuous objections from the company's officers—and shipped to New Guinea—first to Hollandia and then to join the 6th Infantry Division in the Wadke Island–Sarmi area on the northwest coat. The 6th Division had landed on New Guinea in mid-June to relieve the 41st Infantry Division, which had been supported by only a single platoon of the 603d Tank Company. Company C's tanks deployed along the "No Name River" with the GIs, and the tankers settled in for a nervous first night. Shortly after midnight, a jumpy sergeant opened fire on an imagined Japanese gun, which set off a storm of shooting that punctured the drums in the company's fuel depot.

Serious business followed. The 1st and 20th Infantry Regiments attacked vigorously westward on 20 June to capture an objective known as Lone Tree Hill, which overlooks the north coast between the Snaky River and the Maffin Airfield and which was defended by elements of the Japanese 36th Infantry Division, who had beaten off an attempt in May by the 41st Division to take the heights. An LST transported two tank platoons across the Tor River, one of which was attached to the 1st Infantry and the other the 20th Infantry. The next day, the 3d Platoon worked with the 1st Infantry Regiment's 3d Battalion, destroying Japanese pillboxes, while the 1st Platoon knocked a path through the jungle for the 20th

Infantry's 3d Battalion toward Lone Tree Hill. The 1st Platoon tanks were held up by the Snaky River just east of Lone Tree Hill until engineers arrived to fill in the cut, and then the Shermans plowed through to the far side ahead of the infantry.

Here the tanks encountered fierce resistance, and the five tanks opened fire on the green-clad flanks of Lone Tree Hill to cover the infantry. The company's history recorded the outfit's baptism of fire: "The tanks destroyed all active pillboxes, machine guns, plus numerous Japs. Carl Fisher as bow gunner in *Death Dealer*, Sgt. [Paul] Elkins's tank, sighted a Jap leaving his foxhole to seek better security behind a tree. Halfway to the tree, tracers from Fisher's gun finally caught up with the Jap, almost tearing him in half." One tank threw a track, and sniper and mortar fire was so heavy that the crew had to remove the firing mechanism of the gun and abandon the Sherman.

The 3d Battalion was unable to form a perimeter and pulled back across the Snaky River for the night. The next day, the 3d Battalion, followed by the 1st Battalion, seized positions on Lone Tree Hill. The 3d Platoon tankers were sent alone into enemy territory, an action that amounted to a raid, after which the tanks returned.

The Japanese began a series of vicious counterattacks that succeeded in cutting off the 3d Battalion, and the 20th Infantry Regiment's GIs became embroiled in the toughest fight of their lives—bereft of tank support because no suitable route to the top of the hill was available. On 24 June, the 1st Infantry Regiment's 3d Battalion joined the 20th Infantry with orders to conduct a flanking amphibious operation around Rocky Point, which extended into Maffin Bay from Lone Tree Hill, to force the withdrawal of the enemy to the west.

The 6th Cavalry Reconnaissance Troop, which had been equipped with amtanks and amtracs, ferried Companies I and K to a beach below a cliff honeycombed with caves hiding Japanese guns, where the doughboys were pinned down with heavy losses. The 3d Platoon tankers received a call for help. The tanks were ferried by boat to the beach, where they offloaded but could not advance beyond the sand because of an embankment. The company's history recorded, "The only alternative was to line the tanks on the beach facing into the jungle. From this position, they fired into the jungle with 75s and machine guns. . . . The tanks stayed on the beach with the infantry all that night. We could not open the hatches because of mortar fire, and the tanks became so warm inside that the men could hardly stand it. Several got sick from the heat, and each crew drank over five gallons of water each." The next day, other infantry elements reached the trapped men; the fight around Lone Tree Hill had cost 700 casualties.[3]

The physical misery experienced by these tankers in conditions of high heat and humidity was to prove common in the Pacific theater. A postwar study of ten armored battalions by the Pacific Warfare Board concluded that carbon-monoxide buildup from gun fumes played a major role in making crewmen sick, which was a particular problem when the turret was buttoned up. Malaise, nausea, and vomiting were common, and almost every unit reported cases of men passing out in combat. The most common firing pattern contributed by rapidly building up fumes:

gunners typically fired five to ten bursts as quickly as possible—one minute or less—as targets were spotted, and firing forty rounds in ten to fifteen minutes was common.[4]

Company C next supported the drive toward Maffin Airfield, just beyond Hill 265. The company history recorded an example of how decisive tanks could be against the often lightly armed Japanese:

> [Hill 265] was a large hill covered by dense jungle and high grass. The grass made perfect camouflage for enemy machine guns and snipers. Dug in on this hill, the Japanese commanded every approach and were effectively supported with artillery and mortars. There were no enemy guns large enough to be dangerous to our tanks, so we moved forward spraying the grass with machine guns. At the foot of the hill, we turned our guns upward and raked the hilltop with 75mm and machine-gun fire. This was too much for the Japs, and they beat a hasty retreat. The infantry quickly took up the chase. . . .

After weeks of combat, the company was moved to Maffin Bay for rest and relaxation. Four Australian officers appeared to study the use of medium tanks in the jungle and learn about the company, especially discipline and morale. "Our discipline was poor," noted the company's history, "but morale was quite high." Morale jumped higher when the crews received their first beer since leaving the States.[5]

SUPPORTING THE MARINES ON GUAM

In the Pacific Ocean Area, the 3d Marine Division and 1st Marine Provisional Brigade landed on Guam on 21 July while the 77th Infantry Division and 706th Tank Battalion waited on transports in the floating reserve. Beginning on D+3, the reserve debarked into a sea of mud created by constant downpours. The tankers first saw action on 28 July, when a platoon of light tanks from Company D and two mediums from the battalion headquarters were sent to support the 4th and 22d Marine Regiments on Orote Peninsula on the southwest corner of the island.

The light tanks destroyed four pillboxes, numerous dugouts, and accounted for approximately 250 Japanese dead, while the medium tanks destroyed a pillbox and an artillery piece. The next day, the tanks supported the marines during the capture of the airstrip on the peninsula. Late in the day, the army tankers were combined with four marine medium tanks and some M10 tank destroyers and carried a detachment of infantry to the end of the peninsula.

"The tank crews were very enthusiastic about their successes," recorded the battalion history, "and the Marines had shown their appreciation to these men by loading them down with souvenirs of all sorts." A memo from the Marines to the 77th Infantry Division G-3 said, "[The tanks] worked most of the day in the fire fight and were exceptionally outstanding. . . . It is requested that the outstanding actions and aggressiveness of this Army tank platoon be brought to the attention of higher Army authority."

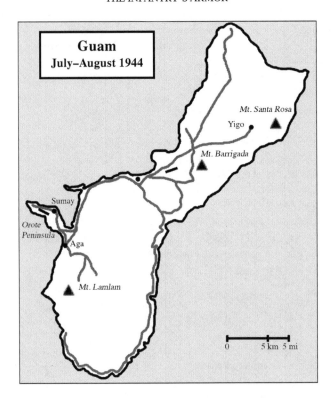

Meanwhile, the 77th Infantry Division put the light tanks to use on reconnais-sance missions that bore no relationship to doctrine. On 2 August, Capt. Leonard Seger led his company on a mission two miles behind enemy lines. The tankers could get away with it because the Japanese had few antitank weapons, and the M5A1s simply drove through rifle and machine-gun fire.

Company A's 2d Platoon went into battle on 3 August supporting the 3d Bat-talion, 307th Infantry, which attacked north of the Barrigada Road. The tankers accounted for several machine-gun nests and an ammunition dump. The 3d Pla-toon joined the 3d Battalion the next day, and the tanks were used to trailblaze routes through thick jungle during the assault on Mount Barrigada on the north-ern end of Guam, which proved successful enough that the infantry employed other tank platoons that way over the coming days.

On 4 August, a section of the 1st Platoon plowed through two Japanese road-blocks to establish contact with the marines to the flank. The tankers had been told that the marines would use colored smoke to identify themselves, but tankers saw no smoke, and a friendly-fire incident erupted in which five marines were wounded. They had never been told about the colored smoke plan.

On 7 August, Lt. Col. Charles Stokes, commanding the 706th Tank Battalion, directed the tanks from Companies C and D and the headquarters section against a Japanese strongpoint near Yigo in one of the largest tank attacks to take place in the Pacific theater. The tankers were to move ahead of the 307th Infantry and seize the high ground 200 yards north of Yigo. After an artillery barrage and attacks by dive-bombers, the tankers moved out with the light tanks in the lead in a column of wedges, followed by two platoons of medium tanks. Three Company A tanks and an M10 provided covering fire.

The tanks advanced at noon, destroying Japanese machine-gun nests. After covering 400 yards, Capt. Leonard Seger, commanding Company D, noted a flash under one of the tanks and radioed Stokes that there might be mines or antitank guns. Stokes ordered the medium tanks forward.

The Japanese had set up ambushes in the thick jungle growth using machine guns, two tanks, and one antitank gun. Gunners opened fire and quickly knocked out two M5A1s and two Shermans with flank shots. Sgt. Joe Divin, who commanded one of the burning Shermans, was badly wounded in the leg and doubted he could lift himself out of the turret hatch so his crewmates could escape. He tried to traverse the turret to move the gun, which was blocking the driver's hatch, but the mechanism was broken. Divin tied a tourniquet to his leg and through a superhuman effort pulled himself from the turret, clearing the escape route. Outside the armor, Divin fell prey to machine-gun bullets.

Light tanks and mediums returned fire and destroyed the Japanese tanks and the antitank gun. Over the course of one hour, the 706th Battalion crushed the last organized Japanese resistance on the island. Four tanks advanced to the objective and held it until the infantry arrived to relieve them. Mopping up operations continued, but the battle for Guam was officially declared over on 10 August.[6]

ANGAUR AND PELELIU ISLANDS

Fleet operations in the Central Pacific in early September revealed that Japanese strength was far weaker than expected, and commanders decided to move more directly than they had intended into the Philippines. MacArthur and Nimitz nevertheless believed that they could not bypass the Palau Islands, because they judged they would need air bases there to protect lines of communications to the western Pacific.[7] The two first objectives would be two islands that lay cheek-by-jowl: Angaur, which fell to elements of the army's 81st Infantry Division, and Peleliu, which went to the 1st Marine Division.

On 17 September, Company D of the 776th Amphibian Tank Battalion formed up at the line of departure off Angaur with amtracs of the 726th Amphibian Tractor Battalion. The fleet and air arm had been pounding the island since dawn, and the crewmen wondered whether any of the Japanese could possibly have survived. Like the rest of the battalion, which was headed for Leyte in the Philippines, the company was equipped with eleven 75-millimeter LVT(A)(4)s and seven 37-millimeter LVT(A)(1)s. The battalion also had two LVT-M4s, which were outfitted for maintenance crews, and a jeep.

The tankers had trained thoroughly with the 81st Infantry Division back in Hawaii, including practice operating with the GIs off the beach as land tanks. Half the company was attached to the 322d Infantry and the rest to the 321st Infantry.

Angaur ran three miles north to south and only two east to west. Phosphate mines, which produced fertilizer for Japan, had torn a quarter of the island into a

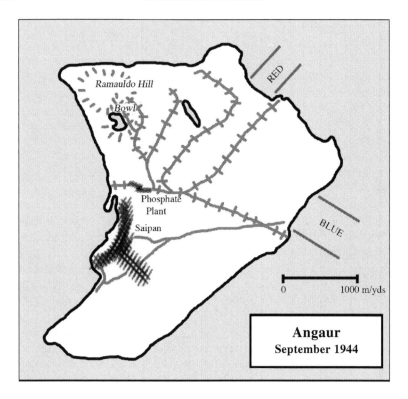

Angaur
September 1944

rugged moonscape. The 1st Battalion of the 59th Infantry Regiment, 14th Division, occupied the isle.

The invasion force headed for shore at about 0815 hours, with the amtanks arrayed on the flanks of the first two waves. Resistance at the beach was surprisingly light, consisting only of small-arms and mortar fire. The amtracs deposited their loads of infantry without a single loss. The amtanks on Blue Beach worked inland with the infantry as planned and stuck with them until noon on D+1. A natural barrier trapped the tanks on Red Beach, where one officer was killed, and by the time engineers had built a road, land tanks from the 710th Tank Battalion had arrived.

The company went into division reserve on D+1 and reported to division artillery for a new mission: indirect supporting fire. This was a concept pioneered by the battalion to take advantage of the 75-millimeter howitzers on the LVT(A)(4)s after initial landings, as the number of tanks in the battalion was equal to the total number of division-level artillery in an infantry division. The battalion had trained at indirect fire and knew how to work with the infantry's fire-control centers. In this case, no missions were tasked, but the concept would soon play out elsewhere.[8]

For the 710th Tank Battalion, in the words of its commanding officer, Lt. Col. W. M. Rodgers, "tanks of the 710th were used under adverse conditions of terrain and weather during a period of groping and 'cut and try' developments in so far as the use of armor in the Pacific was concerned." Tank operations were on the scale of platoons or sections supporting infantry companies. Fortunately, the battalion and infantry had trained extensively together, each tank company with the regiment beside which it was going to fight, and techniques developed on Oahu worked well. Rodgers described the battle for the island as "hard, slow, bitter fighting."

The battalion's after-action report for 18 September offers a representative vignette:

> Because of the extremely heavy jungle growth, it was necessary for the tanks to shoot into the jungle with .30-caliber machine guns and 75mm guns, blasting the foliage away to afford visibility. The infantry followed the tanks [by] from twenty-five to fifty yards. . . . In firing into the jungle growth. . . each tank took an area and searched it; while enemy troops were seldom seen, upon moving forward many dead Japanese were found in the areas fired upon, and in no case had the enemy succeeded in getting close to the tanks with any kind of demolition or antitank mines.[9]

Rodgers observed that because most actions involved two or three tanks, it was hard to construct a history of the fight on Angaur. Cpl. Edward Luzinas, a gunner in a platoon leader's M4A3 in Company C, left one account of his platoon's attempt to support an infantry attack on 21 September into the Lake Salome bowl below Ramauldo Hill, the dominating terrain feature on the northwest corner of the island, where the Japanese had built their key strongpoint. The "Angaur Bowl," as it became known to the 81st Division, was surrounded by cliffs cut by a single rail line for a narrow-gauge mine train. Inside the gap, an embankment of diggings bore the rail line down to the lake.

Heavy Japanese fire stopped the GIs the first time they tried to follow the tanks through the gap, but after liberal doses of friendly artillery and mortar fire, the advance resumed. Intelligence had told the tankers that the Japanese lacked guns that could hurt their tanks, but as the M4A3s crunched through the cut, they found the way blocked by a self-propelled gun that had been knocked out by something. After failing to remove the wreck kinetically (shells, satchel charges), the tankers towed the gun out of the way, the tanks set off down the embankment.

Something hit Luzinas's tank, which was in the lead, and paint chips flew around the turret. The Japanese gun did not, in fact, penetrate the armor, but shells worked over the suspension and tracks on the three tanks stretched out down the embankment. The infantry was stymied.

Luzinas spotted the gun in a cave through his periscope as it fired, emitting a cloud of yellow, brown, and gray smoke. He sprayed the entrance with .30-caliber fire. The tank commander asked him what he was doing and, after Luzinas explained, told him to knock the gun out. Eight high-explosive rounds did the trick.

The infantry moved in, but it was now so close to sundown that the commander did not want to risk being cut off in the bowl by a counterattack after dark, and he ordered a withdrawal. That meant the tanks had to back up the embankment, and steering a tank backwards was no easy task on a flat road.

The two tanks to the rear tried, and each tipped over the side, carrying chunks of the ramp with them. Japanese fire chased the crewmen as they ran for safety, and one man was wounded.

A fourth tank was in the cut, but Luzinas's commander had little faith in relying on directions from there to maneuver. There was, however, the infantry phone on the back of the tank. The loader volunteered to go and slipped out the escape hatch in the belly of the tank. Sheltering as best he could, he directed the driver safely and slowly back up the long embankment to the cut. When a sniper opened up from a palm tree to the rear, the loader pointed Luzinas to the target, and after searching fire from the coax, the shooting stopped.

They didn't teach that at Fort Knox.

The next morning, the crew discovered that the Japanese gun had badly damaged the suspension, and only one connector was holding the track together. Luzinas pondered religious thoughts.[10]

The 710th Tank Battalion relied mainly on liaison personnel with SCR-536 and SCR-509 radios to talk to the infantry. The battalion had put field telephones on the backs of its tanks, but it found that GIs under fire did not replace the handsets, and they were torn off when the tanks moved. The battalion replaced its 105-millimeter howitzers with M10 tank destroyers for the operation, judging the 3-inch gun to have greater penetrating power at longer range.

The battalion had to sit out the last phase of the battle for Angaur from 7 to 22 October because the terrain on the northern tip of the island was too rough for tanks. Company A and other battalion elements moved to Peleliu on 22 September with the 321st Infantry to assist the marines in their bitter fight against the 14th Japanese Division.

For the 710th Tank Battalion, the fighting on Peleliu again featured operations by tank sections with small groups of infantry and lasted until 27 November.[11] Rather than jungle warfare, the tankers fought with the GIs over iron-hard, sun-baked coral rock. Missions generally involved blasting cave entrances and firing slits with the 75-millimeter guns at ranges so short that a commander sticking out of his hatch could be wounded by debris. Ammunition expenditures were high—at times, 100 rounds per day. Eighteen battalion tanks fell prey to mines.[12]

Company B and other elements of the 726th Amphibian Tractor Battalion also shifted to Peleliu on 23 September, where they were attached to the marines' 8th Amphibian Tractor Group to support the 1st Marine Division. Most of the crews engaged in the usual tasks of hauling supplies to the beach and then inland and evacuating the wounded on the way back. The marines mounted heavy flamethrowers in four battalion vehicles, and the amtracs actually spearheaded attacks against several objectives and participated in the final drive through Death Valley, across the China Wall, and into Hell's Pocket.[13] Nevertheless, the LVTs proved to be too fragile for work over rough coral terrain, and the vehicles spent nearly a third of the time under repair for damage such as broken tracks.[14]

CHAPTER 14

The Philippines:
Back to Where It Began

*"Our first impression of the Philippines was that it was a paradise after
being in New Guinea so long. The terrain looked suitable for tank
operations, and that was what we had longed for."*
— Company C History, 44th Tank
Battalion

Physical conditions and relatively advanced economic development made the
Philippines the most European-like of the island battlegrounds in the Pacific
theater, Luzon more so than Leyte, Mindanao, or the lesser islands. Not surprisingly, tank combat there most closely resembled that experienced in Europe. Just
as the Allied armies were grinding to a stop in the European theater and Italy,
armored men in the Pacific were about to stage their biggest operation yet.

LEYTE: RETURN TO THE PHILIPPINES
American planners wanted to capture Leyte, in the heart of the Philippine islands,
to obtain an air and logistical base to support planned operations on Luzon, Formosa, and the coast of China. Leyte offered coastal plains suitable for building
airfields that would guarantee air supremacy over Luzon. The Leyte invasion
would be the largest yet in the Pacific and require the help of ground, air, and
naval assets from the Pacific Ocean Area.

Lieutenant General Krueger's Sixth Army, which was to go ashore along
Leyte's east coast, consisted of the X and XXIV Corps and had 174,000 troops
available for the initial assault phase. Intelligence reports suggested that the Japanese 16th Division had 22,000 men on the island, more than half of them combat
troops. The X Corps was to land on the army's right in the Palo area, with the 24th
Infantry Division (less one regiment) on its left and the 1st Cavalry Division, fighting as an infantry division with four regiments, on its right. The XXIV Corps was to
land fifteen miles to the south in the Dulag area, with its 7th Infantry Division on

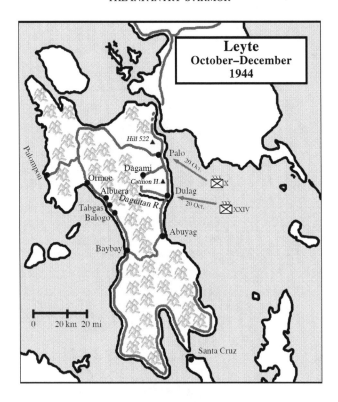

its left and 96th Infantry Division on the right. Japanese combat strength was concentrated in this area. The 32d and 77th Infantry Divisions were available in floating reserve. The two corps were to secure the coastal plain, advance by separate routes to the Ormoc Valley on the west side of the island, and link up.[1]

The XXIV Corps landing force had been scheduled to take Yap as the second phase of the landings conducted on Angaur and Peleliu on 15 September. In light of the absence of effective Japanese air opposition, the High Command decided to abandon the Yap operation and divert the entire landing force, which included half of the available assault shipping in the Pacific Fleet, to the Leyte operation. Plans for Yap had evolved to deal with landing areas protected by a coral reef, so LVTs rather than landing craft were allocated to carry the troops to shore. Leyte offered long, smooth beaches suitable for even LSTs. It was too late to change plans, so the XXIV Corps would conduct a Pacific Ocean Area–style assault, though following waves were to land by boat.[2] This turned out to be fortuitous in the 96th Division's zone.

In terms of armor, there was a remarkable disparity between the corps of the two operating areas arising out of the different campaigns they had waged to date. The XXIV Corps was to attack with two amphibian tank battalions, the X Corps with none. The two XXIV Corps divisions had a complete land tank battalion each, whereas the X Corps divisions shared the equivalent of one battalion.

The XXIV Corps' Tankers Fulfill a Promise

On A-Day, 20 October 1944, the U.S. Navy provided a two-hour preliminary bombardment beginning at 0600 hours, which Task Force 79, off the XXIV Corps' beaches, reported "was increased and maintained at a spectacular intensity during the last half hour." The landings occurred on a broad front, with two regiments abreast in each assault division.[3]

The bulk of the 776th Amphibian Tank Battalion represented the first combat unit to carry out MacArthur's pledge to return to the Philippines. Attached to the 7th Infantry Division, the battalion had three line companies, each with three platoons made up of three LVT(A)(4)s and two LVT(A)(1)s. The company headquarters had two LVT(A)(4)s, which normally operated attached to a platoon during fire missions, as did three LVT(A)(4)s in the battalion's headquarters and service company. Four new LVT(4) amtracs rounded out the battalion amphibians, and a 2.5-ton boom truck, 10-ton wrecker, and two jeeps waited on LSTs for use ashore.[4]

Mortar fire greeted the 776th Amphibian Tank Battalion's LVTs as they churned toward the beach, but there were no hits, and the amtanks clawed their way onto the sand at about 1000 hours, with Companies A, B, and C arrayed from left to right. The tanks pushed inland about 250 yards through small-arms and mortar fire, took up firing positions, and waited for the doughboys to arrive. The infantry-bearing amtracs from the 536th Amphibian Tractor Battalion followed, with the only casualties occurring in one LVT from an air burst that killed three GIs and wounded ten. As planned, the 32d and 184th Infantry Regiments landed abreast behind the amphibian tanks.

The amtank crews had been assigned a fairly complex variety of missions. The battalion had been the first amphibian outfit to undergo comprehensive training in the field artillery role, which had taken place back in Hawaii. The 1st Platoon of Company A immediately deployed into battery formation, and by 1130 hours, the guns were paralleled and a forward observer was in communication, although the 57th Field Artillery Battalion did not order the first fire mission until 1800. The 2d Platoon was to enter the Daguitan River and move upstream to secure the Dao Bridge, but the current proved too swift. The amtanks tried to reach the bridge overland, but they ran into Japanese infantry and a swamp that blocked further progress, and the platoon received orders to pull back and fire under the control of the 49th Field Artillery Battalion.

The 3d Platoon entered the village of Dulag, where it encountered retreating Japanese infantry and cut them down. The platoon fired indirectly out to 2,000 yards and helped the infantry by destroying two pillboxes. An LVT(A)(1), commanded by the battalion's S-3 and specially equipped with a Canadian-made Ronson flamethrower, arrived too late to do any good in Dulag.

Company B suffered the battalion's only fatality of the day when a 40-millimeter round—judged to be friendly fire—struck the company commander's LVT and killed one crewman. The 3d Platoon engaged Japanese infantry with machine guns and 37-millimeter canister, and one scarf gunner killed an enemy soldier who charged an amtank with a grenade. The company quickly lashed into the infantry's fire-control system and fired barrages to support troops attacking the Dulag airstrip.

Company C's 3d Platoon was assigned to move up the small Calbasag River, which reached the sea north of Dulag, to secure a bridge, but it, too, was thwarted, in this case by mud and felled logs. Most of the amtanks engaged Japanese infantry in a trench system with point-blank machine-gun, 37-millimeter, and 75-millimeter fire. One tank commander was wounded during the action, but by afternoon, the company had cleared its area and prepared to fire artillery missions.

Maj. Gen. A. V. Arthur, commanding the 7th Infantry Division, would say of the battalion's support, "The spearheading of the assault troops of the division was outstanding. The fire preceding the landing was timely, and the tank action and later fire support contributed largely to our initial success."[5]

The first 767th Tank Battalion Shermans, from Company A, landed at 1015 in the second wave on Beach Violet 2, in the 32d Infantry's zone, just behind the amphibian tanks in the first wave. The 2d Platoon operated independently at first and destroyed targets of opportunity. Five hundred yards from the water, a concealed Japanese 75-millimeter gun put a round through the side of Number 18 tank and wounded three crewmen. Number 17 survived a hit from the same gun. The Japanese weapon was concealed in one of several pillboxes that each contained an antitank gun and machine guns. The remaining tanks laid suppressing fire on the pillboxes while the infantry from Company K, 32d Infantry, closed from the flanks until they were close enough to knock the pillboxes out with grenades.

The 1st Platoon of Company B was unable to establish contact with the infantry at all, so its tanks entered the village of Dulag and destroyed such opposition as they found. Company D's M5s—nine of them mounted with Ronson flamethrowers—followed. Only the 3d Platoon on Yellow Beach 2 was able to coordinate its actions with the infantry. Clearly, some problems that had surfaced on Kwajalein between the tankers and 7th Infantry Division doughboys had not been fixed.

By noon, the 2d Platoon of Company B had moved rapidly off the beach, still without the infantry. An antitank gun destroyed the two tanks in the second section and struck tank number 15 five times before the gunner could destroy the Japanese. This likely would not have happened had the infantry been available to advance on the gun or to place indirect fire on it. Not too long thereafter, three Company A tanks were hit by antitank fire, but the rounds only set waterproofing alight. By about 1300 hours, the 32d and 184th Infantry Regiments had regained some control over the tanks, and some coordination of effort emerged.[6]

The 780th Amphibian Tank Battalion, which was experiencing its first action attached to the green 96th Infantry Division, at first had a similar experience to that of the 776th Battalion. All companies approached the beach in shallow platoon wedges, the LVT(A)(1)s arrayed to the flanks of the LVT(A)(4)s. Tanks opened fire 300 yards from the beach, and they continued shooting after crossing the sand until infantry arrived and blocked the fields of fire. Companies A and B were delayed by antitank obstacles, trees, and stumps but soon found routes inland and advanced to support the 382d Infantry. Plans for the amtanks to stop roughly 500 yards from the water went out the window because the ground was too swampy for land tanks to move up. The amtracs of the 788th Amphibian Tractor Battalion in the first three waves landed without a loss and offloaded the infantry 500 yards inland as foreseen—the army was now using the marine corps' approach—but the following three waves came under intense mortar fire from elements of the Japanese 9th Infantry Regiment, and the GIs dismounted just past the beach.

Amtanks from Companies C and D supported the 1st Battalion, 383d Infantry, in crossing the small Liberanan River, which enters the sea north of Dulag. One platoon secured the division's right flank by swimming down the river and taking up positions on sandbars near the mouth. Most of the amtracs, meanwhile, were able to negotiate the swamp, and they accompanied the infantry until no longer needed.[7]

The 96th Infantry Division had split the attached 763d Tank Battalion for the assault, with the battalion—minus Companies C and D—supporting the 382d Infantry Regiment and C and D supporting the 383d Infantry. The three medium tank companies had arrived offshore loaded into LCTs in the bays of three LSDs, while Company D's light tanks were in the holds of transports. The medium tanks landed behind the infantry in the seventh wave at 1044 hours and moved smartly 1,000 yards inland, where drivers all along the beach pulled back on their brake levers. Ahead stretched a swamp, and invasion planners had provided no clue about how tanks were supposed to cross this morass. This problem remained unresolved three days later.[8]

As a consequence, on A+1, the 780th Amphibian Tank Battalion withdrew and tied into the field artillery, but the next day, most companies were sent forward again to fight as land tanks. Mud proved a greater hindrance than the enemy, and at one point, all of Company B became bogged in a swamp. Tankers constructed bridges from coconut logs and snaked their way through the muck. During the initial approach to Catmon Hill, which dominated the beaches, the entire battalion operated in line, which probably was the only time an amtank battalion maneuvered en masse on land during the war. The tankers remained beside the infantry until A+5 and by then had reached a line some 6,000 yards from the surf. From 1 November, the battalion provided security in the landing area, often sending out small foot patrols.[9]

Apparently, the 96th Infantry Division was becoming a great believer in using tanks as artillery; on 24 October, the 763d Tank Battalion organized Company B into a "tank artillery battalion" to reinforce division artillery, a role the company played for the duration of the Leyte campaign. The division organized Company C into a second artillery battalion on 20 November, plus eight Company A tanks (two batteries) from 20 November until 10 December.

The division's enthusiasm for employing tanks in this fashion derived in part from the fact that on the few occasions early in the campaign when medium tanks had tried to support the infantry, weak bridges and swampy terrain stopped the tanks before the objectives had been reached. The light tanks of Dog Company were able to help the infantry much more often, including during fighting at Catmon Hill on 28 October, near Dagami from 5 to 10 November, and on nearby Mt. Lobi in early December. The company fielded five diesel-engine M3 light tanks with flamethrowers mounted in the turrets in place of M5 tanks, but their effectiveness is not recorded.[10]

The X Corps Goes in Unarmored

The 24th Infantry Division had the misfortune to go ashore on a stretch of coast that the Japanese had prepared to defend, and it faced the toughest battle of the landings, in part because it had almost no armor support. A wide and deep anti-tank ditch ran the length of the beach, and camouflaged pillboxes with cleared fields of fire overlooked the sand. Swamps and muddy rice paddies lay just beyond the beach. Overlooking the coast was Hill 522, which the Japanese 33d Infantry Regiment had honeycombed with tunnels, trenches, and pillboxes.[11]

Three medium tanks from the 603d Tank Company were loaded on a landing ship, medium, to debark at H+25 to support the 19th Infantry, and a like number was to land with the 34th Infantry. The rest of the company was aboard LSTs and scheduled to reach the beach at H+60.[12]

Elements of Companies A and B, 727th Amphibian Tractor Battalion, carried some of the GIs to the beach, with the remainder of the battalion ready to serve as needed.[13] Other assault elements rode to the sand in landing craft. The Japanese allowed the first five waves to reach shore and then opened up with mortars and 75-millimeter guns on the sixth wave and sank four landing craft. Four LSTs also were hit, and one caught fire. Two LSTs reached the beach and became stuck; the others withdrew, taking most of the tanks and artillery with them.

The doughboys already on land were finding that the preliminary bombardment had not been entirely effective. Without tank support, the GIs had to conduct close assaults on the pillboxes using bazookas, hand grenades, rifles, and BARs. After more than two hours of fighting, the infantry managed to overcome most of the beach defenses about noon. By then, the first medium tanks were available and led the 3d Battalion, 34th Infantry, into the attack at 1230 hours through waist-deep muck to a tree line 150 yards distant. Other elements of the 19th and 34th Infantry Regiments also pressed inland, overcoming strongpoint after strongpoint. Attacks and counterattacks raged on the slopes of Hill 522 into the night.[14]

Lt. Merritt Corbin, who commanded some of the amtracs, recalled, "[That morning] the skies opened and it poured heavy rains. The rice paddies, river, the swamp were flooded. When the LSTs arrived at the beach, no wheeled vehicle could move on the beach because of the wet sand. We spent all days towing wheeled vehicles on the beach."[15]

The amtracs ferried troops, supplies, and casualties for the 19th and 34th Infantry Regiments, but already the infantry could see other uses for the LVTs. The commanding officer of the 34th Infantry commandeered one amtrac for his command-and-reconnaissance vehicle the day after the landing, and several were allocated to carry wire crews.

The 24th Division fought its way westward against stiff resistance. With only a single tank company available to the division, the 34th Infantry employed Cpl. Rade Allen's amtrac to attack a pillbox on A+2. Allen directed his vehicle out of defilade and down Highway 1, and the machine guns raked native houses, ditches, and Japanese machine-gun nests. The tractor had advanced 500 yards on its own when a Japanese soldier charged and slid a mine under one track, which disabled the LVT. Allen and one crewman were wounded, but they stuck to the machine guns until rescued by another amtrac.

The infantry viewed the mission as a great success. Allen and his crew were credited with killing sixty enemy troops, allowing GIs who had been pinned down for twenty-four hours to advance onto the objective and recover casualties who had been lying in the line of fire. Tractors were used subsequently in several other attacks and as reconnaissance vehicles.[16]

The 1st Cavalry Division hit the beach on A-Day in a mix of LVTs from Company A, 826th Amphibian Tractor Battalion, and landing craft, and it encountered almost no resistance at the waterline. The official U.S. Army history asserts that amtanks led the assault, but division records, including the complete field order for the operation, do not indicate that this was the case. The cavalrymen moved inland, soon accompanied by medium tanks from the 44th Tank Battalion. "Landings made on schedule," recorded the battalion journal, "without notable event as pertains to tanks." The tankers were without their Company C, which was fighting with the 6th Infantry Division on distant New Guinea. The remaining companies were attached to the line regiments, and in nearly all cases, complained the battalion's commander, orders concerning employment of battalion elements from higher headquarters were oral and reached the battalion headquarters only after the action had taken place.

The cavalry division was assigned the mission of clearing the mountainous and jungle-clad northern end of Leyte, while the 24th Division advanced toward the west side of the island. The 1st Cavalry Division just could not figure out a good use for its attached tanks in the mountains. "The tanks were road-bound," noted the 44th Tank Battalion's history, "and the front limited to the width of the road." From 24 October to 30 November, the crews from Companies B and D were used on foot to man outposts. Company A was the only line company continuously employed with the infantry, and on A+15, that company was transferred to the 24th Infantry Division in exchange for the 603d Tank Company, only to wind up with the 32d Infantry Division a short time later.[17]

The Ormoc Operation: Daring Amphibian Maneuver

The Japanese had quickly reinforced their troops on Leyte and added by convoy five more infantry divisions and 10,000 tons of material from late October to early

December, mostly through the port of Ormoc. Instead of mopping up, MacArthur was going to have a hard fight for the western part of the island. He committed his own reserve divisions.[18]

By late November, the 7th Infantry Division had clawed its way to the west coast of Leyte, where it faced a grueling fight northward through the hills and along a narrow coastal plain toward Ormoc. Terrain made the movement of land tanks and artillery extremely difficult, but the infantry needed the support of both. Japanese warships operating off the coast made transport by water risky without heavy naval escort. During October and November, the 24th and 32d Infantry Divisions, working with the 727th Amphibian Tractor Battalion, had demonstrated the effectiveness of battalion-size and larger subsidiary amphibious landings as a way to bypass Japanese resistance.

Sitting back at the Leyte beachhead engaged in security duties was an amphibian tank battalion that could function as both armor and artillery, and one visionary officer figured out a way to get that outfit back into the war. Lt. Col. O'Neill Kane, who had just moved from the 776th Amphibian Tank Battalion to take command of the 767th Tank Battalion, was an old cavalryman, as were most of the officers in the 776th Amphibian Tank Battalion, which only three years earlier had been part of the 2d Cavalry Regiment. He conceived of using amphibians in a cavalry role, mainly on unsupported raids deep into the enemy's rear.[19] In proposing the operation to the 7th Infantry Division, Kane had suggested, "The amphibian tank battalion has a better than even chance of success in any engagement with enemy surface craft and could give a good account of itself in an engagement, close ashore, with one or two destroyers." He had conducted water marches of up to twenty miles back at Fort Ord in California.

In late November, the 776th Amphibian Tank Battalion contributed, on corps orders, its Company C—minus all LVT[A][1]s—and the LVT(A)(4)s of two of Company B's platoons, which were to become the combat element of a Provisional Amphibian Battalion organized to provide amtank support to the 7th Infantry Division on the west coast of Leyte. The amtank element had three platoons of six LVT(A)(4)s each. The 718th Amphibian Tractor Battalion contributed a provisional company of twenty amtracs. Kane took command.

The provisional battalion was loaded onto landing ships, medium, on 27 November and transported to a spot off Santa Cruz near the southern tip of Leyte. There the LVTs disembarked and traveled under their own power 100 miles to the 7th Infantry Division's zone of action north of Baybay, the longest water march ever conducted to that point by LVTs under their own power. An LCM led, followed by the amtanks in three columns and then the amtracs, with an LCM bringing up the rear to assist with any maintenance problems. "The ever-droning roar of radial engines purring and the sound of tracks churning the water were constant reminders that the battalion was moving onward," recalled Lt. Charles Shock. Upon arrival, the battalion set up a camp and defensive perimeter against enemy waterborne attack.

On 4 December, the 7th Division ordered the battalion to support an attack northward by the 184th Infantry Regiment by enveloping the Japanese line by sea. Kane made an aerial reconnaissance of the area of operations and coordinated planning carefully with the infantry.

Early on 5 December, Company C's LVT(A)(4)s set off. The battalion's after-action report described the action at Balogo:

> At 0635 the company, which was in column formation headed north, executed a movement by the right flank and advanced toward the shore in line formation firing howitzers and machine guns. About 200 yards from shore, on radio command of the battalion commander, the company executed a movement by the left flank and continued to move north in column. Turrets were swung to the right, and the shelling of Balogo and Tabgas continued. The company arrived at the mouth of the Tabgas River at 0700 and made an unsupported landing by maneuvering from column to line formation. . . . As the amtanks landed, Jap infantrymen were observed evacuating beach positions under the company's machine-gun fire. Ravines, reverse slopes of hills 380 and 910, and other likely areas of enemy concentration were taken under howitzer fire with HE and smoke shells.

By 1045, the raid was over—with not a single loss—and the infantry reported that the tankers had helped unhinge the Japanese line.[20]

The 77th Infantry Division landed on the west coast of Leyte on 7 December in a maneuver designed to deny the Japanese the use of Ormoc's port; attract Japanese reserves, which would hasten the linkup of the X and XXIV Corps; and cut off the Japanese 26th Infantry Division. Company A of the 776th Amphibian Tank Battalion, reinforced by a platoon of Company B, provided the amtank force for the landings by the 305th Infantry in Ormoc Bay, while a provisional amphibious force from the 536th and 718th Amphibian Tractor Battalions carried GIs and supplies.

Ironically, the division's landing disrupted a second amphibian attack by the provisional battalion ordered by the 7th Infantry Division. Company C's amtanks executed the planned attack on Albuera the next day instead and recorded, "At 0650 the amtanks landed in line formation on the north edge of Albuera and shelled the town at point-blank range. Jap infantry was dug in under many of the houses, and most of the structures in the town were burned or damaged by amtank shelling. . . . The amtanks received hostile mortar and gunfire from the vicinity of the town, but this fire caused no casualties. One enemy gun northeast of town was silenced by a direct hit. By 0745, the mission was accomplished." On the way back south, Kane received orders to pull into shore, where his men directed 7th Division artillery fire.[21]

The Japanese had been surprised by the 77th Infantry Division's landing, and the division turned north to push up the coast and took Ormoc on 10 December.

On the eighth, the Company A amtanks conducted amphibious reconnaissance ahead of the division's advance and, the next day, rolled northward along the beach to protect the flank of the advancing infantry. The crews spotted Japanese roadblocks along the coast road and shelled them to clear the way for the GIs. At 0900 on 10 December, the company was the first American unit to enter Ormoc. The 2d and 3d Platoons moved through the streets blasting snipers hidden in the buildings until the infantry arrived to secure the village. The company then took over beach defense, destroying a Japanese LST on 12 December and firing artillery missions.

The Japanese moved reserves into the area, and the 77th Division experienced in the fight north to the Palompon road what has been described as the bitterest American troops had yet encountered in the Pacific. Ten medium tanks from Company A, 706th Tank Battalion, and all of Company D were moved by landing craft to Ormoc Bay on 20 December to support the infantry. Capt. Leonard Seger led nine light tanks against entrenched Japanese infantry on 21 December, but mortar fire was so intense that three tanks were hit, one of which was destroyed.

The plan to advance a fast armored column to Palompon had to be abandoned because of the lack of bridges along the road, so in order to complete the operation, a special amphibian task force—this time consisting of Company A, 776th Amphibian Tank Battalion; a platoon of Company B, 718th Amphibian Tractor Battalion; Company B, 536th Amphibian Tractor Battalion; a platoon of 706th Tank Battalion light tanks; and the 1st Battalion, 305th Infantry—was created to advance to Palompon by water.[22]

After intensive briefings, the task force set off on 24 December for an overnight, thirty-eight-mile journey to the objective—the longest march over open sea yet attempted. The LVTs led, carrying the infantry. While the moon was out, the vehicles swam under blackout restrictions and thereafter with only hooded taillights. PT boats guarded the herd like sheepdogs, and LCMs carrying light tanks, equipment, and supplies brought up the rear.

On 25 December, the task force made an amphibious landing north of Palompon. The amtanks shelled the beach during the approach, but the landing was unopposed. Amtanks, M5A1s, infantry, and engineers quickly moved inland and secured the port, at which point the amtanks took up artillery duties. During this operation, the amtanks provided the only artillery support available to the GIs other than mortars. With the capture of Palompon, MacArthur declared that organized resistance on Leyte had ended, which was not true.

The amphibians continued to work with the infantry, conducting reconnaissance missions, envelopments, and raids, until mid-January, when the attachment to the 77th Division was terminated. Amphibian operations by the elements attached to the 7th Infantry Division continued until 5 February.[23] Meanwhile, the 706th Tank Battalion continued working with the 77th Infantry Division. The light tanks were by far the busiest—and suffered the only losses—probably because the mediums had great difficulty getting around because of destroyed bridges.[24]

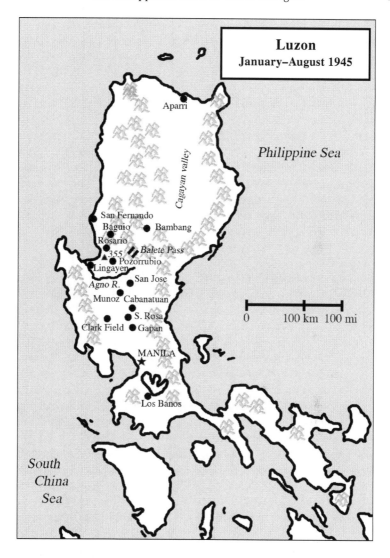

LUZON: THE FIRST REAL TANK COUNTRY

MacArthur intended to invade Luzon right where the Japanese had conducted their main landings in 1941—for the same reason: the Lingayen Gulf provided direct access to the central plains and Manila. He gave the task to Lieutenant General Krueger and his Sixth Army, supported by the air and naval forces of the Southwest Pacific Area.[25] Once ashore, the Sixth Army's I Corps was to protect the beachhead's left flank while the XIV Corps drove south to Clark Field and then Manila.[26]

Gen. Tomoyuki Yamashita, the Japanese commander, did not intend to defend the central plains–Manila Bay area with his 260,000 troops because American superiority in armor and mobility would have its greatest advantage there. He sought only to pin down MacArthur's forces in order to delay Allied progress toward Japan.

The invasion of Luzon began at 0700 on S-Day, 9 January 1945, with a massive naval bombardment. One hour later, the 40th Infantry Division landed at Lingayen on the right wing near the town of that name, with the 37th, 6th, and 43d Infantry Divisions strung out to the left.[27] As this was a southwest Pacific endeavor, no amtank battalions were available, but some officers evidently had been persuaded of their utility, because all of the assault divisions except the 43d formed provisional amtank companies for the operation. As usual, amtracs carried the doughboys to a hostile shore: the 658th Amphibian Tractor Battalion carried the 40th Division, the 672d Amphibian Tractor Battalion the 37th Division, the 727th Amphibian Tractor Battalion the 6th Division, and the 826th Amphibian Tractor Battalion the 43d Division. There was no Japanese resistance on shore.

Luzon was not an amphibian story, but one of land tanks. It was to be the most Europe-like of the Pacific campaigns, but even the American side was just a bit different from counterparts in Europe.

The 6th Infantry Division displayed the haphazard nature of armored attachments in the Pacific. Assigned to it were Company C of the 44th Tank Battalion and Company A of the 716th Tank Battalion, plus a detachment of the latter battalion's service company.[28] The division, therefore, had half the number of tanks assigned to it that a division in Europe could expect, and the tank companies were completely unfamiliar with one another. Meanwhile, the 716th Tank Battalion was split among the 6th and 43d Infantry Divisions, and the 44th Tank Battalion was shared with the 1st Cavalry Division.

Company C, 44th Tank Battalion, landed at H+40. *Old Faithful* (with two tank dozers), *Snafu*, and *Bright Eyes* were the first three tanks to land in the 6th Division's zone. One dozer suffered a mechanical failure, dropped its blade, and turned to supporting the infantry, but the second filled in a large fishpond to create a causeway for the rest of the tanks to move inland. By 1200 hours, three tanks had reached the company's objective at the Binloc River, and the company was withdrawn into division reserve. The rest of the battalion began landing two days later with the 1st Cavalry Division.[29]

There was little Japanese resistance inland at first, either, and within a few days, the Sixth Army had 175,000 men in a twenty-mile beachhead. While the I Corps protected the left flank, the XIV Corps set off to capture Manila.[30]

On 11 January, the I Corps pushed eastward into the defenses of the Japanese 23d Infantry Division. The 43d Infantry Division, with the separate 158th Infantry and the 6th Division's 63d Infantry Regiments attached, made the main effort in the direction of Rosario.[31]

The 716th Tank Battalion landed on S-Day, but other than being shelled, it had seen no action until 15 January, when Company B fought alongside the 43d Infantry Division at Hill 355 near Mount Alava. The Japanese had constructed defensive positions, including log and earth-covered pillboxes, in low, rolling hills and ridges covered with bamboo thickets and scrub, which offered the first good defensive terrain above the Agno River. Artillery pieces were dug in and skillfully hidden.

The 716th Tank Battalion had trained intensively with the infantry, which was the good news. The bad news was that its three medium tank companies had been farmed out to three separate divisions for that training, had landed split between two divisions, and were destined to fight with ten different divisions in the Philippines.

Still, Companies C and D and a platoon of Company B were present when, on 15 January, the battalion supported the 169th Infantry's assault on Hill 355 overlooking Route 3 southwest of Rosario. The Japanese 64th Infantry Regiment held the ground, and the 43d Infantry Division's advance had come to a sudden stop a day earlier in the face of resistance from Japanese troops on a series of hills. The 716th Tank Battalion's assault gun and mortar platoons took positions on a nearby hill to provide fire support. The terrain turned out to be virtually impassable to tanks, and the frustrated men were able to account for only four pillboxes.

Two days later, the battalion went into battle near Pozorrubio, not far from where American and Japanese tanks had first clashed in 1941. This time, the tanks—parceled out by platoons to infantry battalions—crushed Japanese resistance wherever it appeared. Maneuver was rapid, and morale was high. The only tank lost was an assault gun, and tragically, the battalion commander was mortally wounded while helping the crew evacuate.

Things soon turned ugly again, as the battalion on 22 January supported an attack by the 169th Infantry on Hill 355 from a different direction, and a breakdown in cooperation between tankers and infantry was the cause. The battalion's history recorded:

Company B's 2d Platoon attacked Hill 355 from the southwest. . . . [Lt. Eugene Farley's] tanks overran enemy infantry positions, forcing them into the open and machine-gunning them as they fled. In one instance, a 75mm shell uncovered a trench system. Two tanks astride the trench swept its length with enfilading fire, killing a large number of enemy troops. This climaxed a wild fight in which fanatical Japanese rushed at the tanks with bayonets and hand grenades. In one case, an enemy soldier climbed onto the back deck of a tank with a forked stick and attempted to stuff dry grass into the grillwork to fire the tank's engine. He was shot off the tank by a machine gun. . . .
Sergeant Leo Smith, a tank commander, was killed instantly by a sniper's bullet, which penetrated his skull. Lieutenant Farley fell wounded while attempting to reestablish contact with infantry forces, which was broken during the melee. Toward sunset, the tanks' supply of fuel and

ammunition was dangerously low. . . . The infantry commander refused to
release the tanks because of the fluid situation. . . .

Captain [Edward] Stork and Lieutenant Munelly with the 3d Platoon
moved out to support the 2d Platoon. . . . Immediately a fire fight began.
Tank guns hurled great quantities of 75mm and machine-gun shells while
the enemy fired on the six tanks with hidden antitank guns, mortars, and
machine guns. One tank stopped short of the enemy to fix a faulty hatch.
Captain Stork's tank was damaged and forced to withdraw. He mounted
a second tank to remain in the fight. Sergeant [Clarence] Reese's was the
only tank of the remaining four that withdrew undamaged. At great risk
to himself, he dismounted under heavy fire to rescue a wounded comrade
from a knocked-out tank. After evacuating him, he returned to rescue
Captain Stork from death, after Captain Stork had been dazed by a mortar
burst and walked toward the enemy firing a pistol.

The Japanese on Hill 355 withstood combined tank-infantry attacks for
twelve days, and the 43d Division finally secured the prominence on 29 January.
Well-camouflaged antitank guns claimed more Shermans. The action was to prove
the most costly the battalion would endure during the entire campaign in the
Philippines.

Over the preceding four years, the United States had become a global player
in armored warfare, whereas Japanese tank development, which had held the
advantage at the start of the war, had stagnated. This became evident almost as
soon as the 716th Tank Battalion went into battle. On 17 January, Company C
was operating with the 103d Infantry Regiment when it encountered four tanks
from the 2d Japanese Tank Division and destroyed all of them. The Japanese may
have learned a lesson from this, as when the company again encountered tanks on
19 January at San Manuel, the tankers found that the enemy had dug them in as
pillboxes, which deprived them of mobility but offset their thin armor plate.[32]

Elsewhere in the I Corps' zone, Company A, 716th Tank Battalion, was not
far away working with the 6th Infantry Division approaching Rosario during this
period. These tankers also destroyed a number of Japanese tanks and tankettes.
Company C of the 44th Tank Battalion fought beside the 20th Infantry to clear the
Cabaruan Hills, which required cleaning the Japanese from every single hole they
occupied. Tanks were used in small numbers to fire at point-blank range into
Japanese positions, sometimes in vegetation so thick the crews could see no farther than a few yards. At the end of the fight, the 6th Infantry Division counted
1,432 Japanese killed and 7 captured.[33]

The 6th Infantry Division had not left its amtracs at the water's edge and was
exploiting the capabilities of the 727th Amphibian Tractor Battalion inland. On 19
January, for example, twenty-six Company B tractors conducted an assault crossing of the Agno River with GIs from the 1st and 20th Infantry Regiments. The fol-

lowing day, the amtracs hauled supplies across the river to the bridgehead and through rice paddies on the far side.[34]

The Race to Manila

After consolidating its part of the beachhead, the XIV Corps crossed the Agno River unmolested on 15 January. Two days later, MacArthur told Krueger that he wanted the XIV Corps to roll south to capture the Clark Field air base complex with alacrity. The following day, Krueger gave the XIV Corps the green light. The Americans rolled toward Manila, as the Japanese had already largely evacuated the central plain.[35]

Oral tradition holds that MacArthur was so impressed by a raid conducted on 30 January by the 6th Ranger Battalion at Cabanatuan—resulting in the liberation of 500 prisoners of war—that he ordered the 1st Cavalry Division, which had arrived from Leyte on 27 January, to accomplish a similar rescue of 3,700 American and other Western civilians interned at the University of Santo Tomas in Manila. "Go to Manila! Go over the Japs, go around the Japs, bounce off the Japs, but go to Manila!"[36]

MacArthur ordered creation of a "flying column" for the mission, and the 1st Cavalry Division organized a mechanized task force under its 1st Cavalry Brigade. The column was broken into three smaller columns or "serials." Marine corps aviation was to support the operation. With the inevitable twists and turns, the men would have to cover about 100 miles to reach the objective. Fortunately, Santo Tomas lay on the north side of Manila, which the Americans would reach first.[37]

The 44th Tank Battalion—minus Companies A through C—and the 302d Cavalry Reconnaissance Troop formed the spearhead for the flying column, called the Provisional Reconnaissance Squadron. Starting on the night of 31 January, the battalion's commander, Lt. Col. Tom Ross, reached Santa Rosa and pressed on the next day to Gapan. There heavy automatic-weapons fire greeted the column, and Ross was killed. That same day, Company B, working with the 2d Cavalry Brigade, secured the river crossing at Cabanatuan, where heavy street fighting took place, and the tanks proved their worth by destroying the enemy's prepared positions.

The 1st Cavalry Division rolled on, swatting aside resistance here and there, with its flanks protected only by marine corps flyers. On 3 February, tanks from Company B that were operating with the the 1st Brigade's 5th Cavalry Regiment were the first element to enter Manila at about 1830 hours, blasting at all positions suspected of hiding Japanese soldiers. The tanks rolled through streets crisscrossed by sniper bullets and reached the internment camp at Santo Thomas University at about 2100 hours. The Sherman *Battlin Basic*, followed by *Georgia Peach*, knocked down the gates. The bold gambit had succeeded.[38]

Getting into Manila had been easy, but securing the capital proved difficult indeed. Strong Japanese forces, primarily naval, disregarded General Yamashita's plan to hold out in the mountains and fought for possession of the city. On 4 February, Manila was divided into two sectors under the responsibility of the 1st Cavalry Division to the east and the 37th Infantry Division to the west; while the former gathered its strength, its 8th Cavalry Regiment began to push toward the Pasig River that ran roughly east to west through the city's center. The 37th Infantry Division easily secured the river line in its zone the next day, hindered mainly by cheering crowds and burning buildings set alight by the Japanese.

Meanwhile, Company B of the 44th Tank Battalion turned to clear the area northeast of the city center, attached to the 7th Cavalry Regiment. On 7 February, the company was ordered to sweep the eastern suburbs, turn south, and then jog west toward the Pasig River.

In a display of complete incompetence, the division assigned no foot troops to work with the tanks. The tankers ran into strong resistance near the San Juan reservoir, where 5-inch naval and 20-millimeter guns engaged the company, while Japanese infantry closed in with Molotov cocktails and mines. In one platoon, three tanks were destroyed and the other two damaged. The next day, six tanks reached the reservoir but were again set upon by Japanese suicide troops with Molotov cocktails and had to pull back. The infantry finally arrived at 1330 hours, and together, the GIs and tankers secured the reservoir.

The company then moved into the heart of the city, where the other three regiments of the 1st Cavalry Division and the 37th Division's 148th and 129th Infantry Regiments were fighting to clear the area south of the Pasig that the Japanese had converted into a fortress. Company A tankers were already there, working through the streets with the 8th Cavalry Regiment's troopers and blasting bunkers and other positions, sometimes under fire from Japanese naval guns. One tank was lost to a naval depth charge rigged as a landmine; there were 154 such bombs along the road where the tank was destroyed. Some of the tanks were equipped with bow-gun mounted E4-5 flamethrowers, which proved useful against Japanese troops barricaded in buildings. The 1st Cavalry Division reported that the tanks were instrumental in the advance.

The 37th Division's 148th Infantry, meanwhile, put its first troops across the Pasig River on 7 February using assault boats, followed by troops carried by the 672d Amphibian Tractor Battalion, which had accompanied the 37th Infantry Division all the way from Lingayen Gulf. The next day, LVTs carried the 1st Battalion, 129th Infantry, across the river.[39]

The 1st Cavalry Division crossed the Pasig several days later. On the south bank, tankers, doughs, and troopers became embroiled in urban warfare like that in Cassino and Aachen. One journalist who covered the 44th Tank Battalion's engagements reported:

It was a crazy kind of fighting in Manila south of the Pasig River. A tank commander's fire order to his gunner would not designate a particular building to be shelled, but instead a specific window on a certain floor of a particular structure. Instead of normal 75mm gun ranges, they were firing sometimes at twenty-five to fifty yards. On one occasion, U.S. troops held the lower floors of a tall building, the Nips remaining in the upper stories. In the narrow street alongside, one tank paused just long enough for a Japanese to toss a dynamite charge from the roof. His aim was perfect, and it landed on the helmet of the tank commander, Sgt. Albert Kramer. . . . Serious injury, of course, resulted. . . .

The reporter noted that this was a result of the 44th Battalion's having to fight with the hatches unbuttoned so the commander could see the battlefield.[40]

"The fighting was the toughest yet encountered by our troops," recorded the 129th Infantry Regiment. "It was like Bougainville in reverse but instead of attacking log and sand pillboxes, we were up against concrete emplacements thoroughly fortified and prepared and strategically emplaced to offer the best fields of fire." The Japanese had constructed pillboxes in the thick-walled concrete structures at nearly every corner, and the GIs advanced from building to building, clearing each one top to bottom. Artillery and antiaircraft guns were often hidden in doorways or behind second-story windows.

The cavalrymen and tankers had to work out ad hoc tactics that greatly resembled those developed in the first big urban battles in Italy and Germany. "For the tanks as well as the infantry, this was a new type of warfare," recorded the 754th Tank Battalion. "Our tactics were revised and became more flexible to meet the change in conditions. The tanks were used primarily as mobile artillery, firing at strong points at very close range."

The importance of tight control over who was on which street was demonstrated on 11 February, when two tanks from the 754th Battalion—still stuck north of the Pasig because all bridges were down—pounded the 129th Infantry's Company E, an event the regiment termed a "debacle." Massed artillery fire against single buildings increasingly became the tactical fix at first.

The 37th Infantry Division did not even use medium tanks from the 754th Battalion in a direct-fire, close-support role until 14 February, when Shermans and M7 assault guns from the infantry's cannon company pounded the new police station, built of heavily reinforced concrete, to weaken the defenses for an assault by the 129th Infantry Regiment. Thereafter, the division used tanks aggressively to support infantry attacks.

The assault gun platoon from the 711th Tank Battalion was attached to the 37th Division on 17 February to provide even more tactical firepower. By 19 February, the infantry also brought up 155-millimeter howitzers to blast openings in the thickest walls, just as had the 1st Infantry Division in Aachen.[41]

Tank company and platoon attachments within the cavalry division, meanwhile, changed frequently, and the 44th Tank Battalion was scattered once again on 13 February, when Company A was sent to the 11th Airborne Division south of Manila.[42] The grinding battle in Manila wore on. Many tanks expended between three and four units of fire per day.[43] Tanks fell victim to antitank guns, landmines, and satchel charges, and for once, many of them were burning.[44] One was hit on the right sponson by a 120-millimeter dual-purpose gun from only seventy-five yards away. Another was penetrated four times by 47-millimeter fire and then hit by a 120-millimeter high-explosive round. A satchel charge was dropped into the turret of another, and one more was destroyed by a shaped charge placed against the armor.[45]

The battle for Manila effectively ended on 24 February, when the 37th Infantry Division fully occupied the old walled city of Intramuros, though fighting dragged on for another week.

Lessons Drawn

"On the plains of Luzon," concluded a U.S. Army Forces Far East board report on battle experiences, "our forces for the first time operated in open, firm terrain. The failure of our armor to ride rough-shod over the Japanese defenses may be attributed largely to the Jap's skillful use of antitank weapons to bolster fortified positions. . . . On Luzon, the Jap has invariably placed his antitank guns well forward and has displayed skill in siting and camouflaging them. His fire discipline has been excellent, in many cases fire being held until U.S. vehicles were within fifty yards."

In and around Manila, Japanese troops had laid well-designed minefields. "Magnetic mines, lunge mines, and satchel charges," the board report continued, "in the hands of suicidal Jap soldiers were a constant threat. These soldiers, working in pairs and usually covered by antitank guns, would conceal themselves along avenues of approach and attack as our tanks passed by. Tank stalking squads were [also] employed but in most cases were unsuccessful and were killed before they could reach our tank."

Tankers in Manila encountered 37-millimeter, 47-millimeter, and 75-millimeter antitank guns and dual-use antiaircraft guns up to 120 millimeters in size, plus the occasional 120-millimeter naval gun. The 47-millimeter gun could penetrate the M4's turret front at short range and its flanks at medium range. The 75-millimeter gun could penetrate the turret from 500 yards and normally destroyed the tank. Every tank hit by the 120-millimeter naval gun was destroyed.[46]

Tankers and GIs on Luzon learned that the Japanese monitored the return of tanks to a laager to refuel and perform maintenance. The solution was to withdraw tanks before dark and then to disperse them 100 to 200 yards apart and as far from the perimeter as possible. Experience showed that Japanese demolition teams would come after tanks if they were sited at the outer edge.[47]

A Second Rescue Mission

The 672d Amphibian Tractor Battalion, meanwhile, had been attached to the 11th Airborne Division, elements of which had made an amphibious landing sixty miles south of Manila on 31 January. The 511th Parachute Infantry Regiment dropped on 3 February at Tagatay Ridge, and the two forces quickly linked up.

On 18 February, the division headquarters issued orders to the 1st Battalion of the 511th Parachute Infantry to liberate 2,000 civilians from an internment camp at Los Banos, about twenty-five miles south of Manila.

The plan was daring and was executed with only minor glitches. On 21 February, the division's reconnaissance platoon infiltrated the Los Banos area by crossing the Laguna (Lake) de Bay in locally procured boats to make contact with Filipino guerrillas who were to help attack the camp. Division engineers reconnoitered the shore of the lake at the objective to identify places where tracked amphibians would be able to climb the bank. Intelligence collected by guerrillas and from escaped internees revealed that the Japanese garrison gathered without arms at 0700 to perform calisthenics. This fact became a key element to the plan.

At 0500 hours on 23 February, the 672d Amphibian Tractor Battalion's fifty-four amtracs set off across the lake carrying two companies of parachute infantry. At roughly 0700, as Japanese soldiers exercised in the internment camp, Company B of the 1st Battalion jumped from nine C-47s winging overhead and aimed for a drop zone about 800 yards from the perimeter. To at least one internee, the paratroopers descending under their canopies looked like angels from heaven. Working with the recon platoon and guerrillas, who had taken the stunned garrison under fire as soon as the jump began, Company B stormed and secured the camp. By the time the amphibians arrived, the fight was almost over.

Planners had intended to evacuate some of the internees overland, and the 188th Glider Regiment had attacked toward Los Banos to open a route to safety. The gilder infantry made slower progress than expected, and the 672d Battalion instead ferried the 2,147 internees to safety across the lake in two shuttle runs. By 1500, the tankers had evacuated the last of the civilians and their rescuers. "But for the troopers of the 11th Airborne, the men of the 672d Amphibian Tractor Battalion, and those army C-47 pilots, I would not have survived Los Banos Internment Camp," recalled one internee.[48]

Pacific Tank Battles

Back in the I Corps' zone, the 44th Tank Battalion's Company C was still attached to the 6th Infantry Division, which on 1 February pushed off with its running mate, the 25th Infantry Division, to capture San Jose. If the Americans could secure the city, they would cut the last land link between the Japanese Shobu battle group—responsible for the defense of northern Luzon—and the Shimbu battle group defending the south. The Japanese planned a holding action at San Jose using the 2d Tank Division and elements of the 10th and 105th Divisions in hopes of shifting more supplies and the 105th Division northward over the route.[49]

The Japanese 2d Tank Division on Luzon constituted the most formidable armored force faced by the Americans in the Pacific theater. By now, the Japanese clearly had no intention of pitting their undergunned and thinly armored Type 97 medium and Types 95 and 97 light tanks against American M4s, and they used their tanks defensively to stiffen defenses in villages in groups of nine or more

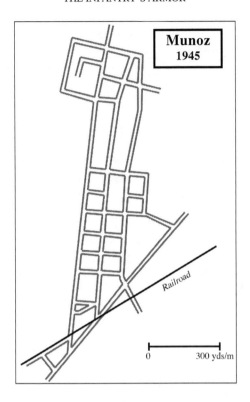

vehicles. The tanks were well dug in and camouflaged, though they could be moved to alternate firing positions. The only times that tanks supported infantry attacks were during last-gasp "banzai charges" when it was clear the defense was collapsing.[50]

Company C of the 44th Tank Battalion, an attached light tank platoon from the 716th Tank Battalion, and the 6th Infantry Division's doughboys ran into the largest of these strongpoints at Muñoz, which lies southwest of San Jose, on 1 February. Some 2,000 Japanese troops defended the village with orders to resist to the last man, including the 6th Tank Regiment (less one company) and elements of the 2d Tank Division's antitank unit armed with 47-millimeter guns.[51]

To the GIs of Company K, 20th Infantry Regiment, approaching Muñoz at 0730 on 31 January, the bomb-shattered buildings that provided excellent camouflage for Japanese emplacements looked just like any other battered town. When the company tried to enter Muñoz from the southwest along a rail line, fierce automatic-weapons fire pinned the assault platoons down and kept them immobile the entire day. Other elements of the 3d Battalion moved up to Company K's line, but it was clear that Muñoz was going to be a problem. Probes over the next two days confirmed that in spades.[52]

The 3d Platoon's medium tanks worked with the 20th Infantry Regiment during its fight to take Muñoz. Company C's battle report described the situation:

Tank operations were limited by flat terrain, boggy ground, and deep water-filled irrigation ditches. The town of Munoz was fortified with antitank guns, 105[-millimeter] artillery pieces, and fifty-seven light and medium tanks, all of which were dug in with a three-feet-thick top of logs and sandbags over them. In addition, numerous alternate positions were available so that the tanks that were in one place one day would be in an alternate position the next.

As a result of constant reconnaissance by the platoon leader, the 3d Platoon was able to move to a somewhat defiladed position on the southwest corner of Munoz, from which point the platoon was able to support the infantry. Movement of tanks was definitely restricted. One false move and a tank was lost. Whenever any armored vehicle attempted to move into the town, it was knocked out by antitank fire. One tank of the 3d Platoon was lost in this manner. Even though limited to almost stationary support, the 3d Platoon gave the infantry considerable support, knocking out six Jap medium tanks, one 105mm artillery piece, four 47mm, and much enemy equipment and personnel.[53]

The 20th Infantry's attack failed in the face of intense fire, and two more days of slugging appeared to bring the Americans no closer to clearing the village.

The rest of Company C's tanks worked with the 63d Infantry, which bypassed Muñoz, reentered the highway on 2 February, and drove on toward San Jose. At the barrio of Abar, the Americans ran into the main defenses before San Jose. The Japanese had emplaced antitank guns and machine guns to cover a water barrier, and tank gunnery that knocked out five 47-millimeter guns was not enough to secure a crossing. The 2d Platoon finally crossed under cover of smoke and then tore up the Japanese defenses, aided by fire from the assault guns, light tanks, and company headquarters, which had enveloped the Japanese line and opened up on the enemy's right flank and rear.[54] The 1st Infantry, which also bypassed Muñoz, entered San Jose on 4 February almost unopposed.

While the 1st and 63d Infantry Regiments mopped up, the 20th Infantry continued its exhausting fight to capture Muñoz. On 3 February, the regiment cracked the first Japanese line running east to west across the south edge of town, which provided a good indication of why the going was so tough. Six medium tanks were dug in forty to eighty yards apart with interlocking fields of fire. Two 47-millimeter antitank guns and two 105-millimeter howitzers were integrated into the line as well. Machine-gun nests and rifle pits covered the tanks and guns.

A very similar Japanese position claimed a Company C tank on 5 February, by which time the 20th Infantry held roughly the southern third of town, as described by infantry officer Capt. Michael Kane, whose Company B was fighting on the east side of Muñoz:

Company B located a tank seventy-five yards to the front. Immediately they requested one of our supporting tanks to engage the enemy tank.

Our tank came up to ten yards east of the storage building and, after the crew had been oriented as to the location of the enemy tank, they fired a 75mm round at the Jap tank, hitting and destroying it. However, our tank, before it could withdraw, was hit by a 47mm shell from a supporting enemy tank. This enemy tank was about eighty yards north of the Jap tank that had just been destroyed. Our tank burst into flames, but the crew escaped safely.

By 6 February, the 20th Infantry had taken only half the town. That day, withdrawal orders reached the defenders.[55]

On the morning of 7 February, the Japanese attempted to break out of Muñoz. Company C's battle report recorded, "The [American] infantry knocked out eleven tanks . . . but the majority of tanks got through."[56] The company's history added:

About three AM, several men woke up as they heard a tractor coming down the highway. It sounded like an American Caterpillar going full speed. Crouching in the dark, they waited and as the vehicle sped by, they recognized it to be a Japanese medium tank. Immediately the alert was sounded, and everyone was up. . . . Soon, more vehicles were heard coming, and we could hear the infantry firing at them but not stopping them. Another medium tank led the convoy, followed by a personnel carrier pulling a 105mm artillery piece. Sergeant Elkins' tank, *Little Anne*, was at the end of the area along the highway covering the direction the Japs were coming from. Corporal [James] Ford jumped into the gunner's seat, Sgt. [Milo] Knowlton into the loader's seat, and T/5 [Charles] Askins stood back of the turret to direct fire. It was impossible to use the gun sights because of the dark. The first tank sped by before the men could fire at it, but when the personnel carrier went by, Askins hollered, "Fire!" and Ford fired. The shell hit dead center on the 105 gun, scattering the Japs that had been sitting on it in all directions. The carrier and gun kept going a few yards down the road, burst into flames, and stopped. Then came another medium tank. *Little Anne*'s gun spoke again and sent an armor-piercing shell clean through the tank.[57]

The battle report continues,

After blocking the highway by destroying one truck and one medium tank, the company fought it out in the dark with seven other Jap tanks plus Jap foot troops. The company area was first riddled with tank fire from the Japs, and then the foot troops attempted to infiltrate our perimeter. In order to avoid firing into our own infantry troops and to have the advantage of the coming daylight in back of the Jap tanks, it was necessary to move one platoon out to the flank of the Jap tanks and take them under fire [which] enabled the company to eliminate all remaining Jap tanks and personnel. . . . Upon checking at daylight, 245 Jap bodies were located, eleven tanks and five trucks had been destroyed.[58]

A physical count revealed the hulks of 48 medium and 4 light tanks in and around Muñoz, plus 4 armored cars, 16 47-millimeter antitank guns, and 4 105-millimeter howitzers.[59] By mid-March, American forces had destroyed 203 medium and 19 light tanks—95 percent of the 2d Tank Division's strength—mostly in the Muñoz–San Jose area.[60]

The fight in Muñoz had, in many ways, resembled the 741st Tank Battalion's struggle in Krinkelt-Rocherath during the Battle of the Bulge, with the roles of the Americans and the enemy reversed. Patient tank-infantry teamwork had paid off in Muñoz, whereas the impatient SS had thrown themselves into a killing ground in the Ardennes.

In February, the 44th Tank Battalion suffered 106 casualties, including thirteen men killed, and lost nine tanks destroyed plus many damaged. March started out just as difficult: two assault guns were knocked out on 3 March, one by a Japanese soldier with a satchel charge and a second by an antitank gun and infantry throwing white phosphorus.[61] The Japanese in and around Manila, in particular, had proved to be as formidable an enemy for the tankers as the Germans had in Europe, without the benefit of a powerful panzer force.

At the end of March, the exhausted men moved to a rest-and-recreation area to enjoy movies, softball, and a swimming pool. By then, an inspection of the 44th Tank Battalion's Company A showed that all of the tank engines needed to be replaced, as well as sixteen sets of tracks. By the time Company C rejoined the battalion in April, the company had been in combat for seventy-seven days straight, which was believed to be a Pacific theater record.[62]

The Drive into Northern Luzon

Tank operations during the drive into the Cagayan Valley in northern Luzon were probably the most diffuse of any organized corps-scale campaign during the war. Except on the valley floor, the terrain was mountainous and jungle clad, and opportunities for even platoon-size action were rare. In April, for example, the 775th Tank Battalion had its headquarters and Companies C and D attached to the 25th Infantry Division, which was driving through the Balete Pass into the Cagayan Valley to eventually link up with the 11th Airborne Division at Appari; Company B attached to the 37th Infantry Division, which was advancing on Baguio; and Company A attached to the 33d Infantry Division, which also attacking toward Baguio.

Tanks often had to support infantry attacks against Japanese pillboxes and gun positions hidden in literally trackless, sloped jungle. Bulldozers had to create "roads," or the tanks had to smash through the vegetation on their own.[63]

The 25th Division's 27th Infantry Regiment recorded a representative picture of the setting and the role of the tanks:

Some three thousand yards south of Balete Pass, the gateway to the Cagayan valley, the enemy constructed his main line of resistance. These defenses formed a general east-west series of fortifications extending from a right flank west of Highway 5 to some distance beyond the Old Spanish Trail, which parallels Highway 5 approximately 12,000 yards to the east.

To man this main line of resistance, the enemy had formed a provisional force composed of elements of his main infantry reinforced by various service units collected from all sectors of Luzon. Principal enemy units represented were the 10th, 11th, and 63d Infantry regiments; the 10th Engineer Regiment; the 10th Transportation Regiment; the 8th Railroad Regiment; and artillery from the 10th Division reinforced by independent artillery and heavy mortar units.

The terrain south of Balete Pass was especially suited for defense. Perpendicular to Highway 5, the enemy's defenses were constructed along a series of ridges and principal hill-masses to which there were few natural routes of approach. The central anchor of the main line of resistance was formed on Myoko Mountain, the dominating hill-mass of the entire area south of Balete Pass and north of Putlan. . . .

With the 2d Battalion in the lead, the regiment commenced the advance to the north. Company G was assigned the left sector adjacent to the highway, and Companies E and F were directed toward Myoko. The terrain was characterized by steep slopes covered by dense rain forest, which offered many problems and hardships in both maneuver and supply. The enemy was supported by intense mortar and automatic weapon fire, and his riflemen were well dug-in on commanding ground. . . .

The terrain was not "tank country." Rather than the usual flat or gently rolling ground usually associated with armor, Myoko Mountain offered only the sharp, narrow ridgeline to the northeast. Saddles and knolls were impassable, and bulldozers had to cut paths, often pushing the tanks into position. . . . When terrain was reached over which the tanks could not move, infantrymen moved ahead to secure the next favorable ground, and the bulldozers followed to improve the ground for further employment of the tanks. Often the path of the tanks was so narrow that a small portion of each track extended over the edge of the ridge.[64]

Lt. Col. Eben Swift described how his 3d Battalion, 27th Infantry, put just a few 775th Tank Battalion Shermans to work in early April to take a feature nicknamed "the Pimple," the highest point on the main Myoko hill-mass. The Japanese were dug in and supported by 150-millimeter and 90-millimeter guns. Swift obtained an armored bulldozer and cut a trail to the Japanese main line of resistance, opening the way for two Shermans that advanced protected by infantry against Japanese suicide attacks. Swift described the scene:

> The tanks labored forward up the narrow bulldozer road to the crest. The Japs knew that something was in the wind and dropped mortar fire; however, most of it passed harmlessly overhead and exploded in the draw behind the tanks. The first tank reached the end of the road almost at the crest of the knoll but stalled when it reached the lip projecting from the crest. . . . The tracks started spinning in the soft dirt. . . .
>
> The bulldozer crawled up behind the tank and pushed it over the top as both engines roared and sputtered. The tank maneuvered into position and fired its 75 and machine guns point-blank at the Jap positions on the Pimple. As fast as the Japs crawled out of their foxholes to fire at the tank, our BAR and rifles cut them down. The 75s not only knocked out the enemy's pillboxes, but also blasted away undergrowth and camouflage in front so they could be plainly seen. After the first tank was set, the bulldozer pushed the next tank up. Together, the two tanks and Company B's riflemen methodically plastered the area.

The next day, the battalion kept two Shermans on a nearby hill firing continuously all day long as the riflemen dug the Japanese off the objective. When one ran out of ammunition, it would pull back and the other would take its place. At the end off the day, commented Swift, "We had squeezed the Pimple."[65]

The regiment noted regarding its advance, "The psychological effect [of tanks] on the enemy was very strong, and the absence of antitank guns proved that he had not remotely expected or considered that tanks could be employed in this sector. . . . [T]he support of the medium tanks was invaluable."[66]

The 775th Tank Battalion concluded at the end of the campaign in northern Luzon, "No one ever conceived that [medium tanks] would or could operate over the rugged terrain which characterized most of the fighting after the enemy was beaten from the central plain into the mountains."

While the 775th Tank Battalion fought its way through northern Luzon, widely scattered elements of the 711th, 716th, and 754th supported the infantry who reclaimed the area east of Manila, the small islands southwest of Luzon, and Mindanao. On some of the smaller islands, no more than a platoon of tanks would be committed to the entire operation.

In terms of duration, the campaign on Luzon most closely approximated the war in Europe. Company C of the 775th Tank Battalion had been in combat for six months and eleven days by the time it was over, and the rest of the battalion had been in combat for nearly five months. Losses, however, were much lighter than in Europe. Only twelve men of the 775th were killed in action, and only four tanks were damaged beyond repair.[67]

American tanks on Luzon did not cover the kind of distances that tanks in Europe did, but conditions were just as hard on the equipment. By summer 1945, the 754th Tank Battalion was suffering from critical shortages of tracks and spark plugs, and it banned movement of the tanks except in emergencies.[68]

CHAPTER 15

Okinawa: The Last Battlefield

"The enemy appears to be making a last-ditch stand, and several times cases of Hari-Kari were observed."
—S-3 Periodic Report, 763d Tank
Battalion, 19 June 1945

The directive for American forces in the Pacific Ocean Area to capture the Ryukyu Islands, of which Okinawa is the largest, dated to 3 October 1944. MacArthur's forces were first to secure Leyte and Luzon in the Philippines, while Adm. Chester Nimitz's forces occupied Iwo Jima. After the capture of the Ryukyus, which constituted Japan's innermost ring of defenses, the final step was to be the invasion of the Japanese Home Islands.[1]

The 77th Infantry Division was instructed to capture the Kerama Islands west of Okinawa a week before the main landings on L-Day to provide the fleet with protected anchorage to support its sustained naval bombardment of Okinawa and with 155-millimeter batteries with firing positions to support the assault wave.[2] On 15 February, the division had established the Provisional Armored Group (Amphibious) to control the operations of the 708th Amphibian Tank and the 715th and 773d Amphibian Tractor Battalions in the upcoming operations.[3]

Beginning on 26 March, the 708th Amphibian Tank Battalion, generally assigning one platoon per rifle company, led a series of small-scale assaults around the Kerama Islands by the 305th Infantry Regiment. This battalion still philosophically viewed amtanks as tanks and not just as mobile artillery, which was evident in the fact that it mounted .30-caliber machine guns in the side hatches of its LVT(A)(4)s to deal with Japanese infantry. The tanks supported the GIs inland from the beaches where the terrain allowed and knocked out pillboxes, shelled

287

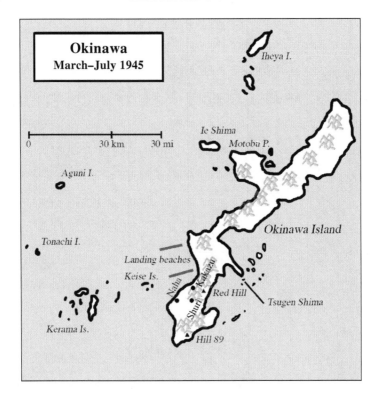

Okinawa
March–July 1945

0   30 km   30 mi

Iheya I.

Ie Shima
Motobu P.

Aguni I.

Okinawa Island

Tonachi I.

Landing beaches

Keise Is.

Naha

Shuri

Kakazu

Red Hill

Tsugen Shima

Kerama Is.

Hill 89

caves, destroyed suicide boats, and engaged enemy infantry. Opposition was light, and only five tankers were wounded.[4]

Okinawa is some sixty miles long and ranges from two to eighteen miles wide. The northern two-thirds are mountainous and cloaked in pine forests. The southern third is covered by rolling hills studded with villages and limestone ridges containing many natural caves. It is excellent defensive country, and an estimated 66,000 Japanese troops were thought to be on the island to exploit that terrain. This estimate was low.

Two army and two marine infantry divisions under the Tenth Army, reinforced by amphibian tank and tractor battalions—about 116,000 men in all—made the initial landings on 1 April after weeks of preparatory destruction by air and naval assets. The invasion beaches were located on the west coast roughly a third of the way up the island. The III Amphibious Corps landed on the left, with its 1st and 6th Marine Divisions, and XXIV Corps on the right, with the 7th Infantry Division just to the north of the 96th Infantry Division. The vast American force charged ashore amidst an earth-shaking bombardment only to find that there were almost no Japanese troops there to resist them.

The 776th Amphibian Tank Battalion was attached to the 7th Infantry Division and led the assault wave. Its orders indicated that as soon as its amtanks reached shore, they were to establish contact with forward observers and shift to artillery missions. This was the culmination of the doctrine the battalion had been creating since Angaur. With the agreement of the 7th Division, the battalion had gotten rid of most of its LVT(A)(1)s, and its platoons now consisted of four LVT(A)(4)s—the size of a field artillery battery. During the landings, battalion amtanks fired 41,297 rounds in support of infantry operations.[5]

Company B of the 711th Tank Battalion had been equipped with T6 pontoon flotation devices, which turned a Sherman into an ungainly raft, and launched from LCMs 500 yards from the beach as part of the 7th Infantry Division's assault wave. All tanks reached the sand west of Kadena, and LCMs brought Company A in shortly thereafter. The remainder of the battalion landed later in the day.[6]

The eighty-eight LVT(4)s and five LVT(2)s of the 536th Amphibian Tractor Battalion carried the 32d Infantry's assault troops to the beach without incident. The LVT(2)s had been allocated as command vehicles for the infantry battalion and amtrac company commanders.[7]

The 780th Amphibian Tank Battalion, again attached to the 96th Infantry Division, landed abreast of the 776th Battalion, as it had at Leyte. The battalion's orders were essentially the same as in the Philippines: to lay down intense fire during the landing, work through the seawall, support initial infantry operations as land tanks; then reinforce division artillery. The battalion had judged that its training and equipment for indirect fire had been inadequate on Leyte, and it had taken care of these deficiencies while preparing for Okinawa. There was no opposition at the water's edge, as things turned out, and the amtanks easily moved inland and supported the infantry with direct fire.[8]

The 763d Tank Battalion joined the 96th Division just behind the infantry assault waves, and unlike on Leyte, the tankers saw country that they could handle. The only tank lost during the landing was one that tipped into a shell hole on a reef, and Japanese fire claimed a second Sherman during the initial advance off the beach. The battalion was well equipped to work with the GIs: tanks carried both SCR-300 radios and sound-powered telephones on the back.[9]

The Tenth Army quickly cut the island in two. The men in the 711th Tank Battalion had the luxury of easing into combat during the push across the island, knocking out the occasional strongpoint and losing not a single tank.[10]

The first signs of serious resistance emerged only after the 96th Infantry Division, on 2 and 3 April, wheeled to advance southward into the rolling hills abreast of the 7th Infantry Division, while the marines turned to clear the north. The Japanese had concentrated their forces, some 100,000 strong, in the southern third of the island and were waiting in their caves and bunkers for the Americans to come to them.[11]

In the 96th Division's zone, the 763d Tank Battalion reported increasing resistance on 2 April, though mines initially posed the main threat to the tanks.

Working with the infantry, the tanks' 75-millimeter fire destroyed Japanese pill-boxes and roadblocks. On 4 April, the 383d Infantry used Company C to spearhead its advance, and the tankers ran into 75-millimeter antitank fire that struck two Shermans and disabled one of them. This was an ominous sign that the Okinawa fight was going to be different than the one the battalion had experienced on Leyte.

The next day, the 763d Tank Battalion recorded in its after-action report, "Strong Japanese fortifications encountered along entire front. Beach, terra cotta, and improvised minefields were extensive. Tank traps, well constructed, were placed on all avenues of approach. 47mm antitank fire was accurate, and guns well placed and concealed. The enemy had excellent observation, and accurate and intense artillery fire was directed at our tanks." Tank losses were heavy from mines and antitank guns, and by 9 April, only forty-three of the fifty-four medium tanks were still in action.[12]

In the 7th Division's zone, the 711th Tank Battalion's Company A experienced its first heavy artillery bombardment during the night of 3 April, and several attempts by suicide squads to reach the tanks with satchel charges were repulsed. Still, the 7th Infantry Division's advance continued, and the division used the tanks to perform reconnaissance in force missions up to two miles ahead of the closest infantry support.

The tankers paid the price for this operating philosophy on 7 April. The 2d Platoon, Company C, was sent ahead of the 2d Battalion, 184th Infantry, down a road that wound past Red Hill. Heavy machine-gun and mortar fire prevented the infantry from following, so on division order, all of Company C and a platoon of light tanks were instructed to take up positions atop Red Hill and neutralize the valley beyond by fire.

The terrain canalized movement, and trouble began when the tenth tank in the column struck an aerial-bomb mine and blocked the rest from passing. While the tankers set to work clearing the minefield with 75-millimeter fire, the 3d Platoon and the light tanks continued up the hill. Soon the lead tank was blown up by another mine, and a suicide squad rushed in and knocked out a light tank with a satchel charge. Only two medium and several light tanks made it to the top of Red Hill.

The Japanese, who had been waiting on the reverse slope, laid down an artillery concentration and counterattacked. Two more light tanks were knocked out. The tankers atop the hill fired all weapons and resorted to grenades and small arms as the Japanese closed in while the wounded crews were evacuated. The Americans retreated.

The 3d Platoon, Company C, then moved down a route west of Red Hill to a point some three miles ahead of the infantry. The Japanese offered no resistance until suicide squads infiltrated between the first and second sections, but the tankers spotted the enemy and drove them off. The platoon pulled back, showered with mortar and artillery fire that the Japanese had withheld while drawing the tanks into their trap.

Meanwhile, Lt. Joseph Gallagher, commanding Company C, sent another light tank platoon followed by an M8 assault gun and a platoon of Shermans up a narrow road with cave-studded hills on both sides. The lead tanks fired their bow machine guns to blow up any mines in the path (this had actually worked once), while the next ones in line sprayed the hillsides and caves. Artillery fell among the light tanks, shaking up two of the crews. Then the lead M5 struck a mine that knocked off the right track. The road was blocked.

The second tank in line moved forward to provide cover. The men in the following vehicles watched Japanese infantry appear and swarm over the advancing M5, but because of obstructing terrain, they could not fire at the enemy soldiers. The Japanese placed a satchel charge that disabled the moving tank and wounded the driver. The watching crewmen to the rear could just make out Japanese troops putting flaming rags on the turret of the second tank. Ignoring the burning rags above, the bow gunner killed a Japanese soldier trying to place a satchel charge on the first tank. Little did he know that an alert crewman in the M8 assault gun who had apparently dismounted with his Tommy gun was just then blowing away a Japanese soldier trying to put a bomb on the bow gunner's vehicle.

The men from the stricken tanks bailed out and scrambled onto the decks of the remaining two, and the platoon pulled back, as did the medium tanks. The exposed men traded shots with Japanese snipers during their escape.

Japanese documents captured near Red Hill made it clear that the 711th Tank Battalion had run into a well-planned antitank defense. Artillery was to separate the infantry from the tanks, making them vulnerable to close assault.[13] The 7th Infantry Division's willingness to push tanks far ahead of the infantry just made things easier for the Japanese.

The next several days were a continuing nightmare for the tankers. During one Japanese counterattack, another tank was destroyed by a satchel charge, and two crewmen were bayoneted while trying to escape. The infantry still pushed the tanks out 600 yards ahead of the riflemen, and direct fire from artillery damaged five tanks, while mines knocked out four more. On 10 April, tanks from Company C, 713th Tank Battalion (Armored Flamethrower), joined each assault company. Only punishing rains that made vehicular movement impossible finally gave the men a break.[14]

THE BATTLE BEGINS IN EARNEST

Six army and marine corps separate tank battalions fought on Okinawa, which allowed each infantry division to have one attached at all times. The extremely rugged terrain prevented the use of armor en masse, and typically, a platoon or two of tanks was committed with each rifle battalion. This was a higher density of armor than had been the case on Luzon—indeed, it was on par with Europe—and on Okinawa, platoons were rarely broken down into sections as they had been in the Philippines.[15]

Each army division in the line also normally had one company of flame-thrower tanks available for use. The 713th Tank Battalion (Armored Flame-thrower) was equipped with Shermans in which the main gun was replaced by a navy flame weapon that fired through the old gun barrel. Normally, the battalion's companies were attached to standard tank battalions (or at times split between two battalions), and in combat, two or three flame tanks operated with a standard tank platoon. When the battalion had converted from a standard to a flamethrower battalion in Hawaii back in January, no doctrine for its use had existed, so the battalion staff had written one.

The E12-7R1 flamethrower was supplied by a 280-gallon fuel tank. A three-quarter-inch nozzle discharged burning fuel at a rate of 4.4 gallons per second to a range of 155 yards. The modified tank required a crew of only four as no loader was needed. The flamethrower proved extremely effective against bunkers and caves and could clear an entire hillside with a full fuel load.[16]

Moreover, flamethrowers in the bow gunner's position had been mounted in all army separate tank battalions on the basis of two per platoon before the landings. As in Europe, crews found the range to be inadequate and the equipment dangerous when tanks were hit by antitank fire.[17]

The Japanese expected to face overwhelming American superiority in tanks and anticipated facing large-scale operations involving up to 300 tanks at a time. Japanese planners drew on lessons learned, especially in the Marianas, Palaus, and Philippines and on Iwo Jima, and spent more time planning and building anti-tank defenses than they had on any other island in the Pacific. Countermeasures included mines, artillery and 47-millimeter guns, artificial and natural obstacles, construction of concealed positions, and use of close-assault attack groups. Before the landings, the close-assault squads were at the center of Japanese thinking. But as the campaign progressed and the enemy realized that tank-infantry cooperation made the tactic extremely difficult to execute, emphasis shifted to the use of mines.[18]

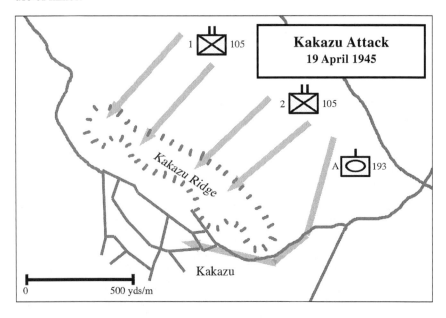

Catastrophe at Kakazu

"The nature of the Japanese defense of Okinawa was first revealed in the heavy fighting of 8–11 April when the Kakazu Ridge position held against a furious American onslaught," recorded the Tenth Army.[19] This obstinate Japanese position was to serve as a harbinger of the costly fight American tankers and GIs were going to face on Okinawa, and it would raise baffling questions about how cooperation between infantry and armor could break down so thoroughly so late in the war.

The package of outfits assigned to overcome the Japanese should have been perfect. The 193d Tank Battalion, which arrived on Okinawa on 8 April, had undergone intensive tank-infantry training with the 27th Infantry Division. The battalion fielded twenty-eight AN/VRC-3 radios to communicate with the infantry's tactical net, and the tanks commanded by the platoon leader and platoon sergeant had been wired with sound-powered telephones.

The 193d Tank Battalion had also modified its tanks to boost survivability. A device called a "back-scratcher" had been installed on sixteen tanks and assault guns. This consisted of four electrically detonated antipersonnel mines mounted around the turret that the crew could trigger to ward off close assaults by infantry. Extra armor plate had been welded over each sponson on the medium tanks.[20]

Yet, though the battalion had been one of the first to reach the Pacific and had been the first battalion to see action in the central Pacific, it was in some ways an untried outfit. The four-day battle on Makin had been one of low intensity against an enemy who lacked much in the way of antitank defenses. The 27th Infantry Division, which had come ashore on 9 April, nevertheless had plenty of experience, including the meat grinder of Saipan. Its planners should have known better.

Whatever the reasons, the plan formulated for the battalion's first action on Okinawa on 19 April completely separated the tanks from the infantry they were to support, with disastrous consequences. Company A of the 193d Tank Battalion and the 1st Platoon of Company B, 713th Tank Battalion (Armored Flamethrower)—the latter in its first action—were detailed to support the 105th Infantry Regiment's attack against the stubborn Japanese defenses along Kakazu Ridge and take the eponymous town on the far side. A bypass had been constructed that would allow tanks to cross a gorge before the ridge, swing by the ridge to its east, and enter town behind the Japanese line. Meanwhile, the 1st and 2d Battalions were to attack directly toward Kakazu and link up there with the tanks.

The tanks were split into two groups. Two Company A platoons and a section of flamethrowers were to push off first, simultaneously with the 1st Battalion. The second group consisted of the third medium tank platoon, the second section of flamethrowers, and all six of the battalion's assault guns working as a six-gun platoon. These tanks were to provide fire support to the first group and then push off at the same time as the 2d Battalion.[21]

The plan was too clever by half, but prisoner interrogations later revealed that it just happened that the Japanese had anticipated such an attack and again designed a defense aimed at separating the tanks from the infantry. The Japanese 272d Independent Infantry Battalion positioned guns, mortars, and machine guns to cover the likely avenues of advance for the infantry, and ten-man squads hid to engage them from ambush. Suicide squads and 47-millimeter antitank guns secured the routes useable by tanks.[22]

The 193d Tank Battalion's after-action report describes the events of 19 April:

The crossing of the first tank elements began at 0730 as scheduled and was executed with difficulty due to the steep slope of the bypass. One tank slipped off the [dirt] fill and overturned. One tank and one flamethrower hit one-horned mines . . . and were disabled. As the first tanks entered [map coordinates], they were taken under fire by a 47mm antitank gun from the left flank. Two flamethrowers and three tanks were hit by this gun before it was spotted and destroyed by the assault gun platoon.

[The Japanese account of the action indicated that suicide squads attacked under cover of smoke at this time and immobilized six tanks, pried open the hatches, and killed the crews with grenades. An inspection of the site revealed that several crews had actually gotten under their tanks and fired small arms until their ammunition ran out. Sixteen tankers died in this area.[23]]

[The surviving tanks made their way into the village, which they shelled and flamed into an inferno.] From approximately 0830, when the movement of all tanks across [the gorge] was completed, to 1200, the remaining tanks, assault guns, and flamethrowers remained around the town of Kakazu, moving to various firing positions and firing on enemy installations and personnel [along the ridge]. During this time, five tanks, one flamethrower, and two assault guns were disabled by mines of various types that were buried indiscriminately over the entire area. One assault gun stuck in a bog, and the crew was later forced to abandon it. . . . [Note: A Tenth Army analysis indicated that a suicide squad destroyed one tank with a box mine.[24]]

The 1st Battalion, 105th Infantry, never reached the top of Kakazu Ridge and subsequently shifted to the [flank] and advanced around the west of Kakazu Ridge. The tank platoon leader of the 1st Platoon, Company A, was in a position [to see] several infantrymen appear over the hill, but an artillery concentration began falling and the infantrymen either became casualties or withdrew. No infantrymen physically contacted those tanks. The platoon was at times in SCR-300 radio contact with elements of the 1st Battalion, but no physical contact was made.[25]

The 2d Battalion had likewise fallen back under artillery and mortar fire. Tank communication with the 2d Battalion was a mess anyway because the latter's commander had been killed shortly after the attack began, and then an artillery round had destroyed the tank battalion's liaison radio and wounded one of the operators.

At 1330, the 193d Tank Battalion's operations officer convinced the regimental commanding officer to permit the tanks to withdraw. Because so many command tanks had been knocked out, nobody was certain that everyone had gotten the message, so the S-3 set out in his Sherman to make sure. All tanks were pulling back, but by the time that was clear, the S-3's tank had hit a mine behind Japanese lines and had to be abandoned.[26] The grand total of twenty-two knocked-out tanks was the greatest loss suffered in a single engagement on Okinawa and in the Pacific theater.[27]

Only two days later, on 21 April, Lt. Col. John Behrns, the 193d Tank Battalion's commander, attempted to lead a column consisting of one platoon of medium tanks from Company C, a platoon of light tanks, and a section from the 713th Armored Flamethrower Battalion past a blown bridge to support Company K, 105th Infantry. Under heavy sniper fire, Behrns dismounted with seven men and used hand tools carve out a suitable bypass. At 1530 hours, Behrns climbed back into the command tank and moved out. About 100 yards beyond the bypass, an antitank round pierced the left side armor of Behrns's tank, followed in quick succession by half a dozen more. Every man in the tank except one was wounded or dead, and the mortally wounded Behrns just managed to climb from the turret and reach the ground before he died.

The platoon leader from Company C took over and moved forward until he reached another blown bridge. Three 47-millimeter shells struck his tank, but this time, the crews in the following tanks spotted the gun and destroyed it. Nevertheless, further advance was impossible, and the infantry commander released the tanks.[28]

The 193d Tank Battalion's experience was echoed elsewhere. According to the 763d Tank Battalion's after-action report,

> From 9 to 19 April, stalemate due to mud and shifting zone of action. The attack on "Tombstone" and "Sawtooth" ridges was spearheaded by Companies A and C, with assault and flamethrower tanks attached. This being an enemy strong point, enemy resistance was the strongest yet encountered. Heavy concentrations of artillery and mortar fire were encountered. Minefields and antitank fire made tank progress slow and costly. The enemy attempted to separate the infantry from the tanks, and then satchel-charge them by suicide attempts. His attempts were unsuccessful due to good mutual tank support. Tanks were instrumental in marking up sizeable gains for the infantry.

During this period, Company B was attached to the 921st Field Artillery Battalion, where it reprised its role on Leyte as an artillery battalion. The battlefield was so lethal that Company D's light tanks were held in reserve. By the time the 96th Division pulled back for rest and rehabilitation on 30 April, the battalion had lost eighteen medium tanks—or roughly a third of its strength—as well as a light tank and an assault gun.[29]

Cave Warfare

Evidence accumulated during mid-April beyond Kakazu that the Japanese held a "tight, coast-to-coast, dug-in, fortified defense line in depth," recorded the Tenth Army. The failure of attacks against the Shuri Line on 19 April ended American hopes that the weight of three infantry divisions and massed artillery could produce a quick victory in southern Okinawa. Maj. Gen. Andrew Bruce, commanding the 77th Infantry Division, proposed conducting an amphibious envelopment of the Japanese line similar to the Ormoc operation on Leyte, but the Tenth Army rejected the idea, saying it lacked sufficient supplies of ammunition for such a venture. The approach was to be brute force.[30]

For the tankers, this meant that much of the fighting on Okinawa involved routing the enemy out of caves—a twist on medieval tales of knights and dragons because this time, the flame-spewing armored beasts were on the outside.

Col. Grant Schlieker, who spoke to Army Ground Forces Headquarters on his return from Okinawa, characterized the development and improvement of cave warfare as the most outstanding feature of the enemy's tactics on the island. The Japanese had adopted cave warfare as a response to overwhelming American firepower on other islands, but on Okinawa, they for the first time consistently covered the approaches to caves with interlocking fields of fire from nearby caves and open emplacements. Machine guns were well camouflaged and far enough away that they were difficult to detect. Mortars provided effective supporting fire from defilade, and artillery often chimed in from distances longer than the Japanese had used before. Infantry in a cave almost always fought to the last man.

The usually well-camouflaged caves were natural but augmented by human construction. Connecting tunnels ran among many of them, and a cave might have two or three exits. Some were large enough to house heavy artillery; one 150-millimeter piece nicknamed "Pistol Pete" fired every night but was so well hidden that it was not spotted until L+45. Mines usually protected caves that housed 47-millimeter antitank guns, and the caves had been selected for good fields of fire against the flanks of tanks canalized by ditches or natural obstacles. The Japanese had responded to American use of flamethrowers by installing ventilations shafts, steel or wooden doors, wet mats, and asbestos curtains.

The infantryman typically was the first one to know that a cave lay ahead, because he came under fire. The first step was to spot the opening and any supporting field positions. The doughboy then turned the job over to the artillery, mortars, or aircrews dropping napalm to destroy the camouflage. If practicable, a colored smoke round would be fired into the entrance to reveal adjacent openings. The easy fix was to shell the area above the opening to jar loose enough earth to cover the entrance.

The hard solution was the tank-infantry team. Schlieker described the team play:

> Neutralization is normally effected by a small infantry group and a tank or armored flamethrower. The tank boys lay [their] direct-fire weapon on the cave mouth as the infantry team works close. Hostile fire from the cave is immediately returned by the tank, while fire from adjacent positions receives retaliatory fire from the members of the infantry group who cover the advance of their comrades armed with flamethrowers and demolition charges. . . . When it is possible to approach the cave with an armored flamethrower, a few short blasts from its flame gun cause the enemy to make a hurried retreat [or be] destroyed by the fire or lack of oxygen caused by the flame.[31]

On 29 April, for example, Company C, 713th Tank Battalion, which was attached to the 96th Infantry Division and the 763d Tank Battalion, committed only eight tanks to support attacks on caves yet was credited by the infantry with killing 90 percent of the 290 Japanese dead counted that day.[32]

Tankers learned that there was an up side to Japanese fire discipline that kept antitank gunners from shooting their 47s until an American tank had come within a few hundred yards. The guns were usually easy to spot, and the close range meant that return fire usually dispatched the gun with a speed that surprised the Japanese. Meanwhile, the simple solution of putting a few GIs in front of a tank to look for suicide squads left the Japanese without an obvious solution, according to captured reports. The gradual destruction of Japanese artillery—which tended to fire at tanks—made the American countermeasure ever less dangerous to the doughboys involved.[33]

By this time, production was underway back in the States of a rugged waterproofed phone, the External Interphone Station RC-298, to permit the tank crews and infantry to communicate. It had taken the army a year and a half to regularize this critical tactical tool from the first ad hoc field experiments.[34]

THE SMALL ISLANDS

While the land tankers sweated through the first weeks of fighting on Okinawa, the last amphibian tank operations of the war were underway just off shore. On 10 April, the 780th Amphibian Tank Battalion's Company B supported elements of the 27th Infantry Division that seized Tsugen Shima off the east coast of Okinawa. Before the amphibians left the line of departure, an artillery round struck one of the LVT(A)(4)s and wounded four crewmen. Mortar and small-arms fire greeted the invading force, but a high bank just off the beach allowed the infantry to dismount safely from their LVTs. Once ashore, the amtanks supported the GIs with direct fire against machine-gun emplacements and one coastal gun. Amtracs from the 728th Amphibian Tractor Battalion's Company B, meanwhile, formed a skirmish line and advanced with the infantry they had carried ashore through small-arms fire to capture the village of Tsugen. The operation was more costly for the amtank battalion than had been the main landing on Okinawa: two men were killed and eighteen wounded. Company D and another 27th Infantry Division assault force captured Tori Shima on 10 May.[35]

The III Amphibious Corps had made such rapid progress securing northern Okinawa that Tenth Army decided to occupy Ie Shima, which stands to the west off Okinawa's Motobu Peninsula, earlier than planned, mainly to make use of the three landing strips there to support operations in southern Okinawa. The 77th Infantry Division got the word to conduct landings on 16 April.

Ie Shima is five miles long and two miles wide and is surrounded by a coral reef, which meant that amphibians would be needed. The island itself is covered by tall grass and scrub, with scattered cultivated plots. The Japanese had thoroughly fortified the island with pillboxes, cave positions, and trenches, which were defended by 2,000 men. The Japanese had cut antitank trenches across the airstrips and mined the area thoroughly.

The 77th Infantry Division decided to land on the southwest corner of the island, the farthest point from the town of Ie and the nearby "pinnacle" promontory, which formed the heart of the Japanese defenses. The 306th Infantry was to land on the left over Green Beach and overrun a nearby airfield, and the 305th Infantry on the right on Red Beaches 1 and 2. Systematic bombardment of the island began on 13 April.[36]

Company C of the 708th Amphibian Tank Battalion supported the 1st and 3d Battalions at Green Beach. The 1st and 3d Platoons formed the first wave. Crossing the line of departure, the tankers found the beach obscured by the dust raised during the bombardment, but the LVT(A)(4)s opened timed fire over the coast with their 75-millimeter howitzers at 500 yards from shore. The tanks crawled over the coral reef and reached the sand. Both platoons had drifted too far left, and the 3d Platoon maneuvered to its proper landing site before making shore. There the company commander ordered the tanks to stop. The beach was laced with mines constructed from powerful aerial bombs. The 3d Platoon's leader ordered his tank to advance gingerly toward an exit through the bluff, but several large-caliber shells struck around the tank, and shrapnel punched through the side armor and severely wounded one man.

The infantry in their LVTs soon reached shore, and engineers started clearing the mines and improving the beach exits. The amtanks from the 2d Platoon arrived with the second wave. After forty-five minutes, the amtanks moved inland, with each tank commander walking in front of his tank to guide the driver around remaining mines.

Upon reaching the GIs, the tank-infantry team pushed off to capture the airfield. In the 3d Platoon, the tankers found it was still necessary for the commanders to lead their tanks because of the mines around the airstrips. The 1st Platoon on the left came under fire from a 47-millimeter gun but could not destroy it because friendly infantry were in the area. These GIs pointed the gun out to the 3d Platoon, and after the amtanks put several 75-millimeter rounds on the emplacement, the infantry overran the gun. "Many pillboxes were found on this flat terrain," recorded the 3d Platoon, "but the fields of fire were very good, and the pillboxes on open terrain were difficult to conceal and quite easy to destroy with our tank 75mms."[37] The 306th Infantry secured the airfield and by evening had covered two-thirds of the length of the island.

Companies A and B of the 708th Amphibian Tank Battalion formed the 305th Infantry's assault wave at Red Beaches 1 and 2. Company A encountered no mines on the beach and pushed up a bluff to a 300-yard stretch of level ground before the next bluff. This ground was heavily mined, and the Japanese covered it with small-arms and machine-gun fire. The amtanks neutralized the machine-gun nests and then gingerly worked their way across the small plain and up the next bluff with the infantry. The 3d Platoon moved eastward while the rest of the company shelled caves in the next bluff to the front.

The 3d Platoon outpaced the infantry and encountered heavy machine-gun fire, which the tankers suppressed. Spotting Japanese infantry in tall grass 700 yards away, the platoon hit them with 75-millimeter fire. At this point, the infantry caught up, and the team pushed on, only to be held up again after 200 yards by fire from strongpoints on a nearby ridge. While reducing these positions with the GIs, the tankers encountered Japanese infantry attacking with magnetic mines, but no tanks were lost.

The 1st Platoon, meanwhile, blasted strong points manned by infantry along the top of the second bluff. The company commander's tank struck a mine, and he and a crewman were wounded when they bailed out under fire. The crippled tank blocked the only route across a steep ravine and stopped further progress by the armor.

During the day, Company B was completely stymied by mines and able to contribute only by firing indirectly. The company learned just how deadly the aerial-bomb mines were when the left track of an amtank triggered one. The left section of the final drive, the left track, the hatches over the driver and assistant driver, and sections of armored plate were torn away, and the tank itself was flipped into the air and landed on its turret. Within minutes, it was a blazing inferno. The only survivors were the turret crew, who were thrown from the tank; the driver, who miraculously was blown clear; and a scarf gunner, who got out of a hatch before the vehicle erupted into flames.

On 17 April, Companies A and B conducted assaults with the 307th Infantry on Red Beaches 3 and 4 on the southeast corner of the island but were unable to move off the beaches because of extremely dense minefields. Meanwhile, Company C spent the next two days fighting with the infantry as land tanks. On W+2,

Company C tanks spotted and destroyed Japanese mortar positions on the pinnacle but lost a platoon leader shot while engaging a machine-gun nest that had stopped the infantry.[38]

Land tanks arrived when, beginning on 18 April, the majority of the 706th Tank Battalion came ashore. The heavier armor provided the decisive edge to the infantry, and in the course of four days, the tankers destroyed pillboxes, fortified caves, gun positions, and Japanese infantry. Land mines destroyed three medium tanks, and suicide squads with satchel charges took out two more.

"'Sherman's march to the sea' was the phrase someone used in describing the final [Company C] action on 22 April," recorded the 706th Tank Battalion's history. "Stretching almost three-quarters the width of the island, the company, supporting the 2d Battalion, 307th Infantry, moved in line formation across the eastern third of the island and reached the sea. Resistance was not very heavy, [and] all tanks completed the mission. . . ."[39]

THE TANK CRUNCH

By the end of May, the four army separate tank battalions and the 713th Tank Battalion (Armored Flamethrower) had lost 221 tanks, of which 94 tanks (43 percent) had been totally destroyed. Gunfire had claimed 111, mines 64, and satchel charges 25 of the destroyed or damaged tanks. The 221 tank casualties amounted to 57 percent of the 338 tanks of all kinds that were available and included 12 flamethrower tanks.[40] The 193d Tank Battalion, which had suffered the highest losses in its twelve days of combat, calculated that it had had 18 tanks disabled by gunfire and artillery, 14 by mines, and 2 by hand-thrown charges. All but 3 medium tanks and 2 assault guns were salvageable, however. Two officers and eighteen men were killed in action, and total casualties amounted to seven officers and fifty-six men.[41]

Tank commanders protested that these losses were too high, but Lt. Gen. John Hodge, the XXIV Corps' commander, had no sympathy. Tanks were made to attack, and up until Okinawa, few outfits had had to face heavy, sustained fighting in the Pacific. Hodge thought that tank losses were proportionate to those of other arms.[42]

The army had not anticipated the high levels of tank attrition that the Japanese were inflicting, and it literally had no reserve stocks available. An order was sent to Oahu for thirteen medium tanks that were stored on Saipan, but they would not arrive until 10 June, when the campaign was virtually over. An additional requisition of sixty-five medium tanks and twenty-five tank recovery vehicles could not be filled until 15 July.[43]

After the bloody April fighting around Kakazu, the Tenth Army pulled the 193d Tank Battalion from the line on 1 May. The next day, the Tenth Army ordered it to turn over all of its serviceable medium tanks to the 706th, 711th, and 763d Tank Battalions as replacements. From that point on, battalion personnel conducted motor and foot patrols, conducted airfield security, and swept areas for

Japanese stragglers. In late June, several detachments were sent to garrison small offshore islands.[44]

The 706th Tank Battalion had just arrived at the front on the main island on 30 April with the 77th Infantry Division, and it went into action the next day. Companies A and B, supporting the 307th and 306th Infantry Regiments, respectively, got a quick jolt of Okinawa's reality. Japanese 47-millimeter guns knocked out two Company A tanks, and one Company B tank was lost behind Japanese lines to unrecorded causes. The targets were again pillboxes, caves, and other fortifications. One platoon of flamethrowers from the 713th Tank Battalion worked with each line company of mediums. That dreary pattern repeated day after day for three weeks. Every few days, another tank or two fell victim to antitank guns, artillery, or mines.

On 21 May, the 1st Platoon of Company A destroyed six Japanese medium tanks while supporting the 307th Infantry. Heavy rainfall began, and by 23 May, the tanks were unable to maneuver through the muck and were largely taken out of the battle except for occasional fire missions. On 2 June, the battalion pulled back to a rest area, and its part in the battle was over.[45]

The 711th Tank Battalion remained engaged in heavy action throughout May. The battalion appears to have developed something of a specialty in using its tankdozers with the lead tanks and flamethrower to create routes to firing positions best suited to help the infantry.

When the 763d Tank Battalion returned to the line with the 96th Division on 10 May after a ten-day rest, its after-action report recorded, "Action during this period was characterized by huge numbers of Japs being destroyed by tanks, after being flushed out of caves by flamethrowers." Cave warfare was dangerous for the attackers, too; between 10 and 22 May, the battalion lost fourteen mediums to guns, mines, and satchel charges.[46]

Finally, on 14 June, the men could sense the end was near. The battalion's history recorded:

For the remainder of the operation, the tanks had a field day. . . . Tanks pushed out in front and took targets under fire as they were designated from regimental OPs, by company commanders, and from battalion CPs. . . . Caves were sealed by tank gun fire; rocky crags, wooded areas, and towns were burned by flame-throwing tanks, which forced the Japanese out into the open to be destroyed by 75mm and machine-gun fire. Some heavy weapons were encountered, but only slight damage was inflicted on our tanks. . . . As the last strong point, Hill 89, was approached, the resistance was practically broken. . . . [T]he Japs started to surrender in large groups.[47]

In three months on Okinawa, the 711th Tank Battalion had lost thirty men killed and eighty-six wounded, twenty-two tanks permanently destroyed (ten by satchel charges), and forty-two tanks damaged but repaired.[48] The 763d Tank Battalion over the same period had lost twenty-seven medium, one light, and two assault gun tanks destroyed.[49]

With no amphibian armored missions to perform, outfits were directed to other tasks. As early as 20 April, the 536th Amphibian Tractor Battalion had been assigned to coordinate defense against amphibious, airborne, and ground attacks in the XXIV Corps' service area.[50] In mid-June, the 20th Armored Group dismounted the 780th Amphibian Tank and 773d Amphibian Tractor Battalions to defend the Minutago area against infiltration. Each platoon, in addition to personal weapons, carried one .50- and four .30-caliber machine guns. In mid-August, the 780th Amphibian Tank Battalion was put in XXIV Corps reserve, with one company mounted and the rest on foot to fight as infantry.[51]

The Japanese commanding general, Lt. Gen. Mitsuru Ushijima, and his chief of staff committed suicide on 22 June, but scattered resistance lasted another week and claimed more than 700 additional American casualties. The campaign formally ended on 2 July. In the bloodiest battle yet against Japan, 12,520 Americans had lost their lives or gone missing, while another 36,361 had been wounded. Approximately 110,000 Japanese personnel had died, and only 7,400 had surrendered.

During the battle for Okinawa, 153 Tenth Army tanks were destroyed and many more damaged. According to the U.S. Army's Center of Military History, the overall loss rate among armored vehicles (army and marines) was about 60 percent, although this figure almost certainly does not include amphibian outfits, where attrition was much lower.[52]

But the tankers had made a vital, if costly, contribution. Colonel Yahara, a senior staff officer of the Japanese 32d Army captured in the last days of the campaign, stated that the most important single factor in deciding the battle on Okinawa was American superiority in tanks. The men in those tanks had generally fought as they had throughout the Pacific war—in platoons, working closely with the infantry. The largest concentration of tanks in a single attack took place in the final days of fighting, when twenty tanks were used on a 1,000-yard front.[53]

RELIEF AS MUCH AS TRIUMPH

The suicidal Japanese resistance on Okinawa seemed to foreshadow an even more costly fight for the Home Islands, and more armor arrived in the Pacific to prepare for that struggle. This included the 28th, 779th, and 785th Tank Battalions and the 720th Amphibian Tractor Battalion. Other outfits, including the 795th Amphibian Tank Battalion and 764th Amphibian Tractor Battalion, were in the pipeline back in California. In Europe, several veteran units, including the 737th, 738th, 739th, and 747th Tank Battalions converted to amphibian tractor battalions and shipped westward toward the Pacific theater.

Operations against the Home Islands were going to require all the amphibian strength available, plus tank support for an unprecedented number of infantry divisions for the Pacific theater. MacArthur's plans foresaw putting three corps ashore simultaneously on Kyushu on 1 November. The initial landing force for Honshu, circa March 1946, was to consist of ten infantry divisions, three marine divisions, and two armored divisions.[54] Planners in Washington, looking at losses suffered so far in the Pacific, expected the number of Americans killed to total at least 500,000, plus many times that in wounded. The army minted so many Purple Heart medals for the operation that they were still being handed out in 1995.[55]

The tankers doubtless were as relieved as anybody else when, on 14 August, the White House announced that Japan had capitulated after the horrifying twin blows of the atomic bombs dropped on Hiroshima and Nagasaki and a Soviet declaration of war. Now, instead of invading the Home Islands, the boys could go home.

CHAPTER 16

A Mission Accomplished and Legacy Secured

"[I]n future wars, the tank-infantry team will be the great striking force. Such a team should not be made up on the battlefield but must be trained long before battle. Its men must know each other well, must work together, and must learn each other's capabilities and limitations."

—Maj. William Campbell,
745th Tank Battalion

The concept of infantry-support tank battalions had been thoroughly vetted and proved in all theaters of operations. "The mission of tanks in support of infantry as laid down in FM 17-33 is substantially correct," concluded the European theater's General Board set up after VE-Day. Looking back at the reality that tanks had often fought tanks, it added, "Tanks should be assigned the role presently assigned to tank destroyers."[1]

The General Board endorsed the continued use of separate battalions fielding special tanks, specifically mentioning "super-heavy" tanks but presumably including the panoply of equipment seen during the war, including mine-clearing, amphibian, and flame-throwing tanks. It concluded that such battalions should be consolidated under the control of a special-equipment headquarters.[2] Given that the United States had not fielded any super-heavy tanks during the war, one wonders whether this reference was a nod to the effectiveness of German Tiger battalions.

Opinion among infantry division commanders in Europe overwhelmingly favored making tank battalions an organic part of the infantry division, and the Pacific Warfare Board reported that armor officers in that theater also endorsed the idea. The General Board recommended that a tank regiment of three battalions be made organic to the infantry division, with one battalion assigned to each infantry regiment. Division commanders favored keeping some general headquarters tank battalions in existence and available to the army commander, but the board rejected this idea.[3]

The army decided to split the difference between a battalion and a regiment. In 1948, it established a new table of organization for the infantry and National Guard divisions that included an organic tank battalion, plus one medium tank company per infantry regiment.[4]

There was a remarkable degree of consistency regarding equipment preferences between the European and Pacific theaters. In Europe, officers from separate tank battalions showed little enthusiasm for the M26 heavy tank, expressing a desire for some variant of the M4A3E8—or a new tank entirely. Officers in the Pacific were open to using some M26s, but they also made clear their desire for the Easy 8. The 13th Armored Group proposed a battalion consisting of one company of M26s, two of Easy 8s, one of M24 light tanks, two platoons of flamethrower tanks, and a platoon of 105-millimeter howitzer tanks. In the Korean War, as things worked out, both the M26 and M4A3E8 played major roles.

Sentiment in both theaters favored making formal the usual field practice of consolidating all six assault guns in a platoon.[5] The army's postwar net assessment of their utility in tank battalions was ambiguous, however: "The use of howitzer tanks (10 percent of gun tanks) as an accompanying support gun was not conclusively shown to be required or desired in World War II. They were largely used in roles which can be far better performed by self-propelled artillery."[6] Tankers nevertheless used the 105-millimeter howitzer Sherman in Korea.

Amphibian tankers were basically pleased with their equipment. The World War II–vintage LVT(4) amtrac served in the Korean War. The main complaint about the LVT(A)(4) amtank was addressed with an updated version, the LVT(A)(5), which incorporated a ball-mounted machine gun at the assistant driver's position and two machine guns mounted atop the turret. The turret top was armored to protect the crew from airbursts. Amtank units also received AN/VRC-3 radios so they could tie in to the infantry net, although amtrac units did not.[7]

POSTWAR DOCTRINE

Postwar doctrine for tank battalions reflected the lessons learned during the war and was to mold the armored battalions that fought in Korea. The 1949 field manual for the tank battalion (FM 17-33) in one simple paragraph captured the retention of the World War II–era separate battalion's mission. The two substantial changes were incorporating the battalion into the infantry division and giving it the mission assigned to tank destroyers:

Each infantry division has an organic tank battalion. The role of the battalion in the infantry division is to support the over-all division mission. The battalion is used in the greatest possible concentration consistent with the situation. It may be reinforced or may be used to reinforce infantry units. The battalion increases the strength and firepower of the attack and counterattack, exploits successes, and adds depth to the anti-tank defense in both the offense and defense.[8]

Tank-infantry communication was hard-wired into the doctrine, including an assumption that the old field-expedient telephone would be available, as was infantry tactical control over attached tanks:

> The voice radio between infantry commanders and individual tanks, and the external interphone on each tank, provide the means of communication between the dismounted infantrymen and the tanks in the attack. . . . Infantry small-unit commanders control the target designation and assist in the selection of terrain for tanks, to ensure coordinated action by the tanks in neutralization or destruction of targets. The tanks act aggressively to fire on such targets. Likewise, the infantry must continue their forward movement to retain the integrity of the team. . . .

Newly formed tank battalions in infantry divisions were to get two weeks of intensive training with an infantry regiment.

The tank battalion organization looked quite similar to the pre-1943 medium tank battalion. There were three line companies, a headquarters and service company, and a medical detachment. Gone were the assault gun and mortar platoons. The medium tank battalion in an armored division had a fourth line company and an assault gun platoon.

The armored group concept had not gone away. In theory, corps-level armored cavalry groups controlled separate tank battalions that could be attached to an infantry division, and division commanders were urged to use such battalions en masse and to avoid superimposing one tank unit on another. Specialized battalions, such as mine-clearing, flamethrower, and bulldozer units, could be subordinated to a group.

Finally, doctrine included an acceptance that tanks might have to fight just about anywhere, and it pulled together the lessons painfully learned by tankers and doughs in the many places they had fought. The 1949 field manual on the tank battalion covered fighting in towns and cities, and the tactics mandated came straight out of the 26th Infantry Regiment's operations in Aachen. Other sections addressed using tanks against fortifications, such as pillboxes; fighting in woods; use of tanks in desert, mountains, and jungles; and amphibious assaults, including the use of flotation devices for tanks.[9]

The de facto amphibian battalion doctrine developed in the Pacific theater was enshrined in postwar field manuals, too. By 1950, amphibian tank and tractor battalions had been renamed amphibious battalions, but the theory and practice were the same. The battalions remained administratively independent units that supported infantry in amphibious landings. The vision for the use of amphibious tanks reflected that pioneered by the 776th Amphibian Tank Battalion, which saw amtanks as self-propelled artillery rather than tanks but acknowledged the reality that operating as land tanks might be unavoidable. Even the "sea cavalry" operations on Leyte became enshrined in doctrine, which specified that amtanks and amtracs could be used for raids behind enemy lines.[10]

The lessons and legacy of the World War II tankers were solid and remain relevant to the present day. Tankers in Korea fought much like the men in the preceding war and often were some of the same men. Lt. Col. Welborn Dolvin, who had fought in Italy with the 756th Tank Battalion and then commanded the 191st Tank Battalion in the European theater, organized the 8072d (later 89th) Tank Battalion in two weeks, and then led his tanks into battle against the North Korean invaders near Pusan on 1 August 1950. His tanks were salvaged and rebuilt wrecks from Pacific war battlefields—in theory, no match for the enemy's T-34s. Dolvin's force lost half its tanks, but the tankers—many of whom had had no training with armor—and GIs of the 27th Infantry stopped the Communist drive. "For the first time, they had met firepower that would knock them out," said Dolvin.[11] By late August, an amphibious tank company and several tank battalions shipped from the States, including the storied 70th Tank Battalion, were in action. Tankers again proved they could operate in terrain that had been deemed unsuitable for armor before the war.[12]

The armored cavalry, part of the armor branch since 1950, served extensively in Vietnam and convinced Gen. William Westmoreland that he had been wrong when he thought the armored troopers unsuitable for his war.[13] The 1st Squadron of the 4th Cavalry accompanied the 1st Infantry Division to Vietnam in 1965 and proved so effective that earlier convictions that tanks could not be used in Vietnam collapsed. When the 25th Infantry Division arrived in early 1966, the 69th Armored Regiment's 1st Battalion came, too. An army monograph concluded, "The myth that armor could not be used in the jungle had been destroyed."[14] Had the army asked the tankers who had fought their way across the Pacific, there would have been no such myth.

By the time of the second war with Iraq, the integration of tanks into infantry divisions was so complete that the Americans were able to use the 3d Infantry Division in April 2003 to spearhead the thrust to Baghdad, a mission that in World War II probably would have fallen to an armored division. Echoes of the past reverberated through the engagements that soldiers and marines fought in the cities of Iraq, including the use of "grunt phones" attached to the back of M1A1 Abrams tanks to enable the marines to talk to the tank crews. The men likely had no idea they were using a technique first tested by the army on Kwajalein seven decades earlier.[15]

The day of massed, heavy armor action may or may not be over. But almost wherever the infantryman fights, he is probably going to want to have his partner in the tank right beside him.

Battalion Profiles

44TH TANK BATTALION

The 2d Battalion, 44th Armored Regiment, 12th Armored Division, redesignated as 44th Tank Battalion, 12th Armored Division, on 11 November 1943. Departed States 22 March 1944, arrived New Guinea 7 May and attached to XI Corps. Company C attached 41st Infantry Division 1 June for combat duty, later to 6th Division, with which fought on New Guinea and Morotai. Remainder of battalion participated in landings on Leyte, Philippine Islands, on 20 October. Company A shunted among three divisions in a month. Companies B and D served mainly dismounted on outpost duty from 23 October to 30 November. Shifted to Luzon 11 January 1945, where rejoined by Company C, which had landed with 6th Division on S-day, 9 January. Entered Manila on 3 February. Company C engaged Japanese 2d Tank Division at San Jose in early February. Battalion fought in Southern Luzon through April as XIV Corps asset. Attachments: 6th, 24th, 32d, 41st, 43d Infantry Divisions; 1st Cavalry Division; 11th Airborne Division. (History, 44th Tank Battalion; Martin.)

70TH TANK BATTALION

First GHQ medium tank battalion in U.S. Army. Formed from 67th Infantry (medium tanks) at Fort Meade, Maryland, on 15 June 1940 under Lt. Col. Stephen G. Henry. Redesignated the 70th Tank Battalion (Medium) 15 July 1940, and as the 70th Light Tank Battalion 7 October 1941. Company C detached 15 February 1942, sent to Iceland; new Company C formed 19 May. Company A landed at Algiers 8 November 1942 as part of 39th ICT (infantry combat team, regimental), 1st Infantry Division. Landed in Sicily July 1943. Arrived England in November 1943, reequipped as standard tank battalion; former Company C reattached as Company D. Landed D-Day on Utah Beach supporting 4th Infantry Division. Companies A and B used amphibious DD Shermans. Joined drive on Cherbourg and breakout at St. Lo. Fought at St. Pois, Villedieu, and Mortain, and entered Paris. Spearheaded 4th Infantry Division's drive into Belgium, entered Germany on 13 September 1944. Moved to Hürtgen Forest in November, where the battalion experienced some of the worst fighting of the war. Moved to Ardennes with the 4th Infantry Division in December, fighting in Battle of the Bulge. Crossed Rhine near Worms 29 March 1945, pursued retreating German forces. With TF Rodwell stormed SS stronghold in Aalen on 21 April. Crossed Danube 25 April at Langen. Ended war near Austrian border at Gmund, Miesbach, and Holz. Attachments: 1st, 9th Infantry Divisions (North Africa); XIX French Corps (North Africa); 1st Infantry Division (Sicily); 4th, 63d, 83d Infantry

Divisions, 101st Airborne Division (ETO). (*Soixante-Dix*, official history of the 70th Tank Battalion; History, 70th Tank Battalion.)

191ST TANK BATTALION

Organized 1 September 1940 out of four National Guard tank companies from New York, Massachusetts, Virginia, and Connecticut. Assembled at Fort Meade, Maryland, in February 1941 under Maj. Littleton A. Roberts. Reorganized as medium tank battalion June 1942. Sailed to North Africa but saw first combat in Italy, landing at Salerno on 9 September 1943. Landed at Anzio January 1944 and joined drive on Rome, during which battalion suffered high losses. Landed in southern France 15 August 1944. Usually attached to 45th Infantry Division, battalion battled north to the Vosges Mountains. Fought in Lorraine and Alsace in November 1944. Slashed through Homburg and Kaiserslautern to Rhine with TF Dolvin March 1945. Company B DD tanks led river crossing on 25 March. Battalion entered Bamberg, Nürnberg, and Munich, where it ended war. Attachments: 3d, 34th, 36th, 45th Infantry Divisions (Italy); 36th, 42d, 45th, 70th, 79th, 103d Infantry Divisions (ETO). (*191 Tank Bn.*, contained in the battalion's official records.)

192D TANK BATTALION

Organized September 1940 out of four National Guard tank companies from Wisconsin, Illinois, Ohio, and Kentucky. Arrived Luzon circa 25 November 1942. Fought delaying actions after Japanese invasion of Philippines in December, retreated to Bataan, surrendered with garrison 9 April 1943. Attachments: Provisional Tank Group.

193D TANK BATTALION .

Organized 1 September 1940 out of four National Guard tank companies from Georgia, Alabama, Texas, and Colorado. Inducted into active service 6 January 1941, all companies converged at Ft. Benning. Attached to 2d Armored Division for training. Moved to California in December and sailed on the 27th for the Philippines to reinforce 192 and 194th Tank battalions. Delivered to Hawaii when mission deemed impossible, arriving 7 January 1942, where companies attached to 24th and 25th Infantry Divisions to defend Oahu. Participated with 27th Infantry Division in the assault on Makin and Tarawa islands in the Gilberts on 20 November 1943 partially equipped with amphibian tractors. Went ashore on Okinawa 8 April 1945. Attachments: 24th, 25th, 27th Infantry Divisions. (History, AARs, 193d Tank Battalion.)

194TH TANK BATTALION

Organized September 1940 out of three National Guard tank companies from California, Minnesota, and Missouri. Arrived Luzon circa 26 September 1942. Fought delaying actions after Japanese invasion of Philippines in December, retreated to Bataan, surrendered with garrison 9 April 1943. Attachments: Provisional Tank Group.

534TH AMPHIBIAN TRACTOR BATTALION

Redesignated from the 534th Armored Infantry Battalion on 28 October 1943 at Ft. Ord, California, under the command of Lt. Col. Paul Bryer. Shipped from San Francisco, California, 8 February 1944, arrived Oahu 15 February, where assigned to 4th Armored Group for training with 27th Infantry Division. Departed 29 May, participated in assault on Saipan 15 June, Tinian 24 July. Departed for Oahu 11 August. Shipped out 20 May 1945, arrived Okinawa 14 July. Attachments: 27th Infantry Division; 4th Marine Division. (History, 534th Amphibian Tractor Battalion.)

536TH AMPHIBIAN TRACTOR BATTALION

Redesignated from the 536th Armored Infantry Battalion on 29 January 1944 at Ft. Ord, California, under the command of Lt. Col. Russell Smith. Shipped from Seattle, Washington, 7 June 1944 arriving Oahu 15 February, where assigned to 4th Armored Group for training with 7th Infantry Division. Departed 11 September, participated in assault on Leyte, Philippine Islands, 20 October. Formed bulk of provisional amphibious force that landed 77th Infantry Division south of Ormoc on 7 December. Departed Leyte 25 March 1945, participated in landings on Okinawa 1 April. Attachments: 7th, 77th Infantry Divisions. (History, AARs, S-3 journal, 536th Amphibian Tractor Battalion.)

539TH AMPHIBIAN TRACTOR BATTALION

Activated on 14 April 1944 at Ft. Ord, California, under the command of Maj. George Emrick and with personnel mainly drawn from tank and tank destroyer battalions. Shipped from Ft. Lawton, Washington, 16 October 1944 arriving Oahu 24 October, where assigned to 19th and in December 4th Armored Group for training. At some point, arrived at Leyte, Philippine Islands, but apparently saw no combat. Attachments: None. (History, 539th Amphibian Tractor Battalion.)

540TH AMPHIBIAN TRACTOR BATTALION

Activated on 14 April 1944 at Ft. Ord, California, under the command of Capt. Robert Byrns. Shipped from Ft. Lawton, Washington, 26 October 1944 arriving Oahu 4 November. Departed Hawaii February 1945, eventually arriving Leyte, Philippine Islands, on 22 June. Saw no combat. Attachments: None. (History, 540th Amphibian Tractor Battalion.)

658TH AMPHIBIAN TRACTOR BATTALION

Redesignated from the 658th Tank Destroyer Battalion on 15 April 1944 at Ft. Ord, California, under the command of Lieutenant Colonel Brownell. Shipped from San Francisco, California, 23 September 1944 arriving New Britain 28 October. Departed 7 December, participated in landings on Luzon, Philippine Islands, 9 January 1945 with 40th Infantry Division. Supported landings by 24th, 40th, and Americal Divisions on other Philippine islands, including Mindanao, Negros, Panay, and Cebu, through April. Attachments: 24th, 40th, 41st Infantry, Americal Divisions. (History, AARs, S-3 journal, 658th Amphibian Tractor Battalion.)

672D AMPHIBIAN TRACTOR BATTALION

Redesignated from the 672d Tank Destroyer Battalion on 15 April 1944 at Ft. Ord, California, under the command of Lt. Col. J. W. Gibbs. Shipped from San Francisco, California, 22 September, arrived Bougainville 9 October, where attached to 37th Infantry Division. Landed on Luzon, the Philippines, on 9 January 1945. Company A attached 1st Cavalry Division 31 January. Reached Manila 5 February, where ferried troops in multiple river crossings under fire. Attached to 11th Airborne Division 20 February, participated in rescue of internees from Los Banos. Supported 1st Cavalry Division operations through June. Attachments: 37th Infantry Division; 1st Cavalry Division; 11th Airborne Division. (History, AARs, 672d Amphibian Tractor Battalion.)

701ST TANK BATTALION

Activated 1 March 1943 at Camp Cambell, Kentucky, under Lt. Col. F. J. Simpson. Originally organized as special battalion equipped with CDL spotlight tanks. Landed in Liverpool on 1 May 1944 and shipped to France in August, where battalion stayed until reorganized as standard tank battalion after 23 October. Moved to front on 19 December 1944 in Ubach, Germany, attached to 102d Infantry Division. Joined the assault across Roer River on 23 February 1945. Attacked northward, reaching Rhine at Krefeld. Crossed Rhine beginning 26 March attached to the 75th Infantry Division. Reattached to 102d Infantry Division for drive through Munster and across Weser River. Ended the war in Gardelegen. Attachments: 75th, 84th, 102d Infantry Divisions. (Edward C. Hassett, ed., *701st Tank Battalion* (Nürnberg: Sebaldus-Verlag, 1945). AARs, 701st Tank Battalion; *Armored Special Equipment.*)

702D TANK BATTALION

Activated 1 March 1943 at Camp Cambell, Kentucky, under Maj. Ralph Talbott III. Transited England, debarked at Utah Beach 6 August 1944; confusingly, a 702d Tank Destroyer Battalion already deployed in same area. Attached to the 80th Infantry Division on 8 August, operated in Argentan-Bordeaux area during closure of Falaise Gap. Fought along Moselle River September and October 1944. Supported 80th Infantry Division offensive in vicinity of Metz November. Moved to Luxembourg City upon outbreak of Battle of the Bulge. Joined 80th Infantry Division attack across Our and Sauer rivers into Siegfried Line in February 1945. Briefly attached to 76th Infantry Division in late February and advanced toward Trier. Advance to Rhine in March with TF Onaway, then shifted to Luxembourg to rejoin 80th Infantry Division. Crossed Rhine near Mainz on 28 March. Advanced rapidly through Germany, including Kassel, Gotha, Erfurt, Jena, Weimar, Gera, Bamberg, Nürnberg, and Regensburg. Attachments: 76th, 80th Infantry Divisions. (Battalion records, 702d Tank Battalion.)

706TH TANK BATTALION

Activated 10 September 1943 out of 3d Battalion, 37th Armored Regiment, 4th Armored Division at Camp Bowie, Texas, under Lt. Col. Charles Stokes. Attached to 4th Armored Division for training. Underwent amphibious training in Texas with 77th Infantry Division in November and December. Sailed from Seattle 28 March 1944, arrived Hawaii 3 April, where underwent jungle training. Moved to Guam 25 July, where Company D supported Marines; helped 77th Division crush last resistance beginning 8 August. Disembarked at Leyte 23 November. Elements moved by water to Ormoc Bay 20 December in vicinity Valencia. Majority of battalion landed on Ie Shima, Ryukyus, 18 April 1945. Moved to Okinawa 25 April. Attachments: 77th Infantry Division. (History, AARs, 706th Tank Battalion.)

707TH TANK BATTALION
Activated 20 September 1943 out of 3d Battalion, 81st Armored Regiment, 5th Armored Division at Pine Camp, New York, under Lt. Col. Richard W. Ripple. Landed in France 1 September 1944. Committed to battle near Krinkelt, Germany, 10 October 1944 attached to 28th Infantry Division. Participated in 28th Infantry Division's disastrous attack on Schmidt in November, during which Company A was destroyed. Withdrew to Luxembourg 20 November for intensive rehabilitation. On 16 December, battalion found itself in path of the German Ardennes offensive and shattered. Company C put into defensive positions on Meuse River on 1 January 1945 attached to 17th Airborne Division, battalion then moved to Belgium. Battalion deployed to Germany in April near Seebachin attached to the 89th Infantry Division. Last action at Neu Wursohnitz on 6 May. Attachments: 28th, 65th, 76th, 89th Infantry Divisions, 17th Airborne Division. (Official History, S-3 Journal, and AARs, 707th Tank Battalion.)

708TH AMPHIBIAN TANK BATTALION
Activated as 708th Tank Battalion on 20 September 1943 from 3d Battalion, 69th Armored Regiment, 6th Armored Division under command of Lt. Col. J. T. Mozley. Redesignated 708th Amphibian Tank Battalion 27 October 1943. Landed at Kwajalein beginning 31 January 1944, Saipan on 15 June. Company D shifted to Tinian 25-27 July. Assaulted small islands off Okinawa beginning 26 March 1945. Attachments: 7th, 77th Infantry Divisions, 4th Marine Division. (General Orders, AARs, 708th Amphibian Tank Battalion; "Army Amphibian Tank and Tractor Training in the Pacific.")

709TH TANK BATTALION
Activated on 20 September 1943 from 3d Battalion, 40th Armored Regiment, 7th Armored Division under command of Lt. Col. Odis L. Harmon. Landed at Liverpool, England, 11 March 1944. Debarked at Utah Beach 10 July 1944. Attached to 8th Infantry Division, fought in Normandy during breakout and into Brittany. Much of battalion joined 83d Infantry Division in fighting at St. Malo, Dinard, and Brest. Performed "occupation" duty in Luxembourg in October and November 1944. Entered Hürtgen Forest on 19 November. On 12 December, 709th was attached to 78th Infantry Division for attack near the Kesternich-Simmarath

Ridge. Participated in fighting in Colmar Pocket in February 1945. Joined race to Rhine in March. Crossed river on 3 April and fought in Ruhr industrial region. Entered military government status in late April 1945. Attachments: 2d, 8th, 28th, 29th, 75th, 78th, 83d, 95th Infantry Divisions. (Official History, S-3 Journal, and AARs, 709th Tank Battalion.)

710TH TANK BATTALION
Activated on 23 September 1943 from 3d Battalion, 80th Armored Regiment, 8th Armored Division. Shipped from States 11 June 1944, arrived Hawaii 22 June. Landed on Angaur Island, Palau Group, on 17 September 1944 attached to 81st Infantry Division; elements moved to Peleliu Island on 22 September. Moved to New Caledonia in December, shipped to Leyte in May 1945 but saw no action. Attachments: 81st Infantry Division. (History, 710th Tank Battalion.)

711TH TANK BATTALION
Activated on 9 October 1943 from 3d Battalion, 14th Armored Regiment, 9th Armored Division, at Camp Ibis, California, under the command of Lt. Col. Robert Collins. Shipped from States 22 March 1944, arrived Hawaii 27 March. Departed 27 December for Leyte, landed on Okinawa 1 April 1945. Attachments: 7th, 27th Infantry Divisions. (History, 711th Tank Battalion.)

712TH TANK BATTALION
Activated on 20 September 1943 at Camp Gordon, Georgia, out of 3d Battalion, 11th Armored Regiment, 10th Armored Division, Maj. William E. Eckles commanding. Landed in France 29 and 30 June 1944. Battalion less Company A committed 2 July near St. Jore attached to 90th Infantry Division; Company A attached to 82d Airborne Division. After breakout, battalion crossed Seine near Mayenne. Joined drive on Le Mans and closing of Falaise Pocket in August 1944. On 8 September near Landres, France, battalion had rare encounter with large German armored force (thirty-five tanks) and destroyed about half. Advanced to the Moselle near Metz in mid-September. Participated in fight for Maizières-les-Metz in October and in Metz offensive in November. Deployed to Rippweiler, Luxembourg, on 7 January 1945 to join fighting around the Bulge. Battalion CO Lt. Col. George B. Randolph KIA 9 January. Reentered Germany in February in 90th Division and SHAEF reserve. Engaged in elimination of German forces west of Rhine in March, crossing Moselle River yet again. Advanced through series of small German towns in April, ending up at border with Czechoslovakia. Entered the Sudetenland in May 1945. Attachments: 90th Infantry Division, 82d Airborne Division. (Official History, S-3 Journal, and AARs, 712th Tank Battalion.)

713TH TANK BATTALION, ARMORED FLAMETHROWER
Activated 23 September 1943 at Camp Barkeley, Texas, out of 3d Battalion, 42d Armored Regiment, 11th Armored Division under Lt. Col. Thomas McCrary.

Arrived in California in May 1944 for amphibious training, shipped to Hawaii in September. Reorganized as the 713th Armored Flamethrower Provisional, on 11 January 1945. Arrived Okinawa 7 April. Attachments: 7th, 27th, 77th, 96th Infantry Divisions; 1st, 6th Marine Divisions. (History, 713th Tank Battalion, Armored Flamethrower.)

715TH AMPHIBIAN TRACTOR BATTALION
Redesignated from 715th Tank Battalion on 27 October 1943 at Ft. Ord, California. Shipped from San Francisco, California, for Oahu 5 January 1944. Participated in landings on Saipan 15 June, Tinian 24 July. Landed elements of 77th Infantry Division on small islands around Okinawa, Ryukyus Islands, from late March into April 1945. Attachments: 77th Infantry Division; 2d, 4th Marine Divisions. (History and AARs, 715th Amphibian Tractor Battalion.)

716TH TANK BATTALION
Activated 20 September 1943 at Chaffee, Arkansas, out of 3d Battalion, 48th Armored Regiment, 14th Armored Division. Arrived New Guinea 3 July 1944; shipped out in November, companies split between 6th and 43d Infantry Divisions for Luzon operations. Landed on S-day, 9 January 1945. Fought on central plain, in Manila, and in and Cagayan valley. Participated in capture of Cebu, Negros, and Panay islands from March through May 1945. Company A landed on Mindanao on 10 March, joined later by rest of battalion. Attachments: 6th, 24th, 25th, 31st, 32d, 37th, 38th, 40th, 41st, 43d, Americal Infantry Divisions. (History, 716th Tank Battalion.)

717TH TANK BATTALION
Activated 10 September 1943 at Camp Chaffee, Arkansas, out of 16th Armored Division under Lt. Col. Raymond W. Odor. Assigned to Armored Board, Fort Knox, Kentucky, testing new equipment, including M26 Pershing. Sailed for Europe 26 December 1944 and landed in France February 1945. Fired first shot 24 March at Rhine River, attached to 79th Infantry Division. After crossing Rhine, participated in operations in Ruhr Valley during April, including assault on Essen in support of 17th Airborne Division. Ended the war in Bottrop, Germany. Attachments: 75th, 79th Infantry Divisions, 17th Airborne Division. (*717th Tank Battalion Record* [1945?].)

718TH AMPHIBIAN TRACTOR BATTALION
Redesignated from 718th Tank Battalion on 15 April 1944 under the command of Lt. Col. John Behrns. Participated in assault landing at Leyte, Philippine Islands, 20 October 1944, amphibious operations around Leyte and neighboring islands through February 1945. Landed on Okinawa, Ryukyus Islands, 1 April 1945. Attachments: 7th, 77th Infantry Divisions. (History and AARs, 718th Amphibian Tractor Battalion.)

726TH AMPHIBIAN TRACTOR BATTALION
Activated on 26 January 1944 at Ft. Ord, California. Shipped from Ft. Lawton, Washington, 8 June, arrived Oahu, Hawaii, 14 June. Departed 8 August, conducted final training on Guadalcanal, and participated in assault on Angaur, Palau Islands, on 17 September. Company A carried 323d Infantry Regiment to Ulithi Island 20 September, other elements supported Army and Marine forces on Peleliu beginning 23 September, where attached to 8th Amphibian Tractor Group (Marines). Departed 17 April, landed elements of 8th Marines on small islands off Okinawa beginning 3 June. Attachments: 81st Infantry Division; 1st, 2d Marine Divisions. (History, 726th Amphibian Tractor Battalion.)

727TH AMPHIBIAN TRACTOR BATTALION
Activated on 26 January 1944 at Ft. Ord, California, under the command of Maj. Frank McLavy. Shipped from San Francisco, California, 16 June, arrived Hollandia 16 July, where assigned to Sixth Army. Assigned Eighth Army 12 October, participated in Landings on Leyte, Philippine Islands, 20 October. Landed on Luzon 9 January 1945. Shipped to Morotai 27 March, where attached to 1st Australian Corps. Conducted assault landings in Brunei Bay 10 June, on Borneo 15 June. Attachments: 6th, 24th, 32d Infantry Divisions; 9th Australian Division. (History, 727th Amphibian Tractor Battalion.)

728TH AMPHIBIAN TRACTOR BATTALION
Converted from 728th Tank Destroyer Battalion on 14 April 1944 at Camp Forrest, Tennessee. Trained at Ft. Ord, California, April-July, shipped from Ft. Lawton, Washington 6 August, and arrived Oahu 14 August. Participated in assault landings on Leyte, Philippine Islands, 20 October, Okinawa, Ryukyus Islands, 1 April 1945, and Tsugen Shima and other small islands beginning 10 April. Attachments: 7th, 27th, 96th Infantry Divisions. (History and AARs, 728th Amphibian Tractor Battalion.)

735TH TANK BATTALION
Activated on 10 January 1943 at Fort Lewis, Washington, under Lt. Col. Ralph Alexander, commanding. Committed on 15 July 1944 in Normandy near Sallen. After breakout, fought at Angers, Chartres, and Reims. Crossed the Moselle in early September and became embroiled in fighting around Metz. Joined fruitless assault on Fort Driant in October 1944. In November, supported 5th Infantry Division's drive into Metz and reduction of forts still holding out. Relieved elements of 778th Tank Battalion in Saarlautern east of Saar River On 17 December. Deployed northward to join fighting in Ardennes beginning 21 December. Remained in Luxembourg until February 1945, during which month the battalion conducted limited offensive operations against Siegfried Line with the 87th Infantry Division. Reached Rhine near Koblenz 13 March and crossed 25 March on rafts as part of the 87th Infantry Division assault. Dash across Germany, reach-

316 THE INFANTRY'S ARMOR

ing Saale River on 13 April. Crossed the Weisse Elster near Brockav on 16 April and went onto defensive. Attachments: 5th, 26th, 35th, 76th, 87th, 95th Infantry Divisions. (General Orders and AARs, 735th Tank Battalion.)

736TH TANK BATTALION

Activated 1 February 1943 at Camp Rucker, Alabama, Maj. William H. Dodge, commanding. Organized as special battalion equipped with top secret CDL spotlight tanks. Arrived in the United Kingdom on 1 April 1944 and Utah Beach in August. Reorganized as standard tank battalion November and attached to 94th Infantry Division in St. Nazaire-Lorient sector. Again selected for special equipment-DD tanks to be used for crossing of the Rhine-to which one company was devoted. Moved to front on 26 January 1945 and joined attack on Kesternich. Reached Rhine March with 83d Infantry Division. Company C DD tanks supported Rhine crossing. Reached Elbe River at Barby on 13 April. Contacted Russian forces 4 May 1945. Attachments: 30th, 78th, 83d Infantry Divisions. (History, AARs, and S-3 Journal, 736th Tank Battalion; *Armored Special Equipment*.)

737TH TANK BATTALION

Activated 1 February 1943 at Fort Lewis, Washington, with Col. S. L. Buracker, commanding. Arrived in England 12 February 1944. Debarked at Omaha Beach 12 July and attached to 35th Infantry Division. While with that division, fought at St. Lo, Mortain, and Le Mans. First tank battalion of Third Army to cross Moselle and Meurthe rivers. Entered Germany east of Sarreguemines on 15 December 1944. On 22 December, redeployed to the Ardennes and joined 5th Infantry Division. Supported division's crossing of Sauer River January 1945 and drive through Siegfried Line to Bitburg in February. Drove along Moselle to the Rhine and then south as part of envelopment of German forces in March. Crossed Rhine 25 March near Russelheim, raced to Frankfurt am Main. Turned north toward Ruhr Pocket in April, then conducted 520-mile road march to return to the Third Army, reaching Bavaria on 1 May. Entered Czechoslovakia south of Winterberg on 3 May 1945. Attachments: 5th, 35th, 76th Infantry Divisions. (History, AARs, and S-3 Journal, 737th Tank Battalion.)

738TH TANK BATTALION

Activated on 16 February 1943 at Fort Benning, Georgia, under command of Lt. Col. Raymond W. Odor. Reorganized on 19 November 1943 as special battalion equipped with top secret CDL spotlight tanks. Arrived in England April 1944. In September, mission changed to operation of special equipment for breaching and clearing minefields. On 12 October 1944, redesignated 738th Medium Tank Battalion, Special (Mine Exploder). Debarked at Le Havre, France, on 11 November 1944 and moved to Aachen, Germany. On 7 December 1944, Company A attached to 3d Armored Division, cleared roads during capture of Obergeich. Performed almost daily missions attached to diverse units thereafter. Attachments: 78th Infantry Division, 3d Armored Division. (Unit journal, history, and AARs, 738th Tank Battalion; *Armored Special Equipment*.)

739TH TANK BATTALION

Activated on 1 March 1943 at Fort Lewis, Washington, under command of Maj. Bethuel M. Kitchen. Reorganized in December 1944 as special battalion equipped with CDL spotlight tanks. Arrived in England August 1944. On 12 October, mission changed to operation of special equipment for breaching and clearing minefields; battalion redesignated 739th Medium Tank Battalion, Special (Mine Exploder). One company obtained flamethrower tanks-probably British Crocodiles supplied for evaluation. Departed for Netherlands on 28 November 1944. On 18 December, one platoon of Company C detonated mines near Suggerath. Beginning in January 1945, mine-clearing elements performed almost daily missions attached to diverse units. Flamethrower platoon first used in Jülich, Germany, on 7 February. In late February, battalion supplied tank drivers to operate LVTs used to ferry personnel and equipment across Roer River during assault. In March, one company detached for training in use of DD tanks. Company B deployed CDLs on 23 March during Rhine crossing. CDL tanks used again twice in April, once in failed effort to capture bridges near Henrichenburg and again to illuminate bridge construction across Dortmund-Ems Canal and Lippe River. Attachments: 29th, 78th, 102d Infantry Divisions. (Unit journal, history, and AARs, 739th Tank Battalion; *Armored Special Equipment.*)

740TH TANK BATTALION

Activated on 1 March 1943 at Fort Knox, Kentucky, under command of Maj. Harry C. Anderson. Reorganized 10 September 1943 as special battalion to be issued CDL spotlight tanks, but never received equipment despite considerable special training. Arrived in Belgium November 1944 with no tanks but with order to convert to standard tank battalion. Clashed with Peiper's spearhead in December 1944 in first action. Attached to 82d Airborne Division in January 1945, attacked north side of the Bulge. Assaulted Siegfried Line in February. Crossed the Ruhr with 8th Infantry Division on 24 March and joined drive on Cologne. After reaching the Rhine, transferred 350 miles south and attached to 63d Infantry Division for another attack through Siegfried Line toward Saarbrucken. Returned to 8th Infantry Division to hammer at Ruhr Pocket in April 1945, after which took on occupation duties in Düsseldorf. Attachments: 8th, 30th, 63d, 70th, 86th, 106th Infantry Divisions, 82d Airborne Division. (Unit history and AARs, 740th Tank Battalion; Rubel; *Armored Special Equipment.*)

741ST TANK BATTALION

Activated on 15 March 1942 at Fort Meade, Maryland, under command of Lt. Col. Jacob R. Moon. Two companies equipped with DD tanks, and battalion formed part of assault wave at Omaha Beach on 6 June 1944 attached to 1st Infantry Division. Reattached to 2d Infantry Division in Normandy and participated in breakthrough at Vire River in July and August. Reached Paris 27 August. Advanced through France and Belgium, reaching Siegfried Line on 13 September. Attacked toward Roer River with 2d Infantry Division on 13 December 1944, turned south at outbreak of German Ardennes Offensive. Supported 2d Infantry Division push to eliminate Bulge and drive into Germany in January and February 1945. Crossed Rhine at Remagen in March, reached Weser River on 5 April. Entered Leipzig 19 April and Czechoslovakia 5 May near Pilsen. Attachments: 1st, 2d, 99th Infantry Divisions. (Unit history and AARs, 741st Tank Battalion.)

743D TANK BATTALION

Activated as a light tank battalion on 16 May 1942 at Fort Lewis, Washington, under command of Maj. John Upham. Redesignated as medium tank battalion on 19 August 1942. Arrived in England November 1943. Two companies equipped with DD tanks, and battalion formed part of the assault wave at Omaha Beach on 6 June 1944 attached to 1st Infantry Division. On 14 June, attached to 30th Infantry Division, with which battalion fought for rest of war. Participated in St. Lo Breakout in July and Battle of Mortain in August 1944. Entered Belgium on 3 September 1944. Company A supported capture of Fort Eben Emael on 10 September. Supported operations against Siegfried Line in October and attack to Roer River beginning 16 November 1944. Shifted to Ardennes on 17 December, fighting in Malmedy, Stavelot, and Stoumont. Took part in attack on Bulge from the north in January 1945. Shifted back to Aachen area in February and supported Roer River crossing. On 24 March, with one DD-equipped company of 736th Tank Battalion attached, crossed the Rhine near Spellen. Raced across Germany, entering Magdeburg (the last major city on autobahn to Berlin) on 16 April 1945. Ended war there. Attachments: 1st, 29th, 30th Infantry Divisions. (Unit history and AARs, 743d Tank Battalion.)

744TH LIGHT TANK BATTALION

Activated on 27 April 1942 at Camp Bowie, Texas, under command of Maj. Richard J. Hunt. Arrived in England 9 January 1944. Debarked at Utah Beach on 29 June 1944. First combat on 26 July near St. Germain in support of 2d Infantry Division. After breakout, attached to 28th Infantry Division for drive to the Seine. On 19 September 1944, moved to Netherlands where it supported 113th Cavalry Group and Belgian Brigade for two months. Moved to Frelenberg, Germany, in November 1944 and joined attacks on fortifications near Suggerath, after which entered Corps reserve. Crossed the Roer with 30th Infantry Division on 24 February 1945, fighting through Hambach Forest. Crossed Rhine on 23 March and fought in Ruhr area with 75th Infantry Division. Took up occupation in Olpe. Attachments: 2d, 28th, 29th, 30th, 75th, 79th, 102d Infantry Divisions. (*The 744th Light Tank Battalion's VE Day Reminiscence*, 744th Tank Battalion.)

745TH TANK BATTALION

Activated on 15 August 1942 at Camp Bowie, Texas, under command of Maj. Thomas B. Burns. Formed part of the assault echelon at Omaha Beach on D-Day, landing its first company on 6 June 1944 in support of 1st Infantry Division. Fought in St. Lo breakout and envelopment of Falaise Pocket. Raced east in wake of 3d Armored Division. Supported 1st Infantry Division near and in Aachen in

September 1944 and attack toward Roer River beginning 16 November. Ordered south with 1st Infantry Division on 16 December to help stop Ardennes offensive, continued to support division against Bulge and Siegfried Line through February 1945. Participated in assault across Roer River on 25 February. Reached Rhine at Bonn on 11 March. Crossed Rhine into Remagen bridgehead. Took part in Ruhr Pocket envelopment in April. Crossed Weser River and advanced into Harz Mountains and then to the Czechoslovakian border, where further movement eastward was halted on 7 May 1945. Attachments: 1st, 9th Infantry Divisions. (Unit history and AARs, 745th Tank Battalion.)

746TH TANK BATTALION
Activated on 20 August 1942 at Camp Rucker, Alabama, under command of Maj. Loveaire A. Hedges. Shipped to England January 1944. Formed part of the assault echelon at Utah Beach on D-Day, landing on 6 June 1944 in support of 82d Airborne Division and 4th Infantry Division. Participated in capture of Cherbourg and the defense of Carentan. Supported 9th Infantry Division breakthrough near Villedieu-les-Poeles in August 1944 and race across France to the Belgian border. Fought in Hürtgen Forest September and October. Transferred to Belgium and supported attack toward Roer River in November. Attacked again toward Roer River in January 1945. Advanced to Rhine in March crossing Remagen bridge (first separate tank battalion to cross the river). Advanced to Ruhr Pocket in April 1945. Shifted east to Harz Mountains, ending war along Mulde River. Attachments: 9th, 83d, 90th Infantry Divisions, 82d Airborne Division. (Unit history and AARs, 746th Tank Battalion.)

747TH TANK BATTALION
Activated on 10 November 1942 at Camp Bowie, Texas, under command of Maj. Sidney G. Brown Jr. Shipped to England February 1944. Landed at Omaha Beach on 7 June 1944 and joined 29th Infantry Division. Aided in closing Falaise Pocket in August. Attacked toward Brussels and then Bastogne in September, entering Germany near Sevenig. Supported 29th Infantry Division's attack toward Roer River in November. Mopped up, fired across river December 1944 and January 1945. Supported assault across the Roer on 23 February. In March, trained to operate LVTs. On 24 March, battalion LVTs attached to 30th Infantry Division participated in Rhine assault crossing. One company conducted brief operations against Ruhr Pocket in April, after which battalion took on military government duties, ending war in Schnega. Attachments: 1st, 2d, 4th, 28th, 29th, 75th Infantry Divisions. (Unit history and AARs, 747th Tank Battalion.)

748TH TANK BATTALION
Activated on 20 August 1942 at Camp Rucker, Alabama. On 20 April 1943, reorganized as a special battalion equipped with CDL spotlight tanks. Shipped to Wales April 1944 and disembarked at Utah Beach on 24 August. Reorganized as standard tank battalion after 23 October. Moved to front on 20 January 1945 near

Buschdorf, Germany, attached to 94th Infantry Division. Fought through West Wall defenses in February. Trained with DD and CDL tanks 1-15 March. Moved to Saarlautern area to support 65th Infantry Division operations against Siegfried Line defenses. Withdrawn again on 20 March to draw DD tanks, attached to 5th Infantry Division near Bad Kreuznach, Germany. Long road marches damaged many DDs, but a few crossed the Rhine on 23 March 1945. CDL tanks deployed to support bridging operations. Turned in all special tanks by mid-April 1945. Advanced with 65th Infantry Division to Danube at Gundelhausen. Entered Regensburg on 27 April. In early May, took Passau and entered Austria, ending war near Linz. Attachments: 5th, 65th, 89th, 94th Infantry Divisions. (Unit history and AARs, 748th Tank Battalion; *Armored Special Equipment*.)

749TH TANK BATTALION

Activated on 2 December 1942 at Camp Bowie, Texas, under command of Maj. Donald Donaldson. Debarked at Utah Beach from England on 29 June 1944 and joined 79th Infantry Division. In August, raced across France, passing through Laval to Le Mans; 79th Infantry Division was first American division to cross the Seine. Entered Belgium on 2 September, fighting near Neufchateau and vicinity of the Foret de Parroy. Months of grinding fighting against prepared defenses followed in drive to Saar River near Sarreguemines. Battled German Nordwind offensive in January 1945. On 13 March, attached to 71st Infantry Division for Seventh Army offensive through Siegfried Line to the Rhine. Crossed Rhine on 30 March at Mainz. Crossed the Weisse River on 13 April near Zeitz and went into defensive posture near Limbach until V-E Day. Attachments: 42d, 44th, 63d, 65th, 70th, 71st, 76th, 79th, 83d, 100th Infantry Divisions. (Unit history and AARs, 749th Tank Battalion.)

750TH TANK BATTALION

Activated on 1 January 1943 at Fort Knox, Kentucky. Served as tank test unit. On 8 July, newly arrived CO Lt. Col. Sidney T. Telfords unofficially christened battalion the "Seven-five-zero," a name that stuck. Sailed to England and then to Omaha Beach in September 1944. Attached to the 104th Infantry Division near Aachen, Germany, in October 1944. First real combat on 16 November in operations against Siegfried Line; spent next month pushing toward Roer River. Participated in counterattack against Bulge December 1944 and January 1945. Supported crossing of Roer River on 23 February. Reached Cologne on Rhine River on 5 March. Crossed into Remagen bridgehead and swung north toward Ruhr Pocket in he wake of 3d Armored Division. Crossed Weser River and reached Halle in April. Encountered Russian forces on Mulde River after 21 April 1945. Attachments: 75th, 99th, 104th Infantry Divisions. (Unit history and AARs, 750th Tank Battalion.)

751ST TANK BATTALION

Designated for activation as 71st Tank Battalion (M) 25 April 1941, activated as 751st Tank Battalion (M) 1 June 1941 at Ft. Benning, Georgia, under the command of Lt. Col. Fay Ross. Arrived UK 20 August 1942. Arrived Tunisia 17 January 1943, entered battle near Sbiba 15 March. Landed with assault force at Salerno, Italy, 9 September. Reorganized as standard tank battalion December 1943. Landed at Anzio 22 January 1944. Participated in breakout and advance on Rome in June. Held defensive positions over the winter, fought in the Po valley offensive in April and May 1945. Attachments: 9th, 34th Infantry Divisions (North Africa); 3d, 34th, 36th, 45th, 85th, 92d Infantry Divisions, 10th Mountain Division, 1st (Brazilian) Infantry Division (Italy). (Unit history and AARs, 751st Tank Battalion.)

752D TANK BATTALION

Activated 1 June 1941 at Fort Lewis, Washington, under the command of Lt. Col. G. H. Anderson. Arrived UK 17 August 1942, Oran, Algeria, 17 January 1943. Inactivated under mistaken reading of orders 15 March, converted to 2642d Armored Force Replacement Battalion, reactivated 16 September. Arrived Italy 12 January 1944, where continued training replacements. Finally committed to battle 27 May north of Gustav Line. Entered Rome 4 June with 88th Infantry Division. Attacked across Cecina River in late June. Deployed for defense of Arno River line in mid August. Supported 85th Division attack on Gothic Line beginning 12 September. Fired mainly artillery missions after stalemate in October. Participated on spring offensive bin April 1945, reached the Po River 23 April. Ended war in vicinity of Vicenza. Attachments: 34th, 88th Infantry Divisions; First Special Service Force. (Unit history and AARs, 752d Tank Battalion. History, 1st Armored Group.)

753D TANK BATTALION

Constituted on 16 December 1940 as 73d Tank Battalion (Medium), activated as 753d Tank Battalion on 1 June 1941 at Fort Benning, Georgia, under command of Lt. Col. Robert B. Ennis. Arrived in North Africa on 26 May 1943 but saw no action. Landed on Sicily as part of Operation Husky on 10 July 1943, drove north across island split between 1st and 45th Infantry Divisions. Debarked at Salerno, Italy, on 15 September 1943, fought up peninsula to the Rapido. Supported the French Expeditionary Corps during breakthrough of Gustav Line in May 1944. Landed in southern France as part of Operation Dragoon assault force on 15 August 1944. Participated in drive toward Germany. In December, supported both the 3d and 36th Infantry Divisions in fierce fighting in the Selestat-Ribeauville-Kaysersberg area, then moved with the 36th into the Strasbourg area. Fought against German Nordwind offensive in January 1945. On 15 March, jumped off in support of 36th's attack through Siegfried Line toward Rhine River. Crossed Rhine under Corps control in April, attached to 63d Infantry Division for limited pursuit of enemy and cleaning up bypassed strong points, including Heilbronn. Located in Kufstein, Austria, when cease-fire orders received on 7 May 1945. Attachments: 1st, 45th Infantry Divisions (Sicily); 34th, 36th, 45th Infantry Divisions; New Zealand Corps; French Expeditionary Corps (Italy); 36th, 63d, 70th, 100th Infantry Divisions (ETO). (Unit history and AARs, 753d Tank Battalion. The records for the period of attachment to the French Expeditionary Corps are missing.)

754TH TANK BATTALION

Activated as medium tank battalion on 1 June 1941 at Pine Camp, New York, under the command of Lt. Col. Robert Wallace. Converted to a light tank battalion on 29 December 1941. Arrived Australia 27 February 1942 and joined the Americal Division on New Caledonia in March. Attached to XIV Corps in August. Reorganized as a standard tank battalion 7 November 1943. Defended perimeter at Augusta Bay, Bougainville, beginning 6 January 1944 as corps reserve. First action with the Americal Division's 132d Infantry on 30 January. Landed at Lingayen Gulf, Luzon, 9 January 1945, with Company A attached to 37th Infantry Division and Company B attached to 40th Infantry Division. Remaining companies attached to 37th Division 28 January, all elements fought at Clark Field. Companies B and D supported 40th Division beginning 8 February while other elements, later joined by Company B, supported 37th Division and 1st Cavalry Brigade in battle for Manila into March. Elements shifted among 6th, 38th, and 43d Infantry Divisions through end of Luzon campaign. Companies B and C moved to Panay Island 28 July with 40th Infantry Division. Attachments: 6th, 37th, 38th, 40th, 43d, Americal Infantry Divisions. (History, 754th Tank Battalion.)

755TH TANK BATTALION

Activated as medium tank battalion on 1 June 1941 at Camp Bowie, Texas. Arrived North Africa January 1943, reorganized as standard tank battalion 15 September, debarked in Italy 27 October. Entered battle 15 December near Venafro with 45th Infantry Division. Attached to French Expeditionary Corps 9 January 1944, supported crossing of Rapido River 24 January, assault on Gustav Line 12 May. Attached to various Divisions along the defensive line over the winter. Trained on LVTs, reorganized into three squadrons, in March. Carried British troops in amphibious operation across flooded area near Ravenna beginning 12 April. Reequipped with tanks by 23 April, except Company C, which ferried troops across the Po River on 24 April. Ended war near Turin. Attachments: 34th, 45th, 85th, 91st Infantry Divisions; 10th Mountain Division; British 56th Division; French 2d Moroccan Infantry, 3d Algerian Infantry, 4th Moroccan Mountain Divisions. (Unit history and AARs, 755th Tank Battalion.)

756TH TANK BATTALION

Activated as light tank battalion on 1 June 1941 at Fort Lewis, Washington. Companies A and C participated in Operation Torch landings in Morocco 8 November 1942. Battalion landed in North Africa on 24 January 1943, Italy on 17 September 1943. Reorganized as a standard tank battalion on 15 December 1943. Fought at Cassino, crossed the Rapido River in January 1944. Landed in southern France on 15 August partially equipped with DD amphibious tanks. Companies A and B equipped with DD tanks for landing near St. Tropez. Drove to Belfort Gap with 3d Infantry Division. Fought in Vosges Mountains, entered Strasbourg on 26 November 1944. Fought in Colmar Pocket January and February 1945. Supported 3d

Infantry Division in late March through Siegfried Line and across Rhine near Worms, crossing on 26 March. Company C supported crossing with DD tanks. Participated in assault on Nürnberg 17-20 April. Attacked south through Augsburg and Munich, formed part of the spearhead that seized Berchtesgaden and Salzburg in early May 1945. Attachments: 3d Infantry Division (North Africa); 34th, 45th, 85th, 88th Infantry Divisions; French 3d Algerian Infantry Division, 4th Moroccan Mountain Division (Italy); 3d, 103d Infantry Divisions, French 2d Armored Division (ETO). (Unit history and AARs, 756th Tank Battalion. Roger Fazendin, *The 756th Tank Battalion in the Battle of Cassino, 1944* [Lincoln, Nebraska: iUniverse, Inc., 1991], xiii.)

757TH TANK BATTALION
Activated as light tank battalion on 1 June 1941 at Fort Ord, California. Arrived in Italy in late 1943, reorganized in January 1944 from a light to standard tank battalion at Agata, Italy. Entered defensive positions attached to the 2d Moroccan Infantry Division on 28 February near Venafro. Broke through Gustav Line in May attached to French 1st Infantry Division, remained attached to French divisions through July. Fired missions along IV Corps front in early August, then moved to II Corps near Florence with 34th Infantry Division, where operated north of Arno River. Generally remained on the line as infantry divisions rotated in and out. Supported 88th and 91st Infantry Divisions in Spring Offensive in April 1945. Ended war near Treviso. Attachments: French 1st Infantry, 2d Moroccan Infantry, 3d Algerian Infantry, 4th Moroccan Mountain Divisions; 34th, 88th, 91st Infantry Divisions. (Unit history and AARs, 757th Tank Battalion.)

758TH LIGHT TANK BATTALION
Activated on 1 June 1941 at Fort Knox, Kentucky. Arrived Italy 25 November 1944. Entered line attached to 760th Tank Battalion with 92d Infantry Division near Lido di Camiore on 1 January 1945. Participated in spring offensive in April, generally under the control of the 760th Tank Battalion, drove along coast toward Genoa. Entered division reserve 29 April, ended war at Voltri. Attachments: 92d Infantry Division. (Unit history and AARs, 758th Tank Battalion.)

759TH LIGHT TANK BATTALION
Activated on 1 June 1941 at Fort Knox, Kentucky, under command of Lt. Col. Kenneth C. Althaus. Stationed in Iceland for eleven months and finally shipped to the United Kingdom in August 1943. Landed in Normandy on 16 June 1944 and was committed attached to 2d Infantry Division. From 21 August 1944 until end of the war, attached to 4th Cavalry Group. Passed through Chartres and crossed the Seine on 26 August 1944; crossed the Meuse River at Dinant and liberated Celles, Rauersim, Stavelot, and Malmedy. Entered Germany on 13 September. Ordered into the Ardennes in December. Spent early 1945 in defensive positions or out of the line. Reached Rhine River on 5 March at Zons. Captured series of

obscure German towns in April, ending month in Aschersleben, where occupation duty began. Attachments: 2d, 4th Infantry Divisions, 101st Airborne Division. (Unit history and AARs, 759th Tank Battalion.)

760TH TANK BATTALION

Activated as a light tank battalion on 1 June 1941 at Camp Bowie, Texas, under command of Lt. Col. Donald Spalding. Redesignated as medium tank battalion in November. Arrived Casablanca January 1943, assigned to I Armored Corps and saw no action. Arrived Italy 26 October, reorganized as standard tank battalion in November. Entered line in Cassino sector on 5 January 1944, supported 36th Division's failed attack across Rapido River. Participated in drive to Rome beginning 11 May, entered city on 4 June. Fought along Arno River beginning 8 July. Moved to Florence sector in late August, where crossed Arno River. Joined IV Corps in coastal sector in late December. Supported 10th Mountain Division during capture of Mt. Belvedere in March 1945, participated in spring offensive in April split between IV Corps and Brazilian Expeditionary Force. Attachments: 3d, 34th, 36th, 85th, 88th, 91st, 92d Infantry Divisions; 10th Mountain Division; 1st Armored Division; British 4th Indian Division; Brazilian Expeditionary Force. (Col. John Krebs, WW II Survey 10,865, Military History Institute, Carlisle, Pennsylvania.)

761ST TANK BATTALION

Activated on 1 April 1942 at Camp Claiborne, Louisiana, as a light tank battalion manned by black enlisted personnel. Major Edward E. Cruise assumed command. First black officers joined in July 1942. Converted to medium tank battalion in September 1943. Arrived in England in September 1944 and France on 10 October. Saw first action on 8 November with Third Army. Entered Germany on 14 December. Participated in American counteroffensive after the Battle of the Bulge from 31 December 1944 to 2 February 1945. In March served as spearhead of 103d Infantry Division in penetrating Siegfried Line. Among first American units to link with Soviet forces, doing so on 5 May 1945 in Steyr, Austria. Attachments: 26th, 71st, 79th, 87th, 95th, 103d Infantry Divisions, 17th Airborne Division. (Trezzvant Anderson; Ulysses Lee Wilson, *U.S. Army In World War II: The Employment of Negro Troops* [Washington, D.C.: Office of the Chief of Military History, United States Army, 1966], 661 ff.)

762D TANK BATTALION

Activated on 23 April 1942 at Schofield Barracks, Oahu, as a medium tank battalion. Reorganized as standard tank battalion 22 November 1943. Companies B and D landed on Saipan beginning 17 June 1944. Sailed for Oahu 5 August. Attachments: 27th Infantry Division. (History, Company A, 762d Tank Battalion; "Army Tanks in the Battle for Saipan"; AAR, 762d Tank Battalion.)

763D TANK BATTALION

Activated on 22 April 1942 at Schofield Barracks, Oahu, as a medium tank battalion. Reorganized as standard tank battalion, date unknown. Embarked Oahu 13 September 1944, landed at Leyte, Philippine Islands, 20 October. Assaulted Okinawa 1 April 1945. Attachments: 32d, 96th Infantry Divisions. (AAR, 763d Tank Battalion.)

766TH TANK BATTALION

Activated on 8 February 1943 at Schofield Barracks, Oahu, under the command of Major H. R. Edmondson. Despite designation, both Companies C and D equipped with light tanks. Companies B and C departed Hawaii 19-23 January 1944 for Marshall Islands; remained in reserve off Kwajalein. Company C landed on Eniwetok on 19 February, Parry Island 22 February. Company D attached to 762d Provisional Tank Battalion, disembarked on Saipan 17 June. All officers and men transferred to 767th Tank Battalion 10 April 1945. Attachments: 27th Infantry Division. (History, AARs, 766th Tank Battalion.)

767TH TANK BATTALION

Activated on 6 February 1943 at Schofield Barracks, Oahu, originally as a light tank battalion. Reorganized as a standard tank battalion on 20 November. Landed at Kwajalein Atoll 31 January 1944, Leyte on 20 October, where remained through 25 December. Transferred to Hawaii, where where absorbed personnel and equipment of deactivated 766th Tank Battalion in April 1945, prepared for invasion of Japan. Attachments: 7th Infantry Division. (History, AARs, 767th Tank Battalion.)

771ST TANK BATTALION

Activated on 10 September 1943 at Camp Bowie, Texas, as part of reorganization of 4th Armored Division. Lieutenant Colonel Jack C. Childers assumed command. Probably landed in France in October 1944. Saw first combat attached to 102d Infantry Division on 21 November. Fought along Roer River until 21 December, when sent to Ardennes with 84th Infantry Division. Joined breakthrough from Metzerath, Germany, in February 1945. Reached Rhine at Homburg on 4 March. On 19 March, attached to 17th Airborne Division, with which battalion was to link after paratroopers landed as part of Rhine River assault. Crossed river night of 25 March, linked up, attacked eastward. Reached Hanover on 10 April. Reached vicinity of Elbe River by midmonth. Took up occupation duties in the vicinity of Salzwedel, Germany, on 4 May 1945. Attachments: 84th, 102d Infantry Divisions, 17th Airborne Division. (General orders and AARs, 771st Tank Battalion.)

772D TANK BATTALION

Activated on 20 September 1943 at Pine Camp, New York, under temporary command of Maj. L. L. Willard. Disembarked at Le Havre, France, on 8 February

1945. Crossed Rhine on 27 March and saw first real combat at Mannheim. Marched along Main River to Werbachhausen and across the Danube to Ulm in April. Operating in area of Imst, Austria, when hostilities in sector ended on 5 May 1945. Attachments: 4th, 44th, 70th Infantry Divisions. (Unit history and AARs, 772d Tank Battalion.)

773D AMPHIBIAN TRACTOR BATTALION

Redesignated from 773d Tank Battalion on 27 October 1943 at Ft. Ord, California, under the command of Lt. Col. Arnold Wall. Shipped from Pittsburg, California, 8 February 1944, arrived Hawaii 15 February. Participated in assault on Saipan 15 June, Tinian 24 July. Supported landings on small islands around Okinawa, Ryukyus Islands, in March and April 1945. Attachments: 27th, 77th Infantry Divisions; 2d, 4th Marine Divisions. (History and AARs, 773d Amphibian Tractor Battalion.)

774TH TANK BATTALION

"Blackcat" battalion activated on 20 September 1943 at Fort Benning, Georgia, from 1st Battalion, 31st Armored Regiment, 7th Armored Division, under command of Lt. Col. N. K. Markle Jr. Arrived in Scotland on 12 July 1944; disembarked at Utah Beach on 24 August. Helped 83d Infantry Division protect Patton's right in September. Entered Luxembourg in October, then participated in operations along Moselle River. Moved to Hürtgen Forest in December 1944 to support the 83d Infantry Division's drive toward Roer River. Supported 83d Infantry Division operations against north flank of the Bulge in January 1945 and the 78th Infantry Division capture of the Roer River dams. Crossed Rhine via the Remagen bridge in March, then attacked Ruhr Pocket in April. Raced 280 miles southeastward to join 101st Airborne Division in drive toward mythical Nazi National Redoubt in Alps near Berchtesgaden. Ended war near Kempfenhausen, Germany. Attachments: 78th, 83d Infantry Divisions; 82d, 101st Airborne Divisions. (Unit history and AARs, 774th Tank Battalion.)

775TH TANK BATTALION

Activated from 1st Battalion, 36th Armored Regiment, 8th Armored Division, on 20 September 1943 at Camp Polk, Louisiana. Departed San Francisco 28 May 1944 for New Guinea. Disembarked on Luzon, Philippine Islands, 11 January 1945, placed in Sixth Army reserve. Attached I Corps 7 February. Companies parceled out to Divisions through 1 June. Attachments: 6th, 25th, 32d, 33d, 37th, 43d Infantry Divisions. (Unit history, 775th Tank Battalion.)

776TH AMPHIBIAN TANK BATTALION

Activated as 776th Tank Battalion from 1st Battalion, 2d Armored Regiment, 9th Armored Division, on 9 October 1943 at Ibis, California under the command of Lt. Col. O'Neill Kane. Redesignated 776th Amphibian Tank Battalion on 8 January 1944, transferred to Ft. Ord. Battalion less Company D departed States 9 September, arrived Oahu, Hawaii, 14 June; Leyte Island, the Philippines, 20 October, where participated in amphibious assault. Company D departed States attached to 81st Infantry Division 13 October for assault on Angaur Island, Palau Group, 17 September. Battalion (-) conducted deep amphibious reconnaissance, envelopments, and raids along island's west coast from November through 5 February 1945. Reunited battalion participated in assault on Okinawa 1 April. Attachments: 7th, 77th, 81st Infantry Divisions. (Unit history and AARs, 776th Tank Battalion.)

777TH TANK BATTALION

Activated on 20 September 1943 at Fort Gordon, Georgia, from 1st Battalion, 3d Armored Regiment, 10th Armored Division. Arrived in England on 27 December 1944; disembarked at Le Havre, France, on 6 February 1945. Took part in Operation Damnation in April attached to 69th Infantry Division, in turn attached to 9th Armored Division. Crossed Weser River, and Company C entered Colditz on 15 April, liberating five hundred French officers and Stalin's son. Other tanks entered Leipzig on the 18 April. Moved to Thrana in early May 1945. Attachments: 28th, 69th Infantry Divisions. (Unit history and AARs, 777th Tank Battalion.)

778TH TANK BATTALION

Activated on 20 September 1943 at Camp Barkeley, Texas, under command of Lt. Col. Frank J. Spettel. Shipped to France in September 1944. Joined battle around Metz attached to 95th Infantry Division on 15 November, including fighting in Maizières-les-Metz. Supported 95th Infantry Division's attack across Saar River in December and helped clear Saarlautern; held defensive positions in this area into February 1945. Beginning 6 February, most of battalion attached to 94th Infantry Division to support its operations against the Siegfried Switch line of fortifications. Crossed Rhine with 26th Infantry Division on 25 March. Supported the division's advance across Germany behind 11th Armored Division in April in direction of Linz, Austria. Advanced toward Prague until 7 May 1945. Attachments: 26th, 65th, 94th, 95th Infantry Divisions. (Unit history, AARs, and S-3 journal, 778th Tank Battalion.)

780TH AMPHIBIAN TANK BATTALION

Activated as 780th Tank Battalion on 22 December 1943 at Camp Beale, California, from 1st Battalion, 43d Armored Regiment, 13th Armored Division. Assigned to Ft. Ord 31 March 1944, redesignated 780th Amphibian Tank Battalion on 8 April. Transferred to Hawaii in July. Departed 10 September, arrived at Leyte, Philippine Islands, 20 October and participated in assault landings, fought inland. From 1 November, secured landing area. Formed part of assault wave at Okinawa on 1 April 1945. Patrolled as foot troops in June. Attachments: 27th, 96th Infantry Divisions. (General orders, field orders, history, AARs, and journal, 780th Tank Battalion.)

781ST TANK BATTALION

Activated (originally as light tank battalion) on 2 January 1943 at Fort Knox, Kentucky, under command of Lt. Col. Harry L. Kinne Jr. Arrived at Marseille in October 1944. Entered combat in Alsace on 7 December attached to 100th Infantry Division, which was attacking toward Maginot Line stronghold of Bitche. From December 1944 to January 1945, battalion supported five different Infantry Divisions, entering Germany attached to 79th. Battled Nordwind offensive in January. Supported 100th Infantry Division attack that finally captured Bitche in March, then drove to Rhine near Mannheim. Crossed the river on 31 March and seized Heilbronn in April. Crossed Neckar River and swung toward Munich. Most of battalion entered Austria near Innsbruck in May, while Company C entered Brenner Pass with 103d Infantry Division. Attachments: 70th, 79th, 100th, 103d Infantry Divisions; 101st Airborne Division. (*Up from Marseilles.*)

782D TANK BATTALION

Activated (originally as light tank battalion) on 1 February 1943 at Camp Cambell, Kentucky. Converted to standard tank battalion on 16 October. Shipped to France in January 1945, arriving at Le Havre. Moved into Germany at Aachen on 8 April. Attached to 97th Infantry Division on 23 April and saw first real action on 30 April at Wittichsthal. Entered Czechoslovakia on 4 May 1945 and ceased operations in vicinity of Sluzetin on 7 May. Attachments: 97th Infantry Division. (Battalion history and AAR, 782d Tank Battalion.)

784TH TANK BATTALION

Activated (originally as light tank battalion) on 1 April 1943 at Camp Claiborne, Louisiana, under command of Maj. George C. Dalia. One of three separate tank battalions with black enlisted personnel and mostly white officers. Reorganized as regular tank battalion on 15 September. Shipped to England in November 1944 and landed on Continent 25 December. Committed on 30 December attached to 104th Infantry Division near Eschweiler, Germany. Reattached to 35th Infantry Division on 4 February 1945 and crossed Roer River on 26 February. Formed part of Task Force Byrnes, which linked up with Canadian forces in Venlo, Netherlands, in early March. Crossed Rhine on 26 March and fought in Ruhr Pocket. By 15 April, was helping to clear woods west of Elbe River. Took on occupation duties in vicinity of Immensen on 27 April. Attachments: 35th, 104th Infantry Divisions; 17th Airborne Division. (AARs, 784th Tank Battalion.)

786TH TANK BATTALION

Activated on 20 September 1943 at Camp Chaffee, Arkansas, out of 1st Battalion, 47th Armored Regiment, 14th Armored Division. Major Charles F. Ryan assumed command. Shipped to United Kingdom, arriving December 1944, and landed at Le Havre, France, on 22 January 1945. Attached to 99th Infantry Division in February and moved to front near Weisweiler, Germany. Supported division's attack to Rhine near Düsseldorf in early March. Crossed Rhine at Remagen on 10

March. Advanced to Weid River, then conducted fast-moving operations along the Frankfurt-Düsseldorf autobahn. Conducted mop-up operations in Ruhr Pocket in April. On 17 April, transferred with 99th Infantry Division to Third Army and advanced to Bamberg. Ceased combat operations on 1 May 1945 near Landshut. Attachments: 99th Infantry Division. (Battalion history and AARs, 786th Tank Battalion.)

787TH TANK BATTALION
Activated on 10 September 1943 at Camp Chaffee, Arkansas, out of 3d Battalion, 16th Armored Regiment, 16th Armored Division. Major David L. Hollingsworth assumed command. Shipped to France, arriving in March 1945. Due to collision off Bermuda, ship carrying the battalion's equipment did not arrive until April 1945, by which time battalion had moved to Wurzburg, Germany. Between 3 and 6 May, conducted road march to join 86th Infantry Division near Erding. Entered Austria on 6 May 1945. Experienced no contact with the enemy. Attachments: 86th Infantry Division. (Battalion history, and AARs, 787th Tank Battalion.)

788TH AMPHIBIAN TRACTOR BATTALION
Redesignated from 788th Tank Battalion on 10 September 1943 at Camp Campbell, Kentucky, under the command of Lt. Col. Francis Hufford. Shipped from Seattle, Washington, 28 July 1944 for Oahu. Participated in assault on Leyte, Philippine Islands, 20 October, and amphibious operations elsewhere on the island. Participated in assault landings on Okinawa, Ryukyus Islands, 1 April 1945. Supported Marine amphibious operations on Okinawa in June. Attachments: 24th, 96th Infantry Divisions; 6th Marine Division. (History and AARs, 788th Amphibian Tractor Battalion.)

826TH AMPHIBIAN TRACTOR BATTALION
Redesignated from 826th Tank Destroyer Battalion on 18 April 1944 at Ft. Ord, California, under the command of L. Col. T. T. Houghton. Departed States 15 August 1944, arrived Admiralty Islands 19 September. Company A participated in landings on Leyte 20 October, operated with 1st Cavalry Division in November and December. Remainder of battalion landed on Luzon 9 January 1945, operated on that island until end of hostilities. Attachments: 43d Infantry Division; 1st Cavalry Division. (History and AARs, 826th Amphibian Tractor Battalion.)

Separate Armored Battalions
by Campaign

TK = Tank Battalion (includes special battalions)
ATK = Amphibian Tank Battalion
ATR = Amphibian Tractor Battalion

EUROPEAN THEATER

Normandy (6 June to 24 July 1944)
70th TK, 709th TK, 712th TK, 735th TK, 736th TK, 737th TK, 741st TK, 743d TK, 744th TK (Light), 745th TK, 746th TK, 747th TK, 749th TK, 759th TK (Light), 774th TK

Northern France (25 July to 14 September 1944)
70th TK, 701st TK, 702d TK, 707th TK, 709th TK, 712th TK, 735th TK, 736th TK, 737th TK, 741st TK, 743d TK, 744th TK (Light), 745th TK, 746th TK, 747th TK, 748th TK, 749th TK, 759th TK (Light), 761st TK, 774th TK, 778th TK

Southern France (15 August to 14 September 1944)
191st TK, 753d TK, 756th TK

Rhineland (15 September 1944 to 21 March 1945)
70th TK, 191st TK, 701st TK, 702d TK, 707th TK, 709th TK, 712th TK, 717th TK, 735th TK, 736th TK, 737th TK, 738th TK, 739th TK, 740th TK, 741st TK, 743d TK, 744th TK (Light), 745th TK, 746th TK, 747th TK, 748th TK, 749th TK, 750th TK, 753d TK, 756th TK (Light), 759th TK (Light), 761st TK, 771st TK, 772d TK, 774th TK, 777th TK, 778th TK, 781st TK, 784th TK, 786th TK

Ardennes-Alsace (16 December 1944 to 25 January 1945)
70th TK, 191st TK, 702d TK, 707th TK, 709th TK, 712th TK, 735th TK, 736th TK, 737th TK, 738th TK, 739th TK, 740th TK, 741st TK, 743d TK, 744th TK (Light), 745th TK, 746th TK, 748th TK, 749th TK, 750th TK, 753d TK, 756th TK, 759th TK (Light), 761st TK, 771st TK, 774th TK, 778th TK, 781st TK

Central Europe (22 March to 11 May 1945)
70th TK, 191st TK, 701st TK, 702d TK, 707th TK, 709th TK, 712th TK, 717th TK, 735th TK, 736th TK, 737th TK, 738th TK, 739th TK, 740th TK, 741st TK,

743d TK, 744th TK (Light), 745th TK, 746th TK, 747th TK, 748th TK, 749th TK, 750th TK, 753d TK, 756th TK, 759th TK (Light), 761st TK, 771st TK, 772d TK, 774th TK, 777th TK, 778th TK, 781st TK, 782d TK, 784th TK, 786th TK, 787th TK

NORTH AFRICA AND MEDITERRANEAN THEATERS

Algeria-French Morocco (8 November 1942 to 11 November 1943)
70th TK (Light), 756th TK(Light)

Tunisia (17 November 1942 to 13 May 1943)
70th TK (Light), 751st TK, 752d TK

Sicily (9 July 1943 to 17 August 1943)
70th TK (Light), 753d TK

Naples-Foggia (9 September 1943 to 21 January 1944)
191st TK, 751st TK, 752d TK, 753d TK, 755th TK, 756th TK, 757th TK, 760th TK

Anzio (22 January 1944 to 24 May 1944)
191st TK, 751st TK

Rome-Arno (22 January 1944 to 9 September 1944)
191st TK, 751st TK, 752d TK, 753d TK, 755th TK, 756th TK, 757th TK, 760th TK

North Apennines (10 September 1944 to 4 April 1945)
751st TK, 751st TK, 752d TK, 755th TK, 757th TK, 758th TK (Light), 760th TK

Po Valley (5 April 1945 to 8 May 1945)
751st TK, 752d TK, 755th TK, 757th TK, 758th TK (Light), 760th TK

PACIFIC THEATER

Philippine Islands (7 December 1941 to 10 May 1942)
192d TK (Light), 194th TK (Light)

Central Pacific (7 December 1941 to 6 December 1943)
193d TK

New Guinea (24 January 1943 to 31 December 1944)
44th TK, 672d ATR, 716th TK, 727th ATR, 775th TK, 826th ATR

Northern Solomons (22 February 1943 to 21 November 1944)
672d ATR, 754th TK

Bismark Archipelago (15 December 1943 to 27 November 1944)
44th TK, 658th ATR, 826th ATR

Eastern Mandates (31 January to 14 June 1944)
708th ATK, 766th TK, 767th TK

Western Pacific (15 June 1944 to 2 September 1945)
534th ATR, 706th TK, 710th TK, 715th ATR, 726th ATR, 762d TK, 766th TK, 773d ATK, 776th ATK

Leyte (17 October 1944 to 1 July 1945)
44th TK, 536th ATR, 539th ATR, 540th ATR, 658th ATR, 706th TK, 710th TK, 716th TK, 718th ATR, 727th ATR, 728th ATR, 763d TK, 767th TK, 776th ATK, 780th ATK, 788th ATR, 826th ATR

Luzon (15 December 1944 to 4 July 1945)
44th TK, 658th ATR, 672d ATR, 716th TK, 727th ATR, 826th ATR, 754th TK, 775th TK

Southern Philippines (27 February 1945 to 4 July 1945)
658th ATR, 708th ATK, 716th TK, 826th ATR

Ryukyus (26 March 1945 to 2 July 1945)
193d TK, 536th ATR, 706th TK, 708th ATK, 711th TK, 713th TK, 715th ATR, 718th ATR, 728th ATR, 763d TK, 773d ATK, 776th ATK, 780th ATK, 788th ATR
        Sources: James A. Sawicki, *Tank Battalions of the U.S. Army* (Dumfries, Va.: Wyvern Publications, 1983); Shelby Stanton, *World War II Order of Battle* (New York: Galahad Books, 1991).

NOTES

CHAPTER 1: GENERAL MCNAIR'S CHILDREN

1. "The Historical Combat Effectiveness of Lighter-Weight Armored Forces: Final Report," the Dupuy Institute, 6 August 2001, www.dupuyinstitute.org/pdf/mwa-2lightarmor.pdf, accessed May 2007. Untitled memorandum on infantry tank strength from Lt. Col. William Crittenberger to the Chief of Cavalry, 16 June 1939, records of the Chief of Cavalry.

2. Brig. Gen. Adna Chaffee, "Mechanized Cavalry: Lecture Delivered at the Army War College, Washington, DC, September 29, 1939."

3. Matthew Darlington Morton, "Men on 'Iron Ponies:' The Death and Rebirth of the Modern U.S. Cavalry," doctoral dissertation, Florida State University, 2004, 167, 178.

4. Robert Stewart Cameron, "Americanizing the Tank: U.S. Army Administration and Mechanized Development Within the Army, 1917-1943," doctoral dissertation, Temple University, August 1944, 492–93; Donald E. Houston, *Hell on Wheels: The 2d Armored Division* (Novato, California: Presidio Press, 1977), 33–34.

5. Cameron, "Americanizing the Tank," 492–93; Houston, *Hell on Wheels*, 33–34.

6. Cameron, "Americanizing the Tank," 492–93.

7. Cameron, "Americanizing the Tank," 493. David E. Johnson, *Fast Tanks and Heavy Bombers: Innovation in the U.S. Army, 1917–1945* (Ithaca, NY: Cornell University Press, 1998), 121.

8. Records of the 13th Armored Regiment; History, 70th Tank Battalion; FM 17-33, *The Armored Battalion*, September 1942, 7; "Redesignation of Units," memorandum AG 320.2, War Department, 8 May 1941.

9. History, 70th Tank Battalion; Marvin Jensen, *Strike Swiftly: The 70th Tank Battalion from North Africa to Normandy to Germany* (Novato, Ca.: Presidio Press, 1997), 7–8.

10. *History and Role of Armor*, ST 17-1-2, US Armor School, April 1974, 13; Cameron, "Americanizing the Tank," 500.

11. Jensen, *Strike Swiftly*, 7–8; Chester Hall, *History of the 70th Tank Battalion: June 5, 1940 . . . May 22, 1946* (Louisville, KY: Southern Press, 1950?), 17–19.

12. History, 193d Tank Battalion.

13. Roger Fazendin, *The 756th Tank Battalion in the Battle of Cassino, 1944* (Lincoln, Nebraska: iUniverse, Inc., 1991), xv.

14. "Trends in Organization of Armored Forces," memorandum from Lt. Gen. Leslie McNair to the acting chief of staff, G-3, War Department, 28 January 1943; Kent Roberts Greenfield, et al., *United States Army in World War II, The Army Ground Forces: The Organization of Ground Combat Troops* (Washington, D.C.: Historical Division, Department of the Army, 1947), 56–61, 321–26.

15. Rich Anderson.

16. *Armored Special Equipment*, The General Board, United States Forces, European Theater, 14 May 1946; "Leaflet Tank," 21 July 1945, General Staff G-2 Section Intelligence Reports, Numerical File, 1943–46, folder 481, NARA.

17. *Armored Special Equipment*, 35–38.

18. Rich Anderson.
19. *Staff Officers' Field Manual for Amphibious Operations*, Fleet Marine Force, Pacific, 10 September 1944; "Landing Vehicle Board Questionnaire," Pacific Warfare Board Report No. 70, 5 October 1945, NARA, RG 407, Special File, 4-7.70/45, box 24464.
20. History, 28th Tank Battalion.
21. T/4 Verne Mauer, et al., *Tank Tracks: 44th Tank Battalion, Tennessee to Tokyo* (Japan: The Battalion, 1945), 3–4; S/Sgt. William Martin, ed., *History of Company "C", 44th Tank Battalion, 1942–1945* (Tokyo: The Battalion, 1945), not paginated.
22. AAR, 713th Tank Battalion, Armored Flamethrower; "713th Flame Throwing Tank Battalion," The 11th Armored Division Association, www.11tharmoreddivision.com, accessed January 2004; "Future Organization and Employment of Main Armament Flamethrower Tanks," Pacific Warfare Board Report No. 76, 6 November 1945, NARA, RG 407, Special File, 4-7.76/45, box 24464.
23. James A. Sawicki, *Tank Battalions of the U.S. Army* (Dumfries, Va.: Wyvern Publications, 1983), 14.
24. Sawicki, *Tank Battalions*, 32 and *passim*; Steven Zaloga, et al., *Amtracs* (Botley, UK: Osprey Publishing Ltd., 1999), 13.
25. History, 70th Tank Battalion.
26. Col. George Hallanan Jr., "The Go-Anywhere Tank Company," *Army* (January 1991): 42.
27. Johnson, *Fast Tanks and Heavy Bombers*, 120ff.
28. *Operations*, FM 100-5, 22 May 1941, 278.
29. Cameron, "Americanizing the Tank," 796; *Armored Force Field Manual: Tactics and Technique*, FM 17-10, 7 March 1942.
30. *Armored Force Field Manual: Tactics and Technique*, FM 17-10, 7 March 1942; *Armored Force Field Manual: The Armored Battalion, Light and Medium*, FM 17-33, 18 September 1942.
31. Wayne Robinson, *Move Out, Verify: The Combat Story of the 743d Tank Battalion* (Frankfurt am Main, Germany: The Battalion, 1945), 30–31.
32. *Organization, Equipment and Tactical Employment of Separate Tank Battalions*, The General Board, United States Forces, European Theater, 14 May 1946, Appendix 2.
33. Memorandum, "Antitank Doctrine and Development," Maj. Gen. George A. Lynch, Chief of Infantry, to the Assistant Chief of Staff, G-3, 3 July 1940, RG 337, box 341, NARA.
34. Brig. Gen. Lesley J. McNair to Adjutant General, AG 320.2 (7-3-40) M-C, 29 July 1940, RG 337, box 341, NARA.
35. *Armored Force Field Manual: Tactics and Technique*, FM 17-10, 7 March 1942.
36. 2d Armored Division report to General Eisenhower.
37. *Tank Gunnery*, The General Board, United States Forces, European Theater, 14 May 1945.
38. Lt. Col. George Rubel, *Daredevil Tankers: The Story of the 740th Tank Battalion, United States Army* (Göttingen, Germany: The Battalion, 1945), 157; AAR, October 1944, 702d Tank Battalion.
39. William S. Triplet, *A Colonel in the Armored Divisions* (Columbia, Missouri: University of Missouri Press, 2001), 46.
40. "Army Amphibian Tank and Tractor Training in the Pacific," 1st Information and Historical Service, records of the 708th Amphibian Tank Battalion, NARA.

41. Headquarters Armored Force, AG 320.2/58, *Reorganization of GHQ Reserve Tank Battalions, and Enlisted Cadres for Newly Activated Battalions*, 16 March 1942.
42. W. J. Blanchard Jr., "Home page of the 746th Tank Battalion," Battalion History, home.hiwaay.net/~blan/Blanchard.
43. William Folkestad, *The View from the Turret* (Shippensburg, PA: Burd Street Press, 2000), vi.
44. History, 726th Amphibian Tractor Battalion.
45. Diary of the 747th Tank Battalion.
46. Robinson, *Move Out, Verify*, 14; History, 775th Tank Battalion.
47. Lt. Col. Raymond Fleig, *707th Tank Battalion in World War II* (Self-published, not dated), 26.
48. History, 767th Tank Battalion.
49. History, 706th Tank Battalion; History, 193d Tank Battalion; History, 713th Tank Battalion, Armored Flamethrower.
50. "Organization of the Armored Units," memorandum from the Special Projects Branch, Army Ground Forces, to the acting chief of staff, Army Groeund Forces, 18 July 1942.
51. "Tanks and Doughboys," *Infantry Journal* (July 1945): 8; "Report of Observations at the European Theater of Operations and North African Theater of Operations," 1 August 1943, General Staff G-2 Section Intelligence Reports, Numerical File, 1943-46, folder 22, NARA.
52. Homer D. Wilkes, *747th Tank Battalion* (Scottsdale, Ariz.: self-published, 1977?), 6.
53. *Tank Gunnery*, 18.
54. Vice Adm. George Carroll Dyer, *The Amphibians Came to Conquer: The Story of Admiral Richmond Kelly Turner*, online version, Hyperwar website, www.ibiblio.org/hyperwar/USN/ACTC/index.html, accessed November 2007, 209-16.
55. Hall, *History of the 70th Tank Battalion*, 18, 21.
56. Fazendin, *The 756th Tank Battalion in the Battle of Cassino*, xv.
57. David Redle, letter to author, January 2008.
58. "Army Amphibian Tank and Tractor Training in the Pacific."
59. Ibid.
60. Cameron, "Americanizing the Tank," 494; Houston, *Hell on Wheels*, 35.
61. Memorandum from Chief of Ordnance to Gen. Jacob L. Devers, Chief, Army Field Forces, 3 August 1948, NARA, RG 337, Army Field Forces Headquarters, Box 9, folder 470.8. Greenfield, et al., *Organization of Ground Combat Troops*, 56–61, 321–26; Cameron, "Americanizing the Tank," 521–22.
62. Armored Force Board report 138, 30 June 1941, NARA, RG 156, Chief of Ordnance, Box J-358.

CHAPTER 2: FIRST BLOOD

1. Al Zdon, *War Stories: Accounts of Minnesotans Who Defended Their Nation* (St. Paul, Minnesota: Stanton Publications: 2002), 115.
2. Burton Anderson, "A History of the Salinas National Guard Company: 1895–1995," Monterey County Historical Society, www.mchsmuseum.com/guard.html, accessed February 2007; "Operations of the Provisional Tank Group, United States Army Forces in the Far East—1941–1942," Bataan Was Hell! website, bataanwashell.blog-city.com, accessed February 2007; Proviso East High School Bataan Commemorative

336 THE INFANTRY'S ARMOR

Research Project, www.proviso.k12.il.us/Bataan%20Web/index.htm, accessed February 2007.

3. *Philippine Islands*, the U.S. Army Campaigns of World War II Series, Washington, D.C.: Center of Military History, n.d., online reprint of CMH Pub 72-3, www.army.mil/cmh-pg/brochures/pi/PI.htm, accessed February 2007.
4. Anderson, "History of the Salinas National Guard Company"; "Operations of the Provisional Tank Group, United States Army Forces in the Far East—1941–1942"; Bataan Commemorative Research Project.
5. *Philippine Islands*.
6. "Operations of the Provisional Tank Group, United States Army Forces In The Far East—1941–1942"; Bataan Commemorative Research Project, which contains a filmed interview with Ben Morin.
7. "Operations of the Provisional Tank Group, United States Army Forces in the Far East—1941–1942"; Bataan Commemorative Research Project.
8. *Philippine Islands*.
9. History, 193d Tank Battalion.
10. Anderson, "History of the Salinas National Guard Company"; "Operations of the Provisional Tank Group, United States Army Forces in the Far East—1941–1942"; *Philippine Islands*; Gene Eric Salecker, *Rolling Thunder against the Rising Sun: The Combat History of U.S. Army Tank Battalions in the Pacific in World War II* (Mechanicsburg, PA: Stackpole Books, 2008), 36–37.
11. Bataan Commemorative Research Project.
12. "Operations of the Provisional Tank Group, United States Army Forces in the Far East—1941–1942"; Anderson, "History of the Salinas National Guard Company"; Bataan Commemorative Research Project.
13. "Operations of the Provisional Tank Group, United States Army Forces in the Far East—1941–1942"; Bataan Commemorative Research Project; Salecker, *Rolling Thunder against the Rising Sun*, 39–41.
14. "Operations of the Provisional Tank Group, United States Army Forces in the Far East—1941–1942."
15. Bataan Commemorative Research Project.
16. "Operations of the Provisional Tank Group, United States Army Forces in the Far East—1941–1942."
17. *Philippine Islands*.
18. "Operations of the Provisional Tank Group, United States Army Forces in the Far East—1941–1942"; Anderson, "History of the Salinas National Guard Company"; *Philippine Islands*.
19. Zdon, *War Stories*, 116.
20. "Operations of the Provisional Tank Group, United States Army Forces in the Far East—1941–1942."
21. Louis Morton, *The Fall of the Philippines: United States Army In World War II: The War in the Pacific* (Washington, D.C.: Center of Military History, United States Army, 1953), 341; Bataan Commemorative Research Project.
22. *Philippine Islands*.
23. Bataan Commemorative Research Project.
24. Ibid.
25. Zdon, *War Stories*, 116–17.
26. *Philippine Islands*.

27. Bataan Commemorative Research Project.

28. Ibid.

29. *Landing Operations on Hostile Shores*, FM 31-5, 2 June 1941.

30. Dyer, *Amphibians Came to Conquer*, 224–25.

31. Lt. Gen. Lucian K. Truscott, *Command Missions* (New York: E. P. Dutton and Company, Inc., 1954), 18ff.

32. "US Army Military History Research Collection, Senior Officers Debriefing Program: Conversation between General Theodore J. Conway and Col. Robert F. Ensslin," U.S. Army Heritage Collection OnLine, www.ahco.army.mil/site/index.jsp, accessed August 2007 (hereafter cited as Conway interview).

33. Hall, *History of the 70th Tank Battalion*, 30.

34. Jensen, *Strike Swiftly*, 19; "The 756th Tank Battalion" website, photographs, www.756tank.com, accessed October 2007. Col. Harry Roper, "Report on Observations Made as Observer with Task Force Brushwood (3d Division Landing at Fedala and Subsequent Attack on Casablanca, French Morocco)," undated, included in "Report of Observers: Mediterranean Theater of Operations," vol. 1, 22 December 1942–23 March 1943.

35. Redle letter.

36. George F. Howe, *Northwest Africa: Seizing the Initiative in the West: United States Army in World War II, The Mediterranean Theater of Operations* (Washington, DC: Center of Military History, United States Army, 1993), 40–41.

37. AAR, 1st Infantry Division. "Summary of Lessons Derived from Amphibious Operations, November 8–11 1942, at Casablanca and Oran," 25 February 1943.

38. "Observer Report," 5 March 1943, included in "Report of Observers: Mediterranean Theater of Operations," vol. 1, 22 December 1942–23 March 1943.

39. Howe, *Northwest Africa*, 49.

40. Ibid., 53.

41. Dyer, *Amphibians Came to Conquer*, 208, 342–43.

42. Roper, "Report on Observations Made."

43. Hall, *History of the 70th Tank Battalion*, 20.

44. Howe, *Northwest Africa*, 103–7.

45. History, 70th Tank Battalion; Capt. Joseph B. Mittelman, *Eight Stars to Victory: A History of the Veteran Ninth U.S. Infantry Division* (Washington, DC: The Ninth Infantry Division Association, 1948), 64; Hall, *History of the 70th Tank Battalion*, 25–26; Howe, *Northwest Africa*, 147ff.

46. "US Army Military History Research Collection, Senior Officers Debriefing Program: Conversation between General Ben Harrell and Col. Robert T. Hayden," U.S. Army Heritage Collection OnLine, www.ahco.army.mil/site/index.jsp, accessed August 2007 (hereafter cited as Harrell interview); Redle letter.

47. Howe, *Northwest Africa*, 124.

48. Conway interview.

49. Fazendin, *The 756th Tank Battalion in the Battle of Cassino*, xxi.

50. Howe, *Northwest Africa*, 125–27.

51. Roper, "Report on Observations Made"; Rick Atkinson, *An Army at Dawn* (New York: Henry Holt and Company, 2002), 156.

52. Account contained in folder "Rpts of Units of 3rd Div in the Casablanca Opns," 3d Infantry Division history files, NARA.

53. Howe, *Northwest Africa*, 128; Medal of Honor citation.

54. AAR, 7th Infantry Regiment; AAR, 30th Infantry Regiment.
55. Jensen, *Strike Swiftly*, 25–28.
56. Howe, *Northwest Africa*, 247.
57. Ibid., 138.
58. Col. James Taylor, "Narrative of Observer's Tour with W.T.F., French Morocco," not dated, included in "Report of Observers: Mediterranean Theater of Operations," vol. 1, 22 December 1942–23 March 1943. Hall, *History of the 70th Tank Battalion*, 25–26. Howe, *Northwest Africa*, 161–62.
59. Howe, *Northwest Africa*, 252, 263–64.
60. "Narrative of Observer's Tour with W.T.F., French Morocco."
61. Ernest Harmon letter to "Dave," 27 December 1942, records of the Armored Board, Army Ground Forces, classified correspondence, RG 337, NARA.
62. "Eisenhower Report on 'Torch'," scanned copy from the Command and General Staff College Combined Arms Research Library's digital library, cgsc.leavenworth.army .mil/carl/contentdm/home.htm, accessed August 2007. B. H. Liddell Hart, *History of the Second World War* (New York: G. P. Putnam's Sons, 1970), 329, 335.
63. "Eisenhower Report on 'Torch'."
64. Helmuth Greiner, Minesterialrat Custodian of the War Diary in Hitler's Headquarters, "Greiner Diary Notes, 12 Aug 1942–12 Mar 1943 (English Copy)," MS # C-065a, not dated (hereafter cited as Greiner diary.)
65. "Minutes, Meeting of the General Council," the War Department, 7 December 1942 and 1 February 1943.
66. "Narrative Report of Antiaircraft Observer in North Africa Theater Lt. Col. Arthur L. Fuller, 27 December, 1942, to 13 January 1943," not dated, included in "Report of Observers: Mediterranean Theater of Operations," vol. 1, 22 December 1942–23 March 1943.
67. History, 1st Armored Group.
68. History, 70th Tank Battalion; Hall, *History of the 70th Tank Battalion*, 26–30; Jensen, *Strike Swiftly*, 57.
69. History, 70th Tank Battalion.
70. Howe, *Northwest Africa*, 376–77.
71. "Eisenhower Report on 'Torch'."
72. Jensen, *Strike Swiftly*, 57–58.
73. Howe, *Northwest Africa*, 378–79.
74. Ralph Ingersoll, *The Battle Is the Payoff* (New York: Harcourt, Brace and Company, 1943), 31–33.
75. Howe, *Northwest Africa*, 380–82.
76. *Tunisia* (CMH Pub 72-12) (Washington, DC: Center of Military History, not dated), 17.
77. Operations report, 1st Armored Division; Operations report, Combat Command B, 1st Armored Division.
78. History, 70th Tank Battalion.
79. Jensen, *Strike Swiftly*, 62–67.
80. Ingersoll, *Battle Is the Payoff*, 33.
81. Jensen, *Strike Swiftly*, 61–63.
82. "Eisenhower Report on 'Torch'"; Howe, *Northwest Africa*, 595ff.
83. Jonathon Forsey, "For the Honour of France," Flames of War website, www.battle-front.co.nz/Article.asp?ArticleID=568, accessed May 2007; "La 1ère DFL, 'noyau

dur' des Forces françaises libres." France-Libre.net website, www.france-libre.net/ forces_francaises_libres/1_1_2_3_1re_DFL_campagne_tunisie.htm, accessed May 2007.

84. History, 70th Tank Battalion. Hall, *History of the 70th Tank Battalion*, 26–30.
85. History, 70th Tank Battalion.
86. Jensen, *Strike Swiftly*, 79.
87. History, 1st Armored Group.
88. History, 751st Tank Battalion.
89. Manuscript by PFC Francis Sternberg, WWII Survey 4792, Military History Institute, Carlisle, Pennsylvania (hereafter cited as Sternberg survey).
90. History and AAR, 751st Tank Battalion.
91. "Eisenhower Report on 'Torch'"; Howe, *Northwest Africa*, 578–82.
92. Sternberg survey.
93. History and AAR, 751st Tank Battalion; *Tankers in Tunisia*, Headquarters, Armored Replacement Training Center, 31 July 1943, online version at the Lone Sentry website, www.lonesentry.com, accessed July 2007.
94. Sternberg survey.
95. Journal, 135th Infantry Regiment; History and AAR, 751st Tank Battalion.
96. *Tankers in Tunisia*.
97. Ibid.; Journal, 135th Infantry Regiment.
98. Journal, 135th Infantry Regiment.
99. History, 751st Tank Battalion.
100. *Tankers in Tunisia*.
101. History, 751st Tank Battalion; AAR, 9th Infantry Division.
102. "Report of Observations at the European Theater of Operations and North African Theater of Operations," 1 August 1943, General Staff G-2 Section Intelligence Reports, Numerical File, 1943–46, folder 23, NARA.
103. Ernest Harmon memorandum to Lt. Gen. Jacob Devers, Chief of the Armored Force, 2 March 1943, records of the Armored Board, Army Ground Forces, classified correspondence, RG 337, NARA (hereafter cited as Harmon memorandum).
104. "Report of Observations at the European Theater of Operations and North African Theater of Operations," 1 August 1943, General Staff G-2 Section Intelligence Reports, Numerical File, 1943–46, folder 23, NARA.
105. Harmon memorandum.
106. Memorandum 319.1/37, "Observer Report," Headquarters, Army Ground Forces, 5 March 1943.
107. "Examination of Tank Casualties," undated memo, folder 091, records of the Armored Board, Army Ground Forces, classified correspondence, RG 337, NARA.
108. "Operational Information on M-4 Series Medium Tanks," Headquarters, 26th Infantry Division, 1 December 1944.
109. "Lessons from the Tunisian Campaign," memorandum, Allied Forces Headquarters, 4 August 1943, records of II Corps.

CHAPTER 3: BEACHHEADS AND MOUNTAINS
1. Field Marshal Lord Carver, *The Imperial War Museum Book of the War in Italy, 1943–1945* (London: Pan Books, 2002), 4–10; *Sicily* (CMH Pub 72-16) (Washington, DC: Center of Military History, 1999), 6–9.

2. General Staff Col. Hellmut Bergengruen, Ia of the Hermann Göring Panzer Division, "Kampf der Pz. Div. 'Hermann Goering' auf Sizilien vom 10.–14.7.1943," MS # C-087a, 31 December 1950, National Archives.
3. Lt. Col. Albert N. Garland, et al., *Sicily and the Surrender of Italy: United States Army in World War II, The Mediterranean Theater of Operations* (Washington, DC: Center of Military History, 1993), 104–5.
4. The Historical Board, *The Fighting Forty-Fifth: The Combat Report of an Infantry Division* (Baton Rouge, Louisiana: Army & Navy Publishing Company, 1946), 17.
5. Truscott, *Command Missions*, 196.
6. C.O.H.Q. Bulletin no. Y/1, "Notes on the Planning and Assault Phases of the Sicilian Campaign by a Military Observer," October 1943.
7. Truscott, *Command Missions*, 198.
8. Journal, 45th Infantry Division; Journal, II Corps.
9. "Report of Observations at the European Theater of Operations and North African Theater of Operations," 1 August 1943, General Staff G-2 Section Intelligence Reports, Numerical File, 1943–46, folder 23, NARA.
10. "Report of the Mission Headed by Lieutenant General Jacob L. Devers to Examine the Problems of Armored Force Units in the European Theater of Operations," undated memorandum, records of the headquarters, Army Ground Forces.
11. "Notes on Operations of 1st Armored Division," 2 April 1943, General Staff G-2 Section Intelligence Reports, Numerical File, 1943–46, folder 45, NARA.
12. Rick Atkinson, *The Day of Battle* (New York: Henry Holt and Company, 2002), 60.
13. Maj. Ellsworth Cundiff, "The Operations of the 3d Battalion, 179th Infantry (45th Infantry Division) 13–14 July 1943 South of Grammicele, Sicily (Personal Experience of a Regimental S-2)," submitted for the Advanced Infantry Officers Course, 1947–1948, the Infantry School, Fort Benning, Georgia.
14. Garland, et al., *Sicily and the Surrender of Italy*, 10–11.
15. The Historical Board, *The Fighting Forty-Fifth*, 21.
16. Cundiff, "Operations of the 3d Battalion"; Bergengruen, "Kampf der Pz. Div. 'Hermann Goering'."
17. The Historical Board, *The Fighting Forty-Fifth*, 22.
18. History, 70th Tank Battalion.
19. Ibid.; Jensen, *Strike Swiftly*, 83.
20. History, 70th Tank Battalion.
21. Ibid.
22. *Combat Lessons Number 1*, War Department, nd, 31.
23. History, 70th Tank Battalion.
24. Carver, *Imperial War Museum Book of the War in Italy*, 48, 54.
25. Ibid., 59–60.
26. History, Fifth Army.
27. "Outline Plan—Operation Avalanche," Fifth Army records.
28. Truscott, *Command Missions*, 247.
29. Field Marshal Albert Kesselring and Gen. of Cavalry Siegfried Westphal, "Questions Regarding the General Strategy during the Italian Campaign," MS # B-270, November 1950, National Archives.
30. C. S. D. I. C. (U.K.) G. G. Report S.R.G.G. 1332(c), 9 July 1945, record group 407, miscellaneous lists, NARA.

31. Martin Blumenson, *Salerno to Cassino: United States Army in World War II, The Mediterranean Theater of Operations* (Washington, DC: Center of Military History, 1993), 159.

32. AAR, 45th Infantry Division.

33. "Outline Plan—Operation Avalanche," G-2 assessment, 21 August 1944, Fifth Army records; History, Fifth Army. Blumenson, *Salerno to Cassino*, 49.

34. AAR, 751st Tank Battalion; "Outline Plan—Operation Avalanche, A-Allotment of Shipping," Fifth Army records; "Report of Observation Trip, NATO," Maj. Gen. W. H. H. Morris, Jr., 27 November 1943, General Staff G-2 Section Intelligence Reports, Numerical File, 1943–46, folder 57, NARA; Operations report, 601st Tank Destroyer Battalion. Blumenson, *Salerno to Cassino*, 56–57.

35. Western Naval Task Force, Operation Plan No. 7-43, Short Title "AVON/W1." "Outline Plan—Operation Avalanche," Fifth Army records.

36. History, Fifth Army.

37. Ibid.

38. Ibid.; Blumenson, *Salerno to Cassino*, 73–77.

39. AAR, 751st Tank Battalion.

40. History and AAR, 191st Tank Battalion.

41. History, Fifth Army.

42. AAR, 751st Tank Battalion.

43. History, Fifth Army.

44. AAR, 751st Tank Battalion.

45. AAR, 751st Tank Battalion.

46. AAR, 191st Tank Battalion.

47. "Report of Observation Trip, NATO," Maj. Gen. W. H. H. Morris, Jr., 27 November 1943, General Staff G-2 Section Intelligence Reports, Numerical File, 1943–46, folder 57, NARA.

48. History, Fifth Army.

49. Ibid.; AAR, 45th Infantry Division.

50. AAR and S-3 journal, 191st Tank Battalion; Journal, 45th Infantry Division.

51. AAR, 751st Tank Battalion.

52. Journal, 45th Infantry Division.

53. AAR, 191st Tank Battalion; Journal, 45th Infantry Division.

54. AAR, 45th Infantry Division.

55. Thomas E. Griess, ed., *The Second World War: Europe and the Mediterranean* (Wayne, NJ: Avery Publishing Group, 1984), 234.

56. "Report of Observation Trip, NATO," Maj. Gen. W. H. H. Morris, Jr., 27 November 1943, General Staff G-2 Section Intelligence Reports, Numerical File, 1943–46, folder 57, NARA.

57. Ibid.; "Observers Notes on the Italian Campaign during the Period 25 August 1943 to 7 October 1943," 5 December 1943, General Staff G-2 Section Intelligence Reports, Numerical File, 1943–46, folder 59, NARA.

58. AAR, 756th Tank Battalion.

59. AAR, 191st Tank Battalion.

60. History, Fifth Army.

61. "From the Volturno to the Winter Line: 6 October–15 November 1943," Washington, DC: Center of Military History, United States Army, 1990, online reprint of CMH Pub 100-8, itself a reprint of a 1945 American Forces in Action Series publication,

www.army.mil/cmh/books/wwii/volturno/volturno-fm.htm#cont, accessed August 2007, 16–18, 28–32.

62. History, Fifth Army; Gen. of Panzer Troops Frido von Senger und Etterlin, "War Diary of the Italian Campaign (1943-45)," MS # C-095A to 095G, 1952, National Archives.
63. Ibid.
64. Maj. Gen. Martin Schmidt, "Panzer Units, Employment in Central Italy, 1944," MS # D-204, 1947, National Archives.
65. History, Fifth Army.
66. AAR, 751st Tank Battalion.
67. History, Fifth Army.
68. Ibid.
69. AAR, 751st Tank Battalion.
70. History, 2d Armored Group.
71. History, Fifth Army.

CHAPTER 4: THE BATTLE FOR ROME

1. Operation Instruction No. 34, H.Q. 15 Army Group, 12 January 1944.
2. Field Order 20, II Corps, 16 January 1944.
3. AAR on Cassino operation, Fifth Army.
4. Field Order 42, 36th Infantry Division, 18 January 1944. AAR, Combat Command B, 1st Armored Division.
5. Field Order 11, 34th Infantry Division, 21 January 1944.
6. Field Order 20, II Corps, 16 January 1944.
7. AAR on Cassino operation, Fifth Army; History, Fifth Army; AAR, 760th Tank Battalion.
8. AAR, Combat Command B, 1st Armored Division.
9. Fazendin, *The 756th Tank Battalion in the Battle of Cassino*, 10, 76, 81.
10. AAR, 756th Tank Battalion; G-2 monthly report, 34th Infantry Division, January 1944; Senger und Etterlin, "War Diary"; Griess, *Second World War*, 242. Fazendin, *The 756th Tank Battalion in the Battle of Cassino*, 20.
11. AAR, 756th Tank Battalion.
12. Ibid.
13. Ibid.; Fazendin, *The 756th Tank Battalion in the Battle of Cassino*, 13, 21–24, 28–32; David Redle, letter to author, January 2008.
14. AAR, 756th Tank Battalion; Fazendin, *The 756th Tank Battalion in the Battle of Cassino*, 38.
15. Legion of Merit citation, Maj. Edwin Arnold.
16. Silver Star citation, T/4 Earl Hollon.
17. AAR, 756th Tank Battalion.
18. Silver Star citation, Capt. French Lewis. Fazendin, *The 756th Tank Battalion in the Battle of Cassino*, 49–51.
19. AAR, 756th Tank Battalion. Fazendin, *The 756th Tank Battalion in the Battle of Cassino*, 61ff, 84.
20. Fazendin, *The 756th Tank Battalion in the Battle of Cassino*, 89–101, 114–17, 124; David Redle, letter to author, January 2008; "History" (actually the journal), 133d Infantry Regiment; AAR, 760th Tank Battalion.

21. "Action by 756 Tank Bn (US) in support of 133 Infantry Regiment (US) During the Crossing of the Rapido River and Subsequent Fighting in the Northeast End of Cassino," Lieutenant Colonel Grenfell, Director of Military Training (Brit) Observer Staff, not dated.

22. Fazendin, *The 756th Tank Battalion in the Battle of Cassino*, 126–27.

23. Ibid., 111.

24. AAR, Combat Command B, 1st Armored Division.

25. Martin Blumenson, *Anzio: The Gamble That Failed* (New York, NY: Cooper Square Press, 2001), 33–40.

26. Ibid., 43ff.

27. Ibid., 56.

28. Ibid., 61–63.

29. "Operation Instruction No. 32," H.Q. 15 Army Group, 2 January 1944.

30. Griess, *Second World War*, 239.

31. Harrell interview.

32. "Shingle Intelligence Summary No. 9," Headquarters, Fifth Army, 16 January 1944.

33. History, Fifth Army.

34. "Shingle Intelligence Summary No. 8," Headquarters, Fifth Army, 11 January 1944.

35. AAR, 751st Tank Battalion.

36. History, Fifth Army.

37. AAR, 751st Tank Battalion.

38. Blumenson, *Anzio*, 75–76.

39. AAR, 751st Tank Battalion; AAR, 3d Cavalry Reconnaissance Troop; History, Fifth Army.

40. AAR, 751st Tank Battalion.

41. History, Fifth Army; "The German Operation at Anzio: A Study of the German Operations at Anzio Beachhead from 22 Jan 44 to 31 May 44," GMDS by a combined British, Canadian, and U.S. staff, not dated.

42. History, Fifth Army; "The German Operation at Anzio."

43. AAR, 191st Tank Battalion.

44. Ibid.

45. History, Fifth Army.

46. AAR, 751st Tank Battalion.

47. "The German Operation at Anzio."

48. AAR, 191st Tank Battalion.

49. *Anzio* (CMH Pub 72-19) (Washington, DC: U.S. Army Center of Military History, not dated), 18–19.

50. AAR, 751st Tank Battalion.

51. AAR, 191st Tank Battalion.

52. AAR, 751st Tank Battalion.

53. Ibid.

54. "Report, Trip to NATOUSA, Modification of Medium Tanks," 3 May 1944, General Staff G-2 Section Intelligence Reports, Numerical File, 1943–46, folder 78, NARA.

55. "Report of Trip to North African Theater of Operations," 5 April 1944, General Staff G-2 Section Intelligence Reports, Numerical File, 1943–46, folder 78, NARA.

56. "Report, Trip to NATOUSA, Modification of Medium Tanks."

57. Ibid.

58. "Report of Trip to North African Theater of Operations."

59. "Observers Notes on the Italian Campaign during the Period 4 October 1943 to 29 December 1943, Inclusive," 7 February 1944, General Staff G-2 Section Intelligence Reports, Numerical File, 1943–46, folder 64, NARA.
60. History, Fifth Army.
61. *Outline History of II Corps* (Italy: 12th Polish Field Survey Company, 1945), 6–7.
62. History, Fifth Army.
63. AAR, 2d Armored Group.
64. History, Fifth Army.
65. Jack Hay, *Italian Campaigns as Witnessed through the Eyes of a U.S. Tank Driver* (Newton, Kansas: Mennonite Press, Inc., 2006), 17–18.
66. AAR, 755th Tank Battalion; History, Fifth Army.
67. History, Fifth Army.
68. AAR, 2d Armored Group.
69. AAR, 756th Tank Battalion.
70. Fazendin, *The 756th Tank Battalion in the Battle of Cassino*, 193–98.
71. AAR, 2d Armored Group.
72. AAR, 2d Armored Group.
73. History, Fifth Army.
74. History and journal, 91st Cavalry Reconnaissance Squadron; Maj. Gen. E. N. Harmon, with Milton MacKaye and William Ross MacKaye, *Combat Commander: Autobiography of a Soldier* (Englewood Cliffs, NJ: Prentice-Hall, 1970), 191; AAR, 760th Tank Battalion.
75. Harmon, *Combat Commander*, 182–83.
76. *Anzio*, 24–25.
77. AAR, 751st Tank Battalion.
78. *191 Tank Bn.* (Germany: The Battalion, 1945); AAR, 191st Tank Battalion; AAR, First Special Service Force.
79. History, Fifth Army.
80. Hamilton Howze, *A Cavalryman's Story* (Washington, DC: Smithsonian Institution Press, 1996), 112–13.
81. Fazendin, *The 756th Tank Battalion in the Battle of Cassino*, 170–71.
82. Howze, *Cavalryman's Story*, 112–14. Fazendin, *The 756th Tank Battalion in the Battle of Cassino*, 171–72.
83. AAR, 756th Tank Battalion; AAR, First Special Service Force; Howze, *Cavalryman's Story*, 115; Fazendin, *The 756th Tank Battalion in the Battle of Cassino*, 173–75.
84. AAR, 191st Tank Battalion.
85. AAR, 760th Tank Battalion.
86. AAR, 756th Tank Battalion.
87. History, 752d Tank Battalion.
88. AAR, 1st Armored Group.
89. History, Fifth Army.
90. Fazendin, *The 756th Tank Battalion in the Battle of Cassino*, 178–79, 206–7.
91. AAR, 191st Tank Battalion.
92. "Extract from an Armored Commanders Narrative on the Italian Campaign," 7 February 1944, General Staff G-2 Section Intelligence Reports, Numerical File, 1943–46, folder 180, NARA.
93. AAR, 756th Tank Battalion.
94. AAR, 760th Tank Battalion.

95. "Tank-Infantry-Artillery Team," 1 July 1944, General Staff G-2 Section Intelligence Reports, Numerical File, 1943–46, folder 128, NARA.
96. Kesselring and Westphal, "Questions Regarding the General Strategy."
97. Griess, *Second World War*, 275.
98. Conway interview.
99. History, 752d Tank Battalion.

CHAPTER 5: LETHAL SEA TURTLES

1. T/5 Clair Polites, WW II Survey 4533, Military History Institute, Carlisle, Pennsylvania.
2. "World War II (Asia-Pacific Theater)," Center of Military History Online, www.army .mil/cmh-pg/reference/apcmp.htm, accessed July 2006.
3. "Observers Report," 29 August 1943, General Staff G-2 Section Intelligence Reports, Numerical File, 1943–46, folder 14, NARA.
4. History and AAR, 193d Tank Battalion.
5. "APM-2/LSD-2 Belle Grove," NavSource Online: Amphibious Photo Archive, www.navsource.org/archives/10/12/1202.htm, accessed May 2007; "History of USS Belle Grove (LSD-2)," www.USSBelleGrove.org website, http://www.ussbellegrove .org/shipshistory/ihistory.html, accessed May 2007.
6. "Participation of Task Force 52.6, 27th Division, in GALVANIC (MAKIN) Operation," 15 January 1944, General Staff G-2 Section Intelligence Reports, Numerical File, 1943–46, folder 63, NARA; Dyer, *Amphibians Came to Conquer*, 626, 660–61, 681.
7. AAR, 193d Tank Battalion.
8. "Participation of Task Force 52.6, 27th Division, in GALVANIC (MAKIN) Operation."
9. AAR, 193d Tank Battalion.
10. "The Tank Infantry Engineer Team in Jungle Operations," memorandum, Headquarters, XIV Corps, 20 January 1944.
11. Journal, 132d Infantry Regiment.
12. "Combined Infantry-Tank-Engineer Operations in the Jungle," memorandum, Headquarters XIV Corps, 4 April 1944; John Miller, *Cartwheel: The Reduction of Rabaul: United States Army in World War II, The War in the Pacific* (Washington, D.C.: Office of the Chief of Military History, Department of the Army, 1959), 351ff.
13. "Questions on Operation of All Types of Military Vehicles in Mud—Ordnance Technical Letter #24."
14. "Combined Infantry-Tank-Engineer Operations in the Jungle," memorandum, Headquarters XIV Corps, 4 April 1944; *Combat Lessons Number 2*, War Department, nd, 62.
15. Lt. Col. James Rogers, "Amphibian Tank Battalion in Combat," *The Cavalry Journal* (March–April 1946): 26.
16. Zaloga, et al, *Amtracs*, 6–10.
17. "Army Amphibian Tank and Tractor Training in the Pacific."
18. Triplet, *Colonel in the Armored Divisions*, 64.
19. Rogers, "Amphibian Tank Battalion in Comat," 26–28; "Army Amphibian Tank and Tractor Training in the Pacific."
20. Triplet, *Colonel in the Armored Divisions*, 64.

21. History, 767th Tank Battalion; *Combat Lessons Number 4*, War Department, nd, 82–83.
22. Rogers, "Amphibian Tank Battalion in Combat," 29–30; "Amphibious Operations: The Marshall Islands, January–February 1944," COMINCH P-002, United States Fleet.
23. Rogers, "Amphibian Tank Battalion in Combat," 30.
24. *Army Amphibian and Tractor Training in the Pacific*, 1st Information and Historical Service, not dated.
25. Triplet, *Colonel in the Armored Divisions*, 48.
26. History, 726 Amphibian Tractor Battalion.
27. AAR, 708th Amphibian Tank Battalion; "History: World War II Part II," Kwajalein Atoll, Republic of the Marshall Islands, website, www.angelfire.com/hi2/kwa/0his_ww2b.html, accessed February 2007; "Extracts from Observers' comments on Flintlock Operation," Office of the Commander, Fifth Amphibious Force, Pacific Fleet, 12 April 1944.
28. Rogers, "Amphibian Tank Battalion in Combat," 30–31; Journal, 767th Tank Battalion.
29. "The Marshall Islands Operations," Historical Division, U.S. Marine Corps, online version, www.au.af.mil/au/awc/awcgate/usmchist/island.txt, accessed February 2007.
30. "The First Armored Amphibian Battalion in World War II," The First Armored Amphibian Battalion, www.marineamphibians.com, accessed January 2007.
31. "Landing Vehicle Board Questionnaire."
32. Lt. Col. S. L. A. Marshall, "One Day on Kwajalein," *Infantry Journal* (August 1944): 14.
33. Journal and history, 767th Tank Battalion; Journal, 767th Tank Battalion.
34. "Amphibious Operations: The Marshall Islands, January-February 1944," COMINCH P-002, United States Fleet; Lt. Col. Robert Heinl and Lt. Col. John Crown, *The Marshalls: Increasing the Tempo, USMC Historical Monograph*, Historical Branch, G-3 Division, Headquarters, U.S. Marine Corps, 1954 (online version at Hyperwar: A Hypertext History of the Second World War, http://www.ibiblio.org/hyperward, accessed February 2007.), 117.
35. Heinl and Crown, *The Marshalls*, 128; Rogers, "Amphibian Tank Battalion in Combat," 32.
36. "Eniwetok Operations, Report of," Commander, Eniwetok Expeditionary Group, 7 March 1944; Heinl and Crown, *The Marshalls*, 128; Rogers, "Amphibian Tank Battalion in Combat," 32–33.
37. AAR, 708th Amphibian Tank Battalion; Rogers, "Amphibian Tank Battalion in Combat," 33.
38. Sgt. Merle Miller, "Surprise Party at Eniwetok," *Yank* (31 March 1944): 5.
39. "Eniwetok Operations, Report of," Commander, Eniwetok Expeditionary Group, 7 March 1944. AAR, Task Group 1, V Amphibious Corps.
40. "Development of Tactical Doctrine for Employment of Amphibian Tanks, 19 June 1945, General Staff G-2 Section Intelligence Reports, Numerical File, 1943–46, folder 394, NARA.
41. "Army Amphibian Tank and Tractor Training in the Pacific"; Rogers, "Amphibian Tank Battalion in Combat," 34.
42. "Amphibious Operations: The Marshall Islands, January–February 1944," COMINCH P-002, United States Fleet.

43. AAR, 767th Tank Battalion.

CHAPTER 6: SAIPAN: BOOKEND TO NORMANDY

1. Maj. Carl Hoffman, *Saipan: The Beginning of the End, USMC Historical Monograph*, Historical Branch, G-3 Division, Headquarters, U.S. Marine Corps, 1950 (online version at Hyperwar: A Hypertext History of the Second World War, www.ibiblio.org/ hyperward, accessed February 2007), 1–12.
2. Lt. Russell Gugeler, "Army Amphibian Tractor and Tank Battalions in the Battle of Saipan: 15 June–9 July 1944," 20 January 1945 (online version of document contained in file 8-5.3 BA, Historical Manuscripts Collection, U.S. Army Center of Military History, www.army.mil/cmh-pg/documents/wwii/amsai/amsai.htm, accessed February 2007).
3. Lt. Col. James Rogers, "Command Control of an Armored Amphibian Battalion," *The Cavalry Journal* (January–February 1945): 5.
4. "Army Amphibian Tank and Tractor Training in the Pacific"; Journal, 708th Amphibian Tank Battalion.
5. Lt. Harry Semmes, "Amtanks at Saipan," *The Cavalry Journal* (May–June 1945): 30; Rogers, "Command and Control of an Armored Amphibian Battalion," 35.
6. Journal, 708th Amphibian Tank Battalion; Gugeler, "Army Amphibian Tractor and Tank Battalions in the Battle of Saipan."
7. Semmes, "Amtanks at Saipan," 30.
8. Journal, 708th Amphibian Tank Battalion; History, 534th Amphibian Tractor Battalion; Hoffman, *Saipan*, 48ff.
9. Semmes, "Amtanks at Saipan," 30.
10. Journal, 708th Amphibian Tank Battalion; History, 534th Amphibian Tractor Battalion. Gugeler, "Army Amphibian Tractor and Tank Battalions in the Battle of Saipan"; Hoffman, *Saipan*, 51, 55ff.
11. Semmes, "Amtanks at Saipan," 30.
12. Rogers, "Command and Control of an Armored Amphibian Force," 35.
13. Hoffman, *Saipan*, 61–62; History, 534th Amphibian Tractor Battalion.
14. Gugeler, "Army Amphibian Tractor and Tank Battalions in the Battle of Saipan."
15. Gugeler, "Army Amphibian Tractor and Tank Battalions in the Battle of Saipan"; Hoffman, *Saipan*, 50.
16. Maj. Richard Adams, "The Operations of Company 'B,' 715th Amphibian Tractor Battalion during the Assault Landing on Saipan Island, 15 June 1944 (Marianas Campaign) (Personal Experience of Company Commander)," submitted for the Advanced Infantry Officers Course, 1949–1950, the Infantry School, Fort Benning, Georgia.
17. Gugeler, "Army Amphibian Tractor and Tank Battalions in the Battle of Saipan"; Hoffman, *Saipan*, 50; Adams, "The Operations of Company 'B,' 715th Amphibian Tractor Battalion."
18. Journal, 708th Amphibian Tank Battalion; Gugeler, "Army Amphibian Tractor and Tank Battalions in the Battle of Saipan."
19. Journal, 708th Amphibian Tank Battalion; Gugeler, "Army Amphibian Tractor and Tank Battalions in the Battle of Saipan."
20. Hoffman, *Saipan*, 50.
21. Gugeler, "Army Amphibian Tractor and Tank Battalions in the Battle of Saipan."
22. Hoffman, *Saipan*, 77, 85–86.

23. Capt. Roy E. Appleman, 1st Information and Historical Service, "Army Tanks in the Battle for Saipan," manuscript, records of the 762d Tank Battalions.
24. Hoffman, *Saipan*, 95; Gugeler, "Army Amphibian Tractor and Tank Battalions in the Battle of Saipan"; Rogers, "Command and Control of an Armored Amphibian Force," 36; "Army Tanks in the Battle for Saipan."
25. Gugeler, "Army Amphibian Tractor and Tank Battalions in the Battle of Saipan."
26. "Army Tanks in the Battle for Saipan."
27. Ibid.
28. Ibid.
29. Ibid.
30. Journal, 708th Amphibian Tank Battalion; History, 534th Amphibian Tractor Battalion.
31. Rogers, "Command and Control of an Armored Amphibian Force," 36.
32. "Army Amphibian Tank and Tractor Training in the Pacific."
33. Memorandum, 762 Tank Battalion, 7 September 1944.

CHAPTER 7: DDS AT D-DAY

1. Peter Chamberlain and Chris Ellis, *Churchill and Sherman Specials* (Windsor, England: Profile Publications, n.d); Memo by Maj. William Duncan, 743d Tank Battalion, "Results of Training, Tests, and Tactical Operations of DD Tanks at Slapton Sands, Devon, England, during Period 15 March–30 April 1944," dated 30 April 1944 and contained in the records of the 753d Tank Battalion.
2. "Armor in Operation Neptune (Establishment of Normandy Beachhead)," Committee 10, Officers Advanced Course, The Armored School, 1949. Online edition posted at Axis History Forum, forum.axishistory.com/viewtopic.php?t=51896, accessed April 2007.
3. Joseph Balkoski, *Beyond the Beachhead, The 29th Infantry Division in Normandy* (Mechanicsburg, PA: Stackpole Books, 1999), 124.
4. "Tanks and Doughboys," 8.
5. Jensen, *Strike Swiftly*, 125.
6. Capt. Charles H. Kidd, "Operations of Company M, 116th Infantry (29th Inf. Div.), in the Landing on Omaha Beach, 6–13 June 1944 (Normandy Campaign)," submitted for the Advanced Infantry Officers Course, 1946–1947, the Infantry School, Fort Benning, Georgia.
7. Unit History for March 1944, 746th Tank Battalion.
8. S-3 Journal, 743d Tank Battalion.
9. Al Heintzleman, *We'll Never Go Over-Seas* (self-published, 1982), 26.
10. Jensen, *Strike Swiftly*, 134.
11. Griess, ed., *Second World War*, 295.
12. Ibid.
13. Seventh Army war diary, record group 407, miscellaneous lists, NARA.
14. Griess, ed., *Second World War*, 296.
15. History of the 6th Armored Group; AAR, 70th Tank Battalion; "Armor In Operation Neptune."
16. Griess, ed., *Second World War*, 296.
17. Ibid., 144; "Armor in Operation Neptune."

18. Maj. Roland Ruppenthal, *American Forces in Action: Utah Beach to Cherbourg (6 June–27 June 1944)* (Washington, DC: Center of Military History, United States Army, 1990), online edition at www.army.mil/cmh-pg/books/wwii/utah/utah.htm, accessed June 2006, 53; Maj. Robert Tincher, "Reconnaissance in Normandy—In Support of Airborne Troops," *The Cavalry Journal* (January–February 1945): 12.

19. Griess, ed., *Second World War*, 297.

20. *Omaha Beachhead (6 June–13 June 1944)*, American Forces in Action Series, (Washington, D.C.: Center of Military History, 1984), online reprint of CMH Pub 100-1, www.army.mil/cmh-pg/books/wwii/100-11/100-11.HTM, 38.

21. AAR, 3d Armored Group.

22. Interview with Sgt. Maj. Paul Ragan (ret.), 22 December 2001.

23. AAR, 741st Tank Battalion; Heintzleman, *We'll Never Go Over-Seas*, A14.

24. Heintzleman, *We'll Never Go Over-Seas*, 28.

25. Hand-written interviewer notes on reverse of "Company H, 16th Infantry," Combat Interviews, 1st Infantry Division, NARA.

26. Interview with Paul Ragan; Unit journal, 741st Tank Battalion.

27. Heintzleman, *We'll Never Go Over-Seas*, 28.

28. Interview with Paul Ragan.

29. Hand-written interviewer notes on reverse of "Company H, 16th Infantry," Combat Interviews, 1st Infantry Division, NARA; Heintzleman, *We'll Never Go Over-Seas*, 24–25.

30. Griess, ed., *Second World War*, 297.

31. Alfred Whitehead, "The Diary of a Soldier," the Second Infantry Division Photo Web Pages website, home.thirdage.com/Military/friends2idww2/Combat_Journal.html, accesed November 2007.

32. "16-E on D-Day," Combat Interviews, 1st Infantry Division, NARA. "Company H, 16th Infantry," Combat Interviews, 1st Infantry Division, NARA. "Armor In Operation Neptune."

33. Personal reports, records of the 741st Tank Battalion.

34. Ibid.

35. AAR, 741st Tank Battalion.

36. Ibid.; "Armor in Operation Neptune"; "The D-Day Experiences of Company L, 16th Infantry," Combat Interviews, 1st Infantry Division, NARA; "Company H, 16th Infantry," Combat Interviews, 1st Infantry Division, NARA; "The Story of Company F, 16th Infantry, on D-Day," Combat Interviews, 1st Infantry Division, NARA; "Company H, 16th Infantry," Combat Interviews, 1st Infantry Division, NARA.

37. Unit Journal, 741st Tank Battalion; Hand-written interviewer notes on reverse of "Company H, 16th Infantry," Combat Interviews, 1st Infantry Division, NARA; Heintzleman, *We'll Never Go Over-Seas*, 25, 28–29.

38. *Omaha Beachhead*, 39.

39. AAR, 743d Tank Battalion.

40. Folkestad, *View from the Turret*, 4.

41. Account of Lt. Jack Shea, Combat Interviews, 29th Infantry Division, NARA (hereafter cited as Shea account).

42. Gordon A. Harrison, *Cross-Channel Attack: United States Army in World War II, The European Theater of Operations* (Washington, D.C.: Center of Military History, 2002), 319–20.

43. Robinson, *Move Out, Verify*, 26–27.

44. Shea account; Journal, 741st Tank Battalion.
45. S-3 Journal, 743d Tank Battalion. Interview with Capt. Joseph Ondre, Combat Interviews, 29th Infantry Division, NARA.
46. S-3 Journal, 743d Tank Battalion.
47. *Omaha Beachhead*, 81.
48. Charles Kidd, "Operations of Company M."
49. *Omaha Beachhead*, 107–8.
50. AAR, 3d Armored Group.
51. AAR, 745th Tank Battalion.
52. AAR, 747th Tank Battalion.
53. Sawicki, *Tank Battalions*, 22.
54. Ruppenthal, *American Forces in Action*, 53.

CHAPTER 8: THE BOCAGE: A SCHOOL OF VERY HARD KNOCKS

1. David Heathcott, "The 749th Tank Battalion: World War II Memories," personal.pitnet.net/heathde/749, accessed November 2007.
2. Robinson, *Move Out, Verify*, 52–53.
3. Martin Blumenson, *Breakout and Pursuit: United States Army in World War II, The European Theater of Operations* (Washington, D.C.: Office of the Chief of Military History, Department of the Army, 1961), 177.
4. Griess, ed., *Second World War*, 307–8.
5. Seventh Army war diary, record group 407, miscellaneous lists, NARA.
6. Lt. Col. Richard Langston Jr., WW II Survey 12,268, Military History Institute, Carlisle, Pennsylvania.
7. Ibid.; AAR, 746th Tank Battalion; History of the 6th Armored Group; Interviews with Col. Francis F. Fainter, Capt. Richard M. Langston, S-3, 746th Tank Battalion, and Lt. Huston Payne, 746th Tank Battalion, Combat Interviews, 4th Infantry Division.
8. W. J. Blanchard Jr., *Our Liberators: The Combat History of the 746th Tank Battalion during World War II* (Tucson, Arizona: Fenestra Books, 2003), 12–13.
9. Interviews with Maj. McKericher, S-3, 70th Tank Battalion, and Lt. John Casteel, Company B, 70th Tank Battalion, Combat Interviews, 4th Infantry Division.
10. Harrison, *Cross-Channel Attack*, 344–45.
11. Wilkes, *747th Tank Battalion*, 11 ff, supplement; conversation with Mrs. Wilkes by author, 10 November 2001.
12. "Combat Interviews, 29 Inf Div, Col S. L. A. Marshall," Combat Interviews, 29th Infantry Division, NARA; "Company H, 16th Infantry," Combat Interviews, 1st Infantry Division, NARA.
13. Harrison, *Cross-Channel Attack*, 352–53.
14. "Armor in Operation Neptune."
15. 746th Tank Battalion Report, 10 July, 83d Div. G-2, G-3 Journal File, cited by Blumenson, *Breakout and Pursuit*, 132.
16. AAR, 6th Armored Group.
17. History of the 6th Armored Group; Jensen, *Strike Swiftly*, 147.
18. AAR, 746th Tank Battalion.
19. 1st Division assault maps.
20. Jensen, *Strike Swiftly*, 144.
21. Stephen E. Ambrose, *Citizen Soldiers* (New York: Touchstone, 1997), 34.

22. Ira Wolfert, "Sure Surprised Hell Out of the Germans!" *Tulsa Tribune* (24 July 1944).
23. Blumenson, *Breakout and Pursuit*, 205; AAR, 749th Tank Battalion.
24. AAR, 749th Tank Battalion.
25. Jensen, *Strike Swiftly*, 144.
26. Blumenson, *Breakout and Pursuit*, 96.
27. Charles Kidd, "Operations of Company M."
28. Blumenson, *Breakout and Pursuit*, 43.
29. S-3 journal, November 1944, 774th Tank Battalion.
30. S-3 journal, 743d Tank Battalion.
31. Robinson, *Move Out, Verify*, 56.
32. AAR, August 1944, 741st Tank Battalion.
33. AAR, July 1944, 6th Armored Group.
34. AAR, 6th Armored Group.
35. Battle Report, 747th Tank Battalion.
36. *From D + 1 to 105: The Story of the 2nd Infantry Division* (Paris: Stars and Stripes, 1944); "The Enemy and His Defenses," Combat Interviews, 2d Infantry Division; Richard Schimpf, "Fighting of the 3rd Parachute Division during the Invasion of France from June to August 1944," MS # B-020, translated by Janet E. Dewey, November 1989 at the US Army Military History Institute and for the Center of Military History.
37. Maj. Lee M. Ray, "Operations of the 23d Infantry Regiment, 2d Infantry Division, in the attack on Hill 192, east of St. Lo, 11–12 July 1944 (Normandy Campaign)," submitted for the Advanced Infantry Officers Course, 1947–1948, the Infantry School, Fort Benning, Georgia.
38. Schimpf, "Fighting of the 3rd Parachute Division."
39. Journal, 741st Tank Battalion.
40. "Planning and Preparation," Combat Interviews, 2d Infantry Division.
41. Schimpf, "Fighting of the 3rd Parachute Division."
42. AAR, 747th Tank Battalion.
43. Robinson, *Move Out, Verify*, 40.
44. Maj. William R. Campbell, "Tanks With Infantry," *Armored Cavalry Journal* (September–October 1947): 49.
45. Combat interviews, 30th Infantry Division, NARA.
46. AAR, 3d Armored Group.
47. Robinson, *Move Out, Verify*, 48.
48. AAR and S-3 Journal, 747th Tank Battalion.
49. Wilkes, *747th Tank Battalion*, 18.
50. S-3 Journal, 747th Tank Battalion.
51. Ray, "Operations of the 23d Infantry Regiment."
52. AAR, 741st Tank Battalion.
53. AAR, 743d Tank Battalion.
54. Wolfert, "Sure Surprised Hell Out of the Germans!"
55. "Extracts from Overseas reports," 28 July 1944, General Staff G-2 Section Intelligence Reports, Numerical File, 1943–46, folder 132, NARA.
56. AARs, 741st and 749th Tank Battalions.
57. "Visit to Armored Units of VIII Corps," memorandum, Twelfth Army Group Armored Section, 15 February 1945.
58. AAR, 749th Tank Battalion.

59. Wilkes, *747th Tank Battalion*, 27.
60. S-3 journal, 3d Armored Group.
61. S-3 journal, 745th Tank Battalion; Blumenson, *Breakout and Pursuit*, 43.
62. Blumenson, *Breakout and Pursuit*, 85.
63. *Tank Gunnery*, 11.
64. AARs, June–July and November 1944, 745th Tank Battalion; AARs, June 1944, January 1945, 756th Tank Battalion.
65. Harrison, *Cross-Channel Attack*, 479; AAR, 746th Tank Battalion.
66. "Entry into Cherbourg and the Taking of the Arsenal: 25–26 June," interview with Captain Hilbert, Combat Interviews, 9th Infantry Division, NARA.
67. Blumenson, *Breakout and Pursuit*, 36–39, 178.
68. Ibid., 175.
69. AAR, 741st Tank Battalion. Ray, "Operations of the 23d Infantry Regiment."
70. AAR, 3d Armored Group.
71. "Planning and Preparation," Combat Interviews, 2d Infantry Division.
72. "Narrative of the Attack—38th Infantry Regiment, 1st Bn.," Combat Interviews, 2d Infantry Division; "Planning and Preparation"; Heintzleman, *We'll Never Go Over-seas*, A17, 33; Schimpf, "Fighting of the 3rd Parachute Division."
73. Heintzleman, *We'll Never Go Over-Seas*, 39.
74. "Narrative of the Attack—38th Inf. Regt., 2d Bn.," Combat Interviews, 2d Infantry Division; Heintzleman, *We'll Never Go Over-Seas*, 34.
75. "Narrative of the Attack—38th Infantry Regiment, 1st Bn."
76. Ray, "Operations of the 23d Infantry Regiment."
77. Interview with Col. Dwyer, Combat Interviews, 29th Infantry Division, NARA.
78. Interview with Maj. Sydney V. Bingham Jr., Combat Interviews, 29th Infantry Division, NARA.
79. Interview with Col. Godwin Ordway Jr., Combat Interviews, 29th Infantry Division, NARA.
80. AARs, 743d Tank Battalion.
81. Michaeel Green, *M4 Sherman: Combat and Development History of the Sherman Tank and All Sherman Variants* (Osceola, WI: Motorbooks, 1993), 40.
82. S-3 Journal, 3d Armored Group.
83. AAR, November 1944, 756th Tank Battalion.
84. Maj Budd W. Richmond, "Operations of the 3d Battalion, 137th Infantry, 35th Infantry Division, in the Attack on Hill 122, north of St. Lo, France, 11–15 July 1944 (Normandy Campaign) (Personal Experience of a Battalion Operations Officer)," submitted for the Advanced Infantry Officers Course, 1949–1950, the Infantry School, Fort Benning, Georgia.
85. History, 737th Battalion, 3–4.
86. Unit Journal and History, 737th Tank Battalion.
87. Richmond, "Operations of the 3d Battalion."
88. Rubottom, Maj. Don C., "Operations of the 1st Battalion, 134th Infantry, 35th Infantry Division, in the Attack on Hill 122, north of St. Lo, France, 15–17 July 1944 (Normandy Campaign) (Personal Experience of a Company Commander)," submitted for the Advanced Infantry Officers Course, 1949–1950, the Infantry School, Fort Benning, Georgia.

89. "Report on Operations of XIX Corps in Normandy and Comments based upon Interviews and Personal Observations," 2 August 1944, General Staff G-2 Section Intelligence Reports, Numerical File, 1943–46, folder 141, NARA.

CHAPTER 9: OPEN-FIELD RUNNING

1. Blumenson, *Breakout and Pursuit*, 181.
2. The following description of Cobra relies heavily on Blumenson, *Breakout and Pursuit*, 218–40.
3. *Northern France* (CMH Pub 72-30) (Washington, DC: U.S. Army Center of Military History, not dated), 7; Report of operations, First Army. AAR, VIII Corps.
4. Robinson, *Move Out, Verify*, 64; Combat interviews, 30th Infantry Division, NARA.
5. Blumenson, *Breakout and Pursuit*, 240; Griess, ed., *Second World War*, 331
6. Interviews with Maj. Robert H. Herlong and Capt. Clayborn Wayne, 119th Infantry Regiment, combat interviews, 30th Infantry Division, NARA.
7. Interviews with Col. Hammond D. Birks and other officers, 120th Infantry Regiment; and Lt. Col. William Duncan and Lt. Ernest Aas, 743d Tank Battalion, combat interviews, 30th Infantry Division, NARA.
8. Robinson, *Move Out, Verify*, 66.
9. Seventh Army war diary, record group 407, miscellaneous lists, NARA.
10. Blumenson, *Breakout and Pursuit*, 243.
11. Christopher J. Anderson, *Hell on Wheels: The Men of the U.S. Armored Forces, 1918 to the Present* (London: Greenhill Books, 1999), 29.
12. Heintzleman, *We'll Never Go Over-Seas*, 36–37.
13. Griess, ed., *Second World War*, 317.
14. S-3 journal, 745th Tank Battalion.
15. Blumenson, *Breakout and Pursuit*, 268.
16. Ibid., 253–54.
17. Ibid., 251–52.
18. Interview with Maj. A. V. Middleworth, S-3 of the 18th Infantry Regiment, "The 1st Division in the Breakthrough of July 25th," Combat Interviews, 1st Infantry Division, NARA.
19. Interview with Lt. Col. E. F. Driscoll and Maj. W. R. Watson, "Normandy Breakthrough: 1st Battalion, 16th Infantry, 1st Infantry Division," Combat Interviews, 1st Infantry Division, NARA; interview with Lt. Col. Chas. T. Horner and Maj. Eston T. White, "Normandy Breakthrough: 27–31 July 1944, 3d Bn., 16th Inf., 1st Division," Combat Interviews, 1st Infantry Division, NARA.
20. Col. Robert S. Allen, *Patton's Third Army: Lucky Forward* (New York: Manor Books Inc., 1965), 71–74.
21. AAR, 749th Tank Battalion.
22. Ibid.
23. Jensen, *Strike Swiftly*, 190–91; AAR, 70th Tank Battalion; Report of operations, First Army.
24. Blumenson, *Breakout and Pursuit*, 308.
25. Col. Roy Moore Jr., *Chariots of Iron: The 735th Tank Battalion (M), World War II, Europe* (Lopez Island, WA: Island Graphics and Advertising, 1991), 70.
26. Ibid., 72–73.
27. AAR, 747th Tank Battalion.

28. Allen, *Patton's Third Army*, 83.
29. Ibid., 87.
30. Chester Wilmot, *The Struggle for Europe* (Ware, England: Wordsworth, 1997), 424.
31. "The Gap at Chambois—Aug 15–22, 1944," Combat Interviews, 90th Infantry Division, NARA; "1st Bn Action at Le Bourg St. Leonard," interview with Maj. Leroy Pond and other battalion officers, Combat Interviews, 90th Infantry Division, NARA.
32. Aaron Elson, *Tanks for the Memories: An Oral History of the 712th Tank Battalion from World War II* (Hackensack, NJ: Chi Chi Press, 1994), 66–68.
33. "The Gap at Chambois—Aug 15–22, 1944," Combat Interviews, 90th Infantry Division, NARA.
34. History, 12th Army Group Armored Section.
35. S-3 Journal, 3d Armored Group; S-3 Journal, 70th Tank Battalion; S-4 Reports, 774th Tank Battalion.
36. S-3 Journal, 737th Tank Battalion.
37. S-3 Journal, 741st Tank Battalion.
38. AAR, 743d Tank Battalion.
39. S-3 Journal, 3d Armored Group.
40. AAR, 756th Tank Battalion.
41. Green, *M4 Sherman*, 102.
42. History, 12th Army Group Armored Section.
43. S-3 Journal, 6th Armored Group.
44. S-3 Journal, 3d Armored Group.
45. Johnson, *Fast Tanks and Heavy Bombers*, 192–93.
46. Griess, ed., *Second World War*, 338–40.
47. Blumenson, *Breakout and Pursuit*, 689.
48. AAR, August 1944, 746th Tank Battalion.
49. AAR, 743d Tank Battalion.
50. AAR, August and September 1944, 743d Tank Battalion.
51. Homer D. Wilkes, *APO 230* (Scottsdale, AZ: self-published, 1982), 115.
52. Griess, ed., *Second World War*, 342.
53. Jensen, *Strike Swiftly*, 205ff.
54. Heintzleman, *We'll Never Go Over-Seas*, 49.
55. S-3 journal, 741st Tank Battalion.
56. AAR, 70th Tank Battalion; Jensen, *Strike Swiftly*, 216.
57. Elson, *Tanks for the Memories*, 74–81; AAR, September 1944, 712th Tank Battalion; "The Battle of the CPs," Combat Interviews, 90th Infantry Division, NARA; "Interview of the Assembled Members of the 712th Tank Battalion (- 1st Platoon Co C) at the Battalion CP (U619802) Concerning the Enemy Attack on the 90th Infantry Division CP the Morning of 8 September," Combat Interviews, 90th Infantry Division, NARA.
58. AAR, 749th Tank Battalion.
59. Charles B. MacDonald, *The Siegfried Line Campaign: United States Army in World War II, The European Theater of Operations* (Washington, D.C.: Office of the Chief of Military History, Department of the Army, 1963), 386.
60. S-3 Journal, AARs, 743rd Tank Battalion.
61. Allen, *Patton's Third Army*, 107.
62. AAR, 743d Tank Battalion. Robinson, *Move Out, Verify*, 86, 89.
63. S-4 Report, 702d Tank Battalion.

64. Dr. Steven E. Anders, "POL on the Red Ball Express," *Quartermaster Professional Bulletin* (Spring 1989), Quartermaster Museum on-line, www.qmfound.com/pol_on _the_red_ball_express.htm.
65. AARs, 743d, 745th, and other tank battalions.
66. AARs, 191st and 753d Tank Battalions.
67. AARs, 191st and 753d Tank Battalions.
68. Redle letter.
69. "Summary of Lessons Learned in Combat," Headquarters 1st Armored Group, 6 November 1944.
70. Redle letter.
71. Maj. Percy Ernst Schramm, "OKW War Diary (1 Apr–18 Dec 1944," MS # B-034, not dated. NARA, 84ff, 104; Obkdo. Armeegruppe G: "Kriegstagebuch Nr. 2 (Führungsabteilung)" 1.7.–30.9.1944; Bennett, 159.
72. Truscott, *Command Missions*, 414ff.
73. Ibid., 407; G-3 journal, VI Corps. Brig. Gen. Frederic Butler, "Butler Task Force," *Armored Cavalry Journal*, published in two parts (January–February 1948, March–April 1948): 13.
74. AAR, 753d Tank Battalion; Samsel.
75. AAR, 753d Tank Battalion.
76. Butler, "Butler Task Force," 36.
77. AAR, 753d Tank Battalion; Butler, "Butler Task Force," 36; Combined G2 and G3 journal, Task Force Butler.
78. Field Message #3, Headquarters Task Force Butler, 22 August 1944.
79. Clarke and Smith, 153.
80. AAR, 753d Tank Battalion. Butler, 37.
81. Schramm, "OKW War Diary (1 Apr–18 Dec 1944)," 107.
82. F. W. von Mellenthin, *Panzer Battles* (New York: Ballantine Books, 1971), 382.
83. AAR, 191st Tank Battalion.
84. *Southern France*, 13 ff; Charles Whiting, *America's Forgotten Army: The True Story of the U.S. Seventh Army in WWII and an Unknown Battle that Changed History* (New York: St. Martin's Paperbacks, 1999), 49 ff.
85. AAR, 756th Tank Battalion.
86. Ibid.
87. Ibid.
88. Ibid.
89. *Southern France*, 28.
90. AARs and S-3 journal, 753d Tank Battalion.
91. "Summary of Lessons Learned in Combat," Headquarters 1st Armored Group, 6 November 1944.
92. AAR, 753d Tank Battalion.
93. AAR, 756th Tank Battalion.

CHAPTER 10: HITTING THE WEST WALL

1. Allen, *Patton's Third Army*, 115–20.
2. MacDonald, *Siegfried Line Campaign*, 35.
3. AAR, October 1944, 737th Tank Battalion.
4. MacDonald, *Siegfried Line Campaign*, 106.

5. Whiting, *America's Forgotten Army*, 100.
6. Wilmot, *Struggle for Europe*, 478–79; MacDonald, *Siegfried Line Campaign*, 31ff.
7. MacDonald, *Siegfried Line Campaign*, 34–35.
8. Campbell, "Tanks with Infantry," 50.
9. MacDonald, *Siegfried Line Campaign*, 37ff.
10. AAR, 746th Tank Battalion.
11. MacDonald, *Siegfried Line Campaign*, 48.
12. AAR, 747th Tank Battalion.
13. Interview with Al Heintzleman, 8 December 2001. Letter from Thornton's nephew, Mr. Paul McDaniel, 6 June 2001; interview with Paul McDaniel, 22 December 2001.
14. MacDonald, *Siegfried Line Campaign*, 55ff.
15. *Armored Special Equipment*, 26-27.
16. Chamberlain and Ellis, *Churchill and Sherman Specials*.
17. Jensen, *Strike Swiftly*, 225.
18. S-3 journal, 3d Armored Group.
19. "The Flame Thrower in the Pacific: Marianas to Okinawa."
20. S-3 journal, 3d Armored Group.
21. AAR, 70th Tank Battalion.
22. Jensen, *Strike Swiftly*, 226.
23. Wilkes, *747th Tank Battalion*, 44, 58.
24. *Armored Special Equipment*, 28.
25. *Rhineland*, the U.S. Army Campaigns of World War II Series (Washington, D.C.: Center of Military History, n.d.), online reprint of CMH Pub 72-25, www.army.mil/cmh-pg/brochures/rhineland/rhineland.htm, 13.
26. MacDonald, *Siegfried Line Campaign*, 231ff.
27. Ibid., 260ff; AAR, 743d Tank Battalion.
28. MacDonald, *Siegfried Line Campaign*, 306.
29. AAR, 743d Tank Battalion.
30. "Clearing Area South of the Rail Road Tracks," Combat Interviews, 1st Infantry Division, NARA.
31. Ibid.
32. Ibid.; MacDonald, *Siegfried Line Campaign*, 310; Campbell, "Tanks with Infantry," 50–51.
33. "Clearing Area South of the Rail Road Tracks," Combat Interviews, 1st Infantry Division, NARA.
34. Desmond Hawkins, ed., *War Report, D-day to VE-day* (London: British Broadcasting Corporation, 1985), 212–13.
35. "Clearing Area South of the Rail Road Tracks," Combat Interviews, 1st Infantry Division, National Archives; *Gefechtsbericht des I.SS-Btl. (Kampfgruppe Rink) für die Zeit vom 9.–22.10.44, Ia KTB, LXXXI Armee Korps*, National Archives; *Rhineland*, 15.
26. *Rhineland*, 17.
37. AAR, 746th Tank Battalion.
38. *Soixante-Dix: A History of the 70th Tank Battalion*, 11. *Soixante-Dix* is an informal battalion history contained in the 70th's official records.
39. Omar N. Bradley and Clay Blair, *A General's Life* (New York: Simon and Schuster, 1983), 343.
40. AAR, 746th Tank Battalion.

41. Peter Chamberlain and Chris Ellis, *Pictorial History of Tanks of the World, 1915–45* (Harrisburg, PA: Stackpole Books, 1972), 182.
42. AARs or S-3 Journals of units cited and of 3d Armored Group.
43. *Armored Special Equipment*, 5–8.
44. AAR, 12th Army Group Armored Section.
45. AARs and S-3 Journal, 3d Armored Group.
46. AARs, 709th and 743d Tank battalions.
47. *Organization, Equipment, and Tactical Employment of Separate Tank Battalions*, 6.
48. Unit History, December 1944, 781st Tank Battalion.
49. Wilkes, *747th Tank Battalion*, 44; Undated memorandum, "Method of Operation: 737th Tank Battalion," 5.
50. AAR, 707th Tank Battalion; S-3 journal, 3d Armored Group; "Vossenack-Kommerscheidt-Schmidt (2-8 November 1944) Action of the 28th Division," interview with S/Sgt. Eugene Holden, Combat Interviews, 28th Infantry Division, NARA; Interview with Sgt. Tony Kudiak, Combat Interviews, 28th Infantry Division, NARA; Raymond Fleig, telephone interview with author, February 2008; Fleig, *707th Tank Battalion in World War II*, 80ff; MacDonald, *Siegfried Line Campaign*, 341ff; Edward G. Miller and David T. Zabecki, "Battle of Hürtgen Forest: Fight for Schmidt and Kommerscheidt," Historynet.com, www.historynet.com/wars_conflicts/world_war_2/3033146 .html?page=1&c=y, accessed February 2008.
51. AAR, 712th Tank Battalion.
52. Hugh M. Cole, *The Lorraine Campaign: United States Army in World War II, The European Theater of Operations* (Washington, D.C.: Historical Division, Department of the Army, 1950), 264–65.
53. Ibid., 266.
54. *Armored Special Equipment*, 10.
55. Cole, *Lorraine Campaign*, 275.
56. Battalion History, 737th Tank Battalion; Allen, *Patton's Third Army*, 122.
57. Cole, *Lorraine Campaign*, 278; Elson, *Tanks for the Memories*, 82ff.
58. Battalion History, 737th Tank Battalion; Allen, *Patton's Third Army*, 122.
59. Allen, *Patton's Third Army*, 125.
60. Ibid., 128ff; Wilmot, *Struggle for Europe*, 565–66.
61. AAR, 737th Tank Battalion.
62. S-3 Journal, 11 November 1944, 737th Tank Battalion.
63. Battalion History, 737th Tank Battalion.
64. Ulysses Lee Wilson, *U.S. Army in World War II: The Employment of Negro Troops* (Washington, D.C.: Office of the Chief of Military History, United States Army, 1966).
65. "Lorraine Campaign," interview with Lt. Edmund T. Tierney, 101st Infantry Regiment, 26th Infantry Division, NARA; Trezzvant W. Anderson, *Come Out Fighting: The Epic Tale of the 761st Tank Battalion, 1942–1945* (Salzburg, Austria: Salzburger Druckerei und Verlag, 1945), 31; David J. Williams, *Hit Hard* (New York: Bantam Books, 1983), 190–91; Gina DiNicola, "Come Out Fighting," *Military Officer* (February 2006), reprinted at the 761st Tank Battalion website, www.761st.com/index .php?page=DiNicolo, accessed January 2008.
66. Cole, *Lorraine Campaign*, 421.
67. Ibid., 380 ff.

68. Ibid.; "Assault of Metz: 5th Infantry Division Operations from the South, 9 to 20 November 1944," interview with Lt. Col. Randolph Dickens, G-3, and Maj. H. A. McGuire, G-2, Combat Interviews, 5th Infantry Division, NARA; "Assault of Metz: 2d Regimental Combat Team, November 9–21, 1944," interview with officers of the 2d Infantry Regiment and 735th Tank Battalion, Combat Interviews, 5th Infantry Division, NARA; "11th Regimental Combat Team: Assault of Metz, 9–24 November 1944," interview with officers of the 11th Infantry Regiment, Combat Interviews, 5th Infantry Division, NARA; "Metz Operation: 735th Tank Battalion," interview with Lt. Col. Bock and other officers of the 735th Tank Battalion, Combat Interviews, 5th Infantry Division, NARA.
69. Cole, *Lorraine Campaign*, 447–48.
70. AAR, 735th Tank Battalion.
71. *Rhineland*.
72. Wilmot, *Struggle for Europe*, 569; Griess, ed., *Second World War*, 230.
73. AARs, 702d and 743d Tank Battalions; *Armored Special Equipment*, 41.
74. Steven J. Zaloga, *The Sherman Tank in U.S. and Allied Service* (London: Osprey Publishing, 1982), 17.
75. AAR, February 1945, 737th Tank Battalion; AAR, January 1945, 702d Tank Battalion.
76. AAR, February 1945, and S-3 journal, March 1945, 737th Tank Battalion.

CHAPTER 11: HITLER'S LAST GAMBLE

1. Wilmot, *Struggle for Europe*, 577.
2. Ibid., 576.
3. Gerald Astor, *A Blood-Dimmed Tide: The Battle of the Bulge by the Men Who Fought It* (New York: Dell, 1992), v.
4. AAR, S-3 journal, 771st Tank Battalion, unless otherwise noted.
5. Waffen-SS Maj. Gen. Hugo Krass, "The 12th SS Panzer Division 'Hitler Jugend' in the Ardennes Offensive," MS # B-522, 1 May 1947, National Archives; Maj. Gen. Viebig, "Operations of the 277th Volksgrenadier-Division in November and December 1944: During the Ardennes Offensive," MS # B-273, 10 November 1946, National Archives.
6. Waffen-SS Col. Rudolf Lehmann, "The I SS Panzer Corps during the Ardennes Offensive," MS # B-779, not dated, National Archives. Viebig, "Operations of the 277th Volksgrenadier-Division."
7. AAR, 741st Tank Battalion. Heintzleman, *We'll Never Go Over-Seas*, 61–63.
8. Journal and AAR, 741st Tank Battalion. "The German Breakthrough—V Corps Sector," interview with Maj. Gen. Walter M. Robertson, Combat Interviews, 2d Infantry Division, NARA (hereafter cited as Robertson interviews); "The German Breakthrough (V Corps Sector)," interview with Col. Jay B. Lovless, CO, 23d Infantry, Combat Interviews, 2d Infantry Division, NARA; "The German Breakthrough—V Corps Sector," interview with Maj. William A. Smith, executive officer, 2d Battalion, 23d Infantry, Combat Interviews, 2d Infantry Division, NARA; "The German Breakthrough (V Corps Sector)," interview with Lt. Col. Tom Morris, executive officer, 38th Infantry Regiment, Combat Interviews, 2d Infantry Division, NARA (hereafter cited as Morris interview).
9. Lehmann, "The I SS Panzer Corps during the Ardennes Offensive."

10. "The German Breakthrough (V Corps Sector)," interview with Maj. Vern L. Joseph, executive officer, 3d Battalion, 23d Infantry Regiment, Combat Interviews, 2d Infantry Division, NARA (hereafter cited as Joseph interview); Charles B. MacDonald, *The Battle of the Bulge* (London: Guild Publishing, 1984), 375ff; Journal, 741st Tank Battalion.

11. Morris interview; Joseph interview.

12. Journal, 38th Infantry Regiment; "The German Breakthrough (V Corps Sector)," interviews with Capt. Fred L. Rumsey, Maj. Martin B. Coopersmith, and Sgt. Grover C. Farrell, 1st Battalion, 38th Infantry Regiment, Combat Interviews, 2d Infantry Division, NARA.

13. Wiliam C. C. Cavanagh, *The Battle East of Elsenborn & the Twin Villages* (Barnsley, UK: Pen & Sword Books, 2004), 127.

14. Heintzleman, *We'll Never Go Over-Seas*, 63. Hubert Meyer, *The 12th SS: The History of the Hitler Youth Panzer Division*, vol. 2 (Mechanicsburg, PA: Stackpole Books, 2005), 259–60.

15. "The German Breakthrough (V Corps Sector)," interview with Capt. Ralph H. Stallworth, Combat Interviews, 2d Infantry Division, NARA; AAR, 741st Tank Battalion; Heintzleman, *We'll Never Go Over-Seas*, 61, 67–68; Lehmann, "The I SS Panzer Corps during the Ardennes Offensive"; Cavanagh, *Battle East of Elsenborn & the Twin Villages*, 127.

16. AAR and journal, 741st Tank Battalion. Journal, 38th Infantry Regiment; "The German Breakthrough (V Corps Sector)," interviews with Capt. Fred L. Rumsey, Maj. Martin B. Coopersmith, and Sgt. Grover C. Farrell, 1st Battalion, 38th Infantry Regiment, Combat Interviews, 2d Infantry Division, NARA; "The German Breakthrough (V Corps Sector)," interviews with Lt. Col. Olinto Barsanti and Capt. John L. Murphy, 3d Battalion, 38th Infantry Regiment, Combat Interviews, 2d Infantry Division, NARA; Heintzleman, *We'll Never Go Over-Seas*, 67–68.

17. Heintzleman, *We'll Never Go Over-Seas*, 64.

18. "The German Breakthrough (V Corps Sector)," interviews with Maj. William F. Hancock, 1st Battalion executive officer, and S/Sgt. Norman Bernstein, 9th Infantry Regiment, Combat Interviews, 2d Infantry Division, NARA.

19. Heintzleman, *We'll Never Go Over-Seas*, 64–65; Journal, 38th Infantry Regiment; Morris interview. Lehmann, "The I SS Panzer Corps during the Ardennes Offensive."

20. Map study, Combat Interviews, 2d Infantry Division, NARA.

21. Battle casualty reports, 741st Tank Battalion.

22. Robertson interviews.

23. AAR, 707th Tank Battalion.

24. Fleig, *707th Tank Battalion in World War II*, 137.

25. Griess, ed., *Second World War*, 379.

26. "The German Breakthrough: Operations of the 28th Division, 16 December to 31 December 1944," Combat Interviews, 28th Infantry Division, NARA; Journal, 109th Infantry Regiment; "Notes taken from the S-2 unit report [112th Infantry Regiment], made available to me Jan 20 1945, having been recently written," Combat Interviews, 2d Infantry Division, NARA; John C. McManus, *Alamo in the Ardennes* (Hoboken, NJ: John Wiley & Sons, 2007), 48, 63.

27. Fleig, *707th Tank Battalion in World War II*, 137.

28. AAR, 707th Tank Battalion; Fleig telephone interview with author, February 2008; Fleig, *707th Tank Battalion in World War II*, 140ff; McManus, *Alamo in the Ardennes*, 92.
29. Fleig telephone interview with author, February 2008.
30. Griess, ed., *Second World War*, 379.
31. *Soixante-Dix*; AAR, 70th Tank Battalion.
32. The following account is taken from the AAR, 743d Tank Battalion, unless otherwise noted.
33. "The German Offensive of 16 December: The Defeat of the 1st SS Panzer Division Adolf Hitler," Combat Interviews, 30th Infantry Division, NARA; Robinson, *Move Out, Verify*, 126–27.
34. AAR, 743d Tank Battalion.
35. Ibid.
36. "The German Offensive of 16 December: The Defeat of the 1st SS Panzer Division Adolf Hitler."
37. Unless otherwise noted, the following account is taken from Rubel, *Daredevil Tankers*, and Paul L. Pearson, *Into the Breach: The Life and Times of the 740th Tank Battalion in World War II* (Cyberworld: Trafford Publishing, 2007), 51ff.
38. Interview with Harold Bradley, 29 December 2001 (hereafter cited as Bradley interview).
39. Ibid.
40. Ibid.
41. "The German Offensive of 16 December: The Defeat of the 1st SS Panzer Division Adolf Hitler." Rubel, 67.
42. AAR, 745th Tank Battalion. Wilmot, 594.
43. AAR, 750th Tank Battalion.
44. Bradley interview.
45. Rubel, *Daredevil Tankers*, 72–73
46. Allen, *Patton's Third Army*, 174–79.
47. Wilmot, *Struggle for Europe*, 599.
48. The following account is drawn from the AAR of the 735th Tank Battalion.
49. Lt. Gen. George S. Patton Jr., War as I Knew It (New York: Bantam Books, 1980), 187.
50. AAR, 735th Tank Battalion.
51. "Meeting Engagement CT-104," Memorandum, Headquarters 104th Infantry Regiment, 18 February 1945, Combat Interviews, 26th Infantry Division, NARA.
52. History, 737th Tank Battalion.
53. "Excerpts from the Diary of Maj. Gen. S. Leroy Irwin, Commanding General, 5th Infantry Division, 20–28 December 1944," Combat Interviews, 5th Infantry Division, NARA.
54. Griess, ed., *Second World War*, 384.
55. AAR, 743d Tank Battalion.
56. Charles B. MacDonald, *The Last Offensive: United States Army In World War II, The European Theater of Operations* (Washington, D.C.: Office of the Chief of Military History, United States Army, 1973), 1; Griess, ed., *Second World War*, 385.
57. MacDonald, *Last Offensive*, 27.
58. AAR, 712th Tank Battalion.
59. AAR, January 1945, 750th Tank Battalion.

60. Rubel, *Daredevil Tankers*, 92–93.
61. AARs, 741st Tank Battalion.
62. AARs, 743d Tank Battalion.
63. AARs, 749th Tank Battalion.
64. AAR, Company A, 753d Tank Battalion.
65. AAR, 743d Tank Battalion.
66. AAR, 750th Tank Battalion.
67. AAR, 741st Tank Battalion.
68. Rubel, *Daredevil Tankers*, 101.
69. MacDonald, *Last Offensive*, 43.
70. AAR, January 1945, 70th Tank Battalion.
71. MacDonald, *Last Offensive*, 46; AAR, 743d Tank Battalion.
72. MacDonald, *Last Offensive*, 42ff.

CHAPTER 12: THE REICH OVER-RUN

1. *Rhineland*, 28–33.
2. Battle casualty report, 741st Tank Battalion; AAR, 743d Tank Battalion.
3. John Walker, "The 750th Tank Battalion," www.104infdiv.org/750TANK.HTM, accessed March 2007; History, 750th Tank Battalion.
4. AAR, 709th Tank Battalion, Annex 3.
5. AAR, March 1945, Company C, 753d Tank Battalion.
6. AAR, 12th Army Group Armored Section.
7. Allen, *Patton's Third Army*, 263; Battalion history, 737th Tank Battalion.
8. Liddell Hart, *History of the Second World War*, 678.
9. Ibid., 678-79.
10. Robinson, *Move Out, Verify*, 156–57.
11. Whiting, *America's Forgotten Army*, 181ff; AAR, 756th Tank Battalion.
12. AAR, 756th Tank Battalion; *Armored Special Equipment*, 19–20.
13. *Armored Special Equipment*, 23.
14. Ibid., 38.
15. Wilmot, *Struggle for Europe*, 684; Belton Y. Cooper, *Death Traps: The Survival of an American Armored Division in World War II* (Novato, CA: Presidio Press, 2000), 247ff.
16. MacDonald, *Last Offensive*, 364.
17. Rubel, *Daredevil Tankers*, 177.
18. Ibid., 180–81.
19. Ibid., 183.
20. Ibid., 172ff. Griess, ed., *Second World War*, 407.
21. Rubel, *Daredevil Tankers*, 203.
22. Cornelius Ryan, *The Last Battle* (New York: Simon and Schuster, 1966), 280.
23. AAR, 737th Tank Battalion.
24. Griess, ed., *Second World War*, 406-7
25. Ryan, *Last Battle*, 285 ff; Macdonald, *Last Offensive*, 387; AAR, 736th Tank Battalion; AAR, 709th Tank Battalion.
26. AAR, April 1945, 702d Tank Battalion.
27. *Soixante-Dix*.
28. AAR, 741st Tank Battalion; "Leipzig Environs," interview with Maj. James H. King and Capt. Henry S. Hopkins, Combat Interviews, 2d Infantry Division, NARA.

29. History, 781st Tank Battalion; *Up from Marseille: 781st Tank Battalion* (Camp Campbell, KY: The Battalion, 1945), 22; Whiting, *America's Forgotten Army*, 193ff.
30. AAR, 756th Tank Battalion; Whiting, *America's Forgotten Army*, 197ff.
31. AAR, 760th Tank Battalion; AAR, 751st Tank Battalion.
32. AAR, 757th Tank Battalion; History, 752d Tank Battalion.
33. History and training memos, 752d Tank Battalion.
34. History, 755th Tank Battalion.
35. History, 752d Tank Battalion.
36. Ibid.
37. AAR, 755th Tank Battalion.
38. Clement, et al, 22–24. AAR, 804th Tank Destroyer Battalion.
39. AAR, 751st Tank Battalion. AAR, 701st Tank Destroyer Battalion.
40. History, 752d Tank Battalion.
41. Kesselring and Westphal.
42. Griess, ed., *Second World War*, 406–7
43. Ibid., 408.
44. *Up from Marseilles*, 25.
45. History, 752d Tank Battalion.
46. Redle letter.
47. Fazendin, *The 756th Tank Battalion in the Battle of Cassino*, xxx.

CHAPTER 13: JUNGLE HEAT

1. *New Guinea*, the U.S. Army Campaigns of World War II Series (Washington, D.C.: Center of Military History, n.d., online reprint of CMH Pub 72-9, www.army.mil/cmh-pg/brochures/new-guinea/ng.htm, accessed February 2008), 1–9.
2. M. Hamlin Cannon, *Leyte: The Return to the Philippines: The United States Army in World War II, The War in the Pacific* (Washington, DC: U.S. Army Center of Military History, 1993), 3.
3. "The Battle of Lone Tree Hill," manuscript, records of the 20th Infantry Regiment; AAR, 6th Cavalry Reconnaissance Troop; Mauer, et al, *Tank Tracks*, 5–10. Martin, *History of Company "C"*; Hallanan, "The Go-Anywhere Tank Company," 45; Robert Ross Smith, *The Approach to the Philippines: The United States Army in World War II, The War in the Pacific* (Washington, DC: Office of the Chief of Military History, Department of the Army, 1996), 252ff.
4. "Requirements of Tank Design and Operation in Relation to Effectiveness of Armored Personnel," Pacific Warfare Board Report No. 60, 9 September 1945, NARA, RG 407, Special File, 4-7.60/45, box 24464.
5. Mauer, et al, *Tank Tracks*, 5–10; Martin, *History of Company "C"*.
6. History, 706th Tank Battalion.
7. Smith, *The Approach to the Philippines*, 492.
8. AAR, Company D, 776th Amphibian Tank Battalion. AAR, 776th Amphibian Tank Battalion. History, 726th Amphibian Tractor Battalion. Capt. Jerry V. Keaveny, "Operations of Company A, 322d Infantry (81st Infantry Division) in the Cleanup Phase of the Capture of the Island of Angaur, 11–22 October 1944 (Western Pacific Campaign) (Personal Experience of a Company Commander)," submitted for the Advanced Infantry Officers Course, 1949–1950, the Infantry School, Fort Benning, Georgia.
9. AAR, 710th Tank Battalion.

10. Edward C. Luzinas, *Tanker: Boys, Men, and Cowards* (London: Athena Press, 2004), 71–79.
11. Lt. Col. W. M. Rodgers, "Armor in Angaur-Peleliu Campaign," The Armored School, Fort Knox, 1950.
12. History, 710th Tank Battalion. Luzinas, *Tanker*, 89–104.
13. History, 726th Amphibian Tractor Battalion.
14. "The Flame Thrower in the Pacific: Marianas to Okinawa."

CHAPTER 14: THE PHILIPPINES: BACK TO WHERE IT BEGAN

1. Cannon, *Leyte*, 1–4, 22–33; "Seizure of Leyte—Report of the Participation of Task Force Seventy-Nine," memorandum FE25/A16-3(3) from Commander, Task Force 79, to Commander, Seventh Fleet, 18 November 1944.
2. "Seizure of Leyte—Report of the Participation of Task Force Seventy-Nine," memorandum FE25/A16-3(3) from Commander, Task Force 79, to Commander, Seventh Fleet, 18 November 1944.
3. Ibid.
4. AAR, 776th Amphibian Tank Battalion.
5. AAR, 776th Amphibian Tank Battalion; S-3 journal, 536th Amphibian Tractor Battalion; Maj. John Collier, "Amphibians in Leyte Operations: Amtanks," *The Cavalry Journal* (May–June 1945), 38; "The Flame Thrower in the Pacific: Marianas to Okinawa." Cannon, *Leyte*, 77.
6. Journal, 767th Tank Battalion; "The Flame Thrower in the Pacific: Marianas to Okinawa." Cannon, *Leyte*, 77.
7. Journal and AAR, 780th Amphibian Tank Battalion; AAR, 788th Amphibian Tractor Battalion.
8. AAR, 763d Tank Battalion; AAR, 96th Infantry Division.
9. Journal and AAR, 780th Amphibian Tank Battalion.
10. AAR, 763d Tank Battalion; AAR, 96th Infantry Division.
11. AAR, 24th Infantry Division; Cannon, *Leyte* 67.
12. Hallanan, "The Go-Anywhere Tank Company," 46.
13. AAR, 727th Amphibian Tractor Battalion.
14. AAR, 24th Infantry Division.
15. Lt. Merritt Corbin, WW II Survey 8888, Military History Institute, Carlisle, Pennsylvania.
16. AAR, 727th Amphibian Tractor Battalion.
17. G-3 daily operations report, 1st Cavalry Division. AAR, 7th Cavalry Regiment; History, 44th Tank Battalion.
18. *Leyte*, the U.S. Army Campaigns of World War II Series (Washington, D.C.: Center of Military History, n.d., online reprint of CMH Pub 72-27, www.army.mil/cmh-pg/brochures/leyte/leyte.htm, accessed July 2006), 20–21.
19. Collier, "Amphibians in Leyte Operations," 38–39; AAR, 727th Amphibian Tractor Battalion.
20. AAR, 776th Amphibian Tank Battalion; Lt. Charles Shock, "Amphibians in Leyte Operations: Amtracs," *The Cavalry Journal* (May–June 1945): 42.
21. AAR, 776th Amphibian Tank Battalion; AAR, 536th Amphibian Tractor Battalion.
22. "Lessons Learned in the Leyte Campaign," 16 May 1945, General Staff G-2 Section Intelligence Reports, Numerical File, 1943–46, folder 204, NARA; AAR, 77th

Infantry Division. AAR, 776th Amphibian Tank Battalion; History, 706th Tank Battalion; AAR, 536th Amphibian Tractor Battalion.

23. AAR, 776th Amphibian Tank Battalion; History, 706th Tank Battalion. Collier, "Amphibians in Leyte Operations, 40; Cannon, *Leyte*, 361.

24. History, 706th Tank Battalion.

25. Robert Ross Smith, *Triumph in the Philippines: The United States Army in World War II, The War in the Pacific* (Washington, DC: Office of the Chief of Military History, Department of the Army, 1963), 18–19.

26. *Luzon*, the U.S. Army Campaigns of World War II Series (Washington, D.C.: Center of Military History, n.d., online reprint of CMH Pub 72-28, www.army.mil/cmh-pg/brochures/luzon/72-28.htm, accessed July 2006).

27. Ibid.; "World War II."

28. AAR, 6th Infantry Divisions.

29. History, 44th Tank Battalion; Martin, *History of Company "C"*.

30. *Luzon*, 9.

31. Smith, *Triumph in the Philippines*, 105.

32. History, 716th Tank Battalion; Smith, *Triumph in the Philippines*, 108–9.

33. History, 716th Tank Battalion; AAR, 6th Infantry Divisions; Smith, *Triumph in the Philippines*, 110–11.

34. AAR, 727th Amphibian Tractor Battalion.

35. Smith, *Triumph in the Philippines*, 142; *Luzon*, 9.

36. Peter R. Wygle, "Santo Thomas Raid," 1st Cavalry Division Association, www.1cda.org/santo_Thomas_raid.htm, accessed March 2007.

37. *Luzon*, 11; Wygle, "Santo Thomas Raid."

38. Wygle, "Santo Thomas Raid"; History, 44th Tank Battalion; Smith, *Triumph in the Philippines*, 220. AAR, 1st Cavalry Division.

39. History, 44th Tank Battalion; "The Flame Thrower in the Pacific: Marianas to Okinawa"; Smith, *Triumph in the Philippines*, 258–59.

40. "Tanks Go Places 'Tanks Can't Go' on Luzon," *Armored News* (18 June 1945): 4; AAR, 1st Cavalry Division; AAR, 37th Infantry Division; AAR, 129th Infantry Regiment.

41. AAR, 129th Infantry Regiment; AAR, 37th Infantry Division; AAR, 754th Tank Battalion.

42. History, 44th Tank Battalion.

43. "Requirements of the Tank Design and Operation in Relation to Effectiveness of Armored Personnel," Pacific Warfare Board Report No. 60, 9 September 1945, NARA, RG 407, Special File, 4-7.60/45, box 24464.

44. History, 44th Tank Battalion.

45. "Questionnaire for Armored (Tank) Units," Pacific Warfare Board Report No. 74, 26 October 1945, NARA, RG 407, Special File, 4-7.74/45, box 24464.

46. "Battle Experiences Against the Jap," USAFFE Board, 4 June 1945, General Staff G-2 Section Intelligence Reports, Numerical File, 1943–46, folder 425, NARA.

47. Ibid.

48. History, 672d Amphibian Tractor Battalion. Sam McGowan, "World War II: Liberating Los Banos Internment Camp," HistoryNet.com, www.historynet.com/magazines/world_war_2/3036481.html, accessed April 2007; Robert A. Wheeler, "The Angel's [sic] Came at Dawn," Drop Zone Virtual Museum, thedropzone.org/pacific/Finalraids/wheeler.htm, accessed April 2007. Maj. Robert E. Kennington, "The Oper-

ations of the Los Banos Force (1st Battalion, 511th Parachute Infantry, and 1st Battalion, 188th Glider Infantry), 11th Airborne Division, in the Liberation of Internees from the Los Banos Internment Camp, Luzon, Philippine Islands, 23 February 1945 (Luzon Campaign) (Personal Experience of a Battalion Operations Officer)," submitted for the Advanced Infantry Officers Course, 1947–1948, the Infantry School, Fort Benning, Georgia.

49. Smith, *Triumph in the Philippines*, 190.
50. "Battle Experiences Against the Jap," USAFFE Board, 4 June 1945, General Staff G-2 Section Intelligence Reports, Numerical File, 1943–46, folder 425, NARA.
51. AAR, 6th Infantry Divisions; Smith, *Triumph in the Philippines*, 192.
52. *The 6th Infantry Division in World War II: 1939–1945* (Washington, DC: Infantry Journal Press, 1947), 90.
53. History, 44th Tank Battalion.
54. Smith, *Triumph in the Philippines*, 198; History, 44th Tank Battalion.
55. Smith, *Triumph in the Philippines*, 199; Capt. Michael Kane Jr., "The Operations of the 20th Infantry 96th Inf. Div. at Munoz, Luzon, Philippine Islands 30 Jan. to 8 Feb. 1945," submitted for the Advanced Infantry Officers Course, 1946–1947, the Infantry School, Fort Benning, Georgia.
56. History, 44th Tank Battalion.
57. Martin, *History of Company "C"*.
58. History, 44th Tank Battalion.
59. Kane, "Operations of the 20th Infantry."
60. "Battle Experiences Against the Jap," USAFFE Board, 4 June 1945, General Staff G-2 Section Intelligence Reports, Numerical File, 1943–46, folder 425, NARA.
61. History, 44th Tank Battalion.
62. Ibid.
63. AAR, 775th Tank Battalion.
64. "Battle Report: Luzon Campaign, Twenty-Seventh United States Infantry," reproduced at the 27th Infantry Regiment "Wolfhounds" website, www.kolchak.org/History/WWII/Luzon.htm, accessed May 2007.
65. Lt. Col. Eben Swift, "Tanks over the Mountains," *Infantry Journal* (October 1945): 32–33.
66. "Battle Report: Luzon Campaign, Twenty-Seventh United States Infantry."
67. AAR, 775th Tank Battalion.
68. AAR, 754th Tank Battalion.

CHAPTER 15: OKINAWA: THE LAST BATTLEFIELD

1. Roy E. Appleman, et al., *Okinawa: The Last Battle: United States Army in World War II, The War in the Pacific* (Washington, D.C.: Center of Military History, United States Army, 1993), 1–4.
2. Appleman, et al., *Okinawa*, 27–32.
3. AAR, Provisional Armored Group (Amphibious).
4. AARs, Companies A–D, 708th Amphibian Tank Battalion.
5. Field Order 1, Operation Iceberg, files the 776th Amphibian Tank Battalion; AAR, 776th Amphibian Tank Battalion.
6. History, 711th Tank Battalion.
7. AAR, 536th Amphibian Tractor Battalion.
8. History and AAR, 780th Amphibian Tank Battalion.

9. AAR, 763d Tank Battalion.
10. History, 711th Tank Battalion.
11. Appleman, et al., *Okinawa*, 27–32.
12. AAR, 763d Tank Battalion.
13. History, 711th Tank Battalion.
14. Ibid.
15. "Information on the Use of Armor in the Ryukyus Operation," Headquarters Tenth Army, 3 September 1945, General Staff G-2 Section Intelligence Reports, Numerical File, 1943–46, folder 615, NARA.
16. "Future Organization and Employment of Main Armament Flamethrower Tanks"; "Questionnaire for Armored (Tank) Units"; AAR, 713th Tank Battalion, Armored Flamethrower.
17. "Information on the Use of Armor in the Ryukyus Operation," Headquarters Tenth Army, 3 September 1945, General Staff G-2 Section Intelligence Reports, Numerical File, 1943–46, folder 615, NARA.
18. "Drafts for History," manuscript, Tenth Army Records.
19. Ibid.
20. AAR, 193d Tank Battalion.
21. Ibid.
22. Appleman, et al., *Okinawa*, 203.
23. "Drafts for History," manuscript, Tenth Army Records.
24. Ibid.
25. AAR, 193d Tank Battalion.
26. Ibid.
27. Appleman, et al., *Okinawa*, 204.
28. History and AAR, 193d Tank Battalion.
29. AAR, 763d Tank Battalion.
30. "Drafts for History," manuscript, Tenth Army Records.
31. "Combat Information Received from Theater Representatives," 18 June 1945, General Staff G-2 Section Intelligence Reports, Numerical File, 1943–46, folder 413, NARA.
32. AAR, 713th Tank Battalion, Armored Flamethrower.
33. "Drafts for History," manuscript, Tenth Army Records.
34. "Special Equipment for Armored Vehicles," Pacific Warfare Board Report No. 26, 18 July 1945, NARA, RG 407, Special File, 4-7.26/45, box 24463.
35. History and AAR, 780th Amphibian Tank Battalion; AAR, 7828th Amphibian Tractor Battalion.
36. Appleman, et al., *Okinawa*, 149ff.
37. AAR, 708th Amphibian Tank Battalion.
38. Ibid.
39. History, 706th Tank Battalion.
40. "Drafts for History," manuscript, Tenth Army Records.
41. AAR, 193d Tank Battalion.
42. "Drafts for History," manuscript, Tenth Army Records.
43. Sawicki, *Tank Battalions*, 32.
44. AAR, 193d Tank Battalion.
45. History, 706th Tank Battalion.
46. AAR, 763d Tank Battalion.
47. History, 711th Tank Battalion.

48. AAR, 711th Tank Battalion.
49. AAR, 763d Tank Battalion.
50. AAR, 536th Amphibian Tractor Battalion.
51. Field orders, 780th Amphibian Tank Battalion.
52. *Ryukyus*, the U.S. Army Campaigns of World War II Series (Washington, D.C.: Center of Military History, n.d.), online reprint of CMH Pub 72-35, www.army.mil/cmh-pg/brochures/ryukyus/ryukyus.htm, accessed May 2007, 28–31.
53. "Drafts for History," manuscript, Tenth Army Records.
54. *Reports of General MacArthur* (Washington, DC: Center of Military History, 1993), online reprint of CMH Pub 13-3, www.army.mil/cmh/books/wwii/MacArthur%20Reports/MacArthur%20V1/index.htm, accessed April 2007, 211–23.
55. D. M. Giangreco, "Casualty Projections for the U.S. Invasions of Japan, 1945–1946: Planning and Policy Implications," *Journal of Military History* (July 1997): 521–82, online reprint at home.kc.rr.com/casualties, accessed April 2007.

CHAPTER 16: A MISSION ACCOMPLISHED AND LEGACY SECURED

1. *Organization, Equipment and Tactical Employment of Separate Tank Battalions*, 12.
2. Ibid.
3. Ibid.
4. Sawicki, *Tank Battalions*, 34; "Combat Divisions in the European Theater," U.S. Army, Europe, website, www.usarmygermany.com/Units/USAREUR_Divisions.htm#Pentomic, accessed April 2007.
5. *Organization, Equipment and Tactical Employment of Separate Tank Battalions*, 12; "Questionnaire for Armored (Tank) Units," Pacific Warfare Board Report No. 74, 26 October 1945, NARA, RG 407, Special File, 4-7.74/45, box 24464; "Questionnaire for Armored (Tank) Units."
6. Memorandum from Gen. Jacob L. Devers, Chief, Army Field Forces, to Maj. Gen. E. S. Hughes, Chief of Ordnance, not dated, NARA, RG 337, Army Field Forces Headquarters, Box 9, folder 470.8.
7. *Amphibious Tank and Tractor Battalions*, FM 17-34, June 1950.
8. *Tank Battalion*, FM 17-33, September 1949.
9. Ibid.
10. *Amphibious Tank and Tractor Battalions*, FM 17-34, June 1950.
11. "US Army Military History Research Collection, Senior Officers Debriefing Program: Conversation Between Lieutenant General Welborn Dolvin and Lieutenant Colonel William Gerald Willis," U.S. Army Heritage Collection OnLine, www.ahco.army.mil/site/index.jsp, accessed August 2007; Roy E. Appleman, *South to the Naktong, North to the Yalu: United States Army in the Korean War* (Washington, DC: U.S. Army Center of Military History, 1992, online edition at www.history.army.mil/books/korea/20-2-1/toc.htm, accessed January 2008), 259.
12. *History and Role of Armor*, 20.
13. "The Legacy of the Mechanized Cavalry," Combat Reform, www.combatreform.com/mechanizedcalvary5.htm, accessed August 2006; *Blood and Steel! The History, Customs, and Traditions of the 3d Armored Cavalry Regiment* (Fort Carson, CO: Fort Carson Office of Historical Programs, 2002), online edition, www.carson.army.mil/

UNITS/3RD%20ACR/main%20pages/3d%20ACR%20History.pdf, accessed August 2006.

14. Gen. Donn A. Starry, *Mounted Combat in Vietnam* (Washington, DC: Department of the Army, 1989), online edition, www.history.army.mil/books/Vietnam/mounted, accessed January 2008, 64.

15. Bing West and Owen West, "Lessons from Iraq, Part II," *Popular Mechanics* (August 2005), www.popularmechanics.com/technology/military_law/1675286.html, accessed January 2008.

GLOSSARY

AAR	After-action report
AP	Armor-piercing
Capt.	Captain
CDL	Canal Defense Light, code for spotlight tanks
CG	Commanding general
CO	Commanding officer
Cpl.	Corporal
DD	Duplex Drive amphibious Sherman tank
Gen.	General
HE	High-explosive
HEAT	High-explosive antitank
HVAP	Hyper-velocity armor-piercing
KO	Knock out, destroy
LCM	Landing craft, mechanized
LCT	Landing craft, tank
LCVP	Landing craft, vehicle and personnel
LD	Line of departure
LSD	Landing ship, dock
Lt.	Lieutenant
Lt. Col.	Lieutenant colonel
LVT	Landing vehicle, tracked
Maj.	Major
MLR	Main line of resistance
MX	Mine exploder
NCO	Noncommissioned officer
OP	Observation post
Pvt.	Private
PW or POW	Prisoner of war
S-2	Intelligence staff
S-3	Operations staff
Sgt.	Sergeant
S/Sgt.	Staff sergeant
SHAEF	Supreme Headquarters Allied Expeditionary Force
SNAFU	Situation normal, all [fouled] up
SP	Self-propelled
RCT	Regimental Combat Team
TAC	Tactical Air Command

BIBLIOGRAPHY

BOOKS AND BOOKLETS

191 Tank Bn. Germany: The Battalion, 1945.

The 6th Infantry Division in World War II: 1939–1945. Washington, DC: Infantry Journal Press, 1947.

Allen, Col. Robert S. *Patton's Third Army: Lucky Forward.* New York: Manor Books, 1965.

Ambrose, Stephen E. *Citizen Soldiers.* New York: Touchstone, 1997.

Anderson, Christopher J. *Hell on Wheels: The Men of the U.S. Armored Forces, 1918 to the Present.* London: Greenhill Books, 1999.

Anderson, Trezzvant W. *Come Out Fighting: The Epic Tale of the 761st Tank Battalion, 1942–1945.* Salzburg, Austria: Salzburger Druckerei und Verlag, 1945.

Anzio (CMH Pub 72-19). Washington, DC: U.S. Army Center of Military History, not dated.

Appleman, Roy E., et al. *Okinawa: The Last Battle: United States Army In World War II, The War in the Pacific.* Washington, D.C.: Center of Military History, United States Army, 1993.

The Armored Group. The General Board, United States Forces, European Theater, 14 May 1946.

Armored Special Equipment. The General Board, United States Forces, European Theater, 14 May 1945.

Astor, Gerald. *A Blood-Dimmed Tide: The Battle of the Bulge by the Men Who Fought It.* New York: Dell, 1992.

Atkinson, Rick. *An Army at Dawn.* New York: Henry Holt and Company, 2002.

———. *The Day of Battle.* New York: Henry Holt and Company, 2007.

Balkoski, Joseph. *Beyond the Beachhead: The 29th Infantry Division in Normandy.* Mechanicsburg, PA: Stackpole Books, 1999.

Blanchard, W. J. *Our Liberators: The Combat History of the 746th Tank Battalion during World War II.* Tucson, Arizona: Fenestra Books, 2003.

Blumenson, Martin. *Breakout and Pursuit: United States Army in World War II, The European Theater of Operations.* Washington, D.C.: Office of the Chief of Military History, Department of the Army, 1961.

———. *Salerno to Cassino: United States Army in World War II, The Mediterranean Theater of Operations.* Washington, DC: Center of Military History, 1993.

Bradley, Omar N., and Clay Blair. *A General's Life.* New York: Simon and Schuster, 1983.

Cavanagh, Wiliam C. C. *The Battle East of Elsenborn & the Twin Villages.* Barnsley, UK: Pen & Sword Books, 2004.

Chamberlain, Peter, and Chris Ellis. *Churchill and Sherman Specials.* Windsor, England: Profile Publications, n.d.

———. *Pictorial History of Tanks of the World 1915–45.* Harrisburg, PA: Stackpole Books, 1972.

Cannon, M. Hamlin. *Leyte: The Return to the Philippines: The United States Army in World War II, The War in the Pacific.* Washington, DC: U.S. Army Center of Military History, 1993.

Carver, Field Marshal Lord. *The Imperial War Museum Book of the War in Italy, 1943–1945.* London: Pan Books, 2002.

Cole, Hugh M. *The Lorraine Campaign: United States Army in World War II, The European Theater of Operations.* Washington, D.C.: Historical Division, Department of the Army, 1950.

Cooper, Belton Y. *Death Traps: The Survival of an American Armored Division in World War II.* Novato, CA: Presidio Press, 2000.

Dick, Robert C. *Cutthroats: The Adventures of a Sherman Tank Driver in the Pacific.* New York: Ballantine Books, 2006.

Elson, Aaron C. *Tanks for the Memories: An Oral History of the 712th Tank Battalion from World War II.* Hackensack, N.J.: Chi Chi Press, 1994.

Fazendin, Roger. *The 756th Tank Battalion in the Battle of Cassino, 1944.* Lincoln, NE: iUniverse, Inc., 1991.

Fleig, Lt. Col. Raymond. *707th Tank Battalion in World War II.* Self-published, not dated.

Folkestad, William. *The View from the Turret.* Shippensburg, PA: Burd Street Press, 2000.

From D + 1 to 105: The Story of the 2nd Infantry Division. Paris: Stars and Stripes, 1944.

Garland, Lt. Col. Albert N., et al. *Sicily and the Surrender of Italy: United States Army in World War II, The Mediterranean Theater of Operations.* Washington, DC: Center of Military History, 1993.

Gilbert, Oscar E. *Marine Tank Battles in the Pacific.* Conshohocken, PA: Combined, 2001.

Green, Michael. *M4 Sherman: Combat and Development History of the Sherman Tank and All Sherman Variants.* Osceola, WI: Motorbooks, 1993.

Greenfield, Kent Roberts, et al. *United States Army in World War II, The Army Ground Forces: The Organization of Ground Combat Troops.* Washington, D.C.: Historical Division, Department of the Army, 1947.

Griess, Thomas E., ed. *The Second World War: Europe and the Mediterranean.* West Point Military History Series. Wayne, NJ: Avery Publishing Group, Inc., 1984.

Hall, Chester. *History of the 70th Tank Battalion: June 5, 1940 . . . May 22, 1946.* Lousiville, KY: Southern Press, 1950.

Harmon, Maj. Gen. E. N., with Milton MacKaye and William Ross MacKaye. *Combat Commander, Autobiography of a Soldier.* Englewood Cliffs, New Jersey: Prentice-Hall, Inc., 1970.

Harrison, Gordon A. *Cross-Channel Attack: United States Army in World War II, The European Theater of Operations.* Washington, D.C.: Center of Military History, 2002.

Hassett, Edward C., ed. *701st Tank Battalion.* Nürnberg: Sebaldus-Verlag, 1945.

Hawkins, Desmond, ed. *War Report, D-day to VE-day.* London: British Broadcasting Corporation, 1985.

Hay, Jack. *Italian Campaigns as Witnessed Through the Eyes of a U.S. Tank Driver.* Newton, KS: Mennonite Press, 2006.

Heintzleman, Al. *We'll Never Go Over-Seas.* Self-published, 1982.

The Historical Board. *The Fighting Forty-Fifth: The Combat Report of an Infantry Division.* Baton Rouge, LA: Army & Navy Publishing Company, 1946.

History and Role of Armor, ST 17-1-2, US Armor School, April 1974.

Houston, Donald E. *Hell on Wheels: The 2d Armored Division*. Novato, CA: Presidio Press, 1977.

Howe, George F. *Northwest Africa: Seizing the Initiative in the West: United States Army in World War II, The Mediterranean Theater of Operations*. Washington, DC: Center of Military History, United States Army, 1993.

Howze, Hamilton. A Cavalryman's Story. Washington, DC: Smithsonian Institution Press, 1996.

Hughes, Dale Adams. *331 Days: The Story of the Men of the 709th Tank Battalion*. Tucson: Self-published, n.p., 1980.

Ingersoll, Ralph. *The Battle is the Payoff*. New York: Harcourt, Brace and Company, 1943.

Jensen, Marvin. *Strike Swiftly: The 70th Tank Battalion from North Africa to Normandy to Germany*. Novato, CA: Presidio Press, 1997.

Johnson, David E. *Fast Tanks and Heavy Bombers: Innovation in the U.S. Army, 1917–1945*. Ithaca, NY: Cornell University Press, 1998.

Liddell Hart, Sir B. H. *History of the Second World War*. New York: G. P. Putnam's Sons, 1970.

Linderman, Gerald F. *The World Within War*. Cambridge, MA: Harvard University Press, 1997.

Luzinas, Edward C. *Tanker: Boys, Men, and Cowards*. London: Athena Press, 2004.

MacDonald, Charles B. *The Battle of the Bulge*. London: Guild Publishing, 1984.

———. *The Last Offensive: United States Army In World War II, The European Theater of Operations*. Washington, D.C.: Office of the Chief of Military History, United States Army, 1973.

———. *The Siegfried Line Campaign: United States Army in World War II, The European Theater of Operations*. Washington, D.C.: Office of the Chief of Military History, Department of the Army, 1963.

Martin, S/Sgt. William, ed. *History of Company "C", 44th Tank Battalion, 1942–1945*. Tokyo: The Battalion, 1945.

Mauer, T/4 Verne, et al. *Tank Tracks: 44th Tank Battalion, Tennessee to Tokyo*. Japan: The Battalion, 1945.

McManus, John C. *Alamo in the Ardennes*. Hoboken, NJ: John Wiley & Sons, 2007.

Mellenthin, F. W. von. *Panzer Battles*. New York: Ballantine Books, 1971.

Meyer, Hubert. *The 12th SS: The History of the Hitler Youth Panzer Division*, vol. 2. Mechanicsburg, PA: Stackpole Books, 2005.

Miller, John. *Cartwheel: The Reduction of Rabaul: United States Army In World War II, The War in the Pacific*. Washington, D.C.: Office of the Chief of Military History, Department of the Army, 1959.

Mittelman, Capt. Joseph B. *Eight Stars to Victory: A History of the Veteran Ninth U.S. Infantry Division*. Washington, DC: The Ninth Infantry Division Association, 1948.

Moore, Col. Roy. *Chariots of Iron: The 735th Tank Battalion (M), World War II, Europe*. Lopez Island, WA: Island Graphics and Advertising, 1991.

Morton, Louis. *The Fall of the Philippines: United States Army In World War II, The War in the Pacific*. Washington, D.C.: Center of Military History, United States Army, 1953.

Northern France (CMH Pub 72-30). Washington, DC: U.S. Army Center of Military History, not dated.

Patton, Lt. Gen. George S. *War as I Knew It*. New York: Bantam Books, 1980.

Pearson, Paul L. *Into the Breach: The Life and Times of the 740th Tank Battalion in World War II*. Cyberworld: Trafford Publishing, 2007.

Reardon, Mark. *Victory at Mortain: Defeating Hitler's Panzer Counteroffensive*. Lawrence, KS: University Press, 2002.

Reynolds, Michael. *Steel Inferno: 1st SS Panzer Corps in Normandy*. New York: Dell, 1997.

Robinson, Wayne. *Move Out, Verify: The Combat Story of the 743d Tank Battalion*. Frankfurt am Main, Germany: The Battalion, 1945.

Rubel, Lt. Col. George. *Daredevil Tankers: The Story of the 740th Tank Battalion, United States Army*. Göttingen, Germany: The Battalion, 1945.

Ryan, Cornelius. *The Last Battle*. New York: Simon and Schuster, 1966.

Salecker, Gene Eric. *Rolling Thunder Against the Rising Sun: The Combat History of U.S. Army Tank Battalions in the Pacific in World War II*. Mechanicsburg, PA: Stackpole Books, 2008.

Sawicki, James A. *Tank Battalions of the U.S. Army*. Dumfries, VA: Wyvern Publications, 1983.

Sicily (CMH Pub 72-16). Washington, DC: Center of Military History, 1999.

Smith, Robert Ross. *The Approach to the Philippines: The United States Army in World War II, The War in the Pacific*. Washington, DC: Office of the Chief of Military History, Department of the Army, 1996.

———. *Triumph in the Philippines: The United States Army in World War II, The War in the Pacific*. Washington, DC: Office of the Chief of Military History, Department of the Army, 1963.

Stanton, Shelby. *World War II Order of Battle*. New York: Galahad Books, 1991.

Tank Gunnery. The General Board, United States Forces, European Theater, 14 May 1945.

Triplet, William S. *A Colonel in the Armored Divisions*. Columbia, MO: University of Missouri Press, 2001.

Truscott, Lt. Gen. Lucian K. *Command Missions*. New York: E. P. Dutton and Company, 1954.

Tunisia (CMH Pub 72-12). Washington, DC: Center of Military History, not dated.

Up from Marseille: 781st Tank Battalion. Camp Campbell, KY: The Battalion, 1945.

Whiting, Charles. *America's Forgotten Army: The True Story of the U.S. Seventh Army in WWII and an Unknown Battle that Changed History*. New York: St. Martin's, 1999.

Wilkes, Homer D. *747th Tank Battalion*. Scottsdale, AZ: self-published, 1977.

———. *APO 230*. Scottsdale, AZ: self-published, 1982.

Williams, David J. *Hit Hard*. New York: Bantam Books, 1983.

Wilmot, Chester. *The Struggle for Europe*. Ware, England: Wordsworth, 1997.

Wilson, Ulysses Lee. *U.S. Army In World War II: The Employment of Negro Troops*. Washington, D.C.: Office of the Chief of Military History, United States Army, 1966.

Zaloga, Steven J. *The Sherman Tank in U.S. and Allied Service*. London: Osprey Publishing, 1982.

———. *US Armored Units in the North African and Italian Campaigns, 1942–45*. New York: Osprey Publishing, 2006.

———. *US Tank and Tank Destroyer Battalions in the ETO, 1944–45*. Oxford, England: Osprey Publishing, 2005.

Zaloga, Steven, et al. *Amtracs*. Botley, England: Osprey Publishing, 1999.

Zdon, Al. *War Stories: Accounts of Minnesotans Who Defended Their Nation*. St. Paul, Minnesota: Stanton Publications: 2002.

ARTICLES AND INTERNET RESOURCES

"133rd Infantry History—World War II." 34th Infantry Division Association website, www.34infdiv.org/index.html, accessed July 2007.

"713th Flame Throwing Tank Battalion." The 11th Armored Division Association, www.11tharmoreddivision.com, accessed January 2004.

Anderson, Burton. "A History of the Salinas National Guard Company: 1895–1995." Monterey County Historical Society, www.mchsmuseum.com/guard.html, accessed February 2007.

Anderson, Rich. "The United States Army in World War II." Military History Online. www.militaryhistoryonline.com/wwii/usarmy, accessed February 2004.

Anders, Dr. Steven E. "POL on the Red Ball Express." Quartermaster Professional Bulletin, Spring 1989. Quartermaster Museum online, www.qmfound.com/pol_on_the _red_ball_express.htm, accessed February 2002.

"APM-2 / LSD-2 Belle Grove." NavSource Online: Amphibious Photo Archive, www.navsource.org/archives/10/12/1202.htm, accessed May 2007.

Appleman, Roy E. *South to the Naktong, North to the Yalu: United States Army in the Korean War*. Washington, DC: U.S. Army Center of Military History, 1992, online edition at www.history.army.mil/books/korea/20-2-1/toc.htm, accessed January 2008.

"Armor in Operation Neptune (Establishment of Normandy Beachhead)." Committee 10, Officers Advanced Course, The Armored School, 1949. Online edition posted at Axis History Forum, forum.axishistory.com/viewtopic.php?t=51896, accessed April 2007.

"Battle Report: Luzon Campaign, Twenty-Seventh United States Infantry." Reproduced at the 27th Infantry Regiment "Wolfhounds" website, www.kolchak.org/History/WWII/ Luzon.htm, accessed May 2007.

Butler, Brig. Gen. Frederic. "Butler Task Force," *Armored Cavalry Journal*, published in two parts, January–February 1948, 12–18, and March–April 1948, 30–38.

Campbell, Maj. William R. "Tanks With Infantry." *Armored Cavalry Journal* (September–October 1947): 49–51.

Collier, Maj. John. "Amphibians in Leyte Operations: Amtanks." *The Cavalry Journal* (May–June 1945): 38–40.

"Combat Divisions in the European Theater." U.S. Army, Europe, website, www.usarmygermany.com/Units/USAREUR_Divisions.htm#Pentomic, accessed April 2007.

DiNicola, Gina. "Come Out Fighting." *Military Officer* (February 2006), reprinted at the 761st Tank Battalion website, www.761st.com/index.php?page=DiNicolo, accessed January 2008.

Duncan, Lt. Col. William. "Tanks and Infantry in Night Attacks." *Armored Cavalry Journal* (January–February 1948): 56–61.

Dyer, Vice Adm. George Carroll. *The Amphibians Came to Conquer: The Story of Admiral Richmond Kelly Turner*. Online version, Hyperwar website, www.ibiblio.org/ hyperwar/USN/ACTC/index.html, accessed November 2007.

"The First Armored Amphibian Battalion in World War II." The First Armored Amphibian Battalion, www.marineamphibians.com, accessed January 2007.

"The Flame Thrower in the Pacific: Marianas to Okinawa." Center of Military History website, www.army.mil/cmh-pg/books/wwii/chemsincmbt/ch15.htm, accessed November 2007. This is a fragment of a publication not formally listed as being resident on the website.

Forsey, Jonathon. "For the Honour of France." Flames of War website, www.battlefront.co .nz/Article.asp?ArticleID=568, accessed May 2007.

"From the Volturno to the Winter Line: 6 October–15 November 1943." Washington, DC: Center of Military History, United States Army, 1990. (Online reprint of CMH Pub 100-8, itself a reprint of a 1945 American Forces in Action Series publication, www.army.mil/cmh/books/wwii/volturno/volturno-fm.htm#cont, accessed August 2007.)

Giangreco, D. M. "Casualty Projections for the U.S. Invasions of Japan, 1945–1946: Planning and Policy Implications." Journal of Military History, July 1997, 521–582. Online reprint at home.kc.rr.com/casualties, accessed April 2007.

Gugeler, Lt. Russell. "Army Amphibian Tractor and Tank Battalions in the Battle of Saipan: 15 June–9 July 1944," 20 January 1945. (Online version of document contained in file 8-5.3 BA, Historical Manuscripts Collection, U.S. Army Center of Military History, www.army.mil/cmh-pg/documents/wwii/amsai/amsai.htm, accessed February 2007.)

Hallanan, Col. George, Jr. "The Go-Anywhere Tank Company." *Army* (January 1991): 42–47.

Heathcott, David. "The 749th Tank Battalion: World War II Memories," personal.pitnet .net/heathde/749, accessed November 2007.

Heinl, Lt. Col. Robert and Lt. Col. John Crown. *The Marshalls: Increasing the Tempo, USMC Historical Monograph*. Historical Branch, G-3 Division, Headquarters, U.S. Marine Corps, 1954. (Online version at Hyperwar: A Hypertext History of the Second World War, www.ibiblio.org/hyperward, accessed February 2007.)

"The Historical Combat Effectiveness of Lighter-Weight Armored Forces: Final Report." The Dupuy Institute, 6 August 2001, www.dupuyinstitute.org/pdf/mwa-2lightarmor .pdf, accessed May 2007.

"History of USS Belle Grove (LSD-2)." www.USSBelleGrove.org website, www.ussbellegrove.org/shipshistory/ihistory.html, accessed May 2007.

"History: World War II Part II." Kwajalein Atoll, Republic of the Marshall Islands, website, www.angelfire.com/hi2/kwa/0his_ww2b.html, accessed February 2007.

Hoffman, Maj. Carl. *Saipan: The Beginning of the End, USMC Historical Monograph*. Historical Branch, G-3 Division, Headquarters, U.S. Marine Corps, 1950. (Online version at Hyperwar, www.ibiblio.org/hyperward, accessed February 2007.)

Holt, Robert, and Daniele Guglielmi. "The 752nd Tank Battalion in the Battle for Cecina," The 752nd Tank Battalion in World War II website, www.752ndtank.com/cecina.html, accessed October 2007.

Ingles, Maj. Gen. H. C., Chief Signal Officer. "Signal Equipment and the Armored Forces," *The Cavalry Journal* (May–June 1946).

"La 1ère DFL, 'noyau dur' des Forces françaises libres." France-Libre.net website, www.france-libre.net/forces_francaises_libres/1_1_2_3_1re_DFL_campagne_tunisie .htm, accessed May 2007.

Leyte. The U.S. Army Campaigns of World War II Series. Washington, D.C.: Center of Military History, n.d. (Online reprint of CMH Pub 72-27, www.army.mil/cmh-pg/ brochures/leyte/leyte.htm, accessed July 2006).

Luzon. The U.S. Army Campaigns of World War II Series. Washington, D.C.: Center of Military History, n.d. (Online reprint of CMH Pub 72-28, www.army.mil/cmh-pg/ brochures/luzon/72-28.htm, accessed July 2006).

Marshall, Lt. Col. S. L. A. "One Day on Kwajalein." *Infantry Journal* (August 1944): 14–25.

"The Marshall Islands Operations." Historical Division, U.S. Marine Corps, online version, www.au.af.mil/au/awc/awcgate/usmchist/island.txt, accessed February 2007.

McGowan, Sam. "World War II: Liberating Los Banos Internment Camp." HistoryNet.com, www.historynet.com/magazines/world_war_2/3036481.html, accessed April 2007.

Miller, Edward G., and David T. Zabecki. "Battle of Hürtgen Forest: Fight for Schmidt and Kommerscheidt." Historynet.com, www.historynet.com/wars_conflicts/world_war_2/3033146.html?page=1&c=y, accessed February 2008.

Miller, Sgt. Merle. "Surprise Party at Eniwetok." *Yank* (31 March 1944): 3–5.

New Guinea. The U.S. Army Campaigns of World War II Series. Washington, D.C.: Center of Military History, n.d. (Online reprint of CMH Pub 72-9, www.army.mil/cmh-pg/brochures/new-guinea/ng.htm, accessed February 2008.)

Omaha Beachhead (6 June–13 June 1944). American Forces in Action Series. Washington, D.C.: Center of Military History, 1984. (Online reprint of CMH Pub 100-1, www.army.mil/cmh-pg/books/wwii/100-11/100-11.HTM, accessed February 2002.)

"Operations of the Provisional Tank Group, United States Army Forces in the Far East—1941–1942." Bataan Was Hell! website, bataanwashell.blog-city.com, accessed February 2007.

Philippine Islands. The U.S. Army Campaigns of World War II Series. Washington, D.C.: Center of Military History, n.d. (Online reprint of CMH Pub 72-3, www.army.mil/cmh-pg/brochures/pi/PI.htm, accessed February 2007.)

Proviso East High School Bataan Commemorative Research Project. www.proviso.k12.il.us/Bataan%20Web/index.htm, accessed February 2007.

Reports of General MacArthur. Washington, DC: Center of Military History, 1993. (Online reprint of CMH Pub 13-3, www.army.mil/cmh/books/wwii/MacArthur%20Reports/MacArthur%20V1/index.htm, accessed April 2007.)

Rogers, Lt. Col. James. "Command Control of an Armored Amphibian Battalion." *The Cavalry Journal* (January–February 1945): 5–7.

———. "Amphibian Tank Battalion in Combat." *The Cavalry Journal* (March–April 1946): 26–36.

Rhineland. The U.S. Army Campaigns of World War II Series. Washington, D.C.: Center of Military History, n.d. (Online reprint of CMH Pub 72-25, www.army.mil/cmh-pg/brochures/rhineland/rhineland.htm, accessed February 2002.)

Rowan-Robinson, Maj. Gen. (ret.) H. "Lessons of a Blitzkrieg." *Infantry Journal* (May–June 1940): 210–22.

Ruppenthal, Maj. Roland. *American Forces in Action: Utah Beach to Cherbourg (6 June–27 June 1944).* Washington, DC: Center of Military History, United States Army, 1990, online edition at www.army.mil/cmh-pg/books/wwii/utah/utah.htm, accessed June 2006.

Ryukyus. The U.S. Army Campaigns of World War II Series. Washington, D.C.: Center of Military History, n.d. (Online reprint of CMH Pub 72-35, www.army.mil/cmh-pg/brochures/ryukyus/ryukyus.htm, accessed May 2007).

Semmes, Lt. Harry. "Amtanks at Saipan." *The Cavalry Journal* (May–June 1945): 30–31.

Shock, Lt. Charles. "Amphibians in Leyte Operations: Amtracs." *The Cavalry Journal* (May–June 1945): 41–45.

Southern France. The U.S. Army Campaigns of World War II Series. Washington, D.C.: Center of Military History, n.d. (Online reprint of CMH Pub 72-31, www.army.mil/cmh-pg/brochures/sfrance/sfrance.htm, accessed February 2002.)

Starry, General Donn A. *Mounted Combat in Vietnam.* Washington, DC: Department of the Army, 1989, online edition, www.history.army.mil/books/Vietnam/mounted, accessed January 2008.

Swift, Lt. Col. Eben. "Tanks Over the Mountains." *Infantry Journal* (October 1945): 32–34.

Tankers in Tunisia. Headquarters, Armored Replacement Training Center, 31 July 1943, online version at the Lone Sentry website, www.lonesentry.com, accessed July 2007.

"Tanks and Doughboys." *Infantry Journal* (July 1945): 8–10.

"Tanks Go Places 'Tanks Can't Go' on Luzon." *Armored News* (18 June 1945): 4.

Tincher, Maj. Robert. "Reconnaissance in Normandy—In Support of Airborne Troops." *The Cavalry Journal* (January–February 1945): 12–17.

Walker, John. "The 750th Tank Battalion," www.104infdiv.org/750TANK.HTM, accessed March 2007.

West, Bing, and Owen West. "Lessons from Iraq, Part II." *Popular Mechanics* online edition, August 2005, www.popularmechanics.com/technology/military_law/1675286.html, accessed January 2008.

Wheeler, Robert A. "The Angel's [*sic*] Came at Dawn." Drop Zone Virtual Museum, the-dropzone.org/pacific/Finalraids/wheeler.htm, accessed April 2007.

Whitehead, Alfred. "The Diary of a Soldier." The Second Infantry Division Photo Web Pages website, home.thirdage.com/Military/friends2idww2/Combat_Journal.html, accessed November 2007.

Wilson, Joseph E. Jr. "Black Panthers Go to Combat in World War II." The History Net on About.com, www.afroamhistory.about.com/library/prm/blblackpanthers1.htm, accessed February 2002.

Wolfert, Ira. "Sure Surprised Hell Out of the Germans!" *Tulsa Tribune* (24 July 1944).

Wygle, Peter R. "Santo Thomas Raid." 1st Cavalry Division Association, www.1cda.org/santo_Thomas_raid.htm, accessed March 2007.

UNPUBLISHED STUDIES

Adams, Maj. Richard. "The Operations of Company 'B,' 715th Amphibian Tractor Battalion During the Assault Landing on Saipan Island, 15 June 1944 (Marianas Campaign) (Personal Experience of Company Commander." Submitted for the Advanced Infantry Officers Course, 1949–1950, the Infantry School, Fort Benning, Georgia.

Bergengruen, Col. Hellmut, Ia of the Hermann Göring Panzer Division. "Kampf der Pz. Div. 'Hermann Goering' auf Sizilien vom 10.–14.7.1943." MS # C-087a, 31 December 1950. National Archives.

Bernstorff, Lt. Col. Douglas Graf. "Operations of the 26th Panzer Division in Italy: 7 September 1943–1 November 1944." MS # D-316, October 1947. National Archives.

Cameron, Robert Stewart. "Americanizing the Tank: U.S. Army Administration and Mechanized Development within the Army, 1917–1943," doctoral dissertation, Temple University, August 1944.

Cundiff, Maj. Ellsworth. "The Operations of the 3d Battalion, 179th Infantry (45th Infantry Division) 13–14 July 1943 South of Grammicele, Sicily (Personal Experience of a

Regimental S-2)." Submitted for the Advanced Infantry Officers Course, 1947–1948, the Infantry School, Fort Benning, Georgia.

Greiner, Helmuth, Minesterialrat Custodian of the War Diary in Hitler's Headquarters. "Greiner Diary Notes, 12 Aug 1942–12 Mar 1943 (English Copy)." MS # C-065a, not dated.

Kane, Capt. Michael Jr. "The Operations of the 20th Infantry (6th Inf. Div.) at Munoz, Luzon, Philippine Islands 30 Jan. to 8 Feb. 1945." Submitted for the Advanced Infantry Officers Course, 1946–1947, the Infantry School, Fort Benning, Georgia.

Keaveny, Capt. Jerry V. "Operations of Company A, 322d Infantry (81st Infantry Division) in the Cleanup Phase of the Capture of the Island of Angaur, 11–22 October 1944 (Western Pacific Campaign) (Personal Experience of a Company Commander)." Submitted for the Advanced Infantry Officers Course, 1949–1950, the Infantry School, Fort Benning, Georgia.

Kennington, Maj. Robert E. "The Operations of the Los Banos Force (1st Battalion, 511th Parachute Infantry, and 1st Battalion, 188th Glider Infantry), 11th Airborne Division, in the Liberation of Internees from the Los Banos Internment Camp, Luzon, Philippine Islands, 23 February 1945 (Luzon Campaign)(Personal Experience of a Battalion Operations Officer)." Submitted for the Advanced Infantry Officers Course, 1947–1948, the Infantry School, Fort Benning, Georgia.

Kesselring, Field Marshal Albert and Gen. of Cavalry Siegfried Westphal. "Questions Regarding the General Strategy During the Italian Campaign." MS # B-270, November 1950. National Archives.

Kidd, Capt. Charles H. "Operations of Company M, 116th Infantry (29th Inf. Div.), in the Landing on Omaha Beach, 6–13 June 1944 (Normandy Campaign)." Submitted for the Advanced Infantry Officers Course, 1946–1947, the Infantry School, Fort Benning, Georgia.

Kidd, Maj. Giles. "The Operations of the 37th Infantry Division in the Crossing of the Pasig River and Closing to the Walls of Intramuros, Manila, 7–9 February 1945 (Luzon Campaign)." Submitted for the Advanced Infantry Officers Course, 1949–1950, the Infantry School, Fort Benning, Georgia.

Krass, Waffen SS Maj. Gen. Hugo. "The 12th SS Panzer Division 'Hitler Jugend' in the Ardennes Offensive." MS # B-522, 1 May 1947. National Archives.

Lehmann, Waffen SS Col. Rudolf. "The I SS Panzer Corps During the Ardennes Offensive." MS # B-779, not dated. National Archives.

Morton, Matthew Darlington. "Men on 'Iron Ponies:' The Death and Rebirth of the Modern U.S. Cavalry," doctoral dissertation, Florida State University, 2004.

Ray, Maj. Lee M. "Operations of the 23d Infantry Regiment, 2d Infantry Division, in the attack on Hill 192, east of St. Lo, 11–12 July 1944 (Normandy Campaign)." Submitted for the Advanced Infantry Officers Course, 1947–1948, the Infantry School, Fort Benning, Georgia.

Richmond, Maj. Budd W. "Operations of the 3d Battalion, 137th Infantry, 35th Infantry Division, in the Attack on Hill 122, north of St. Lo, France, 11–15 July 1944 (Normandy Campaign) (Personal Experience of a Battalion Operations Officer)." Submitted for the Advanced Infantry Officers Course, 1949–1950, the Infantry School, Fort Benning, Georgia.

Rodgers, Lt. Col. W. M. "Armor in Angaur-Peleliu Campaign." The Armored School, Fort Knox, 1950.

Rubottom, Maj. Don C. "Operations of the 1st Battalion, 134th Infantry, 35th Infantry Division, in the Attack on Hill 122, north of St. Lo, France, 15–17 July 1944 (Normandy Campaign) (Personal Experience of a Company Commander)." Submitted for the Advanced Infantry Officers Course, 1949–1950, the Infantry School, Fort Benning, Georgia.

Schimpf, Richard. "Fighting of the 3rd Parachute Division during the Invasion of France from June to August 1944." MS # B-020, translated by Janet E. Dewey, November 1989 at the US Army Military History Institute and for the Center of Military History.

Schmidt, Maj. Gen. Martin. "Panzer Units, Employment in Central Italy, 1944." MS # D-204, 1947. National Archives.

Schramm, Maj. Percy Ernst. "OKW War Diary (1 Apr–18 Dec 1944)," MS # B-034, not dated. National Archives.

Viebig, Major General. "Operations of the 277th Volksgrenadier-Division in November and December 1944: During the Ardennes Offensive." MS # B-273, 10 November 1946. National Archives.

Von Senger und Etterlin, General der Panzertruppen Frido. "War Diary of the Italian Campaign (1943–45)." MS # C-095A to 095G, 1952. National Archives.

ACKNOWLEDGMENTS

I would like to thank my wife, Nancy, who is first in my book and makes me better in every endeavor, including this one. I would like to acknowledge again the folks who were so helpful when I began researching separate tank battalions: "Wild Bill" Wilder, John Walker, Mark Reardon, Mrs. Betty Wilkes, Mrs. Hilda Rubel, Al Heintzleman, Whit Blanchard, Harold Bradley, Phil Fitts, Henry Peters, and Paul Ragan. To these fine people, I gratefully add Raymond Fleig, 707th Tank Battalion; Jeff Danby, 756th Tank Battalion enthusiast and historian; David Redle, 756th Tank Battalion; Aaron Elson, oral historian for the 712th Tank Battalion; John McDaniel, 712th Tank Battalion; and Don Patton, the spark plug in the Dr. Harold C. Deutsch World War II History Roundtable. David Keogh at the U.S. Army's Military History Institute was of great assistance in uncovering material from veterans. The 2d Battalion, 5th Marines, helped me realize via the unit's website that historical information on tank-infantry coordination could be highly relevant to today's warrior, which influenced how I tackled this project.

I would also like to acknowledge the cheerful and efficient public servants at the National Archives and Records Administration's document and still-photo reading rooms in College Park, Maryland. The taxpayer is getting a good deal.

INDEX